THE COMPLETE NOTEBOOKS OF
HENRY JAMES

THE COMPLETE NOTEBOOKS OF
HENRY JAMES

Edited with introductions and notes by

LEON EDEL
and
LYALL H. POWERS

OXFORD UNIVERSITY PRESS
New York   Oxford

Oxford University Press

Oxford   New York   Toronto
Delhi   Bombay   Calcutta   Madras   Karachi
Petaling Jaya   Singapore   Hong Kong   Tokyo
Nairobi   Dar es Salaam   Cape Town
Melbourne   Auckland

and associated companies in
Berlin   Ibadan

Copyright © 1987 by Leon Edel and Lyall H. Powers

First published in 1987 by Oxford University Press, Inc.,
200 Madison Avenue, New York, New York 10016

First issued as an Oxford University Press paperback, 1988

Oxford is a registered trademark of Oxford University Press

Library of Congress Cataloging-in-Publication Data

James, Henry, 1843–1916.
The complete notebooks of Henry James.

Includes index.
1. James, Henry, 1843–1916—Notebooks, sketchbooks,
etc.   I. Edel, Leon. 1907–   II. Powers, Lyall
Harris, 1924–
PS2123.A3   1987   818'.403   86-21680
ISBN 0-19-503782-0 (alk. paper)
ISBN 0-19-504397-9 (PBK.)

2 4 6 8 10 9 7 5 3 1
Printed in the United States of America

Acknowledgments

We wish to express our thanks to the President and Fellows of Harvard College for generous access to the Henry James papers in the Houghton Library and our particular debt to Rodney G. Dennis, the curator of manuscripts in that library. Henry James's holograph notes in nine composition books—as distinct from the notes he later dictated, or from his pocket diaries—were originally edited by F. O. Matthiessen and Kenneth B. Murdock and published by Oxford University Press in 1947. They believed the interest of the notebooks was "not primarily historical or biographical." In their editing, they dealt almost exclusively with the ways in which the notes finally became the finished novels or tales, and they supplied digests of the finished works. We have, in the present volume, used the more traditional editorial forms, that is we deal with the text and its context; it is clear to us that the notebooks are primarily historical, biographical, geographical and psychological, and that their ultimate outcome is the concern of literary criticism.

The senior editor of this volume recalls with pleasure his discussion of these matters with Matthiessen and Murdock in the late 1940s when he checked the proofs of the original book and made certain suggestions to the editors. He wishes also to renew his thanks to the late Henry James III for original access to the James family papers before they were given to Harvard; to the late William James III and his wife for the hospitality (of the last James family seat in Cambridge) at 95 Irving Street, and for maintaining his priorities in the material; and to the late John James for much assistance in the later stages of his biographical work.

The editors of the present volume are indebted also to Alexander R. James, and thank him for timely interest and assistance.

We are also indebted to certain suggestions given us by Professor Daniel R. Fogel, editor of the *Henry James Review,* and to the assistance of Nancy Glover, former librarian at the Hatcher Library of the University of Michigan.

Professor Powers re-explored Rye and Lamb House in Sussex for this edition and expresses a particular debt to Antony Worham; also to Sir Brian and Lady

Batsford, the present tenants of Lamb House; Geofrey Bagley, Honorary Curator of the Rye Museum, and Rosemary Bagley; Ann Hamilton, Maurice and Jennifer Amendt and Edwin Gibson; Dr. Alec Vidler of Friars of the Sack, Rye; The Reverend Mr. David Maundrell, vicar, and G. D. Bateman, beadle, the Parish Church of St. Mary the Virgin, Rye; Mary Owen, editor of the *Rye Gazette;* the staff of Radio Sussex; Sheila Draffin, Master Mariner Jack R. Fletcher, Victoria Gammon, and Peter Kingdon.

L.E.
L.H.P.

Contents

III   Dictated Notes   433

Appendices   585

Introduction: Colloquies
with His Good Angel

LEON EDEL

The Sea Chest: I first came on Henry James's surviving notebooks in 1937. They were in what looked like an old sea chest or footlocker sequestered in the basement of Harvard's Widener Library where the James family papers had been deposited for safekeeping before they would be finally presented to Harvard. I was then editing Henry James's unpublished plays, and the novelist's executor, William James's oldest son, whose name was also Henry, gave me access to the papers and such manuscripts as survived. The papers were spread out in great abundance on a series of long tables. The chest stood in a corner of the large room. It was the kind of wooden box nineteenth century travellers took with them on the old, slow, sea-tossed Cunarders: they needed enough clothes and accessories for all the seasons of the Grand Tour. Did this well-made, time-darkened chest accompany Henry James on his youthful voyages abroad in quest of fame and fortune?—on the China, the Algeric, the Atlas, the Gallia, the Werra, the terse names of voyage. It seemed very likely.

When I inspected the coffin-shaped box and lifted its neatly carpentered lid, I saw that it contained the residue of James's personal papers which death had prevented him from destroying: there were the late plays in variant versions, the dictated notes for his unfinished novels, and miscellaneous writings now reproduced in this volume. These bundles were neatly tied with red and blue cotton strips and had been labelled by James's secretary, Theodora Bosanquet: I knew her and was familiar with her small, neat handwriting. They clearly had not been disturbed for a quarter of a century, having been shipped to America from Lamb House or Carlyle Mansions and deposited with the family papers in some storeroom or attic of the William James house in Irving Street, Cambridge.

I surveyed the tables and saw a dazzling array of documents—boxes containing William's, Henry's and Alice's letters to their parents; the parents' to the children; their letters to one another. There were documents going back to the first William James, who had made his large fortune in Albany. These papers had recently been used by Ralph Barton Perry for his two-volume study, *The Thought and Character of William James* (1935). The entire basement room seemed to speak of a great irony, like one of Henry James's stories of the posthumous life. The novelist had burned his papers and reduced himself to the chest in the corner; but he had forgotten that as the writing son, he was all over the place in the family archive—still a member of the James family.

At the bottom of the coffin-box, when I examined the contents, I noticed the edge of a composition book protruding from under the play manuscripts. It was crammed with HJ's scrawl, right up to the edges. There were other such scribble-books, one partially filled and written in indelible pencil—a journal of James's 1881 visit to America. Professor Powers, in the ensuing pages of this book, describes the physical shape of these precious notebooks. I remember thinking that my experience of that moment resembled that of an archaeologist. I piled up the nine notebook-journals and began to read them. I read slowly and with considerable awe and surprise for several days: now I knew the sensations of the tomb-openers and the diggers in old cities. At last I was peering into James's old work-shops of the novel—the great desk or table by the west window, high above the flushed London sunsets at 34 De Vere Gardens, or the tranquil Garden Room of Lamb House, filled with the songs of birds and the hum of insects in the little brown port of Rye. The notes began curiously enough with the sketch for what turned out to be a novel called *Confidence,* written into the notebook in 1878 and published as a finished work in 1880. The title seemed prophetic: it is a key word in the notebooks. These were concerned with the act of finding self-assurance, self-reliance, belief in persons and things, but also things private and confidential. James said that he was taking blank sheets of paper into his confidence; and he complained, when he read Hawthorne's notebooks, that "he rarely takes his note-book into his confidence."

Note-taking: From his first maturity until his death—and even on his deathbed—note-taking was at the heart of James's creation. The process of observation, for a novelist, was "the business of his life," James wrote in "The Art of Fiction." He defined that business in one of his late prefaces as "the rich principle of the Note," saying, "if one was to undertake to tell tales and to report with truth on the human scene, it could but be because notes had been from the cradle the ineluctable consequence of one's greatest inward energy . . . to take them was as natural as to look, to think, to feel, to recognise, to remember."

Reviewing Hawthorne's French and Italian notebooks in 1872—just about the time his own notebooks were getting under way—James expressed surprise at their flatness and objectivity. They threw little light on Hawthorne's personal feelings and diminished our sense of his intellectual power. Their charm was irresistible; but they had little distinctive force. With a certain sense of being betrayed, James said bluntly that Hawthorne's notebooks represented him as "superficial, uninformed, incurious, inappreciative." They offered "no adequate explanation of him." We see in these strictures James's requirements for an author's written notations. His own possess a singular beauty of statement and the very qualities he felt his American predecessor lacked. The sketches for stories are fresh and full of constant invention, acute in their grasp of personal relations and the tyrannies of the social contract. Many of his pages deal strictly with the business of story-telling, but hardly ever with the necessities of plot; the characters provide the plot, not the plot the characters. We are taken from the germ of a story, some odd little fact or remark at a dinner table, some brief incident or anecdote, into human behavior and human motivation. We watch James in his workshop building narratives brick by brick with a kind of Olympian mastery. Often he is impatient about the details; he will set up some trite machinery as a substitute for a plot; he will dabble in melodrama and offer us the obvious. Reading these notes we say to ourselves, "Isn't he taking an easy way out?," only to find, in the finished story, that much has been changed, the clutter swept away, the proper meaning, the delicate touch applied. Many of the notes are skeletal. It is obvious he carries so much more in his imagination than he can begin to set down. He speaks indeed of "vague dim forms of imperfect conceptions." Other notes, in his later postdramatic phase, are full-blown scenarios during which he seeks to account for every step, as a dramatist must do when he moves his personages on and off the stage. We have full accounts for the pivotal novel in his artistic career, *The Spoils of Poynton,* and he feels his way to new forms in *What Maisie Knew.* These are the exceptions to his more schematic notes in this volume.

However, we become aware, with rhythmic certainty, that the notes exist for other purposes as well. They begin to emerge as a continuing conversation with himself. Certain of the most eloquent and explicit passages are full colloquies and generalizations about the artist's task and role; they reveal profound moments of misgiving and hesitation and other problems never discussed by him elsewhere since these pages were intended for his fireplace. They become a private mode of confession, a discourse on the tribulations as well as the blessings of art. Those accustomed to James's legendary power may find it curious to discover the master saying to himself (I lift phrases at random):

> A strange nervous fear of letting myself go . . .
>
> All one's manhood must be at one's side . . .
>
> . . . to affirm one's self . . . to justify one's self . . .
>
> Ah, once more to let myself go . . .
>
> Courage, courage, and forward, forward . . .

These are brief explosive quests for confidence; and then, at other moments, peace descends and once more there is complete self-assurance. His rhetoric glistens with definitions of the "law of the artist"—but it becomes also "the terrible law"—a law "of fructification," of fertilization, the law by which everything is grist to his mill—"the law of acceptance of all experience, of all suffering, of *all* life, of all suggestion and sensation and illumination."

We can find James's own description of the kind of confidentiality he sought in his story "The Death of the Lion," where the young narrator describes one of the "lion's" scenarios:

> Loose, liberal, confident [the word continues to appear] it might have passed for a great gossiping, eloquent letter—the overflow into talk of an artist's amorous plan

. . . The subject I thought singularly rich, quite the strongest he had yet treated; and this familiar statement of it, full too of fine maturities, was really in summarised splendour a mine of gold, a precious independent work.

And yet with the dust—the gold dust—James throws in our eyes with such extravagance and splendor, with all his self-urging, these colloquies reveal a vague underlying pathos—the reachings out of a lonely bachelor for companionship, for some anodyne to solitude: the very fact that he devises this way of talking to himself is suggestive. We are reminded of his early story "Benvolio" about a talented young poet-playwright who divides his life into two chambers—an immense room hung with pictures and lined with books, draped with rugs and tapestries, possessing a large view of urban existence outside its windows, and a rear room "almost as bare as a monastic cell," which looks out on a tangled moss-grown garden. The divided house, the divided self, was Henry James. In another later story, called "The Private Life," he again created a schizoid individual, a playwright, who "sat at a table all alone, silent and unseen, and wrote admirably brave and intricate things; while the gentleman . . . regularly came forth to sit at a quite different table and substantively and promiscuously and multitudinously dined." This "whimsical theory of two distinct and alternate presences," of a celebrity who was "double," speaks not only for celibacy and loneliness but colors his push for "courage" and his drive to let himself go. One critic wondered, in discussing the tale of Benvolio, whether this character, alternating between the great world and his monk's cell, wasn't "whistling to keep his courage up," and we may wonder whether this could not be said of Henry James himself.

In some passages the novelist is candid about his underlying depression that remains with him not only after the failure of his play-writing but is a part of his mood swings in his daily life. He speaks of his failures, as all writers do, of "indolence, vagueness, inattention," and in one exalted passage his "discouragements and lapses, depressions and darknesses." In all writers there are resistances to work; the words won't come, the mind sinks into a bog of inertia and staleness. And yet even in his deepest depression—after his theatrical failures—James is able to pursue his work. Criticism has failed to recognize that depression itself can be a driving force to powerful creation. I think of T. S. Eliot writing *The Waste Land* when he felt his own life to be a waste; the depression may have caused some of his misjudgments which Pound corrected, but the creative power was generated by despair. Another modern instance is Virginia Woolf, who created her novels as a defence against melancholy and relapsed into her manic state when they were done. This is the *tristimania* described by the first great American psychiatrist, Benjamin Rush, and we see its presence in Proust, in Joyce, in Gide—whose long narcissistic journals he himself published frequently; or in the endless journalizing of Anaïs Nin who began her notebooks as a long letter to an absent father. Notebooks, diaries, journals are often repositories of grief and despair—Kafka told us that writing was for him a form of prayer. Even the more camera-like journals of Edmund Wilson, or earlier the nature-mirror journals of Thoreau, reflect existential struggles, an overpowering need to write the book of the Self in order to find peace of the soul.

James's colloquies reveal distinct fantasies of ritual. There is first the Benvolio ambivalence and withdrawal; he talks ardently of "the Great Good Place" as he did in his tale of that name. He moves into "the luminous paradise of art," the "cool cloister and warm garden." His father's word *sacred* is constantly on the tip of his pen—"sacred hours," "sacred days," "sacred silence," "sacred refuge"—a memory of his father's preoccupation with Blake and Swedenborg. And we remind ourselves that Swedenborg, in his obsessions, recorded his conversations with angels.

━━━━━ ᥫᦡ ━━━━━

The Demon of Patience: There came a moment in James's notebooks when he began to speak of his "good angel" and to invoke his attendant Genius, using the word in its original Greek sense as a protecting spirit. The Greeks called such tutelary spirits δαίμων—daimon—and the poets described them as dwelling on earth, unseen by mortals, ministers of the gods, guardians of men and justice. Daimons, the Greek philosophers taught, were allotted from birth and for life. Henry James accepted this Graeco-Roman mythology for himself, as we can read in a note he sets down while staying at the Coronado Beach Hotel in California in 1905:

> I sit here after long weeks . . . in front of my arrears, with an inward accumulation of material of which I feel the wealth, and as to which I can only invoke my familiar demon of patience, who always comes, doesn't he? when I call. He is here with me, in front of this green Pacific—he sits close and I feel his soft breath, which cools and steadies and inspires, on my cheek . . .

The Good Angel is by no means new to him; it is mentioned for example in "The Art of Fiction," where James tucks it into a sentence about creating characters—how a novelist should make a character "is a secret between his good angel and himself." The good angel in the notebooks is also James's "blest Genius" and on occasion the gallicized spirit *"mon bon"* whom James addresses in French. We remember that Thoreau created some such alter ego in his journals, and one critic described this as a kind of ventriloquism. James's Good Angel never plays the role of a ventriloquist's dummy: he remains silent, invisible—and presumably attentive—in the solitary room, "this quiet, this blessed and uninvaded work room." The monkish oath of silence is broken only by the scratching pen on those clean white sheets receiving the anchorite's confidences:

> *Plus je vais, plus je trouve* that the only balm and the only refuge, the real solution of the pressing question of life, are in this frequent, fruitful, intimate battle with the particular idea, with the subject, the possibility, the place. It's the anodyne, the escape, the boundlessly beneficent resort. No effort in this direction is vain, no confidence [again!] is idle, no surrender but is victorious.

Balm, refuge, fruitful, intimate, anodyne—words of release and relief, accompanying the seed-planting—"fertilization," "fruition," "fructification." When peace comes and the tumult is calmed, the pulse beats regularly again within the "sacred refuge." The moment of mellow fruitfulness seems to be both agricultural and sexual—the two are in any event linked. Percy Lubbock unquestionably responds to one of the passages in this way when he speaks of it as a "wonderful unbosoming."

The magic is achieved as if James were a Zen Buddhist emptying his mind before his private altar, relieving himself of its clutter and its anxieties, pressures, stress. There are indeed moments when the novelist seems on the brink of ecstasy. An unforgettably vivid colloquy is recorded one January dawn of 1910; James has awakened from his sleep and sought the calm of his workroom. He is toying with his ideas for his novel *The Ivory Tower* (within *his* own peaceful ivory tower) and he lapses, as he did earlier, into French: "let us talk, let us talk, my Good One"— but it is James who talks—

> *Causons, causons, mon bon*—oh celestial soothing, sanctifying process . . . Let me fumble it gently and patiently out—with fever and fidget laid to rest—as in all the old enchanted months! It only looms, it only shines and shimmers, *too* beautiful and too interesting; it only hangs there too rich and too full and with too much to give and to pay; it only presents itself too admirably and too vividly, too straight and square and vivid, as a little organic and effective Action . . .

The "old enchanted months" alludes to the time when in De Vere Gardens he enjoyed all the excitement of his "dramatic years"—scenario-writing, play-planning, the working out of dialogue, plot, exits, entries, characters and scenes, when he acquired the key that he could use in the joint lock of drama and fiction.

> Thus just these first little wavings of the oh so tremulously passionate little old wand (now!) make for me, I feel, a sort of promise of richness and beauty and variety; a sort of portent of the happy presence of the elements . . . I seem to emerge from these recent bad days—the fruit of blind accident—and the prospect clears and flushes, and my blest old Genius pats me so admirably and lovingly on the back that I turn, I screw round, and bend my lips to passionately, in my gratitude, kiss its hands.

James's "turn of the screw" in his celebrated tale was a turn of pain and evil. The turn in this passage derives from the pleasure principle and the search for catharsis and purge. The kiss is warm and tender, a kiss of love and gratitude. The orgasmic overtones suggest an extraordinary state of exaltation behind which lay years of immense devotion and industry. Perhaps here James has "let go," and we read it only because we are in reality eavesdropping. The gesture of love would have been denied us if James had had his way.

It would be only too easy to make fun of such artistic piety, to mock and satirize this old writer, performing his ritual of affection and fidelity toward his invisible Good Angel. But the ritual is endowed with the dignity of James's language, the power of his belief, the sincere worship of his art. H. G. Wells did indeed mock the novelist, although not this passage, which wasn't published until 1920 by Lubbock. Wells described the ponderous James as "leviathan retrieving pebbles." He was "a magnificent but painful hippopotamus resolved at any cost, even at the cost of its dignity, upon picking up a pea which has got into a corner of its den." Yet even after several pages of this kind of satire, Wells had to pay tribute to James's "artistic singleness of mind."

The Invaded Sanctuary: If there is a subject for comedy in the history of James's novel-workshop, it resides in the strange and high irony that occurred in the mid-nineties, a kind of industrial revolution in the novelist's life of labor. He had spoken earlier of "this quiet, this blessed and uninvaded work room." The blessings ceased to flow: fate and the machine brought about an invasion. And in this invasion, the colloquies with the Good Angel ceased or were transformed, the privacy went out the window as the typists walked through the study's door. *Mon bon,* the "blest Genius," the Good and Guardian Angel, spread their classic wings and flew away. The machinery could not provide their inspiration or protection. Crude daylight and the typewriter's click invaded the anchorite's cell.

The change came actually in an evolutionary rather than revolutionary way, a series of logical steps which we deduce from certain circumstances and actions. First, James developed writer's cramp, in the very middle of *What Maisie Knew;* this was understandable. He had written for hours, day after day, through three decades. William James had been urging him to get a stenographer. But what was suitable for a Harvard's professorial office could not be applied to a writer's soaring imagination. The shorthand expert James hired, a young Scot, went off to type up the day's dictation; and the novelist had to wait for his copy. Accustomed to rereading promptly what he wrote, to referring back to it as he went on with the story, he found himself the slave of his typist's transcribing. This simply wouldn't do. He did not hesitate. He bought a brand new Remington, then a large clumsy machine. It never occurred to him to learn to type: his job wasn't to get involved with machinery. The portable typewriter—which James would never have accepted—had not yet been created. Instead of having his words taken down in shorthand, he planted his Scot in front of the typewriter and began to practice dictating directly to it—to him: this supplied copy promptly. There was a period of adjustment; a stranger—not a Guardian Angel—a flesh and blood Scot, who showed no emotional reaction to James's prose, gave him back whatever he said. In this there was a certain kind of word-by-word ventriloquism, right down to the punctuation and the spelling out of words. I remember telling this to Marshall McLuhan one day and the enthusiasm it aroused in him long before his later fame—how James moved from the pen to the typewriter, to what he called his "fierce legibility." Even then, McLuhan was challenged by the idea of medium and message.

Could it be the typewriter typed James via the silent medium of William MacAlpine? The novelist denied it. Morton Fullerton had inquired whether the machine might alter James's style. The response was emphatic: "I can be trusted, artless youth, not to be simplified by any shortcut or falsified by any facility."

The real changes occurred in the rituals of his notebooks. For the rest of his days James relied on typists; after a while James found MacAlpine too expensive and, what with the first stirrings of feminism, female typists came cheaper. They proved quiet, efficient, and were almost as invisible as his Good Angel. His assistants had to accustom themselves to long pauses and meditation, starts, fidgets. But the meditations were no longer articulated. After a while, the writer's cramp disappeared, but James did not revert to his older methods; he was by now too accustomed to the sound of the Remington and the ministrations of impersonal skills. He could still scribble in his notebooks at night, when he also wrote personal correspondence in longhand; but even some letters were now typed, with elaborate preludes asking forgiveness for being so "discernible."

The shift from the written notes to the dictated notes made for striking changes. He was no longer bent double over his desk. The presence of a second person to do the manual work gave James a sense of freedom: he could move around his Garden Room, pace up and down—"I'm on my feet a great part of the time" he told his nephew. Communication with the self was at an end during working hours: there was direct communication to a living, receiving person. And then in the evenings, when he had the day's typed sheets before him, he could revert to his privacy, add corrections, revise with great ease, knowing that his pages would be retyped in their revised state as often as he wished. Human ears now received his stories. The procedure came to seem so natural that sometimes verbalized reverie and narrative became mixed: we have an example (see page 536) of James moving into notebook dictation in the midst of an article his typist was taking down. But that was late in life. What posterity lost to the machine and to the human presence in the workroom were the intimate self-exhortations, the continual quest for confidence—if *mon bon* was present he was reduced beyond the invisible to the inaudible.

The Social Frame: The Pocket Diaries, published in this volume for the first time, originally gave us pause. We asked ourselves whether they were not too trivial. Appointment books are commonplace, and at a glance these relics of James's last years seemed sufficiently mundane. The diaries were filled with names that needed explaining and were a record of social engagements, many lunches, dinners, teas, visits, dates kept and dates cancelled. Also they were a record of illness, pill-taking, cash reserves, and the income tax. However the old and practiced note-taker could not exclude himself from his appointment book. Suddenly we came on a bit of landscape; a cloud drifted by in the background; a strange person made a strange remark. The tip of a tail of a notion flitted through his mind. Entries grew more abundant even if the space forced James to unusual brevity. We were in the presence of mini-notebooks in the seven pocket diaries and it seemed to us that they offered a great deal of the worldly Benvolio side of James; they enabled us to extrapolate the life of his earlier, his middle years, when he kept up his social life strenuously. The life in these diaries seemed strenuous enough, considering it was the life of an old man. And then there was a great deal of social history buried in these entries—Edith Wharton and her bittersweet romance with Morton Fullerton; Ethel Sands and her salon at Newington; "Howdie" Sturgis and his embroidery and life with his friend "the Babe" at Qu'Acre; Hugh Walpole seeking out the old master—himself then no more than a young puppy wagging a pleased tail. The visits to the dentists, the summons to the doctors, the long walks, the illnesses: and names of odd persons who were being touched in this way by genius, given a moment of posthumousness in a pocket diary! If James's social reach seems remarkable and crowded in these documentary relics, we must remind ourselves they are also the touching testimony of a literary bachelor's need for company, especially as his creative energy waned and loneliness crowded his hours.

James's note-taking endured to the end. After his first stroke he summoned Miss Bosanquet: he needed the sound of the old Remington. He was delirious; pneumonia had set in. The doctors had no objection: and indeed after dictating certain sentences, James fell into a quiet peaceful sleep—the anodyne, the balm, had worked. He conquered his pneumonia and ruggedly survived for a few weeks but he could not conquer the damage of the repeated strokes. The deathbed dictation, which had not been in the sea chest but was among the papers on the Widener tables, enables us to conclude with his very last notebook-style dictation. There seem to me to be remote echoes of *War and Peace* as the dying James invokes the Napoleonic legend, the Imperial style, the battlefields. Remarkable that the disintegrating mind could frame a vivid sentence such as "They pluck in their terror handfuls of plumes from the imperial eagle, and with no greater credit in consequence than that they face, keeping their equipoise, the awful bloody beak that he turns round upon them."

But James's colloquies with his Guardian or Good Angel had ended before this last dramatic moment—and in his final dictation his colloquy—in the midst of the First World War—was with history.

LEON EDEL

A Note on the Notes

LYALL H. POWERS

This volume brings together all of Henry James's notebooks, sketches, scenarios, dictations, and diaries that escaped accidental loss or intentional destruction. It is difficult to say just what the omissions amount to. Occasionally the extant notebooks refer specifically to entries in notebooks no longer with us; the notebook for 1904–05 opens in the middle of a sentence which must have begun in a notebook long defunct; the style and format of several pieces in *Transatlantic Sketches* (1875)—coupled with James's letter of 9 April 1873 to his brother William— encourage the assumption that they had their source in an "Italian Notebook," a "French Notebook," etc., which no longer exist. A letter James wrote to H. G. Wells late in 1902 mentions his destruction of an indeterminate number of items— and one, his "Project for *The Wings of the Dove*," quite specifically.

There nevertheless remains a rich abundance of material, the result of James's inveterate note-taking in various modes over nearly half a century. Some of this material has been published before, much of it scattered in long out-of-print volumes and in out-of-the-way corners; a good deal of it is published here for the first time. The gathering of this variety into one holding seems necessary and salutary. This collection contains all of the *extant* notes; it is in that sense *The Complete Notebooks of Henry James*.

The notes illustrate the entire spectrum of James's note-taking "habit," from the briefest jottings of a "germ"—the simple kernel of an idea—through the various stages of their development, to the penultimate version of a piece; the ultimate is the version for publication. It is instructive to compare the raw material with the finished literary work and, when possible, to contemplate the intervening steps. Yet it is also useful to ponder those other entries, less specifically the sources for particular novels, tales, or essays, but more general—philosophical, moral, social (or perhaps sociological)—in tone, revealing the ambiance, the quality of mind, out of which the particular works emerged.

The rich and varied abundance of extant notes calls urgently for some clarifying system of arrangement to underline their distinctiveness and significance. Implicit in the very nature of the notes themselves are some strong guidelines. We have sought to follow them. First, we have included only items that are clearly *preparatory* in nature—nothing more "finished" than the penultimate stage of development; we rejected manuscript and typescript versions of the ultimate stage, on which publication directly depended. Second, the apparent distinction between manuscript notes and typescript seemed to offer a useful division; chronology was a constant consideration. Another quality of the material, however, demanded attention. James evidently intended very little of this material for any sort of public consumption: not only is it preliminary in nature, but most of it is distinctly private and personal—instances of James's having "taken a sheet of paper, as it were, into my confidence" (see the beginning of the entry for 25 November 1881). To that category belong the Notebooks, Journals, Detached Notes, and Pocket Diaries—all pen-and-ink or pencil manuscripts. This is an important distinction.

Of these manuscripts, the nine surviving notebooks (Journals I–IX as they are now denominated by the Houghton Library at Harvard) constitute the largest collection, covering the period from November 1878 to March 1911. While the earliest entry opens the first Notebook (Houghton Journal I) and the latest closes the last (Houghton Journal IX), the entries do not follow strict chronological arrangement. James would occasionally pick up the notebook nearest at hand—without regard for dates—to jot down an item; the most arresting example is the *"Verena"* entry in the 1878–88 Notebook (see that headnote). The Notebooks resemble, with one exception, old-fashioned exercise-books or "scribblers" of the kind schoolchildren would buy for a few pennies; the exception is the "little red book," a small pocket notebook so similar to James's Pocket Diaries that it had, until recently, been shelved with them in the Houghton Library. These nine manuscripts provided most of the text for F. O. Matthiessen and Kenneth B. Murdock's 1947 edition of *The Notebooks of Henry James,* in which the system of organization was fairly consistently chronological.

Research during the ensuring forty years has accumulated information that makes it possible now to identify many of the persons and places vaguely alluded to or hidden behind mere initials that the earlier editors chose to overlook;[1] it has also made possible the identification of additional works that derive from the notes. Careful reperusal of the notebooks has enabled us to correct misreadings of James's often difficult script and to identify properly a number of persons and places. "⟨Buxril?⟩" of 6 August 1884, for example, is actually "Bassett," the home of the Charles Darwin family; beside the bank of names between entries for 9 August and 11 September 1900 James's marginal note is not "Essex local" but "Sussex local" (not surprisingly, as Sussex is the county in which James's home, Lamb House, Rye, is located). We have also removed the pointed brackets from several words of which the earlier editors were unsure. No critical commentary on the stories has been offered here; that activity is left to the alert reader. Finally, while the demand of chronology is not neglected, it has not been given the priority in our arrangement of the notebook material that it enjoyed in the 1947 volume.

In addition to the personal and confidential notebook entries, arranged chrono-

---

1. See Matthiessen and Murdock, p. xxiii, "A Note on the Text."

logically in the first section of this volume, we have distinguished three manuscripts in recognition of their evident *purpose*. The notebook for 1881–82 is not merely autobiographical, it exposes James's reflections on his native land and confirmation of his decision to become an expatriate. It is distinguished here as the first American Journal. The notebook for 1904–05 contains James's account of America revisited; and while it is tinged with a warm nostalgic tone, the sense is unmistakable that James has been reconfirmed in his expatriation. This is American Journal II. The two anticipate, and indeed helped James prepare for, *The American Scene* (1907), *A Small Boy and Others* (1913), and *Notes of a Son and Brother* (1914). To mark their difference from the other notebooks and to emphasize their integrity, they are here given a category of their own. Similar in purpose but more sharply focused in intent—more so even than the second American Journal—is the "little red book" (Houghton Journal VIII). From 1907 to 1909 James entered notes in this small journal (almost the size of a pocket diary—the significance of its size will be considered below) for a book on London—not just the business heart, the "City" proper (James was careful to indicate), but the larger metropolis that is officially Westminster—or "London Town," as he called it. These notes have been placed at the end of the first section.

Three other substantial items in manuscript—separate from the notebooks—are gathered as Detached Notes. The third of these, "The K. B. Case and Mrs. Max," was included in the earlier edition of James's Notebooks.

James's Pocket Diaries, published now for the first time, are of the same personal and confidential nature as the notebooks. Seven of them have survived, one each for the years 1909 to 1915. An obvious difference from the notebooks is the physical size of these little books, which tends to encourage (at least at first) a more laconic mode of expression. The majority of the entries are extremely brief, but they are richer than their brevity would suggest; they are, indeed, often the mere tips of icebergs. The initial entries in the Diary for 1909 well illustrate that feature (see headnote and the introduction to this volume).

On the other hand, James by no means confined himself to the bald brevity of typical "date book" entries. On occasion he can be as expansive and revealingly autobiographical in the diaries as he allowed himself to be in the notebooks. A critical moment in the lives of both Henry and his brother William prompts James to use the space for the last week of June 1910 to describe their excursion to Nauheim (where William sought the curative effect of the baths), thence through the Black Forest to Switzerland. A rich little passage of some 400 words, it is a record of family drama: James's memory of the death of their youngest brother Robertson, his fears for his brother William, his own suffering, and so on.

Slightly less personal and confidential than the notebooks and diaries are the items (with three exceptions) contained in section III, Dictated Notes. Because they are "dictated," the confidence into which James takes these sheets is necessarily shared with his typist. They are otherwise quite comparable to the notebook entries—all but the longest similar enough to the notebook developments of *The Spoils of Poynton* and *What Maisie Knew*. They are also perhaps a touch more formal. The note for "Mr. and Mrs. Fields" will do to exemplify the distinction: the rather "finished" tone of most of the piece quite clearly lapses on two different occasions into what Theodora Bosanquet (James's typist from autumn 1907 until his death) aptly termed "jawbation," as he digresses from creative composition to discussing how he will manage the rest of the essay, what he must remember to include, and so forth.

Rather distinctly different in intention and mode from the other manuscript and typescript material are the Notes for Publishers. In a letter to H. G. Wells (15 November 1902) James nicely indicates the difference. Wells had apparently asked to see some (at least two) of "those wondrous and copious preliminary *statements*" of James's works, and intimated that he knew they had been seen (James showed Joseph Conrad the Project for *The Wings of the Dove*). James replies that they no longer exist "in any form in which they can be imparted," and then ofers this helpful comment:

> I shall not again draw up detailed and explicit plans for unconvinced and ungracious editors. . . . A plan for *myself,* as copious and developed as possible, I always do draw up—that is the two documents I speak of were based upon, and extracted from, such a preliminary *private* outpouring. But this latter voluminous effusion is, ever, so extremely familiar, confidential and intimate—in the form of an interminable garrulous letter addressed to my own fond fancy—that, though I always, for easy reference, have it carefully typed, it isn't a thing I would willingly expose to any eye but my own.[2]

One of the "two documents" is the "Project" for *The Ambassadors,* the first of the Notes for Publishers. The quite exceptional nature of "The Deathbed Dictation" requires its singular location at the end of all the notes.

Chronology has been easily honored. It has been, however, if not impossible then highly undesirable to escape chronological overlapping altogether. The Detached Notes (1893–1910) roughly parallel the American Journals (1881–1905). The diaries overlap slightly with the last notebook entries but are themselves in strict chronological order. The first two Dictated Notes overlap with other notes and the remainder of them with the last two years of the diaries. But the system of organization here, implicitly indicated by the varied nature of the notes themselves—manuscript or typescript, in notebooks and diaries or separate—turned out to accommodate the incessant demand of chronology well enough. It has furthermore yielded a possible clarification of James's note-taking practice as his life and career developed, and perhaps throws some new light on the problem of lost notebooks and diaries.

A change in note-taking, discernible as early as 1901, is confirmed in 1909. If we except the specifically focussed second American Journal (1904–05) and Notes for "London Town" (1907–09)—neither of them particularly freighted—we are left with comparatively few and rather thin notebook entries from 19 October 1901 to 3 August 1909. The initial diary entry is 15 February 1909. The role of the notebook in James's life seems to have been taken over by the diary during 1909.

---

2. *Henry James and H.G. Wells,* ed. Leon Edel and Gordon N. Ray (1958), pp. 83–85.

There is some further overlapping: the latest surviving notebook has three entries for 1911—the first quite substantial. Nevertheless, James's reliance on the notebooks has evidently diminished and would apparently soon cease.

An explanation of this phenomenon is that James felt increasingly as he moved into his sixties that he had in hand all the *données*—of whatever degree of development—that his remaining strength and talent could manage. An ancillary point to consider is that not all of James's notebooks have survived, that he may have kept diaries before 1909 and that they too are lost. Yet the nature of the entries in the latest of the surviving notebooks and certain other data would seem to argue against that possibility.

The most persuasive explanation would seem to be found in James's gradually turning from the use of pen or pencil to the practice (soon exclusive) of dictating his material to a typist. That change was instigated by the onset of writer's cramp in the winter of 1896–97. Henceforth James undertakes the preparation and development of his ideas orally rather than scripturally. The lengthy discussion of his subjects and the careful and often detailed working-out of attendant problems which we find quite regularly in the notebooks are now replaced by "jawbation": he would begin by talking about his subject, mulling it over orally as though in soliloquy or in dialogue with his daimon, *"mon bon"* (as he had so often done, scripturally, in the notebooks), until he was ready to attack the story or essay in hand. The relief provided by a typist allowed him to resume writing his letters (and so avoiding the "fierce legibility" for which he would elaborately beg the pardon of his correspondents). But reliance on the "music" of the Remington meant, in those days before "portables," that he could not work when he travelled. As a kind of compensation, it would seem, he turned to the use of the size of notebook he could easily carry with him—the pocket diary and, on at least the one occasion, the little red book.

This is not to "explain away" additional missing notebooks and diaries, but to recognize that if, in 1909, the apparent dwindling use of notebooks and the simultaneous appearance of the earliest diaries is a coincidence, it is nevertheless a rather arresting one.

There remain our Appendices. The story fragment "Hugh Merrow" is obviously a preliminary version in that it is incomplete, yet it is quite "finished" in style. Rather an anomaly, it seems to require a special category.

The Cash Accounts offer insight into James's financial situation during the last years of his life—the dwindling royalties, his management of taxes, the domestic expenses of Lamb House and 21 Carlyle Mansions, etc. The Addresses provide a modest additional source of supplementary biographical information.

———ে∞ু———

Our editorial aim in this volume has been to provide as accessible a text as possible, not to achieve the fidelity of facsimile reproduction. We have silently attended to omitted or repeated words, spelling mistakes, vagaries of punctuation, and errors of dating, except where it has seemed important to retain the original. We have similarly dealt with James's peculiarities. For his habitual use of the ampersand we have substituted "and"; for his "&c.," "etc." He tended to punctuate within parentheses (like this,); we have followed standard practice (like this). We have regularized his haphazard underlining of foreign words; his abbreviations "shd.," "wh.," and so on we have written out as "should," "which," etc. We have usually left untouched his creative Anglicizations, such as adding an "s" to a French infinitive verb to make an English indicative verb: "the Shelley fanatic . . . *couvers* the treasure . . ." (12 January 1887). We have retained James's antiquated past tense of the verb "to stay"—"staid."

Scholarly apparatus has been held to a minimum and kept as unobtrusive as possible. Headnotes to sections and subsections of the text give information necessary to understand the particular features and provenance of what follows, describe the original manuscript or typescript which is the source, offer additional information to "situate" the material historically within James's life and career.

We regularly identify in square brackets persons (and sometimes places) James refers to by initials only. We also use square brackets to indicate our insertion of a missing word or syllable. James very rarely uses square brackets, but where he does so we have identified them as his by footnote. Footnotes, where necessary, provide the minimum of essential information; we hope the few large and full ones are justified by their interest. In section I (The Notebooks) footnotes are numbered consecutively for each entry date. The footnotes often indicate sources of further information.

Abbreviations

For the sources frequently mentioned in the notes we have used the following abbreviations.

Life	Leon Edel, *Henry James: A Life* (New York: Harper and Row, 1985).
Letters I	*Henry James Letters 1843–1875*, ed. Leon Edel (Cambridge, Mass.: Harvard University Press, 1974).
Letters II	———*1875–1883* (1975).
Letters III	———*1883–1895* (1980).
Letters IV	———*1895–1916* (1984).
Lubbock I, II	*The Letters of Henry James,* ed. Percy Lubbock, 2 vols. (New York: Charles Scribner's Sons, 1920).
Complete Plays	*The Complete Plays of Henry James,* ed. Leon Edel (Philadelphia and New York: J. B. Lippincott Company, 1949).
LA II	*Henry James: Literary Criticism; Essays on Literature, American Writers, English Writers* ed. Leon Edel with Mark Wilson (New York: Library of America, 1984).
LA III	———; *French Writers, Other European Writers, The Prefaces to the New York Edition* (1984).
Bibliography	*A Bibliography of Henry James,* ed. Leon Edel and Dan H. Laurence with James Rambeau, 3rd ed. (Oxford: Oxford University Press, 1982).

Certain initials appear so frequently in the Diaries (and with some variation) that we have not identified them at every appearance. Here is a helpful list with variations and identifications:

J. A.	Jessie Allen
B. J. (usually "Phil. B. J.")	Philip Burne-Jones
Rhoda B.	Rhoda Broughton
L. C.	Lucy Clifford
M. F. (or "W. M. F.")	William Morton Fullerton
M. C. J. (or "M. J." or "Mary Cadwal.")	Mary Cadwalader Jones
J. P.	Jocelyn Persse
J. S. (or "Jonathan S.")	Jonathan Sturges
H. S. (or "Howard S.")	Howard Sturgis
E. W.	Edith Wharton
H. W. (or "Hugh W.")	Hugh Walpole
L. H.	Lamb House
R. C.	The Reform Club (105 Pall Mall)

The almost ubiquitous address "74 Eaton Terrace" was the London home of Jessie Allen.

Chronology

1843	Born 15 April at 21 Washington Place, New York City.
1843–4	Taken abroad by parents to Paris and London: period of residence at Windsor.
1845–55	Childhood in Albany and New York.
1855–8	Attends schools in Geneva, London, Paris and Boulogne-sur-mer and is privately tutored.
1858	James family settles in Newport, Rhode Island.
1859	At scientific school in Geneva. Studies German in Bonn.
1860	At school in Newport. Receives back injury on eve of Civil War while serving as volunteer fireman. Studies art briefly. Friendship with John La Farge.
1862–3	Spends term in Harvard Law School.
1864	Family settles in Boston and then in Cambridge. Early anonymous story and unsigned reviews published.
1865	First signed story published in *Atlantic Monthly*.
1869–70	Travels in England, France and Italy. Death of his beloved cousin Minny Temple.
1870	Back in Cambridge, publishes first novel in the *Atlantic, Watch and Ward*.
1872–4	Travels with sister Alice and aunt in Europe; writes impressionistic travel sketches for the *Nation*. Spends autumn in Paris and goes to Italy to write first large novel. Begins systematic notebook-keeping.
1874–5	On completion of *Roderick Hudson* tests New York City as residence; writes much literary journalism for the *Nation*. First three books published: *Transatlantic Sketches*, *A Passionate Pilgrim* (tales) and *Roderick Hudson*.

1875–6	Goes to live in Paris. Meets Ivan Turgenev and through him Flaubert, Zola, Daudet, Maupassant and Edmond de Goncourt. Writes *The American.*
1876–7	Moves to London and settles in 3 Bolton Street, Piccadilly. Revisits Paris, Florence, Rome.
1878	"Daisy Miller," published in London, establishes fame on both sides of the Atlantic. Publishes first volume of essays, *French Poets and Novelists.*
1879–82	*The Europeans, Washington Square, Confidence, The Portrait of a Lady.*
1882–3	Revisits Boston: first visit to Washington. Death of parents.
1884–6	Returns to London. Sister Alice comes to live near him. Fourteen-volume collection of novels and tales published. Writes *The Bostonians* and *The Princess Casamassima,* published in the following year.
1886	Moves to flat at 34 De Vere Gardens West.
1887	Sojourn in Italy, mainly Florence and Venice. "The Aspern Papers," *The Reverberator,* "A London Life." Friendship with grandniece of Fenimore Cooper—Constance Fenimore Woolson.
1888	*Partial Portraits* and several collections of tales.
1889–90	*The Tragic Muse.*
1890–1	Dramatizes *The American,* which has a short run. Writes four comedies, rejected by producers.
1892	Alice James dies in London.
1894	Miss Woolson commits suicide in Venice. James journeys to Italy and visits her grave in Rome.
1895	He is booed at first night of his play *Guy Domville.* Deeply depressed, he abandons the theater.
1896–7	*The Spoils of Poynton, What Maisie Knew.*
1898	Takes long lease of Lamb House, in Rye, Sussex. Writes "The Turn of the Screw."
1899–1900	*The Awkward Age, The Sacred Fount.* Friendship with Conrad and Wells.
1902–4	*The Ambassadors, The Wings of the Dove* and *The Golden Bowl.* Friendships with H. C. Andersen and Jocelyn Persse.
1905	Revisits the United States after twenty-year absence, lectures on Balzac and the speech of Americans.
1906–10	*The American Scene.* Edits selective and revised "New York edition" of his works in 24 volumes. Friendship with Hugh Walpole.
1910	Death of brother, William James.

1913	Sargent paints his portrait as 70th birthday gift from some 300 friends and admirers. Writes autobiographies, *A Small Boy and Others* and *Notes of a Son and Brother*.
1914	*Notes on Novelists*. Visits wounded in hospitals.
1915	Becomes a British subject.
1916	Given Order of Merit. Dies 28 February in Chelsea, aged 72. Funeral in Chelsea Old Church. Ashes buried in Cambridge, Massachusetts family plot.
1976	Commemorative tablet unveiled in Poets' Corner of Westminster Abbey, 17 June.

I
The Notebooks

The Notebooks
1878–1911

1878–1888

Notebook I (7 November 1878 to ? December 1888), $6\frac{1}{4}''$ × $7\frac{5}{8}''$, has black leatherette covers and wine marbled endpapers; two blank pages are followed by 176 lined pages, all with marbled edges. Pages 71–72 (between the entries for 2 January 1884 and 19 January 1884) have been cut out. All entries are in black ink, except for the final item, on *Verena*, which is in red ink and upside down—it became *The Bostonians* (see note for September 1884).

The first two years of this notebook cover the end of HJ's journeyman period. His untried years of apprenticeship, during which he also took notes, are well behind him. We find there a substantial entry for his masterpiece *The Portrait of a Lady*. Following the entry for 18 January 1881 there is a gap of ten months. (The first American Journal intervenes, and HJ resumed use of this particular notebook after his year in the United States.) The subsequent entries (22 December 1882 to ? December 1888) confirm his decision to quit his native land and illustrate his ambivalence to America and Americans as he assiduously works the vein of his "international" theme. Anticipation of his theatrical experiment, implicit in the latest entry in this notebook, is echoed in the last entry of his first American Journal.

3 Bolton St., W., November 7th, 1878.

A young Englishman, travelling in Italy twenty years ago, meets, in some old town—Perugia, Siena, Ravenna—two ladies, a mother and daughter, with whom he has some momentary relation: the mother a quiet, delicate, interesting, touching, high bred woman—the portrait of a perfect lady, of the old English school,

5

with a tone of sadness in the picture; the daughter a beautiful, picturesque high-tempered girl; generous, ardent, even tender, but with a good deal of coquetry and a certain amount of hardness. As the incident which constitutes this momentary contact of Harold Stanmer and Bianca Vane—their names are perhaps provisional—the former may be imagined, in the course of making a sketch of some picturesque old nook in the Italian city, to have found the young girl's figure in the line of his composition, and to have appealed to her as she stands there, to kindly remain a moment and suffer him to introduce it. She consents and he makes a hasty sketch of her—which he presents to her. They are thus in a manner introduced; but they separate without learning each other's names; she however, having made a certain appreciable impression—not exclusively agreeable—on the young man.

2. Stanmer shortly afterwards receives a letter from an intimate friend, Bernard Longueville, begging him to come and join him at Baden Baden (or some other German watering-place), which Harold presently does. The two men are old friends—closely united friends. The interest of the story must depend greatly upon this fact of their strong, deep friendship and upon the contrast of their two characters. They are, in effect, singularly different. Harold must be represented as the (roughly speaking) complex nature of the two—the subtle, the refined, the fanciful, the eminently modern; as he is also, by four or five years, the younger. Longueville is simpler, deeper, more masculine, more easily puzzled, less intellectual, less imaginative. He is greatly under the influence of his friend and has a great esteem for his judgement He concludes his letter, asking Harold to join him, with telling him he has something momentous to consult him about. A certain rigid, formal element must be made appreciable in Longueville—a certain English deference to all the conventions and decencies of life; but it must not be made in any way contemptible, or ridiculous, for one must feel that at bottom his nature is rich and tender, and that when he is once moved, he is moved forever. Stanmer, on joining him, finds that he is with the two ladies whom he himself has met in Italy—and that it is on a subject connected with them that he wishes to consult him. Longueville, in a word, is in love with Bianca Vane, but is rather struggling with his passion. He has a certain indefinable mistrust of the young girl, at the same time that he is deeply smitten. He has proposed to her and she has refused him; but he has reason to believe that if he proposes again she will accept him. Longueville wants to know what Stanmer thinks of her and Stanmer is a good deal embarrassed. This appeal on the part of Longueville can be made natural only by the great simplicity and conscientiousness of the young man, and by his habit of putting faith in his friend's impressions and opinions. There has been recognition, of course, between Stanmer and the two ladies, but it has not gone far; before Longueville there has been nothing more than an allusion to his having seen them at Siena. Harold does not mention the episode of the portrait; he waits, by a natural instinct, for Miss Vane to do so; and, finding that she has not done so, he says nothing. On the whole, seeing more of her, he inclines not to like her; there is something in her that displeases him. He reserves judgement, however, and of course is in no hurry to talk of her unfavourably to his friend. It befalls that the latter is suddenly summoned away for a short time; he is obliged to go to

England. He asks Stanmer to remain near the ladies while he goes—to give them his care and protection; and he adds that it will be [a] capital occasion for Harold to form an opinion about Miss Vane. He will expect him to be ready with one on his own return—and with this he takes his departure. Harold accepts the charge—rather protesting, but interested in the proposal that is made him. Longueville remains absent three weeks, and in his absence Stanmer attempts to study Bianca Vane. The result of his observations is that he perceives her, as he believes, to be a coquette—that she attempts to engage in a flirtation with him. I think it may be made very interesting here to mark the degree in which Stanmer—curious, imaginative, speculative, audacious, and yet conscientious, and believing quite in his own fair play—permits himself to *experiment* upon Bianca—to endeavor to draw her out and make her, if possible, betray herself. He holds that she does so—she makes a painful impression upon him. Longueville comes back and asks him what he thinks—candidly, literally—of Blanche. Stanmer hesitates; but then tells the simple truth. He thinks she is charming, interesting—but dangerous. She is false—she has tried to entangle him. He tells him, as a friend, what has passed between them. Longueville is greatly affected by it—greatly shocked.

'But after all,' says Stanmer, 'there was no literal infidelity, since she had given you no pledge. She had listened to you, but she had refused you.'

Longueville looks at him a moment. 'She had accepted me. After I had spoken to you—the evening before I went away, I proposed to her again. She then accepted me.'

Stanmer, in a good deal of horror, 'Ah, why didn't you tell me?'

Longueville. 'I'm glad I didn't.'

Stanmer. 'Ah, but my dear fellow.'

Longueville, turning away, 'I'm sorry I didn't!'

And Stanmer learns, the next day, that there has been a rupture; but that it has come from Bianca—not from Longueville. The latter gives him no explanation of it and he is a good deal perturbed. The parties separate; Harold has, on the whole, a certain compassion for Miss Vane; and a certain sense that he has done her an injury.

3. They separate, I say, and Stanmer parts from Longueville, as well [as] from the two ladies, who return to England, to live for a long time in the country, in seclusion. Time elapses and the intimacy of the two men suffers a sensible falling-off. There is no rupture nor quarrel—no acknowledged alteration; but, in fact, something has come between them and they see much less of each other than formerly. At last, at the end of three or four years, Stanmer learns that Longueville is on the point of marrying. The marriage takes place—Stanmer is present. The figure of the bride to be studied—an opposition to Bianca. At the end of a couple of years, Harold hears, and has reason to believe, that Longueville's marriage is not a happy one—though he does not learn it from Longueville himself. Then occurs the great stroke of the story: Stanmer meets Bianca Vane again—in England—and falls violently in love with her. This may be made, I think, both very striking and very natural. She is older—she is still unmarried—she is altered—she is sad. He has the sense of having wronged her—she seems to him deeply touching. His friend's marriage leaves him at liberty to address her, and

she listens to him—accepts him. At this moment, before he has had time to let Longueville know of the situation, they learn that the latter has departed from his wife, who has been cruelly unfaithful to him; and immediately afterwards Longueville turns up. He presents himself—he learns that they are on the point of marrying. Then a terrible sense of outrage, out of the past, comes over him—he breaks out in reproaches against Stanmer, whom he calls the falsest, the most treacherous, of friends. Stanmer vainly protests that he has acted with integrity— that it was with no ulterior or disinterested view that he set his friend against Miss Vane at Baden. He had no love for her at that time—it has all come since—since Longueville's own marriage. But in Longueville the sense of injury—the force of resentment—overmasters every other feeling; he continues to protest—he *forbids* Stanmer the marriage. He discloses that he himself has been *always* in love with her—that he has never ceased to dream of her, to long for her; that only the stubbornness and folly of pride has led into his other, this miserable, union.

Stanmer. 'But married you are, unfortunately, nevertheless! What good would [it] be to you that I should renounce Miss Vane? *You* wouldn't be able to marry her.'

Longueville. 'I shouldn't? You will see!'

Three days afterwards he comes and tells them that he is free—that his wife is dead. Here is a terribly dangerous and delicate point. It is left to be supposed—it is not made definitely clear—that he has himself been the means of his wife's death. (The circumstances of this affair to be determined—most carefully.) Bianca guesses the horrible truth and of course, in bewilderment and terror, repudiates Longueville. But she also, almost as inevitably, breaks with Stanmer and flings herself back into retirement—into a religious life. Stanmer is left with Longueville and with the latter's terrible secret. He watches over them both.—The violence of this denouement does not I think disqualify it. It can, I believe, be made strongly dramatic and natural. There are of course very many details to be studied, and I have said, here, nothing about the character of Blanche, which is of the first importance.

A name: Mrs. Portier.

Mrs. Bullivant. Mrs. Almond.

[This note resulted in *Confidence*, serialized in *Scribner's Monthly* August 1979 to January 1880; published in London (1879) and Cambridge, Mass. (1880).]

December 12th. It has often occurred to me that the following would be an interesting situation.—A man of a certain age (say 48) who has lived and thought, sees a certain situation of his own youth reproduced before his eyes and hesitates between his curiosity to see at what issue it arrives in this particular case and the prompting to interfere, in the light of his own experience, for the benefit of the actors. Mortimer, for instance, goes abroad and in some foreign town he finds the daughter of a lady—the Contessa G.—whom, when he was five and twenty, on a visit to the same place, he had known and fallen in love with. That episode of his youth comes back to him with peculiar vividness—the daughter is a strange, interesting reproduction of the mother: The mother had been a dangerous woman and had entangled him in a flirtation; an unscrupulous charmer—an imperious Circe—on the brink of whose abysmal coquetry he trembled for an hour; or rather for many days. After a great struggle he took himself off, escaped from his danger by flight and breathed more freely. Then he had greatly regretted his discretion— he wished that he might have known what it was to love such a woman. Afterwards, however, he hears things that make him think he has had a great escape. The Contessa G. has an intrigue with another man, with whom, in consequence, her husband fights a duel. The Conte G. is killed and the Countess marries her lover. She is now dead—all this, for Mortimer, is a memory. But her daughter, as I say, strongly resembles her and stirs up in Mortimer's mind the depths of the past. She is a beautiful dangerous coquette. Hovering near her Mortimer finds a young Englishman who is evidently much in love with her, and who seems to Mortimer a sort of reproduction of himself at twenty-five—the image of his own early innocence—his own timid and awkward passion. The young man interests him and he watches the progress of his relations with the lady. They seem to him to correspond at all points with his own relations with the mother—so that at last he determines to warn him and opens his eyes. x x x x x (The above sketch worked out and finished Jan. 17th.—*The Diary of a Man of Fifty.*)

x   x   x   x   x

[*Harper's New Monthly Magazine* and *Macmillan's Magazine* July 1879; published in New York (1880).]

January 18th. [1879]

  A. 'Don't you hate the English?'
  B. 'Hate the English—how?'
  A. 'Don't you hate them as a nation?'
  B. 'Hating a nation is an expensive affair. I have taken too much stock in the human race to be able to do so. I can't afford it. It would ruin me.'
  A. 'Ah, if you regulate your emotions upon economical principles. . . !'

January 22d. I heard some time ago, that Anthony Trollope had a theory that a boy might be brought up to be a novelist as to any other trade. He brought up— or attempted to bring up—his own son on this principle, and the young man became a sheep-farmer, in Australia. The other day Miss Thackeray (Mrs. Ritchie)[1] said to me that she and her husband meant to bring up their little daughter in that way. It hereupon occurred to me (as it has occurred before) that one might make a little story upon this. A literary lady (a poor novelist)—or a poor literary man either—(this to be determined)—gives out to the narrator that this is their intention with regard to their little son or daughter. After this the narrator meets the parent and child at intervals, about the world, for several years—the child's peculiar education being supposed to be coming on. At last, when the child is

1. See 27 February 1889. Anne Isabella Thackeray (1837–1919), novelist-daughter of William Makepeace Thackeray and sister-in-law to Leslie Stephen, married in 1877 her cousin Richmond Ritchie (1854–1912), later the permanent Under Secretary of State for India.

grown, there is another glimpse; the intended novelist has embraced some extremely prosaic situation, which is a comment—a satire—upon the high parental views.

["Greville Fane," *Illustrated London News* September 1892; published in *The Real Thing and Other Tales*, London (1893).]

January 22d. Subject for a ghost-story.

Imagine a door—either walled-up, or that has been long locked—at which there is an occasional knocking—a knocking which—as the other side of the door is inaccessible—can only be ghostly. The occupant of the house or room, containing the door, has long been familiar with the sound; and, regarding it as ghostly, has ceased to heed it particularly—as the ghostly presence remains on the other side of the door, and never reveals itself in other ways. But this person may be imagined to have some great and constant trouble; and it may be observed by another person, relating the story, that the knocking increases with each fresh manifestation of the trouble. He breaks open the door and the trouble ceases—as if the spirit had desired to be admitted, that it might interpose, redeem and protect.[2]

x   x   x   x   x

Another theme of the same kind.

A young girl, unknown to herself, is followed, constantly, by a figure which other persons see. She is perfectly unconscious of it—but there is a dread that she may cease to be so. The figure is that of a young man—and there is a theory that the day that she falls in love, she may suddenly perceive it. Her mother dies, and the narrator of the story then discovers, by finding an old miniature among her letters and papers, that the figure is that of a young man whom she has jilted in her youth, and who therefore committed suicide. The girl *does* fall in love, and sees the figure. She accepts her lover, and never sees it again!

["Sir Edmund Orme," *Black and White* 25 November 1891 (first Christmas issue); published in *The Lesson of the Master*, London and New York (1892).]

January 27th. A story upon some such situation as this. Henry Irving, the actor, broke with the Batemans and got rid of Isabel B. in order to get up *Hamlet* on a great scale, and replace poor Isabel by Ellen Terry,[1] a much more brilliant attraction. Ellen Terry appears with immense *éclat* and the thing is a great success. Isabel lapses into obscurity and is quite forgotten. One may imagine that Ellen Terry falls ill, and that Irving is suddenly in want of a substitute. Casting about for one he bethinks himself of Isabel B.—rejected and wounded, having witnessed

---

2. The closed door and ghostly knocking anticipate "The Jolly Corner" (the *English Review* December 1908) and also the opening of the third chapter of *The Portrait of a Lady*, where Isabel Archer alludes to a ghost. The motif is repeated in the entry for 16 May 1899.

1. John Henry Brodribb Irving (1838–1905), later Sir Henry, eminent British actor and theater manager. The Bateman sisters, Kate (1843–1917), Virginia (1853–1940), and Isabel (1854–1934), American actresses, appeared on both sides of the Atlantic. Virginia (Mrs. Edward Compton) played Mme de Cintré in HJ's *The American*, Kate was Mme de Bellegarde in the play's London production. Ellen Terry (1848–1928), famous British actress, later Dame Ellen.

the triumph of the other, and brooding over her wrong. Suppose then that, after a short struggle with her wounded pride, she responds to Irving's appeal—she sacrifices her resentment—makes herself little—and resumes the part in which Ellen T. has so completely effaced her. The sacrifice is an heroic one—that of a woman's most passionate personal vanity. Explanation and revelation—because she is secretly in love with the great actor. These *circumstances* might easily be changed; the idea, otherwise arranged, would remain the special sort of sacrifice made by a woman—and its motive.

January 27th. A story told in letters[2] written alternately by a mother and her daughter and giving totally different accounts of the same situation. The mother and daughter are closely united—there has never been a shadow between them. Both are very gentle and refined—and each is very subtle and resolute. Both also are highly conscientious. The girl is devoutly in love with a young man who is also in love with her—though no declarations or confessions have passed between them. The young man at last makes known his feelings to the mother and asks leave to pay his suit. The mother, thinking him an undesirable match, refuses consent, assuring him and herself that the girl doesn't care for him. He declares that she does—that he feels it, knows it; but the mother insists that she knows her daughter best, that she has watched her, studied her; that the girl is perfectly fancy-free. And she makes up [her] mind to this—desiring and determined to believe it. The young man writes to the girl—three times; and the mother intercepts the letters. The girl, suspecting nothing of this, cherishes her secret passion, and keeps up, out of pride and modesty, that appearance which confirms her mother's theory of her indifference. Mutual attitude of the mother and daughter, with this secret between them and yet with their apparent affection for each other unchanged. Attitude of the daughter in particular, desirious not to *pain* her mother.

x   x   x   x   x

February 21st. Mrs. Kemble[1] told me last evening the history of her brother H.'s engagement to Miss T. H.K. was a young ensign in a marching regiment, very handsome ('beautiful') said Mrs. K., but very luxurious and selfish, and without a penny to his name. Miss T. was a dull, plain, common-place girl, only daughter of the Master of King's Coll., Cambridge, who had a handsome private fortune (£4000 a year). She was very much in love with H.K., and was of that slow, sober, dutiful nature that an impression once made upon her, was made forever. Her father disapproved strongly (and justly) of the engagement and informed her that if she married young K. he would not leave her a penny of his money. It was only in her money that H. was interested; he wanted a rich wife who would enable

2. HJ published two epistolary stories: "A Bundle of Letters" in the *Parisian* December 1879, included in *The Diary of A Man of Fifty;* and "The Point of View" in the *Century Magazine* December 1882, included in *The Siege of London,* Boston (1883). Neither story develops the theme sketched here. See last item, 16 March 1879.

1. Frances Anne Kemble (1809–93), actress and writer, had been divorced by her husband, the Georgia planter and slave owner Pierce Butler. She met HJ in Rome in 1873; they remained close friends to her death.

him to live at his ease and pursue his pleasures. Miss T. was in much tribulation and she asked Mrs. K. what she would advise her to do—Henry K. having taken the ground that if she would hold on and marry him the old Doctor would after a while relent and they should get the money. (It was in this belief that he was holding on to her.) Mrs. K. advised the young girl by *no means* to marry her brother. 'If your father does relent and you are well off, he will make you a kindly enough husband, so long as all goes well. But if he should not, and you were to be poor, your lot would be miserable. *Then* my brother would be a very uncomfortable companion—*then* he would visit upon you his disappointment and discontent.' Miss T. reflected a while; and then, as she was much in love with [him], she determined to disobey her father and take the consequences. Meanwhile H.K., however, had come to the conclusion that the father's forgiveness was not to be counted upon—that his attitude was very firm and that if they should marry, he would never see the money. *Then* all his effort was to disentangle himself. He went off, shook himself free of the engagement, let the girl go. She was deeply wounded—they separated. Some few years elapsed—her father died and she came into his fortune. She never received the addresses of another man—she always cared in secret for Henry K.—but she was determined to remain unmarried. K. lived about the world in different military stations, and at last, at the end of 10 years (or more), came back to England—still a handsome, selfish, impecunious soldier. One of his other sisters (Mrs. S.)[2] then attempted to bring on the engagement again—knowing that Miss T. still cared for him. She tried to make Mrs. K. join her in this undertaking, but the latter refused, saying that it was an ignoble speculation and that her brother had forfeited every claim to being thought well of by Miss T. But K. again, on his own responsibility, paid his addresses to Miss T. She refused him—it was too late. And yet, said Mrs. K., she cared for him—and she would have married no other man. But H.K.'s selfishness had over-reached itself and this was the retribution of time.

[*Washington Square, Cornhill Magazine* June–November 1880 and *Harper's New Monthly Magazine* December 1880; published in New York (1880) and London (1881).]

Names. Mrs. Parlour—Mrs. Sturdy—Silverlock—Dexter Frere—Dovedale.

In a story, some one says—'Oh yes, the United States—a country without a sovereign, without a court, without a nobility, without an army, without a church or a clergy, without a diplomatic service, without a picturesque peasantry, without palaces or castles, or country seats, or ruins, without a literature, without novels, without an Oxford or a Cambridge, without cathedrals or ivied churches, without latticed cottages or village ale-houses, without political society, without sport, without fox-hunting or country gentlemen, without an Epsom or an Ascot, an Eton or a Rugby. . . !!'[3]

2. Henry Kemble (1812–57) met Mary Anne Thackeray, daughter of George Thackeray of King's College, Cambridge (no kin to the novelist), in Germany in 1830. He returned to England in 1850 to resume his suit of Mary Anne, who refused him. Mrs. Edward Sartoris ("Mrs. S."), née Adelaide Kemble (1816–79), sister of Fanny and Henry, was a successful operatic diva.

3. HJ incorporated this list of social "absences" almost verbatim in his critical biography of Hawthorne (1880) to illustrate items lacking in American life for the novelist of manners.

March 16th. The figure of an American woman (in London), young, pretty, charming, clever, ambitious and conscious of her merits, desiring immensely to get into society, but handicapped by a common, vulgar, *impossible* husband. Her struggles—her appeals to the American minister, etc. (Mrs. H.L.)

A subject—The Count G. in Florence (Mme T.[1] told me the other night) married an American girl, Miss F., whom he neglected for other women, to whom he was constantly making love. She, very fond of him, tried to console herself by flirting with other men; but she couldn't do it—it was not in her—she broke down in the attempt. This might be related from the point of view of one of the men whom she selects for this purpose and who really cares for her. Her caprices, absences, preoccupations, etc.—her sadness, her mechanical, perfunctory way of doing it—then her suddenly breaking it off and letting him see that she has a horror of him—he meanwhile being very innocent and devoted.

Names. Dainty—Slight—Cloake—Beauchemin—Lord Demesne.

Description of a situation, or incident, in an alternation of letters, written from an aristocratic, and a democratic, point of view;—both enlightened and sincere.[2]

Names. Osmond—Rosier—Mr. and Mrs. Match—Name for husband in *P. of L.:* Gilbert Osmond—Raymond Gyves—Mrs. Gift—Name in *Times:* Lucky Da Costa— Name in Knightsbridge: Tagus Shout—Other names: Couch—Bonnycastle—Theory—Cridge—Arrant—Mrs. Tippet—Noad.

P. of a L.[1] After Isabel's marriage there are *five* more instalments, and the success of the whole story greatly depends upon this portion being well conducted or not. Let me then make the most of it—let me imagine the best. There has been a want of action in the earlier part, and it may be made up here. The elements that remain are in themselves, I think, very interesting, and they only need to be strongly and happily combined. The weakness of the whole story is that it is too exclusively psychological—that it depends to[o] little on incident; but the complete unfolding of the situation that is established by Isabel's marriage may nonetheless be quite sufficiently dramatic. The idea of the whole thing is that the poor girl, who has dreamed of freedom and nobleness, who has done, as she believes, a generous, natural, clear-sighted thing, finds herself in reality ground in the very mill of the conventional. After a year or two of marriage the antagonism between her nature and Osmond's comes out—the open opposition of a noble character and a narrow one. There is a great deal to do here in a small compass; every word, therefore, must tell—every touch must count. If the last five parts of the story appear crowded, this will be rather a good defect in consideration of the perhaps too great diffuseness of the earlier portion. Isabel awakes from her sweet delusion—oh, the art

---

1. Madame Nikolai Turgeneff, widow of a Russian political exile and a distant relative of Ivan Turgenev. See *Letters* II, 27–30.
2. See 27 January 1879. This idea was developed in "The Point of View."

---

1. This undated sketch for the long last section of *The Portrait of a Lady* was probably written in late December 1880 or early January 1881. There would be six (not five) more installments after Isabel's marriage. The preceding list of names is of some months earlier—perhaps late summer 1880.

required for making this delusion natural!—and finds herself face to face with a husband who has ended by conceiving a hatred for her own larger qualities. These facts, however, are not in themselves sufficient; the situation must be marked by important events. Such an event is the discovery of the relation that has existed between Osmond and Madame Merle, the discovery that she has married Madame Merle's lover. Madame Merle, in a word, is the mother of Pansy. Edward Rosier comes to Rome, falls in love with Pansy and wants to marry her; but Osmond opposes the marriage, on the ground of Rosier's insufficient means. Isabel favours Pansy—she sees that Rosier would make her an excellent husband, be tenderly devoted and kind to her—but Osmond absolutely forbids the idea. Lord Warburton comes to Rome, sees Isabel again and declares to her that he is resigned, that he has succeeded in accepting the fact of her marriage and that he is not disposed, himself, to marry. He makes the acquaintance of Pansy, is charmed with her, and at last tells Isabel that he should like to make her his wife. Isabel is almost shocked, for she distrusts this sentiment of Lord Warburton's; and the reader must feel that she mistrusts it justly. This same sentiment is a very ticklish business. It is honest up to a certain point; but at bottom, without knowing it, Lord W.'s real motive is the desire to be near Isabel whom he sees, now, to be a disappointed, and unhappy woman. This is what Isabel has perceived; she feels that it would [be] cruel to Pansy, dangerous to herself, to allow such a marriage—for which, however, there are such great material inducements that she cannot well oppose it. Her position is a most difficult one, for by begging Lord Warburton to desist she only betrays her apprehension of him—which is precisely what she wishes not to do. Besides, she is afraid of doing a wrong to Pansy. Madame Merle, meanwhile, has caught a glimpse of Warburton's state of mind and eagerly takes up the idea of his marrying the girl. Pansy is very much in love with Rosier—she has no wish to marry Lord W. Isabel is [so] convinced at last of this that she feels absolved from considering her prospects with Lord W. and treats the latter with such coldness that he feels the vanity of hope and withdraws from the field, having indeed not paid any direct attention to Pansy, whom he cannot in the least be accused of jilting. Madame Merle, very angry at his withdrawal, accuses Isabel of having dissuaded him, out of jealousy, because of his having been an old lover of hers and her wishing to keep him for herself; and she still opposes the marriage with Rosier, because she has been made to believe by Lord Warburton's attentions that Pansy may do something much more brilliant. Isabel resents Madame Merle's interference, demands of her what she has to do with Pansy. Whereupon Madame Merle, in whose breast the suppressed feeling of maternity has long been rankling, and who is passionately jealous of Isabel's influence over Pansy, breaks out with the cry that she alone has a right—that Pansy is her daughter. (To be settled later whether this revelation is to be made by Mme Merle herself, or by the Countess Gemini. Better on many grounds that it should be the latter; and yet in that way I lose the 'great scene' between Madame Merle and Isabel.) In any event this whole matter of Mme Merle is (like Lord W.'s state of mind about Pansy) a very ticklish one—very delicate and difficult to handle. To make it natural that she should have brought about Isabel's marriage to her old lover—this is in itself a supreme difficulty. It is not, however, an impossibility, for I honestly believe it rests upon nature. Her old interest in Osmond remains in a modified form; she wishes to do something for him, and she does it through another rather than by herself. That, I think, is perfectly natural. As regards Pansy the strangeness of her conduct is greater; but we must remember that we see only its surface—we don't see her reasoning. Isabel has money, and Mme Merle has great confidence in her benevolence, in her generosity; she has no fear that she will be a harsh stepmother, and she believes she will push the fortunes of the child she herself is unable to avow and afraid openly to patronize. In all this Osmond sinks a little into the background—but one must get the sense of Isabel's exquisitely miserable revulsion. Three years have passed—time enough for it to have taken place. His worldliness, his deep snobbishness, his want of generosity, etc.; his hatred of her when he finds that she judges him, that she morally protests at so much that surrounds her. The uncleanness of the air; the Countess Gemini's lovers, etc. Caspar Goodwood of course must reappear, and Ralph, and Henrietta; Mrs. Touchett, too, for a moment. Ralph's helpless observation of Isabel's deep misery; her determination to show him nothing, and his inability to help her. This to be a strong feature in the situation. Pansy is sent back to the convent, to be kept from Rosier. Caspar Goodwood comes to Rome, because he has heard from Henrietta that Isabel is unhappy, and Isabel sends him away. She hears from Ralph at Gardencourt, that he is ill there (Ralph, himself), that indeed he is dying. (The letter to come from Mrs. Touchett who is with him; or even it would be well that it should be a telegram; it expresses Ralph's wish to see her.) Isabel tells Osmond she wishes to go; Osmond, jealously and nastily, forbids it; and Isabel, deeply distressed and embarrassed, hesitates. Then Madame Merle, who wishes her to make a *coup de tête,* to leave Osmond, so that she may be away from Pansy, reveals to her her belief that it was Ralph who induced her father to leave her the £70,000. Isabel, then, violently affected and overcome, starts directly for England. She reaches Ralph at Gardencourt, and finds Caspar Goodwood and Henrietta also there: i.e., in London. Ralph's death—Isabel's return to London, and interview with Caspar G.—His passionate outbreak; he beseeches her to return with him to America. She is greatly moved, she feels the full force of his devotion—to which she has never done justice; but she refuses. She starts again for Italy—and her departure is the climax and termination of the story.

x   x   x   x   x

With strong handling it seems to me that it may all be very true, very powerful, very touching. The obvious criticism of course will be that it is not finished—that I have not seen the heroine to the end of her situation—that I have left her *en l'air.*—This is both true and false. The *whole* of anything is never told; you can only take what groups together. What I have done has that unity—it groups together. It is complete in itself—and the rest may be taken up or not, later.

—I am not sure that it would not be best that the exposure of Mme Merle should never be complete, and above all that she should not denounce herself. This would injure very much the impression I have wished to give of her profundity, her self-control, her regard for appearances. It may be enough that Isabel should believe the fact in question—in consequence of what the Countess Gemini has told her. Then, when Madame Merle tells her of what Ralph has done for her of old—tells it with the view I have mentioned to precipitating her defiance of Osmond—Isabel may charge her with the Countess G.'s secret. This Madame Merle will deny— but deny in such a way that Isabel knows she lies; and *then* Isabel may depart.— The last (October) installment to take place wholly in England. At the very last Caspar Goodwood goes to Pratt's hotel, and is told that Mrs. Osmond has left it the night before. Later in the day he sees Henrietta who has the last word—utters the last line of the story: a characteristic characterization of Isabel.

[The novel ran in *Macmillan's Magazine* (fourteen installments) October 1880 to November 1881 and the *Atlantic Monthly* November 1880 to December 1881; published in three volumes, London, in one volume, New York (1881).]

January 17th, 1881. I heard an allusion yesterday to a matter in the history of Mme de Sévigné, which suggested the germ of a story. Mrs. Ritchie (Thackeray), who has been writing a little book about her, was mentioning her unbecoming conduct in siding with her daughter against the poor little *demoiselle de Grignan*, who was being forced into a convent, because her father, during her minority, had spent all her property and didn't wish to have to give an account of it. (It was more probably her stepfather: I don't remember.) This suggested to me a situation; unfortunately the convent has to come into it, and the convent is rather threadbare. The guardian or trustee of a young girl—he might be a distant blood-relation— has charge of her property for some time and perverts it to his own use, so that it is impossible to render it up when she comes of age or to give a faithful account of his stewardship. He tries to make her go into a convent (whereby however he would not really [be] absolved from handing in his accounts)—so that he shall be rid of her and of the danger of her making a noise. To his surprise—though he has strong reason to believe that she suspects his infidelity (she must be yet in her minority), she consents with great meekness—with a peculiar kind of sadness and sweetness that touch him. They touch him so much—her want of resentment and readiness to forgive him are so affecting—that, combined with his sense of having wronged her, they produce a great commotion in his mind, the result of which is a sudden consciousness that he has fallen in love with her. He then tries to keep her from executing her step, from retiring from the world; beseeches and implores her not to do so. But she persists, with the same sad gentleness, and turns away from him forever. Then he discovers that she had been in love with him and that her love had made her eager to forgive the wrong he had done her, and to forego all reparation. But his dishonourable act had made her also blush for her passion and desire to bury it in the cloister.[1]

---

1. Mrs. Ritchie's study of Mme de Sévigné (1626–96), née Marie de Rabutin-Chantal, famous French letter writer, was published in 1881. The "demoiselle de Grignan" was Mme de Sévigné's granddaughter Marie Blanche (b. 1670), whose profligate father, the Comte de Grignan (1632–1714), was quite capable of squandering her patrimony. See 30 May 1883.

January 18th, 1881. Mrs. T., living in America (say at Newport), has a son, young, unmarried, clever and selfish, who persists in living in Europe, and whom she therefore sees only at long intervals. He prefers European life, and takes his filial duties very lightly. She goes out to see him from time to time, but dares not fix herself permanently near him, for fear of boring him. At last, however, he comes home, to pay a short visit, and all her desire is to induce him to remain with her for some months. She has reason to believe that he will grow very tired of her quiet house; and in order to enhance its attraction she invites a young girl— a distant relative, from another part of the country—to stay with her. She has not the least desire that her son shall fall in love, seriously, with the girl; and does not believe that he will—being of a cold and volatile disposition and having a connection with some woman abroad. She simply thinks that the girl will make the house pleasant, and her son will stay the longer. That *she* may be sacrificed— that is, that *she* may become too much interested in the son, is an idea which she does not allow to stand in her way. The son arrives, is very pleasant for a week— then very much bored and disposed to depart. He stays a while longer, however, at the mother's urgency, and then does become interested in the girl. The latter, who is very intelligent and observant, has become aware of the part that she has been intended to play, and, after a little, has enough of it and departs. The son meanwhile is seriously in love; he follows the girl, leaves his mother alone, and spends the rest of the time that he is in America in vainly besieging the affections of the young lady—so that the mother, as a just retribution, loses his society almost altogether. The girl refuses him, and he returns in disgust and dudgeon to Europe, where he marries the other person, before-mentioned, while the mother is left lamenting!—The subject is rather trivial, but I think that something might be made of it. If the denouement just suggested appears too harsh, it may be supposed that the girl at last accedes to the son's passion and that he marries her— the separation from his mother being none the less complete. The story may be told as a journal of the mother.[1]

'As to myself, I have learned to be cosmopolitan, but I cannot shake off the feeling that the Latin races need no longer to be reckoned with, even if they should conquer the world, which they won't.'
                    E. Gryzanowski to W.J.,[1] Livorno, December 18th, 1882.

'English things and ways don't impress me nearly as much as they did three years ago. England is all clogged and stuffed with the great load of superfluities, the

---

1. See 30 May 1883.
1. Dr. E. Gryzanowsky (or Grisanowski), a former diplomat of Polish extraction and German education, professor of his own peripatetic medical school in Rome, Pisa, and Leghorn; in Florence a neighbor of Francis Boott, two of whose nephews (Edward Loring and Frank Greenough) had been Gryzanowsky's students until the Civil War. He married a Miss Wright of Exeter, England. William James, HJ's elder brother (1842–1910), the psychologist and philosopher of pragmatism, had taken a year's leave of absence from Harvard—just after the birth of his second son—to meet with fellow psychologists in Europe.

great rubbish-heap and sweepings of centuries that she drags after her, smeared in the fog and smoke. All other nations seem so light and intelligent in the Balance.'

W.J., Letter to his wife, from London, December 22nd, 1882.

'I must on Saturday save my life by escaping to Paris. Never did a place seem to agree with me less than London, strange to say. I like the people more and more. Of all the *Kunst-produkte* of this globe the exquisitely and far-fetchedly fashioned structure called the English Race and Temperament is the most precious. I should think a poor Frenchman would behold with a kind of frenzy the easy and genial way in which it solves, or achieves without needing to solve, all those things which are for his unfortunate people the impossible.'

W.J., London, January 22nd, 1883.

À *propos* of Sarah B. in Sardou's *Fédora:*

'She is a wonderful creature, but how a being as intelligent as she can so elaborate what has so little moral stuff in it to work upon, I don't comprehend. The play is hard, and sinister, and horrible, without being in the least degree tragic or pathetic: one felt like an accomplice in some cold-blooded bit of cruelty when it was over. I feel like giving up the French and calling to my own species to stand from under and let their fate overtake them. Such a disproportionate development of the external perceptions and such a perversion of the natural feelings, must work its nemesis in some way.'[1]

W.J., Paris, February 19th, 1883.

Boston, April 8th, 1883. I transcribe here part of a letter I have just written to J. R. Osgood, my publisher, in regard to a new novel.

'The scene of the story is laid in Boston and its neighborhood; it relates an episode connected with the so-called "woman's movement." The characters who figure in it are for the most part persons of the radical reforming type, who are especially interested in the emancipation of women, giving them the suffrage, releasing them from bondage, co-educating them with men, etc. They regard this as the great question of the day—the most urgent and sacred reform. The heroine is a very clever and "gifted" young woman, associated by birth and circumstances with a circle immersed in these views and in every sort of new agitation, daughter of old abolitionists, spiritualists, transcendentalists, etc. She herself takes an interest in the cause; but she is an object of still greater interest to her family and friends, who have discovered in her a remarkable natural talent for public speaking by which they believe her capable of moving large audiences and rendering great aid in the liberation of her sex. They cherish her, as a kind of apostle and redeemer. She is very pleasing to look upon, and her gift for speaking is a

1. Sarah Bernhardt (1844–1923), star of the French stage. HJ wrote to Grace Norton: "I regard her as the great humbug of the age" (*Letters* II, 324). He incorporated WJ's comment in his essay on Pierre Loti; see *LA* III, 482–505. Victorien Sardou (1831–1908), French dramatist admired by HJ, and *Fédora*, his play of 1882.

kind of inspiration. She has a dear and intimate friend, another young woman, who, issuing from a totally different social circle (a rich conservative exclusive family), has thrown herself into these questions with intense ardour and has conceived a passionate admiration for our young girl, over whom, by the force of a completely different character, she has acquired a great influence. She has money of her own, but no talent for appearing in public and she has a dream that her friend and she together (one by the use of her money and the other by her eloquence) may, working side by side, really revolutionize the condition of women. She regards this as a noble and aspiring task, a mission to which everything else should be sacrificed, and she counts implicitly on her friend. The latter, however, makes the acquaintance of a young man who falls in love with her and in whom she also becomes much interested, but who, being of a hard-headed and conservative disposition, is resolutely opposed to female suffrage and all similar alterations. The more he sees of the heroine the more he loves her, and the more determined he is to get her out of the clutches of her reforming friends, whom he utterly abominates. He asks her to marry him, and does not conceal from her that if she does so, she must entirely give up her "mission." She feels that she loves him, but that the sacrifice of the said mission would be terrible, and that the disappointment inflicted on her family and friends, and especially on the rich young woman, would be worse. Her lover is a distant relative of the rich young woman, who in an evil hour, by accident, and before she was acquainted with his opinions (he has been spending ten years in the West) has introduced him. She appeals to her friend to stand firm—appeals in the name of their intimate friendship and of all the hopes that are centred on the young girl's head. The tale relates the struggle that takes place in the mind of the latter. The struggle ends, after various vicissitudes, with her letting everything go, breaking forever with her friend, in a terrible final interview, and giving herself up to her lover. There are to be several other characters whom I have not mentioned—types of radical agitators—and as many little pictures as I can introduce of the woman's rights agitation.'—So much to Osgood.[1] I must return to this, with more details. The subject is strong and good, with a large rich interest. The relation of the two girls should be a study of one of those friendships between women which are so common in New England. The whole thing as local, as American, as possible, and as full of Boston: an attempt to show that I *can* write an American story. There must, indispensably, be a type of newspaper man—the man whose ideal is the energetic reporter. I should like to *bafouer* the vulgarity and hideousness of this—the impudent invasion of privacy—the extinction of all conception of privacy, etc. Dau-

1. The letter continues: "I propose that the story shall be of the length of 150 pages of the 'Atlantic'; and I desire to receive $4500 for it. (This means that I shall definitely make it of the length of what I called six 'parts.' I first spoke of five, that is 125 pages of the 'Atlantic.') As regards the period at which I should be able to give it (or the greater part of it) to the printers, I am afraid that November first is the earliest date. The reason of this is partly that I wish to write something else first; and this other production I shall also make the subject of a proposal to you which I here subjoin [see note 3 below]." See Caroline Ticknor, *Glimpses of Authors* (Boston and New York, 1922), 248. On Osgood's bankruptcy and HJ's subsequent financial dilemma, see *Life* 314. See also entries for 6 August 1884, August to September 1884, and 10 August 1885.

det's *Évangéliste*[2] has given me the idea of this thing. If I could only do something with that *pictorial* quality! At any rate, the subject is very national, very typical. I wished to write a very *American* tale, a tale very characteristic of our social conditions, and I asked myself what was the most salient and peculiar point in our social life. The answer was: the situation of women, the decline of the sentiment of sex, the agitation on their behalf. x x x x x

[*The Bostonians*, serialized in *Century Magazine* February 1885 to February 1886; published in London and New York (1886).]

x x x x x In this same letter to Osgood, I gave a sketch of the plan of a short story of the 'international' family (like *Daisy Miller*, the *Siege of London*, etc.). 'The name of the thing to be *Lady Barberina* I have already treated (more or less) the subject of the American girl who marries (or concerning whom it is a question whether she *will* marry) a British aristocrat. This story reverses the situation and presents a young *male* American who conceives the design of marrying a daughter of the aristocracy. He is a New Yorker, a good deal of an Anglomaniac and a "dude"; and as he has a good deal of money she accepts him and they are united. The 1st half of the tale goes on in England. In the 2d the parties are transported to New York, whither he has brought his bride, and it relates their adventures there, the impressions made and received by the lady, and the catastrophe.' So much to Osgood.—I think something very good might be made of this—I see it quite vividly.[3]

A good (American) comparison: 'As . . . and as silent as a chiropodist.'

["The Siege of London," *Cornhill Magazine* January–February 1883; reprinted in *The Siege of London*. "Lady Barberina," *Century Magazine* May–July 1884; reprinted in *Tales of Three Cities*, London (1884). In volume XIV of the New York edition the title is changed to "Barbarina."]

---

2. Alphonse Daudet (1840–97), French novelist and friend of HJ; *L'Évangéliste* appeared in 1883.
3. The full text of the continuation (as given in Ticknor, 248–49): "I wish to write before beginning the novel above described another 'international episode'; i.e., a story of the same length and character as 'Daisy Miller,' the 'International Episode,' and the 'Siege of London' (the length to be that of two installments of the 'Cornhill'—the form in which those other tales appeared). The name to be 'Lady Barberina.' I have treated (more or less) in these other things the subject of the American girl who marries (or concerning whom it is a question whether she will marry) a British aristocrat. This one reverses the situation and presents a young male American who conceives the design of marrying a daughter of the aristocracy. He is a New Yorker, a good deal of an Anglomaniac and a 'dude,' and as he has a good deal of money she accepts him and they are united. The first half of the tale takes place in England, and in the second the parties are transported to New York, whither he has brought his bride, and it relates their adventures there, the impressions made and received by the lady, and the catastrophe. I don't know exactly the relation of the 'Atlantic' page to that of the 'Cornhill'; but I call it roughly (about) 50 pages of the 'Atlantic.' I will give you this to do what you choose with (reprint etc.), for $1000. And that you may conveniently reprint it, I will undertake to furnish you later with two short stories, of the length of the 'Pension Beaurepas' and the 'Point of View,' which could make up a volume with it. I should propose to include in this volume the little story (reprinted some time ago in England) entitled 'Four Meetings,' which I spoke of to you the other day when I said that it might have appeared with the 'Siege of London.' "

Lady Barberina: Notes.   *(May 17th, 1883)*

He must be a young physician, the youth who marries the earl's daughter, for that will be very national and typical. It is only here that the son of a rich man—of a man as rich as his father—would have entered that profession, and that the profession itself is capable of being considered 'rather aristocratic.' His father leaves him a great fortune—but he is still 'Doctor Jeune' (say). He doesn't practice but he cares for medicine, and is very generous and beneficient to the suffering poor. He has a brother who is vulgar, and a mother who is charming; and the relations of these two with Lady Barberina after she gets to N.Y. are of course a feature in the story. Lady B.'s expectation of going before Mrs. Jeune (her mother-in-law, etc.). Of course the difficulty will [be] to make the marriage natural: but this difficulty is inspiring. On her part (Lady B.'s) his large fortune will go far toward explaining it. She is not a beauty, though a very fine creature, and she has no fortune to help her to marry in England. She is twenty-six years old, her father is a poor peer, and she has four sisters and five brothers. Her mother thinks that for her to marry a rich man *là-bas* will be a *pied à l'étrier* for the rest of the brood—that the boys in particular, some of them yet young, will be accommodated with ranches and monied wives in the U.S.—Besides Barberina likes the young man, and he must be made attractive. The novelty, the change, takes her fancy, everything American is so the fashion. The 'Dr.' is a big dose to swallow; and I think I must concede that, in London, as he has quite ceased to practice, he doesn't put forward the title. It is only after she is married and reaches New York that she finds every one giving it to him—his own brother always calling [him by] it, etc. One of her sisters, by the way, must come with them to America, and must be recommended as liking it awfully. She must marry a poor young man: a handsome minister of N.Y. The thing is to make the marriage with Lady B. seem natural and possible to my hero, without making him appear snobbish. But it surely can be done. To begin with, there is nothing in life to prevent him from falling in love with her. She must strike him as a splendid young woman—responding completely to his ideal of physical completeness, happy development, perfect health, etc., for all of which he must have an immense appreciation. He must be a great admirer of the physique of [the] English race and think her a beautiful specimen of it. He is a little fellow himself—not a physique which he wishes to perpetuate *telle quelle;* but very cool, very deliberate, very obstinate, and very much attached to his own ideas: opposition always puts him on his mettle; and his marriage to Lady B. is opposed. It is a point that *his* friends and relations, some of them, think it as strange that he should wish to marry her, as hers do that she should unite herself to him. He declines to see *why* it should be difficult for him to marry any woman in the world whom he may fancy; and he is really urged to prosecute his suit by the determination that she *shall* find it natural and comfortable. Damn it, if he fancies an earl's daughter he will have an earl's daughter. The attitude of his mother to be defined, and the details of the episode in New York worked out. Then the *entrée en matière* in London. He must have a pair of confidants there, who bring him accidentally into relation with Lady B., and who watch his proceedings with amusement and dread. In addition to this he must have a friend—a Boston M.D. (of the type of J.P.).

'The self-made girl'—a very good subject for a short story. Very modern, very local; much might be done.[1]

May 30th, 1883. I have promised to furnish three short stories to Osgood (for the *Century*); and Gilder[1] now writes me that they want the two shorter ones first, before *Lady Barberina,* which I had begun and half finished. I have written to him that I will keep back this, and send him the little ones as soon as possible. Accordingly, I must select my tales—my subjects. A short time since I thought of a sufficiently picturesque little *donnée* which I was to call *The Impressions of a Cousin.*[2] It is a modification of the thing suggested to me some time ago by Miss Thackeray and chronicled here—the history of the little *demoiselle de Grignan* who was forced into a convent because her father or stepfather didn't wish to give an account of his false stewardship of her property. I won't go into the details of it here: sufficient that the false trustee here is a gentleman with whom the young girl owning the property is (very secretly) in love; and that his wish is to get her to marry his stepbrother who has a fortune of his own; so that the couple will not insist upon an exposure which will ruin him—deterred therefrom by near relationship, family pride, etc. The girl refuses the cousin absolutely, yet insists on no exposure, and puts up in silence with the injury she has suffered. Her trustee thus, *à qui ceci donne à penser,* discovers that she has loved *him* for three years and that if he had not been such an ass *he* might have married her and enjoyed her property honestly. Now she knows what he has done, she won't prosecute—but of course she can't marry him in his dishonour and she doesn't go into a convent (my tale is too modern); but she retires, as it were, from the world with her property, her wound and her secret. The 'Cousin' of the title is a young woman who relates the story (in the form of a journal), living with her kinswoman as a companion, observing these events and guessing the secret. It is only in her journal that the secret 'transpires.' She herself of course to be a 'type.' I thought of infusing a little American local colour into it by making the story take place in New York and representing the Cousin as a Bostonian, with the Boston moral tone, etc. But that would be pale—the heroine living in 37th St., etc. The New York streets are fatal to the imagination. At all events, I have lost my fancy for the theme, which is rather thin and conventional, and wanting in actuality. Actuality must be my line at present. I may work it with infinite profit. The thing is to do so!

[''Impressions of a Cousin,'' *Century Magazine* November–December 1883; reprinted in *Tales of Three Cities.* The third story is ''A New England Winter,'' *Century Magazine* August–September 1884; reprinted in *Tales of Three Cities.*]

1. See 29 January 1884.

1. Richard Watson Gilder (1844–1909), assistant editor of *Scribner's Monthly* after 1870; when it was succeeded by the *Century* in 1881 he remained as editor until his death.

2. See 17 January 1881 and 18 January 1881.

London, January 2d, 1884.

Names. Daintry—Vandeleur—Grunlus—*Christian names:* Florimond—Ambrose—Mathias—*Surnames:* Benyon—Pinder—Vallance—Nugent—Maze—Dinn—Fiddler—Higgs. Most of them are out of the *Times* of the above date. Very rich.—*Chancellor—Ambient.*

January 29th, 1884. I heard the other day at Mrs. Tennant's[1] of a situation which struck me as dramatic and a pretty subject. The story was told of young Lord Stafford, son of the Duke of Sutherland. It appears he has been for years in love with Lady Grosvenor whom he knew before her marriage to Lord G. He had no expectation of being able to marry her, however, her husband being a young, robust man of his own age, etc. Yielding to family pressure on the subject of taking a wife, he offered his hand to a young, charming, innocent girl, the daughter of Lord Rosslyn. He was gratefully accepted, and the engagement was announced. Suddenly, a very short time after this, and without any one's expecting it, Lord Grosvenor dies and his wife becomes free.[2] The question came up—'What was Lord S. to do?'—to stick to the girl—or to get rid of her in the best way he could and—after a decent interval—present himself to Lady G.? The question, as a matter of ethics, seems to me to have but one answer; if he had offered marriage to Miss Rosslyn (or whatever her name) by that offer he should abide. But the situation might make, as I say, a story, capable of several different turns, according to the character of the actors. The young man may give up Miss R. and betake himself to Lady G., who may then refuse him, on account of his having done an act she deems dishonourable. Or Miss R., guessing or learning the truth, may sacrifice herself, and liberate him of her own free will. Or she may still, knowing the truth, cling to him because she loves him, because she cannot give him up, and because she knows that Lady G. has refused to marry him. (I use these initials simply as convenient signs—knowing nothing of the people.) This attitude Miss R. may maintain until she meets Lady G., when a revulsion may take place, born simply of her fears. She may feel, as the impression of the older more brilliant woman is stamped upon her, that though the latter refuses to marry him at the cost of his tergiversation, she *must* be queen of his thoughts and will finally end by becoming his mistress. A conviction of this—a real presentiment of it—may take possession of her; so that she renounces her brilliant marriage, her noble suitor, rather than face this danger. There is another line which one may imagine another sort of girl taking: a girl, ambitious, tenacious, *volontière,*[3] unscrupulous, even slightly cynical. The state of things becomes apparent to her—

---

1. Née Gertrude Collier (b. 1819), daughter of a naval attaché at the British Embassy in France, Mrs. Tennant met Flaubert in the 1840s; their association was resumed in 1876 and continued to the end of his life. HJ met Mrs. Tennant and her daughter, "Dolly," in 1877.

2. Sibell Mary Lumley, youngest daughter of the ninth Earl of Scarborough, first married Lord Grosvenor, eldest son of the first Duke of Westminster; he died in 1884. That year Lord Stafford married Lady Millicent Fanny St. Claire Erskine, daughter of the fourth Earl of Rosslyn. Sibell Lady Grosvenor married the Right Honorable George Wyndham (1863–1913) in 1887.

3. A slip of the pen on HJ's part: the word is *"volontaire."*

she *has* to recognize that her suitor would give millions to break off his engagement. But she says, 'No, I won't give you up, I can't, it would kill me, for I have set my heart on everything that a marriage with you would bring me—But I don't ask for your affection—if I hold you to our betrothal, I leave you free in conduct. Let me be your wife, bear your name, your coronet, enjoy your wealth and splendour; but devote yourself to Lady G. as much as you like—make her your mistress, if you will. I will shut my eyes—I will make no scandal.'—If I were a Frenchman or a naturalist, this is probably the treatment I should adopt.— These things all deal with the matter from the point of view of the girl. As I began by saying, the quandary of the man is dramatically interesting; and one may imagine more than one issue, though only one is rigidly honourable. Lord S. may determine to stick to the girl. He may resist the temptation and he may have a frank understanding with Lady G. about it; in which she (in love with him) even adds to the height of his own lofty view of the matter, agrees that they must give each other up, that he *must* marry Miss R. and that he and she (Lady G.) must see each other in future as little as possible. The girl, in this, remains innocent and unconscious, but the light of the pathetic is projected upon her by the narrator of the story. It might be told by a friend and confidant of Lord S., who is in the secret throughout. *He* knows the force of Lord S.'s passion for Lady G., he knows that his engagement to Miss R. was merely perfunctory, because a man in his position *must* marry and have an heir and his father has badgered him till he has done so. *He* knows also a good deal about Lady G., and what she is capable of. Therefore when they plan together this noble renunciation, he doubts and fears and he thinks it is of bad omen for the poor little bride and is sure that it is only a question of time that Lord S. shall become the other woman's lover. 'Ah, they have agreed to give each other up!—Poor little woman!' That is the note on which this particular story would close. This arrangement would be congenial to the characteristic manner of H.J.—I shall probably try it. In this case the whole story might be told by Lord S.'s friend, who has observed it while it went on. He may relate it to an American visitor. The *point de départ* of this might be the sight of Lord S. and Lady G. together somewhere, in public; which is an intimation that what the friend has foreseen has happened.[4]

["The Path of Duty," the *English Illustrated Magazine* December 1884; reprinted in *The Author of "Beltraffio,"* Boston (1885).]

I don't see why I shouldn't do the 'self-made girl,' whom I noted here last winter, in a way to make her a rival to D[aisy] M[iller]. I must put her into action, which I am afraid will be difficult in the small compass (16 magazine pages which I now contemplate). But I don't see why I shouldn't make the thing as concise as *Four Meetings*. The concision of *Four Meetings,* with the success of *Daisy M.*; that is what I must aim at! But I must first invent the action! It must take place in New York. Perhaps indeed Washington would do. This would give me a chance to *do* Washington, so far as I know it, and work in my few notes, and my very lovely memories, of last winter. I might even *do* Henry Adams and his wife. The hero

4. See 17 May 1883.

might be a foreign secretary of Legation—German—inquiring and conscientious. New York *and* Washington, say. The point of the story would naturally be to show the contrast between the humble social background of the heroine, and the position which she has made—or is making for herself and, indirectly, for her family. He must meet her first in New York, then in Washington, where she has come to stay (with Mrs. Adams), and is seeing the president's cabinet, etc.; then again in New York; then finally in the country, in summer. Her people—her impossible father and mother—the way she carries them, etc. The picture admiring and appreciative. It must be a case of 'four meetings,' each with its little chapter, etc., each a picture. The thing must have the name of the girl (like D.M.) for its title—carefully selected. Each chapter (if there are 4) 20 pp. of MS.—I may make the thing a 'little gem'—if I try hard enough.[5]

[The "little gem" became "Pandora," *New York Sun* June 1884; reprinted in *The Author of "Beltraffio."* "Four Meetings," *Scribner's Monthly* November 1887; reprinted in *Daisy Miller, A Study,* New York (1878) and London (1879).]

March 26th, 1884. Edmund Gosse mentioned to me the other day a fact which struck me as a possible *donnée.* He was speaking of J.A.S., the writer (from whom, in Paris, the other day I got a letter),[1] of his extreme and somewhat hysterical aestheticism, etc.: the sad conditions of his life, exiled to Davos by the state of his lungs, the illness of his daughter, etc. Then he said that, to crown his unhappiness, poor S.'s wife was in no sort of sympathy with what he wrote; disapproving of its tone, thinking his books immoral, pagan, hyper-aesthetic, etc. 'I have never read any of John's works. I think them most *undesirable.*' It seemed to me *qu'il y avait là un drame—un drame intime;* the opposition between the narrow, cold, Calvinistic wife, a rigid moralist; and the husband, impregnated—even to morbidity—with the spirit of Italy, the love of beauty, of art, the aesthetic view of life, and aggravated, made extravagant and perverse, by the sense of his wife's disapproval. *Le drame pourrait s'engager—si drame il y a*—over the education of their child—the way he is to be brought up and to be taught to look at life; the husband drawing him one way and the wife another. The father wishes to make him an artist—the mother wishes to draw him into the church, to dedicate him to morality and religion, in order to expiate, as it were, the countenance that the family have given to godless ideas in the literary career of the father, who, however, is perfectly decent in life. The denouement to be the fate of the child, who either bolts, as he begins to grow up, and becomes a lout and ignoramus, equally removed from both tendencies—leading a stupid and vegetative life; or else, more pathetically, while he is still a boy, dies, a victim to the *tiraillements,* the heavy pressure, of his parents; not knowing what all the pother is about and not finding existence sufficiently simple. If it were not too gruesome, the mother

5. See 17 May 1883. Henry Adams (1838–1918) and his wife, the former Marion "Clover" Hooper (1843–85), appear as Mr. and Mrs. Bonnycastle in "Pandora."

1. Edmund Gosse (1849–1928), essayist, biographer, and finally librarian of the House of Lords, met HJ in 1879. J. A. S. is John Addington Symonds (1840–93), British art historian and poet. HJ met him at the home of Andrew Lang (1844–1912), poet and litterateur.

might be supposed to sacrifice him rather than let him fall under the influence of the father. He has an illness during which they both hang over him, tenderly, passionately, as he apparently sinks, and in the course of which it becomes clear to the mother that her husband, with his pagan beliefs, his absence of Christian hopes, has no expectation of meeting the child in a future life. This brings home to her the sense of his pernicious views, the sense of what the child will be exposed to if he lives. She makes up her mind secretly, that it is better he should die; she determines not to save him. During one critical night she sits watching him sink—holding his hand—but doing nothing—allowing him for very tenderness to fade away. This, of course, does not 'transpire,' as the American newspapers say; the reader knows it (the husband never does) through its being guessed by an admirer and devotee of the father (whose genius is immensely prized by a select few) and who must be the narrator of the tale, as I may in courtesy call it. The story should be told by a young American who comes out to England and calls upon the poet (he should be a poet or novelist or both) to pay his *hommage.* He is very kindly received—he remains near them for some weeks, and it is his impression, afterwards related (*à propos,* say, of the death of the poet), that constitutes the narrative, which ought to be—which would only bear to be—extremely short. He guesses, and the wife sees that he has guessed, that she has let the child go; in her exaltation and excitement she virtually confesses it to him. He keeps his knowledge to himself—never imparts it to the husband. She is more conciliatory to the latter, it may be conjectured, after the death of the boy. All this would require prodigious delicacy of touch; and even then *is* very probably too gruesome—the catastrophe too unnatural. Still, I think I shall try it; for the general idea is full of interest and very typical of certain modern situations. The story should be called *The Author of (So-and-So),* the name of the poet's principal work, for the love of which the young American had come to see him.

x   x   x   x   x

["The Author of 'Beltraffio,' " the *English Illustrated Magazine;* reprinted in *The Author of "Beltraffio."*]

Same date. Mrs. Kemble repeated to me the other night a story told her by Edward Sartoris and told him by his daughter-in-law, Mrs. Algie,[2] in which it seemed to me that there was a 'situation.' The story has only the *tort* to be very incredible, and almost silly: it sounds 'made up.' Mrs. A. relates at any rate that she knew of a young girl, in one of the far western cities of America, who formed an attachment to a young U.S. officer quartered in the town and of whose attentions to her her family wholly disapproved. They declared that under no circumstances would they consent to her marrying him, and forbade her to think of doing so or to hope for a moment for this contingency. Her passion, however, was stronger, and she was secretly married to the officer. But she returned to her father's house, and it was determined to keep the marriage absolutely secret. Both parties appear

---

2. Nelly Grant, daughter of Ulysses S. Grant, married Algernon (Algie) Sartoris, son of Edward Sartoris and the former Adelaide Kemble, sister of Fanny Kemble.

to have repented, to a considerable degree, of what they had done. In the course of time, however, the girl discovers that living is becoming difficult; she has the prospect of being confined. She is in despair, doesn't know what to do, etc.; and takes a friend, a married woman, into her confidence. This lady, pitying her, offers to take her to Europe and see that in some out-of-the-way place, the child is brought secretly into the world. The girl's parents consent to her making the journey, she goes to Europe with her friend, and in some small Italian town the young lady is delivered. The child is made over, with a sum of money, to a woman of the place, and the others go their way. In due time the young lady returns to her native town and her family, and is reinstated as a daughter of the house. The officer has been ordered to a distant post, and relations between them have ceased. After a while another *prétendant* presents himself, who is agreeable to the family and who ends by becoming agreeable to the girl. (I should mention—for it is the most important point of the whole!—that before she married the officer she extracted from him a promise that he would never demand of her to recognize the union, would never claim her publicly as his wife, etc. He has given this promise in the most solemn form.) She marries the new suitor, the officer makes no sign, and she lives for several years with her new husband, in great happiness, and has several children. At the end of this time the officer turns up. He tells her that it is all very well for *her* to be a bigamist, but that he doesn't choose to, and that she must allow him to institute a divorce suit against her, on the ground of desertion, in order that *he* too may marry a second time, being much in love with another woman and desiring to do so. That he may institute this suit she must release him from his old promise not to claim her as his wife, etc. It was not made clear to me, in Mrs. K.'s story, what the heroine did; but I was arrested by the situation I have just indicated: that of two persons secretly married, and one of whom (the husband, naturally) is tied by a promise to be silent, yet wishes to break the marriage in order to recover his freedom—to marry again, to beget legitimate children. The interest of the other is that the marriage never be known—her honour, her safety concerned, etc. The husband pleads that after the vow she has broken, he may surely break his promise, etc. Her entreaties, in opposition, her distress at the prospect of exposure, etc. The only endurable denouement that I can see is in the officer's agreeing to let her off, giving up his own marriage—making this sacrifice to his word. It will add to the tragic impression of this, etc., that he is unable to account to his new fiancée, or, at any rate, his new *inamorata,* for his backing out. He can't tell her why he gives her up—can't explain to her his extraordinary conduct. His only alternatives are to commit bigamy and to wait for the death of his bigamous wife. The situation as presented in the foregoing anecdote (which is impudently crude and incoherent) might be variously modified. The dropping of the child in Europe would be an impossible incident. It isn't necessary that she should have had a child—though, of course, if she has none at first it is almost necessary that she should have none afterwards.

["Georgina's Reasons," *New York Sun* 20 and 27 July, 3 August 1884; reprinted in *The Author of "Beltraffio."*]

Names. Papineau—Beaufoy—Birdseye—Morphy.

Names.   Tester—Frankinshaw—Tarrant—(Italian):   Olimpino—Pagano—Avellana—Ginistrella—*(English):* Lightbody—R(h)ymer—Busk—Wybrow—Bernardistone—Squirl—Secretan—Ransome.

June 19th, 1884. One might write a tale (very short) about a woman married to a man of the most amiable character who is a tremendous, though harmless, liar. She is very intelligent, a fine, quiet, high, pure nature, and she has to sit by and hear him romance—mainly out of vanity, the desire to be interesting, and a peculiar irresistible impulse. He is good, kind, personally very attractive, very handsome, etc.: it is almost his only fault though of course he is increasingly very *light*. What she suffers—what she goes through—generally she tries to rectify, to remove any bad effect by toning down a little, etc. But there comes a day when he tells a very big lie which she has—for reasons to be related—to adopt, to reinforce. To save him from exposure, in a word, she has to lie herself. The struggle, etc.; she lies—but after that she hates him. *(Numa Roumestan.)*[1]

["The Liar," *Century Magazine* May–June 1888; reprinted in *A London Life,* New York and London (1889).]

June 19th. Mrs. H. Ward mentioned the other day to me an idea of hers for a story which might be made interesting—as a study of the histrionic character.[2] A young actress is an object of much attention and a great deal of criticism from a man who loves the stage (he oughtn't to be a *professional* critic) and finally, though she doesn't satisfy him at all, artistically, loves the girl herself. He thinks something may be made of her, though he doesn't quite see what: he works over her, gives her ideas, etc. Finally (she is slow in developing, though full of ambition), she takes one, and begins to mount, to become a celebrity. She goes beyond him, she leaves him looking after her and wondering. She begins where he ends—soars away and is lost to him. The interest, I say, would be as a study of a certain particular *nature d'actrice:* a very curious sort of nature to reproduce. The girl I see to be very crude, etc. The thing a confirmation of Mrs. Kemble's theory that the dramatic gift is a thing by itself—implying of necessity no *general* superiority of mind. The strong nature, the personal quality, vanity, etc., of the girl: her artistic being, so vivid, yet so purely instinctive. Ignorant, illiterate. Rachel.[3]

Another little thing was told me the other day by Mrs. R. about Mrs. D. S.'s[4] little maid (lady's maid), Past, who was with her for years before her death, and whom I often saw there. She had to find a new place of course, on Mrs. S.'s

1. Alphonse Daudet's novel of 1881.
2. Mrs. Humphry Ward, née Mary Augusta Arnold (1851–1920), published a novel about an actress, *Miss Bretherton* (1884). See *Letters* III, 58–60, and 11 March 1888 and 2 February 1889.
3. "Rachel" was the stage name of the extraordinarily gifted French actress Elisa Félix.
4. Mrs. R. is Mrs. James Rogerson (see 25 November 1881)—the "Lady whom I won't name" (*Letters* III, 98), involved in the Sir Charles Dilke scandal of 1885. Mrs. D. S. is Mrs. Duncan Stewart (1797–1884), wife of a Liverpool merchant and mother of Mrs. Rogerson; she was the original of Lady Davenant in HJ's "A London Life" (see 20 June 1887).

death, to relapse into ordinary service. Her sorrow, the way she felt the change, and the way she expressed it to Mrs. R. 'Ah yes, ma'am, you have lost your mother, and it's a great grief, but what is your loss to mine?' (She was devoted to Mrs. D.S.) 'You continue to see good society, to live with clever, cultivated people: but I fall again into my own class, I shall never see such company—hear such talk—again. She was so good to me that I lived *with* her, as it were; and nothing will ever make up to me again for the loss of her conversation. Common, vulgar people now: that's my lot for the future!' Represent this—the refined nature of the little plain, quiet woman—her appreciation—and the way her new conditions sicken her, with a denouement if possible. Represent first, of course, her life with the old lady—figure of old Mrs. D.S. (modified)—her interior—her talk. Mrs. R.'s relations with her servants. 'My child—my dear child.'

["Brooksmith," *Harper's Weekly* and *Black and White* 2 May 1891; reprinted in *The Lesson of the Master*.]

July 9th, 1884. It was told me the other day of Lady Ashburton[1] that she asked a young girl to come and stay with her in Scotland, asseverating to her (the girl's) mother that she would be the best of duennas, etc., and look after her in perfection. On these terms the girl is allowed to go, alone. She arrives, and finds that Lady A., having quite forgotten that she had asked her, has left home, the day before, on a yachting expedition. She is away from railways, etc., there is nothing for her but to stay, especially as the hostess is expected back in a day or two. She stays, and the next day a young man arrives, also invited and forgotten. The *beau jeune homme* and the girl are face to face—it is a situation out of which something might be made. Various developments possible. The thing might be done in letters—from each person concerned: the hostess after she remembers, on the yacht, included. The young man's scruples—yet desire to stay, etc. The girl's fears—yet hopes that he will. It is all perhaps rather cheap—yet may contain something.

July 9th, 1884. This idea has been suggested to me by reading Sir Lepel Griffin's book[2] about America. Type of the conservative, fastidious, exclusive Englishman (in public life, clever, etc.), who hates the U.S.A. and thinks them a contamination to England, a source of *funeste* warning, etc., and an odious country socially. He falls in love with an American Girl and she with him—this of course to be made natural if possible. He lets her know, frankly, that he loathes her country as much as he adores her personally, and he begs her to marry him. She is patriotic in a high degree—a genuine little American—and she has the sentiment of her native land. But she is in love with the Englishman, and though she resists on patriotic grounds she yields at last, accepts him and marries him. She must have a near relation—a brother, say—who is violently American, an *anglophobiste* (in public life in the U.S.A.); and of whom she is very fond. He deplores her marriage, entreats her to keep out of it, etc. He and the Englishman *loathe* each other. After the marriage the Englishman's hostility to the U.S. increases, fostered by

1. HJ's windows in Bolton Street faced the Ashburtons' residence.
2. Sir Lepel Henry Griffin (1840–1908), travel writer and historian.

the invasion of Americans, etc. State of mind of the wife. Depression, melancholy, remorse and shame at having married an enemy of her country. Suicide? There is a certain interest in the situation—the difficulty of choice and resignation on her part—the resentment of a rupture with the brother, etc. Of course internationalism, etc., may be found overdone, threadbare. That is to a certain extent a reason against the subject; but a weak, not a strong one. It is always enough if the *author* sees substance in it.

["Two Countries," *Harper's New Monthly Magazine* June 1888; reprinted as "The Modern Warning" in *The Aspern Papers,* New York and London (1888).]

Names. Greenstreet—Wingrave—Major—Touchstone—Luna—Midsummer—Utterson—Pardon—Monkhouse—Prance—Basil—Blythe—Lancelot—Farrinder—Bigwood—Float—Hendrik—Joscelind—Mummery—Middlemas—Burrage—Prendergast—Scambler—Wager—Baskerville—Langrish—Robina—Crookenden—Pynsent—Loam—Amandus—Vau—Foot—Oriel (Xtian name)—(Lord) Inglefield: or name of a place—Severals (of a place)—Jump—Maplethorpe (place)—Catching—Quarterman—Alabaster—Muniment—Stark—Whiteroy (place)—Middle—Maidment—Filbert—Fury—Trist (person or place—house).

August 6th, 1884. Infinitely oppressed and depressed by the sense of being behindhand with the novel—that is, with the *start* of it, that I have engaged, through Osgood, to write for the *Century.*[1] I go today for 36 hours to Waddesdon[2] and on the 9th for the same stay to the Rallis'. These are old engagements, which I keep very *à contre coeur:* I would so far rather stick to my table and scribble. But it is far better to put them through—it is the braver course; but what a divine relief when I am back from the Rallis', on the 11th, with all this infernal survival of the season at rest, only *one* engagement, a Sunday at Basset, the 16th, ahead of me, and a clear stretch of work to look forward to. Then I shall possess my soul, my faculties, my imagination again, then I shall feel that life is worth living, and shall (I trust) be tolerably calm and happy. *A mighty will,* there is nothing but that! The integrity of one's will, purpose, faith. To wait, when one *must* wait, and act when one can act!

x   x   x   x   x

I haven't even a name for my novel, and fear I shall have to call it simply—*Verena:* the heroine. I should like something more descriptive—but everything that is justly descriptive won't do—*The Newness—The Reformers—The Precursors—The Revealer*—etc.—all very bad, and with the additional fault that people will say they are taken from Daudet's *Évangéliste.* x x x x x The heroine to be called Verena—Verena Tarrant. Her mother had seen the name in a book and liked it. Her father's name is Amariah. Her friend is Olive Chancellor. The hero is Basil Ransom. The 'other fellow' (her other lover) is Mathias Pinder.[3] The little old lady is Miss Birdseye.

1. *The Bostonians.* See 3 April 1883 and 10 August 1885.
2. Waddesdon Manor was built in the style of a French château by Baron Ferdinand James Rothschild (1839–98) between 1874 and 1881 in the Vale of Aylesbury.
3. The father's name became Selah; Pinder became Pardon; Amariah became Mr. Farrender.

Names. Croucher—Smallpiece—Corner—Buttery—Bide—Cash—Medley (place, country-house) — Dredge — Warmington — Probert — Henning — Beadle — Gallex —Bowerbank—Ermelinda—Lonely—Button—Filer—Dolman (Miss Dolman)— Rushout—Chad—Trantum—German (Xtian name)—Audrey (family name)—Ivy (the plant)—Castanet—Bavard—Rust—Plaster—Buxbridge—Peachey—Pillar— Pontifex—Trigg—Suchbury—Pinching—Pulse—Gleed—Constant—Six—Frowd —Terbot—Wherry.

Names. (continued). Gamage—Fluid—Welchford—Fancourt—Trinder—Trender.

Verena. My divisions of installments: pp. of MS.
    2d no. (VI) begins page 86.
    End of IX chapter (and second Part?).
    p. (MS.) 155. In type p. 97.[1]

August 10th, 1885. It is absolutely necessary that at this point I should make the future evolution of the *Princess Casamassima* more clear to myself. I have never yet become engaged in a novel in which, after I had begun to write and send off my MS., the details had remained so vague. This is partly—or indeed wholly— owing to the fact that I have been so terribly preoccupied—up to so lately—with the unhappy *Bostonians,*[1] born under an evil star. The subject of the *Princess* is magnificent, and if I can only give up my mind to it properly—generously and trustfully—the form will shape itself as successfully as the idea deserves. I have plunged in rather blindly, and got a good many characters on my hands; but these will fall into their places if I keep cool and think it out. Oh art, art, what difficulties are like thine; but, at the same time, what consolation and encouragements, also, are like thine? Without thee, for me, the world would be, indeed, a howling desert. The *Princess* will give me hard, continuous work for many months to come; but she will also give me joys too sacred to prate about.—In the 3d installment of the serial Hyacinth makes the acquaintance of x x x x x

[*The Princess Casamassima,* serialized in the *Atlantic Monthly* September 1885 to October 1886; published in London and New York (1886).]

---

1. This is an illustration of HJ's tendency to write on occasion in any convenient notebook without regard for chronology, etc. In this instance he must have opened Notebook I from the back and upside down so that he seemed to be faced with a clean first page for this note in red ink. He later resumed use of this notebook right side up, and when he turned to the last page to complete his note for 11 March 1888 he was forced to crowd his final sentence because of the space already taken by this earlier note in red. It must have been set down shortly after the entry for 6 August 1884—probably early in September: HJ is still calling his novel *Verena* here, and he mailed off the first installments for serial publication by October 1—under the title *The Bostonians.* See 8 April 1883 and illustration.

---

1. "Unhappy" because as soon as the first installment appeared HJ was criticized by his Aunt Kate, WJ, and James Russell Lowell for caricaturing Miss Elizabeth Peabody (Hawthorne's sister-in-law) in the character of Miss Birdseye (see HJ's denial, *Letters* III, 68–72). Also "unhappy" because his American publisher Osgood declared bankruptcy in the spring of 1885; see 8 April 1883.

August 22d. Phrases, of the people.[1]

. . . 'that takes the gilt off, you know.'
. . . a young man, of his *patron,* in a shop . . . 'he cuts it very fine.' . . .
' 'Ere today, somewhere else tomorrow: that's *'is* motto.'

x   x   x   x   x

August 22d. One does nothing of value in art or literature unless one has some general ideas, and if one has a few such, constituting a motive and a support, those flippancies and vulgarities (abusive reviews in newspapers) are the last thing one troubles about.

Names. Gamble—Balm—Stannary (of a place, seat)—Quibbler—Lonsgrove—Chick—Sholto—Ruffler—Booker—Longhurst (place)—Ambler—Campion—Gus (or Guss)—Leolin (boy)—Leolin(e) (girl)—Starling—Lumb—Merryweather—Yeo—Rix—Francina (girl).

x   x   x   x   x

Florence, January 12th, 1887.[1]

A. mentions in a letter that Sir J.R. is to marry the Dowager Lady T.—that 'he blushes whenever her name is mentioned, and that Mrs. S.C. says it is simply forty years of her mother's life wiped out.'[2] There is a little drama here—at least a possible one—between a father and daughter on such an occasion; especially— I mean—when the 1st married life has been a happy one—the 2 have cherished the memory of the wife and mother together. The daughter's sense of the want of dignity of her father's act—as an old, or elderly, man—of the difference between her mother and the new love, etc. It sickens her—she goes to the fiancée, etc. She must have—to make her opposition natural—the worship of her mother's memory—and a kind of horror. I am not sure that there is much of a subject— but a short tale might be made of it. The father may be affected by his daughter's opposition so much as to repent of his engagement. He is *ébranlé,* he is ashamed of it, he wishes to retreat. But he tells her it is there and that he can't get out of it. 'Very well,' says she—*'je m'en charge.'* SHE goes to the fiancée again and there she tells her something about the father—a pure fabrication—she swears her to secrecy—which she flatters herself will prevent the woman from wishing to go

---

1. These jottings seem to have been noted by HJ for use in *The Princess Casamassima.*
1. The hiatus of sixteen months in this notebook may be accounted for by notebooks that no longer exist, or may be due to three features of HJ's life at the time: he was committed to serialization of *The Bostonians* and *The Princess Casamassima;* his ailing sister was in London and required much attention; he was also busy establishing himself in a flat in Kensington, at 34 De Vere Gardens, into which he moved on 6 March 1886. See *Life* 315–24.
2. A. is HJ's sister, Alice (1848–92); Sir J. R. is Sir John Rose (1820–88), widower (in 1883) of Charlotte, née Temple (see 25 November 1881, note 6). Mrs. S. C. is their daughter, Mary Rose, who in 1867 married Col. Stanley Clarke, equerry to Edward, Prince of Wales (1878–1901). Dowager Lady T. is Julia, Lady Tweeddale, daughter of Keith Stewart Mackenzie of Seaforth and widow of the ninth Marquess of Tweeddale; she married Sir John Rose on 24 January 1887.

on with the marriage. (*What* she tells her is a delicate point—to be settled; and of course it must be under the empire of a passionate *idée fixe*.) This communication has its effect—the intended wife shortly afterwards lets the father know that she repents of the engagement and that she releases him. He is pleased at first—pleased that he has pleased his daughter—and she (the daughter) is delighted at what she has done. Before long, however, she begins to see a change in her father—he is sad, brooding, sombre—he looks at her in a different way. In fact, he is beginning to wonder *how* she affected the lady—what she did, what arts she used—and to suspect that she *did* say something that was injurious to him. She perceives this change in him—that he is resentful and unhappy—and suddenly, weary of the whole thing, she gives up her opposition. She determines to go to the lady and tell her that everything she said before was false. She does so, and the latter replies—'I am very sorry—but I have just become engaged to Mr. So-and-So!' It may be represented—to make the daughter's action a little less odious—that the intended wife has not really believed what she said—has seen through it as a manoeuvre—but *has* thought that the father has lent himself to it and despises him accordingly. It wouldn't be a very 'sympathetic' tale.[3]

x   x   x   x   x

["The Marriages," the *Atlantic Monthly* August 1891; reprinted in *The Lesson of the Master*.]

Same date. Hamilton (V.L.'s brother)[4] told me a curious thing of Capt. [Edward] Silsbee—the Boston art-critic and Shelley-worshipper; that is of a curious adventure of his. Miss Claremont,[5] Byron's *ci-devant* mistress (the mother of Allegra) was living, until lately, here in Florence, at a great age, 80 or thereabouts, and with her lived her niece, a younger Miss Claremont—of about 50. Silsbee knew that they had interesting papers—letters of Shelley's and Byron's—he had known it for a long time and cherished the idea of getting hold of them. To this end he laid the plan of going to lodge with the Misses Claremont—hoping that the old lady in view of her great age and failing condition would die while he was there, so that he might then put his hand upon the documents, which she hugged close in life. He carried out this scheme—and things *se passèrent* as he had expected. The old woman *did* die—and then he approached the younger one—the old maid of 50—on the subject of his desires. Her answer was—'I will give you all the letters if you marry me!' H. says that Silsbee *court encore*. Certainly there is a little subject there: the picture of the two faded, queer, poor and discredited old English women—living on into a strange generation, in their musty corner of a foreign town—with these illustrious letters their most precious possession. Then the plot of the Shelley fanatic—his watchings and waitings—the way he *couvers*

---

3. This entry contains a hint that will be developed in the 28 November 1892 and 14 February 1895 entries for *The Golden Bowl*.
4. V. L. is Vernon Lee, pen name of Violet Paget (1856–1935), then a beginning English novelist whom HJ met in London in the spring of 1884. Hamilton is Eugene Lee-Hamilton (1845–1907), half-brother of Vernon Lee and a cultivated literary personality.
5. The usual spelling is "Clairmont," which HJ would later use; she was Mary Jane Clairmont—or Claire Clairmont, as she preferred to be known.

the treasure. The denouement needn't be the one related of poor Silsbee; and at any rate the general situation is in itself a subject and a picture. It strikes me much. The interest would be in some price that the man has to pay—that the old woman—or the survivor—sets upon the papers. His hesitations—his struggle—for he really would give almost anything.—The Countess Gamba[6] came in while I was there: her husband is a nephew of the Guiccioli—and it was *à propos* of their having a lot of Byron's letters of which they are rather illiberal and dangerous guardians, that H. told me the above. They won't show them or publish any of them—and the Countess was very angry once on H.'s representing to her that it was her duty—especially to the English public!—to let them at least be seen. *Elle se fiche bien* of the English public. She says the letters—addressed in Italian to the Guiccioli—are discreditable to Byron; and H. elicited from her that she had *burned* one of them.

x   x   x   x   x

["The Aspern Papers," the *Atlantic Monthly* March–May 1888; reprinted in *The Aspern Papers.*]

Same date. The idea of a worldly mother and a worldly daughter, the latter of whom has been trained up so perfectly by the former that she excels and surpasses her, and the mother, who has some principle of goodness still left in her composition, is appalled at her own work. She sees the daughter, so hard, so cruelly ambitious, so bent on making a great marriage and a great success at any price, that she is almost afraid of her. She repents of what she has done—she is ashamed. The daughter fixes a rich, soft, amiable young man as an object of conquest—and the mother finds herself pitying the lad. She is tempted to go to him and warn him. They may all be Americans—in Europe: since Howells writes to me that I do the 'international' far better than anything else. The story may be told by an elderly American—the uncle, or cousin, of the very rich lad whom the girl considers a *parti* worth her efforts. He has known the 2 ladies of old—he has seen the mother's great worldliness, and he observes the change. The mother shall have been an old flame of his and shall have thrown him over. After that their relations shall have become frank—intensely candid. She knows he knows her views and efforts—and they have openly talked of them. He doesn't like the daughter—he is responsible for his rich young nephew—he warns the mother off—says the boy is not to be their game. The mother takes the warning—or perhaps it's not definitely given, for that after all might be too brutal. However, that's a point to be settled. She may see for herself that her old sweetheart fears their bagging the boy (for the girl is superficially charming), and determines to retrieve herself in the uncle's eyes by preventing the capture. She has always been ashamed of the way she has treated her old admirer. She sees that her daughter is determined to collar the young man. So she goes to the latter clandestinely, denounces the girl (after a fashion), and recommends him to go away. He consents—he is affected by what she says—and escapes. The mother is in a kind of exaltation—she feels as if she

6. The Countess Gamba, reputed to be the natural daughter of the Tuscan satirist-poet Giuseppe Giusti, married a nephew of Lord Byron's last mistress, Teresa Guiccioli.

had purified herself. She goes to the uncle and says—'Ah, well, you must respect me now.' He admires her, and he must describe this in a good tone. But he feels even a little sorry for the girl, and after a little he even expresses this. Then the mother may reply, as a last word—'Oh, after all, I don't know that it matters! She will still get a prince!' The narrator says—'She *is* now the Countess So-and-So.'

This business might begin and indeed take place wholly at some watering place— say Homburg—or perhaps better in Switzerland. No room for description. Perhaps Florence might do. At any rate the narrator meets the ladies after a long interval. The nephew arrives—joins him—later. The narrator must begin this story—'Never say you know the last word about any human heart! I once was treated to a revelation which startled and touched me in the nature of a person whom I knew well, whom I had been well acquainted with for years, whose character I had had good reason, Heaven knows, to appreciate, and in regard to whom I flattered myself I had nothing more to learn. It was on the terrace of the Kursaal at Homburg, nearly ten years ago, one lovely summer night. I was there alone, but I was waiting for my nephew, etc., etc. The band played—the people passed and repassed in front of me; I smoked my cigar and watched them. Suddenly I recognized Mrs. Grift and her daughter. I hadn't seen Linda since she was fifteen, but I had then seen how she was going. She had become exceedingly pretty—and wonderfully like what her mother was twenty years before.' They walk (the mother and daughter up and down together) and he watches them, unseen, for some time before he speaks to them. No one else does so; it is almost as if they were not respectable. (I don't know that that is very important.) I must give his little retrospect while he regards them. Then he gets up and goes to them—and the rest comes on. I don't see why this shouldn't be a little masterpiece of *concision,* all narrative—not too much attempt to *fouiller,* with every word telling. If M. Schuyler[7] doesn't find *Cousin Maria* possible for his 'holiday number' of *Harper,* this might very well serve.

[The note yielded "Louisa Pallant," *Harper's New Monthly Magazine* February 1888; reprinted in *The Aspern Papers.* "Cousin Maria," *Harper's Weekly* August 1887; reprinted as "Mrs. Temperley" in *A London Life.*]

I don't see why the three above things (the 2d and 3d are much the best—and I think the 2d really almost a gem) shouldn't be, if treated at all, treated effectively with great brevity.

Florence, January 21st, 1887. A possible subject for something 'international' might be the situation of an English or American girl (presumably the latter) who has grown up in a polyglot and 'cosmopolite' society, like that of Florence—and

---

7. Montgomery Schuyler (1843–1914), managing editor of *Harper's Weekly* (1885–87), reader for Harper & Bros. (1887–94). He also worked for the *Sun* and the *New York Times;* his sketches for the latter became *Westward the Course of Empire* (1906).

is sick of it all—sick of the coming and going, the absence of roots and responsibilities in the people, the bad French, which is the medium of social intercourse—the absence of all that savours of her own race and tongue. For the latter she has a sort of consuming desire. She might be made a little literary—privately and unsatisfiedly—to carry this out. All around her Russians, Italians, vague French—English and Americans who are also vague. She is thought to have had great 'advantages'—linguistic and other—but she longs for some little corner of England or of the U.S. She must have a sister or two married in foreign lands. Some young Englishman or American meets her. A sketch—a portrait—of this kind, very briefly treated, might be interesting, and give an impression of such a place, 'socially,' as this.

Venice, June 20th, 1887 (Palazzo Barbaro).[1]

Paul Bourget[2] mentioned to me the other day, as the subject of a *nouvelle,* a situation (making it over to me to use if, and as, I liked) which, through alterations, has converted itself in my mind into an idea which I think excellent. The form in which he gave it to me was suggested by the suicide, in Rome, of his beautiful young friend, Mlle S. She jumped out of the window of an hotel at Milan, in her night-dress, at 6 o'clk., in the a.m. while in the delirium of a fever. Bourget had a theory about her—which was that she had believed that her mother had lovers, that this weighed upon her horribly and that she wanted to escape from the house, to get away and cease to be the witness of the maternal *dérèglements.* The only way for her to do this was to marry. A young man came often to the house, seemed to take pleasure in her society, etc. She thought he might rescue her—if an opportunity were given him—by asking for her hand. So one day—and the impulse was strange and desperate—she said to him: 'You come here so much—you seem to like me, etc. Why do you do it? Is it that you want to marry me? Speak if you do.' No sooner had she uttered these words than she perceived her mistake. The young man was evidently taken completely by surprise; he blushed, stared, stammered, said that certainly the honour of her hand was a thing to which one might well aspire—if one dared, etc. In short he was civil, vague—tried to behave gallantly, for a man caught. She looked at him a moment and burst into tears. 'Oh heavens, what have I done? From the moment you don't throw yourself at my feet with joy, I see what my mistake has been. Go away, go away, this instant, and let me *never* see you again!' The young man retired, respectfully, and left the place altogether. The girl relapsed into the situation that surrounded her, saw no issue, and after a short time, disgusted, sick at soul, despairing, destroyed herself. I should add that a day or two after telling me this story, Bourget let me know that his interpretation of the *motive* of the suicide had probably been utterly fanciful. Nothing, in the real history, was clear but the fact that she had killed herself, and the mother's immorality and the appeal to the

1. The residence from 1881 of the Bostonian Daniel S. Curtis and his wife, née Ariana Randolph Wormeley (daughter of a British admiral). See *Life* 341.
2. Paul Bourget (1852–1935), the French "psychological" novelist whom HJ met in the summer of 1884, dedicated his first important novel, *Cruelle Énigme* (1885), to him.

young man, relegated themselves to the vague. The girl simply had typhoid fever—had been cheerful and natural before it, etc. Bourget's version was very
characteristic of himself—the facility of the hypothesis that the mother was an
adulteress, etc. This however doesn't alter the suggestiveness of the drama as he
imagined it. It would have been very possible in this form, whether actual or not.
But to make something of it I must modify it essentially—as I can't, and besides,
don't particularly want to, depict in an American magazine, a woman carrying on
adulteries under her daughter's eyes. That case, I imagine, is in America so rare
as to be almost abnormal. Something of this sort is the shape into which it has
converted itself to my fancy. I see it as an episode in that 'international' series
which, really, without forcing the matter or riding the horse to death, strikes me
as an inexhaustible mine. Something of about the form of *Daisy Miller* or the
Siege of London. An American girl, very pretty, but of a very light substance,
easily depraved, marries a young Englishman and lives in the smart, dissipated
set, the P[rince] of W[ales]'s,[3] etc., in London. She is frivolous *outre mesure,*
and a terrible young person 'for men.' Her husband is an idiot, though not a bad
fellow, leading exclusively the life of amusement, sport, etc. It will be a very
good chance to try and reproduce some of my London impressions of that order.
Lady Davenant (say, for convenience), has a younger sister who has come out
from America to stay with her, to make a long visit, and it must be of the essence
of this girl's position that she has no other home or refuge—no other place to go.
It must also be the essence of her nature that she is as different as possible from
her sister—grave, sensitive, serious, honest, unadapted to the world in which Lady
D. lives, troubled and tormented by it, and above all distressed and alarmed at
the way she sees Lady D. going. She is poor, the parents are dead, she has no
other brother nor sister—the father has 'failed,' characteristically, in New York,
not long after the elder sister's marriage. This fact, by itself, is already a source
of discomfort and humiliation to the younger. It makes her unhappy, uncertain of
her footing. Lady D. has had a considerable *dot* paid down on her marriage; so
that the failure, subsequent, has not compromised *her* fortune, though she and her
husband are both so extravagant that they transcend their means, etc. This is
necessary (the fact that the elder sister has had her portion and that Laura [say][4]
has nothing), to make it possible to represent the latter as living with her, being
supported by her. Laura has before her the spectacle of Lady D.'s frantic frivolity,
and it pains and bewilders her—she doesn't know what to make of it. It is new to
her—she not having come out to London for some years after the marriage; kept
at home by the family troubles, looking after the father, broken by his reverses,
the mother, after his death, ruined, etc. She is twenty-five or six by the time she
comes; Lady D. is about thirty. Meanwhile the latter has had time to fall into the
pace—to become thoroughly *lancée.* Her sister finds her immensely changed and
[is] startled when she comes; but it takes her some time to take it in—to understand what surrounds her. She is too innocent at first—too pure, too accustomed
to optimistic interpretations. Add to this that her sister imposes upon [her] as her
elder, by her beauty, her brilliancy, etc. This point must be insisted upon—that

3. Later King Edward VII (1901–10).
4. HJ's brackets.

Laura has adored Lady D., admired her precisely for being so different from herself. This is necessary, to make the revulsion, the deep pain greater, when she finds what a good-for-nought she has become. She doesn't presume to judge her at first—it is only little by little. There must be an old lady—like Mrs. Duncan S[tewart][5]—only of rank—a genial, clever, worldly, old-fashioned, half comforting, half shocking old lady, whom she goes to see and talk with, and who half enlightens her, half reassures her. This old woman must have taken a great fancy to her—she tries to marry her. But this doesn't succeed—Laura having no money and not being a success in London. Accentuate the fact that she is of the kind, the American kind, that isn't. Lady D. has already had a lover before her sister comes; she is very considerably compromised, but that episode is over. The wretched woman, completely *brouillée* with her husband, who has none of the tact to manage her, and whose own tastes and pursuits only drive her deeper into the mire, *toute dorée qu'elle soit,* is hovering, drifting, all ready for another plunge. This situation gradually becomes clear to Laura—trace the incidents by which she takes it in. It goes hard with her to judge her sister, to warn her, to check her, but at last she does. She remonstrates, pleads, does her best to save her—and Lady D. pretends to listen, to resist, to cling to her, as a salvation. But this all *plaisir* and comedy—she is incorrigibly light. If I can only make a little masterpiece of Lady D.—as the portrait of a little heartless, shallow, *pretending* cat, who is yet capable of running off with a handsome guardsman if she takes a fancy to him. There must be 2 children in whom Laura takes an interest and whom she tries to view in a pathetic light. But she can't do this—they are such sturdy, happy healthy British infants, with the promise of no nerves—no capacity for self-bother: to grow up into the same world, in the same way, not *creuser*-ing anything and thinking everything natural. How the American Lady D.—the little New York scrap—has produced these perfect English youngsters—best both boys. Laura's relations with her brother-in-law, whom she likes, pities, despairs of, and also more or less despises—for his complicity, his acceptance, his inability to keep his wife straight, because it's all a part of the same business, the same life, and he hasn't the courage to give up any of it. He likes *her* greatly—tells her he wishes it had been she that he married. So I get my change—the young girl sore and sick over a sister's, instead of a mother's, irregularities. I think the American magazines can be made to swallow the sister, at least. The remainder very much as in what B. told me—save that I don't want the suicide. It's too rare, and I used it the other day in the *Two Countries. (To be continued.)*

My young girl in her desire to get away, to make a new life for herself, makes the same strange speech to a young man who comes to the house and as to whom it is open to her to believe that he comes to her—the same singular appeal that the heroine of B.'s anecdote is supposed to have made: a scene which it will take great art and tact to render credible and to keep from being displeasing. This can be done, however, and there is nothing inconceivable in the girl's conduct, once her feelings as to the whole situation are definitely marked. She is essentially a *sensitive*—a nature needing help and support and unable to stand alone. She must

5. See 19 June 1884.

be interesting, touching as a tormented, anxious heroine—not as a free, high-stepping one. I must make my young man, an Englishman, a clerk in the foreign office, of the kind I have seen—*compassé,* ambitious, with a great sense of the *parti* and responsibility of his work, etc.; one of those competent, colourless, gentlemanly mediocrities of whom one sees so many in London and who have a career. Laura sees that her sister is going to 'bolt' with her new lover—that a catastrophe is impending—certain that she can't avert it, and that shame and disgrace hang over the house. She feels above all that they hang over *her.* She ceases almost to feel anything for her brother-in-law—he ends by striking her as a poor creature, cynical and abject, deserving of his doom. A desire has taken possession of her to provide for herself *before* the scandal becomes public—for she feels that there will be a horrible divorce case, with odious details—at least 2 correspondents, etc. After everything has come out she will be dishonoured, as the sister, the only sister, of a woman so dreadfully exposed. No one will marry her then—she will have to hide, to bury herself. She has a sort of terror of that fate, and this has been at the bottom of her appeal. She thinks the young man doesn't know—if he will only take her in time. Of course it will all come out *after* he has married her—but then she will be safe; and meantime she will have made her husband love her and esteem her so that he will regret nothing. This is not heroic, but, given the girl, it is natural and touching. She isn't obliged to care too much that her husband will have been taken in if her sister's shame comes out afterwards—for he won't (she knows how little) have been deceived in *her.* He will have acquired a treasure—she will be incomparably good to him—to make up. The scene follows that takes place in the original and she drives the young man from her sight. Meanwhile if I reject the denouement of the suicide I must have another—the following seems to me the best. Laura's remarkable old friend (Mrs. D.S.) takes, as I think I have noted, an interest in marrying her, all the more after having a glimpse of her state of mind in regard to the situation at home. She doesn't know personally the young man of whom I have spoken, at the time the scene between Laura and him takes place, but she knows him afterwards. Perhaps it ought to be that she, knowing how he comes to the house, though she has not seen him, advises the girl to challenge him—tells her that that's all he is waiting for. I think indeed, that that will be much the best—for it will help the denouement. After the scene with the girl has taken place the old lady learns, elicits from Laura, how painfully it has ended and feels that as she has precipitated it, she owes her young friend some reparation—some compensation. She determines to bring the young man back—she guesses that Laura's conduct has made a greater impression upon him than anything relating to her hitherto, and that he may very well be saying to himself—'after all, why not—why not?' She figures to herself that he has begun to be sad and angry at having been *chassé.* She sends to him to come and see her, and she has a very frank and original talk with him, such as she is capable of. She tells him she knows what has happened—praises Laura immensely to him—pleads for her, as it were, with him. Besides, she makes him in a measure responsible—makes him feel that in such a case a man of delicacy *ought* to marry the girl. Of course she can't do this save that of himself he is fermenting, internally: he wants very much to see Laura again. He determines to do so, and succeeds. Meantime her sister's proceedings have reached a climax: she knows that the worst is at hand—has taken place. Her sister has 'bolted' (under the plea of being in Paris): certain information of this has reached her. No one knows it as yet but herself and her brother-in-law—but it will all inevitably come out in a day or two, so that London society will ring with the scandal. She knows that her brother-in-law wants a divorce—to marry another woman; and that he can get it because he hasn't done, flagrantly, provably, what his wife has done. *Type this, particulier*, of the man of his kind who, in his situation, doesn't. Shall she now accept her suitor, who protests that the other day she completely mistook and misconceived him and that his dearest wish, at present, is that she shall be his wife? She feels that now to be impossible—she only wants to get away from it all, and she refuses him and goes off—vanishes—returns, as best she can, to America. That must be my denouement—it will be vulgarly judged—but it is the only possible one.

[''A London Life,'' *Scribner's Magazine* June–September 1888; reprinted in *A London Life*.]

London, Thursday, November 17th, 1887.

Last winter, in Florence, I was struck with the queer incident of Miss McC.'s[1] writing to the New York *World* that inconceivable letter about the Venetian society whose hospitality she had just been enjoying—and the strange *typicality* of the whole thing. She acted in perfect good faith and was amazed, and felt injured and persecuted, when an outcry and an indignation were the result. That she *should* have acted in good faith seemed to me to throw much light upon that mania for publicity which is one of the most striking signs of our times. She was perfectly irreflective and irresponsible, and it seemed to her pleasant and natural and 'chatty' to describe, in a horribly vulgar newspaper, the people she had been living with and their personal domestic arrangements and secrets. It was a striking incident and it seemed to me exactly the theme for a short story. One sketches one's age but imperfectly if one doesn't touch on that particular matter: the invasion, the impudence and shamelessness, of the newspaper and the interviewer, the devouring *publicity* of life, the extinction of all sense between public and private. It is the highest expression of the note of 'familiarity,' the sinking of *manners*, in so many ways, which the democratization of the world brings with it. I was prompted to make use of the incident in question which struck me [as] a very illustrative piece of contemporary life—the opposition of the scribbling, publishing, indiscreet, newspaperized American girl and the rigid, old-fashioned, conservative, still shockable and much shocked little society she recklessly plays the tricks upon. The drama is in the consequences for *her*, and it is of course interesting in proportion as the consequences are great. They are greatest if the thing brings about a crisis and a cataclysm in her 'prospects.' These prospects bear pre-eminently, of course, on the question of her marriage. Imagine the girl engaged to a young

1. Mary Marcy McClellan, daughter of the Civil War General George B. McClellan, whose gossipy letter to the New York *World* (14 November 1886) created a Venetian scandal. See *Life* 341–42 and *Letters* III, 154–56, 166.

Italian or Frenchman of seductive 'position,' and pretty and *dotée* in order to have become so—and then imagine her writing to a blatant American newspaper 'all about' the family and domestic circle of her fiancé, and you have your story. I shouldn't have thought of the incident if in its main outline it hadn't occurred: one can't say a pretty and 'nice' American girl wouldn't do such a thing, simply because there was Miss McC. who did it. One can't say she *isn't* 'nice'—when she belongs to *tout ce qu'il y a de mieux là-bas*—the daughter of an illustrious citizen. She was not indeed engaged to a Venetian, and her case thereby lends itself the less; but she might easily have been—she would have liked to be—and that addition is necessary. I have made up my mind, however, that it wouldn't do to take her case in its actuality—partly because I might seem to be 'copying' and partly because it can be much improved. So I leave it simply as a starting-point— an idea, and imagine different facts. These are quite my own. An American girl, abroad with her father and sister, becomes engaged to a young European who has been brought up and lived wholly *dans les vieilles idées.* (I give the subject in as few words as possible.) A young American admirer of hers, who has tried without success to woo and win her, is a journalist, of the most enterprising, and consequently the most vulgar, character. He has been with her, crossed the Atlantic with her, etc., before her engagement, and comes upon her again, in Paris, after this takes place. He thinks that if he can't get what he originally wanted out of her he may at least get something else; perceiving therefore all her new affiliations he endeavours to interview her—to make her tell him all about the family and the affairs of her intended—so that he may make of it a bright 'society' letter. *His* type and character therefore become almost the more salient one[s]. He of course hasn't a grain of delicacy in his composition (I must do him very well); he has no tradition of reserve or discretion—he simply obeys his gross newspaper instinct and thinks it a piece of uncommon good luck that he has had such a chance: that he is 'in' with a girl who can tell him so much. She likes him—her refusal to marry him has brought with it no rupture of relations—and thinks him wonderfully 'bright,' wonderfully amusing. She is simple, sweet, uncultivated, gentle, innocent, yet with the stamp [of] her antecedents (I must make them of the right— i.e., of the explanatory sort) upon her mind, her ideas. He means no harm in pumping her, and she means none in telling everything she knows about her prospective circle, who have made much of her, treated her charmingly, etc. (they have accepted the marriage), and with whom she has been staying, living. The result is a most fearful letter from the young man to his big catchpenny newspaper—preferably a Western sheet—'giving away' the girl herself and everyone she has mentioned—a letter as monstrous as Julian H[awthorne]'s beastly and blackguardly betrayal last winter of J.R.L[owell].[2] I must arrange that the young fiancé have gone over to America at the moment to look after affairs, property, etc.— which will account the better for the journalist's having access to the girl. The young man, while he is in the 'States,' comes upon the horrible newspaper— opens it—finds himself, his family, his friends, his sisters, and their husbands, the most personal facts, mysteries, etc., including a family secret, proceeding

2. Julian Hawthorne had published an indiscreet account of a private conversation with Lowell, U.S. minister to England, on English affairs. See 22 October 1891, and also *Letters* III, 147.

from a past generation, which no one talks of—blazoned forth in the vulgarest terms. He is appalled, and rushes back to Europe for an explanation. Meanwhile his people have already seen the letter and share all his horror and wonder. The girl is confronted with the consequences of her act—and is amazed at the light in which they are presented to her. She has meant no harm, and scarcely understands the fuss. The attitude of her new family make[s] her indiscretion a little more clear to her—but *she* is resentful, too, of their scandalized tone, the row they make; her pride rises (all the more that the monstrosity of what she has done *does* begin to dawn upon her), and she draws back, after a scene with the fiancé, and throws up the engagement. The rumpus, the scandal, the crisis, in short are immense. Nothing of that sort has ever been known *dans ce monde là:* the newspaper is a thing of loathing to them. The end is a little difficult to determine. I think the truest and best and most illustrative would be this: that the young interviewer who has *his* virtuous indignation too, learning the scandal he has brought about, the rupture of the marriage, etc., threatens the bloated foreigners with a new horror—that is, to publish the scandal itself, with tremendous headings—the way they have treated the girl, etc. Appalled by this possibility they 'come round'— forgive, conciliate, swallow their grievance, etc., so that the marriage takes place. The newspaper dictates and triumphs—which is a reflection of actual fact. Such is the rough contour of my idea. The application has presented a real difficulty, which, however, I think I have solved: that difficulty was where to find people today in Europe who would really be so shocked as that comes to—shocked enough for my dramatic opposition. I don't in the least see them in England, where publicity is far too much, by this time, in the manners of society for my representation to have any verisimilitude here. The *World* and *Truth,* etc.,[3] stare one in the face—people write to the newspapers about everything—it is in short also a newspaperized world, and, allowing for a rather better form, there is about as little delicacy as *là bas.* The poor Venetians, living outside of modern enterprise, were shocked by Miss McC.; but they are too near, and I can't use them. Besides, their feelings are not interesting enough—the race is poor and represents today too little. A Roman or a Florentine lot wouldn't do either, for very much the same reasons (in a minor degree). So I came down to the French—imagined an old *claquemuré* Legitimist circle, as detached as possible from *tout ce que se fait, s'écrit et se pense aujourd'hui.* There would be great difficulties, however, there, not the least of which the difficulty of really making the picture. Besides I have taken a vow never again to do the French in any such collective way (as in the *American*); *à peu près* effects of that sort are too cheap, too valueless. So I found my solution where, with the help of Heaven, I hope to find many others in work to come; viz., in the idea of the Europeanized American. And it is that that represents not simply an easier way, but a greater reality. The thing is under my nose; imagine the ingredients of E. Lee Childe and D. S. Curtis[4] rolled into one— and add a few of my own—and *je tiens mon affaire.* They would really be the people most detached and most scandalized; and in the light of their idea the

3. English gossip publications. *Truth* is mentioned several times in AJ's diary.
4. Edward Lee Childe (1836–1911), a nephew of General Robert E. Lee, spent the greater part of his life in France. See 25 November 1881, note 10.

whole little story straightens out. It fits together—it hangs together. I knew I should find something—and now I SEE it. *Cela se passe en France*—it begins in Paris and goes on mainly in Paris. Old Mr. Probert (call him) is of the oldest American *monde* there: his father will have come out in 1830. He is completely merged—thanks to wealth, sympathies—*dans le monde du Faubourg*. His 2 sisters have married old French names, his daughter and his other son *en ont fait autant*. His elder son is the fiancé of my young lady—he has *never* been willing to do like the others; he has always had the dream of marrying an American— like his mother. His family smile on it—if he will only pick out a nice one. It was not to be expected that he should come across my heroine—but he does, by accident, and falls in love with her. There are also very good elements of money. His people are glad of these latter and accept the girl, making rather a big mouth— especially to swallow her father and sister. These 2 figures I see, and shall see still better.

[*The Reverberator*, serialized in *Macmillan's Magazine* February–July 1888; published in London and New York (1888).]

January 5th, 1888.

The Patagonia. The name of the ship (a slow voyage, though in summer, from Boston—an old Boston Cunarder—to Liverpool); on which I shall place the little tragic story suggested to me by Mrs. Kemble's anecdote of Barry St. Leger[1] and the lady (married and with a husband awaiting her in England) with whom he sailed from India. She was young and pretty and had been placed under the captain's care. At a certain stage of the voyage the captain was notified that the passengers were scandalized by the way she was flirting and carrying on with B.St.L. This came to her knowledge—and one night she jumped overboard. Admirable little dismal subject.

["The Patagonia," *English Illustrated Magazine* August–September 1888; reprinted in *A London Life*.]

Another came to me last night as I was talking with Theodore Child[2] about the effect of marriage on the artist, the man of letters, etc. He mentioned the cases he had seen in Paris in which this effect had been fatal to the quality of the work, etc.—through overproduction, need to meet expenses, make a figure, etc. And I mentioned certain cases here. Child spoke of Daudet—his *30 Ans de Paris,*[3] as an example in point. 'He would never have written that if he hadn't married.' So it occurred to me that a very interesting situation would be that of an elder artist or writer, who has been ruined (in his own sight) by his marriage and its forcing him to produce promiscuously and cheaply—his position in regard to a younger *confrère* whom he sees on the brink of the same disaster and whom he endeavours to

1. The brother of Harriet St. Leger, an intimate of Fanny Kemble.
2. HJ met the British journalist Theodore E. Child, then a young writer for the *Pall Mall Gazette*, in 1876. He was later Paris correspondent to London newspapers and editor of the Anglo-French journal *Parisian*.
3. Daudet's memoirs were published in 1888.

save, to rescue, by some act of bold interference—breaking off the marriage, annihilating the wife, making trouble between the parties.

[''The Lesson of the Master,'' the *Universal Review* July–August 1888; reprinted in *The Lesson of the Master.*]

Sunday, March 11th, 1888. Here I sit: impatient to work: only wanting to concentrate myself, to keep at it: full of ideas, full of ambition, full of capacity—as I believe. Sometimes the discouragements, however, seem greater than anything else—the delays, the interruptions, the *éparpillement,* etc. But courage, courage, and forward, forward. If one must generalize, that is the only generalization. There is an immensity to be done, and, without vain presumption—I shall at the worst do a part of it. But all one's manhood must be at one's side. x x x x x
Let me note a little more in detail one of the subjects just foregoing—the thing I have called *The Patagonia.* In the incident as mentioned to me by Mrs. Kemble the heroine was a married woman in charge of the captain of the ship—who presumably knew her husband and could tell him of her misbehaviour. I shall change that and make her simply 'engaged': not only because of the prejudices of the Anglo-Saxon reader, but because I really think that more touching—think it more touching, that is, that she should jump overboard to escape having to marry (as well as to be denounced to) the man she is going out to Europe to join. And yet, and yet x x x x x
At any rate let us suppose that she is a young woman no longer in her very 1st youth, who has been the victim of a 'long engagement.' Her intended is in Europe and they have never yet had means to marry. He is studying architecture, and his studies never come to an end. She doesn't care for him at the last as she did at first—she is weary, disillusioned, tepid, but she is poor and she feels she *must* marry. Her lover sends for [her] at last, tells her the union must take place, but he can't come home—can't interrupt his studies. She must come out to him; he will meet her at Liverpool.—They haven't met for four years. She goes, in a perfunctory way, but her heart is not in it. I must tell the story as an eye-witness; I am on the ship and partly an actor in the drama. I must have seen her once— just before starting, on shore. It is a slow Boston Cunarder—a summer passage. The ship is changed *la veille,* to an old substitute, as occurred when I went over, in 1874, in the *Atlas.*[1] The girl must have been committed to the charge of a lady—an old lady, an old friend of mine, whom I call on, in Boston, just before sailing. I go to see her to ask if I can be of any use to her—to tell her we are to be fellow-passengers. It is a summer evening, in the empty town—in Mt. Vernon St. She has come up from the country (Beverly, etc.) to sail—to go to her daughter, in Germany—or some other natural pretext. She is alone at 1st—she tells me that there is a question of her son going with her, so that she won't have to count on me. If he doesn't go, however, she will look to me with pleasure. But he can't

---

1. HJ arrived in Liverpool from the United States in May 1872 aboard the Cunarder *Algeria;* he returned at the end of August 1874 aboard the slow Cunarder *Atlas.* To a reader in North America, ''I went over'' suggests an eastward journey; to HJ, writing in England, ''I went over'' would naturally enough suggest a journey westward.

decide—he is wavering—he has just gone round to the club—it seems as if he couldn't make up his mind—wouldn't really know till the morrow. Suggestion of his rather dissipated type. He comes in presently and is still uncertain: he is waiting for a telegram—he doesn't know—he will go round to the club again and see if the telegram has come. No trouble about a cabin—1st of August—old ship— sure to be several free even at the last moment. He is very good-looking, etc. We sit in the dusky room—with fans and ices—the house is dismantled—the windows look on the Back Bay with its lights. Oh, spirit of Maupassant,[2] come to my aid! This may be a triumph of robust and vivid concision: and certainly ought to be. The girl comes in with her mother. Her mother isn't going; she has to send the daughter off alone. She doesn't know my old lady—save through some common friend—and it is a little 'pushing' (the good mother must be slightly vulgar, and also forlorn, poor and nervous) on her part to come and call and make her appeal. She wants my friend to look after the girl—so that she shan't feel she is quite alone. That is her excuse, her maternal tremors. The girl about 28—very handsome and rather proud and stiff. She lets her mother act—*la laisse faire,* with a little silent embarrassment. Attitude of my old lady—very good-natured condescension, mingled with a little sense of intrusion, etc. She consents to have an eye on the young lady—is very poor at sea—but will do her best. The visitors stay a little and have ices. Before they go the son comes back, is introduced to the visitors, talks with the daughter, wanders into the other room with her, etc.— to go on the balcony—there being none to the windows that look on the water. This lasts about half an hour, or less. Then the ladies go, with vows of meeting on the ship, etc. After they have gone the son announces to his mother that he *has* decided to sail. I take my departure and he comes down to the door with me. I have 3 words with him—Miss X. is mentioned. I wonder, as I walk home, if that glimpse of her is what has determined him. I must tell him she is going out to her fiancé—he has not known that—it having been mentioned, in her mother's chatter, only in his absence. His answer to that. This might make I. Then the middle, II; and the denouement, III. I fear that with all the compression in the world I can't do it in so very short a compass as Comyns Carr[3] has demanded. Well, that is my start—and the rest ought to go. I can trust myself. It suddenly occurs to me, however, that to make the girl's dread of exposure a sufficient (partial) motive, I must be represented as knowing her intended—as having known him of old. My impression of him—in ten words. She must know that I know him and be afraid I shall tell him. Something must pass between us, in regard to this, just before she disappears. This knowledge of mine—this apprehension of hers, must play the part played by the scandalized public opinion of the ship (on the long Indian voyage) in Mrs. K.'s anecdote. That lady was known to be mar-

---

2. Guy de Maupasssant (1850–93), French short-story writer and novelist whom HJ met in 1876 at Flaubert's. HJ had just written an analysis of Maupassant's work in the *Fortnightly Review;* a second essay appeared in *Harper's Weekly* October 1889, reprinted as the introduction to *The Odd Number: Thirteen Tales by Guy de Maupassant,* translated by HJ's friend Jonathan Sturges. See *LA* III, 549, 554.
3. J. Comyns Carr (1849–1916), British dramatist-producer and critic for the *Pall Mall Gazette.* See 26 December 1881, note 7.

ried—to be going back to her husband. If my heroine is only engaged I can't make out the visible scandal as so great. But the young man's mother must also be represented as shocked—she talks with me, very distressfully about the matter. She is greatly displeased with her son, etc. It is rather awkward he is her son—that makes her reprobation of the girl direct and therefore less operative. But I must do my best with this—I must of course have some words with the young man—a little as the friend and representative of the injured fiancé. He must tell the girl that I have spoken, indignantly, for *him*—and that will increase her presumption that I *may* betray her when we land. Of course I must be a good deal older than my old lady's son—that is needed to justify my criticism and interference, if interference it may be called. What I mainly do is to remind him that—at the rate he is going on—the girl is engaged, and that if he makes trouble between and her lover he must at least be prepared to marry her. This he is evidently not in the least disposed to. He behaves badly—the fault is primarily his—and the horror of the denouement such as to overcloud him forever more.

Continuation of sketch of XIII of *Tragic Muse*.[1]

[. . .] between them, is peculiar—interesting—dramatic. Julia is delighted with him—this is the way she likes him—she is in love with him—she is ready for anything. She will marry him on the spot if he asks her. He is very conscious of this and he thinks he ought to ask her. She has done everything for him—for his election—she has been charming, effective, wonderful. She hasn't given money, of course—only Mr. C. has given that. But she *will* give money—she will give him her fortune. She tries to seduce him—she is full of bribery. I *must* make 2 scenes of it—one is not enough. Yet perhaps it is—with the 4th section of the instalment (the one scene should be the third) for his visit to Mr. C., to thank him. Mrs. Dallow virtually says to Nick: 'You have great talent—you *may* have a great future. But you have no money, and you can do nothing without that. I have a great fortune and it shall be yours. We will strike an alliance—I will marry you if I can count upon you. I want to be the wife of a great statesman—I am full of ambition—and my ambition is *that*. I will work with you and for you. Moreover I love you—I adore you. Only you must promise me—you are slippery and I must have some pledges. What did you mean that night in Paris? I love you—but I mistrust you. Therefore reassure me. The best way will be to love me—to possess me. See how charming, how enchanting, soothing, sympathetic I can be—whom they call hard.' She appears soft, seductive—but in it all there lurks her *condition*—her terms. He is much *échauffé*—but he feels this—feels the *condition*. Yes, yes—*one* scene—the rest at St. Albans.

1. This introductory line in the manuscript is written in red ink. The undated entry begins on the page on which the preceding entry (11 March 1888) ends, but it obviously continues a note begun in a notebook no longer extant. Reference is to the installment of the novel for May 1889; the entry thus dates from late 1888 or early 1889. Notebook I ends with this entry and the reference to *Verena*, in red ink, of September 1884 (pp. 30–31).

1889–1894

This notebook (Houghton Journal III, 2 February 1889 to 3 November 1894), $6\frac{1}{2}"$ × $8"$, has black leatherette covers with gilt trim, wine marbled end-papers and 204 lined pages, all with marbled edges. All entries are written in black ink. On the last page are several addresses, an account of accommodations and expenses in Lucerne in May 1893, and, in pencil, a brief arithmetic sum (see Cash Accounts, Appendices).

This notebook covers HJ's "dramatic years" to their critical moment, the production of *Guy Domville*. It also reflects his preparation of "plenty of short things."

The notebook begins a series of three "interlocking entries" that connect it with the three that follow: Houghton Journal III ends with an entry for 3 November 1894, and IV begins with an entry for the same day; IV ends in the middle of an entry for 15 October 1895 that is completed in V; the final entry of V is in turn completed in the initial entry of VI. That phenomenon does not argue, however, for unbroken chronology: other notebooks are evidently missing. The detached notes *The Chaperon* and "The E. P. D. Subject" intervene in the chronology of this notebook, between 7 May 1893 and 26 August 1893.

34 De Vere Gardens, February 2d, 1889.

I have been woefully interrupted in the composition of my long novel for the *Atlantic;* and must absolutely get on with it without further delay. I have had to write four articles[1] (it was really stupid, and it was needless, to consent) since I

1. HJ's "articles" published between October 1888 and June 1889 were a long review of "The Journal of the Brothers de Goncourt" in the *Fortnightly Review* October 1888; "London" in the

47

last worked at it, in the autumn, with any continuity or glow. I had at 1st a great deal of that glow; and I must make it come back to me. I can do so soon and effectually with a little *attention suivie*. The first thing is to keep cool and not to worry and get nervous; above all to *think*—as little as I really manage that in general!—and *live back* into the conditions one has tried to imagine. It all comes, thank God, so soon as I give it a barely decent chance. It is there—it lives—it waits; the picture blooms again so soon as I really fix my eyes on it. It is this time really a good subject, I think: save that it's too pale a one. I have undertaken to tell and to describe too much—given my *data*, such as they are—one of the reasons being that I was afraid of my story being too thin. For fear of making it too small I have made it too big. This, however, is a good fault, and I see my way out of it. Variety and concision must be my formula for the rest of the story—rapidity and action. I have of course, as usual, spread myself too much in the 1st chapter—been too complacently descriptive and illustrative. But I can retrieve that if I only *will*—if I will only bring myself to be brief and quick in the handling of the different episodes. Unless I achieve this I can't possibly get them all in. Let me write it as if, at any stage, it were to be a short story. That is the only way to get on and to put it all there. I have very interesting things to relate, but I must only *touch* them individually. *À la Maupassant* must be my constant motto. I must depend on the collective effect. For instance I must make a little masterpiece in 30 pp. of MS. of Nick's visit to Mr. Carteret. How much I must put into this! The same of the next chapter, Sherringham's visit to the Comédie Française with Miriam,—my impression of Bartet,[2] in her *loge*, the other day in Paris. x x x x x

February 27th, 1889. I have promised Archibald Grove to write him a short tale in three parts for his new projected magazine;[1] and I must get at work at it. The conditions are unsatisfactory—I am doing other work, which I have to interrupt, and I don't like the *form* of this task—the break into three parts each of which is very short—4500 words. Any subject will suffer from it: but I will do what I can: make as good a thing of it as possible and let the form of publication (till it's in a book) concern me as little as possible. x x x x x

["The Solution," the *New Review* December 1889 to February 1890; reprinted in *The Lesson of the Master*.]

There comes back to me with a certain vividness of solicitation, an idea that I noted a long time ago, suggested by something that Annie Thackeray once said or repeated to me.[2] That is, her story of Trollope's having had the plan of bringing

---

Century Magazine December 1888; "An Animated Conversation" in *Scribner's Magazine* March 1889 (all three reprinted in *Essays in London and Elsewhere*); "Our Artists in Europe" in *Harper's New Monthly Magazine* June 1889; and "After the Play" in the *New Review* (also June 1889), both reprinted in *Picture and Text*, New York (1893).

2. Julia Bartet (1854–1941), French actress whose real name was Jeanne Julia Regnault, was playing in *L'École des maris* in Paris. HJ's visit to her *loge* occurred in December 1888; see 12 May 1889.

1. Grove was editor of the *New Review*, in which HJ would publish his essay "After the Play" and the short tale in question here, "The Solution."

2. See 22 January 1879.

up his son to write novels, as a lucrative trade. She added (as Mrs. R. Ritchie) that she and her husband had the same idea with regard to her little girl. They would train her up to it as to a regular profession. This suggested to me the figure of a weary battered labourer in the field of fiction attempting to carry out this project with a child and meeting, by the irony of fate, the strangest discomfiture. All sorts of possibilities vaguely occur to one as latent in it. The child is given a chance to 'see life,' etc., that it may have material, and sees life to such a tune that he (or she) is swamped and destroyed. That is one element. Then the mother (this especially if it be a 'lady-novelist') tries to enable the son to go out into the world for *her own* purposes—to see society, hear things, etc. The poor mother describes fashionable life and the upper classes—and wants data and material. She is frowsy and dingy herself—she can't go—and she is too busy. The stupidity of the children, who bring home nothing—have no observation, etc. But there must be an *action,* of some little sort—and this occurs to me. There is a daughter and she has appeared pretty and clever—she is the one (there is a son beside), whom there has been this attempt to *form,* to train. In the early years there must be the dim vision of a handsome, idle father, living upon his wife. The expense of the girl's education, etc.—and also the boy's, who is good-looking and unaddicted to any literary pursuit. The particular drama to be that the girl proves quite useless as a novelist, but grows up, marries a snob on the edge of good society, is worldly and hard and would be smart, and is ashamed of her mother. Thinks her novels are vulgar rubbish—keeps her at a distance—almost ignores her—makes her very unhappy. The poor lady is obliged to go on writing, meanwhile, to meet the demands of her son—whom she has thrown into the world to pick up information for her, and who has simply become idle, selfish, extravagant and vicious. She has all sorts of lurking romanticisms and *naïvetés*—make a very vivid amusing pathetic picture of her mixture of queer qualities, etc.—her immorality, her natural penchant to license *à la Ouida*[3] of which her priggish daughter is ashamed. Her love of splendour, of the aristocracy, of high society—the wealth and beauty which she attributes to her people, etc.—contrasted with the small shabby facts of her own life. She dies at the end, worn out, disappointed, poor. The thing had much best be told by a witness of her life—a friend—a critic, a journalist, etc.: in the 1st person: rapid notes. I speak of the telegram from the editor of one of the big papers when she dies, asking for ½ a column about her. I saw and wrote the ½ column and made it kinder. Then for myself I wrote these other notes—kinder still.—The thing to be called by the *nom de plume* of the poor lady—some rather smart *man's* name.

This little sketch of which I think very well on the whole (Feb. 28th) would gain in effect by the supposititious narrator being himself a novelist but of the younger generation and of the modern psychological type. There would be touches there which might throw the poor woman's funny old art into contrast with his point of view—touches of bewilderment at his work on *her* side and of indulgence and humour on his.

---

3. "Ouida" was the pen name of a popular British novelist, Maria Louisa Ramé (1839–1908), later changed to de la Ramée. She touched the fringes of the social circle HJ knew in Florence.

February 28th. Mightn't I do something fairly good with that idea I made a note of long ago—the idea of the young man on whom some companions impose the idea that he has so committed himself with regard to a girl that he must propose to her—he is bound in honour—and who does propose, credulously, *naïvement,* to do the right thing, and is eagerly accepted, having money and being something of a *parti.*[1] This was suggested to me by an anecdote told me by Mrs. Kemble of something that had taken place years ago—in the diplomatic body in Rome—I think—under her observation. The young man married the girl—not caring for her at all—under this delusion which 2 or 3 of his colleagues (he was a young secretary, I believe) had amused themselves with fastening upon him—he being a naïf, tempting subject. I think the girl was English, one of two or three sisters with a loud, hard, worldly, pushing mother. 'Only not Olympia'—I made a note of that when the little tale was told me: the young fellow's cry when the others told him that there was one of the sisters who had a right to expect of him that he should make up to her. He thought Olympia too like her mother—but it was of course she whom the others pushed him into the arms of. His after life with Olympia, etc. Isn't this situation very considerably dramatic? There is something in it which might be made interesting—surely. The story should be told by one of the actors, one of the *jeunes étourdis* (an Englishman) who carried out the joke. He relates it late in life—as a very old retired diplomatist, full of memories. The old delicious, quiet, sunny, idle Rome of forty or fifty years ago! He has had great remorse since—he had it at the time—he tried to back out when he found how far the game had gone. I noted all this before—but it didn't seem quite enough. There should be a complete drama in it, a sequel and a conclusion. I began to write the story—but I gave it up—I have the commenced fragment somewhere. Perhaps it would serve my turn for the article for A. Grove, better than the idea recorded in this place yesterday. It would have movement but be short and divisible into three parts. The young fellow practiced upon is the American Secretary of Legation. His simplicity, good faith, etc., made natural—he is easily persuaded that he must act in accordance with European customs, and by that canon he has distinctly committed himself and even compromised the girl. The narrator's scare when he finds the consequences are serious. There must be three men in it—himself and two others. But what is the drama—the denouement—*voyons?* It all depends on that. I try to prevent it—I go to the mother—it is too late. She tells me that she will break off the arrangement—the engagement that has been entered into if *I* will 'take over' her daughter instead. But I *can't* bring my mind to that. I struggle—I hesitate—but I can't. x x x x x

I think *je tiens mon dénouement*—and the rest of the action. There must be another woman in the case; a woman whom I am rather in love with—a woman clever, accomplished, independent, etc. She can only be a widow—and that is rather conventional.

---

1. The notebook in which HJ made that initial note has not survived. Here he develops his idea for "The Solution"; see 27 February 1889. HJ also based his play *Disengaged* (1892) on this story; see 24 November 1892.

March 18th. Note here next (no time today) the 2 things old Lady Stanley told me the other day that the former Lady Holland had said to her—and the admirable subject suggested to me yesterday, Sunday, at Mrs. Jeune's by Mrs. Lynn Linton's (and Mrs. J.'s) talk about F.H.: the man marrying for money to serve him for a great political career and public ends.[1]

March 25th, 1889 (Monday).

Last evening before dinner I took a walk with G. Du Maurier, in the mild March twilight (there was a blessed sense of spring in the air), through the empty streets near Porchester Terrace, and he told me over an idea of his which he thought very good—and I do too—for a short story—he had already mentioned [it] to me—a year or two ago, in a walk at Hampstead, but it had passed from my mind. Last night it struck me as curious, picturesque and distinctly usable: though the want of musical knowledge would hinder *me* somewhat in handling it. I can't set it forth in detail here, now; I haven't the time—but I must do it later. It is the history of the servant girl with a wonderful rich full voice but no musical genius who is mesmerized and made to sing by a little foreign Jew who has mesmeric power, infinite feeling, and no organ (save as an accompanist—on some instrument, violin) of his own. He carries her away, about the world—singing, for shillings, in the streets of foreign towns, etc.—she performs wonderfully while he is there, acting upon her. The man who relates the story—a poorish artist—has known her in London as the stupid, handsome daughter of his landlady, or as that of one of his friends. He meets the pair, abroad, follows them, wonders (having recognized her—and having seen *him* once of old—at an artist's supper in Newman St. [given by his friend] where the girl has waited and been noticed—just enough noticed, by the little Jew, for the story). She doesn't know him—she is changed, strange, besides her wonderful singing—which she didn't have before— and he is quite mystified. He has heard, already, after the girl's original unexplained disappearance—two or three years after—of a wonderful voice—that of a mere *chanteuse de café*, etc.—of which a dilettante friend of his has spoken to him with rapture and which (the owner of which) he tries to follow up and put his hand upon in order to capture her for a party of Lady X.'s, a woman he wishes to please. Say she is to have royalty, etc.—and he is keen in pursuit. But he misses—the pair is vanished. It is *after* this that the narrator meets them abroad— and recognizes them, both as the subjects of his friend's anecdote and as the London *fille bête* and the wonderfully *doué* disreputable little foreigner. *Il s'y perd*—because the girl is really all the while only galvanized by her mate. He makes them come to his rooms somewhere—at Nuremburg or at Siena—and they perform wonderfully for him (all this requires tact—in regard to the music) till the

---

1. Lady Stanley was the daughter of the second Baron Stanley of Alderley and sister of Col. Stanley of the Coldstream Guards. Susan Mary Elizabeth Mackenzie of Scotland married Col. Stanley; at his death she married Francis Henry Jeune, later the first Baron St. Helier. Her grandniece, Clementine Hozier, married Winston Churchill. Mrs. Elizabeth Lynn Linton (1822–98) was a novelist and an early pioneer of the vote for women; she also practised spiritualism. F. H. was probably Frank H. Hill, editor of the London *Daily News* (see 25 November 1881, note 14).

1. HJ's brackets.

man drinks too much and is disabled by it. Then *she* can do nothing, becomes helpless—drinks, *chancelle*, behaves as if she were vaguely tipsy herself. She relapses, in short, into impotence. They disappear again—I meet them one more—and now the man is dead or dying. He dies—the girl becomes *Gros-Jean comme devant*—unable to raise a note. She had only been a subject, and the whole thing was mesmerically communicated to her. She had had the glorious voice, but no talent—he had had the sacred fire, the rare musical organization, and had played into her and through her. The *end*, as regards her, miserably pathetic.[1]

34 De Vere Gardens, May 12th, 1889.

I interrupt some other work this moist still Sunday morning to make a few notes on the subject of the play I have engaged to write for Edward Compton.[1] I needn't go over the little history of this engagement and the reasons—they are familiar enough—which led me to respond to the proposal coming to me from him while I was in Paris last December. I had practically given up my old, valued, long cherished dream of doing something for the stage, for fame's sake, and art's, and fortune's: overcome by the vulgarity, the brutality, the baseness of the condition of the English-speaking theatre today. But after an interval, a long one, the vision has revived, on a new and a very much humbler basis, and especially under the lash of necessity. Of art or fame *il est maintenant fort peu question:* I simply *must* try, and try seriously, to produce half a dozen—a dozen, five dozen—plays for the sake of my pocket, my material future. Of how little money the novel makes for me I needn't discourse here. The theatre has sought me out—in the person of the good, the yet unseen, Compton. I have listened and considered and reflected, and the matter is transposed to a minor key. To accept the circumstances, in their extreme humility, and do the best I can *in* them: this is the moral of my present situation. They are the reverse of ideal—but there is this great fact that for myself at least I may make them better. To take what there *is,* and use it, without waiting forever in vain for the preconceived—to dig deep into the actual and get something out of *that*—this doubtless is the right way to live. If I succeed a little I can easily—I think—succeed more; I can make my own conditions more as I go on.

1. The plot outlined here by George Du Maurier (1834–96), the British novelist and illustrator of *Punch,* was that of *Trilby* (1894), which, at HJ's urging, Du Maurier himself ultimately wrote with tremendous success. Du Maurier had provided a dozen illustrations for HJ's *Washington Square* in 1880 and seven for HJ's essay "Du Maurier and London Society" in the *Century Magazine* May 1883 (reprinted without the illustrations in *Partial Portraits*). HJ introduced a catalogue of Du Maurier's drawings in a pamphlet of 1884 and wrote a brief piece on him for *Harper's Weekly* April 1894 (see *LA* II, 870–76). His final tribute, after Du Maurier's death, appeared in *Harper's New Monthly Magazine* September 1897 (see *LA* II, 876–907 and *Life* 454–55). HJ's early fascination with mesmerism is reflected in his short story "Professor Fargo" (in *Galaxy* August 1874), in *The Bostonians* and in his play *The Reprobate* (see 23 October 1891).

1. Compton was the young actor-manager of the Compton Comedy Company, which had been performing mainly in the British provinces. At the prompting of his wife, the American actress Virginia Bateman, Compton wrote to ask HJ about turning his novel *The American* into a play. *The American* ran in the provinces for some twenty-five performances, beginning January 1891, then in London at the Opera Comique Theatre in the Strand from 26 September to 3 December 1891. See *Complete Plays* 47–55, 179–91.

The field is common, but it is wide and free—in a manner—and amusing. And if there is money in it that will greatly help: for all the profit that may come to me in this way will mean real freedom for one's general artistic life: it all hangs together (time, leisure, independence for 'real literature,' and, in addition, a great deal of experience of *tout un côté de la vie*). Therefore my plan is to try with a settled resolution—that is, with a full determination to return repeatedly to the charge, overriding, annihilating, despising the boundless discouragements, disgusts, *écoeurements*. One should *use* such things—grind them to powder.

x   x   x   x   x

His proposal is that I shall make a play of *The American,* and there is no doubt a play in it. I must extract the simplest, strongest, baldest, most rudimentary, at once most humorous and most touching one, in a form whose main *souci* shall be pure situation and pure point combined with pure brevity. Oh, how it must not be too good and how very bad it must be! *À moi,* Scribe; *à moi,* Sardou, *à moi,* Dennery![2]—Reduced to its simplest expression, and that reduction must be my play, *The American* is the history of a plain man who is at the same time a fine fellow, who becomes engaged to the daughter of a patrician house, being accepted by her people on acct. of his wealth, and is then thrown over (by *them*) for a better match: after which he turns upon them to recover his betrothed (they have bullied her out of it), through the possession of a family secret which is disgraceful to them, dangerous to them, and which he holds over them as an instrument of compulsion and vengeance. They are frightened—they feel the screw: they dread exposure; but in the novel the daughter is already lost to the hero—she is swept away by the tragedy, takes refuge in a convent, breaks off her other threatened match, renounces the world, disappears. The hero, injured, outraged, resentful, feels the strong temptation to *punish* the Bellegardes, and for a day almost yields to it. Then he does the characteristically magnanimous thing—the characteristically good-natured thing—throws away his opportunity—lets them 'off'— lets them go. In the play he must do this—*but* get his wife.

Sunday, May 19th, 1889.

Very interesting meeting with Taine yesterday—at a lunch given by Jusserand[1] at the Bristol Restaurant: company, M. and Mme Taine, their daughter, Dr. Jessopp, pleasant, clerical friend of Jusserand—George Du Maurier—myself. The personal impression of Taine remarkably pleasant; much more *bonhomie*, mildness and geniality, than his hard, splendid, intellectual, logical style and manner had led me to expect. Charming talker—renewal of the sense of the high superiority of French talk. He has an obliquity of vision, yet is handsome in spite of it,

---

2. Eugène Scribe (1791–1861), Victorien Sardou (see 19 February 1883), and Adolphe-Philippe Dennery or D'Ennery (1811–99), French dramatists.

1. Hippolyte Taine (1828–93), French literary critic and historian. Between May 1868 and July 1876 HJ published half a dozen reviews (mainly in the *Nation*) of Taine's work. Jules Jusserand (1855–1932), French literary historian and diplomat; he served as French Ambassador to Washington from 1902 to 1925.

with a fine head, a brown complexion, straight, strong, regular features—a fine, grave, masculine type. He talked about many things, and all well: about England with knowledge, friendliness, etc.—great knowledge; but what I wish especially to note here is his tribute to Turgenieff—to his depth, his variety, his form, the small, full perfect things he has left, which will live through their finished objectivity, etc. He rates T. very high—higher in form even than I have done. But his talk about him has done me a world of good—reviving, refreshing, confirming, consecrating, as it were, the wish and dream that have lately grown stronger than ever in me—the desire that the literary heritage, such as it is, poor thing, that I may leave, shall consist of a large number of perfect *short* things, *nouvelles* and tales, illustrative of ever so many things in life—in the life I see and know and feel—and of all the deep and the delicate—and of London, and of art, and of everything: and that they shall be fine, rare, strong, wise—eventually perhaps even recognized.

Taine used the expression, very happily, that Turgenieff so perfectly cut the umbilical cord that bound the story to himself.

January 23d. [1890] Dining last night at the Ch. Lawrences', Condie Stephen,[1] who sat next to me, mentioned an anecdote—a case—of some man he had heard of, who fearing to suffer intensely in his last illness extracted a solemn promise from his wife that she would give him something that, at the last, would put an end to him. He fell ill, in due course, and then his wife's heart utterly failed her and she only did things—covert spoonsful of brandy, etc.—that would keep him alive longer—even from one day to the other. This struck me—a little tale might be made on it: especially with complications. Her promise, for instance, may be known to some other person, and her underhand restoratives (for she is ashamed of breaking it) be suspected to be doses of an opposite intention. In other words she looks as if she were poisoning her husband, while she is really keeping him alive. Denouement!

February 6th, 1890. (Sent the Act 2 of *The Californian*[1] yesterday to E. Compton.) Perhaps the best formula for the fabrication [of] a dramatic piece *telle qu'il nous faut en faire,* in the actual conditions, if we are to do anything at all, is: Action which is never dialogue and dialogue which is always action.

Vallombrosa, July 27th, 1890. Subject for a short tale: a young man or woman who, in a far Western city—Colorado or California—surrounds himself with a European 'atmosphere' by means of French and English books—Maupassant, *Revue des 2 Mondes*—Anatole France, Paul Bourget, Jules Lemaître, etc.;[1] and,

---

1. The Rev. Charles d'Aguilar Lawrence (1847–1935), rector of Lowestoft, 1889–1901. Sir Alexander Condie Stephen (1850–1908), diplomat and translator.

1. The original title for HJ's play version of *The American.*

1. Anatole France (1844–1924), French novelist and critic; Jules Lemaître (1853–1914), French literary critic.

making it really very complete, and a little world, intense world of association and perception in the alien air, lives in it altogether. Visit to him of narrator, who has been in Europe and knows the people (say narrator is a very modern impressionist painter); and contrast of all these hallucinations with the hard western ugliness, newspaperism, vulgarity, and democracy. There must be an American literary woman, from New England, 'pure and refined,' thin and intense. The sketch, picture, vision—*à la Maupassant.* The point that, after all, even when an opportunity offers to go over and see the realities—go to Paris and there know something of the life described—the individual *stays*—won't leave: held by the spell of knowing it all *that* way—as the best. It isn't much of a 'point'—but I can sharpen it; the situation, and what one can bring in, are the point.[2]

Paris, Hotel Westminster, February 22d, 1891.

    In pursuance of my plan of writing some very short tales—things of from 7000 to 10,000 words, the easiest length to 'place,' I began yesterday the little story that was suggested to me some time ago by an incident related to me by George Du Maurier—the lady and gentleman who called upon him with a word from Frith, an oldish, faded, ruined pair—he an officer in the army—who unable to turn a penny in any other way, were trying to find employment as models. I was struck with the pathos, the oddity and typicalness of the situation—the little tragedy of good-looking gentlefolk, who had been all their life stupid and well-dressed, living, on a fixed income, at country-houses, watering places and clubs, like so many others of their class in England, and were now utterly unable to *do* anything, had no cleverness, no art nor craft to make use of as a *gagne-pain*—could only *show* themselves, clumsily, for the fine, clean, well-groomed animals that they were, only hope to make a little money by—in this manner—just simply *being.* I thought I saw a subject for very brief treatment in this *donnée*—and I think I do still; but to do anything worth while with it I must (as always, great Heavens!) be very clear as to what is in it and what I wish to get out of it. I tried a beginning yesterday, but I instantly became conscious that I must straighten out the little idea. It must be an idea—it can't be a 'story' in the vulgar sense of the word. It must be a picture; it must illustrate something. God knows that's enough— if the thing *does* illustrate. To make little anecdotes of this kind real *morceaux de vie* is a plan quite inspiring enough. *Voyons un peu,* therefore, what one can put into this one—I mean how much of life. One must put a little action—not a stupid, mechanical, arbitrary action, but something that is of the real essence of the subject. I thought of representing the husband as jealous of the wife—that is, jealous of the artist employing her, from the moment that, in point of fact, she begins to sit. But this is vulgar and obvious—worth nothing. What I wish to represent is the baffled, ineffectual, incompetent character of their attempt, and how it illustrates once again the everlasting English amateurishness—the way superficial, untrained, unprofessional effort goes to the wall when confronted with trained, competitive, intelligent, *qualified* art—in whatever line it may be a ques-

---

2. Preliminary note for "Europe"; see 14 February 1895.

tion of. It is out of *that* element that my little action and movement must come; and now I begin to see just how—as one always *does*—Glory be to the Highest— when one begins to look at a thing hard and straight and seriously—to fix it—as I am so sadly lax and desultory about doing. What subjects I should find—for *everything*—if I could only achieve this more as a habit! Let my contrast and complication here come from the opposition—to my melancholy Major and his wife—of a couple of little vulgar professional people *who know,* with the consequent bewilderment, vagueness, depression of the former—their failure to understand how such people can be better than *they*—their failure, disappointment, disappearance—going forth into the vague again. *Il y a bien quelque chose à tirer de ça.* They have no pictorial sense. They are only clean and stiff and stupid. The others are dirty, even—the melancholy Major and his wife remark on it, wondering. The artist is beginning a big illustrated book, a new edition of a famous novel—say *Tom Jones:* and he is willing to try to work them in—for he takes an interest in their predicament, and feels—sceptically, but, with his flexible artistic sympathy—the appeal of their type. He is willing to give them a trial. Make it out that *he* himself is on trial—he is young and 'rising,' but he has still his golden spurs to win. He can't afford, *en somme,* to make many mistakes. He has regular work in drawing every week for a serial novel in an illustrated paper; but the great project—that of a big house—of issuing an illustrated Fielding promises him a big lift. He has been intrusted with (say) *Joseph Andrews,* experimentally; he will have to do this brilliantly in order to have the engagement for the rest confirmed. He has already 2 models in his service—the 'complication' must come from *them.* One is a common, clever, London girl, of the smallest origin and without conventional beauty, but of aptitude, of perceptions—knowing thoroughly *how.* She says 'lydy' and 'plice,' but she has the pictorial sense; and can look like anything he wants her to look like. She poses, in short, in perfection. So does her colleague, a professional Italian, a little fellow—ill dressed, smelling of garlic, but admirably serviceable, quite universal. They must be contrasted, confronted, *juxtaposed* with the others; whom they take for people who *pay,* themselves, till they learn the truth when they are overwhelmed with derisive amazement. The denouement simply that the melancholy Major and his wife won't do—they're not 'in it.' Their surprise—their helpless, proud assent—without other prospects: yet at the same time *their* degree of more silent amazement at the success of the two inferior people—who are so much less nice-looking than themselves. Frankly, however, is this contrast enough of a *story,* by itself? It seems to me Yes—for it's an IDEA—and how the deuce should I get *more* into 7000 words? It must be simply 50 pp. of my manuscript. The little tale of *The Servant (Brooksmith)*[1] which I did the other day for *Black and White* and which I thought of at the same time as this, proved a very tight squeeze into the same tiny number of words, and I probably shall find that there is much more to be done with this than the compass will admit of. Make it tremendously succinct—with a very short pulse or rhythm—and the closest selection of detail—in other words *summarize* intensely and keep down the lateral development. It *should* be a little gem of bright, quick, vivid form. I

---

1. Published as "Brooksmith"; see 19 June 1884.

shall get every grain of 'action' that the space admits of if I make something, for the artist, hand in the balance—depend on the way he does this particular work. It's when he finds that he shall lose his great opportunity if he keeps on with them, that he has to tell the gentlemanly couple, that, frankly, they won't serve his turn—and make them wander forth into the cold world again. I must keep them the age I've made them—50 and 40—because it's more touching; but I must bring up the age of the 2 real models to almost the same thing. That increases the incomprehensibility (to the amateurs) of their usefulness. Picture the immanence, in the latter, of the idle, provided-for, country-house habit—the blankness of their *manière d'être.* But in how tremendously few words I must do it. This is a lesson—a *magnificent* lesson—if I'm to do a good many. Something as admirably compact and *selected* as Maupassant.

[*"The Real Thing,"* *Black and White* 16 April 1892; reprinted in *The Real Thing and Other Tales.*]

Names. Beet—Beddington—Leander (surname)—Stormer—Luard—Void (name of a place) or *Voyd* would do for this.—Morn, or *Morne*—Facer—Funnel—Haddock—Windermere—Corner—Barringer—Jay—State—Vesey—Dacca—Ulic (Xtian name)—Brimble (or for a house)—Fade—Eily, the Irish name—good for a girl.

Marine Hotel, Kingstown, Ireland, July 13th, 1891.[1]

I must hammer away at the effort to do, successfully and triumphantly, a large number of very short things. I have done ½ a dozen, lately, but it takes time and practice to get into the trick of it. I have never attempted before to deal with such extreme brevity. However, the extreme brevity is a necessary condition only for some of them—the others may be of varying kinds and degrees of shortness. I needn't go into all my reasons and urgencies over again here; suffice it that they are cogent and complete. I must absolutely *not* tie my hands with promised novels if I wish to keep them free for a genuine and sustained attack on the theatre. That is one cogent reason out of many; but the artistic one would be enough even by itself. What I call *the* artistic one *par excellence* is simply the consideration that by doing short things I can do so many, touch so many subjects, break out in so many places, handle so many of the threads of life. x x x x x

However, I have threshed all this out; it exists, in my mind, in the shape of absolutely digested and assimilated motive—inspiration deep and clear. The upshot of all such reflections is that I have only to let myself *go!* So I have said to myself all my life—so I said to myself in the far-off days of my fermenting and passionate youth. Yet I have never fully done it. The sense of it—of the need of it—rolls over me at times with commanding force: it seems the formula of my salvation, of what remains to me of a future. I am in full possession of accumulated resources—I have only to use them, to insist, to persist, to do something more—to do much more—than I *have* done. The way to do it—to affirm one's self *sur la fin*—is to strike as many notes, deep, full and rapid, as one can. All

---

1. HJ spent a month (7 July to 7 August 1891) at Kingstown, some six miles from Dublin, recuperating from influenza.

life is—at my age, with all one's artistic soul the record of it—in one's pocket, as it were. Go on, my boy, and strike hard; have a rich and long St. Martin's Summer. Try everything, do everything, render everything—be an artist, be distinguished, to the last. One has one's doubts and discouragements—but they are only so many essential vibrations of one's ideal. The field is still all round me, to be won; it blooms with the flowers that are still to be plucked. But enough of the *general*, these things are the ambient air; they are the breath of one's artistic and even of one's personal life. Strike, strike, again and again and again, at the *special;* I have only to live and to work, to look and to feel, to *gather,* to note. My *cadres* all there; continue, ah, continue, to fill them.

x   x   x   x   x

I made, I think, some time ago, a little note on the idea (suggested by a word of Mrs. Earle's on the situation of Mrs. M. and one of her daughters)[2] of the adaptability of that particular little subject to a short tale. The situation is that of a woman who has compromised herself gravely while her child was young—made a scandal and a rumpus, quitted her husband for another man by whom, in turn, she was quitted, and who, living cold-shouldered by the world, though without another lover, ever since, finds herself confronted with her children when they grow up. There must be a daughter, and a couple of sons. The father has had them and brought them up; living separated of course from his wife, whom he has not chosen, or not been able, to divorce. They have occasionally seen her, have been allowed to go to see her, and are vaguely conscious of the peculiarity of her situation. The daughter grows up pretty and charming and people compassionate her, think it a pity she should have over her the cloud of her besmirched mother, whom she resembles—regret its effect on her prospects, etc. The idea, in a word, of the tale, is that the girl proves such a little person that she not only accepts, courageously, gaily, and quietly, keeping her own counsel and opening herself to no one, the facts of her mother's fate, the 'disadvantage' of such an association, etc., but determines to reverse the condition and be herself the poor lady's providence. Her mother can do nothing for her in society, can't 'take her out,' etc.; so she makes it her plan to bestow these services instead of receiving them. She will take her mother out—she will be *her* chaperon and protectress, she will make a place for her. The mother, in a word, is reinstated socially by the daughter's doing for *her* what she is not able to do for the daughter. I think there *must* have been a divorce—it makes the girl's action more difficult and her *tare* more marked. Type of the girl—pretty, very pretty, with charm; clever, quietly resolute, reticent and imperturbable. She is so attractive that she makes people accept her mother in order to have *her*. She becomes attractive to do it—being really serious, indifferent to vulgar success. She is proud, and she is in love with a clever, rather narrow-minded man, who is much taken with her but who has his reserves, is full of implied reservations and conditions. *Je vois tout ça d'ici*—the items and elements multiply and live. It is necessary that the girl must have elected

---

2. Mrs. C. W. Earle, née Maria Teresa Villiers (1836–1925), widow of Capt. Charles William Earle, was the author of a series of "Pot Pourri" books.

to go and live with her mother. The father has died, expressing the strongest wish [that] his children shall do nothing of the kind. There are two others, a younger daughter and a son who don't. There must be a grandmother and an aunt, both paternal of course. So many types and figures—the observed London world— 'Society' *telle que je l'ai vue.* The whole very short—with every touch an image, a step. The contrast between the mother and daughter—the mother flimsy and trivial, in spite of all her pathos and her troubles—the girl wondering at such yearnings—getting invited to parties, etc.—even while she makes herself their instrument. The mother is reinstated, the girl does it all for her; then she marries her *soupirant,* who must be a young soldier, of the peculiarly English moral and religious kind. She is left with a grievance, after all (I mean the mother), as against her daughter; she makes it a reproach to her that the stepson doesn't like or welcome her—a woman in such a position as hers! Can't she make him receive her differently—make him seem to wish more to see her in his house? Last words of the tale: 'The girl turned away, with a sigh; she spoke wearily: "No, mamma, I'm afraid I can't do that too." ' Her only allusion, to her mother, to what she has done.[3]

[''The Chaperon,'' the *Atlantic Monthly* November–December 1891; reprinted in *The Real Thing and Other Tales.*]

Marine Hotel, Kingstown, July 21st, '91.

I have done my best for the foregoingly noted little subject, but it insists—it has insisted—on getting itself treated at somewhat greater length than I intended—in 2 parts, for the *Atlantic.* I have finished one of these sufficiently well, I think, to make it immensely my interest to straighten out to the very best effect the possibilities of the other. If I can make Part II all it may be, the thing will be very good indeed. Make it purely dramatic, make it movement and action. I have set the stage sufficiently in the first act. Make it a vivid London picture—the picture of what Rose Tramore does and how she does it. The idea is pretty enough and odd enough to express completely. But the right formula for the 2d part is a series of *scènes de comédie,* with a strong ironical taste. Plunge into the midst—set it going. There must be, as a core to the little action, some London woman who wants Rose for her son—her vision of the inducements and advantages made clear— but wants her *without* her mother, tries to get her away from her mother, deal with her singly, etc. Rose's absolute refusal, from the first, to be dealt with singly, and comprehension that with this rigid rule she will eventually succeed in her purpose. The chapter must open with some episode of apparent failure. I see it, and I can go on. It must be intensely brief and concise; only 45 pp. of MS.[1]

Names. Wharton—Rosedew—Vaudrey (or Vawdrey)—Grutt—Stack—Fillingham—Smale—Morillion.

---

1. See 27 July 1891.

1. ''The Chaperon''; see 13 July 1891. Not only did HJ make it ''purely dramatic,'' he later tried to turn it into a play with the same title: see May/June 1893 and the dictated note ''Rough Statement'' (1907).

Kingstown, July 27th, 1891.

The Private Life[1] (title of the little tale founded on the idea of F.L. and R.B.)[2] must begin: 'We talked of London, face to face with a great bristling primeval glacier. The hour and the scene were one of those impressions which make up, a little, in Switzerland, for the modern indignities of travel—the promiscuities and vulgarities of the station and the hotel—the struggle for a scrappy attention, the reduction to the numbered state. The high valley was pink with the mountain rose and the pure air as cold as one's submission to nature. The desultory tinkle of the cattle bells seemed to communicate a sociability with innocent things.'

["The Private Life," the *Atlantic Monthly* April 1892; reprinted in *The Private Life*, London and New York (1893).]

Names. Pickerel—Chafer—Bullet—Whitethorne—Dash—Elsinore (place)—Douce—Doveridge (person or place)—Adney—Twentyman (butler)—Firminger—Wayward (place)—Wayworth—Greyswood (place)—Nona (girl's name)—Runting.

Names (continued).—Scruby—Mellifont (a place, or still better, title. Ld. Mellifont)—Undertone (for a countryhouse)—Gentry—Butterton—Vallance—Ashbury—Alsager—Bosco (person or place)—Isherwood—Loder—Garnet—Antram—Antrim—Cubit—Ambler—Urban (Xtian name)—Windle—Trivet—Middleship—Keep—Vigors—Film—Philmor—Champ—Cramp—Rosewood—Rosin—Littlewood—Esdaile—Galleon—Bray—Nurse—Nourse—Reul—Prestige—Poland—Cornice—Gosselin—Roseabel (Xtian name)—Shorting—Sire—Airey—Doubleday—Conduit—Tress—Gallop—Farrington—Bland—Arrand—Ferrand—Dominick—Heatherfield—Teagle—Pam—Locket—Brickwood—Boston-Cribb—Trend—Aryles—Hoyle—Flake—Jury—Porches(place)—Morrish—Gole.

Marine Hotel, Kingstown, August 3d, 1891.

The Private Life—the idea of rolling into one story the little conceit of the private identity of a personage suggested by F.L., and that of a personage suggested by R.B., is of course a rank fantasy, but as such may it not be made amusing and pretty? It must be very brief—very light—very vivid. Lord Mellefont is the public *performer*—the man whose whole personality goes forth so in representation and aspect and sonority and phraseology and accomplishment and frontage

1. See 3 August 1891.
2. F. L. was Sir Frederic Leighton (1830–96), later Lord Leighton, British painter and sculptor and in 1891 President of the Royal Academy. HJ discussed Leighton's work in articles for *Harper's Weekly* January, February, and May 1897, later collected in *The Painter's Eye*, ed. John L. Sweeney, 1956. R. B. was Robert Browning (1812–89). At Browning's death HJ wrote an account of his burial in Westminster Abbey for the *Speaker* January 1890 (reprinted in *Essays in London and Elsewhere* [1893]), and for the centenary celebration of the poet's birth he read "The Novel in *The Ring and the Book*" to the Academic Committee of the Royal Society of Literature in May 1912 (published in their *Transactions* for that year, and in *Notes on Novelists*, London and New York [1914]). See also 25 November 1881.

that there is absolutely—but I *see* it: begin it—begin it! Don't talk *about* it only,
and around it.[1]

x   x   x   x   x

October 22d, 1891, 34 De Vere Gdns. I finished yesterday my difficult paper on
J.R.L. for the January *Atlantic*[1] and I must immediately get into the work promised to Kinloch-Cooke.[2] I am emerging a little from all the *déboires* and distresses
consequent on the production of *The American* by Edward Compton, and I needn't
note them here to remind myself what the episode has been, and still, in a measure, *is;* nor to feel how much it gives me something to live for in the future. I
shall live, I trust, for several things; but a very prominent one, surely, shall be
the firm—the exquisitely still and deep-rooted resolution—to compass, in the theatre, the solid, the honourable (so far as anything can be honourable there!), the
absolute and interesting success. Meanwhile the soothing, the healing, the sacred
and salutary refuge from all these vulgarities and pains is simply to lose myself in
this quiet, this blessed and uninvaded workroom in the inestimable effort and
refreshment of art, in resolute and beneficient production. I come back to it with
a treasure of experience, of wisdom, of acquired material, of (it seems to me)
seasoned fortitude and augmented capacity. Purchased by disgusts enough, it is at
any rate a boon that now that I hold it, I feel I wouldn't, I oughtn't, to have
missed. Ah, the terrible law of the artist—the law of fructification, of fertilization,
the law by which everything is grist to his mill—the law, in short, of the acceptance of all experience, of all suffering, of *all* life, of *all* suggestion and sensation
and illumination. To keep at it—to strive toward the perfect, the ripe, the only
best; to go on, by one's own clear light, with patience, courage and continuity, to
live with the high vision and effort, to justify one's self—and oh, so greatly!—all
in time: this and this alone can be my only lesson from *anything.* Vague and weak
are these words, but the experience and the purpose are of welded gold and ada-
mant. The consolation, the dignity, the joy of life are that discouragements and
lapses, depressions and darknesses come to one only as one stands *without*—I
mean without the luminous paradise of art. As soon as I really re-enter it—cross
the loved threshhold—stand in the high chamber, and the gardens divine—the
whole realm widens out again before me and around me—the air of life fills my
lungs—the light of achievement flushes over all the place, and I believe, I see, I
do.

x   x   x   x   x

What of this idea for a very little tale?—The situation of a married woman who
during her husband's lifetime has loved another man and who, after his death,

1. See 27 July 1891.

1. HJ's long memorial essay on James Russell Lowell appeared in the *Atlantic Monthly* January 1892;
see *LA* II, 516–40. See 17 November 1887.

2. Sir Clement Kinloch-Cooke, editor of the *English Illustrated Magazine.* HJ did not develop this
idea into a story: he sent instead "Nona Vincent" for February-March 1892 (reprinted in *The Real
Thing and Other Tales*).

finds herself confronted with her lover—with the man whom, at least, she has suffered to make love to her, in a certain particular way. The particular way I imagine to be this: the husband is older, stupider, uglier, but she has of course always had a bad conscience. I imagine a flirtation between her and the younger man, who is really in love with her, which she breaks off on becoming aware that her husband is ill and dying. He is kind, indulgent, unsuspicious to her and she is so touched by his tenderness and suffering that she is filled with remorse at her infidelity and breaks utterly with her lover. She devotes herself to her husband, nurses and cherishes him—but at the end of a short time he dies. She is haunted by the sense that she was unkind to him—that he suspected her—that she broke his heart—that she really killed him. In this state she passes 6 months, at the end of which she meets again he man who has loved her and who still loves her. His hope is now that she will marry him—that he has gained his cause by waiting, by respecting her, by leaving her alone. x x x x x

I interrupt myself, because suddenly, in my imagination the clearing process takes place—the little click that often occurs when I begin to straighten things out pen in hand, really tackle them, sit down and look them in the face. I catch hold of the slip of a tail of my action—I see my little drama. There are 4 persons—2 men and 2 women—not 1 woman and 2 men. The revelation about her husband's behaviour is made to the heroine by the 2d woman, not by the man who loves her. This is a calculated act on the 2d woman's part—she being in love with the 2d man. This sounds awfully crude, but it isn't, as I see it all. It is a subject, and I can make it do for the *English Illust.* I needn't take time, with expatiating on it here—but only *begin* it, in good faith—and it will go.

34 De Vere Gdns., October 23d.

To live *in* the world of creation—to get into it and stay in it—to frequent it and haunt it—to *think* intently and fruitfully—to woo combinations and inspirations into being by a depth and continuity of attention and meditation—this is the only thing—and I neglect it, far and away too much; from indolence, from vagueness, from inattention, and from a strange nervous fear of letting myself go. If I vanquish that nervousness, the world is mine. x x x x x

Surely it would be possible to make another and a less literal application of the idea of poor H.W. and the queer tragedy of his relation with Cousin H.[1] I might make a little tale of it in which the motive would really *be* an idea, and a pretty and touching one—the idea of the *hypnotization* of a weak character by a stronger, by a stronger will, so that the former accepts a certain absolute view of itself, takes itself from the point of view of another mind, etc., and then, by the death of the dominant person, finds itself confronted with the strange problem of liberty.[2]

1. These are Henry Wyckoff and his sister, Mrs. Helen Perkins, cousins of HJ's mother. Cousin Helen dominated the men in her life, especially her husband and her brother Henry; she had control of her brother's ample fortune and allowed him a dime a day. See HJ's account in *A Small Boy and Others*, Chapter XI.
2. The phrase "another and less literal application" suggests that HJ had in mind the play "The Reprobate," written for Edward Compton (possibly by October 1891). He planned to write a tale on

February 5th, 1892. I find myself wrenched away from the attempt to get on with the drama—wrenched only for the hour, fortunately—by the necessity of doing *au plus tôt* some short tales. Once I get into this current the spell works, the charm, the faith comes back to me; but the effort—at the start—is great. But there is all the big suggestive, swarming world around me, with all its life and motion—in which I only need to dip my ladle. But I must dip with a free and vigorous hand.

x　x　x　x　x

It is all one quest—in the way of subject—the play and the tale. It is not one *choice*—it is two deeply distinct ones; but it's the same general *enquête*, the same attitude and *regard*. The large, sincere, attentive, constant quest would be a net hauling in—with its close meshes—the two kinds.

x　x　x　x　x

I was greatly struck, the other day, with something M. d'Estournelles, whom I met at Lady Brooke's,[1] said to [me] about P.B.'s life and situation—in regard to his marriage, his prospects: that his only safety—*their* only safety, as a *ménage heureux,* resided in their remaining *loin de France*—abroad—far from Paris. From the moment they should return there their union would *have* to go to pieces—their safety as a *ménage heureux*—their mutual affection and cohesion. It was sad, but it was *comme ça.* Paris wouldn't *tolerate* a united pair; would inevitably and ruthlessly disintegrate it. When Lady B. said, 'C'est bien triste!,' the speaker said, 'Mon Dieu, madame, c'est comme ça!' Something probably to be done with the tragedy, the inevitable *fate,* of this; the prevision of it, on the part of a young couple, the mingled horror and fascination of the prospect.

x　x　x　x　x

Henry Adams spoke to me the other day of the end [of] certain histories of which, years ago, in London he had seen the beginning—poor Lady M.H., who broke off her engagement with X.Y.Z. on the eve of marriage and now trails about at the tail of her mother—or some other fine lady—a dreary old maid. Then the situation of two other girls of the same noble house, one of whom, Augusta, now gives music lessons for a living. The other, the elder sister, was the daughter of a French mistress—dancer or someone—and of Lord A.B. (before his marriage) and was adopted by him and by his wife—it was a clause of the contract—as his own daughter and grew up on this footing. There is the suggestion of a situation in this—that is, in the relation of the sisters. Express it rapidly and crudely thus. The relation is one—for the younger, the legitimate, of jealousy—she is in love with the same man as Cynthia. He comes to the house—has seemed to hesitate

---

a similar theme. "The Reprobate" was not staged during HJ's lifetime but was published in *Theatricals: Second Series,* London and New York (1894). See *Complete Plays* 401–03. On "hypnotization" see March 1889.

1. Margaret Brooke, née Windt (1849–1936), in 1869 married her much older second-cousin, Sir Charles Brooke, who succeeded his father as Rajah of Sarawak, in northeast Borneo; Lady Margaret thus became the Ranee of Sarawak. She was a good friend of, among others, HJ, Paul Bourget (the P.B. of this entry), and later W. Morton Fullerton.

between them, but really is taken by Cynthia. Augusta suffers, resents—but doesn't know the secret of her sister's birth. *Sur ces entrefaites* her mother—her own mother (ill and dying, say), tells her, so as to put into her hand a weapon, as it were, against Cynthia—to enable her to disclose the real fact and thereby disenchant—put off—the valuable suitor. (The idea is that Augusta should tell his sister—trusting *her* to communicate it.) But Augusta is overtaken by better feelings. She does tell his sister, then repents, has herself in horror and afterwards goes back to her and beseeches her not to tell the brother. The lady has no intention of doing so, and as she holds her tongue Augusta, stoically, sees the marriage take place. (She may at least have the temptation to tell the sister herself, I mean Cynthia—to relieve and *soulager* herself—but even this she resists.) But meanwhile the lady whom she has taken into her confidence is so struck with her behaviour that she mentions it, as a *beau trait,* to a friend—a young man (must *she* be in love with him?—YES, and she's a married woman!) on whom it makes such an impression that he is haunted by Augusta, as it were, seeks her acquaintance, falls in love with her and marries her: so that Augusta *is* rewarded for her magnanimity and *does* get a husband. It sounds, all, rather bald and thin here, but as a little homogeneous drama might, I think, be concisely told.[2]

x   x   x   x   x

An *idée de comédie* came to me vaguely the other day on the subject of the really terrible situation of the young man, in England, who is a great *parti*—the really formidable assault of the mothers, and the *filles à marier.* I don't see, quite, my comedy in it yet—but I do see a little tale of about this kind.—A young nobleman—or only (perhaps better) commoner of immense wealth, feels himself, on the eve of the London Season, in such real discomfort and peril that he makes a compact with a girl he has known for years, and likes, to see him through the wood by allowing it to be supposed and announced, that they are engaged. His mother must have put him up to it. He has come into the whole thing suddenly—unexpectedly. He has known the girl before—for years. He doesn't dream he's hurting her. She consents and the device succeeds. But in the middle of the season she gets a real chance to marry—by feeling that there is a man who would marry her if it were not for this supposititious engagement. So she asks the *parti* if she mayn't drop the comedy. She thinks he *may* refuse—ask her to make it a real engagement. But he doesn't refuse—he's inconvenienced, reluctant—but he lets her go. She marries her *real* suitor—though she is secretly in love with the *parti*—and he afterwards finds that they were at cross purposes: she was *really* in love with him—and he has become so with her—but didn't want to press her lest he should have seemed to attribute to her the cupidity they had both thought to *soustraire* him from. Too great delicacy on his part, etc.—Try and do three for M. Morris,[3] with the other little thing—the one I thought of in Ireland—the thing of which I scratched a beginning— the young man who dines out.—

2. HJ returned to this idea on several occasions—see 26 March 1892, 30 August 1893, and 14 December 1899—but seems never to have developed it into a story.
3. Mowbray Morris, editor of *Macmillan's Magazine,* received the story developed from this idea, but HJ published nothing more in that magazine. The idea he "thought of in Ireland" must have been "scratched" in a notebook that has not survived.

["Lord Beauprey," *Macmillan's Magazine* April–June 1892; reprinted as "Lord Beaupré" in *The Private Life.*]

Could not something be done—in the 'international' line—with the immense typical theme of the *manless* American woman, in Europe—the way everything social is in their hands *là bas,* etc.? The suggestions embodied in Mrs. L. of N.Y.[4] The total suppression of the husband. I seem to catch hold of the tail of an action—2 women—2 husbands. Their description of each other: *minus* the husband:—or to each other (of their lives), with the utterly unmentioned husbands turning up afterwards—as revelations, etc. One of the women may describe to the other—then the other meets the husband—likes him (she being unmarried, etc.) and finds that he *is* the appendage of her new acquaintance. There is distinctly, I think, the making of something in this.

February 28th, 1892. A very good little subject (for a short tale), would be the idea—suggested to me in a roundabout way by the dreadful E.D. 'tragedy' in the south of France[1]—of a frivolous young ass or snob of a man, rather rich, and withal rather proper and prim, who marries a very pretty girl and is pleased with the idea of getting her into society—I mean into the world smart and fast, *où l'on s'amuse;* the sort of people whom it most flatters his vanity to be able to live with. There is no harm in him save that he's an ass and a snob. His wife is really much more of a person, clever, independent, whimsical and easily-bored. She tires of him, and of his platitude, and of that of the world thèy live in, and takes a lover. She has already had 2 children. She commits herself, is compromised, discovered and divorced. The lover is an *homme sérieux,* he marries her. Change of scene and situation. She becomes a serious 'earnest' woman—deploring the levity of her 1st husband, the way he brings up their children, whom he has been able to keep. *He* marries again and has another child—as *she* has. 2d wife a goose but 'good.' She *dies.* The 1st wife's deplorings of the sort of people they are. Renewal of relations in which the divorcée has the moral, earnest, superior attitude—trying to rescue the others from their frivolity. *Rapprochement* of the children. She resents the example of her 1st lot, for her second. Lastly her husband's last daughter (of his second wife), wishes to marry her son (that of her 2d husband) and she breaks it off and the tale—purely ironic and satiric—ends. Told by *me*—the friend and observer.

March 16th. Idea of a servant suspected of doing the mean things—the base things people in London take for granted servants do—reading of letters, diaries, peeping, spying, etc.; turning out utterly innocent and incapable of these things—and turning the tables of scorn on the master or mistress, at a moment when, much

---

4. Probably Florence Bayard (1842–98), who married Major Benoni Lockwood; she was a friend of Sarah Butler Wister, who introduced her to HJ in New York at the beginning of 1875. See 5 October 1899.

1. E. D. was the American Edward Parker Deacon (1844–1901), whose daughter Gladys (1881–1977) became the second wife (after Consuelo Vanderbilt) of the ninth Duke of Marlborough (1871–1934). The "tragedy" was Deacon's shooting of his wife's French lover in a hotel in Cannes; see *Letters* IV, 44–45, 54–55. See development, 15 June 1901, and detached note "The E. P. D. Subject" (1893).

depending on it, they are (the servant is) supposed to have committed all the little baseness.[1]

March 26th. The idea of the *responsibility* of destruction—the destruction of papers, letters, records, etc., connected with the private and personal history of some great and honoured name and throwing some very different light on it from the light projected by the public career. Might not a little drama be built on this—on the struggle, the problem, the decision *what* to do, the interest of truth, etc.? The famous personage may have been a high figure in politics—successful to the world—but with a secret history revealed in compromising documents, revelations of insincerity, tortuosity, venality, etc. They must come into the hands of a poor young man—not a relation—a young man poor enough to be tempted by their pecuniary value and having nothing at stake, for his honour, in their being made public. He must—he at least *may*—be a poor young man of letters, discouraged, depressed by his conscious[ness] of failure and intrinsic inability to produce, 'create'—his want of talent and gift. The manner in which he comes into possession of them to be determined—a dramatic accident. He appreciates their value, as well as the damage they will do to a great reputation, and a publisher or editor offers him money for them. There are no *relations*—no one to suffer. He is tempted, strongly, being in want of the money and not in sympathy with the great man's character or opinions—and *almost* consents to let the publisher have them. But a strange indefeasible instinct—a curious inner repulsion holds him back, makes him, each time he is on the point of concluding the bargain, conscious of an insurmountable feeling. The editor—the publisher—puts before him the public duty, the rights of truth, etc., very eloquently and interestedly. Meanwhile he has encountered a girl—a woman—poor like himself, whom he falls in love with. I see it from here—I needn't go on with the details. She is poor like himself—an actress, a singer or an artist. She lives in his house, say; has the rooms below. Her type, her charm for him. She has a little girl, etc. She must, I think, be somewhat more famous and fortunate than he. That constitutes his difficulty in making up to her—little to offer as he has. But he sees her, knows her, talks with her and to a certain extent makes love to her. x x x x x I see the rest of this so clearly now that I will go straight on with it.

["Jersey Villas," *Cosmopolitan Magazine* July–August 1892; reprinted as "Sir Dominick Ferrand" in *The Real Thing and Other Tales*.]

March 26th, 1892. The idea of the *soldier*—produced a little by the fascinated persual of Marbot's magnificent memoirs.[1] The image, the type, the vision, the character, as a transmitted, hereditary, mystical, almost supernatural force, challenge, incentive, almost haunting, apparitional presence, in the life and conscious-

---

1. The theme of suspected servants is treated again in entries for 21 December 1895 (project No. 5, "The lying fine lady"), 16 May 1899, and 5 October 1899.

1. Marcelin Marbot (1782–1854), with Napoleon in Spain, Portugal, and Russia, became a general on the eve of the Battle of Waterloo. His memoirs, written for his children, were published in three volumes in 1891.

ness of a descendant—a descendant of totally different temperament and range of qualities, yet subjected to a supersititious awe in relation to carrying out the tradition of absolutely *military* valour—personal bravery and honour. Sense of the difficulty—the impossibility, etc.; sense of the ugliness, the blood, the carnage, the suffering. All these things make him dodge it—not from cowardice, but from suffering. Get *something* it is enjoined upon him to do—etc. I can't complete this indication now; but I will take it up again, as I see in it the glimmer of an idea for a small subject, though only dimly and confusedly—the subject, or rather the idea, of a brave soldierly act—an act of heroism—done in the very effort to evade all the ugly and brutal part of the religion, the sacrifice, and winning (in a tragic death?) the reward of gallantry—winning it from the apparitional ancestor. This is very crude and rough, but there is probably something in it which I shall extract.

x   x   x   x   x

I get, it seems to me, a really very good little theme, by infusing an important alteration into the idea suggested by Henry Adams *(vide ante)*, the story of Augusta, Cynthia, the *bâtardise,* etc.—making my heroine a hero, my Augusta an Augustus, and making the question hinge upon money—an inheritance. The secret of the bastardy of one of the brothers told in dying by the mother to the other (the illegitimate son is not hers, but the husband's, now dead), and make the motive the desire to prevent a rich relation (her *own* relation), from leaving the bequest to the wrong one—from favouring him—or there are other things, other possibilities in it. The rich possible benefactor may be really the relation of the bastard— his father's brother—and the bastard may be *her* child. Thresh it out, make it at any rate a young man's struggle and the motive the money question.[2]

[This became "Owen Wingrave," the *Graphic* November 1892; reprinted in *The Wheel of Time,* New York (1893). In December 1907 HJ turned the story into a play, *The Saloon,* which opened in London in January 1911; see *Complete Plays* 641–49.]

Yellowley—Chemney—Monier, or Monyer—Branch—Farthing—Perch—Barber—Pudney—Leal—Carrier—Coil—Paramore (place)—Chichley—Pardie—Verus (baptismal name)—Vera—Gerald—Harley—Crisford—Tregant—Pottinger—Drabble—Landsdale—Ryves (place)—Faith—Sisk (place)—Gaye (name of house)—Taunt—Tant (Miss Tant, name of governess)—Carrow—Hardwig—Punchard—Chivers—Bawtry—Massington (place)—German—Germon—Potcher—Dunderdale—Martle.

May 8th, 1892, 34 De Vere Gardens.

Can't I hammer out a little the idea—for a short tale—of the young soldier?—the young fellow who, though predestined, by every tradition of his race, to the profession of arms, has an insurmountable hatred of it—of the *bloody* side of it, the suffering, the ugliness, the cruelty; so that he determines to reject it for him-

2. For the second, see 5 February and 8 May 1892.

self—to break with it and cast it off, and this in the face of every sort of coercion of opinion (on the part of others), of such pressure not to let the family honour, etc. (always gloriously connected with the army), break down, that there is a kind of degradation, an exposure to ridicule, and ignominy in his apostasy. The idea should be that he fights, after all, exposes himself to possibilities of danger and death for his own view—acts the soldier, *is* the soldier, and of indefeasible soldierly race—proves to have been so—even in this very effort of abjuration. The thing is to invent the particular heroic situation in which he may have found himself—show just *how* he has been a hero even while throwing away his arms. It is a question of a little subject for the *Graphic*—so I mustn't make it 'psychological'—they understand that no more than a donkey understands a violin. The particular form of opposition, of coercion, that he has to face, and the way his 'heroism' is *constatée*. It must, for prettiness's sake, be *constatée* in the eyes of some woman, some girl, whom he loves but who has taken the line of despising him for his renunciation—some *fille de soldat,* who is very *montée* about the whole thing, very hard on him, etc. But what the subject wants is to be distanced, relegated into some picturesque little past when the army occupied more place in life—poetized by some slightly romantic setting. Even if one could introduce a supernatural element in it—make it, I mean, a little ghost-story; place it, the scene, in some old country-house, in England at the beginning of the present century—the time of the Napoleonic wars.—It seems to me one might make some *haunting* business that would give it a colour without being ridiculous, and get in that way the sort of pressure to which the young man is subjected. I see it—it comes to me a little. He must die, of course, be slain, as it were on his own battle-field, the night spent in the haunted room in which the ghost of some grim grandfather—some bloody warrior of the race—or some father slain in the Peninsular or at Waterloo—is supposed to make himself visible.[1]

x   x   x   x   x

D. V. G. May 12th, 1892. The idea of the old artist, or man of letters, who, at the end, feels a kind of anguish of desire for a respite, a prolongation—another period of life to do the *real* thing that he has in him—the things for which all the others have been but a slow preparation. He is the man who has developed late, obstructedly, with difficulty, has needed all life to learn, to see his way, to collect material, and now feels that if he can only have another life to make use of this clear start, he can show what he is really capable of. Some incident, then, to show that what he *has* done *is* that of which he is capable—that he has done all he can, that he has put into his things the love of perfection and that they will live by that. Or else an incident acting just the other way—showing him what he might do, just when he must give up forever. The 1st idea the best. A young doctor, a young pilgrim who admires him. A deep sleep in which he dreams he *has* had his respite. Then his waking, to find that what he has dreamed of is only what he has *done.*

1. See entry for 26 March 1892 for initial note on "Owen Wingrave."

[The last sentence is the idea for "The Great Good Place," *Scribner's Magazine* January 1900; reprinted in *The Soft Side,* London and New York (1900). The rest of the note for "The Middle Years," *Scribner's Magazine* May 1893; reprinted in *Terminations,* London and New York (1895).]

34 De Vere Gdns., May 18th, 1892.

Little subject suggested by some talk last night with Lady Shrewsbury,[1] at dinner at Lady Lindsay's[2] about the woman who has been very ugly in youth and been slighted and snubbed for her ugliness, and who, as very frequently—or at least sometimes—happens with plain girls, has become much better-looking, almost handsome in middle life, and later—and with this improvement in appearance, charming, at any rate, and attractive—so that the later years are, practically, her advantage, her compensation, her *revanche.* Idea of such a woman who meets, in such a situation, a man who, in her youth, has slighted and snubbed her—who has refused a marriage perhaps—a marriage projected by the two families, and, out of fastidiousness, and even fatuity and folly, has let her see that she was too ugly for him. Mustn't there be a second woman, the woman he *has* married and who has turned plain, as it were, later in life, on his hands? Mightn't something be done with this little fancy of the *beau rôle* that the other one has—taking her revenge in protecting, assisting, cheering up the man whose own attitude and situation are now so different? Say she has always loved him—and now he is poor. His wife dies—and he has a son of marriageable age, the son of his wife, the ex-beauty, but who, as it happens, is hideous. He gets a chance to marry this son well (some reason for this must be given) if he can only do something for him. Say he has a fine old name which the other people will take as a *part* of the compensation for his being so hideous. The charming woman, who has money, makes up the rest. Or the charming woman (much better this) *has* also, later, married and she has a son who is very handsome. The disappointed man has a daughter, who is nice but very ugly. The magnanimous *revanche* of the charming woman—the way she shows her 'protection'—is by persuading her son (or perhaps only *trying)* to marry the ugly girl. It is probably better to make this only a trial—a vain one. The son *regimbers* too much—says the girl is too ugly.

'She'll grow better-looking when she's older.'

'She? Jamais de la vie!'

'She'll do as I have done. *I* was hideous.'

'I don't belive it—it's false.— Show me your photograph, to prove it.'

'I was too ugly ever to be taken.'

He doesn't believe it. She has to say to her friend: 'Que voulez-vous? My son won't believe it!'—*She* must have had money, or the prospect of money, as a girl. That's why the marriage was planned by his mother—an old friend, say, of her mother. That's why she has been able to marry later. The thing must begin

---

1. This may be the Lady Shrewsbury denounced by AJ in her diary, 1 February 1890.
2. Caroline Blanche Elizabeth FitzRoy (d. 1912), whose mother was Hannah Mayer Rothschild, in 1864 married Sir Coutts Lindsay (1824–1913), 2nd Bt., director of the Grosvenor Gallery.

with *his* mother, years ago, breaking the idea to him—he hasn't yet seen the girl. Then her qualificative:

'But I must tell you she's very plain.—BUT she has, etc., etc.' He promises to try, sees her, tries still, makes her fall in love with him—then finds he *can't!*

["The Wheel of Time," *Cosmopolitan Magazine* December 1892 to January 1893; reprinted in *The Private Life* and *The Wheel of Time.*]

May 22d, 1892. Read last night admirable article in the *Revue des 2 Mondes* of 1st April last on *La Vie Américaine* by André Chevrillon, which somehow gave to my imagination a kind of impulse making it want to do something more with the American character. Another man—not a Newman, but more completely civilized, large, rich, complete, but strongly characterised, but essentially a *product.* Get the action—the action in which to launch him—it should be a big one. I have no difficulty in *seeing* the figure—it *comes,* as I look at it.[1]

Hotel Richemont, Lausanne, August 4th, 1892.

Last evening, at Ouchy, Miss R.[1] said, after the conversation had run a little upon the way Americans drag their children about Europe:

'A girl should be shown Europe—or taken to travel—by her husband—she has no business to see the world before. *He* takes her—*he* initiates her.'

Struck with this as the old-fashioned French view and possible idea for a little tale. The girl whose husband is to show her everything—so that she waits at home—and who never gets a husband. *He* is to take her abroad—and he never comes, etc. The daughter of a conservative 'frenchified' mother, etc. A pretext for the mother's selfishness, neglect, etc.—*she* travelling about. The girl's life—waiting—growing older—death. The husband comes in the form of death, etc.[2]

x   x   x   x   x

Some painter (Pasolini) in Venice said, after painting the Empress Frederick:[3] is only Empresses who know how to sit—to *pose.* They have the habit of it, and of being looked at, and it is three times as easy to paint them as to paint others.'— Idea of this—for another little 'model' story; pendant to the *Real Thing.* A woman comes to a painter as a paid model—she is poor, perfect for the purpose and very mysterious. He wonders how she comes to be so good. At last he discovers that she is a deposed princess!—reduced to mystery! as to earning her living.

x   x   x   x   x

1. An anticipation of Adam Verver of *The Golden Bowl,* sketched out in entries for 28 November 1892 and 14 February 1895. André Chevrillon (1864–1947), French critic of English literature.

1. Henrietta Reubell (1840?–1924), an elegant American expatriate whom HJ met in Paris in April 1867; she maintained a salon for painters and writers at her home, 42 Avenue Gabriel, and was the original of Miss Barrace in *The Ambassadors.*

2. HJ resumes this idea in the entry for 21 December 1895.

3. Victoria, Empress Frederick of Germany, was a daughter of Queen Victoria. Pasolini was perhaps Count Giuseppe Pasolini, a statesman and diplomat in Victorian England and an amateur painter.

Situation of that once-upon-a-time member of an old Venetian family (I forget which), who had become a monk, and who was taken almost forcibly out of his convent and brought back into the world in order to keep the family from becoming extinct. He was the last *rejeton*—it was absolutely *necessary* for him to marry. Adapt this somehow or other to today.[4]

Names. Beague—Vena (Xtian name)—Doreen (ditto)—Passmore—Trafford—Norval—Lancelot—Vyner—Bygrave—Husson—Domville—Wynter—Vanneck—Bygone—Bigwood (place)—Zambra—Negretti—Messer—Coucher—Croucher—Woodwell—Chamley—Dann—Dane—Anderton (place)—Hamilton-finch (or with other short second name)—Byng—Bing—Bing-Bing—Oldfield—Briant—Dencombe — Tyrrel — Desborough — Morland — Bradbury — Messenden — Ashington —Jewel—Billamore—Windle—Chiddle—Vernham—Illidge—Tertius (Xn. name)—Poynton—Monmouth.

34 De Vere Gardens, W., November 12th, 1892.

—Two days ago, at dinner at James Bryce's[1] Mrs. Ashton, Mrs. Bryce's sister, mentioned to me a situation that she had known of, of which it immediately struck me that something might be made in a tale. A child (boy or girl would do, but I see a girl, which would make it different from *The Pupil*) was *divided* by its parents in consequence of their being divorced. The court, for some reason, didn't, as it might have done, give the child exclusively to either parent, but decreed that it was to spend its time equally with each—that is alternately. Each parent married again, and the child went to them a month, or three months, about—finding with the one a new mother and with the other a new father. Might not something be done with the idea of an odd and particular relation springing up 1st between the child and each of these new parents, 2d between one of the new parents and the other—through the child—over and on account of and by means of the child? Suppose the real parents die, etc.—then the new parents marry each other in order to take care of it, etc. The basis of almost any story, any development would be, that the child should prefer the new husband and the new wife to the old; that is that these latter should (from the moment they have ceased to *quarrel* about it), become indifferent to it, whereas the others have become interested and attached, finally passionately so. Best of all perhaps would be to make the child a fresh bone of contention, a fresh source of dramatic situations, *du vivant* of the original parents. *Their* indifference throws the new parents, through a common sympathy, together. Thence a 'flirtation,' a love affair between them which produces suspicion, jealousy, a fresh separation, etc.—with the innocent child in the midst.[2]

["The Pupil," *Longman's Magazine* March–April 1891; reprinted in *The Lesson of the Master*. The note is for *What Maisie Knew*, the *Chap Book* January–August 1897 and the

---

4. HJ's initial note for the play *Guy Domville*, which he wrote during the summer of 1893 at Ramsgate for George Alexander (1858–1918), popular actor-manager of the St. James's Theatre in London.

1. Viscount Bryce (1838–1922), British historical and political writer and diplomat, Regius Professor of Civil Law at Oxford.

2. See 26 August 1893 and 21 and 22 December 1895.

New Review February–September 1897, published in London, Chicago, and New York
(1897).]

Names.   Mackle—Spavin—Alabaster—Pollard—Patent—Waymouth—George—
Allaway (or Alloway)—Barran—Count—Currier—Arden—Damant—Malling—
Coldfield (place)—Malin—Cushion—Merino—Ramage—Helder—Harrish—Mariner (Marriner)—Chuck-(or Check-)borough (title)—Cressage (place)—Eden-
brook—Gravener—Hine—Millard—Linthorne—Mountain—Checkley—Pilling—
Humber — Comrad — Maddock — Benefit — Blankley (or—like 'Mountain'—
place) — Hue — Ashdown — Bycroft — Gunning — Wintle — Port — Braid — Mc-
Bride—Goldring—Beaver—Berridge—Christmas—Pook—Devenish—Clarence
(surname).

34 De Vere Gardens, W., November 24th, '92.

—Surely if I attempt another comedy for Daly, and a 'big part' for A.R.[1] as
I see myself, rather vividly, foredoomed to do, the subject can only be (it is so
designated, and imposed, by the finger of opportunity), the American woman in
London society. I see my figure—my type—it stands before me, and the problem
opening up is of course the question of a great comedy-action. If this action is a
strong one, a right one, a real one, the elements of success ought to be there in
force. But, ah, how *charming,* how interesting, how noble, as it were, the subject
ought to be. It must be something as remote, as *different,* as possible, from that
of my little talc of *The Siege of London;* with its little picture of an innocent
adventuress and its vague *rappel* of the 'situation' in Dumas's *Demi-Monde*[2]—the
situation of a man of honour who has to testify about the antecedents of a woman
he has known in the past. This must be a totally different kind of *donnée*—with
no *rappel* of anything familiar or conventional or already done—fresh, charming,
superior, with a distinct elevation, a great comedy-'lift' in it. My heroine mustn't
be one of the crudities—she must only be (and that with great intensity), one of
the newnesses, the freshnesses, the independences, the freedoms. What I must
show is the great thing, above all, the blank page, the clear fine-grained surface
of the famous 'adaptability.' If I can do the thing I *see,* it will be too good for
Ada R.; but I must thank heaven it be not for some one worse. The *idea* of the
comedy must reside in the fact of the *renversement,* the alteration of the relations
of certain elements of intercourse; the reyersal of what the parties traditionally
represent. (I am stating it very sketchily and crudely.) What my American woman
must represent, at any rate, is the idea of attachment to the past, of romance, of
history, continuity and conservatism. She represents it from a fresh sense, from
an individual conviction, but she represents it none the less—and the action must

1. John Augustin Daly (1838–99), American playwright, theater manager, and producer. A. R. is
Ada Rehan (née Crehan in 1860 in Limerick), who was the leading lady of his company and for whom
he built his London theater. See *Complete Plays* 295–98. The idea for "another comedy" was used
by HJ during 1985 as a one-actor called *Summersoft,* written for Ellen Terry. See 6 February 1895
and *Complete Plays* 519–23, 549–53.
2. Alexandre Dumas the younger (1824–95), French dramatist and novelist. His *Demi-Monde* is of
1855. See "Occasional Paris" in *Portraits of Places* and preface to volume XIV of the New York
edition.

be something in which she represents it effectively—with a power to save and preserve. In other words, she, intensely American in temperament—with her freedoms, her immunity from traditions, superstitions, fears and *riguardi,* but with an imagination kindling with her new contact with the presence of a *past,* a continuity, etc., represents the conservative element among a cluster of persons (an old house, family, race, society) already in course of becoming demoralized, vulgarized, and (from their own point of view), Americanized. She 'steps in,' in a word, with a certain beautiful beneficence and passion. *How* she steps in, how she arrests and redeems and retrieves and appeals and clears up and *saves*—it is in the determination of this that must reside the *action* of my play: a matter as to which the clear and sacred light can only come to me with prayer and fasting, as it were, and little by little. But charming and interesting, it seems to me, should be the problem of representing the combination of this function of hers, this work, this office, this part she plays, and the intensity, the vividness, the unmistakableness and individuality of her American character. There glimmers upon me already an admirable first act—elements—the surging of them before her with their appeal, their fascination for her, and the culmination, at the end of the act, of her sense that she can *do* something—that she *must* undertake and achieve it. Of course— oh, how utterly!—there must be a 'love-interest'—which is one and the same with the other parts of the situation. It dimly shines before me that my heroine ought to love a younger son—a younger brother, a poor cousin, contingent heir or next of kin to a territorial magnate. Perhaps he's an advanced radical, a tremendous theoretic democrat, etc. Rather, I should say, must she be brought into contact and conflict, *not* amorous, with the theoretic one. A chance for a striking satiric picture—the radical English aristocrat, the democrat in a high place, etc., etc.

x   x   x   x   x

November 26th, 1892. Curiously persistent and comically numerous appear to be the suggestions and situations attached to this endless spectacle—the queer crudity of which is a theme for the philosopher—of the Anglo-American marriage. The singular—the intensely significant circumstance of its being all on one side—or rather in one form; always the union of the male Briton to the female American— *never* the other way round.[1] Plenty of opportunity for satiric fiction in the facts involved in all this—plenty of subjects and situations. It seems to me all made on purpose—*on n'a qu'à puiser.* One has only to dip it out. The contrast between the man the American girl marries and the man who marries the American girl. This opens up—or *se rattache* to—the whole subject, or question, about which Godkin,[2] as I remember, one day last summer talked to me very emphatically and interestingly—the growing divorce between the American woman (with her comparative leisure, culture, grace, social instincts, artistic ambitions) and the male

1. The Anglo-American marriage had been treated "the other way round" in "Lady Barberina" (1884).
2. Edwin Laurence Godkin (1831–1902), founder of the *Nation* in 1865 and editor of the *New York Evening Post,* published HJ in the *Nation* from its beginning in July 1865 and remained a lifelong friend.

American immersed in the ferocity of business, with no time for any but the most sordid interests, purely commercial, professional, democratic and political. This divorce is rapidly becoming a gulf—an abyss of inequality, the like of which has never before been seen under the sun. One might represent it, picture it, in a series of illustrations, of episodes—one might project a lot of light upon it. It would abound in developments, in ramifications.

["An International Episode," *Cornhill Magazine* December 1878 to January 1879; reprinted in *An International Episode*, New York (1879).]

x   x   x   x   x

November 28th. Situation, not closely connected with the above, suggested by something lately told one about a simultaneous marriage, in Paris (or only 'engagement' as yet, I believe), of a father and a daughter—an only daughter. The daughter—American of course—is engaged to a young Englishman, and the father, a widower and still youngish, has sought in marriage at exactly the same time an American girl of very much the same age as his daughter. Say he has done it to console himself in his abandonment—to make up for the loss of the daughter, to whom he has been devoted. I see a little tale, *n'est-ce pas?*—in the idea that they all shall have married, as arranged, with this characteristic consequence—that the daughter fails to hold the affections of the young English husband, whose approximate mother-in-law the pretty young second wife of the father will now have become. The father *doesn't* lose the daughter nearly as much as he feared, or expected, for her marriage which has but half gratified her, leaves her *des loisirs,* and she devotes them to him and to making up, as much as possible, for having left him. They spend large parts of their time together, they cling together, and weep and wonder together, and are even *more* thrown together than before. The reason of all this, for the observer (and I suppose the observer, as usual, must tell the tale—or, rather, *No*—this time I see it *otherwise*—especially in the interest of brevity)—the reason, I say, is not far to seek, and resides in the circumstance that the father-in-law's second wife has become much more attractive to the young husband of the girl than the girl herself has remained. *Mettons* that his second wife is nearly as young as her daughter-in-law—and prettier and cleverer—she knows more what she is about. *Mettons* even that the younger husband has known her before, has liked her, etc.—been attracted by her, and would have married her if she had had any money. She was poor—the father was very rich, and *that* was her inducement to marry the father. The latter has settled a handsome *dot* on his daughter (leaving himself also plenty to live on), and the young husband is therefore thoroughly at his ease. Relations are inevitably formed between him and his father-in-law's wife—relations which, in the pleasure they find in each other's society, become very close and very intimate. They spend as much of their time together as the others do, and for the very reason that the others spend it. The whole situation works in a kind of inevitable rotary way—in what would be called a vicious circle. The *subject* is really the pathetic simplicity and good faith of the father and daughter in their abandonment. They feel abandoned, yet they feel consoled, with *each other,* and they don't see in the business in the least what every one else sees in it. The rotary motion, the vicious circle, consists in the reasons which each of the parties give[s] the other. The father marries because he's bereft, but he ceases to be bereft from the moment his daughter returns to him in consequence of the *insuccès* of his marriage. The daughter weeps with him over the *insuccès* of *hers*—but her very alienation in this manner from her husband gives the seond wife, the stepmother, her pretext, her opportunity for consoling the other. From the moment she is not so necessary as the father first thought she would be (when his daughter seemed wholly lost), this second wife has also *des loisirs,* which she devotes to her husband's son-in-law. Lastly, the son-in-law, with the sense of his wife's estrangement from him, finds himself at liberty and finds it moreover only courteous to be agreeable to the other lady in the particular situation that her 'superfluity,' as it were, has made for her. A necessary basis for all this must have been an intense and exceptional degree of attachment between the father and daughter—he peculiarly paternal, she passionately filial. The young husband may be made a Frenchman—*il faut,* for a short tale, *que cela se passe à Paris.* He is poor, but has some high social position or name—and is, after all, morally only the pleasant *Français moyen*—clever, various, inconstant, amiable, cynical, unscrupulous—charming always—to 'the other woman.' The other woman and the father and daughter all intensely American.[1]

[The germ of *The Golden Bowl,* New York (1904) and London (1905).]

34 De Vere Gardens, December 18th, 1892.

Intensely picturesque impression of visit yesterday afternoon to the Tower of London—to the 'Queen's House'—by invitation from Miss M.,[1] whom I found alone. Very English—quite intensely English, impression—the whole thing: the old homely, historic nook in the corner of a military establishment—the charming girl, daughter of the old Governor of the Tower, etc.—the memories, the ghosts, Anne Boleyn, Guy Fawkes, the block, the rack and the friendly modern continuity. *Ah, que de choses à faire, que de choses à faire!*

x   x   x   x   x

December 27th. 'I am disappointed in Greece, as I was disappointed in England'—phrase quoted to me by G.N.—from letter of her nephew (Dick)[1] and commented on by her as example of the joyless vagueness, the want of temperament and (I suppose) 'passion' of the modern youth (American in particular), as she sees them. Interesting view to see taken of it, almost comedy or tragi-comedy view. Suggestion to me of the 'culture' that has no assimilation nor application—the deluge of cultivated mediocrity, etc. The possibility of a little tale on it—the

---

1. See 14 February 1895; the father is anticipated in 22 May 1892. The subjects for *The Golden Bowl* and for ''The Marriages'' were evidently mingled in HJ's mind: see 12 January 1887 and 21 December 1895.

---

1. ''Miss M.'' was Angelina Milman, curator of the Tower museum.

---

1. Grace Norton (1834–1926), sister of Charles Eliot Norton, and a longtime friend of HJ. Richard Norton (1872–1918), an archaeologist, became Director of the School of Classical Studies in Rome in 1899.

reaction against the overdose of education, on the part of a youth *conscious* of his mediocrity—a reaction frantic, savage, primitive and forming a grotesque commentary on all that has been expected of him and pumped into him. The *form* of the reaction to be determined and to constitute, really, the subject. This subject possibly obtainable by introduction of 2d concomitant and contrasted figure—the yearning (for culture) barbarian. A woman?[2]

[''The Tree of Knowledge,'' published (without serialization) in *The Soft Side* (1900).]

Names. Bernal—Veitch (or Veetch)—Arrow—Painter—Melina (Xtian name)—Peverel—Chaillé (de Chaillé) for French person—Brasier—Chattock—Clime—Lys—Pellet—Paraday—Hurter—Collop—Hyme—Popkiss—Lupton—Millington—Mallington—Malville—Mulville—Wiffin—Christopher (surname)—Dark—Milsom—Medway—Peckover—Alum—Braby (or of place)—Longhay—Netterville—Lace—Round—Ferrard—Remnant (noted before)—Polycarp (Xtian name)—Masterman—Morrow (house—place)—Marrast—Usher—Carns—Hoy—Doy—Mant—Bedborough—Almeric (Xtian name)—Jesmond—Bague—Misterton (place)—Pruden—Boys—Kitcat—Oldrey—Dester—Wix—Prestidge.

x   x   x   x   x

Said in defence of some young man accused of being selfish—of self-love: 'He doesn't love *himself*—he loves his *youth!*' or 'It isn't *himself* he loves—it's his *youth*—and small blame to him!'
    'The most beautiful word in the language?—Youth!'

Hotel Westminster, Paris, April 8th, 1893.

The strange *genius* of Pierre Loti—so exquisite even in a thing so *mince,* so comparatively shrunken and limited, as *Matelot,* which I am just reading—and expressed somehow in the beauty of a passage that strikes me (with that indefinable charm of his) so much that I transcribe it.
    'Donc, ils en venaient à s'aimer d'une également pure trendresse, tous les deux. Elle, ignorante des choses d'amour et lisant chaque soir sa bible; elle, destinée à rester inutilement fraîche et jeune encore pendant quelques printemps pâles comme celui-ci, puis à vieillir et se faner dans l'enserrement monotone de ces mêmes rues et de ces mêmes murs. Lui, gâté déjà par les baisers et les étreintes, ayant le monde pour habitation changeante, appelé à partir, peut-être demain, pour ne revenir jamais et laisser son corps aux mers lointaines. . .'[1]

Hotel National, Lucerne, May 7th, '93.

I have been worrying at the dramatic, the unspeakably theatric form for a long time, but I am in possession now of some interposing days (the reasons for which I needn't go into here—they are abundantly chronicled elsewhere), during which

2. See 1 May 1899.
1. ''Pierre Loti'' was the pen name of Julien Viaud (1850–1923), French novelist whose *Matelot* was published in 1893. Further praise of this passage, with qualification, is in Lubbock I, 203. See also *LA* III, 482–520.

I should like to dip my pen into the *other* ink—the sacred fluid of fiction. Among the delays, the disappointments, the *déboires* of the horrid theatric trade nothing is so soothing as to remember that literature sits patient at my door, and that I have only to lift the latch to let in the exquisite little form that is, after all, nearest to my heart and with which I am so far from having done. I let it in and the old brave hours come back; I live them over again—I add another little block to the small literary monument that it has been given to me to erect. The dimensions don't matter—one must cultivate one's garden. To do many—and do them perfect: that is the refuge, the asylum. I must *always* have one on the stocks. It will be there—it will be started—and little by little it will grow. I have among the rough notes of this book ½ a dozen decent starting-points. I don't say to myself, here, a 10th of the things I might—but it isn't necessary. So deeply I know them and feel them.

August 26th, 1893 (34 De Vere Gdns.).

I am putting my hand to the idea of the little story on the subject of the *partagé* child—of the divorced parents—as to which I have already made a note here. The little *donnée* will yield most, I think—most *ironic* effect, and this is the sort of thing mainly to try for in it—if I make the old parents, the original parents, *live,* not die, and transmit the little girl to the persons they each have married *en secondes noces.* This at least is what I ask myself. May I not combine the ironic and the *other* interest (the 'touch of tenderness'—or sweetness—or sympathy or poetry—or whatever the needed thing is), by a conception of this sort; viz.: that Hurter and his former wife each marry again and cease to care for the child—as I have originally posited—as soon as they have her no longer to quarrel about? The new husband and the new wife then take the interest in her, and meet on this common ground. The Hurters quarrel with *them* over this, and they separate: I mean each of the Hurters separate afresh. Make *Hurter* die? His 1st wife survives and becomes extremely jealous of his 2d. I must remember that if Hurter dies, the situation breaks, for his wife then gets the whole care of Maisie; which won't do. No, they both live.[1]

x   x   x   x   x

August 30th. The desire to escape from the cramp of the *too* intensely short possesses me; crowds back upon me and pulls me up—making me ask myself whether I am not creating myself needless difficulties. God knows how dear is brevity and how sacred today is concision. But it's a question of degree, and of the quantity of *importance* that one can give. That importance is everything now. To try and squeeze it into a fixed and beggarly number of words is a poor and a vain undertaking—a waste of time. There are excellent examples of the short novel—and one that has always struck me as a supremely happy instance is poor Maupassant's

---

1. See 12 November 1892 and 22 December 1895, for *What Maisie Knew.*

admirable *Pierre et Jean*.[1] Octave Feuillet[2] is also, with all his flimsiness, singularly wise as to length. I want to do something that I can do in three months—something of the dimensions of *Pierre et Jean*. I should be glad also to make my story resemble it in other ways. The great question of *subject* surges in grey dimness about me. It is everything—it is everything. I have 2 or 3 things in mind, but they happen to be purely ironic. They will serve for some other time: the particular thing I want to do now is not the ironic. I want to do something fine—a strong, large, important human episode, something that brings into play character and sincerity and passion; something that marches like a drama. A truce to all subjects that are not superior! I have two things in mind, and the best thing is for me to thresh them out a little here. It all comes back to the old, old lesson—that of the art of *reflection*. When I practice it the whole field is lighted up—I feel again the multitudinous presence of all human situations and pictures, the surge and pressure of *life*. All passions, all combinations, are there. And oh, the luxury, the value of having time to *read!* As to this, however, the long ache is too deep for speech—sad, hungry silence covers it. x x x x x

One of the things which hangs before me just now, but which needs, in its actual vagueness and mere formal presence, a great deal of vivification, is the subject as to which, in 2 different places, I have scratched a few lines here already—referring to it as suggested by an anecdote, a mention, of Henry Adams's.[3] I have sketched something very dimly *(vide ante)*, which is a large, vague expansion of that suggestion. Then there is the subject that I have been turning over as a theme for a play, and tackled very superficially the 1st act of, under the designation of *Monte Carlo*.[4] It will be no waste of time to straighten these things out a little. The question, as regards the latter, comes up as to how willing one can be to give up to the temporary presence of the need to produce a story, a *donnée*, that has presented itself as valuable for a play—the form as to which good *données* are so rare. That, however, is an independent question. In the 1st case (H.A.'s suggestion), the struggle, the drama, enacts itself round a question of legitimacy. As I have stated it before (as H.A. described the original situation to me), there were two girls brought up as sisters, as equal daughters, of a *cadet* of a good English house. However, I needn't recapitulate this. One of them, the younger, is informed by her mother, on the latter's deathbed, that the other is illegitimate. She is the child of the late father by a former liaison (pre-matrimonial), taken over, adopted by the wife and brought up as her own child. However, I have stated this situation before, with the *variante* of making the sisters brothers, and the matter, the interest at issue, being not a marriage, but an inheritance, a question of money. Let me see a little what this may give. It gives primarily the advantage of a hero, a male central figure, which I prefer. This young man is the younger son. But what force of *deterrence* can the information given, the revelation made, for her reasons, by the dying mother be supposed as having if imparted to the person

1. *Pierre et Jean* by Guy de Maupassant (1887).
2. Feuillet (1821–90), French novelist and dramatist.
3. See 5 February and 26 March 1892.
4. See May/June 1893.

from whom the money is expected? Say it's expected in the form of a daughter
with a fortune and offered to the family by a x x x x x

34 De Vere Gardens, W., December 24th, 1893.

Three little histories were lately mentioned to me which (2 of the 3 in particular),
appear worth making a note of. One of these was related to me last night at dinner
at Lady Lindsay's, by Mrs. Anstruther-Thompson.[1] It is a small and ugly matter—
but there is distinctly in it, I should judge, the subject of a little tale—a little social
and psychological picture. It appears that the circumstance is about to come out
in a process-at-law. Some young laird, in Scotland, inherited, by the death of his
father, a large place filled with valuable things—pictures, old china, etc., etc. His
mother was still living, and had always lived, in this rich old house, in which she
took pride and delight. After the death of her husband she was at first left unmo-
lested there by her son, though there was a small dower-house (an inferior and
contracted habitation) attached to the property in another part of the country. But
the son married—married promptly and young—and went down with his wife to
take possession—possession *exclusive,* of course—according to English custom.
On doing so he found that pictures and other treasures were absent—and had been
removed by his mother. He enquired, protested, made a row; in answer to which
the mother sent demanding still other things, which had formed valuable and interesting features of the house during the years she had spent there. The son and
his wife refuse, resist; the mother denounces, and (through litigation or otherwise), there is a hideous public quarrel and scandal. It has ended, my informant
told me, in the mother—passionate, rebellious against her fate, resentful of the
young wife and of the loss of her dignity and her home—resorting to [the] tremendous argument (though of no real *value* to her) of declaring that the young
man is not the son of his putative father. She has been willing to dishonour herself
to put an affront upon *him.* It is all rather sordid and fearfully ugly, but there is
surely a story in it. It presents a very fine case of the situation in which, in
England, there has *always* seemed to me to be a story—the situation of the mother
deposed, by the ugly English custom, turned out of the big house on the son's
marriage and relegated. One can imagine the rebellion, in this case (the case I
should build on the above hint), of a particular sort of proud woman—a woman
who had *loved* her home, her husband's home and hers (with a knowledge and
adoration of artistic beauty, the tastes, the habits of a collector). There would be
circumstances, details, intensifications, deepening it and darkening it all. There
would be the particular type and taste of the wife the son would have chosen—a
wife out of a Philistine, a tasteless, a hideous house; the kind of house the very
walls and furniture of which constitute a kind of *anguish* for such a woman as I
suppose the mother to be. That kind of anguish occurred to me, precisely, as a
subject, during the 2 days I spent at Fox Warren (I didn't mean to write the

1. Clementine (Kit) Anstruther-Thompson was an intimate friend of Violet Paget's. See *Letters* III,
403.

name), a month or so ago. I thought of the strange, the terrible experience of a nature with a love and passion for beauty, united by adverse circumstances to such a family and domiciled in such a house. I imagine the young wife coming, precisely, out of it. I imagine the mother having fixed on a girl after her own heart for the son to marry; a girl with the same exquisite tastes that *she* has and having grown up surrounded with lovely things. The son doesn't in the least take to this girl—he perversely and stupidly, from the mother's point of view, takes to a girl infatuated with hideousness. It is in this girl's people's house, before the marriage, that the story opens. The mother meets there the other girl—the one that pleases her: the one with whom she discovers a community of taste—of passion, of sensibility and suffering.[2]

["The Old Things," the *Atlantic Monthly* April–October 1896; published as *The Spoils of Poynton,* London and Cambridge, Massachusetts (1897).]

Names. Gisborne—Dessin—Barden—Carden—Deedy—Gent—Kingdon (before)—Peregrine King (name in *Times)*—Brendon—Franking—Crevace—Covington (house)—Ledward—Bedward—Dedward—Deadward—Olguin—Alguin—Gannon—Leresche—Pinhorn—Loynsworth (Loinsworth)—Gallier—Parminter (Parmenter)—Count—Rouch—Carvel—Hilder—Medwick—Rumble (place)—Rumbal (person)—Ariel—Cork—Gulliver—Nesfield—Nest (place, house)—Rainy—Saltrem (or Saltram)—Cline—Stransom—Coxon—Derry—Lupus—Stamper—Creston—Cheston—Berry—Anvoy.

December 26th, 1893 (34 De Vere Gardens).

I have been sitting here in the firelight—on this quiet afternoon of the empty London Christmastide, trying to catch hold of the tail of an idea, of a 'subject.' Vague, dim forms of imperfect conceptions seem to brush across one's face with a blur of suggestion, a flutter of impalpable wings. The prudent spirit makes a punctual note of whatever may be least indistinct—of anything that arrives at relative concreteness. Is there something for a tale, is there something for a play, in something that might be a little like the following? It is the *play* that I am looking for, but it is worth noting, all the same, for the *other* possibility.

Very briefly, I imagine a young man who has lost his wife and who has a little girl, the only issue of that prematurely frustrated union. He has very solemnly, and on his honour, promised his wife, on her deathbed, that, *du vivant* of their child, he will not marry again. He has given her this absolutely sacred assurance and she has died believing him. She has had a reason, a deep motive for her demand—the overwhelming dread of a stepmother. She has had one herself—a stepmother who rendered her miserable, darkened and blighted her youth. She wishes to preserve her own little girl from such a fate. For five years all goes well—the husband doesn't think of marrying again. He delights in the child, consoles himself with her, watches over her growth and looks forward to her future. Then, inevitably, fatally he meets a girl with whom he falls deeply in love—in

2. See 13 May, 11 August, 8 September, and 15 October 1895 and 13 and 19 February and 30 March 1896.

love as he hadn't *begun* to be with his poor dead wife. She returns his affection, his passion; but he sees the phantom of his solemn vow, his sacred promise rise terribly before him. In the presence of it he falters, and while the girl obviously stands ready to surrender herself, he hangs back, he tries to resist the current that sweeps him along. *Or,* there is another figure intensely engaged in the action—and without whom it would present no drama. This is the figure of a young woman who loves him, who has loved him from the moment she has seen him, who has seen him, known him, *du vivant* of his wife. The circumstances of this personage are all questions to determine. What is of the essence is that she was a friend and perhaps even a relation of his wife, who admired and trusted her and who more or less bespoke her sympathy and protection for the little girl that was to be left motherless. *Mettons,* provisionally, supposititiously, that she was a relation, and at the time of the wife's death a married woman—a woman young, ardent, and already, at that time, secretly in love, with my hero. Stay—better still than making her married will it be, I think, to make her *engaged*—engaged to a fine young man whom the dying wife knows, approves of, takes comfort in thinking of as the girl's *futur,* her caretaker through life. In the first chapter of my story this young man is present—the 1st chapter of my story—by which I mean the 1st act of my play! Their engagement is a thing established—their marriage is not to be distant. Well, very briefly, the wife dies, exacting the promise that I have mentioned, and which is imparted to the girl at the time—probably by the wife herself. In the early part of the act the condition of the wife is uncertain—her end not positively near. When her fate *becomes* certain, the girl, by a strange abrupt *revirement,* in face of a renewed importunity of her lover, an 'appeal to name the day,' suddenly *breaks* with him, to his amazement, says she can't, that their engagement is at an end. He goes off in dismay, and it is *after* he goes off that she learns what the vow is that the hero has taken. There are also present in this first act the doctor, and a second young girl—my heroine proper, who has great subsequent importance and who is only introduced in the 1st. This 1st is of the nature of a prologue. Very, very briefly, so as to give the vaguest skeleton and *enclose* the statement in a definite loop, I go on with the mere essence of the story. The curtain rises on Act II, 5 years later. My Hero has never married, of course—no more has my Bad Heroine. She is fearfully in love with my Hero. He meanwhile has fallen in love with my Good Heroine, who ignorantly and innocently returns his passion. My Bad Heroine is frightfully afraid the two will marry; so, knowing what the other girl is, she makes up her mind to tell her of the vow he has made his wife, believing that will make her despise him if he violates it. Then, somehow, *this* is what I saw $\frac{1}{2}$ hour ago, as I sat in the flickering firelight of the winter dusk. The women have a talk—I won't answer, nor *attempt* to, now, here, of course, for links and liaisons—the women have a talk in which the good girl learns with *dismay* that it is the life of the child that keeps her from her lover. The effect of this revelation upon her is not, to the bad girl's sense, what she expected from it. She rebels, she protests, she is far from willing to give him up. Then my young lady takes a decision—she determines to poison the child—on the calculation that suspicion will fall on her rival. She does so—and on the theory of *motive*—suspicion *does* fall on the wretched girl. There are two persons to figure as the *public,* the judging, wondering, horrified world, the doctor and a convenient older woman who has been in the first act. Suspicion descends—it is *constatée* that the child is poisoned: the question is who has done it? The Hero, *seeing* the horrible fact and believing, for the moment, the good Heroine *is* responsible, has a moment of horror and anguish, and then, to *shield* her, takes a sublime decision, tells a noble dramatic lie, assumes the guilt (since the 'motive' may be shown to have all its force for him, too) and says '*I* did it!' That I am supposing to be the end of Act II. But I am also supposing that something has happened in Act I, and something more in Act II, which have combined to lay a magical hand on the gate of the denouement. The dismissed lover of the Bad Heroine has come back at the end of Act II—come back unexpectedly and from afar—in time to catch this last declaration, to be on the spot and astounded by it. Can't I, mustn't I, in the first act, have introduced some incident between himself and his fiancée of that hour, which now comes up again as a solution of the horrible predicament? Can't he have given her something, which she has kept ever since then and used in connection with her attempt on the child's life? May not this object have been found in the child's room, near the child's person, so that he recognizes it when it is again produced? I seem to see something like *this*— that in the 1st act something on the subject of the small object in question may have passed between the doctor and himself—on the subject of its being a strange and little-known poison, of which my young man happens to have brought, from a far country, this rather valuable specimen. It is in a locket, say: some woman gave it to him. *He* gives it to the Bad Heroine, *before* she throws him over. She *uses* it in Act II—he recognizes it in Act III. He has in Act III a scene with her about it. The doctor has also been in love with her—*is* in love with her up to the time of this strange exposure. The doctor's a bachelor. The 2d *amoureux* is the means of disproving the heroic lie of the Hero. In the 1st act either the 2d *amoureux or the doctor* must have emptied the locket and substituted something innocuous for the fatal fluid. The child recovers, demanding the Good Heroine, and the attempt of the Bad One is condoned and covered up by the doctor—who has aspired to her hand!—and the man who first loved her. The Hero at the '*request*' of his little daughter determines on a union with the Good Heroine; and the other woman is got off by the doctor and the 2d *amoureux*. As I so barbarously and roughly jot the story down, I seem to feel in it the stuff of a play, of the particular limited style and category that can only be dreamed of for E.C.[1] But I [am] not so much struck with there being in it a Part for an actor manager. A moment's reflection, however, suggests to me that that is only because of my very imperfect and inarticulated way of stating the matter. *Je me fais fort* to state it again in such a manner as that the Part of the Hero will appear—will take and hold its place.

x   x   x   x   x

34 De Vere Gardens, January 9th, 1894.

Last night, as I worried through some wakeful hours, I seemed to myself to catch hold of the tail of an idea that may serve as the subject of the little tale I

1. Edward Compton (see 12 May 1889, note 1). This idea for a play (or story), which he would call "The Promise" and later *The Saloon*, occupied HJ's mind for two years: see 23 January 1894 and 21 December 1895. See *Complete Plays* 677–79.

have engaged to write for H. Harland and his *Yellow Book.*[1] It belongs—the *concetto* that occurred to me and of which this is a very rough note—to the general group of themes of which *The Private Life*[2] is a specimen—though after all it is a thing of less accentuated fantasy. I was turning over the drama, the tragedy, the general situation of disappointed ambition—and more particularly that of the artist, the man of letters: I mean of the ambition, the pride, the passion, the idea of greatness, that has been smothered and defeated by circumstances, by the opposition of life, of fate, of character, of weakness, of folly, of misfortune; and the drama that resides in—that may be bound up with—such a situation. I thought of the tragic consciousness, the living death, the helpless pity, the deep humiliation, etc., etc., of it all. Then I thought of the forces, the reverses, the active agents to which such an ambition, such pride and passion, may succumb—before which it may have to lay down its arms: intrinsic weakness, accumulations of misfortune, failure, marriage, women, politics, death. The idea of *death* both checked and caught me; for if on the one side it means the termination of the consciousness, it means on the other the beginning of the drama in any case in which the consciousness survives. In what cases *may* the consciousness be said to survive—so that the man is the spectator of his own tragedy? In the cases of defeat, of failure, of subjection, of sacrifice to other bribes or other considerations. There came to me the fancy of a sacrifice to political life—in combination with a marriage.[3] A young man who has dreamed that he has the genius of a poet—a young man full of dreams of artistic glory—full of brilliant gifts as well—makes, in a political milieu, a worldly, showy, advantageous marriage, a marriage that pushes him, commits him, vulgarizes him, destroys his faith in his faculty. He forsakes, for this end, a girl whom he has originally loved and who is poor and intelligent. She has been the confidante of his literary, his poetic dreams; she has listened to his verses, believed in his genius and his future. He breaks with her, in an hour of temptation, and casts his lot the other way. That is the *death* my *donnée* supposes and demands. It hasn't form and value however till one determines the manner, the form in which one imagines his 'consciousness,' his observant life, his spectatorship of his own history, standing over and becoming an element of the case. I suggest this in the shape of the survival of his relation to the woman he had originally loved. He comes back to her, at the very behest of this consciousness. The woman he marries has taken him away; but he has died, as it were, in her hands. His corpse is politically, showily, galvanized; he has successes, notorieties, children, but to himself, in the situation, he is extinct. He meets the first woman again—and the dead part of him lives again. She too has married, after a while—and her husband and her children are dead. She is surrounded with death— and yet she lives with life. The other woman—his wife—is surrounded with life, and yet she lives with death. The thing can only be, like the *Private Life,* impressionistic: with the narrator of the story as its spectator. Stated, pen in hand, the

1. The American writer Henry Harland (1861–1905) had published in the United States, under the pen name ''Sidney Luska,'' a number of novels dealing with the lives of immigrant Jews in America; he came to England in 1890 to write under his own name and became the first editor of the *Yellow Book* in 1894.
2. See 27 July and 3 August 1891.
3. See the note on the F. H. story, 18 March 1889.

whole *concetto* strikes me as thinner and less picturesque than when it first occurred to me. I must think it over a little more and perhaps something more in the nature of an *image*—as in the P.L.—will come out of me. Say (it occurs to me), that my hero dies ½ way through the story—dies really—and that *this,* to the woman who still loves him, becomes the crowning sign of his 'life' for *her.* She is in mourning *pour tous les siens* and at this she goes into radiant colours.* She has him now—he is all hers. He has come to her from his blighting wife. His verses, his poems, the things he has done for *her,* must play a part in the business.

*[James's note] This incident, as the essence of the matter, very possible, I think for a *very short* thing. *Vide* red morocco notebook.[4]

x   x   x   x   x

34 D.V.G., January 23d, 1894.

Plus je vais, plus je trouve that the only balm and the only refuge, the real solution of the pressing question of life, are in this frequent, fruitful, intimate battle with the particular idea, with the subject, the possibility, the place. It's the anodyne, the escape, the boundlessly beneficent resort. No effort in this direction is vain, no confidence is idle, no surrender but is victorious.—I failed the other day, through interruption, to make a note, as I intended, of the anecdote told me some time since by Lady Gregory,[1] who gave it me as a 'plot' and saw more in it than, I confess, I do myself. However, it is worth mentioning. (I mean that I see in it all there is—but what there is is in the rather barren [today],[2] and dreary, frumpy direction of the pardon, the not-pardon, of the erring wife. When the stout middle-aged wife has an unmentionable 'past,' one feels how tiresome and charmless, how suggestive of mature petticoats and other frowsy properties, the whole general situation has become.) At any rate, Lady G.'s story was that of an Irish squire who discovered his wife in an intrigue. She left her home, I think, with another man—and left her two young daughters. The episode was brief and disastrous—the other man left her in turn, and the husband took her back. He covered up, hushed up her absence—perhaps moved into another part of the country, where the story was unknown; and she resumed her place at his *foyer* and in the care and supervision of her children. *But* the husband's action had been taken on an inexorable condition—that of her remaining only while the daughters were young and in want of a mother's apparent, as well as real, presence. 'I wish to avoid scandal—injury to their little lives; I don't wish them to ask questions about you that I can't answer or that I can answer only with lies. But you remain only till they are of such and such ages, to such and such a date. Then you go.' She accepts the bargain, and does everything she can, by her devotion to her children, to repair her fault. Does she hope to induce her husband to relax his rigour—or does she really accept the prospect that stares her in the face? The story doesn't say: what it does say is that the husband maintains his conditions, and the attitude of the wife, maintained also for years, avails in no degree to attenuate them. He has

---

4. This notebook has not survived.

1. Augusta, Lady Gregory (1852–1932), née Persse, Irish dramatist and poet active in the Celtic revival movement with W. B. Yeats; she was long a friend of HJ.

2. HJ's brackets.

fixed a particular date, a particular year, and they have lived *de part et d'autre,* with her eyes upon this dreadful day. The two girls alone have been in ignorance of it, as well as of everything else. But at last the day comes—they have grown up; her work is done and she must go. I suppose there isn't much question of their 'going out'; or else that it is just this function of taking them into the world, at 17, at 18, that he judges her most unfit for. She leaves them, in short, on the stroke of the clock, and leaves them in a bewilderment and distress against which the father, surely, should have deemed it his duty to provide—which he must from afar off have seen as inevitable. The way he meets it, in Lady G.'s anecdote, at any rate, is by giving the daughters the real explanation—revealing to them the facts of the case. These facts *appal* them, have the most terrible effect upon them. They are sensitive, pure, proud, religious (Catholics); they feel stained, sickened, horrified with life, and they both go into a convent—take the veil. That was Lady G.'s anecdote. I confess that as I roughly write it out, this way, there seems to me to be more in it—in fact, its possibilities open out. It becomes, indeed, very much what one sees in it or puts in it; presenting itself even as the possible theme of a rather strong short novel—80,000 to a 100,000 words. Jotting roughly what it appears to *recéler,* or suggest, I see the spectacle of the effect on the different natures of the 2 girls. I see a kind of drama of the woman's hopes and fears. I see the question of the marriage of one of the girls or of both—and the attitude, *là-dedans,* the part played, by the young men whom it is a question of their marrying. I see one of the girls 'take after' her mother on the spot. The other, different, throws herself into religion. The 1st one, say, has *always known* the truth. The revelation has nothing new to teach her. Something doubtless resides in such a subject, and it grows, I am bound to say, as one thinks of it. The character, the strange, deep, prolonged and preserved rigour of the husband—and above all his responsibility: that of his action, his effect upon his daughters. His stupidity, his worthlessness, his pedantry of consistency, his want of conception, of imagination of how they will feel, will take the thing. The absence of imagination his main characteristic. Then the young man—the lover of one of them— and his part in the drama, his knowledge in advance, his dread of it. He is the lover of the girl who goes into religion. The other one—reckless, cynical, with the soul of a *cocotte* has another tie: a secret relation with some bad fellow to whom, say, she gives herself. And the mother—and her lover? What becomes of her? The lover, say, has waited for her?—or the husband relents after he has seen the ravage made by his inhuman action and is reunited to her on the ruins of their common domestic happiness. x x x x x

Quite the subject of a story as well as of a play—it occurs to me—may be the idea, of the dramatic form of which I the other day commenced a rough sketch under the *étiquette* of *The Promise.* Oh yes there is a story in that—a story of from 80,000 to a 100,000 words, which would greatly resemble a play. In the story wouldn't one make the thing begin by a visit to the young wife from her stepmother, the stepmother whom she hated and from whom she had suffered? This lady would meet in the house—it would be the first incident or scene—the other woman, the bad girl, the heroine of the later events.[3]

3. See 26 December 1893 and 21 December 1895.

Another incident—'subject'—related to me by Lady G. was that of the eminent
London clergyman who on the Dover-to-Calais steamer, starting on his wedding
tour, picked up on the deck a letter addressed to his wife, while she was below,
and finding it to be from an old lover, and very ardent (an engagement—a rupture,
a relation, in short), of which he never had been told, took the line of sending
her, from Paris, straight back to her parents—without having touched her—on the
ground that he had been deceived. He ended, subsequently, by taking her back
into his house to live, but *never* lived with her as his wife. There is a drama in
the various things, for her, to which that situation—that night in Paris—might
have led. Her immediate surrender to some one else, etc., etc., etc. x x x x x

It reminds me of something I meant to make a note of at the time—what I heard
of the W.B.'s when their strange rupture (in Paris, too) immediately after their
almost equally strange marriage became known. He had agreed, according to the
legend, to bring her back to London for the *season,* for a couple of months of
dinners—of *showing,* of sitting at the head of his table and wearing the family
diamonds. This, in point of fact, he did—and when the season was over he turned
her out of the house. There is a story, a short story, in that.

x   x   x   x   x

34 De Vere Gdns. February 3d, 1894. Could not something be done with the idea
of the great (the distinguished, the celebrated) artist—man of letters he must, in
the case, be—who is tremendously made up to, *fêted,* written to for his autograph,
portrait, etc., and yet with whose work, in this age of advertisement and newspaperism, this age of interviewing, not one of the persons concerned has the smallest
acquaintance? It would have the merit, at least, of corresponding to an immense
reality—a reality that strikes me every day of my life. If I can devise a little
action, a little story, that will fit and express the phenomenon I mean, I think the
thing would be really worth while. The phenomenon is the one that is brought
home to one every day of one's life by the ravenous autograph-hunters, lion-
hunters, exploiters of publicity; in whose number one gets the impression that a
person knowing and *loving* the thing itself, the work, is simply never to be found
(The little tale might be called *The Lion.*)[1] It should—the whole situation—be
resolved, somehow, into a little concrete drama. The drama must reside in a close,
an intense connection between the author's personal situation and this question of
whether any one (in the crowd of lionizers) does know, really, when it comes to
the point, the first word of the work the hero's reputation for having produced
which is the very basis of their agitation. Something must depend, for him, on
their knowing it—depend, perhaps, for his honour, for his memory (something
important, I mean, something intimate, something vital), and the revelation of
their chattering ignorance only becomes complete. They must *kill him, hein?*—
kill him with the very fury of their selfish exploitation, and then not really have

1. See 9 February 1894.

an idea of what they killed him *for. Trouve donc, mon bon,*[2] an ingenious and compact little action, which will bring all this out. I seem to see, dimly, the possibilities of the thing in the situation of a man to whom public recognition has come late in life. The whole intention of the tale should be admirably satiric, ironic. The bewildered old hero is murdered by the interviewers—but the *consciousness of the moral* should probably reside only in the person telling the story, a friend, a companion, an observer and spectator of the drama. Shouldn't it, the little drama, take, in part, the form of this narrator's defending, attempting to defend—and attempting vainly—his precious friend against this invasion of the interviews, the portraitists and such; to defend him in particular against the appropriation of some arch and ferocious lion-huntress? This part of the story presents itself to me as tolerably easy to conceive; the difficulty is in what one may be able to find to express the crisis, as it were: the *other* half of the action—to embody the *exposure,* as it were, of the mere selfish interests on which the lionization rests. The whole thing might rest on a complete mistake and blunder as to the nature, the *form,* of the man's work.[3] I *see,* however, the essence of the thing; and the party at the country-house, and the ultra-modern hostess, and the autograph hunters and interviewers—and the collapse, the extinction of the hero, and the possible (for the interviewers) simultaneously *rising* star: the alternative of that A.B., the new woman who writes under a man's name, or B.A., the new man who (in order to be in the swim—profit by the predominance of the women) writes under a woman's. Say, too, the battle (of the narrator, the friend, the lover, the knower, the protector) with the destructive horde, with the lion-hunting hostess in particular, be the result of the hero's having imparted to him, read to him, talked of to him, the project of a spendid new unwritten thing which he wants time and strength still to do, and which the young man, said friend, yearns to *save* him, to keep him alive for. x x x x x

I seem to catch hold (Feb. 9th) for the foregoing subject of the two or three indispensable joints or hinges. Suppose I call it *The Death of the Lion,* and make my narrator, my critical *reflector* of the whole thing, a young intending interviewer who has repented, come to consciousness, fallen away. 'I had simply what is called a change of heart—and it began, I suppose, when they sent me back my manuscript'—that's the way I see it begin.

["The Death of the Lion," the *Yellow Book* April 1894; reprinted in *Terminations.*]

34 De Vere Gardens, Sunday, February 17th[1] *1894.*

Last night, at Mrs. Crackanthorpe's, Stopford Brooke[2] suggested to me 2 little ideas.

2. "Mon bon" is the term HJ will use with increasing frequency to refer to his "guardian spirit" and figure of inspiration. When he used the term in conversation he would raise his hat. On at least one occasion he used the Italian equivalent, "caro mio"; see 9 August 1900.

3. An anticipation of "The Figure in the Carpet"; see 24 October 1895.

1. Actually the date of "Last night" for Sunday was the 18th in February 1894.

2. The Reverend Stopford Augustus Brooke (1832–1916), Anglican clergyman and literary scholar.

(1) The man *(à propos* of S.B.) who has become afraid of himself when alone—vaguely afraid of his own company, personality, disposition, character, presence, fate; so that he plunges into society, noise, sound, the sense of diversion, distraction, protection, connected with the presence of others, etc.[3]

(2) The notion of the young man who marries an older woman and who has the effect on her of making her younger and still younger, while he himself becomes her age. When he reaches the age that *she* was (on their marriage), she has gone back to the age that *he* was.—Mightn't this be altered (perhaps) to the idea of cleverness and stupidity? A clever woman marries a deadly dull man, and loses and loses her wit as he shows more and more. Or the idea of a *liaison,* suspected, but of which there is no proof but this transfusion of some idiosyncrasy of one party to the being of the other—this exchange or conversion? The fact, the secret, of the *liaison* might be revealed in that way. The two things—the two elements—beauty and 'mind,' might be correspondingly, concomitantly exhibited as in the history of two related couples—with the opposition, in each case, that would help the thing to be dramatic.[4]

[*The Sacred Fount,* published (without serialization) in New York and London (1901).]

x   x   x   x   x

There came to me a night or two ago the notion of a young man (young, presumably), who has something—some secret sorrow, trouble, fault—to *tell* and can't find the *recipient.* x x x x x [5]

["A Round of Visits," the *English Review* April–May 1910; reprinted in *The Finer Grain,* New York and London (1910).]

March 16th, 1894. Note at 1st leisure the idea suggested to me by George Meredith's amusing picture—the other night (Boxhill, March 11th)—of the bewilderment of A.M. in the presence of the immense pretensions to 'conquest' (to 'having repeatedly overthrown Venus herself') of A.A. It suggested to me a subject—or at any rate a type, a study—the man who celebrates his own great feats and triumphs of love, his irresistibility. The confrontation of another man with it, a man who has really *had* immense successes—in his younger past—and has kept deeply silent about them: the mystification, sadness, comedy, etc., of this (and especially of the A.A. type), seems to contain the germ of something that might be threshed out.—[1]

3. HJ gives another turn to this idea and adds possible titles in his entries of 16 May 1899 and 11 September 1900; he apparently never developed it into a story.

4. See 15 February 1899.

5. See 21 April 1894, 7 May 1898, and 16 February 1899.

1. George Meredith (1828–1909), English poet and novelist and a friend of HJ's since 1878, had made Flint Cottage, Box Hill, Surrey, his home from the beginning of 1868. A. M. is Admiral Frederick Augustus Maxse (d. July 1900), grandson of the Earl of Berkeley. The Admiral was famous for his naval exploits during the Crimean War and was Meredith's most intimate friend. He was the model for Nevil Beauchamp (*Beauchamp's Career,* 1875). A. A. is Alfred Austin (1835–1913), appointed Poet Laureate in 1896 and the *vainqueur de Vénus* of this idea—a theme HJ developed further in the 19, 20, and 21 April 1894 entries. Meredith enjoyed ridiculing Austin's tiny stature and towering

Casa Biondetti, Venice, April 17th, 1894.

Here I sit[1] at last, after many interruptions, distractions, and defeats, with some little prospect of getting a clear time to settle down to work again. The last six weeks, with my 2 or 3 of quite baffling indisposition before I left London, have been a period of terrific sacrifice to the ravenous Moloch of one's endless personal, social relations—one's eternal exposures, accidents, disasters. *Basta.*

x   x   x   x   x

All the little subjects I have lately noted here seem to me good and happy—that is, essentially susceptible of further threshing out and development. x x x x x

In reading Dykes Campbell's book on Coleridge[2]—it is so good that one almost forgets how much better a little more of the power of evocation might have made it—I was infinitely struck with the suggestiveness of S.T.C.'s figure—wonderful, admirable figure—for pictorial treatment. What a subject some particular cluster of its relations would make for a little story, a small vivid picture.[3] There was a point, as I read, at which I seemed to see a little story—to have a quick glimpse of the possible drama. Would not such a drama necessarily be the question of the acceptance by someone—someone with something important at stake—of the general *responsibility* of rising to the height of accepting him for what he is, recognizing his rare, anomalous, magnificent, interesting, curious, tremendously suggestive character, vices and all, with all its imperfections on its head, and *not* being guilty of the pedantry, the stupidity, the want of imagination, of fighting him, deploring him in the details—failing to recognize that one *must* pay for him and that on the whole he is magnificently worth it. The individual whom I have described as having something at stake *does* pay for him, as it were—whereas there is another who doesn't, who won't. The figure of the rare eccentric, the bone of contention himself, is so (potentially) fine, I think, that one must hold one's little story—*je tiens mon effet*—from the moment one puts one's hand on the action that throws him into relief. Does it not seem to one that that action is, to a certain extent and in its general outline, fundamentally designated, indicated—that one puts one's hand on it as soon as one disengages that degree and quantity of it that are *implied* in the very personality and presence, the *obviousness* of fate, of the hero? He has the great Coleridge-quality—he is a splendid, an incomparable *talker.* He has the other qualities—I needn't name them here, I see them admirably, all, with the high picturesqueness of their anomalous, their baffling, despairing, exasperating

---

conceit. Austin's confessed "cult" for Maxse's beautiful daughter Violet inspired Meredith to compose burlesque odes, which he attributed to Austin, and a legendary account of the wooing of Miss Violet in which Austin stands on a chair to kiss her (see Lionel Stevenson, *George Meredith,* 1953). HJ never completed the "Vainqueur de Vénus" story; see 21 April 1894.

1. HJ had rooms on the Grand Canal that had been occupied by American novelist Constance Fenimore Woolson (b. 1840) during the summer and fall preceding her tragic death in January 1894. For details of the "exposures, accidents, disasters" see *Life* 376–78, 390–402.

2. J. Dykes Campbell's biography of the poet Samuel Taylor Coleridge (1772–1834) had just been published.

3. See 18, 25, and 29 April 1894 and 4 June 1895 for allusions to "The Coxon Fund."

cluster round the fine central genius. *Or,* what is 'obvious' in the action required, the action capable of making the thing a little masterpiece in 20,000 words, is precisely the element of opposition in the two modes, the unimaginative and the imaginative, the literal and the constructive manner of dealing with him. If I can embody this opposition in a little drama containing adequately the magic of suspense, [make it] amount effectively to a story, I may do something capable of being admirable. It is just this story, this chaste but workable and evincible young freshness of the inevitable, that I must shut myself up with in the sacredest and divinest of all private commerces. Live with it a little, *mon bon,* and the happy child will be born. x x x x x

The contender, the believer, the acceptor of responsibility, must, tolerably clearly, be a woman. The forces she is opposed to are the man's own belongings. What belongings can these be—on the assumption imperative, I think, as a solution of certain difficulties, of his being *young,* a wonder of *promise,* with all his infirmities already budding and all his genius already sensible to those susceptible of feeling it? (When I say 'young,' can he be less than 40? I must remember that I must give some of the people time for exhausted patience—for the determination of their disbeliefs and chuckings-up.) He must have a wife—a wife who divorces him? Yes, and the girl, the heroine, must incur imputations, by association, by induction, in regard to her own virtue. One of the sacrifices she makes is a big sacrifice of money? Assuredly, and the drama, the story, is the anecdote of this sacrifice, of the determination of it, in the face of scandal, etc.—the money being a high responsible trust. The trust is a bequest—an 'endowment of research' on the part of a rich, well-meaning relative, a woman (Bostonian?), an aunt, a cousin, or even simply a friend who feels her responsibilities to culture. The story may thus be excellently named *The So-and-So Fund,* of which the girl has, in a manner, the administration. Let it be constituted *after* the girl has made the acquaintance of the hero, begun to be interested in him and to wonder privately, secretly, with a certain conscious diffidence, whether he isn't one of those great ones who should have something done for them. She keeps this dawning conception from her relative (in pure innocence), at the time that relative (in dying and perhaps unable to be explicit about all her testamentary intentions) delegates to her summarily, leaving it, as a high expression of affectionate trust in her wisdom, partly to her discretion, the execution, the administration of a certain legacy in a particular spirit already discussed with her, explained to her. *(The Coxon Fund.)* Put Saltram (Coleridge—or something like) on his feet from the first: present him to the girl, make her get her impression. Also his wife and the question of their divorce. He is staying with someone (à la Coleridge) whom she goes to see; the wife (of the host, patron) has been a former friend of hers. She appeals to Mrs. Saltram *not* to divorce him—appeals before her aunt's death: I set down things as they occur to me. She is engaged to a young man approved by her aunt and who is co-administrator of the fund with her. She therefore makes a sacrifice of marriage. He marries sister of Mrs. Saltram. The action, therefore, is the contention between the girl and her young man about the application of the fund—and it must be *d'un serré.* x x x x x

["The Coxon Fund," the *Yellow Book* July 1894; reprinted in *Terminations.*]

It must indeed be *d'un serré!* but after a single morning (April 18th) spent in starting the above *(The Coxon Fund)* and starting it fairly well, I recognize that the theme is far too fine and brave to be spoiled by mutilation—compression into the compass of 20,000 words. Indeed that operation is utterly impracticable—I see the folly of undertaking it. 20,000? A good 100,000 are already required. Some day it shall have them. It is so much to the good. Let it stand there as the admirable subject of a fine short (1 vol.) novel, all ready to my hand; and let me for my present job address myself patiently to something much simpler.

Casa Biondetti, April 19th, 1869. [1894][1]

The idea I noted here the other day[2]—the situation suggested to me by an allusion of George Meredith—to A.A., *Vainqueur de Vénus,* and A.M.'s confused, anxious consideration of him (he, of so different a type, who had *really* been loved), recurs to me as an excellent little theme. It belongs, however, I think, essentially to the ironic, to the order of fine comedy, satiric observation, and is not exactly what I want for a story of emotion, a history of some passion, some tender relation. What it is, and what it is capable of being, I must add, is only determinable after it shall have been mated with some action, some element requisite for making it a tale. As I have it now it is only an idea—and everything is wanting to make it a story. The situation, primarily, is wholly wanting, and the 'moral' wholly to be disengaged. There must of course be a woman in it, or the thing has no sense. It is the action of the little drama that must reveal itself—the relation to the real forces of love (i.e., to some woman or some women) as well as to each other that the 2 men find themselves in. What essentially *takes* me in the *concetto* is, I think, the chance to have a fling at the general attitude of swagger and egotism in this particular matter—to have a dab at the *French* attitude, as I may call it for convenience. What I want to oppose to it dramatically is something that I may call for convenience the English attitude.[3] I must, *voyons,* have something at stake for my genuine man—something in operation, in question; some passion, some devotion, some success—something perhaps that comes back out of the past, the past of his own personal triumph. He WONDERS so at the little man's own achievements, *vanteries,* successes, confidences, exhibitions—is stupefied, mystified, depressed by them (being simple, impressible, etc., in his credulity), so that they make him say that if this is the kind of person that women succumb to, his own history must be all a delusion and a myth. Various little possibilities seem to loom

1. The slip of the pen to 1869 refers back to the year of HJ's first adult voyage to Europe.
2. See 16 March 1894.
3. The concern with "the French attitude" and opposing it dramatically to "the English attitude" foreshadows *The Awkward Age.* See 4 March 1895 and HJ's preface to the novel, volume IX, New York edition.

and hover before me—disengaging themselves faintly in the divine way, the dear old blessed healing, consoling way in which they *always* respond to real solicitation and the pure, generous loyalty of which (one's own grateful sense of it), brings tears to my eyes as I write. Isn't there a potentiality of 3 men instead of 2—to give me the YOUNG man whose aspirations are nipped in the bud—by which I mean discouraged by the spectacle of the anomaly of the prosperous *vantard,* rendered 'mythic' to him in the future, as those of the elder man, originally conceived, are rended 'mythic' *(to him)* in the past. Confraternity of these two men, exchange of bewilderments, mutual communication of melancholies and questions. Doesn't the 'action' become, this way, in *spite* of themselves, in spite of their modesty, their discovery of the falsity of the pretensions of the other? I want to establish, to illustrate, somehow, that these pretensions (i.e., of the kind), are *not* the real thing—that the real thing is silence and sanctity. I want to 'do' the egotist, the self-celebrator. I want to make the women themselves bring about the denouement, testify to my moral: I want it to come *by* them. My elder man is there with something that comes back to him out of his past—my younger one is there with something that *may* come to him out of his future. I seem to see my elder man coming back at some bidding of his conscience, that of some memory of an old wrong done—coming back devoutly and tenderly to repair it. He thinks he has hurt a woman in his youth—he thinks he has hurt two women. He comes back (from India?) to see *which* woman he has hurt (i.e., jilted, disappointed) most, in order that he may, if possible, marry her, make it all up to her now. My notion is that his reflections (upon A.A.) make him think he has exaggerated his responsibility and his compunction. I seem to get hold of the slippery tail of a fine idea in seeing something in the nature of a demonstration of the beauty and virtue of silence, and in particular of this truth that it is in their very movement of flight for *defense,* as it were, that the women have thrown themselves into the PRETENSE of victimization by A.A.—because they know he will betray them. He is their shield against the men who are silent—that is his very function: and it is only because there is nothing to betray that they let him appear to betray it. May I not imagine *this* position—these 2 positions—for my older and my younger man respectively—that the woman whom the former wishes to make the reparation to lends herself to A.A. from pride (precisely because she still so loves her old 'wronger'), and the woman whom the young man wishes to make up to (she must be married), seeks the same refuge from dread—dread of succumbing to the young man, the instinct of letting him think she belongs to another man, so that he may not pursue her. The *vantard* is USED, in the manner the most disrespectful of himself—that is the real ironic fact about him—and that is the moral of my little comedy, which will be difficult, thank God!, to write. The *vantard,* the swaggerer, is *always* used—while it is the silent man who *uses;* that is the generalization, the salient truth. Is it all too alembicated, too subordinate and subtle? I ask myself this, and the right answer seems to be that it *needn't* be, and that if I really take hold of the thing *autant cela qu'autre chose.* If it remains muddled, and vague—abstract and suggested—it will be 'too subtle'; if it is a clear, straight, lucid action, a thing after my own heart, I don't see why the little drama of it shouldn't be fine and interesting. The *form* of this drama is what I have to determine: if it is happily determined the sense of it all will come out, vividly, of itself. Make your little story, find your little story, tell your little story, and leave the rest to the gods! Ah, how the gods are on one's side the moment one enters the enchanted realm! Ah, consoling, clarifying air of *work*—inestimable sacred hours! Every doubt of them is an outrage—every act of faith is a triumph! x x x x x

My two sincere men must be united, somehow—united by a meeting, by a friendship, by a confidence or a series of confidences; and there must not be too great a difference in their age. Say one is fifty-three and the other, the 'young' one, thirty-six. The elder man, I think, must be a soldier; convenient, indispensable attribution! The younger has political aspirations. They must meet first before they both meet the swaggerer. But the swagger[er] must have had some contact with *one* of them—the swaggerer too must have political aspirations. Say he is indeed the only one that has them, and that my young man of 36 is something else, a barrister, even a city man. There is perhaps indeed no particular need of his being something else—they may be different types of the political *genus*. This, however, is manageable enough: what requires consideration is the particular plausibility of circumstance in which the men are brought together. Say the two other men are fellow contributors to a newspaper which the General (or Colonel) has bought. Or say the swaggerer—or one of the others, the man of 36—is a diplomatist. *C'est encore bien* arrangeable—for these are details; what is of the essence is the whole question, difficult to present to English readers, of the 'sexual' side of the business, the element of pursuit, possession, conquest, etc., on the men's part and of danger, response, desire, surender, etc., on the part of the women. However, one makes one's appeal in all this, as one has always made it, to frankness, truth and taste; to the *interesting*, as usual, wherever it resides and abides. I seem, at any rate, to see *both* the women as antecedently connected with the General—the one whom the younger man is in love with as the second of the two women whom he has had compunctions about. x x x x x

Somehow, this morning (April 20th) the whole frank, bright, manly, human little comedy—in its initial steps at least—seems to come to me. Begin it—try it a little; put your hand into the paste!

x   x   x   x   x

Casa Biondetti, April 21st, 1894.

I *have* put my hand to it—I did yesterday, in a morning's limited scribble; but the subject, which is good, doesn't somehow speak to me for this particular purpose. It isn't the quite *objective* thing I want. The thing I want will come[1]—

---

1. The thing never did come, probably because of HJ's inherent inability to manage the details of the *macho* male sexuality—the "swagger and egotism" of the real *"vainqueur."* He is simply not a Jamesian "type."

will come 'in its glory': the quiet, generous, patient mornings will bring it. They are everything; or only want to be, beg to be, so far as they are encouraged and permitted. Oh, soul of my soul—oh, sacred beneficence of *doing! Ohne Hast, ohne Rast!* Consider many things and open the hospitable mind! Look at this, judge of that and turn over the other! It all helps and fructifies and enriches x x x x x

There is apparently something worth thinking of in the idea I barely noted, a few weeks ago,[2] of the young man with something on his mind—the young man with a secret, a worry, a misery, a burden, an oppression, that he carries about with him and suffers from the incapacity to tell—from the want of a confidant, a listening ear and answering heart, an intelligent receptacle for. He *tries* to communicate it, in the belief that it will relieve him. He goes from house to house and from person to person, but finds everywhere an indifference, a preoccupation too visible, a preoccupation, on the part of every one, with other things, with their own affairs, troubles, joys, pleasures, interests—an atmosphere that checks, chills, paralyses the possibility of any appeal. Some have pleasures they're entirely concerned with, others have troubles of their own which he thinks they make a strange excessive fuss about—being so much slighter and smaller than his. So he wanders, so he goes—with his burden only growing heavier—looking vainly for the ideal sympathy, the waiting, expectant, responsive recipient. My little idea has been that he doesn't find it; but that he encounters instead a sudden appeal, an appeal more violent, as it were, more pitiful even than his own has had it in it to be. He meets in a word a *demand* where he had at last been looking for a supply— a demand which embodies the revelation of a trouble which he immediately feels to be greater than his own. In the presence of this communication which he has to receive instead of giving it he forgets his own, ceases to need to make a requisition for it. His own ache, in a word, passes from him in his pity and his sympathy; he is healed by doing himself what he wanted to have done *for* him. Such is the little idea—which is perhaps as pretty as another. The charm and interest of the thing must necessarily be in the picture—the little panorama of his vain contacts and silent appeals, the view of his troubled spirit and of the people, the places, he successively turns to only to find that everywhere his particular grief is a false note. No one says to him—it *occurs* to no one to say: 'You've got something very painful on your mind—do tell us if we can help you—and what it is!' Don't I see that there is one person whom he has been counting upon most, inevitably a woman, a woman whom he has been occupied with, confusedly, anxiously, tenderly, whom he hasn't been sure about and as to his feeling for whom he has been by no means sure? He thinks it clears up that feeling that now, instinctively, it is to *her* his imagination turns most. He takes this as *a sign,* this confidence that he has in her; declaring to himself that if she meets it it will settle the matter for him, prove to him that she *is* the fine creature he has not been certain she is. She is unfortunately absent—away from London, and he is intensely impatient for her return. It is in the meantime, as a substitute, as a resource that *may* meet his case, that he goes to the other places, the other people.

2. See 18 February 1894.

I think I see the little story begin with his visit to her house, after his grief, his disaster: his 1st movement is toward her. I describe, don't I?, his discomfiture, his disappointment as he learns that she is away, has gone to Paris—gone for some time, the servant not knowing when she will be back. The young man has absolutely expected to find her—had reason to count upon it. Her absence is really connected with the great trouble of her own which he doesn't know or suspect. He turns away from her door, deeply dejected and disappointed. He must go about with his burden for a week or ten days—trying vainly to *place* it, to dispose of it. Then a sort of intuition, a hope against hope, after his other failures and discomfitures, prompts him to return, to see if by a miracle she may not have happened to come back. She has—she *has!* and they are so soon face to face. Of extreme moment, and quite the keystone of my little arch, the question of what each of these two 'troubles' consist of. They must both be grave, painful, ugly; belong more or less to the horrors, the shocks, the treacheries, the disillusionments, the real sufferings of life. I must put my hand very exactly upon them; for as I make this blessed little statement I seem to see that my situation does hold something, that the thing is distinctly, within its dimensions, a subject. I seem to see *this* element in it—that the thing on which the woman makes her appeal, her demand to him (turns the tables on him, as it were), proves a matter as to which his participation, his knowledge, his compassion can bring him no profit, no personal advantage. If he is relieved by pity for another it is by pity for the sake of pity— not for the sake of the reward his pity will bring him. To illustrate simply, off-hand, what I mean, let me suppose that she is a married woman, a woman living apart from her husband x x x x x

Casa Biondetti, Venice, April 25th, 1894.

I have committed myself to the *Yellow Book* for 20,000 words, and I swing back, on 2d thought, to the idea of *The Coxon Fund*—asking myself if I can't treat it in a way to make it go into that limited space. I want to do something very good for the Y.B., and this subject strikes me as superior. The formula for the presentation of it in 20,000 words is to make it an *Impression*—as one of Sargent's[1] pictures is an impression. That is, I must do it from my own point of view—that of an imagined observer, participator, chronicler. I must picture it, summarize it, impressionize it, in a word—compress and confine it by making it the picture of what I see. That has the great advantage, which perhaps after all would have been an imperative necessity, of rendering the picture of Saltram an implied and suggested thing. I should probably have had, after all, to have come to this—should have found it impossible to content myself with any literal record—anything merely narrative, with the detail of narrative. But if the thing becomes *what I see*—what is it I see—in the way of action, sequence, story, climax? The subject remains the same, but the great hinge must be more salient perhaps, and the whole thing simplified. A strong subject, a rich subject *summarized*—that is my indispensable formula and memento. x x x x x

1. HJ had met John Singer Sargent (1856–1925), the American painter, in Paris in February 1884.

Casa Biondetti, April 29th. I have begun my little tale, and written neatly enough, upwards of 3000 words—3300 rather say—p. 28 of MS.—stating, putting sufficiently well *en scène* my Frank Saltram and my George Gravener—but having left less than 17,000 to do all the rest. This will be sufficient, however, if I get the proper *grasp* of my drama. *Voyons un peu, mon bon,* what that grasp must be. I don't fail one jot of the faith—nor flinch in it—that the subject is admirable; but that very sense it is that makes me particularly nervous. I want so to squeeze out of it the perfection of a condensed action. Essentially, the pivot and climax of the action is the girl's decision, in circumstances of the highest import for her, that Saltram's 'morality,' i.e., his conduct, don't in such an exceptional case, matter. It seems to me that what I must get is an *intensification* of the drama of her situation by making doubly-much depend and hinge upon her determination. That she forfeits her lover goes without saying; but she must do more than this— she must forfeit money, somehow; forfeit the money of the 'fund.' The manner in which she does this—the special provisions of the founder—I shall arrive at with a little patience. What I must CONSISTENTLY establish is the summarized *exhibition* of Saltram's incorrigibility—make the climax of it, as it were, match with the climax of her exaltation about his deserving the endowment. The picture becomes the picture of the opposition of these two states. I see that my leaps and elisions, my flying bridges and great comprehensive loops (in a vivid, admirable sentence or two), must be absolutely bold and masterly. I see, I think, that the thing must consist, that my safety and facility must reside, in a division into numbered sections which insist on remaining short and succeed in being rich and each one a fine dramatic and pictorial step; so that, each making from 12 to 15 pp. of my MS., there shall be some 15 in all. I think I catch my next step and a happy idea in making *Saltram himself* put the girl in relation with the narrator— that makes a long *enjambée*. That is III—she doesn't then know George Gravener; but she is presented, I introduce her, and she makes her first impression, for me, and gets her 1st as regards Frank Saltram. Four or five years have elapse[d], and *two,* say, must elapse before the next section—the IV. This is a rough computation of everything; but it helps me, divinely, to make it. What it presses to interweave *quickly* is the element of the eccentric will-making aunt; and what it presses above all to render lucid is the terms of her will and the precise nature and degree of Saltram's want of character—the IMAGE of his laxity, his abandonment *des siens,* his want of all the qualities of will, exemplified in some deep vice, some abyss. There must be *one whole brief section* devoted to an impressionism of the beauty of his personal genius and the kindling effect of his talk. Perhaps I can't make IV, at that stage, comprehensive enough without making it both III and IV. The most treatable-in-a-short-compass infirmity that I can give him is his abandonment *des siens*—his intolerance of the family tie. He must endure *no* liens— and he must have NATURAL CHILDREN. The section about his genius must deal with the NOBLENESS of his intellect—his lectures, his *conférences.* May the girl not turn up at a *lecture?*—slip in that way first? I must care about the girl—but I mustn't get her. The girl must have met Mrs. Saltram—must have known her. Mrs. Saltram must have done something for the girl's aunt. That's why she has come to the lecture—to the *conférence.* There must be one at which Saltram himself has failed—through being drunk—through being 'off.' *That* is the one at which the girl and the narrator meet—*that* is III. She must, in regard to her aunt's bequest, have an option—a discretion. She is not *travelling* with her aunt; she has come out to see her. There are certain good little reasons which I think *prevail* for making her American. Though in relation (of help given) with Mrs. Saltram, the aunt never *dreams* of *his* being the sort of person who may be, or become, the object of her bounty. She is vague, highly disapproving about him—as an element in Mrs. Saltram's life. She can *only* be an 'eccentric.' I don't see how I can manage the question of the girl's option unless I make the question of the bequest for the fund come after her engagement, and during it. I must meet her at the (failure) lecture—and she mustn't *there* see Saltram. She must only hear about him from me. I must have a little talk with her—to explain. Then she disappears—the time elapses. I must have put her *au courant*—about everything. The III may open with her appeal to me to know if Mr. Saltram will really come; or with the words: 'If that first night was one of the liveliest, or at any rate was the freshest, of my exaltations, there was another, four years later, that was one of my disgusts. He had been announced to lecture (in the little St. J.'s Wood Assembly Rooms) but he didn't turn up'—or words to that effect. I *tell* the strange young lady—the pretty American girl—more or less about him. That's a short III. She also tells me how she comes to be there—and this strikes the note of the eccentric aunt—all in the III. Oh, the minimum of dialogue! The girl disappears— till IV; or till later. *Je crois que je tiens* my element of the Coxon bequest: Ah, *miséricorde divine,* ah, exquisite art and privilege and joy! The girl has the assurance of money—or thinks she has—and it is on the basis, the basis of what her father will be able to do for her, that she becomes engaged to George Gravener. After her engagement her aunt, who is not very rich and has some other claims, tells her of the provision existing in a will already made, a provision for the endowment of a fund for the disinterested pursuit of truth—the formula to be made perfectly felicitous. It doesn't at first seem to cover Saltram's case at all: it only becomes susceptible of this afterward by the girl's interpretation. The aunt, *on the girl's engagement,* offers to alter her will and give her the money instead— but she *declines* (after a discussion with her lover)—can't bear to deprive struggling merit of the advantage of the endowment. Tension of Gravener's attitude— *he* doesn't like it, and would much rather she would take the money. But he swallows the sacrifice—is consoled by the hopes from the father. The aunt is so pleased with the girl's response that, as a great compliment and honour, she makes her an administrator of the fund—a trustee, an executrix. She then—the aunt— dies and the marriage is retarded a little. Then the girls' father either dies or fails—or both; she loses all her prospects—all save £500—or less—a year. This retards the marriage and produces a certain lukewarmness on Gravener's part. *Then* the girl—or before this—makes the full acquaintance of Saltram's talk. She must do so just *as* her father fails. Gravener wants her at least to dispose of it so that Mrs. Saltram shall get the use of it. But her reflection—objection? 'It's for *him*—how else does it meet the idea of the bequest?' Gravener makes it a condition that she doesn't do that with it. *She may even keep the money*—somehow; ARRANGE THIS. Yes, her knowledge of Mrs. Saltram, her wrongs, her story, her representations, which I work in with *my* corresponding knowledge, must pervade the part stretching from the lecture-night to her real meeting with Saltram; and it must be through Mrs. Saltram that I partly know these dispositions—incidents, conditions. Query?—doesn't this almost dispense with *my* knowing Gravener? No!!

Casa Biondetti, Venice, May 13th, 1894.

I am struck, in reading in the *Fortnightly Review* of May, 1894, an article on 'English and French Manners,' with there being in these lines, perhaps, something of a 'subject.' 'When it is thoroughly understood in England that the majority of French people (exception being made for the Anglomaniacs of advanced society) consider that "flirting" is a dishonourable amusement and that a woman who has once listened to the overtures of a man considers it an act of justice to console him, this side of the French character will be more comprehensible to the English mind.' Make the 2 women—with their *opposed views of 'conduct.'* [1]

["The Given Case," *Collier's Weekly* December 1898 to January 1899; reprinted in *The Soft Side.*]

15 Beaumont St., Oxford, September 29th, 1894. [1]

I seem to see a pretty idea for a short tale in a small fancy to which I should give the name of *The Altar of the Dead.* [2] The name, at least, is happy; if the story may be half as much so! I imagine a man whose noble and beautiful religion is the worship of the Dead. It is the only religion he has; and it is a refuge and a consolation to him. He cherishes for the silent, for the patient, the unreproaching dead, a tenderness in which all his private need of something, not of this world, to cherish, to be pious to, to make the object of a donation, finds a sacred, and almost a secret, expression. He is struck with the way they are forgotten, are unhallowed—unhonoured, neglected, shoved out of sight; allowed to become so much more dead, even, than the fate that has overtaken them has made them. He is struck with the rudeness, the coldness, that surrounds their memory—the want of place made for them in the life of the survivors. The essence of his religion is really to make and to keep such a place. This place I call—he calls—their altar; an altar that, in the obscurity of his spiritual spaces, seems to blaze with lights and flowers. *His* dead, at least, are there, and there is a great perpetual taper for each of them. The situation, the action, that makes the idea a subject, comes to me vaguely as something like this. Let me first say that I had first fancied the 'altar' as a merely spiritual one—an altar in his mind, in his soul, more spendid to the spiritual eye than any shrine in any actual church. But I probably can't get an adequate action unless I enlarge this idea. Let me suppose for the moment, at any rate, that he has set up a spiritual altar—either in some Catholic church or in some apartment or chapel of his own house. The latter alternative is, I think,

1. See 21 December 1895.
1. This was the last English residence of Constance Fenimore Woolson.
2. See next two entries and *Life* 389–99.

much the *least* practicable. The idea of the story, in its simplest expression, is that, loving and cherishing his altar, he feels that it doesn't become complete—that it won't be, can't be, till his *own* taper is lighted there. It's to that end, as a climax, that the little tale must work. I think I see it, and that it comes to me. He begins it with the death of his mother—or at any rate with the loss of some dear friend. The thing takes place in London, vaguely, fancifully, obscurely, without 'realism' or dots upon the *i*'s. He wanders in his bereavement into a Catholic church. He sits there—in the darkness of a winter afternoon—before a lighted altar; and the comfort and the peace are sweet to him. It could all be much better abroad; but that is a detail, and tact, and art, the divine, circumvent everything. Abroad or in London, at any rate, he sees an old woman paying for a taper—for one of *her* poor dead; and that gives him the fancy, the hint. He finds one of the side-altars of the church obscure and neglected—and he makes an arrangement by which, on payment of a sum of money, *he* may establish certain perpetual candles there.

x   x   x   x   x

["The Altar of the Dead," published (without serialization) in *Terminations*.]

34 De Vere Gardens, October 2d, 1894.

I came back to town yesterday—and I see my little subject comparatively clear— I think. My hero's altar has long been a 'spiritual' one—lighted in the gloom of his own soul. Then it *becomes* a material one, and the event is *determined* in a manner that the story relates. He wanders into a suburban (of course, Catholic) church on a winter afternoon. He is under the *coup,* the effect, of some *fresh* perception of the way the Dead are forgotten, dishonoured, in the manner I have hinted at.

x   x   x   x   x

October 24th, 1894. I broke off there—but I wrote the greater part of a very short tale on those lines: with the effect, unusual for me, of quite losing conceit of my subject, within sight of the close, and asking myself it it is worth going on with: or rather feeling that it isn't. I shall put it by—perhaps it will, the humour of it, come back to me. But the thing is a 'conceit,' after all, a little fancy which doesn't hold a great deal. Such things betray one—that I more and more (if possible) feel. *Plus je vais,* the more intensely it comes home to me that solidity of subject, importance, emotional capacity of subject, is the only thing on which, henceforth, it is of the slightest use for me to expend myself. Everything else breaks down, collapses, turns thin, turns poor, turns wretched—betrays one miserably. Only the fine, the large, the human, the natural, the fundamental, the passionate things. It is true, of course, that in the case of a little thing like this *Altar of the Dead,* a short thing, as to which its modest dimensions speak for it, it need not be of much moment, one way or the other, if one *does* go on with it. What one *has* seen in it is probably there, and pressing a little will bring it out.

One's claim for it is, on the very face of the matter, slight. Let me remember that I have always put things through. x x x x x

Meanwhile Henry Harper,[1] the other day at McIlvaine's gorgeous dinner at the Reform (given to *him*, H.H., Oct. 17th), brought me a kind of message from Alden of the *Magazine,* a message strongly backed up by himself, to the effect that they wanted to 'see me in the Magazine again.' Henry Harper, who is a very pleasant, clear-faced fellow, even suggested, as coming (partly) from Alden, the rough idea of a subject for me!—a subject on which an international tale, a tale of the *Daisy Miller* order, might be based. The odd part of it is that there is probably something in it, that it doesn't strike me as very bad, or as very empty! It is—vaguely speaking—the eternal question of American snobbiness abroad; the vividness of which appeared to have been brought home to *ces messieurs* by the situation and proceedings of W.A.[2] I think they were rather out in their example— I should say he wasn't, for various reasons, a good signal instance. But the proposal seems to represent something to me, and I ask myself if it isn't—if it may not be—the moment for me to see something in such an overture? Henry Harper evidently wants another *Daisy Miller;* and *je ne demande pas mieux;* only there are various things to be said; such as that above all, first, I can't (if I *do* thresh the subject out into something good) undertake to handle the thing within the short compass of *Daisy M.* Anything I shall see in it must resolve itself into the form of something of about the length of Daudet's *Immortel*[3]—or it's not worth doing. *L'Immortel* is, to speak vulgarly, upwards of eighty thousand words long. *The Reverberator* is less than 30,000. x x x x x

Innumerable questions and alternatives *(questions d'art,* alternatives of work—of present immersion) have been surging round me all these last days; especially these 2 last—3 last—that I have been shut up with a sickly cold—the cold I brought home from the Millets[1] on the 22d. (I write this Oct. 25th, 1894.) I have felt nervous and embroiled—but that's not worth mentioning here. x x x x x

November 3d, 1894. Isn't there a little drama in the idea of such a situation as A.L.'s—that of an extremely clever and accomplished man, a man much prized and followed up in society, a great favourite there as a talker and a 'brilliant' person, whose interior is 'impossible' through the dreariness of his wife and children, their inferiority to himself, their gross, dense, helpless stupidity and commonplaceness? If one were to give him *one* child—a daughter—who is like him-

1. J. Henry Harper was head of the American publishing house of Harper and Brothers; Henry Mills Alden was the editor of *Harper's New Monthly Magazine.* Clarence W. McIlvaine joined Harper's in 1891 and established the London office at 45 Albemarle Street.

2. Probably William Waldorf Astor (1848–1919), first Viscount, who expressed severely anti-American sentiments on deciding to remove to England in 1891.

3. Daudet's novel of 1888; see also *LA* III, 253–57.

1. Francis D. Millet (1846–1912), American painter and illustrator and associate of Edwin A. Abbey and John Singer Sargent; his English home was at Broadway, Worcestershire, in the Cotswolds. See *Letters* III, 132.

self, bright, intelligent, sympathetic, there would perhaps be more in the little story. One can imagine his fellowship with this child, their sympathy, their fore-gatherings, confidences, mutual *entente* and the rest. Yet that makes, on the whole, another story, and complicates the simple effect that I see in the thing. This effect is that of the almost insoluble problem of his social life with such belongings: the absence of *acute* tragedy in it, yet the presence of all misery. His daughter utterly unmarriageable, his sons mere louts. One would have to consti-tute the picture in some little *action,* build the situation round some climax. The climax his having to give up everything—leave London, take them all off and bury them somewhere in the country—and himself with them. The story might be told, the episode witnessed, by a person, a friend, who has foreseen it from the first of his coming into the London horizon, has been asked advice and has hesi-tated, and been much troubled, seeing the germs of the situation. The poor man comes to take leave of him, to say 'good-bye—I chuck it up—it's impossible.' However, all that would be *à trouver.* What I seem to see is that there is a little subject in the picture, the predicament of such a man, with society catching at him hard, and such a family to carry.[1]

1. This entry concludes Houghton Journal III.

1894–1895

This notebook (Houghton Journal IV, 3 November 1894 to 15 October 1895), 7″ x 9″, has red covers with gilt trim, wine marbled endpapers, a blank flyleaf and 131 lined pages written in black ink. The first three pages, written on both sides, have been torn out of the notebook. The final entry, 15 October 1895, breaks off in the seventh sentence. The continuation (clearly marked as such by HJ) begins on page 13 of the next notebook, following the initial entries, for 8 and 22 September 1895. The two parts of the entry for 15 October 1895 are united in the following notebook.

This notebook traces HJ's facing the climax and nadir of his theatrical experiment—the rehearsal, opening, and failure of *Guy Domville*. It also records his recognition of the sterling gain at the center of the apparent loss: discovery of "the divine principle of the Scenario." We find here the two most extensive series of notes for single works in these notebooks—those for *The Spoils of Poynton* and *What Maisie Knew*.

34 De Vere Gardens, W., November 3d, 1894.

Isn't perhaps something to be made of the idea that came to me some time ago and that I have not hitherto made any note of—the little idea of the situation of some young creature (it seems to me preferably a woman, but of this I'm not sure), who, at 20, on the threshold of a life that has seemed boundless, is suddenly condemned to death (by consumption, heart-disease, or whatever) by the voice of the physician?[1] She learns that she has but a short time to live, and she

1. See 7 November 1894, 14 February, and 21 December 1895.

rebels, she is terrified, she cries out in her anguish, her tragic young despair. She is in love with life, her dreams of it have been immense, and she clings to it with passion, with supplication. 'I don't want to die—I won't, I won't, oh, let me live; oh, save me!' She is equally pathetic in her doom and in her horror of it. If she only could live just a little; just a little more—just a little longer. She is like a creature dragged shrieking to the guillotine—to the shambles. The idea of a young man who meets her, who, knowing her fate, is terribly touched by her, and who conceives the idea of saving her as far as he can—little as that may be. She has known nothing, has seen nothing, it was all beginning to come to her. Even a respite, with one hour of joy, of what other people, of what happy people, know: even this would come to her as a rescue, as a blessing. The young man, in his pity, wishes he could make her taste of happiness, give her something that it breaks her heart to go without having known. That 'something' can only be—of course—the chance to love and to be loved. He is not in love with her, he only deeply pities her: he has imagination enough to know what she feels. His impulse of kindness, of indulgence to her. She will live at the most but her little hour—so what does it matter? But the young man is entangled with another woman, committed, pledged, 'engaged' to one—and it is in that that a little story seems to reside. I see him as having somehow to risk something, to lose something, to sacrifice something in order to be kind to her, and to do it without a reward, for the poor girl, even if he loved her, has no life to give him in return: no life and no personal, no physical surrender, for it seems to me that one must represent her as too ill for *that* particular case. It has bothered me in thinking of the little picture—this idea of the physical possession, the brief physical, passional rapture which at first appeared essential to it; bothered me on account of the ugliness, the incongruity, the nastiness, *en somme,* of the man's 'having' a sick girl: also on account of something rather pitifully obvious and vulgar in the presentation of such a remedy for her despair—and such a remedy only. 'Oh, she's dying without having had it? Give it to her and let her die'—that strikes me as sufficiently second-rate. Doesn't a greater prettiness, as well as a better chance for a story, abide in her being already too ill for that, and in his being able merely to show her some delicacy of kindness, let her think that they might have loved each other *ad infinitum* if it hadn't been too late. That, however, is a detail: what some dim vision of a little dramatic situation seems to attach to is the relation that this encounter places him in to the woman to whom he is *otherwise* attached and committed and whom he has never doubted (any more than this person herself has) that he loves. It appears inevitably, or necessarily, preliminary that his encounter with the tragic girl shall be *through* the other woman: I mean that *she* shall know all about her too (they may be relatives—brought together after an absence or for the first time) and shall be a close witness of the story. If I were writing for a French public the whole thing would be simple—the elder, the 'other,' woman would simply be the mistress of the young man, and it would be a question of his taking on the dying girl for a time—having a temporary liaison with her. But one can do so little with English adultery—it is so much less inevitable, and so much more ugly in all its hiding and lying side. It is so undermined by our immemorial tradition of original freedom of choice, and by our practically universal acceptance of divorce. At any rate in this case, the anecdote, which I don't, by the way, at all yet *see,* is probably more dramatic, in truth, on some basis of marriage being in question, marriage with the other woman, or even with both! The little action hovers before me as abiding, somehow, in the particular complication that his attitude (to the girl) engenders for the man, a complication culminating in some sacrifice for him, or some great loss, or disaster. The difficulty is that the beauty of the thing is precisely in his not being in love with the girl—in the disinterestedness of his conduct. She is in love with him—that is it: she has been already so before she is condemned. He *knows* it, he learns it at the same time that he learns—as *she* has learnt—that her illness will carry her off. Say that she swims into his ken as the cousin—newly introduced—of the woman he is engaged to. Say he *is* definitely engaged to this elder girl and has been engaged some time, but that there is some serious obstacle to their marrying soon. It is what is called a long engagement. They are obliged to wait, to delay, to have patience. He has no income and she no fortune, or there is some insurmountable opposition on the part of her father. Her father, her family, have reasons for disliking the young man; the father is infirm, she has to be with him to the end, he will do nothing for them, etc., etc. Or say they have simply no means—which indeed has the drawback of not being very creditable to the hero. From the moment a young man engages himself he ought to have means: if he hasn't he oughtn't to engage himself. The little story *que j'entrevois* here suddenly seems to remind me of Ed. About's *Germaine,*[2] read long years ago and but dimly remembered. But I don't care for that. If the young couple have at any rate, and for whatever reason, to *wait* (say for her, or for *his,* father's death) I get what is essential. *Ecco.* They are waiting. The young man in these circumstances encounters the dying girl as a friend or relation of his fiancée. *She* has money—*she* is rich. She is in love with him—she is tragic and touching. He takes his betrothed, his fiancée, fully into his confidence about her and says, 'Don't be jealous if I'm kind to her—you see *why* it is.' The fiancée is generous, she also is magnanimous—she is full of pity too. She gives him rope—she says, 'Oh yes, poor thing: be kind to her.' It goes further than she quite likes; but still she holds out—she is so sure of her lover. The poor child *is*—most visibly—dying: what, therefore, does it matter? She can last but a little; and she's so in love! But they are weary of their waiting, the two fiancés—and it is their own prospects that are of prime importance to them. It becomes very clear that the dying girl would marry the young man on the spot if she could.

November 7th, 1894. I dropped the foregoing the other day—I was pressed for time and it was taking me too far. There are difficulties in it—and what I meant was really only to throw out a feeler. I had asked myself if there was anything in the idea of the man's *agreeing with his fiancée that he shall marry the poor girl in order to come into her money and in the certitude that she will die and leave the money to him*—on which basis (his becoming a widower with property) they themselves will at last be able to marry. Then the sequel to that?—I can scarcely

2. Edmond About (1828–85), French novelist and academician; *Germaine* appeared in 1858.

imagine any—I doubt if I can—that isn't ugly and vulgar: I mean vulgarly ugly. This would be the case with the girl's not, after all, dying—and that's not what I want, or mean. Moreover if she's as much in love with the young man as I conceive her, she would leave him the money without any question of marriage. I seem to get hold of the tail of a pretty idea in making that happiness, that life, that snatched experience the girl longs for, BE, *in fact,* some rapturous act of that sort—some act of generosity, of passionate beneficence, of pure sacrifice, to the man she loves. This would obviate all 'marriage' between *them,* and everything so vulgar as an 'engagement,' and, removing the poor creature's yearning from the class of egotistic pleasures, the dream of being possessed and possessing, etc., make it something fine and strange. I think I see something good in *that* solution—it seems dimly to come to me. I think I see the thing beginning with the 2 girls—*who must not love each other.* This idea would require that the dying girl, whom family or personal circumstances have brought into relation with the other, should not be fond of her, should have some reason to dislike her, to do *her* at least no benefit or service. One may see the story begin with them—the two together; brought a little nearer by the younger girl's illness and trouble—so that the *other* is the FIRST witness of her despair and had the FIRST knowledge of her doom. The poor girl breaks out to her, raves, can't help it. The elder girl is privately, secretly engaged to the young man, and the other hasn't seen him when the doom aforesaid is pronounced. She sees him and she loves him—he becomes witness of her state and, as I have noted, immensely pities her. It is with a vision of what she could do for *him* that she renewedly pleads for life. *Then* she learns, discovers—or rather she doesn't discover at first—that the 2 others—her relative and the young man—are engaged. I seem to see what passes between the young man and his fiancée on the subject. The fiancée has a plan—she suddenly has a vision of what may happen. She forbids her lover to tell the girl they are engaged. Her plan is that he shall give himself to her for the time, be 'nice' to her, respond, express, devote himself to her, let her love him and behave as if he loved her. She foresees that, under these circumstances, the girl will become capable of some act of immense generosity—of generosity by which her own life, her own prospect of marriage will profit—and without her really losing anything in the meanwhile. She therefore *checks* her lover's impulse, and he rather mystifiedly and bewilderedly assents. He 'reads her game' at last—she doesn't formally communicate it to him. She knows the girl dislikes her—say she has jilted the girl's brother, who has afterwards died. At any rate there is a *reason* for the dislike—and she, the elder woman, knows it. So much as this the latter tells her lover—for she has, after all, to *give* him a reason—explain to *him,* too, the dislike. In fact, in giving it, she virtually communicates her idea. 'Play a certain game—and you'll have money from her. But if she knows the money is to help you to marry me, you *won't* have it; never in the world!' My idea is that the poor (that is the rich) girl *shall,* at last, know this—learn this. How does she learn it? From the inexorable father? From the jilted brother (if he be *not* dead)? From the man (some other man, that is) whom the inexorable father *does* want her (i.e., want the elder girl) to marry; and who, disgusted with her, turns, in a spirit both vindictive and mercenary, to the rich little invalid? I seem to see, a little, THAT. I seem to see a

penniless peer, whom my elder girl refuses. Her father will help her if she doe
that—if she makes the snobbish alliance. Her merit, her virtue is that she won
make it, and it is by this sacrifice that she holds her lover—*en le faisant valoir*—
and makes him enter, as it were, into her scheme. Lord X. is a poor creature an
has *nothing* but his title. The girl's sacrifice is a sacrifice of that—but of nothin
else. If Lord X. goes, then, rebuffed, mercenarily and vindictively to the dyin
girl and tells her the other woman's 'game' (that is, her presumed, divined, er
gagement, from which she little by little, piece by piece, or in a vivid flash c
divination, *constructs* the engagement), I seem to get almost a little 3-act play—
with the main part for a young actress. I get, at any rate, a distinct and rathe
dramatic *action,* don't I?—*Voyons un peu.* The poor dying girl has an immens
shock from her new knowledge—but her passion, after a little, is splendidly proc
against it. She rallies to it—to her passion, her yearning just to taste, briefly, c
life *that* way—and becomes capable of still clinging to her generosity. She clings
she clings. But the young man learns from her that she *knows*—knows of hi
existing tie. This enables him to measure her devotion, her beauty of soul—and
produces a tremendous effect upon him. He becomes ashamed of his tacit asser
to his fiancée's idea—conceives a horror of it. In that horror he draws close to th
dying girl. He tells his prospective bride that she knows—and yet how she seem
determined to behave. 'So much the better!' says the prospective bride. My stor
pure and simple, very crudely and briefly, appears to be that the girl dies, leavin
money—a good deal of money—to the man she has so hopelessly and generousl
loved, and whom it has become her idea of causing to contribute to her on
supreme experience *by* thus helping, thus, at any cost, testifying to a pure devo
tion to. Then the young man is left with the money face to face with his fiancée
It is what now happens between them that constitutes the climax, the denouemen
of the story. She is eager, ready to marry now, but he has really fallen in lov
with the dead girl. Something in the other woman's whole attitude in the matter—
in the 'game' he consented in a manner to become the instrument of: somethin
in all this revolts him and puts him off. In the light of how exquisite the dead gir
was he sees how little exquisite is the living. He's in distress about what to do—
he hangs fire—he asks himself to what extent he can do himself violence. Thi
change, this regret and revulsion, this deep commotion, his betrothed perceives
and she presently charges him with his infidelity, with failing her now, whei
they've reached, as it were, their goal. Does he want to keep the money fo
himself? There is a very painful, almost violent scene between them. (How i
all—or am I detached?—seems to map itself out as a little 3-act play!) They *break*
in a word—he says, 'Be it so!'—as the woman gives him, in her resentment and
jealousy (of the other's memory, now) an *opening* to break—by offering to le
him off. But he offers her the money and she *takes* it. Then vindictively, in spite
with the money and with her father's restored countenance, she marries Lord X.
while he lives poor and single and faithful—faithful to the image of the dead. O
course in the case of a play that one might entertain any hope of having acted
this denouement would have to be altered. The action would be the same up [to
the point of the girl's apparently impending death—and the donation of money
would be before the EVENT. The rupture between the two fiancés would take plac

also before—he would buy her off with the money, the same way—and the hero would go back to the poor girl as her very own. Under this delight she would revive and cleave to him, and the curtain would fall on their embrace, as it were, and the *possibility* of their marriage and of her living. Lord X. and the betrothed's flunkeyizing father would be characters, and there would have to be a confidant of the hero's *evolution*, his emotions. I seem to see a vivid figure, and perhaps, for the hero, THAT figure—i.e., the 'confidant'—in the dying girl's *homme d'affaires*. I seem to see her perhaps as an American and this personage, the *homme d'affaires*, as a good American comedy-type. His wife would be the elderly woman. I seem to see Nice or Mentone—or Cairo—or Corfu—designated as the scene of the action, at least in the 1st act, and the gatherability of the people on some common ground, the salon of an hotel or the garden of the same. x x x x x

[*The Wings of the Dove*, published (without serialization) in New York and London (1902).]

November 8th, 1894. The other day, when at McIlvaine's dinner, as I have noted *ante* (in another old finished book),[1] Henry Harper told me how he and Alden wanted me to do a little international story on American snobbishness abroad. Three weeks later, meeting H.H. at lunch at the R[eform] C[lub] he returned to the question, urgently, again. I seemed to feel it in me to respond a little—to see it as an idea with which something might be done. But *voyons un peu* what it might possibly amount to. The thing is not worth doing at all unless something tolerably big and strong is got out of it. But the only way that's at all luminous to look at it is to see what there may be in it of most eloquent, most illustrative and most human—most characteristic and essential: what is its real, innermost, dramatic, tragic, comic, pathetic, ironic *note*. The primary interest is not in any mere grotesque picture of follies and misadventures, of successes and sufferings: it's in the experience of some creature that sees it and knows and judges and feels it all, that has a part to play in the episode, that is tried and tested and harrowed and exhibited by it and that forms the glass, as it were, through which we look at the diorama. On the very threshold one sees the difficulty that the subject is too big—too big for treatment on the *Daisy Miller* scale: which is what the *Harper* people have in their mind. And, alas, there is no inspiration or incentive whatever in writing for *Harper* save the sole pecuniary one. They want, ever, the smaller, the slighter, the safer, the inferior thing; and the company one keeps in their magazine is of a most paralysing dreariness.

November 18th, 1894 (34 De Vere Gdns. W.).

Isn't there perhaps the subject of a little—a very little—tale *(de moeurs littéraires)* in the idea of a man of letters, a poet, a novelist, finding out, after years, or a considerable period, of very happy, unsuspecting, and more or less affectionate, intercourse with a 'lady-writer,' a newspaper woman, as it were, that he has been systematically *débiné*, 'slated' by her in certain critical journals to which she

1. See 24 October 1894.

contributes? He has known her long and liked her, known of her hack-work, etc., and liked it less; and has also known that the *éreintements* in question have periodically appeared—but he has never connected them with her or her with them, and when he makes the discovery it is an agitating, a very painful, revelation to him. Or the reviewer may be a man and the author anonymously and viciously— or, at least, abusively—reviewed may be a woman. The point of the thing is whether there be not a little supposable theme or drama in the relation, the situation of the two people after the thing comes to light—the pretension on the part of the reviewer of having one attitude to the writer *as* a writer, and a totally distinct one as a member of society, a friend, a human being. They *may* be—the reviewer may be—unconsciously, disappointedly, *rég[u]lièrement,* in love with the victim. It is only a little situation; but perhaps there is something in it.[1]

x   x   x   x   x

It occurs to me that there may also be a situation, a small drama, in the conception of the way certain persons, closely connected, are affected by an event occurring, an act performed, which reflects strongly and grievously on the unspotted honour of their house, their family—an event embodied presumably in an individual, a dishonoured, dishonouring, misguided, sinning, erring individual—a strong difference as to the treatment of whom breaks out between them and constitutes the action. It must be, somehow, the contrasted opposition of the 2 forms of pride— the pride that can harden and stiffen its heart, its stare, its apparent, studied, unflinching unconsciousness of what has happened, and face out and live down the shame, disown, repudiate, inexorably *sacrifice* the guilty party—and the pride that suffers, and suffers *otherwise,* shrinks, hides, averts itself from the world and yet, while suffering, feels a solidarity with, can't too inhumanly dissociate itself from, the criminal. These things—I mean this situation—would depend wholly on what one should imagine in a way of a relation between the 2 representations, as it were—and on what one should imagine in the way both of a compromising act on the part of the 3d party and of a 'sacrifice' of him or her. The unchaste woman is too stale and threadbare, I think.[2]

Names. Hanmer—Meldrum—Synge—Grundle—Adwick—Blanchett—Sansom— Saunt—Highmore—Hannington (or place)—Medley (house)—Myrtle—Saxon —Yule—Chalkley—Grantham—Farange—Grose—Corfe—Lebus—Glasspoole (or place)—Bedfont, Redfont (places?)—Vereker—Gainer—Gayner—Shum—Oswald—Gonville—Mona (girl)—Mark—Floyer—Minton—Panton—Summervale —Chidley—Shirley—Dreever—Trendle—Stannace—Housefield—Longworth —Langsom—Nettlefold—Nettlefield—Beaumorris—Delacoombe—Treston— Mornington—Warmington—Harmer—Oldfield—Horsefield—Eastmead.

1. HJ gave a title to this idea, "The Publisher's Story" (21 December 1895), and returned to it; see 7 May 1898 and 15 February 1899.
2. See 4 March 1895.

Saturday, January 12th, 1895. Note here the ghost-story told me at Addington (evening of Thursday 10th), by the Archbishop of Canterbury:[1] the mere vague, undetailed, faint sketch of it—being all he had been told (very badly and imperfectly), by a lady who had no art of relation, and no clearness: the story of the young children (indefinite number and age) left to the care of servants in an old country-house, through the death, presumably, of parents. The servants, wicked and depraved, corrupt and deprave the children; the children are bad, full of evil, to a sinister degree. The servants *die* (the story vague about the way of it) and their apparitions, figures, return to haunt the house *and* children, to whom they seem to beckon, whom they invite and solicit, from across dangerous places, the deep ditch of a sunk fence, etc.—so that the children may destroy themselves, lose themselves by responding, by getting into their power. So long as the children are kept from them, they are not lost: but they try and try and try, these evil presences, to get hold of them. It is a question of the children 'coming over to where they are.' It is all obscure and imperfect, the picture, the story, but there is a suggestion of strangely gruesome effect in it. The story to be told—tolerably obviously—by an outside spectator, observer.

[*"The Turn of the Screw," Collier's Weekly*, with illustrations by John LaFarge and Eric Pape, January–April 1898; reprinted in *The Two Magics*, London and New York (1898).]

34 De Vere Gardens, W., January 23d, 1895.

I take up my own old pen again—the pen of all my old unforgettable efforts and sacred struggles.[1] To myself—today—I need say no more. Large and full and high the future still opens. It is now indeed that I may do the work of my life. And I will. x x x x x I have only to *face* my problems. x x x x x But all that is of the ineffable—too deep and pure for any utterance. Shrouded in sacred silence let it rest. x x x x x

January 26th, 1895. The idea of the poor man, the artist, the man of letters, who all his life is trying—if only to get a living—to do something *vulgar*, to take the measure of the huge, flat foot of the public: isn't there a little story in it, possibly, if one can animate it with an action; a little story that might perhaps be a mate to *The Death of the Lion?* It is suggested to me really by all the little backward memories of one's own frustrated ambition—in particular by its having just come back to me how, already 20 years ago, when I was in Paris writing letters to the *N. Y. Tribune*, Whitelaw Reid wrote to me to ask me virtually *that*—to make 'em baser and paltrier, to make them as vulgar as he could, to make them, as he called it, more 'personal.'[1] Twenty years ago, and so it has been ever, till the other

1. Edward White Benson (1829–96), Archbishop of Canterbury from 1882. Addington is the archiepiscopal residence.

1. HJ's five-year foray into the theater had ended with the opening-night fiasco of *Guy Domville* on 5 January. See 4 August 1892 and 26 January 1895.

1. Reid (1837–1912) was publisher of the *New York Tribune*. HJ's response of 30 August 1876 is in *Letters* II, 63–64. For HJ's letters to the *Tribune* see *Parisian Sketches* (ed. Edel and Lind, 1957).

night, Jan. 5th, the *première* of *Guy Domville*. Trace the history of a charming little talent, charming artistic nature, that has been exactly the martyr and victim of that ineffectual effort, that long, vain study to take the measure above-mentioned, to 'meet' the vulgar need, to violate his intrinsic conditions, to make, as it were, a sow's ear out of a silk purse.[2] He tries and he tries and he does what he thinks his coarsest and crudest. It's all of no use—it's always 'too subtle,' always too fine—never, never, vulgar enough. I had to write to Whitelaw Reid that the sort of thing I had already tried hard to do for the *Tribune* was the very worst I *could* do. I lost my place—my letters weren't wanted. A little drama, climax, a denouement, a small tragedy of the *vie littéraire*—mightn't one oppose to him some contrasted figure of another type—the creature who, dimly conscious of deep-seated vulgarity, is always trying to be refined, which doesn't in the least prevent him—or her—from succeeding. Say it's a woman. *She* succeeds—and she *thinks* she's fine! Mightn't *she* be the narrator, with a fine grotesque *inconscience?* So that the whole thing becomes a masterpiece of close and finished irony? There *may* be a difficulty in that—I seem to see it: so that the necessity may be for the narrator to be *conscient,* or SEMI-CONSCIENT, perhaps, to get the full force of certain efforts. The narrator at any rate, a person in the little drama who is trying bewilderedly the opposite line—working helplessly for fineness.

x   x   x   x   x

February 5th, 1895. Last evening, as, by a tremendous clear cold, I rolled along in a rattling four-wheeler (to go to dinner with the Lovelaces, who, by agreement—the only other guest being Miss De Morgan, a person much initiated—showed me some of their extremely interesting Byron papers; especially some of those bearing on the absolutely indubitable history of his relation to Mrs. Leigh, the sole *real* love, as he emphatically declares, of his life)—as I rolled along there came to me, I know not why, the idea of the possible little drama residing in the existence of a peculiar intense and interesting affection between a brother and a sister. It was an odd coincidence that this should have suggested itself when I was in the very act of driving to a place where I was to see the Byron-Leigh letters—some of them.[1] But this (as regards the particular documents) I knew nothing

---

2. HJ uses this phrase to describe his *Guy Domville* failure; see *Letters* III, 509. The phrase appears again in the story developed from this sketch, "The Next Time"; see 4 June 1895.

1. Ralph Gordon Noel King (1839–1906), second Earl of Lovelace and grandson of the poet Lord Byron, was much concerned with history's view of his grandfather's love affair with his half-sister Augusta Leigh and eager to refute certain versions of that affair—e.g., that expressed in Edgecumbe's *Byron: The Last Phase.* At the request of Lady Lovelace in November 1909 HJ and John Buchan (whose wife was Lady Lovelace's niece) agreed to read the letters Byron had written to Lady Melbourne during the three years preceding his marriage and to write an opinion of the contents to be deposited in the British Museum. The small dinner-party recorded here was evidently a precursor to the full reading. HJ thus found himself involved in the continuation of a brouhaha that had enlisted the participation of Harriet Beecher Stowe a quarter of a century earlier. Mrs. Stowe had known Lady Byron in England and had got her version of the story; she took the unpopular position of defendant of Lady Byron—in an article for the *Atlantic* in 1869 and then in her book *Lady Byron Vindicated*— and was consequently reviled by the press. (See Edmund Wilson, *Patriotic Gore* [1962], pp. 50–52.)

about in advance—didn't know I was to see *those*, at all. Also, the little relation that occurred to me presented itself to me with none of the nefarious—abnormal—character of the connection just mentioned. There may be nothing in it—probably is: but what I vaguely thought of (scarcely distinctly enough indeed for the purposes of this note) was the incident of such a union (of blood and sympathy and tenderness) that, on the part of each, it can only operate for intelligence and perception of the other's conditions and feelings and impulses—not in the least for control or direction of them—as is the case with *most* affectionate wisdoms, guiding devotions, which enter into the nature of the loved object *for its good* and to protect it sometimes against itself, its native dangers, etc. I fancy the pair understanding each other too well—fatally well. Neither can protect the character of the other against itself—for the other in each case is, also, equally the very self against whom the protection is called for—can only abound in the same sense, see with the same sensibilities and the same imagination, vibrate with the same nerves, suffer with the same suffering: have, in a word, exactly, identically the same experience of life. Two lives, two beings, and *one* experience: that is, I think, what I mean; with the question of what situations, what drama, what little story, might possibly come of it. The manner in which the thing (the climax) hovered before me was the incident of their dying together as the only thing they *can* do that does not a little fall short of absolutely ideally perfect agreement. I imagined such a feeling about life as that when one, under the influence of it, 'chucks up' the game, the other, from a complete understanding of the sensibilities engaged, the effect produced, must do exactly the same—in a kind of resigned, inevitable, disenchanted, double suicide. It's a reflection, a reduplication of melancholy, of irony. They may be twins, but I don't think it's necessary. They needn't even be brother and sister: they may be 2 brothers or even 2 sisters. Brother and sister, however, probably most recommend themselves—and not as twins. I remember now—it comes back to me—what little image led to the fancy: the idea of some unspeakable intensity of feeling, of tenderness, of sacred compunction, as it were, in relation to the *past*, the parents, the beloved mother, the beloved father—of those who have suffered before them and *for* them and whose blood is in their veins—whose image haunts them with an almost paralysing pathos, an ineffability of pain, a sense of the irreparable, of a tragic reality, or at least a reality of sadness, greater than the reality of the actual. What it is probable that the little *donnée* would rightly present is the image of a deep, participating devotion of one to the other (of a brother to a sister presumably), rather than that of an absolutely equal, a mathematically divided affection. The brother suffers, has the experience and the effect of the experience, is carried along by fate, etc.; and the sister understands, perceives, shares, with every pulse of her being. He has to tell her nothing—she *knows:* it's identity of sensation, of vibration. It's,

---

Buchan recalled his reading the materials with HJ: "The thing nearly made me sick, but my colleague never turned a hair. His only words for some special vileness was 'singular'—'most curious'—'Nauseating, perhaps, but how quite inexpressibly significant' " (*Memory Hold-the-Door*, 1940). Their opinion was that the letters "afford most weighty corroborative evidence" in support of the account Lord Lovelace offered in his *Astarte*. It is signed "Henry James, 7 April 1910 / John Buchan 4 April 1910" (see Janet Adam Smith, *John Buchan: A Biography* [1965], Appendix A). See 12 January 1887.

for *her*, the Pain of Sympathy: *that* would be the subject, the formula. The denouement would be: to what that conducts you—conducts the victim. It conducts to a sharing of the fate of the other, whatever this fate may be. The story is the fate.

February 5th, 1895. What is there in the idea of *Too late*—of some friendship or passion or bond—some affection long desired and waited for, that is formed too late?—I mean too late in life altogether. Isn't there something in the idea that 2 persons may meet (as if they had looked for each other for years) only in time to feel how much it might have meant for them if they had only met earlier? This is vague, nebulous—the mere hint of a hint. They but meet to part or to suffer— they meet when one is dying—'or something of that sort.' They may have been dimly conscious, in the past, of the possibility between them—been groping for each other in the darkness. It's love, it's friendship, it's mutual comprehension— it's whatever one will. They've heard of each other, perhaps—felt each other, been conscious, each, of some tug at the cord—some vibration of the other's heartstrings. It's a passion that *might* have been. I seem to be coinciding simply with the idea of the married person encountering the *real* mate, etc.; but that is not what I mean. Married or not—the marriage is a detail. Or rather, I fancy, there would have been no marriage conceivable for either. Haven't they waited— waited too long—till something else has happened? The only *other* 'something else' than marriage must have been, doubtless, the wasting of life. And the wasting of life is the implication of death. There may be the germ of a situation in this; but it obviously requires digging out.[2] x x x x x

["The Way It Came," the *Chap Book* and *Chapman's Magazine of Fiction* May 1896; reprinted in *Embarrassments*, London and New York (1896) as "The Friends of the Friends."]

There comes back to me, *à propos* of it, and as vaguely and crookedly hooking itself on to it, somehow, that *concetto* that I have jotted down in another notebook[3]— that of the little tragedy of the man who has renounced his ambition, the dream of his youth, his genius, talent, vocation—with all the honour and glory it might have brought him: sold it, bartered it, exchanged it for something very different and inferior, but mercenary and worldly. I've only to write these few words, however, to see that the 2 ideas have nothing to do with each other. They are different stories. What I fancied in this last mentioned was that this Dead Self of the poor man's lives for him still in some indirect way, in the sympathy, the fidelity (the relation of some kind) of another. I tried to give a hint in my former note, of what this vicarious self, as it were, might amount to. It will require returning to; and what I wanted not to let slip altogether was simply some reminder of the beauty, the little tragedy, attached perhaps to the situation of the man of genius who, in some accursed hour of his youth, has bartered away the fondest vision of that youth and lives ever afterwards in the shadow of the bitterness of the regret. My other little note contained the fancy of his *recovering* a

2. See 21 December 1895 and 10 January 1896. This also anticipates "The Beast in the Jungle"; see 27 August 1901.
3. See 9 January 1894.

little of the lost joy, of the Dead Self, in his intercourse with some person, some woman, who knows what that self was, in whom it still lives a little. This intercourse is his real life. But I think I said that there was a banality in that; that, practically, the little situation will have often enough been treated; and that therefore the thing could, probably, only take a form as the story, not of the man, but of the woman herself. It's *the woman's sense of what might [have been] in him* that arrives at the intensity. (The link of connection between the foregoing and this was simply my little feeling that they each dealt with might-have-beens.) *She is his Dead Self: he is alive in her and dead in himself*—that is something like the little formula I seemed to *entrevoir*. He himself, the man, must, *in* the tale, also materially die—die in the flesh as he had died long ago in the spirit, the *right* one. Then it is that his lost treasure revives most—no longer *contrarié* by his material existence, existence in his false self, his wrong one.—But I fear there isn't much in it: it would take a deuce of a deal of following up.[4]

February 6th, 1895. I went yesterday, by appointment, to see Ellen Terry; and I won't pretend here, now, to go into the question of the long, tragic chapter with which my consideration (so troubled, so blighted for the time at least) of the proposal contained in the note of hers which led to our interview, was—and still is—associated. I make this allusion, this morning, simply because it has reference to my talk with her, and to what may come of it, to ask myself *de cette triste plume tâtonnante,* whether, for such a little one-act or two-act play as Ellen Terry wants, there is possibly anything in the idea of *Mme Sans-Gêne,* as it were, turned the other way, reversed, transposed: I mean not a woman of the people, who in consequence of a stroke of fortune has to play the *grande dame,* but a *grande dame* who in consequence of a stroke of fortune has to play a woman of the people. It is by no means impossible that this image may not be void: everything would depend on the story that embodies it, on what the stroke of fortune is, may be conceived as being. This to be admirably figured out.[1]

x x x x x

Another little possibility dances before me—I only just catch the tip of its tail— in the fancy of something faintly suggested by Miss Terry's happening to have said, rather in the air, that she would have a fancy to do an American woman! A couple of years ago, in a note previous to this, in an hour of deep delusion (like perhaps even *this* hour), I jotted down something very vague (with an eye to some part for Ada Rehan), on the subject of an American woman as the beneficent intervening agent in the drama of an English social, an English family, crisis— some supreme dramatic, probably tragic, but possibly some comic, juncture in the affairs of an old English race—her stepping in as the real conservative, more royalist than the king, etc.; stepping in with some charming, clever enthusiasm

4. This "other little note" seems to be the germ of "The Jolly Corner," the *English Review* December 1908, reprinted in the New York edition: see the more definite note 16 May 1899.

1. Reference is to the play *Summersoft;* see 24 November 1892. *Madame Sans-Gêne* (1893) is a play by Sardou.

and infatuation of her own which repairs and redeems—which rescues and re-
stores. The mere tail of the image which I catch hold of for the moment is the
confused vision of the American woman (a rich widow) coming down, *en tour-
iste,* to see an old house she has heard of, seen a photograph or picture of, dreamed
about, and alighting *so* upon the dramatic crisis as to which she becomes a saviour
and redeemer. This will probably permit (God forgive me if it doesn't!) of some
following up; particularly because I seem to see in it the adumbration of a short
tale *aussi bien* as of a play. However, what I see in it as yet is just merely that
figure and its background, with everything else confused and crude; I mean the
bright, kind, comic, clever, charming creature—in the agitated, convulsed, threatened somehow troubled and exposed *show* house. I seem to see the 'show' element—the trooping visitors, the other tourists—salient and usable as an effect of
comedy. Even as I write, just God, something seems to come to me!—seems to
come as a sort of faint ramification of there swimming before me a certain phan-
tasmagory of the charming woman *showing the house herself,* showing it better
than any of *them* can. *Elle s'improvise,* somehow, *cicerone.* I have a confused
dream of a rupture, a breakdown or crisis, on the part of the people of the house,
with regard to this question of farming it out to an *entrepreneur* (as I believe
Knole is farmed), to their want of returns, of proceeds, their immediate need of
the money, their making some better arrangement, necessitated by extreme pressure. *She* takes it over—and the younger son with it. Or—an alternative swims
before me: the presence of some vulgar English people, very new and very dreadful, who, coming down to look at it, think of buying it, want to buy it, propose
for it. She saves it from *them.* I fancy I see a wild ostensible radical of an eldest
son, of an owner, and a sympathetic and sensible younger brother, the 'hero,'
whom she hits it off with. But all this is troubled and confused—very mixed and
crudely extemporized: I must come back to it. All I mean, for the moment, is that
the little picture, the localised and animated *act,* shines out at me. x x x x x

34 D. V. G., W., February 14th, 1895.

I have my head, thank God, full of visions. One has never too many—one
has never enough. Ah, just to let one's self go—at last: to surrender one's self to
what through all the long years one has (quite heroically, I think) hoped for and
waited for—the mere potential, and relative, increase of *quantity* in the material
act—act of application and production. One has prayed and hoped and waited, in
a word, to be able to work *more.* And now, toward the end, it seems, within its
limits, to have come. That is all I ask. Nothing else in the world. I bow down to
Fate, equally in submission and in gratitude. This time it's gratitude; but the form
of the gratitude, to be real and adequate, must be large and confident action—
splendid and supreme creation. *Basta.* x x x x x

I have been reading over the long note—the 1st in this book—I made some time
since on the subject of the dying girl who wants to live—to live and love, etc.;
and am greatly struck with all it contains.[1] It is there, the story; strongly, richly

1. The subject of *The Wings of the Dove;* see 3 November 1894.

there; a thing, surely, of great potential interest and beauty and of a strong, firm artistic *ossature*. It is *full*—the scheme; and one has only to stir it up *à pleines mains*. I allude to my final sketch of it—the idea of the rupture at last between the 2 fiancés: his giving her the money and her taking it and marrying Lord X. Meanwhile I am haunted by the idea of doing something for Henry Harper, as he put it before me in the autumn: something that I may do *now,* soon, in 3 months, and get the money for. In other words, as I sit here, it goes against my grain to relinquish without a struggle the idea of the short 'International' novel the Harpers want—little as H.H.'s suggestion of the particular thing at first appealed to me. Something probably lurks in it—something that I have only to woo forth. Let me live with it a while—let me woo it; even if I have to sit with it here in mere divine *tâtonnement* every patient morning for a week or two. If I don't find it I shall at least find something else, *much* else perhaps, even, by the way. Dimly the little drama looms and looms; and clearly it will come to me at last. Meanwhile in my path stands—appears at least to stand—brightly soliciting, the idea I jotted down a year ago, or more,[2] and that has lain there untouched ever since: the idea of the father and daughter (in Paris, supposably), who marry—the father for consolation—at the same time, and yet are left more together than ever, through their respective *époux* taking such a fancy to each other. This has many of the very elements required: it is intensely international, it is brief, dramatic, ironic, etc.; and this mere touching of it already makes my fingers itch for it. I seem to see in it something compact, *charpenté*, living, touching, amusing. *Everything* about it qualifies it for *Harper* except the subject—or rather, I mean, except the adulterine element in the subject. But may it not be simply a question of *handling* that? For God's sake let me try: I want to plunge into it: I *languish* so to get at an immediate creation. This thing has for my bang-off purpose the immense merit of having no prescribed or imposed length. I seem to see it as a nominal 60,000 words: which *may* become 75,000. *Voyons, voyons:* may I not instantly sit down to a little close, clear, full scenario of it? As I ask myself the question, *with* the very asking of it, and the utterance of that word so charged with memories and pains, something seems to open out before me, and at the same time to press upon me with an extraordinary tenderness of embrace. Compensations and solutions seem to stand there with open arms for me—and something of the 'meaning' to come to me of past bitterness, of recent bitterness that otherwise has seemed a mere sickening, unflavoured draught. Has a *part* of all this wasted passion and squandered time (of the last 5 years) been simply the precious lesson, taught me in that roundabout and devious, that cruelly expensive, way, *of the singular value for a narrative plan too* of the (I don't know *what* adequately to call it) divine principle of the Scenario? If that *has* been one side of the moral of the whole unspeakable, the whole tragic experience, I almost bless the pangs and the pains and the miseries of it. IF there has lurked in the central core of it this exquisite truth—I almost hold my breath with suspense as I try to formulate it; so much, so *much,* hangs radiantly there as depending on it—this exquisite truth that what I call the divine principle in question is a key that, working in the same *general* way fits the complicated chambers of *both* the dramatic and the narrative lock: IF, I say, I have

2. The idea for *The Golden Bowl;* see 28 November 1892.

crept round through long apparent barrenness, through suffering and sadness intolerable, to that rare perception—why my infinite little loss is converted into an almost infinite little gain. The long figuring out, the patient, passionate little *cahier*, becomes the *mot de l'énigme*, the thing to live by. Let me commemorate here, in this manner, such a portentous little discovery, the discovery, probably, of a truth of real value even if I exaggerate, as I daresay I do, its *partée*, its magicality. Now something of those qualities in it vivifies, backwardly—or appears to a little—all the horrors that one has been through, all the thankless faith, the unblessed work. But how much of the precious there may be in it I can only tell by trying. x x x x x

34 De Vere Gardens, February 27th, 1895.

For a very short thing the idea of a Girl—the idea suggested to me, in a word, by learning *par où E.B. a consenti à passer* in the matter of her engagement to C.R.[1] His family would give her, first, no sign whatever—his mother wouldn't write to her: they being Florentines *de vieille souche,* proud, 'stuck up,' etc. They demanded that she should write first—make the overture. She brought a fortune; she brings, in short, almost everything. But she consented—she wrote first. One can imagine a case in which the Girl—an American Girl—wouldn't: would have taken her stand on her own custom—her own people—that of the bride's being *welcomed,* always, by the mother, in the family into which she is to enter. One can imagine a situation arising out of this. The young man, distressed by her refusal, yet having his own family attitude, his mother's stiffness, etc., to count with, tries to make the latter make a concession—write 1st. She may not like the marriage or the girl, though having had reasons not definitely to oppose it; or she may be, merely, stiffly and *bêtement,* inexorably proud. She waits for the girl to write—says that if she does she will then herself do everything proper. But write first herself—never! This is exactly what the girl says: it's an *idée fixe* with her, she can't—she won't—she oughtn't. She takes exactly the same stand as the mother. What comes of the young man, of the engagement, of the marriage, between them? The girl asks him if he wants her to humiliate herself. He says no, and consents to *passer outre.* But she then says she won't come into the family without the letter from the mother. That is perhaps too hard an attitude to attribute to her. Imagine him devoted to his mother, *à l'italienne*—and yet consenting to the girl's not writing. There are the germs of trouble in that. Say the mother writes at last, but writes too late. The state of tension has warped the situation. The relation between the 2 lovers is injured, spoiled: and not less so—not less fatally damaged—the relation of the son to his mother.

[''Miss Gunton of Poughkeepsie,'' *Cornhill Magazine* May 1900 and *Truth* May–June 1900; reprinted in *The Soft Side.*]

X   X   X   X   X

1. E. B. was Edith Bronson, only child of Katherine De Kay Bronson, who become the Countess Rucellai; C. R. was Count Cosimo Rucellai of Florence.

I was greatly struck, the other day, with something that Lady Playfair told me of the prolongation—and the effects of it—of her aunt, old Mrs. Palfrey, of Cambridge, Mass. She is, or was, 95, or some such extraordinary age; and the little idea that struck me as a small *motif* in it was that of the consequences of this fact of the existence of her 2 or 3 poor old maid daughters, who have themselves grown old (old enough to die), while sitting there waiting, waiting endlessly for her to depart. She has never departed, and yet has always been supposed to be going to, and they have had endlessly to be ready, to be near her, at hand—never to be away. So Sarah P., whom I vaguely remember, has come to be 70. They have never been anywhere, never done anything—their lives have passed in this long, blank patience. Some small thing might perhaps be done with the situation, with the picture. One of the daughters—the eldest—might die—of old age; and the thing, all the while, have to be kept from the old woman. She wonders what has become of her, tries to find out; and then, at last, one of the others tells her— tells her So-and-So has died. The old woman stares. 'What did she die of?' She died of old age. This makes the old woman realize—it finishes her. Or 2, the 2 elder, must die (of old age!) and *one* be left simply to watch—to conceal it. Only I think that 2 sisters is the right number originally—there had better not be more.[2]

[''Europe,'' *Scribner's Magazine* June 1899; reprinted in *The Soft Side*.]

x   x   x   x   x

Reading, at the Athenaeum the other night, a little volume of *Notes sur Londres* by one 'Brada,' with a very, and on the whole justly, laudatory preface by that intelligent, but just at the end always slightly vulgar *(ça ne manque jamais)* Augustine Filon,[3] skimming through this, I say, I was greatly struck with all that may be of dramatic, of fertile in subject, for the novel, for the picture of contemporary manners, in 2 features of current English life on which he much insists. One of them is perhaps fuller than the other; but what strikes me in both of them is that they would have as themes, as *données* dealt with, with the real right art, a very large measure of a sort of ringing and reverberating actuality. What I speak of, of course, is manners in this country. What 'Brada' speaks of in particular, as the 2 most striking social notes to him, are *Primo,* The masculinization of the women; and *Secondo,* The demoralization of the aristocracy—the cessation, on their part, to take themselves seriously; their traffic in vulgar things, vulgar gains, vulgar pleasures—their general vulgarization. x x x x x I must go on with that: I must copy the passage out of 'Brada.'

March 4th, 1895. The idea of the little London girl who grows up to 'sit with' the free-talking modern young mother—reaches 17, 18, etc.—comes out—and,

2. Second note for "Europe"; see 27 July 1890 and 7 May 1898. Mrs. Palfrey was the widow of the historian John Gorham Palfrey; her niece, the American-born Edith Russell, became Lady Playfair on her marriage in 1878 to the first Baron Playfair, British scientist and reformer.
3. "Brada" was the pen name of Henrietta Consuelo (Sansom), Contessa di Pulaga. See 4 March 1895. Pierre Marie Augustin Filon (1841–1916), French man of letters and tutor to the Prince Impérial in England, was author of a history of English literature.

not marrying, has to 'be there'—and, though the conversation is supposed to be expurgated for her, inevitably hears, overhears, guesses, follows, takes in, becomes acquainted with, horrors. A real little subject in this, I think—a real little situation for a short tale—if circumstance and setting is really given it. A young man who likes her—wants to take her out of it—feeling how she's exposed, etc. Attitude of the mother, the father, etc. The young man hesitates, because he thinks she already knows too much; but all the while he hesitates she knows, she learns, more and more. He finds out somehow how much she *does* know, and, terrified at it, drops her: all her ignorance, to his sense, is gone. His attitude to her mother— whom he has liked, visited, talked freely with, taken pleasure in. But when it comes to taking *her* daughter—! She has appealed to him to do it—begged him to take her away. 'Oh, if some one would only marry her. I know—I have a bad conscience about her.' She may be an ugly one—who has also a passion for the world—for life—likes to be there—to hear, to know. There may be the contrasted clever, *avisée* foreign or foreignized friend or sister, who has married her daughter, very virtuously and very badly, unhappily, just to get her out of the atmosphere for her own talk and entourage—and takes *my* little lady to task for her inferior system and inferior virtue. Something in this really, I think—especially if one makes it take in something of the question of the non-marrying of girls, the desperation of mothers, the whole alteration of manners—in the sense of the *osé*— and tone, while our theory of the participation, the *presence* of the young, remains unaffected by it. Then the type of the little girl who is conscious and aware. 'I am modern—I'm supposed to know—I'm not a *jeune fille*,' etc. x x x x x

[*The Awkward Age,* serialized in *Harper's Weekly* October 1898 to January 1899; published in London and New York (1899).]

Names. Genneret—Massigny—Mme d'Ouvré (or Ouvray)—Ince—Haffenden— Moro—Snape—Gossage—Goldberg—Vandenberg—Vanderberg—Beauville— Duchy—Pillow—Warry—Garry—Brigstock—Bransby—Gracedew—Tregarthen—Gable—d'Audigny—Callow—Sensechal—Bounce—Bounds (house, place)— Grander—Rix—Bembridge—Waterbath (? place)—Mme de Jaume or Geaume— (Mme J. or G.)—Mordan—Gwither (or Gwyther)—Able—Mme de la Faye—Robeck—Roebeck—Crimble—Birdwhistle—Ardrey—Acherley—Gysander—Gésandre—Heffernan—Considine—Limbert—Mellice—Thane—Turret—Atherfield—Otherfield—Gereth—Vanderbank—Desborough—Markwick—Dedborough —Mysander—Bonnace—Bender (American—might do for the Father [and daughter][1], in the novel of the *Mystification*—even if written Benda)—Messent— Bloore—Cheshire—Shirving—Pelter—Marybourough—Marsac—Russ—Counsel —Smout—Daft   (place—house)—Umber—Umberley—Umberleigh—Ombré— Mme d'Ombré—Rimmington—Roof—Carvick—Corvick—Burbeck—Longdon— Silk—Mme de Vionnet—Iffield—Buddle—Manders—Barningham—Pugsley— Parm—Fradalon—Brere—Vizard.

> 'Donald Macmurdough lies here low,
> Ill to his friends and waur to his foe,
> Leal to his maister in weal and woe.'

1. HJ's brackets.

Some extremely well-said and suggestive things (oh, the common, general French *art de dire,* as exemplified even in a nobody like this!) in *Notes sur Londres* by one 'Brada,' alluded to above. The idea of his little book in the Revolution in English society by the *avènement* of the women, which he sees everywhere and in everything. I saw it long ago—and I saw in it a big subject for the Novelist. He has some very well uttered passages on this and other matters.

'Tel Gladstone, aujourd'hui Anglais jusqu'aux moelles, même dans une salutaire hypocrisie. Oui, assurément salutaire, et elle s'en va, elle disparaît: encore quelques années et il n'en restera plus rien; et ce sera un grand dommage, car c'était une belle chose après tout, que de voir une puissante aristocratie, une société si riche et si forte, tant d'êtres divers tenus en respect par quelques fictions que suffisaient à défendre l'édifice social; c'était une salutaire illusion que de supposer toutes le femmes chastes, tous les hommes fidèles, et d'ignorer, de chasser résolument ceux qui portaient quelque atteinte visible à cette fiction. Ce respect de mots, cette pudeur de convention, provoquaient et développaient néanmoins de réelles vertus: cela s'en va; dans certaines milieux cela a déjà disparu!' x x x x x

And on the excellent subject of the *déchéance* of the aristocracy; its ceasing to have style, to take itself seriously: 'A vouloir être trop libérale et de bon accueil, à se moquer elle-même de ses vieux préjugés, l'aristocratie anglaise joue une grosse partie, et sans être un grand prophète on peut croire que dans sa forme actuelle ses jours sont comptés. Tout est permis à une caste fermée qui est persuadée de sa supériorité, mais du moment qu'elle abdique elle-même, prétend à la liberté d'allures du premier plébéien venu, on ne sait plus très bien ce qu'elle signifie, et il est à craindre qu'un beau jour on ne le lui demande un peu rudement. Assi longtemps' (also) 'que les femmes entretiennent le feu du sanctuaire on peut avoir bon espoir, mais du moment qu'elles se rient et du sanctuaire et du feu sacré, il est probable qu'il ne tardera pas à s'éteindre, et le grand mouvement d'émancipation qui s'accomplit à cette heure en Angleterre vient de la femme. Il y a plusieurs courants, mais tous tendent au même but: s'affranchir de la tutelle de l'homme—vivre d'une vie personnelle.'

'Le succès de l'Américain s'explique par un côté particulier du caractère anglais, cette volonté d'ignorer certaines choses; l'Américain est un personnage anonyme, pour ainsi dire: on peut commodément feindre ne rien savoir de son passé ni de la source de sa fortune, ce qui est moins facile vis-à-vis du nouveau riche qui est de provenance nationale. L'amour propre souffre moins d'avouer une épousée de New York ou de Washington que de la prendre à l'ombre d'une usine; il y a là une nuance qui a été très commode à l'orgueil héréditaire; puis l'Américaine est un être particulier dont, à l'occasion, la vulgarité sera traitée de couleur locale; ce qui n'est pas le cas pour un compatriote. Il ne faut pas oublier non plus que cette uniformité de gens bien élevés n'existe pas en Angleterre—que les manières de voir, les façons, les habitudes de la grande classe moyenne ne sont pas du tout celles de la class supérieure; on ne s'y trompe pas lorsqu'on connaît l'un et l'autre, et par conséquent la fusion est bien plus difficile. x x x x x

Malgré tout l'Américain à Londres ne peut être qu'un accident, et le jour qu'on voudra le boycotter, rien de plus facile.

Les I^{ers} à être corrompus par le changement de la vieille société ont été les jeunes gens; autrefois les bonne[s] grâces des nobles maîtresses de maison leur étaient nécessaires pour faire leur chemin dans le monde, aujourd'hui ce sont eux qui sont nécessaires aux maîtresses de maison. La plupart du temps ils sont invités par des tiers; le sans-façon qu'ils ont apporté chez les parvenus indignes ou étrangers, ils le conservent comme manière définitive; la politesse la plus élémentaire est mise de côté, celle même de se faire présenter à son hôtesse. De l'excès de conventionalité on est tombé à l'excès du cynisme: des fils de famille n'ont pas rougi de servir (moyennant finance) de recruteurs à des tapissiers ou à des couturières; eux-mêmes sont devenus couturiers et recommandent l'article à leurs danseuses; il y a là le plus lamentable renoncement à la dignité personelle, la véritable nécessité n'ayant rien à invoquer là-dedans, et une société aristocratique qui ne saurait pas sauver ses membres d'une telle humiliation serait indigne d'exister.' x

x x x x

I have copied the above for convenience of statement; and it appears to me that the general direction of *all* these observations swarms with subjects and suggestions. As I have noted before there is a big comprehensive subject in the *déchéance* of the aristocracy through its own want of imagination, of nobleness, of delicacy, of the exquisite; and there is a big comprehensive subject in the *avènment,* or rather in the masculinization of women—and their *ingérence,* their *concurrence,* the fact that, in many departments and directions, the cheap work they can easily do is more and more all the 'public wants.' The 'public wants' nothing, in short, today, that they *can't* do. I seem to see the great broad, rich theme of a large satirical novel in the picture, gathering a big armful of elements together, of the *train dont va* English society before one's eyes—the great modern collapse of all the forms and 'superstitions' and respects, good and bad. and restraints and mysteries—a vivid and mere showy general hit at the decadences and vulgarities and confusions and masculinizations and feminizations—the materializations and abdications and intrusions, and Americanizations, the lost sense, the brutalized manner—the publicity, the newspapers, the general revolution, the failure of fastidiousness. *Ah, que de choses, que de choses!*—I am struck with there being the suggestion of something in the *last* lines quoted above from this neat 'Brada'—I mean of something in the way of a little objective tale. She speaks ('Brada,' too, is a She) of the prevention by the general aristocratic body of the *déchéance,* the commercialization, the shopkeeping, the mounting upon *les planches,* etc., of its unfortunate members. She implies that an aristocracy worthy to exist comes to the rescue of that sort of thing and sees that it shall not take place. Well, when it does, it can mainly assist and prevent and interfere by *alms,* by giving money, making the individual dependent, etc. This is what suggests a little situation, and the situation *se rattache* (in my mind—vaguely) to that vague one I hinted at, somewhere, very sketchily (in this *cahier de notes*),[1] that of the different view taken by 2 (or more) members of an 'old family,' of some dishonour or abomination that has overtaken someone *qui leur tient de près:* that is, the different view taken of the question of the treatment of it—the treatment before the world:

1. See 18 November 1894.

the alternatives of disowning, repudiating, sinking the individual, or of covering him (or her) with the mantle of the general honour, being imperturbable and inscrutable, and presenting to the world a marble, unconscious face. It seemed to me that there might be a small drama in the embodiment in 2 opposed persons, on a given occasion, of these conflicting, irreconcilable points of view. One would arrange, one would invent and vivify the particular circumstances—construct the illustrative action. It occurs to me that, with a given little *donnée,* the 'illustrative action,' precisely, might include the picture of such a predicament as those foreshadowed in the aforementioned citation from 'Brada.' There, too, is a chance for the opposed, the alternative views. On the one side the demoralized aristocrat opens a shop, or wants to, engages, in short, or desires to, in some mercenary profession. On the other, he is saved from doing so by accepting 'relief' from the persons who would be ashamed of seeing him do it. Oppose these conflicting theories of relief and of 'vulgarity'—dramatise them by making something depend on them, depend on the question at issue, for certain persons who are actors in the little story. Make the conflict, in other words, a little drama—or make it so perhaps by thickening the situation, interweaving with it pictorially the other element, the situation of the individual who has been guilty (of something or other serious), and of the treatment of whom the family, the relations, the others, take a different view. This individual would be, as it were, the *pretext* of the little drama: the actors, the sufferers, the agents are the conflicting others. x x x x x

May 13th, 1895. I have just promised Scudder[1] 3 short stories for the *Atlantic.* I have a number of things noted here to choose from; but wish, in general, to remind myself that, more and more, every thing of this kind I do must be a complete and perfect little drama. The little idea must resolve itself into a little action, and the little action into the *essential* drama aforesaid. *Voilà.* It is the way—it is perhaps the only way—to make some masterpieces. It is at any rate what I want to do. x x x x x

There comes back to me the memory of a little idea I took up a year or two ago to the extent of writing a few pages—pages which I have just rummaged out of my desk: the idea suggested to me by one Mrs. Anstruther-Thompson, whom I sat next to at a Xmas dinner at Lady Lindsay's. She told me an anecdote that I noted at the time, in another book (than this) and have just hunted up.[2] Reading over my little statement I find the case vividly enough, though very briefly, presented, and I can probably go on with my beginning. What is wanting is a full roundness for the action—the completeness of the drama-quality. I see the action up to a certain point, but what can be the solution, the denouement? The action is the mother's refusal to give up the house, or the things. But that is, in itself,

---

1. Horace Elisha Scudder (1838–1902), Boston novelist and biographer, edited the *Atlantic Monthly* from 1890 to 1898. HJ delivered "Glasses" (see 26 June 1895) and *The Old Things* (i.e., *The Spoils of Poynton*) to Scudder. The intended third blossomed later into *The Awkward Age; see Letters* IV, 22–23.

2. See 24 December 1893. HJ begins to develop *The Spoils of Poynton,* which he first called *The House Beautiful* and then *The Old Things.*

no conclusion, no climax. What is it that follows on that? *(May 15th, 1895.)* I seem to see the thing in three chapters, like 3 little acts, the 1st of which terminates with the son's marriage to one—the dreaded one—of the Brigstocks. In this 1st act Mrs. Gereth takes the girl—her own girl (Muriel Veetch)—to her own house and adopts her there, as it were, shows her its beauty. Her initiation—their relation. A scene with Albert there, before the marriage. Mrs. Gereth's threat of rupture if it takes place. She must have had a scene with Nora Brigstock at Waterbath—the scene that determines her. All this spendidly foreshortened, as it were; as the whole thing must be. Then, Act II, the little drama of Mrs. Gereth's attitude, her preparations to leave the house—her going over it in farewell; then her collapse, her inability to *s'en arracher* and surrender her treasures. Of course in Act I all due prominence given to the element of Albert's 'want of taste'—his terrible, fatal *penchant* to ugliness, the thing that has made his mother precisely *want* so to redeem him, to safeguard, by a union with such a girl as Muriel Veetch—and makes her feel that the union with a Brigstock precisely loses him forever. All this crystalline in Act I. It surely gives me plenty of material for that act. Each act is 50 pages of my MS. Well then, in II, I give her collapse, her refusal to surrender. But I must carry the action on a step, a stride *beyond* that, to get the climax of my Chapter II. What can this climax be? May it be some act or step on the part of the son—some resolution, some violence of his? And then the denouement, the solution, the climax that Chapter III leads up to, may that be something done by Muriel Veetch? I have a dim sense that the denouement must be *through* her. One thing strikes me as certain, that she must really be in love with Albert. The battle between Albert and his mother must be arrayed—and she in some way intervenes. His 'taking up the glove' ends Act II. Muriel takes the field in Act III—she interposes, she achieves. I seem vaguely to disembroil something like THIS: That Mrs. Gereth's *démarche* in II, the circumstance of her deciding to fight, is that she determines to have all the most precious things removed to the dower-house. She not only determines it—she *does* it. The element of her resentment at the way 'the mother' is treated in England is an active force in this. Perhaps she has a sister married in France—a silhouette, a thumbnail sketch chalked in—who sharpens the contrast and eggs her on. She *despoils* Umberleigh, or whatever the name is—she *skims* it, she strips it. She has everything that is really precious and exquisite carted away to her own house. *She does it in Muriel's absence*—while Muriel is away on a family errand (her dying father or something of that sort). She does it too without telling Albert of what she intends. He comes and finds it done—comes back from his wedding-tour—or from some later absence. This discovery, on his part, is the 'climax' of Chapter II. The mother and son are face to face in a 'row.' He threatens to prosecute—his wife eggs him on. Muriel's intervention takes the form of trying to avert all this hideousness, getting Mrs. Gereth to make the terrible concession and restore what she has taken away. She secretly loves the young man—that is why. She prevails, Mrs. Gereth has the things restored. The horrible, the atrocious conflagration—which may at any rate, I think, serve as my working hypothesis for a denouement. x x x x x

34 De Vere Gdns., W., June 4th, 1895.

The question of doing something in a very short compass—10,000 (or 8000) words with the little idea that I noted some time back[1]—the notion of the little drama that may reside in the poor man of letters who squanders his life in trying for a vulgar success which his talent is too fine to achieve. He wants to marry—he wants to do at least once something that will sell; BUT—do what he will—he *can't* make a sow's ear out of a silk purse. It's in this sad little baffled, almost tragically baffled, attempt that the small action must reside. He succumbs, somehow, he has to fail, to give up, to collapse materially, because the worst he can do, as it were, is too good to succeed—too good for the market. It is the old story of my letters to the *N.Y.T[ribune]* where I had to write to Whitelaw R. that they 'were the worst I could do for the money.' It is against a little series of cases of this kind, of dismissals, of misfortunes, of failures to catch the tone in spite of wanting and *needing* to, that the talent incapable of adequate vulgarity *se rompt*—'every time.' The little story would be the story of what depends on it—of what he is prevented from doing (marrying, living, keeping his head above water), by his not hitting it off. I don't know what I can hope to do in my short 8000 words except show 3 or 4 cases. One of them—the one to begin with—might be just a little case similar to, identical with, my adventure with the *Tribune.* I lost that work, that place— so *he* loses it and is left stranded. Only for me everything didn't depend upon it; while for my imagined little hero everything *does.* Has he married on the prospect?—one must figure it out. In 8000 words—which is what I must try for—I probably can't show more than 3 cases. I seem to see them as three striking, crucial ones, observed at intervals by the narrator. In my former note of this I seemed to catch hold of the tail of a dim idea that my narrator might be made the ironic portrait of a deluded vulgarian (of letters too), some striving *confrère* who *has* all the success my hero hasn't, who *can* do exactly the thing he can't, and who, vaguely, mistily conscious that he hasn't the suffrages of the *raffinés,* the people who count, is trying to do something distinguished, for once, something that they will notice, something that WON'T sell. This person, man or woman, has become, *through* selling, rich enough to *se passer cette fantaisie*—which comes to him, or to her, through the stirring of the spirit communicated by contacts with our friend. Is this person the narrator—and do I simplify and compress by making him so? The difficulty is that the narrator must be fully and richly, must be ironically, *conscient:* that is, *mustn't* he? Can I take such a person and make him—or her—narrate my little drama *naïvement?* I don't think so—especially with so *short* a chance: I risk wasting my material and missing my effect. I must, I think, have my real ironic painter; but if I take that line I must presumably include the vulgarian somehow in my little tale. *I* become the narrator, either impersonally or in my unnamed, unspecified personality. Say I chose the latter line, as in the *Death of the Lion,* the *Coxon Fund,* etc. *Voyons un peu* what, saliently, in that case, my little vision of the subject gives me. Say, as the 1st example, the episode of the newspaper correspondence, the letters from London to some provincial sheet. He

1. See 26 January 1895.

has married on this?—or has he only planned to marry? Oh, yes, the latter—that gives me more drama. He is just going to be able to, when the dismissal from the paper comes. He has to put it off—to wait. Then he writes his novel, and it is, for the *raffinés,* so fine, that it's accepted. It is published and has no sale at all; so he again can't marry. His fiancée must have a grim, vulgar, worldly, interfering mother *qui s'y oppose*—makes an income a condition. May not she have pretensions to 'smartness'—to family?—and be broken-down and mercenary and selfish as well, very reluctant to part with the convenience of her daughter; hating her marriage and attaching conditions. She has some money to leave—she holds the girl to a certain extent by it. The girl's a lady and is extremely pretty. Her mother thinks her a beauty and that she might have contracted a much more elegant connection. Or may not the mother be a snobbish, pretentious, tyrannical FATHER, so as not to have 3 women? That's a detail—*nous verrons bien.* I seem, at any rate, to see my vulgarian, the successful novelist, as the sister (or the brother?) of the girl my hero's engaged to. *Mettons, sister,* for the sake of the little ray, the little play of added irony that comes from the question, here, of sex. It is she, started, *lancée,* as a novelist, who brings the young man her sister's engaged to, to my notice as a struggling young writer. I get him the engagement on the provincial paper. The successful sister isn't then—isn't *yet*—the great success she afterwards becomes. She is fearfully ugly. *She* marries perhaps a publisher, or (if that is too like Miss Braddon),[2] a man of business who makes her bargains for her. When she develops the fancy to do something 'literary'—i.e., that won't sell—it sells more than ANYTHING she has done! I seem to catch hold of the tail of a glimpse of my own personality. I am a critic who doesn't sell, i.e., whose writing is too good—attracts no attention whatever. My distinguished writing fairly damages *his* distinguished—by the good it tries to do for [him]. To keep me *quiet* about him becomes one of his needs—one of the features of his struggle, that struggle to manage to do once or twice, remuneratively, the thing that will be popular, the exhibition of which (pathetic little vain effort) is the essence of my subject. I try not to write about him—in order to help him. This attitude of mine is a part of the story. I am supposing, then, that his novel (he must have written 2 or 3 before) fails, commercially, thanks to the attitude of the mother or the father about his marriage. But the marriage must take place, for the sake of what takes place after it. It is AFTER it that he tries to do the work that will meet Whitelaw Reid, etc. Then the pressure, the necessity to do that becomes great. He writes a 2d disinterested novel—and I get a magazine to 'serialize' it. It is on *that* money that he hopefully marries. But (the money having been paid down in a lump!) the serial is a deadly failure; and he is, with his wife and children on his hands, face to face with his future. *Or,* into what 2 or 3 salient, crucial cases can I summarize, to illustrate his vain effort, that future? What are the things that, thanks to his quality, he has successively to give up? There must be one or two of these, and then an illustrative denouement. May it be a question of some place—an editorship that he loses because he will only put in things of quality—and can't get them: won't

2. Mary Elizabeth Braddon (1837–1915) had written thrillers since 1862, when she published her best-selling *Lady Audley's Secret.* HJ had reviewed her as early as 1865 in the *Nation* (9 November).

put in certain vulgarities? He chucks up the thing on the question of a certain vulgar contribution which the publisher wants to force in, and which he can't bring himself to publish. He will himself work to sell, because he knows what he will do, or rather what he *won't* do; but he won't publish the rot of others when it belongs precisely to this class of what he won't do. He sacrifices the editorship—has the courage to do it—because this time, precisely, he holds—*il tient*— the idea that will make the selling novel. He puts the novel through, and it proves (I think it at least) finer than ever. I want to say so—but he begs me to keep my hands off it. He says, 'Can you abuse it? *That* may help it.' I say I will see, I will try. But I find I can't—so I say nothing. I seem to myself to want my denouement to be that in a final case I *do* speak—I uncontrollably break out (without his knowing I'm going to: I keep it secret, risk it); with the consequence that I just, after all, dish him. There is something that must depend, for him, on his book's selling—something that he will get or that he can do: I mean in this final case, which constitutes the denouement. *Voyons.* He is ill and must go abroad— go to Egypt. Then it is that wanting to help him and carried away by the beauty of the thing, I risk it. I secretly—that is without asking his leave, blow my trumpet for him. Yes—I dish him. The book *doesn't* do, this time, any more than the other times (he keeps changing publishers), and on my head is the responsibility. I am the *blighting* critic. He can't go abroad—he has to give it up—he dies for want of it, and his wife, in her frenzy, comes down on me. But she repents, retracts, says now that he is dead I *can* praise him. The good natured, vulgar sister-in-law's effort (she must have a hard stingy husband, who prevents her from charities and *largesses)*—this effort, *not* to sell, for once, and which also fails, must be in some manner synchronous with my hero's. She wants me to praise her, so that THAT may help her not to sell. But I *can't*—so sell she does. I think I may call the thing *The Next Time.* And begin it—'Yes, my notes as I look them over bring it back to me.' Or begin it with the visit of the selling sister-in-law (after his death, on the errand just stated) and hark back from that? This last, I think. Oh, it will take 10,000 words.

[''The Next Time,'' the *Yellow Book* July 1895; reprinted in *Embarrassments.*]

June 26th, 1895, 34 De Vere Gdns., W.

A little idea occurred to me the other day for a little tale that Maupassant would have called *Les Lunettes,* though I'm afraid that *The Spectacles* won't do. A very pretty, a very beautiful little woman, devoted to her beauty, which she cherishes, prizing, and rejoicing in it more than in anything on earth—is threatened, becomes indeed absolutely afflicted, with a malady of the eyes which she goes to see oculists about. She has had it for a long time, and has been told that she must wear spectacles of a certain kind, a big strong unbecoming kind, with a *bar* across them, etc.—if she wishes to preserve her sight. (The little notion of this was given me by my seeing a very pretty woman in spectacles the other day on the top of an omnibus.) She has been unable to face this disfigurement—she has evaded

and defrauded the obligation (wearing them only in secret and sometimes changing them for glasses, etc.) and she has got worse. She *adores* her beauty, and it
has other adorers. The story must be told by a 3d person, as it were, a spectator,
an observer. He knows her case—sees her 1st at the oculist's, where he has gone
for himself. At any rate he is witness of her relations with an adoring young man,
whom she cold-shoulders, makes light of, treats, *du haut de son orgeuil et de sa
beauté*, as not worth her trouble. He must be ugly—rather ridiculously ugly—and
not brilliant in other ways. Then she *has* to take to the spectacles and disfigure
herself. She must have been a married woman—separated from her husband. Or
she may marry—THIS IS BETTER—a rich man from whom she keeps the secret of
her infirmity. May it not be *in order* to catch him, nail him, that she so keeps it?
She is in dread of losing him if she lets him know how she may be afflicted and
disqualified in the future. He marries her (or *doesn't* he?—does he chuck her at
the last, on a suspicion?) and what I, as narrator, see is a poor blind helpless
woman (but beautiful in her blindness still), with the old rejected and despised
lover now tenderly devoted to her, giving up his life to her—in short, as it must
be, married to her. I think one *must* make her MISS the preferred lover—miss him
at the very last, through his getting an accidental glimpse of her doom, and so be
left alone and without fortune, with that doom staring her in the face.

["Glasses," the *Atlantic Monthly* February 1896; reprinted in *Embarrassments*.]

34 De Vere Gardens, W., July 15th, 1895.

Yesterday at the Borthwicks', at Hampstead, something that Lady Tweedmouth [1]
said about the insane frenzy of futile occupation imposed by the London season,
added itself to the hideous realization in my own mind—recently so deepened—
to suggest that a 'subject' may very well reside in some picture of this overwhelming, self-defeating chaos or cataclysm toward which the whole thing is drifting.
The picture residing, exemplified, in the experience of some tremendously exposed and intensely conscious individual—the deluge of people, the insane movement for movement, the ruin of thought, of life, the negation of work, of literature, the swelling, roaring crowds, the 'where are you going?,' the age of Mrs.
Jack, [2] the figure of Mrs. Jack, the American, the nightmare—the individual consciousness—the mad, ghastly climax or denouement. It's a splendid subject—if
worked round a personal action—situation. x x x x x

The Americans looming up—dim, vast, portentous—in their millions—like gathering waves—the barbarians of the Roman Empire.

x   x   x   x   x

1. Algernon Borthwick was proprietor of the *Morning Post*. Lady Tweedmouth, née Fanny Churchill
(d. 1904), daughter of the ninth Duke of Marlborough, in 1873 married Edward Marjoribanks (1849–
1909), second Baron Tweedmouth, Chief Liberal Whip under Gladstone (1892) and Lord President of
the Council under Asquith (1908).
2. "Mrs. Jack" was Isabella Stewart (1840–1924), who married John L. Gardner in 1860 and late in
life built Fenway Court in Boston in the form of a Venetian palace. It is now the Gardner Museum.

Osborne Hotel, Torquay, August 11th, 1895.

Voyons un peu où j'en suis in the little story of the situation between the mother and the son, in the little tale I have called the *House Beautiful* and of which I have hammered out some 70 pp. of MS. It is a question of a concision—for the rest of my 150 pp. in all, my rigid limit, for the *Atlantic*—truly masterly. Mona Brigstock and her mother are down at Poynton, brought by Owen Gereth, who considers that Mona shows to great advantage there and is having a great success. This infatuated density, this singleness and stupidity of perception, so often characteristic of the young Englishman in regard to the inferior woman, is the note of his attitude throughout. It makes Fleda wonder, marvel—and marvel without jealousy—see clearly how much more *doué* he is for marital than for filial affection. He cares, comparatively, nothing for his mother—would sacrifice her any day to his virtuous, Philistine, instinctive attachment to Mona. It is only *for* Mrs. Gereth that Fleda is, as it were, jealous; she says, in the face of Mona: 'Good heavens, if she were *my* mother, how common and stupid she would make, in comparison and contrast, such a girl as that, appear!' What I should like to do, God willing, is to thresh out my little remainder, from this point, tabulate and clarify it, state or summarize it in such a way that I can go, very straight and sharp, to my climax, my denouement. What I feel more and more that I must arrive at, with these things, is the adequate and regular practice of some such economy of clear summarization as will *give* me from point to point, each of my steps, stages, tints, shades, every main joint and hinge, in its place, of my subject—give me, in a word, my clear order and expressed sequence. I can then *take* from the table, successively, each fitted or fitting piece of my little mosaic. When I ask myself what there may have been to show for my long tribulation, my wasted years and patiences and pangs, of theatrical experiment, the answer, as I have already noted here, comes up as just possibly *this:* what I have gathered from it will perhaps have been exactly some such mastery of fundamental statement—of the art and secret of it, of expression, of the sacred mystery or structure. Oh yes—the weary, woeful time has done something for me, has had in the depths of all its wasted piety and passion, an intense little lesson and direction. What that resultant is I must now actively show. x x x x x

What then is it that the rest of my little 2d act, as I call it, of *The House Beautiful* must do? Its climax is in the removal—*must absolutely and utterly be: voilà*—from the house, by Mrs. Gereth, of her own treasures. What are the steps that lead to that? Well, these.

1st. Owen must have a morsel with Fleda in which he shows how happy he is with the result of their visit, and which she doesn't retail to his mother.

2d. Mrs. G., the morning they go (the Brigstocks), does take the alarm, though Owen doesn't give her the news himself. He hasn't got it yet—Mona doesn't speak till they get back to town. But Mrs. Brigstock has spoken more or less, and Owen has shown, does show, to Mrs. Gereth, how pleased he is. There must be a scene of some sort between the young man and his mother—and between Mrs. G. and Mona. Yet surely all this must be very, *very*, VERY brief and rapid—for it is after all preliminary, and the centre of gravity of the piece, which is that Owen marries Mona, is in danger of being thrust much too far forward, out of its place. As it is I've almost no room at all for my people to talk. What I think I want to make take place between Mrs. Gereth and Owen and Mona is the striking utterance on her part of some note of warning—some expression to them of her own ground, of what she expects, how she feels. It must take place before Fleda. Make it, *n'est-ce pas?*, that the pieces follow each other in this order.

(a) Owen shows himself to his mother *and* Fleda in the morning; and Fleda, after a vision of what is going on between them, goes out, leaves them together. She goes out into the grounds and finds Mona there; ten words about what passes between the 2 women. They come in again, and then it is that Fleda has the sense of what Mrs. G. has said to Owen—has probably, dreadfully said—about *her.*

(b) The scene, for Mrs. G., before Owen and Fleda, with Mona—the scene that as Fleda feels, practically settles and clinches Mona. (It is Owen's own indications that have, after the night when they went downstairs, alarmed Mrs. G.) They depart, the ladies and Owen, leaving Mrs. G. under the impression that she has frightened them away. *But Fleda knows better*—though she pretends to agree. It is then—after they are gone—that Mrs. Gereth lets her know or suspect, to her horror, what she has already seemed to divine, to apprehend—that she *did* speak (while F. was in the garden with M.) about her, F., being *her* ideal for a daughter-in-law. This it is that makes F. doubly sure that the engagement to Mona will now be precipitated. Owen comes down alone in a few days, in fact, to announce it. What action does his mother then take? There must be the scene, *before* Fleda, about her surrender of the house—the scene of her, Mrs. G.'s, waiting for him to say, passionately, grievingly giving him a chance to say, that she may stay, that feeling as she does, he won't turn her out—or even that he'll give her up some of the things. But he doesn't say it. x x x x x

Rather, indeed, why may he *not* say this last? Doesn't his mother have, there, her long-smothered outbreak—flash about upon him about Mona's barbarism and the horrors of Waterbath? It's a dreadful, fatal scene: Fleda sees it or knows it. *Then* it is she has the scene with Owen that is to come after her knowing what his mother has said to him about her. It leads to the fact that Owen *does* offer to let his mother keep some of the things. Fleda puts in her own plea for this and makes her own reflection. Owen tells his mother, before he leaves, what he'll do. Before the marriage, however, he retracts—he lets her know that his wife has refused to part with anything. It was as he showed her Poynton, that day, that she wants to have it. It was the sight of it that day, that settled her. Therefore he must keep faith with her—and after all isn't he within his absolute rights? The marriage takes place—all in Act III. Fleda isn't present at it—the young couple go to Italy. But after she is settled in her own house Fleda goes down to see Mrs. Gereth. The 1st thing she perceives in her house—her little dower-cottage—are the things Mrs. G. has removed from Poynton. *Voilà.* That was to have been the climax of my 2d act, as it were; but I don't see how it *can* be, with any feasible adjustment to my space, if I try to make my 2d act one with my second chapter or section—my little 'II.' My only issue, here, is in multiplying, throughout the whole, my divisons. x x x x x

❧

1895–1896

This notebook (Houghton Journal V, 8 September 1895 to 26 October 1896), 7" x 8¾", has black leatherette covers with gilt trim, wine marbled endpapers, 179 unlined pages written in black ink, with some underlining in red ink.

The notebook illustrates the fertility of HJ's middle years; it contains the extensive development of *The Spoils of Poynton* and *What Maisie Knew*, the substantial nurturing of the "germ" of *The Ambassadors*, and the marshaling of sundry ideas into manageable lists. The final entry (26 October 1896) leads directly into the opening of Houghton Journal VI as HJ responds to the urgent demands of his *Maisie*.

Osborne Hotel, Torquay, September 8th, 1895.

I am face to face with several little alternatives of work, and am in fact in something of a predicament with things promised and retarded.[1] I must thresh out my solutions, must settle down to my jobs. It's idiotic, by the way, to waste time in writing such a remark as that! As if I didn't feel in all such matters infinitely more than I can ever utter! x x x x x

My immediate necessity is to tackle again the question of one of the little stories that I have promised to do for Scudder: the question round which, in general, as I have found before this, such tragic little accidents are apt to cluster. By tragic little accidents, I mean the tragic accident of the waste of labour to which I have often found myself condemned in trying to do the short (the really, I mean, the

---

1. In addition to three short stories promised to the *Atlantic* (see 13 May 1895), HJ had agreed to write two novels for Heinemann and a short story for the first number of *Cosmopolis*, January 1896 (see 4 November 1894).

129

very short) thing. I am just crawling out of one of them, in this particular connection: the attempt, in *The House Beautiful,* to meet Scudder on the basis of 10,000 words—an attempt that has ended, irremissibly, incurably, in almost 30,000— leaving on my hands a production that *he* doesn't want and that I must try to make terms for in some other way, terms bad, terms sadding, at the best. Ah, but let me not go, here, into the question of the reason for which this larger manner now imposes itself upon me—as it has every right and power to do: reasons with which my spirit is sufficiently saturated! Suffice it that I'm simply face to face with the little question: 'Can I do the thing in 10,000 words or can I not?' The answer to it is surely that I'm not prepared to say I can't. The difficulty has been, I think, when I've failed, that I haven't tried *right.* I've lost sight too much of the necessary smallness, necessary singleness of the subject. I've been too proud to take the very simple thing. I've almost always taken the thing requiring developments. Now, when I embark on developments I'm lost, for they are my temptation and my joy. I'm too afraid to be *banal.* I needn't be afraid, for my danger is small. I must try now, to do the thing of 10,000 words (which there is *every* economic reason for my recovering and holding fast the trick of). I must try it, I say, on the basis of rigid limitation of subject. That is, I must take, and take only, the single incident. I know what I mean by the single incident. *The Real Thing, The Middle Years, Brooksmith,* even, *The Private Life, Owen Wingrave,* are what I call single incidents. Many others are essentially ideas requiring development. *Cherchons, piochons, patientons—tenons-nous-en* to the opposite kind. Try to make use, for the brief treatment, of nothing, absolutely *nothing,* that isn't ONE, as it were—that doesn't begin and end in its little self. x x x x x

I noted the other day the little *concetto* that I might call *The Spectacles.*[2] *Voyons,* let me consider a little how to turn it. It has the needed singleness, hasn't it? Surely, if anything *can* have. x x x x x

Torquay, September 22nd, 1895.

Note here more fully, later, 2 little *sujets de nouvelle* suggested to me, one by Mme Bourget, the other by both P.B. and his wife.—[1] The 1st came up through our talking of Hugues L[e Roux][2] and his elaborate imitation—personal, manual, literary and other—of Bourget. The idea of such an imitation—of the person making it—operating as a source of disenchantment (through accentuation of the points least liked) to a person deeply interested in the model—in the individual imitated. More concretely a woman, say, is in love with the great artist (poet, soldier, orator, actor—whatever), A. She doesn't know him well, but has been taken, smitten, though protesting—and has had, somehow, to lose him, to give him up. She meets B., the imitator, and, being struck with the great analogy, hails him at 1st as a source of interest, a consoler, a substitute. Then the way he brings out all the sides of the other man that she has liked least rises before her and creates a disillusionment—a dislike. It must be on *them* the imitation most bears. The imi-

2. See 26 June 1895.

1. Paul and Minnie Bourget.

2. Hugues LeRoux (1860–1925), French journalist and friend of Paul Bourget's.

tator must *make* it so bear—in his fatuity and also (oh yes!) his *sincerity,* with the very design of pleasing, capturing her. He wants to get her for himself—his attempt upon her is a conscious one. But his admiration of his model is real—profound. He thinks he sees resemblances—is sure he does, and very artfully cultivates them. The Denouement, it strikes me, offhand, must be determined by the chance—by *a* chance the woman has to recover the great man—meet him again, have him again—know him better. *He* wants to give it to her—he has liked her. Unexpectedly, etc.—somehow—he has come back. But now she doesn't want him—she refuses, flees, waves him off, hides herself: the imitator has been fatal. *This,* at least, strikes me, offhand, as a case in which the narrator may be personal—first-personal. I seem to see that 'I' may figure. I seem to see that the thing may begin with my meeting the imitator 1st and being the source. of his contact with the woman. I go on to see her somewhere, after this meeting—I find my friend under the impression of her separation from, her loss of, the original. I mention to her the other man who is such an extraordinary reproduction of him, and that *he* is coming, also, in a day or two. Isn't that a good beginning? I assist, there, at the little drama. I must, of course, have had my own independent knowledge or observation of the original. And I have a glimpse of the *finis*—the FINAL finish. The original *does* 'come on'—to the place, wherever it is—and only disappointedly to find the woman missing, absent, or whatever it may be—having, as it were, chucked him up. I meet him, I am with him, I explain.—'Well, you see So-and-So—the Imitation—was here.' 'Oh, I see! She has taken *him!*' 'On the contrary—she has him in horror.' The Great Man is puzzled. 'And yet he is awfully like me.' 'He is too much so!' But the great man never understands.[3]

x   x   x   x   x

Note here, at. leisure, the other small subject—the situation of Cazalis and Jean Lahor: the *médecin de ville d'eau* with his great *talent de poète,* changing his name to a 'pen-name'—at his worldly wife's behest, to write poetry—frivolous and compromising for a doctor who has to make his way and feed his children, etc.—and then when the poetry brings him honour, some money, etc., having to change back again, so that—in fine the thing is to be figured out. There is a subject. The loss and confusion of identity, etc.[4] Make, later on, a statement of idea for treatment of Gualdo's charming little subject of *The Child.*[5]

Osborne Hotel, Torquay, October 15th, '95.[1]

My little story has grown upon my hands—I am speaking of *The House Beautiful*—and will make a thing of 30,000 words. But though I have been scared at the dimensions it was taking—scared in view of the meagerness of the little subject—

---

3. See 7 May 1898.
4. Dr. Henri Cazalis (1840–1909), medical man and literary amateur, was a minor Parnassian poet and a friend of Stéphane Mallarmé; he used the pen name "Jean Lahor." See 7 May 1898.
5. Luigi Gualdo (b. 1847), Italian novelist. See 7 May 1898, 16 February 1899, 11 September 1900, and 12 June 1901, for development of "Maud-Evelyn."

1. The first six and a half sentences of this entry conclude Houghton Journal IV; see headnote to the notebook of 1894–1895.

yet I think I see the way to make it fill out its skin and be very fairly solid and fine. x x x x x

Fleda Vetch is down at Ricks—has come down to find Mrs. Gereth installed and in possession of most of the treasures of Poynton. I did what I could yesterday to handle her arrival, but I must thresh out finely every inch of the action from that point to the end. The sense of what her friend has done quite appals the girl, and what has now passed between her and Owen prepares her for a great stir of feeling in his favour—a resentment on his behalf and pitying sense of his spoliations. I am here dealing with very delicate elements, and I must make the operation, the presentation, of each thoroughly sharp and clear. If this climax of my little tale is confused and *embrouillé* it will be nothing; if it's as crystalline as possible it will be worth doing. I have, a little, to guard myself against the drawback of having[2] in the course of the story determined on something that I had not intended—or had not expected—at the start. I had intended to make Fleda 'fall in love' with Owen, or, to express it *moins banalement,* to represent her as loving him. But I had not intended to represent a feeling of this kind on Owen's part. Now, however, I have done so; in my last little go at the thing (which I have been able to do only so interruptedly), it inevitably took that turn and I must accept the idea and work it out. What I felt to be necessary, as the turn in question came, was that what should happen between Fleda and Owen Gereth should be something of a certain intensity. My idea was that it should be, whatever it is, determining for *her;* and it didn't seem to me that I could make it sufficiently intense and sufficiently determining without making it come, as it were, *from* Owen. *Je m'entends.*—Fleda suddenly perceives that on the verge of his marriage to Mona— he is, well, what I have in fact, represented. My present question—not to waste words about it—is as to what takes place between them when he comes down to Ricks. For I seem to see it so—that he does come down to Ricks. Mrs. Gereth must have achieved her devastation by a *coup de main*—proceeded with extraordinary celerity: this is made clear as between her and Fleda: the way she proceeded—got off in a night, as it were—is made perfectly distinct. Definite questions and answers about this. Fleda's night, after this, in the 'lovely' room Mrs. Gereth had arranged for her—her suffering under it, hatred of it, hatred of profiting by such things at Owen's cost, as it were. What has happened makes her think only of Owen. His marriage hasn't as yet taken place, but it's near at hand—it's there. She expects nothing more from him—has a dread of its happening. She wants only, as she believes, or tries to believe, never to see him again. She surrenders him to Mona. She has a dread of his not doing his duty—backing out in any way. That would fill her with horror and dismay. But she has no real doubt that he'll go through with his marriage. In going down to Ricks she has only seemed to herself to be going further away from him. She has had no prevision— she *could* have none—that he would turn up there. All she has wanted is to hear of his marriage. Touch the note that it has seemed to her even unduly delayed—

2. This point marks the end of Houghton Journal IV. At the top of page 13 of V, following the two entries for September 1895, HJ wrote: "(continuation from last page of Red Book: Osborne Hotel, Torquay: Oct. 15, '95) in the course of the story. . . ."

delayed in a way to act on her nerves. She has got no invitation, but she hasn't expected that. The light on Mrs. Gereth's action, however, that she encounters at Ricks, changes the whole situation; causes her to hold her breath—making her not know exactly WHAT may happen. Now, *voyons un peu, mon bon:* the whole idea of my thing is that Fleda becomes rather fine, DOES something, distinguishes herself (to the reader), and that this is really almost all that has made the little anecdote worth telling at all. It gives me a lift—an air—and I must make it give me as much of these things as it ever possibly can. But I am confronted with a little difficulty which requires my looking it as coolly and calmly as I can in the face and figuring it out. What I have seen Fleda do is operate successfully (to state it as broadly as possible), to the end that the things be mainly sent back to Poynton. Now there are 2 necessary facts in regard to this. One is that a certain event, or certain events, certain forces, *lead up* to it, with their irresistible pressure on the girl. The other resides in the particular way in which she responds to that pressure. She gets the things back. *How* does she get them back? My idea had been that she successfully persuades Mrs. Gereth to send them. That seemed possible and adequate so long as my thought was simply that she had a sentiment for Owen: it seemed in the key of that little suppressed emotion. But now that the emotion is developed more and Owen himself is made, as it were, active, I feel as if I wanted something more—I don't know what to call it except *dramatic*. Let me make out first, however, exactly what precedes, and then I shall see my way a little more into what follows. Owen is brought down to Ricks by his discovery of the spoliation of Poynton. He has gone over, after his mother's departure, and taken in the scene. He has notified Mona, and Mona has then come over with him and seen for herself, and the upshot has been that—having had the matter out between them—he has come down to his mother to demand a surrender. I must *motiver* his coming—his coming in person. Mona has wanted him to communicate only through their solicitor. He won't do that—he will be more tender: but Fleda sees that he takes his own way first because Mona has been strenuous about hers. I must represent Owen as not coming down with a preoccupation about Fleda: he doesn't know she's there—he thinks she in fact isn't. He has come because he simply *has* to. The reason WHY he simply has to, comes out in what takes place between him and Fleda. His mother refuses to see him—he is over at the inn. She makes Fleda see him for her. This takes place the day after Fleda's arrival. The girl thinks of refusing—then she consents. She has tried to refuse—for the trouble and torment the thing inflicts upon her—and because she has made it her rule, now, not to meet him, not to 'encourage' him, not to let herself go to this 'lawless love.' It seems to me I have really here the elements of something rather fine. The fineness is the fineness of Fleda. Let me carry that as far as possible—be consistent and bold and high about it: allow it all its little touch of poetry. She is forced again, as it were, by Mrs. Gereth, to renew a relation that she has sought safety and honour, tried to be 'good,' in *not* keeping up. She is almost, as it were, thrown into Owen's arms. It is the same with the young man. He *too* has tried to be good. *He* has renounced the relation. He has determined to stick to Mona. He is thrust by his mother into danger again. Mrs. Gereth is operating with so much more inflammable material than she knows. The young people meet at first as if that scene in Kensington Gdns. hadn't occurred; and Fleda says to herself that he repents of it, is ashamed of it. But they get into deeper waters. He informs her of the *sommation* he bears to his mother. Then briefly, quickly, *de fil en aiguille,* they come to the question of his alternative—his alternative or contemplated course if Mrs. Gereth refuses. Owen lets her know—practically what it is. It is Mona who now determines it. Mona has insisted on his *insisting*—and if he doesn't insist she will break off their marriage. She has made it a *condition* of their marriage. This is the climax of the 'scene' between the 2. It helps to constitute whatever beauty I may put into the thing. It is Fleda's opportunity—Fleda's temptation. If Mrs. Gereth doesn't surrender Mona will break, and if Mona breaks—*her* opening seems to lie there before her. Well—it's a part of what the girl does that she *resists*. She *sees* this, yet she does her best, heroically, to shut her eyes to it. She sees that Owen is ashamed of his disloyalty to Mona, and she has such a feeling about him that she doesn't want, she can't bear, to see him disloyal. That's about the gist of it. If I want *beauty* for her—beauty of action and poetry of effect, I can only, I think, find it just there; find it in making her heroic. To *be* heroic. To achieve beauty and poetry, she must conceal from him what she feels. I have it then that he shows, but that she doesn't. What's the matter with Owen is that he has never known a girl like her, and that it's a girl like her he wants. She reads it all for him and in him, and we see it as she sees it, without his telling, his coming out with it. It's all on *his* part inarticulate and clumsy; but we *see*—though she doesn't let him give Mona away. What does she do then?—how does she work, how does she achieve her heroism? She does it in the first and highest way by urging him on to his marriage—putting it before him that it must take place without a week's more delay. She settles this, as it were—she fixes it: she says *she'll* take care of the rest. It's the question of *how* she takes care of it that is the tight knot of my *donnée*. She sends Owen off, sends him back to Mona, answers to him for it that what they demand shall be done. At least, rather (for she can't of course really 'answer'), she gives him her word that she will do her utmost to bring the restitution about; and it's on this he leaves her, promising her, as it were, to get married immediately. That confronts me with the question of the action Fleda exercises on Mrs. Gereth and of how she exercises it. My old idea was that she worked, as it were, on her feelings. Well, eureka! I think I have found it—I think I see the little interesting turn and the little practicable form. How a little click of perception, of this sort, brings back to me all the strange sacred time of my thinkings-out, this way, pen in hand, of the stuff of my little theatrical trials. The old problems and dimnesses—the old solutions and little findings of light. Is the beauty of all that effort—of all those unutterable hours—lost forever? Lost, lost, lost? It will take a greater patience than all the others to see!— My new little notion was to represent Fleda as committing—for drama's sake— some broad effective stroke of her own. But that now looks to me like a mistake: I've got hold, very possibly, of the tail of the right thing. Isn't the right thing to make Fleda simply work upon Mrs. Gereth, but work in an interesting way? She proceeds to the execution of Owen's commission *auprès de sa mère,* but she is conscious that she can proceed to it only by an appeal. *She* has no idea of there being anything else she can do. She appeals therefore, frankly, strongly—has the most strenuous and *equal* sort of scene with her friend that she has ever had. She places her behaviour in the light of honour, duty, etc.—of the failure of Owen's contract with Mona, which was to give her the house as Mona came down that day and saw it. She produces an impression—she shakes and influences Mrs. Gereth; but it isn't from the point of view of these special arguments that she uses. It's by the very fact of her urgency, the very accent of her earnestness, of her hidden passion. Mrs. Gereth guesses that hidden passion, and by this she's affected—she throws herself into the possibility. She pricks up her ears—she stares— she exclaims: she suddenly breaks out and charges the girl with the sentiment which is her motive, the sentiment that she had divined in her. Fleda, taken aback at first, upset, bewildered, sees in a moment the chance (towards her ideal end) that it will give her to admit to Mrs. Gereth the truth. She admits then—but admits nothing else; nothing of what has supremely passed between Owen and herself. There must be an absolute definiteness about what *has* passed: the promise, as it were, in exchange for *her* promise to act, that Owen has made her to go and get married. There must have been an opening here for the question of date, of post-ponement. Owen tells Fleda, in their interview, that Mona has postponed, so as to give him time to act and his mother time to restitute. (The *original* date of the marriage was otherwise close at hand.) Fleda makes Owen PROMISE to make Mona fix a day—make it by telling her that she (Fleda) undertakes for what Mrs. Gereth will do, and that she (Fleda) desires him to inform her to that effect. This consti-tutes a definite transaction between him and Fleda. It is on this transaction that the girl, to Mrs. Gereth, observes a studied silence. (Fleda, by the way, has coerced Owen into this agreement, or transaction, as I call it, by being in posses-sion—entering into possession—of his secret, as it were, without having surren-dered to him her own. This secret of his change about Mona is *used* by her in her 'heroism.') She not only keeps Mrs. Gereth off the scent of finding out, of per-ceiving or inferring, Owen's condition, but she tells a virtuous, 'heroic' *lie* on the subject. 'Does he know?' 'Thank God, no!' Fleda can say that with truth; but when—at some turn of her investigation—Mrs. Gereth has a gleam of wonder sufficient to make her say: 'Can it be possible he doesn't feel as he did about Mona—that he likes *you?*,' Fleda emphatically denies this. But Mrs. Gereth in-sists. 'He has not said a word to you that could give colour to such a possibility?' 'He has not said a word to me.' *Reste* the question of the postponement. She learns, Mrs. G., that the wedding *is* postponed. It is really postponed to give her time to send back the furniture; but Fleda doesn't tell her this. She doesn't tell her of Mona's condition, as communicated by Owen; for in her appeal to her she has not put it on that ground—she has put [it] on the ground of Owen's honour, etc. But she *works,* as it were, the fact of the postponement—allows Mrs. Gereth to see a reason, an encouragement and hope in it. 'If he *should* break with her— *should* ask you to marry him, would you take him?'

'I'd take him,' says Fleda, profoundly. After this they *still* don't hear of the marriage. This determines Mrs. Gereth and she takes action in consequence. She sends back all but a few things—sends them all back and goes *abroad.* x x x x x

From the point I have reached (Oct. 16th) it must all be an absolute and unmiti-
gated *action*. I have in VII Fleda's impression of the situation at Ricks. This must
go to p. 210 of MS.—to Owen's arrival and include what passes between the 2
women on the subject of it.

VIII—p. 211–240. The 'Scene' at Ricks between Fleda and Owen, including
the latter's departure.

IX—p. 241–271: the whole business of the Restitution, between Mrs. Gereth
and Fleda, including the former's decision.

X.

x   x   x   x   x

Torquay, October 18th, 1895.

The little subject there may, somehow, be in the study of a romantic mind.—That
term is a very vague and rough hint at what I mean. But it may serve as a reminder.[1]

The idea of the picture, fully satiric, in illustration of the 'Moloch-worship' of the
social hierarchy in this country—the grades and shelves and stages of relative
gentility—the image of some succession or ladder of examples, in which each
stage, each 'party,' has something or someone below them, down to extreme
depths, on which, on whom, the snubbed and despised from above, may wreak
resentment by doing, below, as they are done by. They have to take it from Peter,
but they give it to Paul. Follow the little, long, close series—the tall column of
Peters and Pauls. x x x x x

["The Story in It," the *Anglo-American Magazine* January 1902; reprinted in *The Better
Sort*, London and New York (1903).]

Torquay, October 24th, 1895.

I seem to see a little subject in this idea,[1] that of the author of certain books
who is known to hold—and to declare as much, *au besoin*, to the few with whom
he communicates—that his writings contain a very beautiful and valuable, very
interesting and remunerative *secret*, or latent intention, for those who read them
with a right intelligence—who see *into* them, as it were—bring to the perusal of
them a certain perceptive sense. There's a general idea *qui s'en dégage:* he doesn't
tell what it is—it's for the reader to find out. 'It's there—it's *there,*' he says; 'I
can't—or I won't—tell you what it is; but my books constitute the expression of
it.' I should premise that I think I see these books necessarily to be NOVELS; it is
in fact essentially as a novelist that the personage *se présente à ma pensée.* He
has such qualities of art and style and skill as may be fine and honourable ones
presumably—but he himself holds that they don't *know* his work who don't know,
who haven't felt, or guessed, or perceived, this interior thought—this special *beauty*

1. See 8 May 1898, 15 February and 16 May 1899.
1. See 4 November 1895.

(that is mainly the just word) that pervades and controls and animates them. No reviewer, no 'critic,' has dreamed of it: lovely chance for fine irony on the subject of that fraternity. *Mettons* that he mentions, after all, the fact of the thing to only one person—to *me,* say, who narrate, in my proper identity, the little episode. Say *I'm* a 'critic,' another little writer, a newspaper man. I am in relation with him, somehow—relation, admiring, inquisitive, sympathetic, mystified, sceptical—whatever it may be. *I* haven't, in the books, seen anything, but just certain pleasant and charming things—or whatever these things, merits, features, may superficially and obviously be. No, *I* haven't discovered anything. But he tells *me:* say (yes), I'm the only person he tells. (I can't go into the stages and details here—this is the barest of summaries.) That is, he tells me the fact: the *existence* of the latent beauty: oh, what it *is,* what it consists of, he doesn't tell me or tell anybody, at all. This he confides to no one, and is serenely, happily content not to confide to any one. There it is, there it is: there let it stay! His great amusement in life is really to see if any one will ever see it—if the great race of critics, above all, will ever be sufficiently perceptive for it some day to flash upon them. *'Does* it flash—is that the way it comes—in a sudden revelation?,' I ask him. My worriment, my wonderment—my little torment about what the devil it can be. My questions, my readings-over—and his answers, his indifference, his serenity, his amusement at all our densities and imbecilities: but without a shadow of *real* information. His answers only play with my curiosity—and he doesn't care. It isn't the 'esoteric meaning,' as the newspapers say: 'it's the *only* meaning, it's the very soul and core of the work.' I wonder if he's only joking—or if he's mad. I somehow don't believe he's joking (circumstances contradict it), and if he's mad, how can he have made his work so *perfect?* How can it be, in form and substance, so sane and sound? Decidedly, it must be distinguished, the work, must have the qualities of charm that are patent. That is needed to preclude the idea of madness. *Voyons,* then: after he makes his communication to me (tells me the thing is there), I, immediately, in turn, make it to another friend of mine, a young man of letters, say. He is interested in our author—he is much interested in the fact, in the revelation, imperfect as it is. Just after this the author tells me that I had better not mention or repeat what he has told me—it was for *me:* it wasn't for the vulgar world. I tell him that I *have* already repeated it to my young friend, etc.; but that I will tell him not to tell others. The Author says, 'Oh, it doesn't matter!'—he doesn't seem really to care, after all. I do tell my young friend what he has said to me—his caution about diffusing his statement; and my young friend says: 'I'm very sorry—I've already told So-and-So!' So-and-So is a young lady in whom he is much interested. 'Well, tell her to keep it to herself,' I say. He does so—he tells me afterward that she will. But he tells me also that she is much interested—she is an 'admirer,' and she wants to find out—if she can— what the reference bears upon. The young man, the 2d young man (my friend), does too—and it is *his* torment, *his* worry, *his* study of the pretty books, that I perhaps mainly represent. I have given them up—the game isn't worth the candle. It's all a bad joke and a mystification: *that's* the ground I take. But I know that he talks the matter over with his young lady, goes into it with her, wonders, worries, seeks, renounces, with her. Say *I* take the ground of our hero's madness, or mere persistent pleasantry amounting almost to madness—and that it's he who take[s] the side of the outright beauty and sanity of the work. He too is a critic— only he's the shamed one, the one sensitive to the reproach. I'm not, I don't care, I cling to my vulgar explanation: I've not been a particular admirer of the novels. My friend has always seen more in them than I do. He has his theories—he has his explanations, his clues and glimpses—he puts forward one, then another, then a third—which he successively renounces—they won't hold. The young lady had hers—which he tells me about and which break down, too. They quarrel about them—they are quite possessed with their search. Does the young man, my friend, know the author, meet him, talk with him? A point to be settled, but I think not: he *wants* to, but he wants to wait till he can really say, 'Eureka!,' and then go and submit his solution to him and get a reply: say 'Isn't *that* it?'—and have perhaps at last the great assent. Well, before this, the Author dies—and that test, that light, that disclosure, become forever inaccessible. No one knows, now—he carries the secret away with him. But (to make a long story—it's really—it must be really—of the briefest—short) my young man continues to be haunted by it. At last he lets me know—from a distance—that he has discovered it. He has, he *has*, this time—it's a revelation—it's wonderful. Or I must learn, perhaps from the young woman, that this has occurred. Yes, that's the way I'll have it! He's at a distance and *she* has heard from him. She doesn't at all know what it is—but he's to tell her. I am then devoured with curiosity and suspense. 'When is he to tell you?' 'Well, after we're married,' she replies with some embarrassment. 'You're to be married?' I have thought they had quarrelled—but it appears they have made it up. She tells me *when*—he is coming on to London (he's abroad, or in the East, or in Scotland) and it will then take place. I write to him, however, before that— I ask him to appease my curiosity. He replies that he is coming on to his wedding and will do so then. I write that I shall not be in London, alas, for it, and that he had better make me the revelation by letter. He rejoins that he can do it much better *viva voce*, and would rather so do it; and I have to rest content with that. He has specified some near time at which we *shall* be likely to meet. But we don't meet—we never meet. I leave town before he comes—and he is married in my absence. Three months later, before I get back, he is killed—by an accident. He carries away his discovery with him—save in so far as he *has*, after marriage, told it to his wife. I must KNOW that he *has* so told it. But somehow I feel it to be a thing I can't ask her and she can't tell me. There is evidently, about it, a strange mystifying uncomfortable delicacy. She never offers to satisfy me—though I meet her and she has a chance and knows how curious I am. So I have to go unsatisfied. I do so for a long time. The strange thing is that now, somehow, I feel the mystery to be a reality. I feel that the deceased wasn't mad. I almost want to marry the widow—to learn from her *de quoi*, in the name of wonder, *il s'agit*. I feel as if she might tell me if we should be married—but that she'll never tell me otherwise. But I don't marry her—I *can't*, simply for that! At last she marries some one else. I feel sure she tells *him*. I want to ask him—I hover about him— I come very near it. But I don't—I don't think it, when I come to the point, quite delicate or fair. I don't—I forbear. In the course of time—in childbirth—*she* dies. Then, after an interval, I get my chance. She is the 3d person who has carried the mystery to the grave; but she, at last will have left, in the person of her husband, a depositary. I am able to approach him, and I do so. I put the question to him, ask him if his wife didn't tell him. He stares—he's blank—he doesn't know what I'm talking about. 'So-and-So? The secret of his books—?' He looks at me as if *I* am mad. She has never told him anything: she has carried the mystery uncommunicated to the grave. x x x x x

Two little things, in relation to this, occur to me. One is the importance of my being *sure* the disclosure has been made to the wife by her 1st husband. The other is the importance of *his* having been sure he had got hold of the right thing. The only way for this would be to have made him submit his idea to the Author himself. To this end the Author's death would have *not* to precede his discovery. Say I make him get *at* the Author, with his 'discovery,' and the latter's death occurs, away from London, therefore, between that event and my ascertainment of the intended marriage. The form in which I hear of it from the girl is that her fiancé HAS submitted it to the author. *Then* the Author dies—abroad, ill, in a climate. It's *there* my young man has gone to him—is with him. All this mere suggestion—to be figured out. The thing to be REALLY brief. x x x x x

["The Figure in the Carpet," *Cosmopolis* January–February 1896; reprinted in *Embarrassments.*]

Torquay, October 28th, 1895.

I remember how Mrs. Procter[1] once said to me that, having had a long life of many troubles, sufferings, encumbrances and devastations, it was, in the evening of that life, a singular pleasure, a deeply-*felt* luxury, to her, to be able to *sit and read a book:* the mere sense of the security of it, the sense that, with all she had outlived, *nothing could now happen,* was so great within her. She had, as it were, never had that pleasure in that way or degree; and she enjoyed it afresh from day to day. I exaggerate perhaps a little her statement of her individual ecstasy—but she made the remark and it struck me very much at the time. It comes back to me now as the suggestion of the tiny little germ of a tiny little tale. The thing would be, of course, only a little picture—a little scrap of a vignette.[2] One would tell it one's self, one would have seen it, and would retain it as an impression. There would be an old, or an elderly, a person whom one would have known, would have met—in some contact giving an opportunity for observation. This old person—in the quiet waters of some final haven of rest—would manifest such joy—such touching bliss—in the very commonest immunities and securities of life—in a quiet walk, a quiet read, the civil visit of a friend or the luxury of some quite ordinary *relation,* that one would be moved to wonder what could have been the troubles of a past that give such a price to the most usual privileges of the present. What could the old party (man or woman) have been through, have suffered? This

1. Née Anne Benson Skepper (1798–1888), widow of Bryan Waller Procter (1778–1874)—the poet "Barry Cornwall"—whom she had married in 1824. She had known all the great English poets from Shelley to Browning.

2. See *Les Vieux,* 31 October and 21 December 1895; see also 29 August 1901.

remains a little suggestive mystery. The old party (the time of life a thing to determine properly) is reserved, obscure, uncommunicative about certain things—but ever so weary and ever so rested. One wonders, but one doesn't really want to know—what one is really interested in is guarding and protecting these simple joys. One watches and sympathizes, one is amused and touched, one likes to think the old party is safe for the rest of time. Then comes the little denouement. Isn't the little denouement, must it *not* only be, that some horrid danger becomes real again, some old menace or interruption comes back out of the past? The little safeties and pleasures are at an end. What I seem to see is that somebody, a fatal somebody, turns up. *Voyons:*—I seem to see something like an old fellow whose *wife* turns up. The *mot* of his present ease is that it's his wife who has been the source of the complications, the burdens that preceded. But she comes back as a repentant, reconciled, compunctious, reunited wife. She abounds in this sense—but all the more, on that account, *sein' Ruh ist hin.* She invades him still more with her compunction than with her—whatever it was of old. She has come (genuinely, but selfishly, for peace and quiet—*she* wants to read a book, etc.) but hers, somehow, puts an end to his. I note this, I see it all, I feel for him. It's the old life—in essence—back again. At last, abruptly, he disappears—he vanishes away, leaving the wife in possession. Then I see *her*—having exterminated him—given up to the same happy stillness as *he* was. She is in his chair, by his lamp, at his table: she expresses just the same quiet little joy that he did. 'It's such a luxury to just sit and read a book.' It's the same book—one I have seen *him* read. My old party, let me note, must (it seems to me) be, necessarily and essentially, of the specifically refined and distinguished order—a man of the world, absolutely, in type, a man of quality, as it were, in order to make this contentment with small joys, this happiness in the mere negative, sufficiently striking. It wouldn't *be* adequately striking in a person of very simple or common kind. The same, I suppose, is, or ought to be, true of the type of the wife. Mayn't one imagine them both *raffinés*—who have undergone a considerable loss of fortune?[3]

Names.   Wilverley—Perriam—Boel—Beaudessin—Poyle—Jerram—Stanforth—Overmore—Undermore—Overend.

Torquay, October 31st, 1895.

I was struck last evening with something that Jonathan Sturges, who had been staying here 10 days, mentioned to me: it was only 10 words, but it seemed, as usual, to catch a glimpse of a *sujet de nouvelle* in it.[1] We were talking of W.D.H. and of his having seen him during a short and interrupted stay H. had made 18 months ago in Paris—called away—back to America, when he had just come—at the end of 10 days by the news of the death—or illness—of his father. He had

---

3. See 11 May 1898, 15 February and 9 October 1899.

1. Sturges (1864–1909), Princeton graduate, was crippled in childhood by polio but led an active expatriate life in London and numbered HJ and Whistler among many friends. It was in Whistler's Paris garden that he received the advice from William Dean Howells ("W. D. H."). The *nouvelle* became *The Ambassadors.* See "Project of Novel" under "Notes for Publishers."

scarcely been in Paris, ever, in former days, and he had come there to see his domiciled and initiated son, who was at the Beaux Arts. Virtually in the evening, as it were, of life, it was all new to him: all, all, all. Sturges said he seemed sad—rather brooding; and I asked him what gave him (Sturges) that impression. 'Oh—somewhere—I forget, when I was with him—he laid his hand on my shoulder and said *à propos* of some remark of mine: "Oh, you are young, you are young—be glad of it: be glad of it and *live*. Live all you can: it's a mistake not to. It doesn't so much matter what you do—but live. This place makes it all come over me. I see it now. I haven't done so—and now I'm old. It's too late. It has gone past me—I've lost it. You have time. You are young. Live!" ' I amplify and improve a little—but that was the tone. It touches me—I can see him—I can hear him. Immediately, of course—as everything, thank God, does—it suggests a little situation. I seem to see something, of a tiny kind, springing out of it, that would take its place in the little group I should like to do of *Les Vieux*—The Old. (What should I call it in English—*Old Fellows?* No, that's trivial and common.) At any rate, it gives me the little idea of the figure of an elderly man who hasn't 'lived,' hasn't at all, in the sense of sensations, passions, impulses, pleasures— and to whom, in the presence of some great human spectacle, some great organization for the Immediate, the Agreeable, for curiosity, and experiment and perception, for Enjoyment, in a word, becomes, *sur la fin*, or toward it, sorrowfully aware. He has never really enjoyed—he has lived only for Duty and conscience— his conception of them; for pure appearances and daily tasks—lived for effort, for surrender, abstention, sacrifice. I seem to see his history, his temperament, his circumstances, his figure, his life. I don't see him as having battled with his passions—I don't see him as harassed by his temperament or as having, in the past, suspected, very much, what he was losing, what he was not doing. The alternative wasn't present to him. He may be an American—he might be an Englishman. I don't altogether like the *banal* side of the revelation of Paris—it's so obvious, so usual to make Paris the vision that opens his eyes, makes him feel his mistake. It might be London—it might be Italy—it might be the general impression of a summer in Europe—abroad. Also, it *may* be Paris. He has been a great worker, a local worker. But of what kind? I can't make him a novelist—too like W.D.H., and too generally *invraisemblable*. But I want him 'intellectual,' I want him *fine*, clever, literary almost: it deepens the irony, the tragedy. A clergyman is too obvious and *usé* and otherwise impossible. A journalist, a lawyer—these men WOULD in a manner have 'lived,' through their contact with life, with the complications and turpitudes and general vitality of mankind. A doctor—an artist too. A mere man of business—he's possible; but not of the intellectual grain that I mean. The Editor of a Magazine—that would come nearest: not at all of a newspaper. A Professor in a college would imply some knowledge of the lives of the young—though there might be a tragic effect in his seeing at the last that he hasn't even suspected what those lives might contain. (They had passed by him— he had passed them by.) He has married very young, and austerely. Happily enough, but charmlessly, and oh, so conscientiously: a wife replete with the New England conscience. But all this might be—oh, so light, so delicately summarized, so merely touched. What I seem to see is the possibility of some little illustrative action. The idea of the tale being the revolution that takes place in the poor man, the impression made on him by the particular experience, the incident in which this revolution and this impression embody themselves, is the point *à trouver.* They are determined by certain circumstances, and they produce a situation, his issue from which is the little drama. I am supposing him, I think, to have 'illustrated,' as I say, in the past, by his issue from some *other* situation, the opposite conditions, those that have determined him in the sense of the sort of life and feeling I have sketched and the memory, the consciousness of which roll over him now with force. He has sacrificed some one, some friend, some son, some younger brother, to his failure to feel, to understand, all that his new experience causes to come home to him in a wave of reaction, of compunction. He has not allowed for these things, the new things, new sources of emotion, new influences and appeals—didn't realize them at all. It was in communication with *them* that the spirit, the sense, the nature, the temperament of this victim (as now seems to him) of his old ignorance, struggled and suffered. He was wild—he was free—he was passionate; but there would have been a way of taking him. Our friend never saw it—never, never: he perceives that—ever so sadly, so bitterly, now. The young man is dead: it's all over. Was he a son, was he a ward, a younger brother—or an elder one? Points to settle: though I'm not quite sure I like the *son.* Well, my vague little fancy is that he 'comes out,' as it were (to London, to Paris—I'm afraid it *must* be Paris; if he's an American), to take some step, decide some question with regard to some one, in the sense of his old feelings and habits, and that the new influences, to state it roughly, make him act just in the opposite spirit—make him accept on the spot, with a *volte-face,* a wholly different inspiration. It is a case of some other person or persons, it is some other young life in regard to which it's a question of his interfering, rescuing, bringing home. Say he 'goes out' (partly) to look after, to bring home, some young man whom his family are anxious about, who won't *come* home, etc.—and under the operation of the change *se range du côté du jeune homme,* says to him: 'No; STAY:—*don't* come home.' Say our friend is a widower, and that the *jeune homme* is the son of a widow to whom he is engaged to be married. *She* is of the strenuous pattern—she is the reflection of his old self. She has money—she admires and approves him: 5 years have elapsed since his 1st wife's death, 10 since his own son's. He is 55. He married at 20! Displeasing the strenuous widow is a sacrifice—an injury to him. To marry her means rest and security *pour ses vieux jours.* The 'revolution' endangers immensely his situation with her. But of course my denouement is that it takes place—that he makes the sacrifice, does the thing I have, vaguely, represented him, *supra,* as doing, and loses the woman he was to marry and all the advantages attaching to her. It is too late, too late *now,* for HIM to live—but what stirs in him with a dumb passion of desire, of I don't know what, is the sense that he may have a little super-sensual hour in the vicarious freedom of another. His little drama is the administration of the touch that contributes to—that prolongs—that freedom.

[*The Ambassadors,* the *North American Review* January–December 1903; published in London and New York (1903).]

34 De Vere Gardens, November 4th, 1895.

I am thinking of trying the little *sujet de nouvelle*[1] I noted the other day at Torquay—the one on the Author's Secret—for the 1st no. of the new review, *Cosmopolis,* to which the editor has asked me to contribute; but I must make it fit neatly into 11,000 words or, in other words, into a hundred *(close)* pages of my MS. *Voyons, voyons.* x x x x x I must make 10 little chapters of 10 pages of my MS. each. So! x x x x x

I. The visit from my friend who, owing to his *empêchement* (specify) asks me to do—to oblige him—a review of the Author's new novel, which he has made himself responsible for. He has to go off—to meet the girl who subsequently figures—meet her and her mother—returning from abroad: strike—yes—the note of the appearance of the girl here. He hasn't time—I must do it; and besides, it's a chance for me. I recognize the chance—I introduce the incident, in the very 1st words of my narration—as my FIRST real or good chance: the beginning of my little success or little career. I accept; we speak a moment or two of the Author— during which out note of divergence appears—and I mention, as a coincidence, that I have accepted an invitation to go from the following Saturday to Monday down to a place in the country where it has been mentioned to me that I may meet him. 'Oh, then, you'll write handsomely—if you are going to look him in the face.—You must tell me about him.' 'Yes, I'll tell you: I *will* look him in the face!' He goes off—I write my notice—I go down to the place. But I needn't detail here, so much, the points—only broadly indicate them.

II. I report to Corvick—I communicate: I set, in a word, the ball in motion. I see Vereker again and he warns me. I repeat this to Corvick and he tells me he has told the girl. x x x x x

I have brought the little subject treated of in the foregoing to p. 68 of my MS. (Nov. 22d), and must be sharply definite as to the skeleton of the rest. I have at the most 40 pages more. But they are, thank God, enough. *These,* at the point I've reached, are the facts still to be handled:—

Corvick has gone to the East on a commission from a newspaper.

Mrs. Erme is still alive and he is not yet engaged to Gwendolen.

She tells me that he writes to her from (Bombay?) that he has 'found it.'

What is it?

She doesn't know—he hasn't told her. (He says he'll tell her 'when we're married.') (She marries to find out [?])[2] He's to stop and see Vereker at Mentone and submit his idea to him. THEN he'll tell—if it's *right*—if it proves so. I hasten to Gwendolen to learn. Yes—it's right. Vereker says so. He's *with* Vereker. 'Then what is it?' 'He says he'll tell me when we're married.' 'You're engaged?' 'We've become so—but we can't marry in my mother's lifetime.' I don't ask after her mother's health, but I wonder—just wonder—! Corvick has told me before leaving England that they're *not* engaged. I write to him—he replies, telling me to

1. This became "The Figure in the Carpet"; see 24 October 1895.
2. HJ's brackets.

wait. I am called away before his return: so I haven't the chance to see him face to face. I go to America—Vereker dies. Corvick dies 4 months after his marriage. The foregoing in 2 sections—leaving the last one for all that follows. Each to be of 12 pp. MS.

Names. Rotherfield—Fresson—Count—Delafield—Ash—Burr—Barb—Faber—Beale—Venning—Dandridge—Overmore—Balbeck—Bulbeck—Armiger—Gibelin—Beddom—Gerse—Nish—Bath—Brookenham—Fernanda ('Nanda')—Maliphant—Sneath.

December 21st, 1895, 34 De Vere Gardens.

The idea, for a scrap of a tale, on a scrap of a fantasy, of 2 persons who have constantly heard of each other, constantly been near each other, constantly *missed* each other. They have never met—though repeatedly told that they ought to know each other, etc.: the sort of thing that so often happens. They must be, I suppose, a man and a woman. At last it has been arranged—they really *are* to meet: arranged by some 3d person, the friend of each, who takes an interest in their meeting—sympathetically—officiously, blunderingly, whatever it may be: as also so often happens. But before the event one of them dies—the thing has become impossible forever. The other then comes, after death, to the survivor—so that they do meet, in spite of fate—they meet, and if necessary, they love.—They see, they know, all that would have been possible if they *had* met. It's a rather thin little fantasy—but there is something in it perhaps, for 5000 or 6000 words. There would be various ways of doing it, and it comes to me that the thing might be related by the 3d person, according to my wont when I want something—as I always do want it—intensely objective. It's the woman who's the ghost—it's the woman who comes to the man. I've spoken to them of each other—it's through me, mainly, that they know of each other. I mustn't be too much of an *entremetteur* or an *entremetteuse:* I may even have been a little reluctant or suspicious, a little jealous, even, if the mediator is a woman. If a woman tells the story she may have this jealousy of her dead friend after the latter's death. She suspects, she divines, she feels that the man, with whom she is herself more or less in love, *continues* to see the dead woman. She has thought, she has believed, he cares for *her;* but now he is sensibly detached. Or if I don't have the '3d person' narrator, what effect would one get from the impersonal form—what peculiar and characteristic, what compensating, effect *might* one get from it? I should have in this case—shouldn't I?—to represent the *post-mortem* interview? Yes—but not necessarily. I might 'impersonally' include the 3d person and his (or her) feelings—tell the thing even so from his, or her, point of view. Probably it would have to be longer so—and really 5000 words is all it deserves.[1]

x   x   x   x   x

Thus I come back, inveterately—or at any rate necessarily—to the little question of the really short thing: come back by an economic necessity.

1. Development of "The Way It Came" ("The Friends of the Friends"). See 5 February 1895 and 10 January 1896.

I can *place* 5000 words—that is the coercive fact, and I require, obviously, to be able to do this. It will help me so much to live that—really—I must make a more scientific trial of the form—I mean, of the idea of this extreme brevity. I needn't take time to make that formal declaration here: God knows I know what I mean, what I think, what I see, what I feel. My troubled mind overflows with the whole deep sense of it all—overflows with reflection and perception. The little things to do will all come to me—things of observation and reflection and fancy: life is full of them—they meet me at every turn. One thing is certain—they will come more and more the more I want them. Let them all proceed from my saturation—let them all be handed me straight by life. They'll come—they'll come: they *do* come: they have come: illustrations, examples, figures, types, expressions—I hold out my arms to them, I gather them in. À *l'oeuvre, mon bon, à l'oeuvre—roide!* x x x x x

Note, at my 1st leisure, briefly and concisely *all* the subjects for 'short' novels (80,000 to 100,000 words) I have *en tête,* and especially the 2 things that lately came to you: *The Advertiser* (magnificent, I think—[H(all) C(aine) etc.][2] and the thing suggested by what was told me the other day of the circumstances of the W. K. Vanderbilt divorce:[3] his engaging the *demi-mondaine,* in Paris, to *s'afficher* with him in order to force his virago of a wife to divorce him. I seem to see all sorts of things in that—a comedy, a little drama, of a fine colour, either theatrised or narrated: a subject, in short, if one turns it in a certain way. The way is, of course, that the husband doesn't care a straw for the *cocotte* and makes a bargain with her that is wholly independent of real intimacy. He makes her understand the facts of his situation—which is that he is in love with another woman. *Toward* that woman his wife's character and proceedings drive him; but he loves her too much to compromise her. He can't let himself be divorced on *her* account—he can on that of the *femme galante,* who has nothing—no name—to lose: a conspicuity the more, indeed, only to gain. The *femme galante* may take, of course, a tremendous, disinterested fancy to him: at any rate the thing has the germ of the *point de départ* of something—I think.

[''The Special Type,'' *Collier's Weekly* June 1900; reprinted in *The Better Sort* (1903).]

x   x   x   x   x

I was greatly struck, the other day, with Sargent's account of McKim, the American architect, given me in the train while we went together to Fairford (Wednesday, Dec. 18). I mean of his princely gallantry *(de procédés)* to women—to ladies—with whom his relations are irreproachable, etc.: the scale of it, the practical chivalry of it, etc., etc. It might be something to *do*—as very characteristically American. Do the old *grand seigneur* in a 'new bottle'—Frank H.'s cabling his

2. Thomas Henry Hall Caine (1853–1931), British author of romantic-sentimental novels. HJ's brackets.

3. William Kissam Vanderbilt I (1849–1920), grandson of Commodore Cornelius Vanderbilt, divorced his wife of twenty years in 1895 (she had been instrumental in arranging the marriage of their daughter Consuelo to the ninth Duke of Marlborough). The *''demi-mondaine''* was Nellie Neustretter of Eureka, Nevada, then established in Paris.

eloping wife £100,000, a case in point: the sort of thing which a 1000 French pens would have commemorated of the Duc de Richelieu.[4] x x x x x

Here, by the way, are the approximate or provisional labels of the *sujets de roman* that I just alluded to one's having *en tête*.

1° *La Mourante:* the girl who is dying, the young man and the girl he is engaged to.

2° *The Marriages* (what a pity I've used that name!): the Father and Daughter, with the husband of the one and the wife of the other entangled in a mutual passion, an intrigue.

3° *The Promise:* the *donnée* that I sketched (I have it all), as a 3-act play for poor E.C.[5]

4° *The Awkward Age:* to be completely ciphered out. It exists as yet only in a brief, former note and in my head—but I can produce it the moment I sit down to it—certainly with the help of my former note.

5° *The Advertiser* (Hall Caine): The idea, as I hinted it, the other night when I was dining with the former, to Colvin and Barrie[6] (it came to me on the spot roughly and vividly), strikes me as really magnificent.

6° Call it, for the moment, *The Vanderbilt Story: vide supra.*

Let me just jot down, in this remnant of a beguiled morning, 3 or 4 things that I have noted before and may identify with a small label—3 or 4 less ideas that I can put a *present* hand on in 5000 words apiece: 50 pages of my MS. The very essence of such a job is—let me with due vividness remember it—that they consist each, substantially, of a *single incident,* an incident definite, limited, sharp. I must *cultivate* the vision, the observation and notation of that—just as I must sternly master the *faire,* the little hard, fine, repeated process.

[1.] I have, to begin with, *Les Vieux*—the thing noted, at Torquay, on the memory of something said to me by Mrs. Procter.

[2.] I have the suggestion found in the Frenchman's article in the *Fortnightly Review* about the opposition of view of the *Française* and the *Anglaise* as to the responsibility incurred by a flirtation: one thinking of the compensation *owed* (where the man is really touched), the other taking the exact line of backing out. 'It's serious'—they both see—but the opposed conclusion from that premise. This seems to me *exactly* treatable in my small compass. In a correspondence—in a series of colloquies that reflect the facts—or in some other way? Shall I put the 2 men together?—or shall I put the 2 women? The law of EVERY job of this kind can only be intensely, *powerfully,* to simplify. I shall come to the treatment—the

4. Charles Follen McKim (1847–1909), leader of the neoclassical revival in architecture and member of the influential firm of McKim, Mead and White. Frank Harrison Hill (1830–1910), editor of the London *Daily News* until 1886, later with the *World.* Armand Jean du Plessis, Duc de Richelieu (1585–1642), French cardinal and statesman.
5. *La Mourante* became *The Wings of the Dove* (see 3 November 1894), *The Marriages* became *The Golden Bowl* (see 28 November 1892), and *The Promise,* sketched for Edward Compton, became *The Other House* (see 26 December 1893).
6. Sidney Colvin (1845–1927), Slade Professor of Fine Art at Cambridge and then Keeper of Prints and Drawings at the British Museum until 1912; Sir James Matthew Barrie (1860–1937), Scottish novelist and playwright.

subject, at any rate, *y est*. I can't get brevity here—or anywhere—obviously, save by some tremendous foreshortening; but that effort, so remunerative, is part of the general high challenge of the whole business. Don't I see my *biais* here, don't I see my solution, in my usual third person: the observer, the *knower,* the confidant of either the 2 women or the 2 men? The 2 women seem, decidedly, the really designated characters. That gives me the *notes,* the confidences, the reflections, the sharp, bright anecdote of some acute and clever person, some elderly woman, presumably, who was in relation with them—*devant laquelle la chose se passa. Voilà.*

3. The mother who takes the line that her daughter's husband must show her everything—the husband who never comes. (The little idea suggested by a remark of Miss Reubell.)

4. The child whose parents divorce and who makes such an extraordinary link between a succession of people. (Suggested by something mentioned to me several years ago, at dinner at the J. Bryces', by Mrs. Ashton, Mrs. Bryce's sister-in-law.)

5. The lying fine lady who *assumes* that her maid has spied on her, has read her letters—knows certain things about her doings 'because maids always do.' The figure of the maid: innocent, incapable of such tortuosity, and losing her place—*mise à la porte*—because, in a crisis of some misconduct of the mistress, she can't—*à l'improviste*—help her—save her—by acting for her as if—without explanation—she has the knowledge—the nefarious clue—which she could only have got by nefarious watching and peeping.

6. The reviewing woman who *éreinters* her friend—the man of letters who comes to see her—in the paper for which she does novels, *because she is RA-GEUSEMENT* in love with him. The publisher finds it out—it might be called *The Publisher's Story.* There must be, of course, some climax: the idea must be: '*What is the way to make her stop?*' 'Try a sweet review of her, and let her know it's yours.' 'But I hate her work.' 'Well, nevertheless, pump out something.' The novelist tries this—it has no effect.—I check myself: there may be something in the *concetto* (a very small something indeed—even for 5000 words), but it doesn't lie in that direction. *Laissons cela* till something more seems to come out of it. x x x x x [7]

December 22d. Promising H. Harland a 10,000 (a *real* 10,000) for the April *Yellow Book,* I have put my pen to the little subject of the child, the little girl, whose parents are divorced, and then each marry again, then die, leaving her divided between the 2d husband of the one and the 2d wife of the other.[1] But the thing, before I go further, requires some more ciphering out, more extraction of the subject, of the drama—if such there really *be* in it. *Voyons un peu*—what little

---

7. For *Les Vieux* see 28 and 31 October 1895 and 29 August 1901; the *Fortnightly Review* article led to "The Given Case" (see 13 May 1894); Miss Reubell's remark is noted in the entry for 4 August 1892; the fourth item, the idea for *What Maisie Knew,* echoes the entry for 12 November 1892 (and cf. 28 December 1895); the "spying maid" idea appears in 16 March 1892; *The Publisher's Story* appears in 18 November 1894 and 7 May 1898.

1. *What Maisie Knew;* see 12 November 1892.

drama *does* reside in it?—I catch it, I catch it: I seize the tail of the little latent action *qu'il recèle*. I made a mistake, above, in thinking—in speaking—of the divorced parents as 'dying': they live—the very essence of the subject is in that. Make my point of view, my *line*, the consciousness, the dim, sweet, sacred, wondering, clinging perception of the child, and one gets something like *this*. The parents become indifferent to her as soon as they cease to have her to quarrel about; then each marry again. The father *first*—it's *his* new spouse who first takes an interest in the child. But let me state it, rather [in] 8 or 10 little chapters.

I. 12½ pages about the parents.

II. 10 pages: the child's perceptions of the situation at first—its wonderings, bewilderments, then gradual clever little perception of what it must do. Boyd first takes her—his pretended arrangement of his life for it, his playing at being occupied with her and devoted to her. His talk to her about her mother—her dread and awe of going to her. Then her going—the mother's wild caresses, and her getting from the child all the father has said of her. The results of this—her behaviour on going back to her father, etc. The results don't show the *1st* time: she repeats to her father what her mother has said, as she has repeated to her mother what her father has said. Then, on her 2d visit to her mother, she takes the line of *not* telling—she gets a glimpse, in her little prematurely troubled and sharpened mind, of what she can do in the way of *peace*. This disappoints and angers her mother on the second visit—so that, with her vicious activity dropping, her mother neglects her, neglects her badly, and she is eager to return to her father. On her return she finds a governess. Or does her MOTHER get her the governess? I seem to see reasons for that. The mother hires the governess for the last three months of the visit—but under penalty of her displeasure if she goes to the other place with the child. She's to wait and take her six months later—that had been the arrangement under which she is hired. But she takes such a fancy to Maisie that she breaks the vow and goes, knowing what displeasure she incurs, and offers herself to Boyd. He is horrified, learning that she comes from his wife—from Maisie under that roof. But he relents on finding what promise she has broken, and binds her by another not to go back there. *She* gives it—her line is now, secretly, to keep the child at the father's. She falls in love with Boyd. The scene between Boyd and the governess takes place before Maisie. This is all in II.

III. Relation between Maisie and the governess. Then Maisie goes back once again to her mother, and stays there without the governess—with another, who also gets embroiled about her. Her mother *drops* her, after this third period, and she stays on—on and on. A young man comes to her father's, in the latter's absence, to see about her. He proves to be her mother's new husband. He has been put up to it—egged on by the embroiled governess—who adores the child and wants to get her back or get back *to* her. Essence of the little drama this—the strange, fatal, complicating action of the child's lovability. It occurs to me, however, that instead of making the young man come himself, outright (a little unnatural and *invraisemblable*), I had better make the 'embroiled governess'—the second, elder, plain one—come herself, hungrily, desperately, to see if the child *isn't* coming back to her mother. She has come to see Boyd Farange, but he is away. She sees *his* governess, the pretty one, my second 'heroine'; and the scene between the 2 women takes place before Maisie. The plain governess, the honest frump, *tells* of Mrs. Farange's marriage—this is the 1st they know of it. She has married Captain So-and-So—she tells who: she is abroad—it has taken place at Florence. She has written to the frump, characteristically—enclosing the portrait of her *sposo*—younger than herself, very handsome. (The 'Pretty' governess must not be very handsome—too much beauty—only a marked type.) The SPOSI *are coming home*—hence the poor woman's officious, pathetic errand. Her passion for the child—it breaks out. She catches her up, hugs her. She must be a widow—MRS. Something: she has lost her only little girl. Movement between the women precipitating the younger one's announcement of the kind of place she holds—the authority with which she speaks: she is engaged to be married to Boyd Farange.

IV. I must handle freely and handsomely the years—treat my *intervals* with art and courage; master the little secrets in regard to the expression of duration—be superior I mean, on the question of time. Maisie does go back to her mother— she sees her new stepfather—she stays a year. Her new stepfather—the Captain— attaches himself to her tenderly. Simple, good, mild chap, bullied, hustled by his wife, and not destined, as he is already sure, or at any rate definitely apprehensive, to have a child of his own: the thing he has almost predominantly married for—and not *been* married, grabbed and appropriated, by Mrs. Farange. (I must get a name, a Xtian name, for Mrs. F. early—so as not to speak of her by a *changed* surname.) It occurs to me that it will be well to make Ida have a confinement—a *very*, VERY prompt one—which is what, in its results, dashes the Captain's hope of paternity. She is awfully ill—the child dies—her convalescence is long—her attitude about another episode of the same kind unmistakable. It is during this—for him—worried and lonely time that the Captain fraternizes and foregathers with Maisie, who is as 'lonely' as himself—*délaissée* in a way that touches him. The year that she is now by way of staying with her mother is to make up for the time that Ida DIDN'T insist, antecedently to that event. It is the Captain, really, who, from his fancy for the child, carries out the rule of the time to be made up, stickles for it, puts it through. Trace as vividly as may be, *mark strongly*, the *drop*, the cynical surrender, on each side of the *real parents'* responsibility—of their sense of it and pretension *to* it, and tolerance of the trouble of it. Mark the point of the *full change*—the change that leaves only the step-parents to keep the matter up. It is, e.g., the Captain who now keeps Maisie—the Captain only. All this in section IV. Section IV must terminate with the second wife's visit to the Captain, to *get back* the child. This is their MEETING—their 1st being brought face to face over Maisie. It takes place before Maisie—EVERYTHING TAKES PLACE BEFORE MAISIE. That is a part of the essence of the thing—that, with the tenderness she inspires, the rest of the essence, the second of the golden threads of my *form*. Maisie is really more—much more—than a year with the Captain and her mother. It is as married to Boyd Farange—married now *depuis bientôt 2 ans*—that the pretty governess presents herself. She has realised, too, that she will have no children. She may have been confined (yes, that is right) and lost her little girl. Yes, yes, she *tells* that to the Captain. This 1st meeting marks practically the middle of my tale. I am not SURE, now, that it will be well for her—at the end of III—to have ANNOUNCED to the frumpy governess her engagement to

Boyd. And yet why not? When I can prepare so little, and must take such jumps, so much preparation as that may be valuable to me. *Nous verrons bien.* This relation established between the 2 step-parents evidently, at any rate, flows over into section V.

SECTION V consists, therefore, of the sharp, vivid establishment of the contact in question and of:—

(b) The second wife's second visit to the Captain to *continue* the effort to get Maisie. Ida is away—Boyd is away: this marks what has become of *their* duty. The Captain is at the seaside somewhere—in lodgings—with the child: say at Brighton. The second wife, this second time, comes down to Brighton. The frumpy governess is back again with the little girl—now 10 years old. She has come to her [in spite of everything?][2]—she clings to her: she is her only REAL guardian. Sound that note in her feeling—in her sense, her deep foreboding. She sees what is to happen between the younger pair—SHOW that she sees it.

(c) Maisie's return to her father and her stepmother.

(d) The Captain's going to see her there. *Boyd consents* to this—is jolly over it, seeing how unhappy he too is with Ida. This *rapprochement* between the 2 men takes place in the child's presence. The frumpy governess is meanwhile forbidden the house by the second wife—who is jealous and suspicious of her, has *her* vague foretaste and foreknowledge of what may happen, and an intuition of the old woman's perception of it which makes her keep her at a distance. The old woman gets in once—to express this to Maisie. That is, she formulates to the child exactly what *I* have just formulated. Everything is forumulated and formulatable to the child. May not V terminate with this formula?—leaving VI to consist virtually of the *growth* of the extraordinary relation between the step-parents as witnessed by Maisie? Yes, that is it. The formula from the frump at the end of V *facilitates* my making the child witness the phenomenon in question—prepares the mirror, the plate, on which it is represented as reflected. Therefore we have:—

VI. *(sixth)*[3] The freedom, the facility, of the step-parents together over the child. *Cela se passe chez* Boyd—since the Captain can come there. *Description of it in form of picture of the child's dim sense.* It terminates in irruption of Ida— an outbreak of jealousy. The Captain is out somewhere with Maisie in Kensington Gardens—out with her, *as brought from Boyd's house*—where they suddenly encounter Ida, who is there with a strange gentleman—strange to Maisie, but known, very well, to the Captain. Scene of jealousy from Ida to anticipate, to FORESTALL her 2d husband's (the Captain's) suspicion of her relations with the strange gentleman. The strange gentleman takes Maisie off—at Ida's request—to walk a little. That moment is, in 3 lines, described (*the gentleman* PERFECTLY SILENT—Maisie also), and the situation the child finds on their rejoining the others. VI ends up with Maisie going back to her mother,[4] who has to have her to back up the grievance she has hurled at the Captain, but she really doesn't care for it a bit, *ou* that her being there only keeps the Captain more on the premises—or *may* do so:

2. HJ's brackets.
3. The manuscript has "VI. *(sixth)*" in red ink.
4. The remainder of this sentence is surrounded by a red line in the manuscript; subsequent Roman numerals (VII–X) are underlined in red ink.

a state of affairs that doesn't suit her book, as she has her lover to receive and be with. However, the chapter terminates with the little girl's redomicilement under her mother's roof.

VII embodies:—(a) What I have surrounded with a red line just above. (b) The Captain's veto on the tattling frump. (c) The incident of Maisie being out with her stepmother—out from her mother's house—and meeting (as a counterpart of the incident of VI) her father with a strange lady, a lady strange to Maisie but known, well known, to her stepfather. The same things happen as before. There is the same scene between the 2 *sposi.* Maisie is taken off to walk a little by the strange lady—only the strange lady is extraordinarily loquacious, almost violently chatters. The *bout de scène* that, before the child, Boyd makes his wife, is a scene of *insincere jealousy*—like the scene Ida has made the Captain. But before introducing the incident I must have made it clear that the Captain has forbidden the frumpy governess his house—kept her off. Maisie knows the reason from him—knows that, to be well with Ida and get *at* the child (since Mrs. Farange no. 2 has turned her out—has banged *her* door in her face), she (the frump) has communicated to Ida her idea about the 2 step-parents. This to make Ida bring the child home, where she (the frump) may see her. She has reckoned without the Captain's divination (or knowledge *through* Ida) and resentment, which does not keep her out. He says *he* will teach Maisie.

In VIII, Ida 'bolts' with the strange little gentleman. The Captain formulates this to Maisie. He takes her to her stepmother and there she learns—through the latter's formulation—that Boyd Farange has bolted with the strange little lady.

In IX, Maisie sees her step-parents very definitively come together—unite in devotion to her. *They* will take care of her, take care of her together—they will both be to her everything she has lost. She is wonderstruck and charmed with this—she sees them *really exalted and magnificent over it;* and she accepts the prospect, tells them it's them she prefers, etc., and prepares to give herself altogether to them. Then, with—

X, The old frumpy governess arrives, intervenes, has her great scene with them, *leur dit leur fait,* grandly, vividly (puts everything into her mouth), and carries off the child, to rescue her, to save her. *She* will bring her up.

34 *D. V. G., W., January 10th, 1896.*

I am doing for Oswald Crawford[1]—in 7000 words—the little subject of the 2 people who never met in life.[2] I see it in 5 little chapters, all very, very tiny and intensely brief—with every word and every touch telling. I have only put pen to paper; but before I go further I must be crystal-clear. *Voyons un peu* what must be immitigably brought out. The salient thing, up to the death of the woman, must be the condition, the state of things, or relation between the pair, brought about by its being—there being—so often a question, a lively question of their meeting,

1. Oswald John Frederick Crawford (pen name "Jean Latouche") was editor of *Chapman's Magazine of Fiction* and the author of *Travels in Portugal* (see HJ's review in the *Nation* 21 October 1875, *LA* II, 849–52).

2. "The Way It Came," later "The Friends of the Friends"; see 5 February 1895.

and nothing ever coming of it. They perpetually *miss* each other—they are the buckets in the well. There seems a fate in it. It becomes, *de part et d'autre*, a joke (of each party) with the persons who wish to bring them together: that is (in the small space) with *me*, mainly—the interested narrator. They say, each, the same things, do the same things, feel the same things. It's a JOKE—it *becomes* one—*de part et d'autre*. They each end by declaring that it makes them too nervous, *à la fin*—and that really it won't *do*, for either, at last, to see the other: so possible a disappointment, an anticlimax, may ensue. Each knows that the other knows—each knows just how the other is affected: a certain self-consciousness and awkwardness, a certain preoccupied shyness has sprung up. So it goes. This colours the whole situation so that, necessarily (as it happens), the thing is left very much to accident. It is the *idea* that it shall be so left. It's too *serious* to arrange it in any other way. *Chance* must bring the meeting about. So it's by way of being left to chance. It's a joke, above all for *me:* that is, it's an element of the little action to perceive in the joke a little serious side that makes me say 'Tiens!' Ah, divine principle of the 'scenario!'—it seems to make that wretched little past of patience and gain glow with the meaning I've waited for! I seem to catch hold of the tail of the very central notion of my little *'cochonnerie,'* as Jusserand used to say. The LAST *empêchement* to the little meeting, the supreme one, the one that caps the climax and makes the thing 'past a joke,' *'trop fort,'* and all the rest of it, is the result of *my own act*. I prevent it, because I become conscious of a dawning jealousy. I become conscious of a dawning jealousy because something has taken place between the young man (the man of my story; perhaps he's not in his 1st youth) and myself. I was on the point of writing just above that 'something takes place just before the last failure of the 2 parties to meet—something that has a bearing n this failure.' Well, what takes place is *tout simplement* THAT: I mean that he and the narrator become 'engaged.' It's *on* her engagement that her friend, her woman-friend, wants, more than ever, to see the man who has now become the fiancé. It is this (comparative eagerness) and a vague apprehension that determines her jealousy. It makes her *prevent* the meeting when it really might have (this time) occurred. The other failures have been by accident: this one, which might have come off (the narrator sees that there would have been no accident), has failed from active interference. What do I do? I write to my fiancé not to come—that *she* can't. (She mustn't live in London—but [say][3] at Richmond.) So he doesn't come. *She* does—and she sits with me, vainly waiting for him. I don't tell *her* what I have done; but, that evening, I tell *him*. I'm ashamed of it—I'm ashamed, and I make that reparation. She, in the afternoon, has gone away in good faith, but almost painfully, quite visibly disappointed. She is not well—she is 'odd,' etc. I am struck with it. The form my reparation takes is to take him the next day straight out to see her. Is she then, as we find, dead—or only very ill—i.e., dying? The extreme brevity of my poor little form doubtless makes it indispensable that she shall be already dead. I can't devote space to what passes while she is dying, while her illness goes on. I must jump that—I must arrive (with all the little *merveilleux* of the story still to come) at what happens *after* this event.—Or rather, on second thoughts, have I got this—this last bit—

3. HJ's braclets.

all wrong? Don't I, *mustn't* I, see it, on reflection, in another way? *Voyons, voyons.* Say the narrator with her impulse of reparation (having TOLD her fiancé)—*confessed* to him—in the p.m., as I stated it just now: say she goes ALONE out to Richmond. She does this in the a.m. of the next day. She finds her friend has died that night. She goes home, with the wonder of it; and there befalls the still greater wonder of her interview with him in the afternoon. He tells her his marvellous experience of that evening—how, on going home, he has found her there. BUT that only comes out—is shaken out—in the *secousse*—of *my* announcement that she's dead—that she died at 10 o'clock that evening. Ten o'clk.—the stupefaction, the dismay, the question of the *hour,* etc. I see this—I see this: I needn't detail it here. I see what has (to his sense) happened—how she hasn't spoken, etc.—has visibly only come to see him, to let him see her: as if to say, *'Shouldn't* we, now, have liked each other?' He puts it that way to the narrator. The narrator says, utterly wonderstruck: 'Why, she was dead *then*—she was dead already.' The marvel of this, the comparison of notes. The possible doubt and question of whether it was after or before death. The ambiguity—the possibility. The view we take—the view *I* take. The effect of this view upon *me.* From here to the end, the attitude, on the subject, is mine: the return of my jealousy, the imputation of the difference that seeing her has made in *him;* the final rupture that comes entirely from ME and from my imputations and suspicions. I am jealous of the dead; I feel, or I imagine I feel, his detachment, his alienation, his coldness— and the last words of my statement are: 'He sees her—he sees her: I know he sees her!' x x x x x

The ground on which the idea is originally started and the claim made that they shall know each other is that of this extraordinary peculiarity that each have had in their pretended *(constatée),* recognized, etc., experience of having had, each of them, the premonition, on the announcement of the death of a parent—he of his mother, she of her father after death—had it at a distance, at the moment, or just before, or just after. This known, recognized, etc.—whether generally, publicly or not; at any rate by the narrator. I've had it from each—I've repeated it to each. Others—yes—have done the same. Yes, there must be—have been—sad much publicity as that: to make the needed consensus—the thing that follows them up and amuses and haunts them—the 'point' of the 1st ½ of the *morceau.* If instead of beginning the thing as I began it yesterday I give my first 10 (CLOSE ten) pages to a summary statement of this just-mentioned hearsay-business between them, and how it went on for long, each knowing and knowing the other knows, etc.— then I have my *last* 10 (all of premised closeness) for the state of mind, the imputations, suspicions, interpretations, etc., of the narrator—as a climax. That leaves me thirty for the rest: say, roughly 10 of these for the engagement and what surrounds it relative to *her.* But I've only to reflect to see that under this latter head must come in—then and there—the question of the last occasion for meeting. Perhaps I must make *10* little chapters. Try it so: each of 25 close pages. Let us see what this gives. But isn't, on the other hand, the best way to do so to see first what *five* give? FIRST. The statement of the peculiarity of the pair, and the way in which, for 3 or 4 years, it was followed by their dodging, missing, failing. SECOND. The narrator's engagement. Her jealousy. The day the 2d woman comes, when she (the narrator) has put off the man. THIRD. Her compunction, her confession to the man. Her going to Richmond. Her return with the news—with a certain relief. Her seeing her fiancé. FOURTH. His story to her. The recrudescence of her jealousy. FIFTH. Their going on with their engagement—her wonder and *malaise* about him. Then its coming over her—the *explanation's* coming over her (of what she sees). Her imputation. The rupture. Now let me try the little subdivisions into smaller fractions—a series of tenths.

1–10. 1st. The 2 persons and their story.

10–16. 2d. The long, odd frustration of their encounter.

16–20. 3d. The engagement. The others to meet because of it. The nearing of the day—my jealousy. I'm engaged—if now at the last moment something should intervene! I will—putting him off.

20–25. 4th. Her visit—her waiting—my dissimulation—her departure.

25–30. 5th. My compunction, my confession—scene with him—pendant to preceding.

30–35. 6th. My going to Richmond. What I learn there; and my return with the news—with a certain relief.

35–40.[4] 7th. My scene with him—his revelation. My stupefaction.

8th. The ambiguity—the inquiry (mine). The return of my jealousy.

9th. Our approaching marriage—my theory—my suspicions—my imputations.

10th. The rupture. He goes on, unmarried, for years. Then I make up to him (?)—seek a reconciliation. *Il s'y soustrait par la mort* (?).

34 D. V. G., W., February 13th, '96.

R. U. Johnson's letter to me the other day, returning my little paper on Dumas[1] as shocking to their prudery, strikes me as yielding the germ of a lovely little ironic, satiric tale—of the series of *small* things on the life and experiences of men of letters, the group of the little 'literary' tales. Isn't there an exquisite little subject in his sentence about their calculation that my article on A.D. would have been unobjectionable through being merely personal? It's the beauty of that, when one thinks of it, that is suggestive and *qui paraît se prêter* to the ironic representation of some illustrative little action—little action illustrative of the whole loathsomely prurient and humbugging business. The wondrous matter is their conception, their representation of their public—its ineffable sneakingness and baseness. Oh, the whole thing *does* open up as a *donnée!* Their hope that one would have given a 'personal' account of a distinguished man, a mere brief, reserved, simply intelligible statement of the subject matter [of] whose work is too scandalous to print. They want to *seem* to deal with him because he is famous—and he is famous because he wrote certain things which they won't for the world have intelligibly mentioned. So they desire the supreme though clap-trap tribute of an *intimate* picture, without even the courage of saying on what ground they desire any

4. These seven sets of page numbers (from 1–10 to 35–40) are underlined in red ink in the manuscript.

1. Robert Underwood Johnson (1853–1937) was editor of *Century Magazine*. The rejected article on Alexandre Dumas *fils* appeared in the *Boston Herald* and the *New York Herald* in February and in the *New Review* in March 1896; it was reprinted in *Notes on Novelists* (1914). See *Life* 280–81.

mention of him at all. One must figure out a little story in which that *bêtise* is presented. There must be the opposition—embodied in 2 young men, the serious, intelligent youth who, *à propos* of a defunct great, fine, author, makes an admirable little study or statement; and the other fellow who, canny, knowing, vulgar, having the instinct of journalistic vulgarity, doesn't say a valuable thing, but goes in for superficial gossip and twaddle. The success of the latter, the failure of the former. The whole thing must of course reside in some little objective, concrete, DRAMA—which I must cipher out. This is a mere bald hint. I seem to see something like the DAUGHTER of the great defunct (who has only come up, say, into *vulgar* recognition, after, or at the moment of, his death). Don't I see a furious magazine-hunt, newspaper-hunt for a PORTRAIT, and the 2 men, the 2 attitudes, presented to, confronted with HER—the clear, loyal, ardent daughter—over the question of the obtention of the photog. for engraving—publishing. The story, this time, not told in the 1st person—but presented from outside.—There has never been but that sole photog. x x x x x

["John Delavoy," *Cosmopolis* January–February 1898; reprinted in *The Soft Side*.]

February 13th, '96. I am pressingly face to face with the FINISH, for the *Atlantic,* of *The Old Things,* as the *House Beautiful* seems now destined, better, to be called.[2] I must cipher out here, to the last fraction, my last chapters and pages. As usual I am crowded—my first two-thirds are too developed: my third third bursts my space or is well nigh squeezed and mutilated to death in it. But that is my problem. Let me state first, broadly, what I have now to show. The crude *essence* of what I have to show is this: that Mrs. Gereth sends back the things, that the marriage of Owen and Mona then takes place and that after the treasures are triumphantly relodged at Poynton the house takes fire and burns down before Fleda's eyes. Those are the bare facts. *Voyons un peu les détails.* Mrs. Gereth surrenders the things partly because she believes—has reason to—that Fleda will eventually come into them. But that calculation won't—doesn't—appear a sufficient motive: she must have another to strengthen it. She surrenders them therefore, furthermore, because she appears to see that the knowledge of their being back again at Poynton, as an incentive, a heritage, a reward, a future (settled there again immutably, this time), will operate to make Fleda do what she has so passionately appealed to her to do—get Mona away from Owen. She, Mrs. G., is seeing if Mona WON'T break. She does at first what the end of X shows her as doing—she keeps on the things as she threatens. XI must begin, I think, this way. It is that same evening.

FLEDA: 'Well, then what answer am I to write Mr. Owen?'
MRS. G.: 'Write him to come up to town to meet you there.'
FLEDA: 'For what purpose?'
MRS. GERETH: 'For any purpose you like!'
She sets the girl on him—cynically, almost, or indecently (making her feel AGAIN how little account—in the way of fine respect—she makes of her. Touch

2. This and the following two entries (19 February and 30 March) complete the notes for *The Spoils of Poynton.*

that, Mrs. G.'s unconscious brutality and immorality, briefly and finely). She presses Fleda—yes—upon him: would ALMOST like her, in London, to give herself up to him. She has a vision of a day with him there as 'fetching' him—IN SPITE of Fleda's fine fit about the young man's not caring for her. *She'll* see, Mrs. G. will, if he won't care. The very *essence* of this turn of the story is that the escape of the girl's 'secret,' the revelation to Mrs. G. that she loves Owen, completely alters (in a manner still for the better—as regards at least the mother's attitude) the relations of the two women. It develops them further—develops Mrs. Gereth's feeling *for* Fleda—though not Fleda's (with all her dimnesses and delicacies) for her pushing, urging, overwhelming, hinting, suggesting friend. It is on this basis of her 'love' that Mrs. G. now extravagantly handles her. She is free with her on it, bold, frank, urgent, humorous, cynical with her on it, beyond what Fleda's fineness enjoys. She alludes perpetually, wonderingly, *admiringly* to it—all the while—attributing to her a FIERCER kind of sentiment (judging by herself) than Fleda's sacrificial exaltation really *is*—making her wince and draw back in this flood of familiarity. At the same time I catch for her, here, in this connection—ADMIRABLY, I think—a prime element of my denouement. Fleda is left 'sick' at the end of X by her companion's threatened postponement of the surrender—but that only spurs her to renewed, to confirmed, action and endeavour. It is an *idée fixe* with her that she shall serve Owen—bring about the disgorgement. She becomes hereby capable of lending herself *in appearance* to Mrs. G.'s inflamed view of her possible effect on Owen and routing of Mona. The thing she still cherishes is Owen's secret (his shy, barely revealed feeling for her); everything else has been blown upon and she is willing to accept that condition of things and *use* it as far as she can. What I see is, here, that she MUST have one more personal meeting with Owen. It is the last time she sees him. She must go up to town—with a 'subtle' appearance of profiting by Mrs. Gereth's directions and injunctions and suggestions—she must go up to town and have, somehow and somewhere, an hour with him. Say at her father's in West Kensington. I just suggest to myself that. If I can from this point on only clarify this to the SCENIC intensity, brevity, beauty—make it march as straight as a pure little dramatic action—I shall, I think, really score. What Fleda writes to Owen after that opening bit of dialogue with Mrs. G. is that, 1st, he is to hold on, that it's difficult, but that she is helping him; and that 2d, she will come and meet him in town. It comes to me that her meeting with him in town must be *une scène de passion*—yes, I must give my readers that. Don't I get a glimpse, this way, of the real and innermost mechanism of my end? Fleda breaks down—lets Owen see she loves him. It is all *covert*—and delicate and exquisite: she adjures him to do his literal duty to Mona. They arrive at some definite and sincere agreement about this. That is the ground, the *fond,* the deep ground TONE of their scene. It must be for MONA to break—only for Mona. *He* mustn't—by all that's honourable—do it if she *doesn't*. He agrees to this—he sees it, feels it, understands it, gives her his word on it.

'But she WILL break if mamma doesn't send back the things. Therefore she mustn't NOW,' says Owen. Fleda's *aveu* has changed all.

'You mustn't say that—you mustn't. You so must do your part—impeccably. I've worked your mother up to it.'

'Very good—leave it so. But she won't—she WON'T!' says Owen jubilantly.

What I have my glimpse of as my *right* issue is that even while they are talking, as it were, Mrs. Gereth DOES. She does it because, 1st: she has a visit from Mrs. Brigstock in which she reads a virtual revelation that the marriage is off; and 2d: she does it to fetch Fleda. To make these things possible I must represent the meeting between Owen and Fleda as an incident of an ABSENCE that Fleda makes from Ricks. She goes up to town for a week—goes to her father, goes to escape Mrs. G.'s hounding on, AND to prove to Mrs. G. that she *will* go at Owen in the sense *she* (Mrs. G.) pleads for. So I have roughly something like this.

XI. The new situation at Ricks between the 2 women, on the basis of Fleda's *aveu*. Fleda's attitude on this new footing, and the letter she 1st writes to Owen. It tells him to hold on: she is serving him—it is difficult—he must be patient. She *1st declines* Mrs. G.'s suggestion about meeting him—then at last (after a *fortnight* [?][3]) she turns, changes, can't stand it at Ricks, pleads that she must go up to town. She goes with Mrs. G.'s high approbation. What Mrs. G. sees in it.

XII. Her meeting with Owen in town.

XIII. Her meeting, their meeting, with Mrs. B.

XIV. Her return to Ricks to find everything gone. The last have just left. Mrs. Gereth has ACTED. She shows WHY. Fleda is partly prepared. There has appeared that a.m. in the *Morning Post* an announcement that the marriage, etc., will not take place. Then she describes Mrs. B.'s visit—a stupid frightened visit—*to complain of Fleda*. For it comes to me that they must have had in London—Owen and Fleda—an encounter with Mrs. B. SHE COMES TO SEE FLEDA—for news of Mrs. G.'s intentions and she finds Owen there. As an old acquaintance—her hostess, in Chap. I, at Waterbath, she knows her whereabouts or address. Yes—SHE COMES TO COMPLAIN. That encourages and determines Mrs. G.—she will, I have said, make it sure, 'fetch' Fleda and act on her. There she is—in the nudity of Ricks; but the news in the *Morning Post* rejoices her; and though Fleda, NOW THAT THE THINGS ARE GONE BACK, practically has her doubts and fears *(which she doesn't communicate)* the two women have together, an hour, a week of happiness and hope, *vis-à-vis* of the future. FLEDA MUST NOW HAVE LET OUT OWEN'S SECRET.

XV. The news that the marriage has taken place. This must (with other indispensable things) be a chapter by itself. They wait—the 2 women, first—for Owen to come down—almost immediately to propose for Fleda. The situation altered again—by a further shift—(I mean by Fleda's *aveu*, now, of Owen's 'caring for her') in a degree equivalent to that in which it has been altered *in X* by her *aveu* of her caring for him. They wait, they wait. Fleda tells Mrs. G. of Owen's offer to her of something from Poynton—anything: any small thing she can pick out. She rejoices: she says there is something at Ricks—the Maltese Cross. She will have THAT. [*It occurs to me that she had better not go back to Ricks—but that Mrs. G. comes up to town. The house is despoiled—the packers have been at it. Fleda has been on the POINT of going when she arrives. She learns from her that everything has gone—including the Maltese cross. She arrives the evening of the day the M.P. gives the news of the rupture. She stays at an hotel. Owen is at*

---

3. HJ's brackets.

Poynton.]⁴ It is thus in London that the news comes to them together of the marriage HAVING taken place. It comes at the end of about 10 days. Mrs. G. then (her *state*, just Heaven, her condition) determines to go abroad. But she hears the young couple are going. LAST CHAPTER.—Fleda goes down to rescue the Maltese cross and finds the house in flames—or already burnt down to the ground.

February 19th, 1896.

I shall push (D. V.) bravely through *The Old Things;* but I must, a little, look into the matter of Fleda's second meeting with Owen in London, and Mrs. Brigstock's finding them together. *Il me faut en tirer* everything—especially in the way of beauty—it can possibly give. It *can* give, surely, some little *scène de passion;* but I want also, from this point on, the whole thing closely and admirably *mouvementé.* It must be unmitigatedly objective narration—unarrested drama. It must be in a word a close little march of cause and effect. Fleda is a week in London without anything happening. Then Owen comes to West Kensington. He comes because his mother has let him know she is there. Fleda immediately challenges him—and he gives her that reason. His mother has written to him that Fleda has come up and has something to ask him on her behalf. He tells Fleda this. He has come to see *what* she has to ask him. She, painfully disconcerted, thinks Mrs. G. has been capable of meaning that she (Fleda) shall communicate to Owen *her* (Mrs. G.'s) idea. She is revolted—but Owen gives her a clue—in *his* having, as he shows, taken for granted what his mother *does* mean by Fleda's errand. Fleda actively CHALLENGES him on this—finds out instantly, before she lets him go further, as it were, what he has thus assumed—assures herself in other words that what she has *first* feared is NOT the case—that Mrs. Gereth has not put him up to the idea that she is in love with him. She actually cross-questions him about this; and his answers show—clearly enough—that Mrs. G. has *not* gone so far—that she has been still AFRAID to. Fleda *breathes,* at this—feels more free to receive him. Then *his* communicated vision of what his mother HAS *entendu* by her message gives her the cue for a basis to let him stay a little without her giving herself away by *emotion* of any sort. WHAT Owen has assumed is that his mother has commissioned her to ask him, for her, whether if she engages to send back the things he will break with Mona—on the basis that Mona's delay, Mona's WAITING, seems obviously to have suggested the reality of. Besides, nothing is more natural than that he should *rush* to Fleda for more news than her note and her silence have given, of *où ils en sont, tous,* in the interminable transactions—of *où il en est, lui,* as to what he may really hope. She has been 'working for him,' she has said: 'Well then, has nothing at all been done?' His mother's note has sent him to Fleda to hear what *has* been done. It is of the essence—or at least of the necessity—of this scene, that Fleda shall with real directness question him. She didn't talk of Mona before—she talks of her NOW. She questions him straight—as he questions her. He asks her what has happened, on her side, since their hour together at Ricks—she asks him what has happened on *his*. What does Owen tell her?—Her questions must DRAW OUT what he tells her. He must be categoric. So, on *her* side, to meet and satisfy *him*, HER information must be. What *has* he,

---

4. This passage is bracketed and underlined in red ink in the manuscript.

then, to tell her? What has she to tell *him?* He has to tell her that they are still waiting—that Mona is—and he must speak of that young woman more plainly, as it were, than Fleda has let him do at Ricks. He must speak very plainly indeed. He must tell the extreme and, to him, humiliating tension of the things not coming. AT THE SAME TIME HE MUST let her know that if they DON'T come he is free, he is hers. He must tell her that he hasn't seen Mona for a fortnight—but that he has had to describe to her—*had* described to her fully his scene with Fleda at Ricks, every detail of that visit. Mona knows therefore that he is dealing with Fleda—that Fleda has absolute *charge* of their affairs. This knowledge is part of the tension—of his present trouble and embarrassment and worry. He *must* tell her all—he *tells* her all, every scrap. I mustn't interrupt it too much with elucidations or it will be interminable. IT MUST BE AS STRAIGHT AS A PLAY—that is the only way to do. Ah, *mon bon,* make *this, here,* justify, crown, in its little degree, the long years and pains, the acquired mastery of scenic presentation. What I am looking for is my joint, my hinge, for making the scene between them pass, at a given point, into passion, into pain, into their facing together the truth. Some point that it logically reaches must DETERMINE the passage. I want to give Fleda her little hour. She can only *get* it if Owen fully comes out. Owen can only fully come out if he sees what is really in her. He must offer to give up Mona for her—and she must utterly refuse that. What her response IS is that she will take him if Mona really breaks. Yes, here I get my evolution don't I?—an understanding between them dependent on the things not coming. The difference is now, with the other scene (at Ricks), that they are *really*—morally—face to face and that they *speak* of it all. But *voyons, voyons,* I must be utterly crystalline and complete, and my *charpente* must be of steel. What must be thrown up to the surface is the coming back, through Owen, of Mrs. Gereth's OFFER of Fleda at Poynton. Owen has understood it since—*lived* on it—and it all is *in* him now. Thus it is a prime necessity that Mrs. G.'s attitude shall be absolutely—NOW—recognized between them. Owen must KNOW, from Fleda—must get it out of her, that his mother WILL absolutely surrender if he'll marry Fleda. Now it comes to me, in connection and accordance with this, that I must separate this London episode into 2 chapters, 2 occasions: making the 1st culminate in the arrival of Mrs. Brigstock at West Kensington. She then and there takes Owen away with her. She has come to get information and satisfaction from Fleda. She knows what Mona knows—that Fleda has charge of Owen's case *auprès de sa mère.* Owen, moreover, must have told Fleda that he has told Mona (by letter) of his having learned from Mrs. G. that she, Fleda, is in town. This is how Mrs. Brigstock knows it. She has more faith in the girl than her daughter has; and she comes to say: 'Do you realise this hideous deadlock?' Then she finds her daughter's worst suspicions and her jealousies confirmed, by what she seems to have surprised between the young couple upon whom she comes in. Owen must have told Fleda definitely that Mona is jealous. That is the prompt hinge or joint of his fuller frankness. But what I want to mark just here is the evolution of the second chapter of the pair. *This* is the chapter of passion—determined by Mrs. B.'s intervention. She has made him a scene of jealousy. By the chapter of 'passion' I mean the scene of Fleda's *aveux.* I don't see what it can do but take place the next day. Owen comes back to tell her what has happened between Mrs. Brigstock and himself. HE DOESN'T KNOW *she has made* up her mind to go straight down to Ricks. What overwhelms me, however, is the reflection that I have almost no space. FORTY PAGES of small (my smallest) penmanship[1] (like this) must do it all. There can be almost no dialogue at all. This is an iron law. It is absolute. I can squeeze *what* I can into 40 pp.; but I can't have a line more. Therefore in XIII, at least, it must be pure, dense, summarized narration. How can I bring in Mrs. Brigstock, in the tiny space, if it isn't? But above all what I must fix is what is the basis of emotion on which the 2d meeting between Owen and Fleda takes place? They feel that the situation has altered by Mrs. B.'s intervention. MONA WILL BREAK. Fleda surrenders herself—she tells him that she will marry him if Mona does break. On this they get their little duet. It is their hour of illusion—it is their fool's paradise. But it is indispensable to make clear that Fleda won't listen to anything but freedom by Mona's rupture; and therefore to have made clear antecedently exactly what Mona's actual attitude IS—at the point the affair has reached. Mona—*voyons*—must have given an *ultimatum*—a date: if the things are not sent back by such and such a day she *will* break. This day is near at hand. Mrs. Brigstock has been ANGRY—therefore she will be angering Mona by the description of how she found the pair together in West Kensington. Fleda's *aveux* are all qualified—saddened and refined, and made *beautiful*, by the sense of the IMPOSSIBLE—the sense of the infinite improbability of Mona's not really hanging on—and by the perfectly firm and definite ground she takes on the absolute demand of Owen's honour that he shall go on with Mona if she DOESN'T break.

March 30th, 1896.

I am face to face now with my last part of *The Old Things,* and I must *(D.V.)* put it through with the aid of every drop that can be squeezed from it. It will take 10 days of real application—and then I shall have to get straight at the 65,000 for Clement Shorter.[1] x x x x x

What I have, here, is that, in XVIII, Fleda perceives what it is that Mrs. Gereth has done and why she has done it: the full proportions of the bribe, the bid, the pressure of her friend's confidence. I must do it all in 3 chapters of 35 pages each. In XVIII the impression on Fleda, the overwhelmedness, the sense that everything is lost, and her confession of everything to Mrs. Gereth—their complete intimacy and exchange of all emotion and explanation over the matter. I see the whole instalment as *between* them—but this chapter as especially between them. They have it out together as it were—they are more face to face than they have ever been. What they are together, face to face with, is the question of what Owen will have done—Fleda lets Mrs. Gereth see that *she* believes it's too late, believes that Mona holds him. Mrs. Gereth denounces him with passion—denounces him for a milksop and a muff, declares that he's less than a man and that she's horribly ashamed of him. Fleda defends him, and the chapter (18) which ought, after all,

1. HJ has written "penmanship" about half the size of his usual script in this passage.

1. Clement King Shorter (1857–1926) was editor from 1891 to 1900 of the *Illustrated London News,* which published the longer-than-65,000-word *The Other House.* See 26 December 1893.

to be of 3000 words at most, terminates on their suspense. What I am asking myself is whether I bring back Owen at all. I am not well this a.m. and still shaky from a sick cold, a small assault of influenza; though convalescent, I'm not quite in my *assiette* and must puzzle my little problem out here with a mild patience and a considerable imperfection. But patience and courage—through endless small botherations and interruptions—will see me through—and I have only to *me cramponner*—and add word to word. *Se cramponner* and add word to word, is the endless and eternal receipt. *Owen is married*—that's what has happened; that is what I have to deal with in 19 and 20. HOW do I deal with it? How is the revelation made to the 2 women? It seems to me indispensable that OWEN should NOT come back. That's impossible—absolutely, and gives me ½ a dozen impossibilities and *gaucheries* of every kind. The whole thing *must* be between the two women, and the little problem of art is, finely, inspiringly, keeping it between them, to make it palpitate, make it close and dramatic and full to the very end. Little by little, as I press, as I ponder, it seems to come to me, the manner of my denouement—it seems to fall into its proportions and to *compose*. I see *4* little chapters, rather, of 25 pages each. I think, at any rate, I see Fleda return to Maggie's at the end of XVIII. There, after 2 or 3 days, Mrs. Gereth comes to her. Yes, Mrs. Gereth must *see* her there. This gives me the manner of my revelation to Fleda— it is Mrs. Gereth who makes it. Mrs. Gereth has had it herself from Owen: HE HAS COME TO HER IN TOWN TO THANK HER FOR WHAT SHE HAS DONE: he has been at Poynton and seen the things restored. Yes, that is it. That has clinched Mona, and they have been married at the registrar's on the spot. This scene of reproduction of these occurrences takes place between Mrs. G. and Fleda at Maggie's.

The Vicarage, Rye, September 22d, 1896.[1]

I've brought my little history of 'Maisie' to the point at which I ought to be able to go on very straight with it,[2] the point at which the child comes back to her father and the domesticated Miss Overmore *after* her 1st period with Mrs. Wix at her mother's. The relations between Miss Overmore and Beale exist—she is his mistress. This is my V, I find, and it must include the *prolongation* of Maisie's stay and the visit of Mrs. Wix as noted *supra*. x x x x x

34 De Vere Gardens, October 26th.

I have brought this little matter of Maisie to a point at which a really detailed scenario of the rest is indispensable for a straight and sure advance to the end. Let me not, just Heaven—not, God knows, that I *incline* to!—slacken in my deep observance of this strong and beneficent method—this intensely structural, in-

---

1. The six-month hiatus in this journal may be accounted for by HJ's commitment to finishing *The Spoils of Poynton*, which began serialization in April, and *The Other House*, which began in July. In the midst of this he experienced the first serious attacks of the writer's cramp that would lead to his decision to dictate his work directly to a typist.

2. This and the following entry (26 October) complete the notes for *What Maisie Knew*.

tensely hinged and jointed preliminary frame. In proportion as this frame is vague do I directly pay for the vagueness; in proportion as it is full and finished do I gain, do I rejoice in the strength. Sir Claude—in my VIII—has come for the child to Mrs. Beale and taken her to her mother's. What then is the function and office of my IX? To develop the relation between Maisie and Sir Claude and, through her, between him and Mrs. Beale. It must picture a little Ida's *intérieur*—poor Sir Claude's relation to *her*—her own relation to Maisie, etc. She's very much in love with Sir Claude. She mustn't be too monstrous about Maisie—she must welcome her at 1st. Mrs. Wix is there—Mrs. Wix must explain things to the child. She adores—they BOTH adore—Sir Claude. He must be very nice, very charming to Maisie, but he must get a little tired of her. As the whole thing is an action, so the little chapter is its little *piece* of the action; and to what point must the latter be brought by it? *Voyons, voyons.* Don't I best see the whole thing reflected in the talk, the confidences, the intercourse of Mrs. Wix? Something very pretty may be made of this—her going a little further and further, in the way of communication, of 'crudity,' with the child than her own old dingy decencies, her old-fashioned conscience quite warrants—her helpless pathetic sighs at what she *has*, perforce, to tell her, at what Maisie *already* has seen and learnt—so that *she* doesn't make her any more initiated—any 'worse': etc., etc., and thus serves as a sort of a dim, crooked little reflector of the conditions that I desire to present on the part of the others. The rest of my story—*voyons*—consists of the sharp notation, at a series of moments, of these conditions. Each little chapter *is*, thereby, a moment, a stage. What is this IX, then, the moment, the stage, *of?* Well, of a more *presented*, a more visible *cynisme* on the part of everybody. But what *step* does the action take in it? *That of Sir C.'s detachment from Ida—Mrs. Beale's from Beale—* OVER the little opportunity and pretext of Maisie. Furthermore the distinct indifferent parental surrender of Maisie. Beale has 'surrendered' her practically in VIII— her mother, getting her back through Sir Claude, and putting up with her, to please him, at 1st (exhibit this through Mrs. Wix, to the child), her mother breaks down and resents her presence—or rather resents Beale's shirking—at the last. Yes, I *see* thus, I think, my little *act* of my little drama here. Ah, this *divine* conception of one's little masses and periods in the scenic light—as rounded ACTS; this patient, pious, nobly 'vindictive'[1] application of the scenic philosophy and method—I feel as if it still (above *all*, YET) had a great deal to give me, and might carry me as far as I dream! God knows how far—into the flushed, dying day—*that* is! *De part et d'autre* Maisie has become a bore to her parents—with Mrs. Wix to help to prove it. They must still hate each other, and Ida must be furiously jealous—of Mrs. Beale. Beale is more indifferent, but he won't (if he can help it) have back Maisie. What my IX brings me to is the coming together of Sir Claude and Mrs. B. on the basis of '*What* the devil are they to do with the child?' Sir Claude says that Ida at last demands that Beale shall do, again, his turn; Mrs. Beale says that her husband is tremendously recalcitrant. Then they are *together*—with the child on their hands. *They* have a moment together, to this effect—a moment which seems to me to be the right climax of my IX. I must

---

1. HJ corrects this to "vindicating" in a note at the top of the manuscript page.

enjamber my period—my time for the child with her mother—from the 1st: hold out my cup—of this year—and then pour my little chapter—express my little act—into it. It must 'transpire' that Claude's visit to Mrs. Beale, his snatch at Maisie, has been 'unbeknown' to Ida. This has been his little way of doing it— quite sincere and generous and really tender to the child—in his pretty, pleasant, weak, bullied, finally disgusted nature—disgusted, of course, with Ida. Ida refuses to see Maisie at first—and Mrs. W. puts her *au courant.* Then Ida's relenting and what Maisie does see—the painted Idol, the sharp, showy, fiercely questioning mamma. She 'gets it out' of Maisie—the scene at Mrs. Beale's. It's the way it has been done—his going there to that woman—that she resents. But to the child she is at first pretentiously endearing. She must, however, take Sir Claude AWAY a great deal at 1st—through her absorption in him—her passion for him. He re- sents her neglect of her child and makes up for it to the little girl: comes up to the nursery or schoolroom, rather, to see her, charms Mrs. Wix more and more (she's in love with him), braves ridicule by going out with them when he can, taking them to the theatre, etc. Then comes the transition, the change. Ida be- comes unfaithful. Beale becomes unfaithful. Sir Claude and Mrs. Beale come together on it and on 'What's to be done with Maisie?' I seem to see that I must keep Mrs. Beale AWAY for a year. I show it through Mrs. W.'s presentation of it to the child. Mrs. Wix shows Maisie that it's impossible she should come. Maisie knows fully how jealous her mother is of her (Mrs. B.). So there's an interval after the beginning, that I have shown in VIII, of the relations between Mrs. Beale and Sir Claude. The climax of the act, then, the *resumption* of them, the confron- tation of the pair (at Brighton?), the 'Will *you* take her?' the 'Can't *you* keep her?' etc. They must have been, before this, in correspondence—toward the end of the year—ABOUT her. Mrs. Wix *clutches* her. But Sir Claude, in spite of Mrs. Wix, and not wishing in the least to pain her, but *having* to act, to do something, and wishing to see again—for Maisie's sake—Mrs. Beale, in whose tenderness for her he *believes*—Claude *does act,* takes her off alone, takes her down to Brighton.

X.

What then does my X give me? It gives me primarily 2 things: one of them that Maisie *goes* back to her father's; the other that I get, till the end, rid of Mrs. Wix. I *must* get rid of Mrs. W., to give effect to her return *at* the end, when everything else has failed. And I must replace Maisie at her father's as the only possible basis for the carrying on of the intrigue between her step-parents. Claude can go there—Mrs. Beale could never go to Ida's. Claude is now Mrs. Beale's lover, and it is in this X that I must make the scene in Kensington Gardens occur—the outbreak of 'jealousy' on Ida's part when she—being there with a lover of her own—meets her husband and her daughter. I have sketched this scene *supra*— and here refer myself to it. It must *begin* my X—for the little picture of Sir Claude's *fréquentation* of Beale's house must come *after* it—resting *upon* it. Beale is constantly away—after *his* woman; and this X must contain a passage between him and Maisie. But what's to be its climax? That of the chapter—this passage of the child with her father? Or must that come AFTER the pendant-scene to the foregoing—the scene of Maisie's being out with Mrs. Beale and meeting Beale with a strange lady as, out with Sir Claude, she has *met* Ida with a strange gentleman?[2]

2. Houghton Journal V ends here. The remainder of this entry begins VI and is introduced by HJ's explanatory note, (*"continuation . . . gilt line."*).

1896–1909

This notebook (Houghton Journal VI, 26 October 1896 to 10 February 1909), $7\frac{1}{2}''$ x $9''$, has wine marbled covers trimmed in black, wine marbled endpapers, 208 lined pages with marbled edges, of which 154 are written in black ink, one, the last page of the entry for 7 May 1898, in red, and the remainder blank.

The notebook reflects HJ's mental fertility at the peak of his artistic career, when he is involved with his turn-of-the-century writings. After 1901 there is a marked thinning out before the last entry in 1909. The second American Journal and most of the notes for "London Town," however, help to give some suggestions of his activity during that period. The text here appends the previously unpublished entry for 3 August 1909, which appears at the end of Houghton Journal II, the first American Journal.

(continuation of note on Maisie *of Oct. 26th, 1896, from last page of black covered book with gilt line.)*[1] I think it *must* come after XI (brief), must consist of this second episode and the passage between the child and her father. The latter, it seems to me, can really be *fine* in its picture of the brutality of Beale's cynicism and baseness. It prepares for the 'bolt' and it is the climax of the little chapter. I must now *leave* Maisie under his roof—I can't take her back again to her mother's. But do we *see* Ida again?—after the scene of the meeting? I *think* so—I think I can get an effect from it. Yes, Maisie has her passage with her father—she has her passage with her mother. Then if the former, following the *second* meeting, forms the climax of XI, the latter must be the *beginning* of XII. I imag-

---

1. This explanatory parenthesis is underlined in red in the manuscript.

ine Ida coming—oh yes, oh yes, frankly, brazenly, to see the child *at* Beale's to tell her that—well, she's weary of the struggle—she surrenders her to her father. She is strange—she cries, she lies, she hugs her as she used to do of old—and she disappears. This is my 1st half of XII. The next thing Maisie 'knows' is that her mother has 'bolted.' Sir Claude arrives at her father's, where she is, with this news for Mrs. Beale. He is a 'free man,' but they greet the news as a supreme trick she has played Beale—about the child; unfitting herself—by her act—for further bother about it. Sir Claude, on this, asks Maisie if she will come now and live—stay with him: he will do her mother's turn for her. She must have had, over her mother's flight, a burst of grief and shame—her *one* EXPRESSION of perceptive violence: she cries, she breaks down. Her *one* break down. This *moves* Sir Claude; makes him want more to have her. He *urges* her—but on this Mrs. Beale protests. No—*she'll* keep her: he'll come and see her there. It reaches almost a dispute between them. I must have it that Mrs. Beale *really* clings to her—partly from her old affection, the charm of the child (formulate *to* the child—*for* the reader, *through* Mrs. Wix or Sir Claude, this charm so complicating and entangling for others); and partly because her presence is a way of *attracting* Sir Claude and making a tie *with* him. But he is the person, who, after Mrs. Wix, loves her most and he does get her away from Mrs. Beale—for a week; succeeds in taking her to the empty house, where, abandoned of Ida, they moon about, vaguely and tenderly, together. That is, I *think* he takes her to the empty house: this is to settle, to *creuser. Voyons, voyons—arrangeons un peu cela.* What I seem to want is that a little interval should occur before the revelation that Beale, too, has bolted with a 'paramour.' If I can only keep this—that is, *make* it, really dramatic, it may perhaps be something of a little triumph. Mrs. Beale must come down, somewhere, *to* Sir Claude and Maisie with her great news for the former and her 'Now we're free!' My climax is that what this freedom conveys for them is the freedom to live together—to do now what they like—with the rather perplexed and slightly ashamed consciousness that now, charged with the child, if they keep her they keep her mixed up with their *malpropreté,* their illegitimate tie. The embarrassment, the awkwardness, the irony, the *cynisme,* the melancholy comedy, or whatever one may call it, of this. *Then* poor Mrs. Wix's descent—her indignant rise in her might, her putting before them the horror (for *her,* at least), of what they're doing; the way, in a word, in which *elle leur dit leur fait,* winding up with her *taking* Maisie to her own poor, bare shabbiness of home and life—her rescuing her, declaring that *she* will do for her. That is my clear climax and denouement; BUT what I've been asking myself is whether I may not with effect, whether I, indeed, *must* not, represent a little prior descent of Mrs. Wix's *after* Ida's flight and *before* Beale's—in the interval that I'm obliged to make. (Put it in the episode of the empty house?) It is not only that this interval—the wait for the effect of Mrs. Beale's advent with *her* news, the tidings of what has happened to *her* home—it is not only that this little interval requires to be filled; but, further, that there are 2 other reasons. One of these is that, given the attitude already imputed to Mrs. W. toward Sir Claude, it seems to me she mustn't reprobate him, break with him *tout d'un coup.* The other is that I do well to give her a chance to *appeal* to him—do it well from the point of view of dramatic prettiness and pathos. Isn't there a grotesque *pathos,* in especial, in her turning up on learning (I must settle *how* she learns—with her relation to Ida *that* is manageable very naturally) of her ladyship's flight and hurrying down to him to put his present chance for beauty and virtue (of behaviour) before him. She sees how the event must throw him into Mrs. Beale's arms, and *elle se démène* as *against* that. She pictures to him his chance—his chance to come off now with Maisie and *her.* They will be together—they will make a *trio.* The small touching oddity (with her secret passion for him) of her offering *herself* as a rescue from the temptation, the impropriety of Mrs. Beale. ADMIRABLE, this. He resists—he doesn't see it yet; and she *has* to go off, with her return, her next entrance, prepared for, as it were, and led up to. I seem to see this out of town—at Brighton, at a watering-place *quelconque.* I see Mrs. W. 'come down';—I see Mrs. Beale 'come down';—I see Mrs. W. 'come down' again. She leaves, in snatching up Maisie. Mrs. Beale and Sir Claude to go *abroad.* Yes, she goes back with the child to London. They stay there—behind—together: to embark together for the continent. Don't I get an effect from *Folkestone?* It's to Folkestone Sir Claude has taken Maisie, and after Mrs. Beale, on Beale's 'bolt,' has rushed down, it is *there,* a very good place, I think, that they find themselves with the problem of having her between them in their adulterous relation. I thought of making Mrs. Wix arrive the same day as Mrs. Beale—in the afternoon—but I think I strengthen my effect by making her not come till *3 or 4* days after. A part of the ugly little comedy is their—the 'guilty couple's'—at once exalted and rueful *consideration* of what they are face to face with—and I must give that a little time—a few days—to go on. They go about with her—looking over to France and 'abroad'—meanwhile; and it is this *accomplished* situation that Mrs. Wix breaks into. Susan Ash is also with the child— Susan Ash has accompanied her and Sir Claude down to Folkestone when he goes and possesses himself of *Maisie* after Ida's flight. And Susan Ash *too* is a hussy, whom Mrs. Wix also *dit son fait* to—or about.

December 21st, 34 De Vere Gdns., W.

I realise—none too soon—that the *scenic* method is my absolute, my imperative, my *only* salvation. The *march of an action* is the thing for me to, more and more, *attach* myself to: it is the only thing that really, for *me,* at least, will *produire* L'ŒUVRE, and L'ŒUVRE is, before God, what I'm going in for. Well, the scenic scheme is the only one that *I* can trust, with my tendencies, to stick to the march of an action. How reading Ibsen's splendid *John Gabriel*[1] a day or two ago (in proof) brought that, FINALLY AND FOREVER, home to me! I must now, I fully recognize, have a splendid recourse to it to see me out of the wood, at all, of this interminable little *Maisie; 10,000 more words* of which I have still to do. They can be magnificent in movement if I resolutely and triumphantly take this course with them, and *only if I do so.*

---

1. Henrik Ibsen (1828–1906), Norwegian dramatist and poet; *John Gabriel Borkman* appeared in 1896.

January 6th, 1897 Lamb House

To-day I went out to Harrow to see poor Elly Temple (Mrs. George Hunter),[1] lately, on her arrival from the U. S., settled there, and she lent, to look at, a small packet of old letters, family matters, given us by our cousin, the late Catherine Gourlay, who died last year, at a very advanced age, in Albany. Among them I find an old yellow and faded page on the subject of my great-grandfather (my father's maternal grandfather) John Barber. He died at his residence, Montgomery, Orange County (New York State or New Jersey?) on the *12th February* 1836; aged 87 years. "Another Revolutionary Patriot," says the notice, "is gone." The page is evidently copied from a contemporary local newspaper. "Mr. Barber was an officer in the Revolutionary War, and served with the Clintons and other Patriots of that day in resisting the British arms in storming Fort Montgomery. He occupied in his native county of Orange, during his long and useful life, a very elevated and influential rank. And the spontaneous and repeated testimony of the citizens of that county, in placing him in honourable and responsible stations, evince the esteem and confidence reposed in his judgment and moral worth.—For more than ½ a century he was Elder in the Good-Will church of his native town." If he was 87 years of age in 1836 he was born (at Montgomery) in 1759.[2] But how little I know about him—or his father.————

May 7th, 1898.[1]

1. The thing suggested by what Aug. Birrell mentioned to me the other night, at Rosebery's, of Frank Lockwood[2]—that is, of his writing, so soon after his death and amid all his things, F.L.'s *Life*—past tense—and 'feeling as if he might come in.'

2. *Les Vieux.*

3. 'Vanderbilt' story—the Cocotte (for the Divorce) 'covering' the real woman he wants to marry.[3]

---

1. Ellen James Temple (1850–1920), Minny Temple's younger sister, married Christopher Temple Emmet (1822–84) and after his death the Englishman George Hunter (1847–1914). She was now in England with her daughters Ellen Gertrude (Bay), a painter, Rosina Hubley, and Edith Leslie.
2. An error in arithmetic: he must have been born in 1749.

1. The hiatus of almost a year and a half may perhaps be accounted for by a combination of elements in HJ's life during that time: he was completing *What Maisie Knew* for serialization and then book publication at the end of 1897; he was preparing a series of articles on London for *Harper's Weekly* during the first half of 1897; his writer's cramp had obliged him to resort to an amanuensis at the beginning of 1897; preparation for and celebration of Queen Victoria's Diamond Jubilee had disrupted his routine and driven him out of London to the Channel coast; finally, he had learned that Lamb House (which he had discovered two years earlier) had become available. He leased it and involved himself in moving from London, subletting his flat in De Vere Gardens, etc.
2. Augustine Birrell (1850–1933), essayist whose *Obiter Dicta* (1884, 1887, 1924) were widely read; later president of the Board of Education (1905–07), and Chief Secretary to the Lord Lieutenant of Ireland (1907–16). His *Sir Frank Lockwood: A Biographical Sketch* was published in London in 1898. Lockwood (1846–97), M. P., became Queen Victoria's Solicitor-General in 1895 when Lord Rosebery was Prime Minister. See American Journal I, 20 December 1881, note 2.
3. For *Les Vieux* see 18 October 1895 and 21 December 1895. The "Vanderbilt" story became "The Special Type"; see 21 December 1895 and 19 February 1899.

4. The Lady R.C. (Bourget) vindictive, bad, dressing of young wife incident.[4]

5. The 'Cazalis' wife ('pen-name' and doctor's name) situation.

6. The Miss Balch and Lady G. incident. Imagine the protectress (Respectability) dealing death upon the person coming to denounce. She (Respectability) *must get her money*, etc.

7. The resemblance-of-Hughes-L.-to-Bourget-story—the woman affected.[5]

8. Gualdo's story of the child *retournée*—the acquisition, construction (by portrait, etc. ???) of an ANCESTOR, instead of *l'Enfant*. The setting up of some one who must *have lived: un vrai mort*. Imagine old couple, liking young man: 'You must have married our daughter.'

'Your daughter?'

'The one we lost. You were her fiancé or her *mari*.' Imagine situation for young man (as regards some living girl) who has more or less accepted it. He succumbs to suggestion. He has sworn fidelity to a memory. He ends by believing it. He lives with the parents. They leave him their money. I see him later. *He is a widower*. He dies, to rejoin his wife. He leaves their fortune to the girl he doesn't marry. 35 pages. (Subject—subject.)

[''Maud-Evelyn,'' the *Atlantic Monthly* April 1900; reprinted in *The Soft Side*.]

9. (In same key.) The woman who wants to have *been* married—to *have become a widow. She* may come, *à la Gualdo*, to the painter to have the portrait painted—the portrait of her husband. The painter does it. Very pretty too I think. Young man—friend of painter's: 'Lord, I wish *I* looked like it—or it looked like *me!*' (Extraordinary old girl is rich.)[6]

[''The Tone of Time,'' *Scribner's Magazine* November 1900; reprinted in *The Better Sort*.]

10. *Les Vieux* again or *The Waiters:*—Lady P[layfair]'s story of the Miss Palfreys. The last one—she remains. Or perhaps there is only *one* who waits. The mother survives her. (25 pages.) The daughter dies. The way they put it to the mother, or *she* puts it. 'Oh, I knew, I knew she would: she has gone to Europe!'

11. The young man who can't get rid of his secret—his oppressive knowledge—with solution of his *taking* one—HAVING to, from some one else—to keep it company.

12. Etta R.'s case of maturing, withering daughter. 'Her *husband* will *show* her the world, travel with her—a girl—in *our monde*—waits for *that.*'

13. 'The Publisher's Story.' Mrs. X.—a literary woman—EREINTERS *pendant de longues années* a writer—preferably novelist or poet. I (the Publisher) ask: 'Why can't you let him alone? You *know* him—like him.' 'Yes, but I don't like his work.' Then—about his never seeing what she says: *elle est rageuse.* I put my

---

4. See 16 February 1899. Lady Randolph Churchill (''R. C.'' here), the former Jennie Jerome and mother of Sir Winston, paid a call on the Bourgets at Le Plantier (at Costebelle near Hyères in the South of France) in April 1898, when HJ was visiting; she then persuaded HJ to write a story for the *Anglo-Saxon Review*, which she edited. He complied: see 10 February 1899.

5. For 'Cazalis,' see 22 September 1895. The incident in no. 6 is developed in 15 and 16 February, 16 May, 9 October, and 11 November 1899. For no. 7 see 22 September 1895.

6. No. 8 is ''Maud-Evelyn''; see 22 September 1895. The parenthetical conclusion of no. 8 is written in red ink in the manuscript. No. 9 is ''The Tone of Time''; see 16 February 1899. For HJ's development of a related theme see the unfinished story ''Hugh Merrow'' in the Appendices.

finger on the place: 'You love him.' She has to admit it. 'Well, try another tack.' She writes a euology, which he *sees;* and learns the authorship of, and in consequence of which he does notice her work. x x x x x I see the *other* woman or girl, who, then, on the accident of his seeing at last the back numbers and learning who *has* slated him (it needn't have been for so long; a year or two) says '*I* wrote them'; to save her friend. But *my* thought, on this, of how *she,* the 2d girl, must love. Try 1st (May 7th, 1898) the Frk. Lockwood, the Playfair, Palfrey, the Young Man who has Married the dead Daughter, and the wonderful feat of the poor fine lady (Miss B.) who, taking the money to put the *tarée* one through, *kills* the upsetter who comes to make her job worthless. Only the killing is difficult.[7]

Names. Dedrick—Emerick—Bauker—Flickerbridge—Marsock—Sandbeach—Chirk—Rivory—Reever—Dirling—Catchmere—Catchmore—Cashmore—Pewbury (place)—Gallery—Mitchett—Mitcher—Stilmore (place)—Tribe—Pinthorpe (place)—Cutsome.

34 De Vere Gdns., W., May 8th, 1898.

L'honnête femme n'a pas de roman—beautiful little 'literary (?)' subject to work out in short tale. The trial, the exhibition, the proof:—either it's not a '*roman,*' or it's not *honnête.* When it becomes the thing it's guilty; when it doesn't become guilty it doesn't become the thing.[1]

May 11th. Notion given me by G[aillard] T. L[apsley][1] yesterday on leaving with him a 'drawing-room tea' at the American Embassy. The 2 American girls there (Miss C.'s) whose history led him to touch the American phenomenon of the social suppression of the parents. They had suppressed theirs, etc., etc.—and *de fil en aiguille* the little idea comes to me: a case in which 2 children, daughter and *son,* I think—but the son essentially as his ambitious and 'successful' sister's mandatory and underling, so *conceal* their homely mother—with the aid of her own subjection and effacement—that, having almost, practically, given out that she is *dead*—brought to this by the scare of learning that she's supposed to be concealed because she is compromising—they, in a given case or crisis, are so ashamed and embarrassed at having to show she *isn't,* and they *have* sacrificed her, that they get her—for the occasion—till it's tided over and they are safe, etc.—get her to FEIGN death, to lend herself—which it is part of the pathos and drollery of the thing that she submissively and bewilderedly—*devotedly,* above

---

7. No. 10 is the third note for "Europe"; see 27 July 1890 and 27 February 1895. No. 11 is "A Round of Visits"; see 18 February and 21 September 1894, and 16 February 1899. For Henrietta Reubell's "case" see 4 August 1892 and 21 December 1895. The final two sentences of no. 13 are written in red ink in the manuscript.

1. Idea for "The Story in It"; see 18 October 1895, 15 February and 9 October 1899.

1. Gaillard (pronounced and sometimes spelled "Gilliard") Thomas Lapsley (1871–1949), a graduate of Harvard, taught in California until 1904, when he was elected Fellow and Lecturer of Trinity College, Cambridge. He enjoyed an international reputation for his work in medieval constitutional history.

all—does. The son is WITH her—works it FOR the sister as (also) submissively as he must—and as tenderly as he *can*.[2]

Names. Leon—Brivet (place)—Trete (place)—Ure (place or person)—Hessom—Manger—Hush (person or place)—Mush—Issater—Ister (Icester)—Elbert—Challen—Challice (or *is*)—Challas—Syme—Dyme—Nimm—Etchester—Genrick (Genneric)—Dluce—Bagger—Clarring—Compigny—Cavenham—Grendon—Treck—Randidge—Randage—Bandidge—Neversome—Witherfield—Withermore—Chering (place)—Smarden—Addard—Petherton—Kirl—Rosling—Ulph (place)—Treffry—Curd ('Lucy Curd')—Lutley (or place)—Staverton—Brissenden—Traffle—Verver (or, for place, Ververs)—Heighington—Hington—Hingley—Braddle—Gostrey—Beveridge—Waldash (Waldish)—Dadd—Charl—Chelver—Iddings—Branson—Brinton—Laud—Blessingbourne—Mapleton—Withermore—Shirrs—Damerel—Dreuil (Mme le Dreuil)—Bonair—Keel (Keal)—Tocs.

Lamb House, January 22d, 1899.[1]

George Alexander writes me to ask for *Covering End* for 'him and Miss Davis'[2] to do, and I've just written to him the obstacles and objections. But I've also said I *would* do him a *fresh* one-act thing; and it's strange how this little renewal of contact with the vulgar theatre stirs again, in a manner, and moves me. Or rather, it isn't at all the contact with the theatre—still as ever, strangely odious: it's the contact with the DRAMA, with the divine little difficult, artistic, ingenious, architectural FORM that makes old pulses throb and old tears rise again. The blended anguish and amusement again touch me with their breath. This is a grey, gusty, lonely Sunday at Rye—the tail of a great, of an almost, in fact, *perpetual* winter gale. The wind booms in the old chimneys, wails and shrieks about the old walls. I sit, however, in the little warm white study—and many things come back to me. I've been in London for 3 weeks—came back here on the 20th; and feel the old reviving ache of desire to get back to work. Yes, I yearn for that—the divine unrest again touches me. This note of Alexander's is probably the germ of something. I mean of a little wooing of something ingenious. Ah, the one-act! Ah, the 'short story!' It's very much the same trick! Apropos of the latter, Edmund G. gave me the other night, in town, something that was kindly intended for a possible tip—something retailed lately to himself as such. Some lady had seen an incident and told him. She was in a railway-carriage x x x x x (But note later on Gosse's incident of the *éplorée* mourning widow, observed by narrating fellow-traveller in corner of carriage, who gets into train with relations of dead husband so sympathetically seeing her off, and then at next station with a changed aspect meets handsome gentleman, who gets in and with whom she moves into other carriage—with a sequel, etc.)

2. Development of "Fordham Castle"; see 18 October 1895, 15 February and 9 October 1899.

1. HJ signed a twenty-one-year lease for this house in Rye, Sussex, in September 1897 and took possession in June 1898. See *Life* 460–71 and *Letters* IV, 61–65.

2. George Alexander had produced *Guy Domville*, and Fay Davis was an actress long attached to his company. See 4 August and 24 November 1892 and 5 February 1895 for origins of "Covering End."

Lamb House, January 27th, 1899.

How, through all hesitations and conflicts and worries, *the* thing, the desire to get back only to the *big* (scenic, constructive 'architectural' effects) seizes me and carries me off my feet: making me feel that it's a far deeper economy of time to sink, at *any* moment, into the evocation and ciphering out of *that,* than into any other *small* beguilement at all. Ah, once more, to let myself go! The very thought of it soothes and sustains, lays a divine hand on my nerves, and lights, so beneficently, my uncertainties and obscurities. *Begin* it—and it will grow. Put in now some strong short novel, and come back from the continent, with it all figured out. I must have a long *tête à tête* with myself, a long ciphering bout, on it, before I really start. *Basta.* I've other work to do this a.m. and I only just now overflowed into this from a little gust of restless impatience. I'm somehow haunted with the *American* family represented to me by Mrs. Cameron[1] (à propos of the 'Lloyd Bryces') last summer. Yet that is a large, comprehensive picture, and I long to represent an *action:* I mean a rapid, concrete action is what I desire, yearn, just now, to put in: to build, construct, teach myself a mastery of. But *basta* again. *À bientôt.*

Lamb House, February 10th, '99.

Dear old George Meredith the other day (on Sunday the 5th at Boxhill) threw out an allusion (in something he was telling me) that suggested a small subject— 5000 words. Some woman was marrying a man who knew very little about her. He was in love—intensely: but something came up about her 'past.' 'What *is* it? Is there anything . . .? Anything I ought to know?' 'Give me 6 months,' she answers. 'If you want to know it *then*—I promise you I will tell you.' That was all his allusion—but it made me, on the spot, tie a knot in my handkerchief. There *is* a little subject—but what is it? I seem to see different possibilities. I see the thing, at any rate, as distinctively *ironic.* What appears to come out most is *this:—*

The woman is a woman who *may* have had a past; of an age, of a type. The question, the suspicion, the possibility, the idea, in short, comes up for the man who is making up to her, who has proposed and whom she has accepted. Thence the question, the answer, I have quoted. She is not in love with him—she is in love with another man; a man he knows. Well, he finds he can't accept her condition. 'Tell me *first.* It won't make any difference. I won't mind. Only I want to know. You ought to tell me. If you believe it's something that *will* make no real difference, why *can't* you tell?'

'Ah, but I can't. I won't. Yes, I'll marry you. I believe I shall suit you. But you must trust me so far. I swear that if six months hence you still *want* to know—!'

'Ah, but then I shall be married to you.'

'Yes, but what will you have lost by that—?'

'You mean if I *don't* want to know?'

1. Elizabeth Sherman Cameron (1857–1944), wife of Senator James Donald Cameron (1833–1918), was for years an intimate friend of Henry Adams's. See *Life* 471–74.

'Yes—and if you do. If you care for me *now*—'
'I shall care for you then?—What if it's anything very bad?—*Is* it something very bad?'
'I don't know what you'd think it. If you must know it, you'll estimate it when you do know it. I don't know how it would strike you.' x x x x x

However, I find I can't figure this out today, through extreme seediness from convalescent influenza. I just catch the tail there—the 2d man to whom the 1st tells his predicament. He backs *out*—the first—he can't accept the condition. The '2d man' is a man she does love—and the 1st (not knowing this) has told him (being a friend) of his predicament and then of his collapse. The 2d is so interested and touched that he approaches her—*he* in turn makes up to her—he mentions to her what the 1st has told him. He 'falls in love' with the woman, and intimates that *he* would accept her condition. *This* is what she has dreamed of, and she says 'Well, then—!' and she renews, *with* him, the condition; promises that if, after 6 months, he does want to know *what* there has been in her past, she will then make a clear statement. On this he marries her. They are happy—she charms and satisfies him; he is highly pleased with his own magnanimity and delicacy, and when at the end of 6 months she says to him: 'Now *do* you want to know?' he waves away the thought. He *doesn't*. He wouldn't know for the world. He forbids her to tell him—and she of course (confessing it is quite what she hoped), happily concurs and mildly triumphs. She says still: 'Whenever you like, you know!'—but he *doesn't* like: he won't hear of it. What he *does* like is the beauty of his own trust and confidence, his relinquishment—and on that they go on and on. The 1st man, meanwhile, has vanished into space—has gone off, after the marriage of his friend, the easier suitor, or has heard of it, rather, at a distance. But in time, restless, dissatisfied with himself, he comes *back*. He has been as little pleased with his own insistence as the happy husband has been much so with *his* own generosity: he continues to care for the woman, to be haunted and restless. He has never married another. He thinks of her perpetually—he wonders and wonders. (Oh, divine old joy of the 'Scenario,' throbbing up and up, with its little sacred irrepressible emotion, WHENEVER I give it again the ghost of a chance!) He tries to find out about her—he does get on her trace—comes across traces of her 'past,' looks into it, rakes it up. But nothing he gets a scent of is at all a *guilty* business or a compromising relation: only, really, traces of her courage and *bonne grâce;* difficulties, struggles, patience, solitude—all things to her honour. (Say she's a little music-mistress—a 'lady' adrift or say, even, she 'paints.') He is all the *more* perplexed and dissatisfied—feeling what he perhaps has lost. Yet, too, if she herself has admitted something, what does it mean? In fine he reappears. He comes back to her. The husband is still his friend—so he has a certain freedom. When they meet alone, he and the wife (he has met, again—renewed with—the husband first), he brings it up to her, tries to have it out.
'Have you ever told *him?*'
'Never.'
'And he doesn't want to know.'
'Absolutely not.—*You* wouldn't,' she adds—'if you had only believed it.'

'Well,' the old lover replies, sighing, pained, wretched: 'Will you at least tell me now?'

'Ah, no *par exemple!*' That's too much for him to ask.

'You're afraid I'll go and tell your husband?'

'No—not *that*. He wouldn't let you.'

'Well, what then prevents you?'

He lets her know—*has* let her know—that he is in love with her still; but, at any rate, they separate without her having in any way satisfied him. He comes back; he sees her again; and then at last he brings out his thought. 'I've rifled and ransacked your life—so far as I could get near it and *at* it. But I've found, I *can* find, *nothing*. What was it—when was it? I believe there *was* nothing? Is it so? For god's sake, *tell* me.'

She considers. 'Will you give me a promise?'

'*Any* promise!'

'Will you swear on your sacred honour?'

'I'll swear.' He does so—swears, I mean, to repeat what she says to *no one*.

'Well, then—there *was* nothing.'

'Nothing?'

'Nothing.'

He's overwhelmed with the strangeness—the bitterness. 'What then were you to have told *me?*'

'Nothing. For you wouldn't have wanted it.'

'How could you be *sure*—?'

'Well, I would simply then have told you there *was,* there is, nothing.'

'Then why did [you] speak as if there was?'

'I didn't. It was *you* who did—from the first.'

'Ah, but you left the matter in an obscurity. You were willing to let me think an evil.'

'Certainly—that was your punishment.'

'At your expense? that of your reputation?'

'My reputation for what? For being too proud, simply, to go into explanations—!' x x x x x

—But my developments are carrying me too far at a moment when I'm still sick and seedy. *Basta.* My denouement is the *éclaircissement* between these 2: the explanation, the presentment she gives of the case. He says: 'And you don't want your husband to *know* that there's nothing—?'

'I want the subject left as he prefers to leave it—untouched, again, forever.'

'And let him believe every evil—?'

' "Every?" Why, my dear man, he scarcely believes ANY!'

'I like your scarcely! You mean he doesn't think it was so *very* bad—?'

'Well, he sees I'm, at all events—whatever may have happened—a good creature; and I have the benefit of that. I've been very nice to him.'

Un temps. 'You *really* wouldn't like me to tell him—as from my own belief—that there was nothing . . .?'

Her positive irony of amusement. 'Don't you think it a delicate matter to offer such a reassurance?'

'I mean only as an amends for my former talk with him. I can tell him that with time I've felt that a burden to my conscience.'

'Well, however it may occur to you to put it, I don't recommend you to speak of it to him.'

Un temps. 'Oh, of course I can't—after my vow, my oath, to you.' *Encore un temps.* 'But I see now—of course—why you exacted that vow.' He shows her he sees why; puts his finger on that fact of the husband's 'hugging' his sense of the beauty of his own behaviour and forgiveness which is the psychological *noeud* or *concetto* of the matter.

She *accepts* this interpretation—and, I, so far, *give* it, with my lucidity and authority. Then he tells her, the ex-lover, that he *now, par exemple,* does rage with jealousy, his passion re-excited by the thought of all this peculiar bliss that the husband enjoys. It does make him want to blight it—to spoil the other man's (self-)complacency. He is tempted to break his vow.

'Ah, you can't.'

'No—I can't.'

'That you see is your punishment.'—This speech of hers is the logical last note of the thing—the climax and denouement: but I seem to want to tuck in before it 2 or 3 things. I mean that any other (2 or 3) things I *do* want to tuck in must be *put* before it—so as to leave it in final possession. Above all I 'feel that I feel' that I don't absolutely get what I want in making *her* give up her 'past' *as* simply nothing. *Don't make her formulate that too much.* Let her rather, simply, *take it from* her ex-lover, since this is the way his researchers have made it strike him. 'Oh, well—if you think so . . . .!'—*that* is her attitude. She assents at most. 'Oh, well, if you can't *find* it—!' *That's* the way she puts it, as if with light, vague relief. That he hasn't been able to 'find' it is what he speaks of telling the husband.

[''The Great Condition,'' *Anglo-Saxon Review* June 1899; reprinted in *The Soft Side.*]

February 15th (Lamb House), 1899.

Would the little idea of the 'suppressed (American) mother' be feasible in 5000 words?[1] It would be worth trying—for I seem to see I shall never do it in any other way. Try it so for what it is worth. DO THESE IN 5000 AT WHATEVER COST. IT IS ONLY THE MUTILATED, *the indicated thing that is feasible.* It occurs to me that it would be possible, and make for brevity, to do the thing *from* the vision, as it were, and the standpoint *of* the mother; i.e., make the mother show and present it. I see no effective brevity *but* in that. (I count 30 pages of author's 'pad' MS.) (This makes 5 divisions of 6 pages or 6 little sections of 5.) Oh, if I could only arrive at a definite firm fixed form of that exact dimension. How it *would* help to make the pot boil! Well, *cela ne tient qu'à moi—qu'à ma volonté.*

1. Development of ''Fordham Castle''; see 11 May 1898 and 9 October 1899.

Tâchons, tâchons. It's a question of throwing up, under the pressure of necessity, the right thing.—In this little subject I see the Daughters 1st; see them as I saw them, the pair, the Misses So-and-So, that day at the American Embassy, last spring—fresh from the Drawingroom. I recall my walk away, afterwards, in company with G. T. Lapsley—my stroll, in the budding May—or June—sunshine along the Mall of St. James's Pk. There he told me—charmingly—sounded the note of the sort of thing in which I instantly saw [a] little *donnée*. 'And in all kept their mother so out of the way, somehow—!' It was the way they had done it.— Well, narrating, I have (in I) met the 2 girls. I give my little talk about them— the little talk I have with my (American also) hostess. *They have a chaperon—a dame de compagnie.* 'As usual, after everyone had gone—it was what I always outstaid them all for—my hostess, on her sofa by the fire, answered my questions and met my wonderments.' I begin about in *that* sort of little way. 'The 2 sisters?—oh, the Miss P.'s—they come to be presented.' Lapsley—sketch of them, and note of the ambiguity—obscurity—of the mother question more or less sounded.

II. I meet the mother—in Dresden or Switzerland—at *pension.* She tells me about her daughters. I 'fit' them together.

III. I re-meet the daughters—in London, Paris, Rome, or somewhere, in situation in which I *see* them pass as *without* the appendage. 'Mother?—oh, they *have* none.' I am going to interfere when the *chaperon—D. de C.*—checks me. 'Don't— I'll tell you *why.*' She tells me. [The thing might be told *by* the *dame de compagnie.*][2] x x x x x Pursue this some other time—keeping hold of the idea that the mother consents, for the given occasion, not to exist.

x   x   x   x   x

Don't lose sight of the little *concetto* of the note in former vol. that begins with fancy of the young man who marries an old woman and becomes old while she becomes young.[3] Keep my play on idea: the *liaison* that betrays itself by the *transfer* of qualities—qualities to be determined—from one to the other of the parties to it. They *exchange.* I see 2 couples. One is married—this is the *old-young* pair. I watch *their* process, and it gives me my light for the spectacle of the other (covert, obscure, unavowed) pair who are *not* married.

x   x   x   x   x

Keep in view 'The Publisher's Story.'[4] Also *L'honnête femme—n'a pas de roman* story.[5] Worry something out of that. There is something in it. And for the Publisher's story, revert to what I seem to have (in this vol.) got hold of the tail of— the idea of the 2d woman (girl), who falsely takes upon *herself* the authorship of the 'slatings' and who is *the* one that the narrator attributes the secret passion to. x x x x x

In the 'Honnête Femme' may there not be something like *this?*—very, very short: 3000 or 4000 words. A man of letters, an artist, *represents, expresses,* to a young,

2. HJ's brackets.
3. For *The Sacred Fount;* see 18 February 1894.
4. See 18 November 1894, 21 December 1895, and 7 May 1898.
5. ''The Story in It''; see 18 October 1895 and 8 May 1898.

'innocent,' yearning woman (a widow, say), that contention, in respect of the *honnête femme.* She must have wrestled with him about it—*à propos* of 'the French novel,' books, pictures, etc.—'art' I mean, generally—with her 'Anglo-Saxon' clinging to the impossible thesis. He is very clear. If she's *honnête* it's not a *roman*—if it's a *roman* she's not *honnête. He's* married—he's the artist—the man of frank, firm attitude. All the while she's in love with him—*secretly,* obscurely, with nothing coming out. But she has a relation, a witness, a friend who is also in love with him and is present at, assists at, this innocent contentious relation. *She* has let herself go—the man is her lover. It is successfully hidden. I show, however, that the passion, the relation, ardently, tormentedly, clandestinely, exists. Finally—after scenes and passages—to *confute* her friend (who *agrees,* to her, with the artist), she says: 'And all the while he talks thus he doesn't *know!'* 'Know what?' 'Why, that I *adore* him.' The friend, whose relations with the artist must have been *given,* unmistakeably, to the reader, wonders, winces, but controls herself. 'Then don't you want him to?' *'Never!'* 'Why, then—?' 'Because where then would be my (decency) *honnêteté?'* The other woman's deep, sore, tragic answer: 'But without it, triple idiot, where then is your romance?' *'Here.'* She strikes her heart. 'Oh!' says the other. I seem to wish to require, to have a passage, for finality and lucidity, between the artist *and* his mistress—in which the latter 'gives' him the foregoing. 'She calls *that,'* she says, "a romance. But how, where? A romance is a *relation:* Well—like yours and *mine.* Where is—for *her*—the relation? There *is* none.' The artist turns it over, ponders, feels it. 'A relation—yes. But mayn't it be, after all, also a (sort of) *consciousness?'* 'How? What is there in that? What does it do for her?' *He* must say *he* has one too. 'Well then—constituted as she is—what does *yours* do for her?' He has to take this. 'I see. It only does—what it *can* do—for ME!' *That* I see as the climax. But I see also there must have been—*n'est-ce pas?*—2 or 3 other things. That is, it must be struck out that as *she* (the 'lost' woman) puts it—'It all depends on what you *call* a relation.' Further, oughtn't the thing to *begin* with the fact of the relation (which she *does* call one) existing between the artist and the thoroughgoing woman. But it will be pretty, though, in making that plain, not to crudify the statement of it. Give her acceptance, vision of it, simply, *as* a relation. x x x x x I see it as *London* thing—the above.

x   x   x   x   x

Look also, a little, *mon bon,* into what may come out, further, of the little something-or-other deposited long since in your memory—your fancy—by the queer confidence made you by the late Miss B. (B . . . h) on the subject of what she had undertaken to do for the *tarée* Lady G.—her baffled, defeated undertaking.[6] I say 'look into it a little' because I find I dashed off last summer, at the beginning of this vol., a reference to some gleam it appeared then to have thrown up. Miss B., say (her equivalent) *took* the money—that is, has had *half*—and is to receive the rest when the job is done. Frustration threatens her in the person of some interfering, protesting, fatal marplot of a *revealer,* a maker definite of the facts,

---

6. Development of "Mrs. Medwin"; see 7 May 1898, 16 February, 16 May, 9 October, and 11 November 1899.

of the *tarée* woman's actual history. This is dreadful to Miss B., who is in want of her money. She must oppose it, must prevent it. If she *is* frustrated she won't get her precious money. What does she do? I appear to have been visited by the flight of fancy that she 'kills' her upsetter. There is something fine in that—but 'kills' is soon said. 'The Killing,' I find I remarked, 'is the difficulty.' It is indeed! But I must let it simmer—I must worry it *out!* The whole essence of the thing is of course not in the very *usé* element of the *tarée* woman's desire to creep in—but in the situation of the Miss B. woman, with her *gagne-pain* of these offices, the way she *works* her *relations,* etc., etc. The essence is that she does something bold, big and prompt. x x x x x

It comes to me that she does something better than any 'killing'—comes through the portal of one's seeing how 'boldness' and promptness shows itself as a sort of anticipating, forestalling and turning of the tables. Again, however, the thing becomes a little drama, and from the moment it becomes that, strains for more space. Well, one must only *sacrifice* more: that's all. This would be really a little cynical comedy. Miss B. has a suppressed, disowned appendage of a horrid, disreputable kind—I don't see what he can be but a fearfully *taré* and impossible brother, who turns up sometimes to ask for money, to exasperate and mortify her, to try and beg or bully her into getting him back into society. He has been the subject of a 'scandal' years before, and has more or less vanished—but leaving a name that is known. He can't be a brother—he must be a cousin; of another name. *Mettons* that he isn't a 'sponge'—that he has means, that he's even rich. Only he's out of society. I wish I could make him a murderer! x x x x x

February 16th. I've been ill again (with beastly little trail of influenza)—which was what broke the above off. But let me try to go on with this, and 2 or 3 more things in more or less stammering accents and very briefly. x x x x x

I see the 'appendage' of 'Miss B . . . h' must be—say—a stepbrother—with a different name; and that he must, decidedly, *not* be rich, as that has obvious interference. He is discredited, disgraced, has had to leave England; but he comes back after an interval and wants money from his sister-in-law. I put this crudely and temporarily. He and Lady G. have both been with her the day of the visit of the *protesting* friend. Well—well—I needn't (feeling rather seedy and sickish) worry this out now further than just to state simply that one's little climax and subject consists in the 'light' that comes to Miss B. on seeing her visitor (on some trace or gleam!) suddenly flash into a curiosity, a desire to see, to know, THIS *taré* one. He comes *up* between them. 'And he too—drat them all—wants to get back into society! But I can do nothing for *him.* I wash my hands!' x x x x x Effect of this on visitor. 'You think him hopeless?' 'Utterly'—but she has MENTIONED that it's some of her MONEY he wants, has *told* of this in fact to explain her need for the sum (£300) which the defeat of the effort for Lady G. will deprive her of. This is the beginning. The visitor warms to *him*—the PICTURE of the 'warming' given; and the climax becomes the bargain struck: the intermeddling woman allowing Miss B. to operate in peace on *condition* of her presenting *her* to—allowing her to take in hand the *case* of—the peccant and compromised stepbrother. But *how* must he have been compromised? There's the difficulty. I must leave it vaguish—or put *cards*. Cards will probably do. His poverty a proof of the baselessness of the allegations against him. x x x x x[1]

I pick up for a minute the idea of the portrait *à la* Gualdo—it haunts me: oh, what things, what *swarms* haunt me! (As for instance this little gleam of the notion of a man who, *bourru,* unamiable, ungracious, though absolutely 'straight' in some relation, becomes visibly, increasingly mild, gentle, gracious, GOOD—to the point of attracting the attention of some observer and spectator, who, struck, mystified, finding it strange, too marked, even suspicious, watches him till he finds it is the concomitant just of some adopted vice or pursued irregularity, 'impropriety,' wrong. It's his wishing to *se faire pardonner.* But *what, donc?* The narrator watches, studies, discovers. The thing has to fix on the vice.)[2] (Don't lose, after this, the tail of the little *concetto* of the poor young man with the burden of his personal sorrow or secret[3] on his mind that he longs to work off on some one, roams restlessly, nervously, in depression, about London, trying for a *recipient,* and finding in the great heartless preoccupied city and society, every one taken up with quite other matters than the occasion for listening to *him.* I had thought, for the point of this, of his being suddenly approached by some one who demands *his* attention for some dreadful complication or trouble—a trouble so much greater than his own, a distress so extreme, that he sees the moral: the balm for his woe residing not in the sympathy of some *one* else, but in the coercion of giving it— the sympathy—*to* some one else. I see this, however, somehow, as obvious and banal, *n'est-ce pas?*—'goody' and calculable beforehand. There glimmers out some better alternative, in the form of his making some one *tide over* some awful crisis by listening to him. He learns afterwards what it has been—I mean the crisis, the *other* preoccupation, danger, anguish. [The thing needs working out— *maturing.*][4]) (Don't let me let go either the idea of the 2 artists of some sort— male and female—I seem to see them—as a writer and a painter—who keep a stiff upper lip of secrecy and pride to each other as to how they're 'doing,' getting on, working off their wares, etc., till something sweeps them off their feet and breaks them down in confessions, AVEUX, tragic surrenders to the truth, which have at least the effect of bringing them, for some consolatory purpose, together. Mustn't they have been somehow originally acquainted and separated? The fact, the situation that BREAKS DOWN THEIR MUTUAL PRIDE [that's the *nuance*][5] to be of course worked out. x x x x x)

["Broken Wings," *Century Magazine* December 1900; reprinted in *The Better Sort.*]

At last I come back to the woman who wants a portrait of some non-existent (*never*-existent) person. I've noted the notion before as that of a woman who wants to 'have been' a *widow*—she wants to have in her house the portrait of her husband. What is there *in* it? I seem to catch the glimmer of something. Is she an

---

1. See 15 February 1899.
2. See 22 September 1895 and 7 May 1898.
3. Development of "A Round of Visits"; see 18 February 1894.
4. HJ's brackets.
5. HJ's brackets.

old enriched *femme galante?* I *think* not—I think, though I'm not sure. She must be an odd creature. A mere intense old maid? No—there are reasons, I see immediately, against that. Well, what she is, what she has been, transpires, is implied. She is an *ancienne,* an ex-*femme galante,* but it comes out as it can. She calls on a painter of distinction.

'I want you to paint my husband.'

'*Fort bien.* When will he sit?'

'He can't sit. He's dead.'

'Ah, from some other memorial—from photographs?'

'No—I've *no* photographs: I've *no* other memorial.'

'Then how, Madam—?'

Un temps. 'Can't you do it from a—from a—No—I can't give you that. Can't you do it from imagination?'

In short she has a talk with him, the consequence of which is that he goes to see a friend, a lady artist. In a scene with *her* he tells her of his interview with a visitor—he comes with the visitor's *(final) assentiment,* to hand on the commission. He gives the whole thing—of which, directly, I have only given the opening notes. She wants—the odd lady—to have been married: she wants to be a widow. She wants a tall fine portrait of her late husband. She has no view—he must only be a *très-bel homme.* He must not moreover be a portrait from life of any one in particular: he must be a fancy creation. The artist must invent him—a perfection. *Elle y mettra bien le prix.* Well, this fantastic commission the painter can't take—but he thinks his old friend and comrade *may,* and wanting to give her the benefit of it if it is possible, he comes to her with the story. She is a rare copyist—but she has painted some charming things and that all look old. Who is she—? *What* is she? He says, more or less. (But this to be determined.) The lady-artist paints the picture—doing a thing, as she believes and tries, from imagination. But *what* she does, she does really from memory—the memory of the one man she *herself* has loved. He was the handsomest, the most irresistible: he jilted, forsook her, etc., in youth: she too has never married. She has reason to—more or less— *execrate* him: *aussi* she has thought of him with, always, as much of the passion of bitterness as of the passion of the other thing. She paints it almost in hate. *Bref*—when that woman sees it she recognizes it as a man she too has known and the only one she would have married, or can think of now (so base her view of those men she *has* known) as the one she would have a portrait of. Situation—the lady-artist has really evoked and represented a (dead) reality—the man they both had loved. The *Ancienne* is eager for the picture—but then it is the lady-artist turns. Ah, *now* she can't have it. The other woman doubles the price—offers money, money. Ah, *now* she can't have it—*no.* She refuses the money—keeps the picture for herself. It has taken her resentment, her bitterness to produce, to paint it—it has been painted in hate. And now she sees, moreover, for whom it was he abandoned her. A reality is *added* to his reality for her—the reality of the other woman's connection with him. *But,* all the same, for herself, she now suddenly prizes this image of his cruelty and falsity that she hasn't produced *for* herself—but for another—yet that she can't part with. She refuses everything, keeps the picture, begins to *love* it. One day her comrade, the R.A. is there—it

is over her chimney-piece. A visitor, a sitter, comes and asks, 'Who is it?' 'He's my late husband.' (Though this perhaps a little extravagant and *de trop.*)[6]
    The notion of the Lady R.C.'s little vengeance on the bride might be done this way. The lover who has *lachéd* her, taken to wife the charming simple young girl, comes to me—before going up to town—and says, 'What shall I do? How shall I proceed with her? I'm thinking of playing a very frank, bold game—of throwing myself on her magnanimity. She's generous, she's not *mean*'—and 'Addie'—or whatever—is charming. She can't help liking her. Therefore isn't the really superior policy to ASK her to be kind to her, to appeal to her for guidance, for patronage for his little wife? Hum!—*I* don't know! *I'm* not sure. I'm not so positive of Lady X.'s magnanimity. This takes place—this interview—abroad. I meet them on their wedding-tour. The talk is of what to do when they get to London. Well, I leave my friend to determine for himself. *Je me récuse*—I'm vague and elude the question. Then I see them later, in town. I HAVE the situation in my head—only this has come to me in regard to it: that I make, as a narrator, the point, that *fagotée* by her terrible friend's hands the little bride *is* hideously attired, while Lady X. is consummately so: a revelation of taste and distinction. But the faces! (*The Faces* might [be] the name of the little story.) The bride dimly, vaguely conscious of the trick played on her, pathetically lovely under her hideous toggery—angelic in her bewildered fairness: the other woman infernal in expression over all the perfection of her appearance. The husband speaks to me— we *mark* it so: we formulate and phrase it. Or rather isn't it some *new* lover she (Lady X.) is trying for, that *catches* it, phrases it, puts it to me? Yes—and it's thus *herself* she dishes.[7]

[''The Faces,'' *Harper's Bazar* December 1900 and, as ''The Two Faces,'' *Cornhill Magazine* June 1901; reprinted as ''The Two Faces'' in *The Better Sort*.]

February 19th., 1899

Struck an hour ago by pretty little germ of small thing given out in 4 or 5 lines of charming volume of Miss Jewett—*Tales of N.E.*[1] A girl on a visit to new-found old-fashioned (spinster-gentlewoman) relation, 'idealized her old cousin, I've no doubt; and her repression and rare words of approval, had a great fascination for a girl who had just been used to people who chattered and were upon most intimate terms with you directly, and could forget you with equal ease.' That is all—but they brushed me, as I read, with the sense of a little—a very tiny— subject. Something like *this*. I think I see it—*must* see it—as a young *man*—a young man who goes to see, for the first time, a new-found old-fashioned (spinster-gentlewoman) cousin. He has been ill—is convalescent—doesn't get well very fast—has had infernal influenza. He's a young barrister—young journalist. He's poor—but he's engaged. Well, his old cousin's type and manner and old-

6. ''The Tone of Time''; see 7 May 1898.
7. See 7 May 1898. Lady R.C. is Lady Randolph Churchill.
1. Sarah Orne Jewett (1849–1909), American regionalist whose *Tales of New England* was published in 1879.

fashionedness are a revelation. Her absence of chatter—of excess—of familiarity are a cool bath to him—living as he does in a world of chatter, of familiarity, of exploiting of everything, of *raving* above all. Yes, he lives in that world, and the girl he's engaged to lives in it. *She* chatters, she raves. She writes—she's clever— (she masculine?) she's conscious and appreciative of everything. Well, the form that the effect, the impression his relative makes on the young man, *takes* on the form of wishing to keep her—for his private delectation—just *as* she is; keep her from getting approached, known and spoiled. He has a horrible fear that she'll herself *like* the chatter-element, the chatter people, if once she knows them. And oh, she *rests* him so! She'll think them so clever—and they'll appeal and rave and treat her as enchanting and picturesque and make her conscious. She doesn't *know* what and how she is—and the people actually about her don't know either. So he feels about her as we feel about a little untouched *place* that we want to keep to ourselves—not put in the newspapers and draw a railway and trippers and vulgarities to. So when she asks about his fiancée even, he has a terror. She's the great raver. *She'll* chatter about her and *to* her. She'll write her up. Yet the cousin wants to see her—wants her to come. She has to—he has to consent. Well, she comes, and his worst fears are verified. She does all he fears, and with the effect. The old woman becomes a show old woman. She likes it. He is overwhelmed with melancholy and regret—which the fiancée sees as jealousy and resents. *Bref,* the old cousin becomes completely *public,* exploited and demoralized, and after a rupture with his young woman, he retreats, *flees,* leaving *her* in chattering and raving possession.

["Flickerbridge," *Scribner's Magazine* February 1902; reprinted in *The Better Sort.*]

Take some occasion to cipher out a little further the 'Vanderbilt'—arrangement with *cocotte* to *cover* real preferred woman and enable hated wife to bring divorce suit—subject. There is probably something in it—but to be a great deal pulled out. The *cocotte s'y prête*—from real affection for him: knowing the terms, etc.[2]

Palazzo Barbaro, May 1st, 1899.

Note the 'Gordon Greenough'[1] story told me by Mrs. C[urtis]—the young modern artist-son opening the eyes of his mother (his sculptor-father's *one* believer) to the misery and grotesqueness of the Father's work: he, coming back from Paris (to Florence, Rome, the wretched little *vieux jeu*—of the American and English set, etc.) to 'set her against' the father and unseal her eyes. She *has* so admired him. I must see the son, *also,* I think, as stricken in production—as too intelligent and critical to wish to do anything but what he *can't*—and the mother, between the pair: the son *in fact* NOT consoling her pride for the ridiculousness of the father. The latter serenely and most amiably *content de lui.* G.G. *died.*

2. "The Special Type"; see 21 December 1895 and 7 May 1898.
1. Of the Greenoughs, Gordon was the nephew of the pioneering Horatio (1805–52) who at the age of twenty went to Rome and embraced the rigidities of classical art, carving an unmanageable statue of Washington. He lived in Florence from 1828 to 1851. His youngest brother, Richard Greenough (1819–1904), also sculpted; and Richard's son, Gordon, the subject of HJ's "The Tree of Knowledge," studied painting.

Rome, Hotel d'Europe, May 16th.

Note the idea of the knock at door *(petite fantaisie)* that comes to young man (3 loud taps, etc.) *everywhere*—in all rooms and places he successively occupies—going from one to the other. *I* tell it—am with him: *(he* has told *me); share* a little (though joking him always) his wonder, worry, suspense. I've my idea of what it means. His fate, etc. 'Sometime there *will* be something there—some one.' I am *with* him once when it happens, I am with him the 1st time—I mean the 1st time *I* know about it. (He doesn't notice—I do; then he explains: 'Oh, I thought it was only—' He opens; there *is* some one—natural and ordinary. It is my *entrée en matière.*) The denouement is all. What *does* come—at last? What *is* there? This to be ciphered out.[1]

[''The Jolly Corner,'' the *English Review* December 1908; reprinted in the New York edition, volume XVII.]

Mrs. Elliott (Maude Howe) on Sunday last (while I was at her charming place near St. Peter's—flowered terrace on high roof of Palazzo Rusticucci, with *such* a view) told me of what struck me as such a pretty little subject—her mother's (Julia W. H.'s) *succès de beauté,* in Rome, while staying with her, the previous winter: her coming out *(après)* at the end of her long, arduous life and having a wonderful unexpected final moment—at 78!—of being thought *the* most picturesque, striking, lovely old (wrinkled and *marked*) 'Holbein,' etc., that ever was. 'All the artists raving about her.' AWFULLY good little subject—if rightly worked. *Revanche*—at 75!—of little old ugly, or plain (unappreciated) woman, after dull, small life, in 'aesthetic' perceptive 'European' 'air.' Element in it of situation of some other American woman (who *has* had lots of 'Europe' always)—thought so pretty (and so envied by my heroine) when younger—and now so 'gone.' Work it out.[2]

[''The Beldonald Holbein,'' *Harper's New Monthly Magazine* October 1901; reprinted in *The Better Sort.*]

For W. W. Story. Beginning. 'The writer of these pages—(the scribe of this pleasant history?) is well aware of coming late in the day . . . BUT the very gain by what we see, *now,* in the contrasted conditions, of happiness of old Rome of the old days.' x x x x x[3]

Names. Steen—Steene—Liege—Bleat—Bleet (place)—Crawforth—Masset—Mulroney—Perrow (or place)—Drydown (place)—Harbinge—Belpatrick—Beldonald—Belgeorge—Grigger—Dashley—Belgrave ('Lord B.')—Counterpunt—Prime—Mossom—Birdle—Brash—Fresh—Flore (place)—Waymark—Dundeen—Prevel—Mundham—Thanks (place or person)—Outreau (d'Outreau—Mme d'O.).

1. See 22 January 1879; 5 February 1895.
2. Maud Howe (1854–1948), daughter of Julia Ward Howe (1819–1910), American poet and lecturer (author of ''The Battle Hymn of the Republic''), in 1887 married John Elliott (1858–1925), Scottish-born portraitist and muralist and a founder of the Newport Art Association.
3. This is the only extant note for HJ's biography of the American expatriate sculptor, *William Wetmore Story and His Friends,* published in Edinburgh and Boston (1903).

Names. Pilbeam—Kenardington—Penardington—Ardington—Lindock—Sturch—Morrison-Morgan—Mallow—Newsome—Ludovick—Bream—Brench—Densher—Ilcombe—Donnard—Camberbridge—Marl (or place)—Norrington—Froy (or place)—Trumper—Husk—Vintry—Dunrose—Milrose—Croy—Match—Midmore.

For 'Anecdotes.'

1. 'The Sketcher'—some little drama, situation, complication, fantasy, to be worked into small Rye-figure of woman working away (on my doorstep and elsewhere).

2. The Coward—*le Brave.* The man who by a fluke has done a great bravery in the past; knows he can't do it again and lives in *terror* of the occasion that shall put him to the test. DIES of that terror.[4]

3. 'The Advertiser'—the CLIMAX: (NOT, for 5000 words, told by 'me').[5]

4. The Faces.

5. THE NAME: Cazalis—Jean Lahor: wife's action and effect as told me by Bourget.

6. The idea of the man who looks *like* the other (Hugues L[e Roux]-P.B[ourget]) to the degree of effect on woman. *Vide ante.*

7. The 2 couples (*vide ante:* Stopf. B[rooke]).[6]

8. The *Roman de l'Honnête Femme.*

9. The supposedly (assumedly) letter-reading servant.

10. The Biographer (after death: A.B[irrell] and F.L[ockwood]).

11. The V . . drb . . t (Cocotte-Divorce) thing ["The Special Type"].

12. The (Cocotte) Portrait (of supposed Husband) thing. *Vide ante.*

13. The Mother and Husband (American) Meeting thing.

14. Yes—literally: The Miss B. and Lady G. idea—concentrated*issimo:* 4 sections of 28 pages—7 (with 'talk') each ["Mrs. Medwin"].[7]

The idea of the rich woman *nuancée,* condemned, who *has* everything—so everything to lose and give up—wanting to arrange with little poor woman to *die for* her: the latter having *nothing* to lose—to give up. (Lady R.—the condemned.)

October 5th, 1899. Don't forget the little *Gordon-Greenough-and-his-mother-and-his-father (as to the latter's sculpture, etc.) idea.* Practicable on the rigid Maupassant (at extremest brevity) system.[1]

I seem to see something in the idea of 2 contrasted scenes between (1) a 'corrupt' London pair—friends or lovers—who are treating of something on the basis, the supposition, assumption, that 'one's maid (and one's man) of course read all one's letters'; and (2) a pair of servants (maid and man) who show themselves somehow *not* so depraved, nearly, as their employers assume. The man believes

4. See 18 February 1894; cf. 11 September 1900.

5. For nos. 3, 9, and 11 see 21 December 1895 (etc.).

6. No. 7 is *The Sacred Fount;* see 18 February 1894 (etc.). No. 8 is "The Story in It"; see 18 October 1895 (etc.). No. 13 is "Fordham Castle"—see 28 October 1895 (etc.)—but it is also reminiscent of *The Golden Bowl* idea of 28 November 1892 and 21 December 1895.

7. For the other items (except no. 1) see 7 May 1898.

1. "The Tree of Knowledge"; see 1 May 1899.

his man so good—the woman believes hers so bad. One would like to make some little gleam of an action hinge on it—and something is doubtless to be ciphered out. (Oh, the kind little, sweet little spell, the charm, that still lurks in that phrase and process—small, sacred relic of those strange *scenario* days! To use it at all is really to yearn, quite to let one's self go to it. Well, one does—one *is* letting one's self: oh, it will come again! Lamb House, Oct. 9th, 1899.) One feels in it some small situation—reflected in the up-stairs and the downstairs view. Of course there must be an IRONY—*tout est là*. One must fumble it out.

So one must fumble out the conjunction of the 2 American appendages—the shunted mother (of 'presented,' etc., daughters) and the relegated husband (of presented, etc., wife) who meet somewhere (in the absence of their launched correlatives) and exhibit the situation to each other (unconsciously) in a series of confidences, communications, comparings of notes, etc., of the rarest and most characteristic *naïveté*. They go from one thing to another—they have the IV little passages (for 5000 words). As always, one must disengage an action—something they are respectively *in,* from day to day, in respect to the 2 prominent daughters and the voyaging wife. I work into this in thought, that idea *(vide supra)* of the mother consenting temporarily to be *dead* (as it were) to help the daughter *through* something—some social squeeze, 'country-house,' etc. One seems to see the husband as becoming the subject of some similar convenience for his wife—which mustn't be quite the same, but *matching,* and in the same 'note.' 'Separated?' 'Ill?' —at a 'cure,' which he doesn't require? I feel the pair to be somewhere at an hotel in Switzerland or Germany—in a kind of waiting *perdu* way. It may turn out that the wife of the poor man is in—as chaperon—with the daughters of the poor woman. I think I see Death and 'Separation.' They meet—they talk—the little affair *is* their talk. They learn from EACH OTHER *what each learns that they, respectively, are made, by the correlatives—thus together—to (temporarily) pass for.* That's about the little formula for the very short thing.[2]

['"Fordham Castle,'" *Harper's Magazine* December 1904; reprinted in New York edition, volume XVI.]

I see such chances in these little scenic, self-expository things—dramatic, ironic passages and samples. I seem to see just now, say *4* small subjects as so treatable—on the (that is) 'dialogue' (more or less) plan. The 2 foregoing: the (what I call) 'Miss B . . . h and Lady G . . . ly' situation; and the little thing noted a long time ago as on a word dropped by Miss R.—the way for a woman (girl) to see the world, to travel, being for her husband to show her. The foreignized American mother who takes that line—and the *un*foreignized ditto—or, rather, American girl herself—who represents the idea of the young woman putting in all she can *before*—either to show it herself to her husband, or because she will, *after,* with the shelved and effaced state of so many, precisely, *by* marriage, have no chance. I might give the 3 images: the girl *à la* Miss Reubell (I mean evoked by her word); and the 1st and second, *both,* of these last-mentioned cases. They

2. See October 1895, 11 May 1898, 15 February and 16 May 1899.

would make a little presented 'scenic' trio. *Et puis, vous savez, il n'y a pas de raison pour que je n'arrive pas à me dépêtrer*—in even 3000![3]

["Mrs. Medwin," *Punch* August–September 1901; reprinted in *The Better Sort.*]

Ne lâchez donc pas, vous savez, mon bon, that idea of the little thing on the *roman de l'honnête femme.* It may be made charming—and 5000 words are ample![4]

Note here the little 'ironic' subject of 'H.A.' and the life of countryhouses as against—fill it out—the memorandum. (Suggested by H.A.'s verses among the celebrities in M. de N.'s wonderful album.)[5]

3. See 7 May 1898 (etc.). For Miss Reubell's subject see 21 December 1895.
4. "The Story in It"; see 18 October 1895 (etc.).
5. H. A. here is not Henry Adams, as might be supposed, but rather Charles Hamilton Aïdé (1826–1906), called "the greatest dilettante of his period." Resigning his commission in one of the Guards regiments, the young Aïdé devoted himself to painting, literature (a couple of popular novels, the successful comedy *A Nine Days' Wonder,* and the play *Philip,* acted by Henry Irving), and the composition of music. His regular "at homes" in his London flat in Queen Anne's Mansions were for men only. Mrs. Antonio Fernando de Navarro, née Mary Anderson (1895–1940), an American actress, in 1890 married the engineer son of a shipping magnate of Basque origin; they lived in Broadway, Worcestershire. See HJ's letter of 13 October 1899 to Mrs. Navarro (Lubbock I, 328–30) with its enclosed autobiographical anecdote, "The Golden Dream," for her album. Aïdé's verses in the album which HJ read with such interest are here reproduced from a copy of them taken by Leon Edel at the Navarros' in 1958. They are dated "August 7th 1897":

[Shout!]

i

Shout for the ship that's in sight!
  Weep for the ship that's away!
Grieve for the fallen in fight,
  But honour the victor with bay.
Hope never dies with the light,
      For the night
Hides within it the promise of day.

ii

Shout for the youth that has won!
  Weep for the youth that has failed!
At noontide, the day is not done,
  For the mist that at morning prevailed;
Why should the race that's begun
      Not be won,
Though the boat was nigh wrecked when it sailed?

iii

Shout for the glory of birth!
  Weep for the conquest of death!
With the love and the laughter of mirth,
  Come the sins and the sorrows of breath,
But who shrinks from the fight upon earth
      Is not worth
We should weep for him after his death!

(A version of "Shout" was printed in *Past and Present: Verses* by Hamilton Aïdé, 1903. It substitutes for the next to last lines, "But the man who despairs on this earth is not worth" as a single line.)

Names. Berther—Champer—Server—Yateley—Lender—Casterton—Taker—
Pouncer—Dandridge—Wantridge—Wantrage—Gunton—Medwin—Everina (fem.
Xtian)—Obert—Burbage—Bellhouse—Macvane—Murkle (or place)—Mockbeg-
gar (place)—Cintrey—Kenderdine—Surredge—Charlick—Carrick—Dearth—
Mellet—Pellet—Brine—Bromage—Castle Dean (place).

November 11th, 1899 (L[amb] H[ouse]).

Subject of, for, a one-act thing with *male* part equivalent to what Mrs. Gracedew,
in *Covering End,*[1] is for female, suggested by the idea of *transposing* the small
donnée (transposing *and* developing, *mon bon!*) noted *supra* as the 'episode of
Miss B. and Lady G.'[2] Idea of making Miss B. a *man*—an amiable London
celibate, favorite of ladies, humorous, kindly, ironic, amusing, expert—fond of
them (the ladies), applied to by them in troubles and difficulties and always helping one or another out of some hobble. I seek in the situation, the elements, of
the little 'Miss B[alc]h'[3] incident for an analogue, a similarity, drawn from
circumstances of such a London bachelor; and giving, as in *C.E.,* the whole act,
after effective preparation, to the alert presence and happy performance of that
personage. After all, I brought the subject of *C.E.* from much further away still,
and dug it out of much more unprepared earth. There *is* a man-situation in the 'B.
and Lady G.' affair—I mean there is *the* one, the right one. Dig—dig! *creusons,
fouillons!* The idea of the *exchange* effected by the protagonist in the interest at
once of his encumbrance and of his petitioner—the bargain made as the result of
a happy inspiration to practice on the ravening *Londonism* of the *grande dame*
representing the stronghold the petitioner—applicant for help—(the compromised
Lady G.) wishes to scale: this is more of a nucleus, *much,* than I had to start with
for Ellen Terry. It seems to me that given the general idea—in its most general
form—the successful 'placing' socially of some one he doesn't really care about
by working the acquaintance, availability, of some one else (much worse, etc.,
etc.) as a bribe—sounding, searching, ciphering, from there down—on that *ground*—
MUST, with patience, lead to anything. Difficulties, of course, but that's what it
all means; and *turn and turn and turn about* is the gospel of it. It glimmers before
me as the picture of a situation in which 3 or 4 more or less panting and pushing
little *femmes du monde* all want something of him: all except one who wants
nothing at all. Or perhaps the *clou* lies elsewhere: the thing, only, now is to let
the matter Simmer. *Muse* it out till light breaks.

November 12th. Tiny fantasy of the projected 2 *vols. of posthumous letters* of 2
men who have had their course and career more or less side by side, but been
rivals and unequal successes (one a failure)—watched, recorded by the wife
(widow—or attached woman) of one of them (the failure), who has also known
intimately of old (been loved and misused by) the success. Both die—and the
bitter and sore wife (about her husband's—the failure's—overshadowing) has ever
felt how really more brilliant (for the expert, the knowing) he was than the other.

1. See 24 November 1892.
2. See 7 May 1898 ("Mrs. Medwin").
3. HJ's brackets.

Then she hears the *Letters* of the other are to be published—and this excites, moves her: if it comes to *that*, why not publish the letters of *her* husband (the success's wife—an idiot, *quoi!*—publishes *his*) which *must* have been so far superior and which will so ineffably score. She appeals—right and left—to his friends: and lo! no one has kept any. There *are* none to publish. Beneath this last humiliation—no one *keeping* them—she feels quite crushed: and has only to wait, pale and still more embittered, the issue of the rival's. They appear—and lo, they are an anti-climax, for mediocrity and platitude, a grotesqueness (for his reputation—turning it inside out), that makes it almost seem as if it were *as* grotesques and exposures that they were, by his correspondents, cynically and cunningly preserved. They fall with a flatness—they blast his hollow frame! She feels with a great swing round of her spirit—*avenged!* Then (I am thinking) she publishes the letters of her OWN (her husband's *to* her) that she has kept. *Those* SHE has kept! *(rather!!)* but delicacy, etc., the *qu'en dira-t-on?* has prevailed. Now it goes. She doesn't care. She wants to score. She publishes—and does.—*Or is there anything* ELSE *in it?—in connection with the letters she eventually publishes* ????—???—???

["The Abasement of the Northmores," published (without serialization) in *The Soft Side*.]

December 14th, '99.— In my superficial (as yet) vision of what I call 'the H. Adams story,' the dying mother tells the younger son (her son) that the elder is not legitimate; and with the notice that he shall tell a certain person, a relation and presumable benefactor, who wants to benefit *her* child. The elder son is *not* her child, but a child of her husband (of before marriage) adopted and brought up, by agreement, *as* her own: the son of the father's early mistress in short. Well, my idea is a situation of magnanimity and heroism *(comme qui dirait)* for the young man—a young *man*, oh, at last preferably, instead of girl (2 girls) as in H.A.'s dim little germ of an anecdote. What does the relation propose to do?— seem likely to do? It must be a *definite* thing: say settle money on condition of a marriage x x x x x

Well, I seem to catch hold of the tail of something in supposing his encounter, somehow, with the girl destined to this purpose, through which it 'transpires' that she, too, is illegitimate. That is, a vision dimly rises of the check of his *use* of the knowledge imparted in respect to his brother by the x x x x x[1]

January 28th, 1900. Note at leisure the subject of the parson-and-bought-sermon situation suggested to me by something mentioned by A. C. B[enson].[1] My notion of the unfrocked, disgraced cleric, living in hole, etc., and writing, for an agent, sermons that the latter sells, typewritten, and for which there is a demand.

---

1. Earlier notes for the Henry Adams story are in 5 February and 26 March 1892 and 30 August 1893.

1. Arthur Christopher Benson (1862–1925), Housemaster at Eton and later Master of Magdalen College, Oxford, edited Queen Victoria's selected letters. He was a son of Edward White Benson, Archbishop of Canterbury from 1882.

Names.   Chattle—Voyt—Podd—Tant—Murrum—Glibbery—Wiggington—Gem-
ham—Blay—Osprey—Holder—Dester—Condrip—Cassingham—Dyde—Ques-
—Glint—Stroker—Brothers ('Brothers and Brothers')—Goldridge—Slate (or
place)—Culmer—Frale (place)—Drack—Drook—Gellatly—Gellattly—Wel-
wood—Lauderdale—Bridgewater—Bree—Blint.

L.H., April 17th, 1900

Note the little idea of the 'Jongleur' as I caught it in talking with J[onathan]
S[turges][1] this afternoon—as we lingered, talking, in the dining room after tea:
that of the deluge, the vulgarity, the banality of *print* being at last such that the
'real' artistic thing isn't committed to it: is composed, *parachevé*, then talked, said,
dit: hence idea of artist having his little person to whom he commits his repertory
and who says it, on occasion, before a real audience. What's the situation—little
drama—that can, that might, result from that—this committal of the thing to the
perishable individual?

Name.   Waterworth—Waterway—Pendrel—Pendrin—Cherrick—Varney—Castle-
dene—Castledean—Coyne—Minuet—Fallows—Belshaw—Quarrington—Dam-
mers—Beldm—Deldham—Tangley.

Lamb House, August 9th, 1900.

I've a great desire to see if I can worry out, as I've worried out before, some
possible *alternative* to the 50,000 words story as to which I've been corresponding
with Howells, and as to which I've again attacked—been attacking—*The Sense of
the Past.*[1] I fumble, I yearn, *je tâtonne,* a good deal for an alternative to *that* idea,
which proves in execution so damnable difficult and so complex. I don't mind,
God knows, the mere difficulty, however damnable; but it's fatal to find one's
self in for a subject that one can't possibly treat, or hope, or begin, to treat, in
the space, and that can only betray one, as regards that, after one is expensively
launched. The ideal is something as simple as *The Turn of the Screw,* only different and less grossly and merely apparitional. I was rather taken with Howells's
suggestion of an 'international ghost'[2]—I kindle, I vibrate, respond to suggestion,
imaginatively, so almost unfortunately, so generously and precipitately, easily.
The formula, for so short a thing, rather caught me up—the more that, as the
thing *has* to be but the 50,000, the important, the serious, the sincere things I
have in my head are all too ample for it. And then there was the remarkable
coincidence of my having begun *The Sense of the Past,* of its being really 'international,' which seemed in a small way the finger of providence. But I'm afraid
the finger of providence is pointing me astray. There are things, admirably beau-

---

1. See 31 October 1895.
1. After completing two and a half sections of this novel HJ abandoned it. He returned to it in 1914
to begin a detailed ''sketch'' of a revised version. The unfinished novel and the sketch were published
(ed. Percy Lubbock) in London and New York (1917). See Dictated Notes, pp. 502ff.
2. See Dictated Notes, pp. 502ff and *Letters* IV, 149–52.

tiful and possible things, in the *S. of the P.*, but I can't gouge them out in the space, and I fear I must simply confess to my funk at the danger, the risk, the possibility of the waste of *present*, precious hours. Let me lay the many pages I've worried out of it piously away—where some better occasion *may* find them again. I must proceed now with a more rigorous economy, and I turn about, I finger other things over, asking, praying, feel something that will do instead. I take up, in other words, this little blessed, this sacred small, 'ciphering' pen that has stood me in such stead often already, and I call down on it the benediction of the old days, I invoke the aid of the old patience and passion and piety. They are always there—by which I mean *here*—if I give myself the chance to appeal to them. There are *tails* of things that one must, with one's quick expert hand, catch firm hold of the tip of. They seem to whisk about me—to ask only for a little taking of the time, a little of the old patient mystic pressure and 'push.' Adumbrations of 'little' subjects flash before me, in short, and the thing is to make them condense. I *had* a vague sense, last autumn when I was so deludedly figuring out *The S. of the P.* for 'Doubleday,' that, as a no. 2 thing (in 'Terror') for the same volume, there dwelt a possibility in something expressive of the peculiarly acute Modern, the current polyglot, the American-experience-abroad line. I saw something; it glimmered on me; but I didn't in my then uncertainty, follow it up. *Is* there anything to follow up? *Vedremo bene.* I want something *simpler* than *The S. of the P.*, but I don't want anything, if may be, of less dignity, as it were. *The S. of the P.* rests on an idea—and it's only the idea that can give me the situation. *The Advertiser* is an idea[3]—a beautiful one, if one could happily fantasticate it. Perhaps one *can*—I must see, I must, precisely, sound that little depth. Remember this is the kind of sacred process in which ½ *a dozen days*, a WEEK, of depth, of stillness, are but all too well spent. THAT kind of control of one's nerves, command of one's coolness, is the real economy. The *fantasticated* is, for this job, my probable formula, and I know what I mean by it as differentiated from the type, the squeezed sponge, of *The T. of the S.* 'Terror' *peut bien en être*, and all the effective *malaise*, above all, the case demands. Ah, things swim before me, *caro mio*,[4] and I only need to sit tight, to keep my place and fix my eyes, to see them float past me in the current into which I can cast my little net and make my little haul. Hasn't one got hold of, doesn't one make out, rather, something in the general glimmer of the notion of what the quasi-grotesque Europeo-American situation, in the way of the gruesome, may, *pushed to the full and right expression of its grotesqueness*, has to give? That general formula haunts me, and as a *morality* as well as a terror, an idea as well as a ghost. Here truly *is* the tip of a tail to catch, a trail, a scent, a latent light to follow up. Let me, in the old way that I can't *think* of without tears, scribble things as they come to me, while little by little the wandering needle and the wild stitch makes the figure. I see the *picture* somehow—saw it, that night, in the train back from Brighton—the picture of the 3 or 4 'scared' and slightly modern American figures moving against the background of three or four European *milieux*, different European conditions, out of

3. See 21 December 1895 (etc.).
4. HJ uses the Italian equivalent of his customary term for his guardian angel, *"mon bon."* See 3 February 1894.

which their obsession, their visitation is projected. I seemed to see them *going*—hurried by their fate—from one of these places to the other, in search of, in flight from, something or other, and encountering also everywhere the something or other which the successive *milieux* threw up for them, each with the tone and stamp of its own character x x x x x—an awfully loose expression of something too faintly glimmering. It's only by way of saying that I seemed on the scent of an English, a French, an Italian terror—with an American to wind up? That was as far as I got with my formula—and it's not very far and I am now wondering whether one or other of the little American situations 'abroad' that have been running in my head as things of irony, of satire, *voire* of considerable comedy, may not lend themselves, if one really looks, to some sort of little fantastication that will be effective. x x x x x

What was at the basis, as I thought, of almost the prime beauty of the idea of the *S. of the P.* but the fancy of the *revealed* effect of 'terror,' the fact that the young man had himself become a source of it—or, to speak more lucidly—the fact of the consciousness of it as given, not *received,* on the part of the central, sentient, person of the story? That seemed to me charmingly happy, a real solution and working *biais*—and it seems so still: so that I am not sure that, 'dear God!' as the Brownings would say, I don't still see [it] again as sufficiently vivid to make me feel that by still clinging to the whole *essence* of the conception, I may not ride a wave that will yet float me through. *Voyons un peu* what SIMPLIFICATION of the presentation as originally dreamed of may not be hammered out. It comes over me, for the hundredth time, as really so beautiful—the germ-idea—that I oughtn't even temporarily to shelve it without trying a little more for *all* that simplification can do to it. One of my old flushes and flutters seems to come to me as I begin perhaps to *entrevoir* that one's ingenuity and *expertise* may, God help them, possibly STILL save it. It glimmers before me that it's somehow attackable at a different angle and from a different side altogether—that is *almost.* A difficulty indeed immediately rises—when did I abjure the fond faith that a difficulty stated can, for me, only be a difficulty half solved? When I think of the expedient of making the narrator's point of view that of the persons outside—that of one of them—I immediately see how I *don't* get that way, the presentation by the person who is the source of the 'terror' of his sense of being so. On the other hand I don't, if I tell the thing from his point of view *in* the 'ist person' get, easily, that I can see, the intense simplification. At the same time, I seem clearly to see, I don't get the hope, and the chance, of real simplification save *by* the first-person. What I feel I roughly make out is that if, under this rubric, I can arrange anything simple enough to be told in the first person, I shall manage: but if that, if, it won't go so, there's no use in it. My 'prologue,' it more than ever comes to me, is my overwhelming space-devourer; my exposition encroaches awfully on the time, on the field, of the poor little drama itself. I believe I could *do* my drama itself, if I could only launch my narrator, speaking for himself, straight into it.

Names. Strett (Allan Strett)—Strether—Sound—Wildish—Wickhamborough—Yarm—Crispin—Longhurst.

Names.   Ferring—Leapmere—Longersh—Beddingham—Baberham—Billing-
bury—Warlingham—Poynings—Pallingham—Storrington—Ovingham—Warlingham—Worthingham—Maudling—Lillington—Wittering—Ashling—Bruss—
Bress—Hillingly—Lissack—Mant—Cordner—Bayber—Berridge—Wrent—
MARCHER—Mild—Montravers—Gasper—Brocco—*Rashley*—Darracott—Barrick.[5]

Lamb House, September 11th, 1900.

Two or three small things have struck me as possibilities for the short tale—one
or two in particular mentioned by Alice[1] (not for that purpose!). Let me say first,
by the way, that I learned last month from P.B[ourget] what makes the little
'Gualdo' notion of 'The Child' really, it seems to me, quite *disponible* to me on
my own lines. They know nothing of his ever having *written or published* such a
tale—they only meant in mentioning the thing to me at Torquay, that he had
mentioned it to *them*. That he ever treated it, or what he made if he did, they
wholly ignore—and it is moreover a question for me of a mere *point de départ:*
that a young childless couple comes to a painter and ask him to *paint* them a little
girl (or a child *quelconque*) whom they can have as their own—since they so want
one and can't come by it otherwise. My subject is what I get out of *that*. Several
pretty little things, it seems to me.[2] *Me voilà donc libre. Bon!* x x x x x

Alice, in a little walk with her to-day—the eve of her leaving for the U.S., with
W. at Nauheim—mentioned to me something that had passed between her and
Mme F.[3] at Geneva, on the subject of the possible marriage of her daughter to a
young man, the son [of] old friends, who combined, as regards fortune, position,
etc., *toutes les convenances* save ONE. This one was that he was stone-deaf, and
hereditarily; not born so, I believe (so that he was not dumb), but having become
so early, and now, at 28, or whatever, quite completely so. *Everything good,*
else, was there; only that one stumbling-block. It was grave—very grave; but they
were thinking; and what should they do? Alice *se récria:* but how *can* you think?
how *can* you be willing, with such a terrible *tare?* It was Mme F.'s answer that
gave me my hint. 'Well, there is one side even to THAT, that isn't absolutely
without its compensation or virtue. It will in some respects protect her—it will be
in a manner a guarantee that *elle peut être tranquille* (as to his relations with other
women) as so many of us, *hélas, Madame,* even here, are not—and in *his* family
(where there have been specimens!) that is not to be overlooked.' The idea, in
other words, would be—*comme cela*—that he would be more faithful, *moins coureur,* less attractive to other women, and find *liaisons*, etc., less workable. It

5. The manuscript has a vertical line in the margin, just to the left of this second list of names (Ferring
to Barrick); written in that margin is ''Sussex local.''

1. WJ's wife, the former Alice Howe Gibbens (1849–1922), a Boston schoolteacher of an old New
England family. They were married in July 1879.

2. See the unfinished story ''Hugh Merrow'' in the Appendices, and 22 September 1895 (etc.) for
notes on ''Maud-Evelyn.''

3. Mme Flournoy, wife of the Swiss philosopher Theodore Flournoy. The WJs had lately been guests
in Geneva of the Flournoys.

somehow suggested to me a girl married *so,* on that reasoning, and on those lines, and what might come of it: the one particular thing that would form the little situation. What would this particular thing be? Two things come to one: the irony of the 'sell' (both things are inevitably ironic) for the family, for the wife: it proving that, deaf as he is, he is *coureur* (or rather not that, for that would be compatible) but, rather, *galant* and unfaithful *comme pas un;* so that the wife has all the bore and fatigue of his deafness and none of the safety—and may perhaps be imagined as not *knowing* her lot, pitying him and unconsciously permitting. Or else, better, but *more* 'cynical,' she, *se pivant,* takes advantage of his infirmity to take her own course, he unknowing—so that what the infirmity does protect and assure is just *her* flirtations and her license. He is the sacrificed, thus, the 'pathetic' figure; the fiction being kept up that her happiness is complete in their union and what the deafness does for her ideal of it. Her *mother's* attitude on this. There's *something* in it—very, very ironic. x x x x x

Alice related a day or two ago another little anecdote, of New England, of 'Weymouth' origin, in which there might be some small *very* good thing. Some woman of that countryside—some woman and her husband—were waked at night by a sound below-stairs which they knew, or believed, must be burglars, and it was a question of the husband's naturally going down to see. But the husband declined—wouldn't stir, said he wasn't armed, hung back, etc., and his wife declared that in that case *she* must. But her disgust and scorn. 'You mean to say you'll *let* me?' 'Well, I can't prevent you. But *I* won't—!' She goes down, leaving him, and in the lower regions finds a man—a young man of the place—whom she *knows.* He's not a professional housebreaker, naturally, only a fellow in bad ways, in trouble, wanting to get hold of some particular thing, to sell, realise it, that they have. Taken in the act, and by *her,* his assurance fails him, while hers rises, and her view of the situation. He too is a poorish creature—he makes no stand. She threatens to denounce him (he keeps her from *calling*) and he pleads with her not to ruin him. The little scene takes place between, and she consents at last, this first time, to let him off. But if ever again—why, she'll *this:* which counts all the *more* against him—so, look out! He does look out, she lets him off and out, he escapes, and she returns to her husband. He has heard the voices below, making out, however, nothing, and he knows something has taken place. She admits part of it—says there *was* somebody, and she has let him off. Who was it then?—he is all eagerness to know. Ah, but this she won't tell him, and she meets curiosity with derision and scorn. She will *never* tell him; he won't be able to find out; and he will never know—so that he will be properly punished for his cowardice. Well, his baffled curiosity *is* his punishment, and the subject, the little subject, would be something or other that this produces and leads to. Tormenting effect of this withholding of his wife's—and creation for him, by it, of a sense of a relation with (on her part) the man she found. There is something in it, but for very brief treatment, for the simple reason that the poltroon of a husband can't be made to have a consciousness in wh[ich] the reader will linger long.[4] x x x x x

4. See 21 April 1911; cf. 18 February 1894 and 16 May 1899—"The Coward."

Note on some other occasion the little theme suggested by Lady W.'s[5] account of attitude and behaviour of their landlord, in the greater house, consequent on their beautiful installation in the smaller and happy creation in it—beyond what he could have dreamed—of an interesting and exquisite milieu. Something in the general situation—the resentment by the bewildered and mystified proprietor—of a work of charm beyond anything he had conceived or can, even yet, understand. It's a case—a study [of] a peculiar kind of jealousy, the resentment of supersession. The ugly hopeless, helpless great house—the beautiful, clever, unimitable small one. The *mystification*—the original mistake.

Don't give up—DON'T give up the American girls and their suppressed mother; the meeting of the latter and the man whose wife is to the fore.[6]

Names. Pembrey—Landsbury (place)—Belph—Loveless—Duas—Styart—Tryart—Brabally—Lane-Lander—Nevitt—STANT—Wain—Etcher—Wisper (person)—Wispers (place)—Mora (girl)—Fencer—Dyas—DREED—Churcher—Bartram—Pletch (or place)—Lowsley—Chapple—Perdy—Lewthwaite—Malham—Stanyer—Bilham—Barrace—Anning—Cavitt—Scruce(place)—Went—Crenden—Ferrand—Banyard — Boyer — Borron — Budgett — Rance — Daltrey — Casher — Gadham — Garvey — Pester — Astell — Formle — Assingham — Padwick — Lutch — Marfle — Bross—Crapp—Didcock—Wichells—*Putchin*—Brind—Coxeter—Cockster—Angus—Surrey—Dickwinter—Dresh—Rambridge—Pardew—FAWNS (country-house) — Jakes — Talmash — Bract — Chorner — Chawner — Colledge — Maule — Mawl—Hazel—Chance—Bundy—Flurrey (or place)—Belton—Messiter—Motion—Pannel (place)—Flodgeley—Mitton.

Names. Drewitt—Courser—Tester—Player—Archdean—Manningham—Matcham—Matchlock—Marcher—Everel—Aldershaw (or place)—Leakey—Pemble—Churley (or place)—Wetherend—or Weatherend (place or person)—Larkey—Shrive—Betterman—Say—Shreeve—Gray.

Lamb House, May 23rd, 1901.

I seem to see a little subject in the small idea—tiny enough, no doubt—of some person who discovers after the death of some other person nearly, intimately, related (one seems to see it inevitably as husband and wife), some unsuspected, some concealed, *side* or gift, which the survivor's own personality has had the effect of keeping down, keeping in abeyance, in *their* intercourse, but which has come out in intercourse with others. The form in which this occurs to me is the notion—put it frankly, for convenience, of husband and wife—that the wife may have been a charming *talker*—and the husband never had an inkling of it *because* he has been himself so overwhelming and inconsiderate a chatterbox. Think, in this connection, of F.T.P.[1]: say HE had discovered that his wife *could* talk—

5. Lady Wolseley, née Louisa Erskine, wife of Sir Garnet Joseph, later Field Marshal and Viscount Wolseley (1833–1913), the famous British soldier. The Wolseleys were then near neighbors of HJ, at Glynde.

6. "Fordham Castle"; see 28 October 1895 (etc.).

1. Francis Turner Palgrave (1824–97), British poet and anthologist.

discovered after her death, some relation in which this had come out. But the denouement?—for is *that* enough? Does he marry again—as an atonement—some talkative woman, to give her a chance? But what can come of that? Work it out. It's a little germ—to be possibly nursed. *N.B.* How, after a long intermission, the charm of this little subject-noting for the 'S[hort] S[tory]' glimmers out to me again—lighting up for me something of the old divine light, re-kindling the little old sacred possibilities, renewing the little link with the old sacred days. Oh, sacred days that are still somehow *there*—that it would be the golden gift and miracle, to-day, still to find *not* wasted!

x x x x x

Lamb House, June 12th, 1901.

The other day at Welcombe (May 30th or 31st) the Trevelyans, or rather Lady T.,[1] spoke of the odd case of the couple who had formerly (before the present incumbents) been for a couple of years—or a few—the people in charge of the Shakespeare house—the Birthplace—which struck me as possibly a little *donnée*. They were rather strenuous and superior people from Newcastle, who had embraced the situation with joy, thinking to find it just the thing for them and full of interest, dignity, an appeal to all their culture and refinement, etc.[2] But what happened was that at the end of 6 months they grew sick and desperate from finding it—finding their office—the sort of thing that I suppose it is: full of humbug, full of lies and superstition *imposed* upon them by the great body of visitors, who want the positive impressive story about every object, every feature of the house, every dubious thing—the simplified, unscrupulous, gulpable *tale*. They found themselves *too* 'refined,' too critical for this—the public wouldn't have criticism (of legend, tradition, probability, improbability) at any price—and they ended by contracting a fierce intellectual and moral disgust for the way they had to *meet* the public. That is all the anecdote *gives*—except that after a while they could stand it no longer, and threw up the position. There may be something in it—something more, I mean, than the mere facts. I seem to see them—for there is no catastrophe in a simple resignation of the post, turned somehow, by the experience, into strange sceptics, iconoclasts, positive negationists. They are forced over to the opposite extreme and become rank enemies not only of the legend, but of the historic *donnée* itself. Say they end by denying Shakespeare—say they do it on the spot itself—one day—in the presence of a big, gaping, admiring batch. *Then* they must go.—THAT seems to be arrangeable, workable—for 6000 words. In fact, nothing *more* would be—nothing less simple. It's that or nothing. And told *impersonally,* as an anecdote of *them* only—not, that is, by my usual narrator-observer—an inevitably much more copious way.

1. Lady Trevelyan, wife of Sir George Otto Trevelyan (1838–1928), author of a history of the American Revolution (6 vols., 1899–1914). Their "modern mansion" Welcombe was located near Stratford-on-Avon.
2. The "superior people" from Newcastle-on-Tyne were Joseph Skipsey (1832–1903), a poet of North Country mining life, and his wife, who were custodians of Shakespeare's birthplace from 1889 to 1891. For another version of this anecdote see Ernest Rhys, *Everyman Remembers* (1931).

P.S. I don't quite see why this and the foregoing and the Gualdo ('Child')[3] thing shouldn't make a trio.

["The Birthplace," published (without serialization) in *The Better Sort*.]

Lamb House, June 15th, 1901.

Reading in a small vol. of tales of Howells's a thing called a *Circle in the Water,*[1] I seem to see in a roundabout way a little idea suggested to me. His story deals, not very happily, I think, with the situation of a man released from 10 years in prison for swindling and the question of whether his daughter shall be told about him. She is with relations who have taken her, blinded her, and who wish her never to: but other friends—former friends of the father—are for putting them (*he* wants it so) face to face. There is a difference—an opposition, etc. However, I mention this (of which very little directly comes) only for the notion of small small possibility it made *arrive at* thinking of—*de fil en aiguille.* I seem to see some girl, some woman, in relation to whom, by no fault of her own, some very painful fact exists, and 2 men who 'care for' her and one of whom thinks she should know it, and the other that she shouldn't. Is it something about her mother?—is it the question of her *seeing* her mother? (like the seeing the father in H.'s tale), the latter being discredited and dishonoured, but re-emergent for the occasion. I seem to see something come of it—but not very much. They are each trying to marry her, and each takes a line on the question *in* that interest. The crisis passes—she *doesn't* see her mother (or isn't reached by the knowledge, whatever it is) and she marries the man who has been for this result, whatever the case may have been. Say it is a mother who has been horrid. The father has deeply suffered from her and is dead—partly *by* her. This is what the girl believes. *She* has adored her father. The mother has turned up, wishing, pressing to see her. Shall she, the girl, be told? A. opines Yes—B. insists No. The mother waits. B.'s side carries the day—the mother goes off, dies, disappears. The girl, who has learned, followed this, marries B. Time passes and she isn't very happy with B. The dismissed A. reappears. What she knows about *him* is mainly that he was for her seeing her mother. Her husband, who had been so against it, had not seen her himself. A. had seen her, did see her—continued to see her afterwards. This draws her to A.—draws her *from* B. It becomes A.'s merit now. He had thought ill of her for not wanting, not *re-calling,* the poor woman. They meet on it, grow frequent and intimate on it, on much talk of it. The thing is from a point of view—some old woman (a non-narrator) as in *Miss Gunton of Poughkeepsie.* She is the observer, recipient, confidant. The husband comes to her—has his last word for her—or she hers for *him.* 'Oh, you see, *you* wouldn't let her see her mother.' 'But that was just what she liked me, *married* me, for.' (Say *they* were engaged—and A. what? a cousin, a discarded one?) Then the old lady's reply—which I must get right.— Perhaps the thing isn't very much. But don't lose sight, by the way, of the subject that I know—I've marked it somewhere, as the *E. Deacon* subject.[2]

3. See 22 September 1895 (etc.), "Maud-Evelyn."

1. Howells's short story "A Circle in the Water," first published in *Scribner's* March–April 1895, was reprinted in *A Pair of Patient Lovers,* New York and London (1901).

2. See detached note "The E. P. D. Subject" (1893).

L.H., June 19th. Note the idea, here, suggested to me by Louisa Loring's[1] mention of the girl, 'Chicago girl,' engaged to 'Boston man,' who, making a serious illness (fever) showed herself on recovery to have *forgotten* completely both the man she had been engaged to and the fact of her engagement. He, in face of difficulty of re-establishing his identity for her, *gave her up,* etc.—could only accept the strange accident. But scrabble down here the one or two notions in connection—as sequences—that confusedly occur to you—on the 1st leisure. (No time tonight.)

1st. It's being suggested to her fiancé that it possibly will come back to her (*he* will) if she sees him apparently interested in another woman. 'Ah, but how *can* I be?'—Then the 'apparently,' etc., etc.

2d. The girl *feigns* it as a KIND way of getting rid of him—or there is a question of whether she *isn't* feigning. 'I' tell the story; my suspicion, wonderment, doubt, etc.—thus my *clue* or whatever—the *dénouant* all to be worked out.

L.H., July 28th, 1901.

Scrabble here (happy word!) at 1st leisure some note of the 2 small notions:—

1st. The suggestion (utterly vague) conveyed by passage in Funck-Brentano's *Affaire du Collier* (about the servants of the *ancien régime*) which quote (p. 115).[1]

2d. The suggestion, equally vague, conveyed by passage in recent letter to me from E.F.,[2] which I've destroyed—passage characteristically advising me—and in the strongest good faith—to go to the U.S. and give readings from my work—for the money and the boom. I seem to see *that* possible result and then, as a sequel, a quenching of every other result: the whole interest swallowed up in and annihilated by, the satisfied, sated, gorged curiosity and publicity, and the thing working so into something of my old little notion of *The Advertiser.*[3] Puzzle out—something perhaps in it.

Lamb House, August 22d, 1901.

Note the notion suggested to me by George Ashburner's allusion to something said to Sir J.S.[1] by the man with whom his niece had 'bolted' and was living: 'If I marry her I lose all control of her.' ('I will if you insist, etc.—*but*—etc.') They *did* insist, and what he foretold happened—he lost all control. But imagine the case in which *(given the nature of the girl)* one of the parties interested or con-

---

1. Younger sister of Katharine Peabody Loring (1849–1930), the intimate friend and attendant of AJ from 1880 to her death in 1892.

1. Frantz Funck-Brentano (1862–1947), French historian. *L'Affaire du Collier* was published by Hachette, Paris (1901).

2. Edgar Fawcett (1847–1904), American novelist, poet, and playwright.

3. See 21 December 1895 (etc.).

1. The Ashburners were neighbors of the Jameses in Cambridge, Mass., and related by marriage to the Sedgwick and Norton families in the United States and to the Darwins in England. Sir John Simon became Home Secretary and would be instrumental in arranging HJ's naturalization as a British subject in 1915.

nected *doesn't* insist, while the other does, for the appearance, and the situation springing from that—the opposition, the little drama for short thing.

["Mora Montravers," the *English Review* August-September 1909; reprinted in *The Finer Grain*.]

L.H., August 27th, 1901.

An idea, perhaps a 'first rate' one, seems to me to reside in passing allusion made this p.m., by William[1] to general attitude observed by Mrs. W. (of Boston) to her late husband—he is just dead.[2] He was insignificant, common, inferior, and she was—well, all that one knows. She could scarcely bear it of him; bear above all the way he gave away, as it were, their earlier time, when he *was* good enough for her, *was* a possible match. She had always stuck to him and done the letter of her duty to him, while disliking him and ashamed of him, and, above all, while *showing* that she was. My 'story' seemed struck out in one of the small quick flashes in which such things come, when William, speaking of these things, said, 'Ah, the mistake, in such a case, of the American sort of *honnête femme* tradition! Better for her, surely, to have left him, to have gone her way—that is, as it were, *not* have been faithful, have been perpetually exemplary and, as it were, exasperated.' Those were not perhaps his exact words, but such was the query he threw off. On the spot it suggested to me a little novel of American types and manners, following pretty well the facts, or appearances, of the W. case. I seem to see that case, and to see opposed to it, and dramatically, the case of the woman who *does* take the line of W.'s query, does not stick and 'virtuize' and suffer, but who appears somehow to seek, to have found, *her* solution somewhere other than in the *honnête femme* line, the good conscience *quand même—quand même* she (like Mrs. W.) despises and shows she despises. She does in short the opposite of what Mrs. W. did (though *outwardly* 'sticking'—that is outwardly not 'bolting,' etc.) and she thereby suffers, despises and generally 'minds' less. There seems to me much in this—in the dramatic complexity formed by the 2 cases, etc.—to be gouged out, and it especially strikes me as working rather particularly into my old idea of something to illustrate and *mettre en scène* the big typical American ease of the growing separation of the 2 sexes *là bas* by the growing superiority of the woman, getting all the culture, etc., to the man immersed in business and money. I've wanted a *hinge* for that, a pivot and platform; but wouldn't they here, precisely, appear to be *'archi'*-found? Lots of things, it strikes me, would come in

1. WJ and his wife and daughter Peggy had been guests at Lamb House in April 1901.
2. Sarah Wyman Whitman (d. 25 June 1904), of French ancestry, moved in the best circles of Cambridge society; she was a portraitist, an artist in stained glass, an amateur archaeologist, a female-American version of the Renaissance man—"all one knows." WJ wrote of her to HJ (28 June 1904): "An extraordinary and indefinable creature! . . . her way of taking people as a great society 'business' proceeding, . . . her agitated life of tip-toe reaching in so many directions, of genuinest amiability. . . . She leaves a dreadful vacuum in Boston." See HJ's graceful letter to her, *Letters* II, 425–26. WJ's view of her husband, Henry Whitman (d. June 1901), was more indulgent than HJ's. On Whitman's death WJ wrote (10 July 1901): "Whitman, whom I never knew very well, but whom I always liked thoroughly, and wish I had known better."

under it; and I must hammer at it—that is, turn it round a bit—with more time and a better occasion x x x x x

Meanwhile there is something else—a very tiny *fantaisie* probably—in small notion that comes to me of a man haunted by the fear more and more, throughout life, that *something will happen to him:* he doesn't quite know what. His life *seems* safe and ordered, his liabilities and exposures (as a *result* of the fear) a good deal curtailed and cut down, so that the years go by and the stroke doesn't fall. Yet 'It *will* come, it will still come,' he finds himself believing—and indeed saying to some one, some second-consciousness in the anecdote. 'It will come before death; I shan't die without it.' Finally I think it must be *he* who sees—not the 2d consciousness. Mustn't indeed the '2d consciousness' be some woman, and it be she who *helps* him to see? She has always loved him—yet, *that,* for the story, 'pretty,' and he, saving, protecting, exempting his life (always, really, with and *for* the fear), has never known it. He likes her, talks to her, confides in her, sees her often—*la côtoie,* as to her hidden passion, but never guesses. She meanwhile, all the time, sees his life as it is. It is to her that he tells his fear—yes, she is the '2d consciousness.' At first she *feels* herself, for him, his feeling of his fear, and is tender, reassuring, protective. Then she reads, as I say, his real case, and is, though unexpressedly, *lucid.* The years go by and *she sees the thing not happen.* At last one day they are somehow, some day, face to face over it, and then she speaks. 'It *has,* the great thing you've always lived in dread of, had the foreboding of—it *has* happened to you.' He wonders—when, how, what? 'What is it?—why, it is that *nothing* has happened!' Then, later on, I think, to keep up the prettiness, it must be that HE sees, that he understands. She has loved him always—and *that* might have happened. But it's too late—she's dead. That, I think, at least, he comes to later on, after an interval, after her death. She is dying, or ill, when she says it. He *then* DOESN'T understand, doesn't see—or so far, only, as to agree with her, ruefully, that that very well *may* be it: that nothing has happened. He goes back; she is gone: she is dead. *What* she has said to him has in a way, by its truth, created the need for her, made him want her, *positively* want her, more. But she is gone, he has lost her, and *then* he sees all she has meant. She has loved him. *(It must come for the* READER *thus, at this moment.)* With his base safety and shrinkage he never knew. *That* was what might have happened, and what *has* happened is that it didn't.

["The Beast in the Jungle," published (without serialization) in *The Better Sort.*]

L.H., August 29th, 1801 [*1901*]

SAME DATE.[1] Note more fully than I can now the small *conte* suggested by W.'s mention of Edmund T[weedy] and 'Margaret,' Aunt M.'s[2] *garde-malade* and at-

---

1. "Same Date" may indicate that HJ meant to write "August 27th," the date of his previous entry.
2. Edmund Tweedy had married Mary Temple, who was not actually an aunt to the Jameses but was so called by them because she was the half-sister of their Temple cousins, whom she adopted after the death of their parents.

tendant whom he inherited after the latter's death. She has been with him—or lately *had*—ever since then—and as his eyes were, with his 87th, 88th, and so, year, supposed to be failing, it became a part of her duty to read to him—a part of regular evening routine. *La voilà,* then, settled down to this, feeling it, however, an effort and a charge, until *her* eyes gave out—with the odd and unexpected result that *he* then began to read to *her*. I seem to see the point of tiny *conte* in that situation. I see it told by a friend—the author is the observer. E.T. *likes* to read aloud—on finding that he *can* (with one of those flickers of life in old age that make his previously-incapable sight no longer an obstacle) and they thus sit together with Margaret having to listen and her *corvée* now changed to *that*. It is worse than the other—she tells me—she complains. If *she* could only read now—that would be the less evil. Could I *arrange* it? Could I put it back as it was before? Well, I try, I approach him on it, but he won't *hear* of it—he is so proud of his *ability,* his powers, which are indeed, at his age, uncanny and unnatural. So I have to leave her to her fate. 'He will read to you till he dies.' 'Ah, but when will he die?' 'Well, you must wait. Now—(here he comes) go and sit down.' And he opens the book and I leave her trying to listen.[3]

October 19th, 1901, Lamb House.

Something in reference to man who, like W.D.H[owells] (say), has never known *at all* any woman BUT his wife—and at 'time of life' somehow sees it, is face to face with it: little situation *on* it. *Ça rentre,* however, rather, into the idea (is a small side of it) of *The Ambassadors.* But *never,* NEVER—in any degree to call a relation at all: *and on American lines.* x x x x x

Something like the man who subscribes to an agency for 'clippings'—a Romeike, or whatever, *quelconque,* to send him everything 'that appears about him,' and finds that nothing ever appears, that he never receives anything[1] x x x x x

And connection between that and notion suggested by little case of woman writing to me (to fill in some paper) on behalf of *Outlook.* The case of the newspaper girl or man who *needs* your reply, your taking *some* notice—suggesting once the little antithesis for tale: the would-be newspaperite whom, by a *guignon,* of his, of hers, people never answer (and sadness of that); and the other who finds that they never fail, that they leap, bound at him, press, surge, scream to be advertised; and ugliness of *that.* Awfully good little possibility seems to me to abide in it, as contrast and link between them—different shows of human egotism and the newspaper scramble: or even in the opposition, conjunction, *rencontre* of failure-girl and man first-named.

[*"The Papers," published (without serialization) in *The Better Sort.*]

3. Cf. "Mrs. Procter's Tale," 28 October and 21 December 1895.
1. See 17 August 1901.

August 31st, 1906 Lamb House[1]

Never yet made a record here of the fact that I "took" Lamb House, Rye (where I write this) in October 1897, and came here to live on one of the 1st days of July 1898.[2] I note this after all these years.

Lamb House, December 26th, 1908.

Mrs. F.F. (of Budd's Wittersham, where Aleck[1] and I have just been spending Xmas) mentioned to me little local fact that strikes me as good small 'short-story' *donnée* of the orthodox type. (It was told her of some small working or shop-keeping person there.) The man had engaged himself to a young woman, but afterwards had thought better of it and had backed out, to her great indignation and resentment, so that she threatened him *bel et bien* with an action for breach of promise of marriage—and so menacingly, and with such a prospect or presumption of success that he, scared, afraid of the scandal and injury, etc., agreed to 'compromise' and pay her two hundred Pounds of damages—her own valuation, etc. This he did, but with the effect for years afterward of staggering under the load of the obligations he had contracted to raise the money. His whole life blighted by it, impoverished, etc.—and the years going by. In the Wittersham case—as she heard—he had married somebody else, etc.; after which, his wife dying, he had come round somehow to *her,* his early fiancée again—or she to *him*—and they had patched it up somehow and married. What I seem to see in it is *her* life and behaviour—her subsequent action. She has got her £200—she has been thrifty and canny; she has found work (off perhaps as a domestic servant in London); she has kept her money and added to it—she has led her life. She waited and watched in short—watched the hero of her early episode—from afar—or I seem to see her rather designedly and consciously doing it—almost on a calculation of what may happen. She *sees* him suffer—sees him burdened and collapsing—sees him pay for what he has done to her; and she measures and follows this, as if determined to let it go a certain time. In the little story, as I see it take its turn, they finally meet again—and they then marry. She has kept the money—she has it for him, gives it back to him augmented—she has been keeping it for him till the day when only this will save him. I seem to see her come to him—it isn't that he goes to *her;* never! And at first he won't look at her. They must have met before—he seen her prosperous, etc. Then he has hated her, etc. The thing given him by her in the end as all her own plan, design, etc. She has taken the money because she has known he would want money badly—later on; and she has kept it although other men have made up to her for it. She tells him she has refused to marry—so that the money shouldn't be got at by her husband. He has known of a case—a fellow she has known before she knew him and *whom she*

1. See 6 January 1897.

2. HJ signed the lease before the end of September 1897 and slept in Lamb House for the first time probably on 28 June 1898. See *Life* 462, 468.

1. Alexander Robertson James (1891–1946), WJ's youngest son. They were staying at the home of Francis Ford, the music critic.

has refused or chucked, jilted, in order to become engaged to him—and whom she supposes that now she *will* marry (now that she has the money); he sees her refuse this man just *because* she has, and wishes to keep, the money—and he's mystified and hasn't understood—thinks the money has made her 'proud'—and mean. But she has just thus remained single for him. At last, when he (the 'hero') learns that she has the money, *then* he accepts her charity, then he marries her.

["The Bench of Desolation," *Putnam's Magazine* October-December 1909 and January 1910; reprinted in *The Finer Grain*.]

Same date. Noting this has brought back to me the little *donnée, à la Mary Wilkins,*[2] etc., which I took mental note of here 10 years ago—the situation mentioned to me in relation to W.D. and his drinking-habits, etc., by (I think) Mrs. E.S. That surely is do-able—and I see it from the 'point of view of the woman,' don't I?—effectively enough. She traces, *views,* notes, follows, records, *reflects* (by observations and anxiety) the effect upon her rejected suitor, of the marriage she *has* made—his beginning to be seen to drink, then his getting worse, etc. She sees it herself at her wedding feast—on her wedding day. It makes her glad she *didn't* choose him—yet she yearns over him too till he gets worse. Then she declines responsibility—or assures herself she does. And I seem to see it 'told' through some—through 'certain'—passages between herself and a 'confidant'; not her husband, not the man she has accepted (that *complicates*), but her trustee, adviser, elderly bachelor friend or whatever, *qui lui rapporte* and talks over with him the facts involved. He has hoped she'll 'take' W.D. Then when she doesn't he fears something; and it's only through him she has news of the rejected one (I think). In fact this *has* to be for brevity. It goes on in a series of 'conversations'— or whatever. I see *this, par exemple,* in an 'easy' 5000. Surely I do. It's the very *type,* at least—it has *that* for it. And its predecessor noted here—that *ils ont pour eux* if nothing else. They are rather too much alike to be done as a pair. But I see the one before this in '5 of 5'—five little sections of 5 pages each: 25 in all, and 5000 words, through each section being of 1000 words—200 to a page. The present, the 'W.D.' one, seems to cut itself, say perhaps, rather in 3 or 4 parts. *Voyons alors.*

Same date. I find on loose page an allusion to what I call G.L.G.'s (and 'Colonel' H.'s[3] story. Ah *that!*

Names. Parkyn—Dummett—Sugg—Gaymer (or Gamer)—Properly.

Lamb House, February 10th, 1909.

A sense with me, divine and beautiful, of hooking on again to the 'sacred years' of the old D.V. Gdns. time,[1] the years of the whole theatric dream and the 'work-

2. Mary Eleanor Wilkins (1852–1930), later Mrs. Freeman, author of novels and tales of New England rural life, which HJ found "impossible" because of their "sentimentality" (see *Letters* IV, 223, 260).

3. Sir George Leveson Gower (1858–1951), private secretary to Prime Minister Gladstone, 1880–85, and European editor of the *North American Review,* 1899–1908; "Colonel H." may allude to Col. George Harvey of Harper's.

1. HJ lived at 34 De Vere Gardens, London W., from March 1886 to the end of June 1898.

ing out' sessions, all ineffable and uneffaceable, that went with that, and that still live again, somehow (indeed I *know* how!) in their ashes:—that sense comes to me, I say, over the *concetto* of fingering a little what I call the C.F. and Katrina B. subject[2]—that [of] the Prsa. de M. and de G. connection and of the 'humiliations' of Mrs. B. without her *amanti*—in the midst of the *amanti* of the others— that's what C.F. very intelligently said to me one day, put vividly before me.

August 3rd, 1909, Lamb House[1]

Also never yet (Aug. 3*rd* 1909) made a record of the fact that I went to the United States on the 24*th* or 25*th* (I forget which) of August 1904 (sailing from Southampton in Kaiser Wilhelm der Grosse), and arrived at N.Y. in 5 days (about); and that I sailed again from Boston the following year July 4*th* 1905[2]—in Ivernia—Walter Berry and Elizabeth Robins[3] being fellow-passengers.

2. C. F. is Constance Fletcher (1858–1938), an American novelist who wrote under the pen name "George Fleming"; *Kismet* is her best-known work. She was a longtime resident of Venice, as was Katherine De Kay Bronson—whom HJ called "Katrina" during the last half-dozen years of her life. The "subject" would ultimately be developed into *The Ivory Tower*, left unfinished at HJ's death; see detached note "The 'K.B.' Case" (1909) and dictated notes for *The Ivory Tower* (1914).

1. See 6 January 1897.

2. HJ sailed on 24 August and docked on 30 August 1904. He left Boston for the return on 5 July 1905; it was a nine-day voyage.

3. Walter Van Rensselaer Berry (1859–1927), born in Paris, graduated from Harvard and took a law degree from Columbia. He was appointed to the International Tribunals in Egypt in 1909, was president of the American Chamber of Commerce in Paris (1916–23), and was for years an intimate friend of Edith Wharton. Elizabeth Robins (1863–1952), a Kentucky-born actress, created major Ibsen roles on the London stage with considerable success, and played the role of Mme de Cintré in HJ's play *The American*. The voyage is described in Robins, *Theatre and Friendship* (1932), 251–53.

1911

This notebook (Houghton Journal IX, 21 April 1911 to 10 May 1911), 7″ x 8½″, has brown marbled covers, white endpapers, a blank flyleaf and 152 lined and numbered pages with marbled edges; the entries are on 43 recto pages, first page written in pencil, remainder in black ink. Page 1 has the heading "95 Turning St. Cambridge Nov 16th 1910" but no entry; the first entry is for 21 April 1911. This, the briefest of all HJ's extant notebooks, testifies to the change in his *modus operandi*. During the winter of 1896–97 HJ had begun to dictate most of his work and much of his correspondence. He soon learned to dictate directly to a typist. The change is visible in the closing pages of this notebook. Furthermore, the first entry in HJ's earliest surviving pocket diary, dated 15 February 1909, antedates the last entry in Houghton Journal VI: he seems to have begun to shift from a reliance on notebooks to a new reliance on his pocket diaries for his note-taking habit. Even allowing for the many missing notebooks and pocket diaries, this seems more than coincidental.

April 21st, 1911.

Just to seize the tip of the tail of the idea that I noted a longish time [ago],[1] given me by Alice, a reminiscence of something, I think, that had happened at Weymouth, Mass., in her childhood; the incident of the woman waked up at night by some sound, below stairs, that shows there is someone in the house, on which she wakes up her husband. They listen, they consider—they become convinced that a burglar, a thief, a malefactor of some sort has made his way in and is operating with great precautions, which have yet not prevented their hearing him.

1. See entry for 11 September 1900. Alice is WJ's widow.

It is obvious the husband must go down and see—but the wife perceives, at first with surprise and then with resentment, that he is not at all inclined to. She appeals to him, to his self-respect, to his common courage, but he remains unmoved and unshamed—whereupon she feels that she really now, in the light of this deplorable exhibition, knows him for the first time. It's a shock and a disgust to her, and in the irritation it produces, and by way of putting him to the blush, she determines to go down herself. She does so—though he protests (so not to the point, how- ever, of preventing her by mustering pluck himself); she goes down, she faces the intruder—whom she finds to be a young man of the town whom she knows, whom she *has* known. I seem to see, yes, that they are old acquaintances or friends, that something has passed between them several years before: when she was a girl of twenty, say; she being now 30 and (but) these 2 or 3 years married. He, the man, has had a sort of 'lower-orders' flirtation with her—they've kept company for a little, or whatever—she having given him up or broken with him because of his bad habits, his being wild or idle, his not inspiring her with due confidence. Then she has lost sight of him—he has left the place. Behold then now she sees him again, after the interval, in this extraordinary situation—that of his standing there in her kitchen at 2 o'clk in the morning. I am assuming thus at any rate that they have had this relation—but *il faudra voir;* just as I seem to see that the scene must—had best—be a London suburb. Well, she confronts him— whether recognizing him or not (*as* an old—a young—acquaintance); and in either case their interview is a curious, an odd one. It takes a remarkable, an anomalous turn. Decidedly, they *must* have met before; the economy of the tale as a short thing demands it. The great fact is that he is unexpectedly mild and accommodat- ing and reasonable—he doesn't threaten or bully or browbeat her, and she, on her side, doesn't (after a bit) threaten him with exposure. He attempts to explain and justify—to make out that he only stole in, through the temptation of seeing a window unlatched or whatever, to get some food. (His pretext, apology or what- ever, to be worked out; as also the question of *his* surprise and the question of whether he knew the house to be hers, her husband's, or only *happened* to have, by an extraordinary coincidence, picked out theirs as the subject of his attempt.) Probably he must have *observed* they were there and so chosen: this is what she accuses him of—of resentfully playing on her and on the man she has married this belated vengeance, to make her pay for her old contempt of him. Something of that sort. He a poor *raté,* of course—essentially a vagabond, but with redeeming traits; and of course I can only pretend here to the barest skeleton. She feeds him and gets rid of him—it's of course of the essence that the scene mustn't be too prolonged—as that makes her husband's not coming down quite too unnatural. If she stays below—while he sharply listens above—beyond a certain point, he will of course come down to see what she's doing—unless indeed one can put it that her non-return and apparent non-departure of the burglar constitutes an additional ground for fear by seeming to indicate that she may somehow have been nefar- iously dealt with. At any rate the passage between the two takes place, and the great point of it is that she is *interested.* The young man somehow or other pro- duces that effect; so that though she does give him something to eat and lets him off safely—I mean gets rid of him for a very bad character—she keeps hold of him to the extent of not absolutely refusing to see him again in some wholly different way—and of even getting from him some indication of where and how he can again be got at. His plea is that her old treatment of him had ruined him, that she has been the prime cause of his perversion. She can still help him, he pretends, by being 'Kind' to him, and he leaves her with a measure of assurance that she will be. She goes up again to her husband, flushed, as it were, with the success of the boldness she has shown, and proportionately the more disillusioned and disdainful at the sort of figure that, through it, her lord and master has made. (He is a 'city-clerk' or such like—and they are in the position of keeping a servant who has been that night absent on a necessity of some sort or a holiday.) When he asks his wife what has happened below—who was there and what she—or he—did, she only looks at him from the depths of her disgust—at first without answering, and as if amazed and additionally nauseated at his asking. Then she has an inspiration. 'I won't tell you.' And on his pressure, his urgency: 'Nothing would induce me to.' He has to take it then, and they go to bed; but on the morrow he returns to the question—he wants so abjectly to know. As she sees this it gives her cue—she sees that she can punish him for his poltroonery by balking his curiosity. 'You shall *never* know—you shall never, never, never get it out of me.' As she sees the curiosity work in him she determines that he never shall, and she will attend to it that he shall not in any way find out. To this end she sees her young man again—she judges that she must *tell* him how she is dealing with her husband on the question of what happened between them that night—how he is never to know: so that he, the young man, shall keep *his* mouth absolutely closed about it. I seem to see that I must somehow or other make the irruption comparatively innocuous and innocent—as having some colour of need. He may have thought them absent and come in to help himself to something— only *what?*—that he was very much in want of. They have been absent and just got back—he not knowing of their return (that evening). The idea of the small thing comes out then *there*—in the relation created between the wife and the young man, created *for* her with him, by his thus getting her to help him to conceal his act from the *possibility* of her husband's knowing—and by his know- ing how she was dealing with her husband, and why she was so doing it. Happy thought—the young man isn't a burglar—he's a young man she knows—he thinks they are away. The great thing is that the husband knows the other person, 'the man,' knows what a coward he has been. She tells him she has told the man. Therefore what man is it? His intense curiosity to know. It intensely and horridly works in him. The growth of his suspicion of the 'relation'; not a relation formed, to his imagination, for 'illicit' purposes, but made up of their knowing together, she and the man, the abject little facts about him. If he can only know, if he can only learn, who her participant in this is while the fact that he doesn't, that the other man gives no sign, and the sense therefrom proceeding of the 'hold' she accordingly has upon the unknown only irritates and haunts him the more. Well, so far so good—if 'good' at all: but the question is, what does it, the situation, lead to, and where is one's little issue, climax or denouement? It must arrive somewhere, or it's without form and void. I ask myself, but nothing very much seems to come—and with my small prospect of ever using any such small scrap of a *donnée,* after all the humiliation and pain and inconvenience I've been through over this question of my small pieces—the end of the matter scarce seems worth gouging out now. However, I hate to touch things only to leave them, and the appeal of the little old consecrated idea of the application of the particular firm and gentle pressure that has seen me, in the past, through so many dark quandaries, difficult moments, hours of more or less anguish ('artistic' at least), that appeal throbs within me, or before me, again, and pleads and penetrates. I seem to see it glimmer to me that one's climax here is in some effect of the husband's finding out, identifying the man. He finds out *and*—well, what comes of it and how does he do it? I seem to want it to be somehow to his advantage and not to that of his wife—or at least I seem to want it to be to the advantage of the 'man,' the wife's fellow-conspirator or concealer. *Mettons* that he is bored by the fuss the woman makes over their secret at last—and *mettons* that at this stage the husband 'spots' him as *the* man. The way the husband spots him to be worked out; it would be arrangeable. The husband then lets him know that he has so spotted him, but *asks him not to let the wife know he has* done so. The man consents, promises, and the husband believes him, and that, in a way, makes a case—given the *how and why* the husband recognizes and sees. The man is affected by the husband, pityingly, humorously or however—and I don't see perhaps—or do I see?—why the story shouldn't, as the best economy possibly, and the best vividness, which *is* the best economy, be *told* by the man himself—*of* himself, *of* the wife and the husband. Doesn't the latter somehow show the man that if it's only *he* of whom the wife is so keeping the identity from him—if it's so only *he*—why he doesn't care a bit. Say then that he proposes *this* to the man— that they two now make a compact, as it were, to keep the wife in the dark—in the dark about her husband having spotted the man and brought his identity home to him; about what has passed between them on that head—so that she may still think, still believe, his own, the husband's, obscurity and worriment complete and continuous and continual. Say the 'man' feels, on grounds of his own—these to be presented—the force or the oddity, the 'quaintness,' of this appeal, and that he is somehow touched and tempted (though isn't it all rather thin?) and that, in a word, he agrees to what the husband asks of him, and sees that the husband sees (as *we* see) that he will keep his promise. He does so, and the husband's sense of it is somehow the latter's revenge—on the wife. He has befooled her, taken her in *l'a mise dedans.* For she all the while *thinks,* believes, and the man now deceives her—and that is the husband's *revanche.* Now that I have so threshed it out—*à propos*—I can't say it strikes [me] as much of a matter—but such is the only way to lay these hovering little ghosts of motives. Attempt to *state* them— and then one sees. This *test* of the statement is moreover in any case such an exquisite thing that it's always worth making, if only for the way it brings back the spell of the old sacred days. The more I seem to fix the little stuff, such as it is, the more I seem to make out that the only way is to make the 'man' narrate it, make it *his* adventure. The wife, coming down, TELLS him what has happened above stairs—she gives her husband away to him;—and she may thus have seen him (*he* can make that right) for the 1st time. That, from the 1st, sticks in his crop a little and makes him wonder—even while he consents to do what she asks. He doesn't like it—for she, after all, *needn't* have told him—she might have pretexted, or whatever. Thus it lays a kind of basis, from the 1st, for the evolution of his feeling, and the turn of the climax—though, ah me, perhaps, what grand names! x x x x x

April 25th, 1911, 95 Irving St.

And then there is the little fantasy of the young woman (as she came into my head the other month) who remains so devoted to her apparently chronically invalid Mother, so attached to her bedside and so piously and exhaustedly glued there, to her waste of youth and strength and cheer, that certain persons, the doctor, the friend or two, the other relation or two, are unanimous as to the necessity that something be done about it—that is, that the daughter be got away, that she be saved while yet there is time. Say she is 35—or, perhaps (for the mother's being young enough), 32 or 33, and has been fast at her post for 10, 12, 14 years. She has always refused to move, under whatever pressure; she has been almost sublimely *entêtée* about it; but, visibly, she *is* worn and spent, she is withering on the stem—that is, more or less fading and fainting and perishing, at her post. Thus it is that the others intervene—and again I see that the little story must be told *more mea* by a witness, by an agent and a spectator, by one of the interveners, interferers, man or woman, but most probably by a man—one of those who have been partly responsible. He relates it as an odd, almost as a droll, case. Well, what happens, by my *concetto,* is that the young woman consents under this extreme benevolent and sympathetic pressure, to *take* the holiday, to go away, to go abroad, for a time—say, as the case is put to her, for 6 months. (Of course the locus must be American—New Englandish.) She resigns herself, makes the effort, goes. It is the person who takes her place *auprès de la mère souffrante* who tells the tale—THAT clearly shines out; THAT is the obviously designated economy. So it goes; only *this* identity for the narrator surely, after all, makes that person a woman. 'I' (narrating) then take my place by the mother, and my poor cousin or whatever, my heroine in short, starts for Europe in consonance with arrangements made for her. What happens in 3 words (for I mustn't draggle *this* out here) is that in the first place Betty or whoever (to give her a stopgap name) doesn't come home in 6 months but prolongs her absence to 12 or 15; and that in the second place, when she does come, she shows herself absolutely detached and indifferent. She has been cured of her devotion—the holiday has acted but too well; the world has entered into her, and to see more of it, and thereby shed and shuffle off her burden, is the one thought that now possesses her. She has, in a word, a wholly changed consciousness, and the change is what I chronicle. That is the *subject* of the small stuff—that I see what we have done and that we have produced our effect only too well. 'The state—*of absolute indifference,* ONLY THAT AT 1ST—we have brought about in her by her experiences *là-bas*—so that what in the world can they, can these have been?' That is but the 1st half of the matter, however; for obviously there must be a development and a supplement, complement, to make a drama and a climax—to complete the case. What then shall this be? It has already come to me: the irony of the thing resides in the effect on the mother of this change of Betty's state. It would of course be in the last degree stupid and ugly and uninteresting that it should be simply a *bad* effect—the effect of the mother's sinking or suffering under neglect or cruelty. I see it as quite *another* effect—I assist at it as such; and therein seems to be a very pretty and curious and amusing situation. The mother realises that the daughter doesn't want to come back to her and *is* at 1st wounded, wronged, staggered; but then rallies from that under the effect of circumstances. Won't it be, *inter alia,* that Betty has made a little *héritage,* a sufficient one to give her her freedom if she is disposed to use it? She uses it then—and what the mother rallies under the effects of is the positive fascinations of the new character and new activity that Betty has taken on. Betty's 'heartlessness,' the *degree* of her detachment, itself fascinates her—makes her 'sit up.' She sits up 1st for surprise—then for a sort of resentful and even vindictive curiosity and interest. She becomes in her way as changed, as re-animated (and thereby as capable and convalescent) as Betty herself. My idea, my narrative vision, is that as Betty turns from her she ravenously turns after her. As Betty flees from her she rises from her long sofa and eagerly pursues. The fascinations, the resentment, the bringing B. to justice (partly—and partly the curiosity, the participating) give her that strength. Betty dashes off to Europe again, and before I know it, the mother, shaking *me* clear, has dashed after. I see, I hear of, the elder, following the younger woman like the tail of a kite or a comet. This must go more or less on—it must in fact all go on for 2 or 3 years (I getting echoes, gleams, rumours, reports, glimpses of it) in Europe. Then I see Betty return, breathless, having outstripped her mother. Then I see the mother arrive, breathless also, to overtake, to rejoin, Betty. Then I see Betty start afresh for Europe (dash away absolutely in secret) and, the next thing, see the mother take a following steamer—stream away after her: which makes my climax, the last *recorded* note of the drama and the point where I leave them. The thing necessitates, of course, the *recency* of the record; the narrator's having somehow brought it up to yesterday. That is all there is of it.

May 10th, 1911, 95 Irving St.

Can I catch hold—if it be in the least worth the effort?—of a very small fantasy that came to me the other month in New York?—but which, as I look at [it] a minute or so, seems to say to me that it has almost nothing to give. I mean the little idea about the good little picture in the bad sale, the small true and authentic old thing that the 'hero' of the sale recognizes in a sham collection, a *ramassis* of false attributions that are on show previous to being put up at auction. The idea came to me on my going in to one of the extraordinary places—for the pompous flourishing look in which humbugging masterpieces are offered to view—and recognizing that it was an array of wretched counterfeits and imitations. But the idea seems already to have slipped away—practically. I imagined that in such a show, in such company, after going (very quickly and easily) from one thing to another, I (the person narrating the anecdote) suddenly recognize a little thing which *is* a genuine old master, a primitive, perhaps—or something else, and seeing how lost in the heap, and compromised by its associations it is—pity it for the company it keeps x x x x x But I break down—letting the thing for the moment go.[1]

1. This entry concludes this notebook, the last of the Houghton Journals (IX).

The American Journals
1881–1905

1881–1882

American Journal I (Houghton Journal II, 25 November 1881 to 11 November 1882), $7\frac{1}{2}''$ x 9″, has wine marbled covers, spine and corners reinforced with black trim; wine marbled endpapers; and 186 lined pages, all with marbled edges. The first eight pages are written in indelible pencil, pages 9 to 55 are written in black ink, and the remainder are blank. On the flyleaf are written the names of HJ's clubs—Reform, Athenaeum, and Savile—with the amount and date of annual subscription (see Cash Accounts in the Appendices).

The first American Journal offers an autobiographical review that confirms HJ in his decision to live abroad and strengthens his resolve to work harder as his fortieth birthday approaches. The last entry, in its reference to the play *Daisy Miller,* anticipates the advent of HJ's "dramatic years"—implicit at the close of the earliest surviving scribbler. The last four pages of the manuscript contain entries for 6 January 1897, 31 August 1906, and 3 August 1909; they are published here for the first time, in their proper chronological place in the notebook for 1896 to 1909.

Brunswick Hotel, Boston, November 25th, 1881.

If I should write here all that I might write, I should speedily fill this as yet unspotted blank-book, bought in London six months ago, but hitherto unopened. It is so long since I have kept any notes, taken any memoranda, written down my current reflections, taken a sheet of paper, as it were, into my confidence. Meanwhile so much has come and gone, so much that it is now too late to catch, to reproduce, to preserve. I have lost too much by losing, or rather by not having acquired, the note-taking habit. It might be of great profit to me; and now that I am older, that I have more time, that the labour of writing is less onerous to me, and I can work more at my leisure, I ought to endeavour to keep, to a certain extent, a record of passing impressions, of all that comes, that goes, that I see, and feel, and observe. To catch and keep something of life—that's what I mean. Here I am back in America, for instance, after six years of absence, and likely while here to see and learn a great deal that ought not to become mere waste material. Here I am, *da vero,* and here I am likely to be for the next five months. I am glad I have come—it was a wise thing to do. I needed to see again *les miens,* to revive my relations with them, and my sense of the consequences that these relations entail. Such relations, such consequences, are a part of one's life, and the best life, the most complete, is the one that takes full account of such things. One can only do this by seeing one's people from time to time, by being with them, by entering into their lives. Apart from this I hold it was not necessary I should come to this country. I am 37[1] years old, I have made my choice, and God knows that I have now no time to waste. My choice is the old world—my choice, my need, my life. There is no need for me today to argue about this; it is an inestimable blessing to me, and a rare good fortune, that the problem was settled long ago, and that I have now nothing to do but to act on the settlement.[2]—My impressions here are exactly what I expected they would be, and I scarcely see the place, and feel the manners, the race, the tone of things, now that I am on the spot, more vividly than I did while I was still in Europe. My work lies there— and with this vast new world, *je n'ai que faire.* One can't do both—one must choose. No European writer is called upon to assume that terrible burden, and it seems hard that I should be. The burden is necessarily greater for an American— for he *must* deal, more or less, even if only by implication, with Europe: whereas no European is obliged to deal in the least with America. No one dreams of calling him less complete for not doing so. (I speak of course of people who do the sort of work that I do; not of economists, of social science people.) The painter of manners who neglects America is not thereby incomplete as yet; but a hundred years hence—fifty years hence perhaps—he will doubtless be accounted so. My impressions of America, however, I shall, after all, not write here. I don't need to write them (at least not *à propos* of Boston); I know too well what they are. In many ways they are extremely pleasant; but, Heaven forgive me! I feel as if my time were terribly wasted here! x x x x x

It is too late to recover all those lost impressions—those of the last six years— that I spoke of in beginning; besides, they are not lost altogether, they are buried deep in my mind, they have become part of my life, of my nature. At the same time, if I had nothing better to do, I might indulge in a retrospect that would be interesting and even fruitful—look back over all that has befallen me since last I left my native shores. I could remember vividly, and I have little doubt I could express happily enough, if I made the effort. I could remember without effort with what an irresistible longing I turned to Europe, with what ardent yet timid hopes, with what indefinite yet inspiring intentions, I took leave of *les miens.* I recall

1. HJ was actually 38.
2. HJ did not act on that settlement until 1 September 1883, after which date he did not return to the United States until August 1904.

perfectly the maturing of my little plan to get abroad again and remain for years, during the summer of 1875; the summer the latter part of which I spent in Cambridge. It came to me there on my return from New York where I had been spending a bright, cold, unremunerative, uninteresting winter, finishing *Roderick Hudson* and writing for the *Nation*.[3] (It was these two tasks that kept me alive.) I had returned from Europe the year before that, the beginning of September, '74, sailing for Boston with Wendell Holmes and his wife as my fellow passengers.[4] I had come back then to 'try New York,' thinking it my duty to attempt to live at home before I should grow older, and not take for granted too much that Europe alone was possible; especially as Europe for me then meant simply Italy, where I had had some very discouraged hours, and which, lovely and desirable though it was, didn't seem as a permanent residence, to lead to anything. I wanted something more active, and I came back and sought it in New York. I came back with a certain amount of scepticism, but with very loyal intentions, and extremely eager to be 'interested.' As I say, I was interested but imperfectly, and I very soon decided what was the real issue of my experiment. It was by no means equally soon, however, that I perceived how I should be able to cross the Atlantic again. But the opportunity came to me at last—it loomed before me one summer's day, in Quincy St.[5] The best thing I could imagine then was to go and take up my abode in Paris. I went (sailing about October 20th, 1875) and I settled myself in Paris with the idea that I should spend several years there. This was not really what I wanted; what I wanted was London—and Paris was only a stopgap. But London appeared to me then impossible. I believed that I might arrive there in the fullness of years, but there were all sorts of obstacles to my attempting to live there then. I wonder greatly now, in the light of my present knowledge of England, that these obstacles should have seemed so large, so overwhelming and depressing as they did at that time. When a year later I came really to look them in the face, they absolutely melted away. But that year in Paris was not a lost year—on the contrary. On my way thither I spent something like a fortnight in London; lodging at Story's Hotel, in Dover St. It was November—dark, foggy, muddy, rainy—and I knew scarcely a creature in the place. I don't remember calling on anyone but Lady Rose and H. J. W. Coulson,[6] with whom I went out to lunch at Petersham, near Richmond. And yet the great city seemed to me enchanting, and I would have given my little finger to remain there rather than go to Paris. But I went to Paris, and lived for a year at 29 Rue de Luxembourg (now

3. *Roderick Hudson,* serialized in the *Atlantic Monthly* January-December 1875, published by Osgood, Boston (1875), was actually his second novel; *Watch and Ward,* in the *Atlantic* August-December 1871, published by Osgood (1878) was his first. During 1875 HJ contributed 58 unsigned reviews to the *Nation;* another 13 appeared in the first half of 1876; see *Bibliography.*
4. Oliver Wendell Holmes, Jr. (1841–1935), son of Dr. Oliver Wendell Holmes (author of *The Autocrat of the Breakfast Table,* etc.) and future Supreme Court Justice, was an old friend of HJ's and was then newly married to Fannie Bowdich Dixwell.
5. 20 Quincy Street, Cambridge, Massachusetts was the home of HJ's parents, which he shared until his first attempt at expatriation in October 1875.
6. Lady Rose (d. 1883), née Charlotte Temple, an aunt to HJ's Temple cousins, married Sir John Rose (1820–88); see 12 January 1887. For HJ's account of the meeting with Coulson see *Letters* III, 4–5.

Rue Cambon). I shall not attempt to write the history of that year—further than to say that it was time by no means misspent. I learned to know Paris and French affairs much better than before—I got a certain familiarity with Paris (added to what I had acquired before) which I shall never lose. I wrote letters to the *New York Tribune,* of which, though they were poor stuff, I may say that they were too good for the purpose (of course they didn't succeed). I saw a good deal of Charles Pierce that winter—as to whom his being a man of genius reconciled me to much that was intolerable in him.[7] In the spring, at Madame Turgenieff's, I made the acquaintance of Paul Joukowsky.[8] *Non ragioniam di lui—ma guarda e passa.* I don't speak of Ivan Turgenieff, most delightful and lovable of men, nor of Gustav Flaubert, whom I shall always be so glad to have known; a powerful, serious, melancholy, manly, deeply corrupted, yet not corrupting, nature. There was something I greatly liked in him, and he was very kind to me. He was a head and shoulders above the others, the men I saw at his house on Sunday afternoons—Zola, Goncourt, Daudet, etc. (I mean as a man—not as a talker, etc.) I remember in especial one afternoon (a weekday) that I went to see him and found him alone. I sat with him a long time; something led him to repeat to me a little poem of Th. Gautier's—*Les Vieux Portraits* (what led him to repeat it was that we had been talking of French poets, and he had been expressing his preference for Théophile Gautier over Alfred de Musset—*il était plus français,* etc.)[9] I went that winter a great deal to the Comédie Française—though not so much as when I was in Paris in '72. Then I went every other night—or almost. And I have been a great deal since. I may say that I know the Comédie Française. Of course I saw a great deal of the little American 'set'—the American village encamped *en plein Paris.* They were all very kind, very friendly, hospitable, etc; they knew up to a certain point their Paris. But ineffably tiresome and unprofitable. Their society had become a kind of obligation, and it had much to do with my suddenly deciding to abandon my plans of indefinite residence, take flight to London and settle there as best I could. I remember well what a crime Mrs. S.[10] made of my doing so; and one or two other persons as to whom I was perfectly unconscious of having given them the right to judge my movements so intimately. Nothing is more characteristic of certain American women than the extraordinary promptitude with which they assume such a right. I remember how Paris had, in a hundred ways, come to weary and displease me; I couldn't get out of the detestable *Amer-*

---

7. Charles Sanders Peirce (1839–1914), physicist, mathematician, and one of America's foremost philosophers. His philosophy of pragmatism profoundly influenced WJ.

8. Son of the Russian poet and translator, Vassili Zhukovsky (to give the modern transliteration of the name), and himself an amateur painter; he had been reared in the court of the Tsarina. Ivan Turgenev introduced him to HJ in Paris in April 1876. See *Letters* II, 40–43.

9. Ivan Turgenev (1818–83), Russian expatriate novelist; Gustave Flaubert (1821–80); Emile Zola (1840–1902); Edmond de Goncourt (1822–96); Alphonse Daudet (1840–97); Théophile Gautier (1811–72); and Alfred de Musset (1810–57) were some of the most important figures on the French literary scene, and HJ met and wrote critical commentary on most of them. See *Bibliography.*

10. Mrs. Charles E. Strong, née Eleanor Fearing, of New York. Estranged from her lawyer husband, cousin of the jurist George Templeton Strong, she became a lifelong expatriate with her daughter. HJ first met her in Rome in November 1869. See Louis Auchincloss, *Reflections of a Jacobite* (1961), the essay on "Crisis in Newport—August 1857."

ican Paris. Then I hated the Boulevards, the horrible monotony of the new quarters. I saw, moreover, that I should be an eternal outsider. I went to London in November, 1876. I should say that I had spent that summer chiefly in three places: at Étretat, at Varennes (with the Lee Childes),[11] and at Biarritz—or rather at Bayonne, where I took refuge being unable to find quarters at Biarritz. Then late in September I spent a short time at St. Germain, at the Pavillon Louis XIV. I was finishing *The American*. The pleasantest episode (by far) of that summer was my visit to the Childes; to whom I had been introduced by dear Jane Norton, who had been very kind to me during the winter; and who have remained my very good friends. Varennes is a little moated *castel* of the most picturesque character, a few miles from Montargis, *au coeur de l'ancienne France*. I well recall the impression of my arrival—driving over from Montargis with Edward Childe—in the warm August evening and reaching the place in the vague twilight, which made it look precisely like a *décor d'opéra*. I have been back there since—and it was still delightful; but at this time I had not had my now very considerable experience of country visits in England; I had not seen all those other wonderful things. Varennes therefore was an exquisite sensation—a memory I shall never lose. I settled myself again in Paris—or attempted to do so (I like to linger over these details, and to recall them one by one); I had no intention of giving it up. But there were difficulties in the Rue de Luxembourg—I couldn't get back my old apartment, which I had given up during the Summer. I don't remember what suddenly brought me to the point of saying—'Go to; I will try London.' I think a letter from William had a good deal to do with it, in which he said, 'Why don't you?—That must be the place.' A single word from outside often moves one (moves *me* at least) more than the same word infinitely multiplied as a simple voice from within. I *did* try it, and it has succeeded beyond my most ardent hopes. As I think I wrote just now, I have become passionately fond of it; it is an anchorage for life. Here I sit scribbling in my bedroom at a Boston hotel—on a marble-topped table!—and conscious of a ferocious homesickness—a homesickness which makes me think of the day when I shall next see the white cliffs of old England loom through their native fog, as one of the happiest of my life! The history of the five years I have spent in London—a pledge, I suppose, of many future years—is too long, and too full to write. I can only glance at it here. I took a lodging at 3 Bolton St., Piccadilly; and there I have remained till today—there I have left my few earthly possessions, to await my return. I have *lived* much there, felt much, thought much, learned much, produced much; the little shabby furnished apartment ought to be sacred to me. I came to London as a complete stranger, and today I know much too many people. *J'y suis absolument comme chez moi.* Such an experience is an education—it fortifies the character and embellishes the mind. It is difficult to speak adequately or justly of London. It is not a pleasant place; it is not agreeable, or cheerful, or easy, or exempt from reproach. It is only magnificent. You can draw up a tremendous list of reasons why it should be insupportable. The fogs, the smoke, the dirt, the darkness, the wet,

---

11. The American Edward Lee Childe and his French wife, Blanche de Triqueti. See 17 November 1884, note 4.

the distances, the ugliness, the brutal size of the place, the horrible numerosity of society, the manner in which this senseless bigness is fatal to amenity, to convenience, to conversation, to good manners—all this and much more you may expatiate upon. You may call it dreary, heavy, stupid, dull, inhuman, vulgar at heart and tiresome in form. I have felt these things at times so strongly that I have said—'Ah London, you too then are impossible?'' But these are occasional moods; and for one who takes it as I take it, London is on the whole the most possible form of life. I take it as an artist and as a bachelor; as one who has the passion of observation and whose business is the study of human life. It is the biggest aggregation of human life—the most complete compendium of the world. The human race is better represented there than anywhere else, and if you learn to know your London you learn a great many things. I felt all this in that autumn of 1876, when I first took up my abode in Bolton St. I had very few friends, the season was of the darkest and wettest; but I was in a state of deep delight. I had complete liberty, and the prospect of profitable work; I used to take long walks in the rain. I took possession of London; I felt it to be the right place. I could get English books: I used to read in the evenings, before an English fire. I can hardly say how it was, but little by little I came to know people, to dine out, etc. I did, I was able to do, nothing at all to bring this state of things about; it came rather of itself. I had very few letters—I was afraid of letters. Three or four from Henry Adams, three or four from Mrs. Wister, of which I only, as I think, presented one (to George Howard).[12] Poor Motley,[13] who died a few months later, and on whom I had no claim of *any* kind, sent me an invitation to the Athenaeum, which was renewed for several months, and which proved an unspeakable blessing. When once one starts in the London world (and one cares enough about it, as I did, to make one's self agreeable, as I did) *cela va de soi;* it goes with constantly increasing velocity. I remained in London all the following summer—till Sept. 1st—and then went abroad and spent some six weeks in Paris, which was rather empty and very lovely, and went a good deal to the theatre. Then I went to Italy, spending almost all my time in Rome (I had a little apartment flooded with sun, in the Capo le Case). I came back to England before Xmas and spent the following nine months or so in Bolton St. The club question had become serious and difficult; a club was indispensable, but I had of course none of my own. I went through Gaskell's[14] (and I think Locker's) kindness for some time to the Travellers'; then after that for a good while to the St. James's, where I could pay a monthly fee. At last, I forget exactly when, I was elected to the Reform; I think it was about April, 1878.

12. Sarah Butler Wister (1835–1908), daughter of the actress Fanny Kemble and the Southern planter Pierce Butler, and mother of the novelist Owen Wister, a close and longtime friend of HJ. George James Howard (1843–1911), ninth Earl of Carlisle, of Castle Howard, York.

13. John Lothrop Motley (1814–77), historian and diplomat (Minister to England under President Grant, 1869–70), obtained guest privileges for HJ at the Athenaeum Club. See *Letters* II, 98–100.

14. Charles George Milnes Gaskell (1842–1919) was of a well-to-do Yorkshire family whose houses, Thornes (near Wakefield) and Wenlock Abbey in Shropshire, HJ would frequent: he wrote for the *North American Review*. He and Frederick Locker gave HJ entry to the Travellers' Club. HJ paid a monthly fee for use of St. James's Club. Frank H. Hill, editor of the London *Daily News*, and Charles H. Robarts, with the aid of Sir Charles Dilke, put HJ up for the Reform Club where he was elected in May 1878.

(F. H. Hill had proposed, and C. H. Robarts had seconded, me: or vice versa.) This was an excellent piece of good fortune, and the Club has ever since been, to me, a convenience of the first order. I could not have remained in London without it, and I have become extremely fond of it; a deep local attachment. I can now only briefly enumerate the landmarks of the rest of my residence in London. In the autumn of 1878 I went to Scotland, chiefly to stay at Tillypronie. (I afterwards paid a short visit at Gillesbie, Mrs. Rogerson's,[15] in Dumfriesshire.) This was my first visit to Scotland, which made a great impression on me. The following year, 1879, I went abroad again—but only to Paris. I stayed in London during all August, writing my little book on Hawthorne, and on September 1st crossed over to Paris and remained there till within a few days of Xmas. I lodged again in the Rue de Luxembourg, in another house, in a delightful little *entresol entre cour et jardin,* which I had to give up after a few weeks however, as it had been let over my head. Afterwards I went to a hotel in the Rue St. Augustin (de Choiseul et d'Égypte) where I was staying during the great snow-storm of that year, which will long be famous. It was in that October that I went again to Varennes; I had other plans for seeing a little of France which I was unable to carry out. But I did a good deal of work: finished the ill-fated little *Hawthorne,*[16] finished *Confidence,* began *Washington Square,* wrote a *Bundle of Letters.* I went that Christmas, as I had been, I think, the Christmas before, to Ch. Milnes Gaskell's (Thornes).[17] In the spring I went to Italy—partly to escape the 'season,' which had become a terror to me. I couldn't keep out of it—(I had become a highly-developed diner-out, etc.) and its interruptions, its repetitions, its fatigues, were horribly wearisome, and made work extremely difficult. I went to Florence and spent a couple of months, during which I took a short run down to Rome and to Naples, where I had not been since my first visit to Italy, in 1869. I spent three days with Paul Joukowsky at Posilipo, and a couple of days alone at Sorrento.[18] Florence was divine, as usual, and I was a great deal with the Bootts.[19] At that exquisite Bellosguardo at the Hotel de l'Arno, in a room in that deep recess, in the front, I began the *Portrait of a Lady*—that is, I took up, and worked over, an old beginning, made long before. I returned to London to meet William, who came out in the early part of June, and spent a month with me in Bolton St., before going to the continent. That summer and autumn I worked, *tant bien que mal,* at my novel which began to appear in *Macmillan* in October (1880). I got away from London more or less—to Brighton, detestable in August, to Folkestone, Dover, St. Leonard's, etc. I tried to work hard, and I paid very few visits. I had a plan of coming to America for the winter and even took my passage; but I gave it up. William

15. Mrs. Rogerson, née Christina Stewart, popular informal London hostess at one of whose dinners HJ met the American painter James McNeill Whistler (1834–1903) in March 1878. See 19 June 1884.

16. "Ill-fated" because of its unfavorable reception in the United States. See *Life* 247–48.

17. HJ's account of this visit to Thornes House (*Letters* II, 122–28) was prepared for his "An English New Year," the *Nation* January 1879; reprinted in *Portraits of Places,* London (1883) and Boston (1884).

18. On the Sorrento sojourn see *Letters* II, 281–84 and *Life* 253.

19. Francis Boott (1813–1904), an old friend of the James family and heir to New England textile mills, spent many years as an expatriate in Florence where he reared his daughter Elizabeth, or "Lizzie" (1846–88), who married the Cincinnati painter Frank Duveneck in 1886.

came back from abroad and was with me again for a few days, before sailing for home. I spent November and December quietly in London, getting on with the *Portrait,* which went steadily, but very slowly, every part being written twice. About Xmas I went down into Cornwall, to stay with the John Clarks,[20] who were wintering there, and then to the Pakenhams', who were (and still are) in the Government House at Plymouth. (Christmas day, indeed, I spent at the Pakenhams'— a bright, military dinner at which I took in Elizabeth Thompson [Mrs. Butler], the military paintress,[21] a gentle, pleasing woman, very deaf.) Cornwall was charming, and my dear Sir John drove me far away to Penzance, and then to the Land's End, where we spent the morning of New Year's day—a soft moist morning, with the great Atlantic heaving gently round the outermost point of old England. (I was wrong just above in saying that I went *first* to the Clarks'. I went on there from Devonport.) I came back to London for a few weeks, and then, again, I went abroad. I wished to get away from the London crowd, the London hubbub, all the entanglements and interruptions of London life; and to quietly bring my novel to a close. So I planned to betake myself to Venice. I started about February 10th and I came back in the middle of July following. I have always to pay toll which I didn't much enjoy. Then I traveled down through France, to Avignon, Marseilles, Nice, Mentone and San Remo, in which latter place I spent three charming weeks, during most of which time I had the genial society of Mrs. Lombard and Fanny L. who came over from Nice for a fortnight.[22] I worked there capitally, and it made me very happy. I used in the morning to take a walk among the olives, over the hills behind the queer little black, steep town. Those old paved roads that rise behind and above San Remo, and climb and wander through the dusky light of the olives, have an extraordinary sweetness. Below and beyond, were the deep ravines, on whose sides old villages were perched, and the blue sea, glittering through the grey foliage. Fanny L. used to go with me—enjoying it so much that it was a pleasure to take her. I went back to the inn to breakfast (that is, lunch), and scribbled for 3 or 4 hours in the afternoon. Then, in the fading light, I took another stroll, before dinner. We went to bed early, but I used to read late. I went with the Lombards, one lovely day, on an enchanting drive— to the strange little old mountain town of Ceriana. I shall never forget that; it was one of the things one remembers; the grand clear hills, among which we wound higher and higher; the long valley, swimming seaward, far away beneath; the bright Mediterranean, growing paler and paler as we rose above it; the splendid stillness, the infinite light, the clumps of olives, the brown villages, pierced by the carriage road, where the vehicle bumped against opposite doorposts. I spent

20. Sir John Clark, Bt., and Lady Clark owned what HJ described as "the highest placed laird's house in Scotland" at Tillypronie, Aberdeenshire (mentioned above); see "English Vignettes," *Lippincott's Magazine* April 1879, reprinted in *Portraits of Places.* Lieut.-Gen. Thomas Henry Pakenham (1826–1913), Commander (in the Government House at Devonport, the edge of Plymouth Sound) of what was then one of the great military districts of England; his wife was the former Elizabeth Staples Clark of New York. See *Letters* III, 214.
21. Lady Butler, née Elizabeth Southerden Thompson (1846–1933), an artist whose vivid drawings of military subjects delighted Queen Victoria. HJ's brackets.
22. HJ had known Mrs. Lombard and her daughter Fanny in Florence in 1874.

ten days at Milan after that, working at my tale and scarcely speaking to a soul; Milan was cold, dull, and less attractive than it had been to me before. Thence I went straight to Venice, where I remained till the last of June—between three and four months. It would take long to go into that now; and yet I can't simply pass it by. It was a charming time; one of those things that don't repeat themselves; I seemed to myself to grow young again. The lovely Venetian spring came and went, and brought with it an infinitude of impressions, of delightful hours. I became passionately fond of the place, of the life, of the people, of the habits. I asked myself at times whether it wouldn't be a happy thought to take a little *pied-à-terre* there, which one might keep forever. I look at unfurnished apartments; I fancied myself coming back every year. I *shall* go back; but not every year. Herbert Pratt[23] was there for a month, and I saw him tolerably often; he used to talk to me about Spain, about the East, about Tripoli, Persia, Damascus; till it seemed to me that life would be *manquée* altogether if one shouldn't have some of that knowledge. He was a most singular, most interesting type, and I shall certainly put him into a novel. I shall even make the portrait close and he won't mind. Seeing picturesque lands, simply for their own sake, and without making any use of it—that, with him, is a passion—a passion of which if one lives with him a little (a little, I say; not too much) one feels the contagion. He gave me the nostalgia of the sun, of the south, of colour, of freedom, of being one's own master, and doing absolutely what one pleases. He used to say, 'I know such a sunny corner, under the south wall of old Toledo. There's a wild fig tree growing there; I have lain on the grass, with my guitar. There was a musical muleteer, etc.' I remember one evening when he took me to a queer little wineshop, haunted only by gondoliers and *facchini,* in an out of the way corner of Venice. We had some excellent muscat wine; he had discovered the place and made himself quite at home there. Another evening I went with him to his rooms—far down on the Grand Canal, overlooking the Rialto. It was a hot night; the cry of the gondoliers came up from the Canal. He took out a couple of Persian books and read me extracts from Firdausi and Saadi. A good deal might be done with Herbert Pratt. He, however, was but a small part of my Venice. I lodged on the Riva, 4161, *quarto piano.* The view from my windows was *una bellezza;* the far-shining lagoon, the pink walls of San Giorgio, the downward curve of the Riva, the distant islands, the movement of the quay, the gondolas in profile. Here I wrote, diligently every day and finished, or virtually finished, my novel. As I say, it was a charming life; it seemed to me, at times, too improbable, too festive. I went out in the morning—first to Florian's, to breakfast; then to my bath, at the Stabilimento Chitarin; then I wandered about, looking at pictures, street life, etc., till noon, when I went for my real breakfast to the Café Quadri. After this I went home and worked till six o'clock—or sometimes only till five. In this latter case I had time for an hour or two *en gondole* before dinner. The evenings I strolled about, went to Florian's, listened to the music in the Piazza, and two or three

23. Herbert Pratt, WJ's Cambridge friend and fellow medical school student, spent most of his life as the wanderer depicted in this passage. The character of Gabriel Nash in *The Tragic Muse* derives to some extent from Pratt. See 19 June 1884, 11 March 1888, and 2 February 1889.

nights a week went to Mrs. Bronson's.[24] That was a resource but the milieu was too American. Late in the spring came Mrs. V.R.,[25] from Rome, who was an even greater resource. I went with her one day to Torcello and Burano; where we took our lunch and ate it on a lovely canal at the former place. Toward the last of April I went down to Rome and spent a fortnight—during part of which I was laid up with one of those terrible attacks in my head. But Rome was very lovely; I saw a great deal of Mrs. V.R.; had (with her) several beautiful drives. One in particular I remember; out beyond the Ponte Nomentano, a splendid Sunday. We left the carriage and wandered into the fields, where we sat down for some time. The exquisite stillness, the divine horizon, brought back to me out of the buried past all that ineffable, incomparable impression of Rome (1869, 1873). I returned to Venice by Ancona and Rimini. From Ancona I drove to Loreto, and, on the same occasion, to Recanati, to see the house of Giacomo Leopardi, whose infinitely touching letters I had been reading while in Rome. The day was lovely and the excursion picturesque; but I was not allowed to enter Leopardi's house. I saw, however, the dreary little hill-town where he passed so much of his life, with its enchanting beauty of site, and its strange, bright loneliness. I saw the streets—I saw the views he looked upon . . . Very little can have changed. I spent only an evening at Rimini, where I made the acquaintance of a most obliging officer, who seemed delighted to converse with a *forestiero,* and who walked me (it was a Sunday evening) all over the place. I passed near *Urbino:* that is, I passed a station, where I might have descended to spend the night, to drive to Urbino the next day. But I didn't stop! If I had been told that a month before, I should have repelled the foul insinuation. But my reason was strong. I was so nervous about my interrupted work that every day I lost was a misery, and I hurried back to Venice and to my MS. But I made another short absence, in June—a 5 day's *giro* to Vicenza, Bassano, Padua. At Vicenza I spent 3 of these days—it was wonderfully sweet; old Italy, and the old feeling of it. Vivid in my memory is the afternoon I arrived, when I wandered into the Piazza and sat there in the warm shade, before a *caffe* with the smooth slabs of the old pavement around me, the big palace and the tall *campanile* opposite, etc. It was so soft, so mellow, so quiet, so genial, so Italian: very little movement, only the waning of the bright day, the approach of the summer night. Before I left Venice the heat became intense, the days and nights alike impossible. I left it at last, and closed a singularly happy episode; but I took much away with me. x x x x x

I went straight to the Lake of Como and over the Splügen; spent only a lovely evening (with the next morning) at Cadenabbia. I mounted the Splügen under a splendid sky, and I shall never forget the sensation of rising, as night came (I walked incessantly, after we began to ascend) into that cool pure Alpine air, out

24. Katherine De Kay (Mrs. Arthur) Bronson of New York and Newport entertained HJ often at her Venetian home, Casa Alvisi on the Grand Canal. HJ memorialized her and her home in a preface to "Browning in Venice, Recollections by Katherine De Kay Bronson" (*Cornhill Magazine* October 1902), reprinted as "Casa Alvisi" in *Italian Hours,* London (1888). Mrs. Bronson was probably the original of Mrs. Prest in "The Aspern Papers"; see 27 July 1891.

25. Probably Mrs. Philip Livingstone Van Rensselaer, American expatriate, whom HJ also referred to as "the Rensellina" in letters to Lizzie Boott.

of the stifling *calidarium* of Italy. I shall always remember a certain glass of fresh milk which I drank that evening, in the gloaming, far up (a woman at a wayside hostel had it fetched from the cow), as the most heavenly draft that ever passed my lips. I went straight to Lucerne, to see Mrs. Kemble, who had already gone to Engelberg. I spent a day on the lake, making the *giro;* it was a splendid day, and Switzerland looked more sympathetic than I had ventured to hope. I went up to Engelberg, and spent nearly a week with Mrs. Kemble and Miss Butler,[26] in that grim, ragged, rather vacuous, but by no means absolutely unbeautiful valley. I spent an enchanting day with Miss Butler—climbing up to the Trübsee, toward the Joch Pass. The Trübsee is a little steel grey tarn, in a high cool valley, at the foot of the Titlis, whose great silver-gleaming snows overhang it and light it up. The whole place was a wilderness of the alpine rose—and the alpine stillness, the splendour of the weather, the beauty of the place, made the whole impression immense. We had a little man with us who carried a lunch; and we partook of it at the little cold inn. The whole thing brought back my old Swiss days; I hadn't believed they could revive even to that point. x x x x x

New York, 115 East 20th St., December 20th, 1881.

I had to break off the other day in Boston—the interruptions in the *morning* here are intolerable. That period of the day has none of the social sanctity here that it [has] in England, and which keeps it singularly free from intrusion. People—by which I mean ladies—think nothing of asking you to come and see them before lunch. Of course one can decline, but when many propositions of that sort come, a certain number stick. Besides, I have had all sorts of things to do, chiefly not profitable to recall. I have been three weeks in New York, and all my time has slipped away in mere movement. I try as usual to console myself with the reflection that I am getting impressions. This is very true; I have got a great many. I did well to come over; it was well worth doing. I indulged in some reflections a few pages back which were partly the result of a melancholy mood. I *can* do something here—it is not a mere complication. But it is not of that I must speak first in taking up my pen again—I shall return to those things later. I should like to finish briefly the little retrospect of the past year's doings, which I left ragged on the opposite page. x x x x x I came back from Switzerland to meet Alice,[1] who had been a month in England, and whom I presently saw at the Star and Garter, at Richmond. I spent two or three days with her, and saw her afterwards at Kew; then I went down to Sevenoaks and to Canterbury for the same purpose, spending a night at each place. I paid during July and August several visits. One to Burford Lodge (Sir Trevor Lawrence's); memorable on which occasion was a certain walk we took (on a Sunday afternoon), through the grounds of the Deepdene, an artificial but to me a most enchanting and most suggestive English place— full of foreign reminiscences; the sort of place that an Englishman of 80 years ago, who had made the grand tour and lingered in Italy would naturally construct.

---

26. Frances Butler, Mrs. Kemble's youngest daughter.

1. Alice James (1848–92), HJ's sister.

I went to Leatherhead, and I went twice to Mentmore.[2] (On one of these occasions Mr. Gladstone was there.) I went to Fredk. Macmillan's at Walton-on-Thames, and had some charming moments on the river. Then I went down into Somerset and spent a week at Midelney Place, the Lady Trevilian's. It is the impression of this visit that I wish not wholly to fade away. Very exquisite it was (not the visit, but the impression of the country); it kept me a-dreaming all the while I was there. It seemed to me very old England; there was a peculiarly mellow and ancient feeling in it all. Somerset[3] is not especially beautiful; I have seen much better English scenery. But I think I have never been more *penetrated*—I have never more loved the land. It was the old houses that fetched me—Montacute, the admirable; Barrington, that superb Ford Abbey, and several smaller ones. Trevilian showed me them all; he has a great care for such things. These delicious old houses, in the long August days, in the south of England air, on the soil over which so much has passed and out of which so much has come, rose before me like a series of visions. I thought of a thousand things; what becomes of the things one thinks of at these times? They are not lost, we must hope; they drop back into the mind again, and they enrich and embellish it. I thought of stories, of dramas, of all the life of the past—of things one can hardly speak of; speak of, I mean, at the time. It is art that speaks of those things; and the idea makes me adore her more and more. Such a house as Montacute, so perfect, with its grey personality, its old-world gardens, its accumulations of expression, of tone—such a house is really, *au fond,* an ineffaceable image; it can be trusted to rise before the eyes in the future. But what we think of with a kind of *serrement de coeur* is the gone-and-left-behind-us emotion with which at the moment we stood and looked at it. The picture may live again;; but *that* is part of the past. x x x x x

Cambridge, December 26th.

I came here on the 23rd, to spend Xmas, Wilky[1] having come from the West (the first time in several years), to meet me. Here I sit writing in the old back sitting room which William and I used to occupy and which I now occupy alone— or sometimes with poor Wilky, whom I have not seen in some eleven years, and who is wonderfully unchanged for a man with whom life has not gone easy. The long interval of years drops away, and the edges of the chasm 'piece together' again, after a fashion. The feeling of that younger time comes back to me in which I sat here scribbling, dreaming, planning, gazing out upon the world in which my fortune was to seek, and suffering tortures from my damnable state of health. It was a time of suffering so keen that that face might serve to give its

2. Green Farm, Leatherhead, was the home of the American banker Russell Sturgis (1805–87), senior partner in Baring Brothers; his son, Howard (1855–1920) became an intimate friend of HJ after the turn of the century. Mentmore Towers was part of the vast estate of Archibald Philip Primrose, fifth Earl of Rosebery (1847–1929), British Foreign Secretary and (in 1894–95) Prime Minister; he had married Hannah de Rothschild (1851–90). Mentmore was built in 1851 by her father, Mayer Amschel Rothschild (1818–74), grandson of the original founder of the family fortunes.

3. See *English Hours* (1905), especially the essays on ''North Devon,'' which include HJ's memories of Somerset, and ''Abbeys and Castles.''

1. Garth Wilkinson James (1845–83), HJ's brother, third son of the family.

dark colour to the whole period; but this is not what I think of today. When the burden of pain has been lifted, as many memories and emotions start into being as the little insects that scramble about when, in the country, one displaces a flat stone. Ill-health, physical suffering, in one's younger years, is a grievous trial; but I am not sure that we do not bear it most easily then. In spite of it we feel the joy of youth; and that is what I think of today among the things that remind me of the past. The freshness of impression and desire, the hope, the curiosity, the vivacity, the sense of the richness and mystery of the world that lies before us— there is an enchantment in all that which it takes a heavy dose of pain to quench and which in later hours, even if *success* have come to us, touches us less nearly. Some of my doses of pain were very heavy; very weary were some of my months and years. But all that is sacred; it is idle to write of it today. x x x x x

What comes back to me freely, delightfully, is the vision of those untried years. Never did a poor fellow have more; never was an ingenuous youth more passionately and yet more patiently eager for what life might bring. Now that life has brought something, brought a measurable part of what I dreamed of then, it is touching enough to look back. I knew at least what I wanted then—to see something of the world. I have seen a good deal of it, and I look at the past in the light of this knowledge. What strikes me is the definiteness, the unerringness of those longings. I wanted to do very much what I have done, and success, if I may say so, now stretches back a tender hand to its younger brother, desire. I remember the days, the hours, the books, the seasons, the winter skies and darkened rooms of summer. I remember the old walks, the old efforts, the old exaltations and depressions. I remember more than I can say here today. x x x x x

Again, in New York the other day, I had to break off: I was trying to finish the little history of the past year. There is not much more to be said about it. I came back from Midelney, to find Alice in London, and spent ten days with her there, very pleasantly, at the end of August. Delightful to me is London at that time, after the horrors of the season have spent themselves, and the long afternoons make a cool grey light in the empty West End. Delightful to me, too, it was to see how *she* enjoyed it—how interesting was the impression of the huge, mild city. London is mild then; that is the word. And then I went to Scotland—to Tillypronie, to Cortachy, to Dalmeny, to Laidlawstiel. I was to have wound up, on my way back, with Castle Howard; but I retracted, on account of Lord Airlie's death. I can't go into all this; there were some delightful moments, and Scotland made, as it had made before, a great impression. Perhaps what struck me as much as anything was my drive, in the gloaming, over from Kirriemuir to Cortachy; though, taking the road afterward by daylight, I saw it was commonplace. In the late Scotch twilight, and the keen air, it was romantic; at least it was romantic to ford the river at the entrance to Cortachy, to drive through the dim avenues and up to the great lighted pile of the castle, where Lady A., hearing my wheels on the gravel (I was late) put her handsome head from a window in the clock-tower, asked if it was I, and wished me a bonny good-evening. I was in a Waverly Novel.

Then my drive (with her) to Glamis; and my drive (with Miss Stanley) to Airlie

Castle, enchanting spot! Dalmeny is delicious, a magnificent pile of wood beside the Forth, and the weather, while I was there, was the loveliest I have ever known in the British Isles. But the company was not interesting, and there was a good deal of dreariness in the ball we all went to at Hopetoun for the coming of age of the heir. A charming heir he was, however, and a very pretty picture of a young nobleman stepping into his place in society—handsome, well-mannered, gallant, graceful, with 40,000£ a year and the world at his feet. Laidlawstiel, on a bare hill among hills, just above the Tweed, is in the midst of Walter Scott's country. Reay walked with me over to Ashestiel one lovely afternoon; it is only an hour away. The house has been greatly changed since the 'Sheriffs' day;[2] but the place, the country, are the same, and I found the thing deeply interesting. It took one back. While I was at the Reays' I took up one of Scott's novels—*Redgauntlet:* it was years since I had read one. They have always a charm for me—but I was amazed at the badness of *R.: l'enfance de l'art.*

x   x   x   x   x

Now and here I have only one feeling—the desire to get at work again. It is nearly six months that I have been resting on my oars—letting the weeks go, with nothing to show for them but these famous 'impressions'! Prolonged idleness exasperates and depresses me, and though now that I am here, it is a pity not to move about and (if the chance presents itself) see the country, the prospect of producing nothing for the rest of the winter is absolutely intolerable to me. If it comes to my having to choose between remaining stationary somewhere and getting at work, or making a journey during which I shall be able to do no work, I shall certainly elect for the former. But probably I shall be able to compromise: to see something of the country and yet work a little. My mind is full of plans, of ambitions; they crowd upon me, for these are the productive years of life. I have taken aboard by this time a tremendous quantity of material; I really have never taken stock of my cargo. After long years of waiting, of obstruction, I find myself able to put into execution the most cherished of all my projects—that of beginning to work for the stage. It was one of my earliest—I had it from the first. None has given me brighter hopes—none has given me sweeter emotions. It is strange nevertheless that I should never have done anything—and to a certain extent it is ominous. I wonder at times that the dream should not have faded away. It comes back to me now, however, and I ache with longing to settle down at last to a sustained attempt in this direction. I think there is really reason enough for my not having done so before: the little work at any time that I could do, the uninterrupted need of making money on the spot, the inability to do two things at once, the absence of opportunities, of openings. I may add to this the feeling that I could afford to wait, that, looked at as I look at it, the drama is the ripest of all the arts, the one to which one must bring most of the acquired as well as most of the natural, and that while I was waiting I was studying the art, and clearing off my field. I think I may now claim to have studied the art as well as it can be studied in the contemplative way. The French stage I have mastered; I say that without hesitation. I

2. Sir Walter Scott (1771–1832) was appointed Sheriff of Selkirkshire in 1799. He rented the house of Ashestiel, on the south bank of the Tweed near Selkirk, in 1804.

have it in my pocket, and it seems to me clear that this is the light by which one must work today. I have laid up treasures of wisdom about all that. What interesting hours it has given me—what endless consideration it has led to! Sometimes, as I say, it seems to me simply deplorable that I should not have got at work before. *But it was impossible at the time,* and I knew that my chance would come. Here it is; let me guard it sacredly now. Let nothing divert me from it: but now the loss of time, which has simply been a maturing process, will become an injurious one. *Je me résume,* as George Sand's[3] heroes say. I remember certain occasions; several acute visitations of the purpose of which I write come back to me vividly. Some of them, the earliest, were brought on merely by visits to the theatre—by seeing great actors, etc.—at fortunate hours; or by reading a new piece of Alex. Dumas, of Sardou, of Augier.[4] No, my dear friend[4a], nothing of all that is lost. *Ces emotions-là ne se perdent pas; elles rentrent dans le fonds même de notre nature; elles font partie de notre volonté.* The *volonté* has not expired; it is only perfect today. Two or three of the later occasions of which I speak have been among the things that *count* in the formation of a purpose; they are worth making a note of here. What has always counted, of course, has been the Comédie Française; it is on that, as regards this long day-dream, that I have lived. But there was an evening there that I shall long remember; it was in September, 1877. I had come over from London; I was lodging in the Avenue d'Antin—the house with a *tir* behind it. I went to see *Jean Dacier,* with Coquelin as the hero; I shall certain[ly not] forget that impression. The piece is, on the whole, I suppose, bad; but it contains some very effective scenes, and the two principal parts gave Coquelin and Favart a magnificent chance. It is Coquelin's *great* chance, and he told me afterwards in London that it is the part he values most. He is everything in it by turns, and I don't think I ever followed an actor's creation more intently. It threw me into a great state of excitement; I thought seriously of writing to Coquelin, telling him I had been his school-mate, etc.[5] It held up a glowing light to me—seemed to point to my own path. If I could have sat down to work then I probably should not have stopped soon. But I didn't. I couldn't; I was writing things for which I needed to be paid from month to month. (I like to remind myself of these facts—to justify my innumerable postponements.) I remember how, on leaving the theatre—it was a lovely evening—I walked about a long time under the influence not so much of the piece as of Coquelin's acting of it, which had made the thing so human, so brilliant, so valuable. I was agitated with what it said to me that I might do—what I ought to attempt; I walked about the Place de la Concorde, along the Seine, up the Champs Elysées. That was nothing, however, to the state I was thrown into by meeting Coquelin at breakfast at Andrew Lang's, when the Comédie Française came to London. The occasion, for obvious

3. "George Sand," pen name of Aurore Dupin, Baronne Dudevant (1804–76), French novelist.
4. Alexandre Dumas, the younger (1824–95), Victorien Sardou (1831–1908), and Emile Augier (1820–89), French dramatists.
4a. HJ's earliest vocative for his muse; see "mon bon," Index.
5. Benoît Constant Coquelin (1841–1909), celebrated French actor, creator of Rostand's *Cyrano de Bergerac,* and schoolmate of HJ's in Boulogne in 1858. HJ wrote about Coquelin in "The Théâtre Français," the *Galaxy* April 1877, reprinted in *French Poets and Novelists,* London (1878). Marie Favart, stage name of Pierette Ignace Pingaud (1833–1908), actress at the Théâtre Français.

reasons, was unpropitious, but I had some talk with him which rekindled and revived all my latent ambitions. At that time, too, my hands were tied; I could do nothing, and the feeling passed away in smoke. But it stirred me to the depths. Coquelin's personality, his talk, the way the *artist* overflowed in him—all this was tremendously suggestive. I could say little to him there—not a tittle of what I wished; I could only listen, and translate to him what *they* said—an awkward task! But I listened to some purpose, and I have never lost what I gained. It excited me powerfully; I shall not forget my walk, afterwards, down from South Kensington to Westminster. I met Jack Gardner,[6] and he walked with me to leave a card at the Speaker's House. All day, and for days afterward, I remained under the impression. It faded away in time, and I had to give myself to other things. But this brings it back to me; and I may say that those two little moments were landmarks. There was a smaller incident, later, which it gives me pleasure to recall, as it gave me extreme pleasure at the time. John Hare asked me (I met him at dinner at the Comyns Carrs')—urged me, I may say—to write a play, and offered me his services in the event of my doing so. I shall take him at his word.[7] When I came back from Scotland in October last I was full of this work; my hands were free; my pocket lined; I would have given a £100 for the liberty to sit down and hammer away. I imagined such a capital winter of work. But I had to come hither instead. If that however involves a loss of part of my time, it needn't involve the loss of all!

February 9th, 1882, 102 Mt. Vernon St., Boston.

When I began to make these rather ineffectual records I had no idea that I should have in a few weeks to write such a tale of sadness as today. I came back from Washington on the 30th of last month (reached Cambridge the next day), to find that I should never again see my dear mother. On Sunday, Jan. 29th, as Aunt Kate[1] sat with her in the closing dusk (she had been ill with an attack of bronchial asthma, but was apparently recovering happily), she passed away. It makes a great difference to me! I knew that I loved her—but I didn't know how tenderly till I saw her lying in her shroud in that cold North Room, with a dreary snowstorm outside, and looking as sweet and tranquil and noble as in life. These are hours of exquisite pain; thank Heaven this particular pang comes to us but once. On Sunday evening (at 10 o'clock in Washington) I was dressing to go to Mrs. Robinson's—who has written me a very kind letter—when a telegram came in from Alice (William's)[2]: 'Your mother exceedingly ill. Come at once.' It was a great alarm, but it didn't suggest the loss of all hope; and I made the journey to New

6. John L. "Jack" Gardner, husband of the flamboyant Isabella Stewart Gardner.
7. John Hare (later Sir John) was an enterprising actor-manager in the London theatrical world. HJ offered him, early in 1891, "Mrs. Vibert"—later called *Tenants*—for the Garrick Theatre; but it was never produced. See *Complete Plays* 53–55 and passim.
1. Catherine Walsh (1808?–1889), older sister of HJ's mother, lived in the James household.
2. HJ's sister-in-law, née Alice Howe Gibbens (1849–1922).

York with whatever hope seemed to present itself. In New York at 5 o'clock I
went to Cousin H.P.'s—and there the telegram was translated to me. Eliza Ripley
was there—and Katie Rodgers—and as I went out I met Lily Walsh. The rest was
dreary enough. I went back to the Hoffman House, where I had engaged a room
on my way up town and remained there till 9.30, when I took the night-train to
Boston. I shall never pass that place in future without thinking of the wretched
hours I spent there. At home the worst was over; I found father and Alice and
A.K. extraordinarily calm—almost happy. Mother seemed still to be there—so
beautiful, so full of all that we loved in her, she looked in death. We buried her
on Wednesday, Feb. 1st; Wilkie arrived from Milwaukee a couple of hours before. Bob[3] had been there for a month—he was devoted to mother in her illness.
It was a splendid winter's day—the snow lay deep and high. We placed her, for
the present, in a temporary vault in the Cambridge cemetery—the part that lies
near the river. When the spring comes on we shall go and choose a burial place.
I have often walked there in the old years—in those long, lonely rambles that I
used to take about Cambridge, and I had, I suppose, a vague idea that some of us
would some day lie there, but I didn't see just that scene. It is impossible for me
to say—to begin to say—all that has gone down into the grave with her. She was
our life, she was the house, she was the keystone of the arch. She held us all
together, and without her we are scattered reeds. She was patience, she was wisdom, she was exquisite maternity. Her sweetness, her mildness, her great natural
beneficence were unspeakable, and it is infinitely touching to me to write about
her here as one that *was*. When I think of all that she had been, for years—when
I think of her hourly devotion to each and all of us—and that when I went to
Washington the last of December I gave her my last kiss. I heard her voice for
the last time—there seems not to be enough tenderness in my being to register the
extinction of such a life. But I can reflect, with perfect gladness, that her work
was done—her long patience had done its utmost. She had had heavy cares and
sorrows, which she had borne without a murmur, and the weariness of age had
come upon her. I would rather have lost her forever than see her begin to suffer
as she would probably have been condemned to suffer, and I can think with a
kind of holy joy of her being lifted now above all our pains and anxieties. Her
death has given me a passionate belief in certain transcendent things—the immanence of being as nobly created as hers—the immortality of such a virtue as that—
the reunion of spirits in better conditions than these. She is no more of an angel
today than she had always been; but I can't believe that by the accident of her
death all her unspeakable tenderness is lost to the things she so dearly loved. She
is with us, she is of us—the eternal stillness is but a form of her love. One can
hear her voice in it—one can feel, forever, the inextinguishable vibration of her
devotion. I can't help feeling that in those last weeks I was not tender enough
with her—that I was blind to her sweetness and beneficence. One can't help wishing one had only known what was coming, so that one might have enveloped her
with the softest affection. When I came back from Europe I was struck with her
being worn and shrunken, and now I know that she was very weary. She went

---

3. Robertson James (1846–1910), HJ's youngest brother.

about her usual activities, but the burden of life had grown heavy for her, and she needed rest. There is something inexpressibly touching to me in the way in which, during these last years, she went on from year to year without it. If she could only have lived she should have had it, and it would have been a delight to see her have it. But she has it now, in the most complete perfection! Summer after summer she never left Cambridge—it was impossible that father should leave his own house. The country, the sea, the change of air and scene, were an exquisite enjoyment to her; but she bore with the deepest gentleness and patience the constant loss of such opportunities. She passed her nights and her days in that dry, flat, hot, stale and odius Cambridge, and had never a thought while she did so but for father and Alice. It was a perfect mother's life—the life of a perfect wife. To bring her children into the world—to expend herself, for years, for their happiness and welfare—then, when they had reached a full maturity and were absorbed in the world and in their own interests—to lay herself down in her ebbing strength and yield up her pure soul to the celestial power that had given her this divine commission. Thank God one knows this loss but once; and thank God that certain supreme impressions remain! x x x x x

All my plans are altered—my return to England vanishes for the present. I must remain near father; his infirmities make it impossible I should leave him. This means an indefinite detention in this country—a prospect far enough removed from all my recent hopes of departure.

August 3d, 1882, 3 Bolton St. W. From time to time one feels the need of summing-up. I have done it little in the past, but it will be a good thing to do it more in the future. The prevision with which I closed my last entry in these pages was not verified. I sailed from America on the date I had in my mind when I went home—May 10th. Father was materially better and had the strongest wish that I should depart; he and Alice had moved into Boston and were settled very comfortably in a small, pretty house (101 Mt. Vernon St.). Besides, their cottage at Manchester was rapidly being finished; shortly before sailing I went down to see it. Very pretty—bating the American scragginess; with the sea close to the piazzas, and the smell of bayberries in the air. Rest, coolness, peace, society enough, charming drives; they will have all that.—Very soon after I had got back here my American episode began to fade away, to seem like a dream; a very painful dream, much of it. While I was there, it was Europe, it was England, that was dreamlike—but now all this is real enough. The Season is over, thank God; I came in for as much of it as could crowd itself into June and July. I was out of the mood for it, preoccupied, uninterested, bored, eager to begin work again; but I was obliged, being on the spot, to accommodate myself to the things of the day, and always with my old salve to a perturbed spirit, the idea that I was seeing the world. It seemed to me on the whole a poor world this time; I saw and did very little that was interesting. I am extremely glad to be in London again; I am deeply attached to London; I always shall be; but decidedly I like it best when it is 'empty,' as during the period now beginning. I know too many people—I have gone in too much for society x x x x x

Grand Hôtel, Paris, November 11th. Thanks to 'society,' which, in the shape of various surviving remnants of the season, and to a succession of transient Americans and to several country visits, continued to mark me for its own during the greater part of the month of August, I had not even time to finish that last sentence written more than three months ago. I can hardly take up at this date the history of these three months: a simple glance must suffice. I remained in England till the 12th of September. Bob, whom I had found reclining on my sofa in Bolton St. when I arrived from America toward the last of May—(I hadn't even time, above, to mention my little disembarkation in Ireland and the few days I spent there)— Bob, who as I say was awaiting me at my lodgings in London—greatly to my surprise, and in a very battered and depressed condition, thanks to his unhappy voyage to the Azores—sailed for home again in the last days of August, after having spent some weeks in London, at Malvern and at Llandudno, in Wales. The last days, before sailing, he spent with me. About the 10th of September William arrived from America, on his way to the Continent to pass the winter. After being with him for a couple of days, I came over to Paris via Folkestone (I came down there and slept, before crossing), while he crossed to Flushing, from Queenborough. All summer I had been trying to work, but my interruptions had been so numerous that it was only during the last weeks that I succeeded, even moderately, in doing something. My record of work for the whole past year is terribly small, and I opened this book, just now, with the intention of taking several solemn vows in reference to the future.[1] But I don't even know whether I shall accomplish that. However, I am not sure that such solemnities are necessary, for God knows I am eager enough to work, and that I am deeply convinced of the need of it, both for fortune and for happiness. x x x x x

I scarcely even remember the three or four visits to which, in the summer, I succeeded in restricting my 'social activity.' A pleasant night at Loseley—Rhoda Broughton[2] was there. Another day I went down there to lunch, to take Howells (who spent all August in London) and Bob. Two days at Mentmore; a Saturday-to-Monday episode (very dull) at Miss de Rothschild's, at Wimbledon; a very pleasant day at the Arthur Russells', at Shiere. This last was charming; I think I went nowhere else—having wriggled out of Midelney, from my promised visit to Mrs. Pakenham, and from pledges more or less given to Tillypronie. Toward the last, in London, I had my time pretty well to myself, and I felt, as I have always felt before, the charm of those long, still days, in the empty time, when one can sit and scribble, without notes to answer or visits to pay. Shall I confess, however, that the evenings had become dull? x x x x x

I had meant to write some account of my last months in America, but I fear the chance for this has already passed away. I look back at them, however, with a

1. After completing *The Portrait of a Lady* in mid-1881, HJ worked in the early months of 1882 in the United States on a dramatization of *Daisy Miller*. The play, intended for the Madison Square Theater, was not produced; see *Complete Plays* 117–19. Otherwise he published a book review in June and a piece on "London Pictures and London Plays" in August; "Venice," one of his best-known travel essays, appeared in November, and the short story "The Point of View" in December.
2. Rhoda Broughton (1840–1920), popular Victorian novelist, whom HJ had known from the mid-70s.

great deal of tenderness. Boston is absolutely nothing to me—I don't even dislike it. I like it, on the contrary; I only dislike to live there. But all those weeks I spent there, after Mother's death, had an exquisite stillness and solemnity. My rooms in Mt. Vernon St. were bare and ugly; but they were comfortable—were, in a certain way, pleasant. I used to walk out, and across the Common, every morning, and take my breakfast at Parker's. Then I walked back to my lodgings and sat writing till four or five o'clock; after which I walked out to Cambridge over that dreary bridge whose length I had measured so often in the past, and, four or five days in the week, dined in Quincy St. with Father and Alice. In the evening, I walked back, in the clear, American starlight.—I got in this way plenty of exercise. It was a simple, serious, wholesome time. Mother's death appeared to have left behind it a soft beneficent hush in which we lived for weeks, for months, and which was full of rest and sweetness. I thought of her, constantly, as I walked to Boston at night along those dark vacant roads, where, in the winter air, one met nothing but the coloured lamps and the far-heard jingle of the Cambridge horse-cars. My work at this time interested me, too, and I look back upon the whole three months with a kind of religious veneration. My work interested me even more than the importance of it would explain—or than the success of it has justified. I tried to write a little play *(D[aisy] M[iller])* and I wrote it; but my poor little play has not been an encouragement. I needn't enter into the tiresome history of my ridiculous negotiations with the people of the Madison Square Theatre, of which the Proprietors behaved like asses and sharpers combined; this episode, by itself, would make a brilliant chapter in a realistic novel. It interested me immensely to write the piece, and the work confirmed all my convictions as to the fascination of this sort of composition. But what it has brought [me] to know, both in New York and in London, about the manners and ideas of managers and actors and about the conditions of production on our unhappy English stage, is almost fatally disgusting and discouraging. I have learned, very vividly, that if one attempts to work for it one must be prepared for *disgust,* deep and unspeakable disgust. But though I am disgusted, I do not think I am discouraged. The reason of this latter is that I simply can't afford to be. I have determined to take a year—even two years, if need be—more, in experiments, in studies, in attempts. The dramatic form seems to me the most beautiful thing possible; the misery of the thing is that the baseness of the English-speaking stage affords no setting for it. How I am to reconcile this with the constant solicitation that presses upon me, both from within and from without, to get at work upon another novel, is more than I can say. It is surely the part of wisdom, however, not to begin another novel at once—not to commit myself to a work of *longue haleine.* I must do *short* things, in such measure as I need, which will leave me intervals for dramatic work. I say this rather glibly—and yet I sometimes feel a woeful hunger to sit down to another novel. If I can only *concentrate* myself: this is the great lesson of life. I have hours of unspeakable reaction against my smallness of production; my wretched habits of work—or of un-work; my levity, my vagueness of mind, my perpetual failure to focus my attention, to absorb myself, to look things in the face, to invent, to produce, in a word. I shall be 40 years old in April next: it's a horrible fact! I believe however that I have learned how to work and that it is in moments of forced idleness, almost alone, that these melancholy reflections seize me. When I am really at work, I'm happy, I feel strong, I see many opportunities ahead. It is the only thing that makes life endurable. I must make some great efforts during the next few years, however, if I wish not to have been on the whole a failure. I shall have been a failure unless I do something *great!* x x x x x

1904–1905

American Journal II (Houghton Journal VII, 11 December 1904 to 30 March 1905), 7″ x 8¼″, has brown marbled covers, black spine, white endpapers, and 122 lined pages written, on recto pages only, in grey ink to the middle of the third sentence for 11 December 1904, in blue for the rest of the entry, then back to grey for the rest of the notebook. In addition to the usual title (written always in a hand other than HJ's) the words "Journal III" are written in HJ's hand. The onetime existence of I and II of the series might account for the hiatus of more than three years between the last entry we have (19 October 1901, in VI) and the beginning of this journal.

This American Journal begins with an undated entry probably only a few days antecedent to the next entry, and apparently a continuation from one of the notebooks no longer extant. The journal has clear affinities with American Journal I of the 1880s in the references to deaths in the family and to the general Cambridge scene as it had struck him particularly in 1882. But with all the nostalgic retrospection, the entries here also look forward to *The American Scene* and the autobiographical volumes. HJ had arrived in America on 30 August 1904; he was at WJ's home, 95 Irving Street, Cambridge, Massachusetts, and about to embark on a lecture tour that would take him on a journey of discovery to the four corners of the United States.

. . . expressively (articulatedly) to the kindly eyes: 'See, see, we are getting older, we are getting almost old—old enough; we are taking it on and entering into the beauty of time and the dignity of life—we are at last beginning. We don't look *now* like anything *else,* do we?' —etc., etc. And, then, oh golly!, the question of the Gate and the enclosure,[1] and what that would easily give me if it didn't give me too much. It does—and so does that reference I should like to make to the effect of Sargent's portrait of H[enry] H[igginson], rather dimly made out in the 1st 'gloaming' at the Union,[2] and *se rattachant* so to the still-living vividness of the emotions of 23 years ago, when I was, the winter of Father's death, for a month or two in N.Y. and in Washington.

x   x   x   x   x

December 11th, 1904. I came back from New York last night after (36 hours after) Harvey's Dinner[1] and I snatch this intensely cold, but as intensely sunny, Sunday a.m. to try to catch on a little again to the interrupted foregoing. The lapse of each day, save the last 3 days' rough and lurid vision of N.Y., gives me more and more the sense of what there is to be done, of the affluence of the Impression and the Reflection, of 'the fortune there *is* in it, upon my honour'—I being meanwhile only a little nervous about the amount of overtaking and catching up that I have now upon my hands. As I feared, the 'New England II' gives me a marked *muchness* of material to deal with, but the only way is to let it *all* come— that serves me well; to drop every thing into my pot and then pick out such pieces as I can place. These Cambridge, these Boston *concetti* are already receding things, but let me get back a little to where I broke off, too many days ago—to where I was reaching out to little connections for which I then made, on a loose leaf, for reference today, a brief memorandum—I was fumbling, I was groping through the little Cambridge haze that I was, by the same stroke, trying to make 'golden,' and I noted for my recall 'The Gates—questions of the Gates and of the fact of *enclosure* and of disclosure in general—the so importunate American question (of *Dis*closure—call it so!) above all.' This, with some possible peep (but *how* and *where?*) of my vision of the old high Cambridge and Oxford *grilles* and their admirable office of making things look *interesting*—MAKE so—by their intervention, a *concetto* worth developing just *un brin;* as for instance how, *within* the College Yard, its elements and items gain presence by what has been done (little as it is, of enclosure—with a glance at the *old* misery!) and how I may put it that the less 'good' thing enclosed, approached, *defined,* often looks better than the less good thing *not* enclosed, not defined, not approached. With all of which, too, I was reaching out to Sargent *à propos* of the H.H. portrait[2]—and the impression of the Union—which in its turn is a connection, the vision and sentiment (mine!) of the Union—with other things, and a sort of hook-on, possibly, for use, to that

---

1. HJ was concerned about the absence of a fence around the Harvard Yard: see next entry.
2. Harvard's Student Union contained Sargent's portrait of the donor, Major Henry Lee Higginson (1843–1919), Boston financier and patron of the arts.
1. Col. George Brinton McLellan Harvey (1864–1928), president of Harper & Brothers, was host to a dinner in honor of HJ at the Metropolitan Club on December 8. The thirty guests included the novelists Mark Twain, Booth Tarkington, and Hamlin Garland, and also Elizabeth Jordan, who had made the arrangements for HJ's lecture tour. HJ had signed a contract with Harper for his impressions of America.
2. Sargent's portrait of Higginson; see preceding entry.

small bit about the *Stadium,* the foot-ball (Dartmouth) match,[3] and the way the big white arena *loomed* at me, in the twilight, ghostly and queer, from across the river, during the ½ hour, the wonderful, the unforgettable, that afternoon's end that I spent in the C[ambridge] C[emetery].[4] Do that (the picture) with the pink winter sunset and the ghosts, the others, Lowell's, Longfellow's and Wm. Story's.[5] I swim a little, in fancy, in imagination, in association, in the Sargent connection—for its other ramifications—but there are so many of these. There is the one with the Boit picture, and there is the one with Mrs. G[ardner]'s portrait, and there is above all the one with the Boston Pub[lic] Lib[rary][6] making—this one perhaps—a bridge straight across to the *Boston* compartment of my little subject, into which I so, with a happy economy, plunge in the midmost manner—though I don't want to be there till I have got quite out of Cambridge. I mustn't come *back* to C., with all that there is waiting, and with all there is to do for these other matters: therefore tack Cambridge in as you can, *mon bon;* make of it something pretty that you won't have, by the time you cross that bridge, to touch again. Surely the different little *clous* (for C.) *doivent*—with my imperative economy—*tous y'être.* I seem to hang over the 'massing larger' and what that means; I seem to hang over the *concetto* of the largeness, all the great largeness of development before the University, and for which I should like some SPECIAL FIGURE, of a fine high application; something about the way such an (American) institution sits and looks across the high unobstructed table-land of its future in a manner all its own—with a kind of incalculability in the probable, the logically-unsolved extent of its resources—and an horizon so receding, so undetermined, that one sees not—scarce sees—the lowest or faintest blue line. THAT, something of that—which calls up within me, however, such a desire for the glimmer of a glance at the 'sinister,' the ominous 'Münsterberg' possibility[7]—the sort of class of future phenomena repres[en]ted by the 'foreigner' coming in and taking possession; the union of the large purchasing power with the absence of prejudice—of certain prejudices; the easy submission to foreign imposition (of attitude, etc.) and the very sovereign little truth that no branch, no phase, no face, nor facet is perhaps more 'interesting' (than this) of the question that hangs so forever before one here, and *more and more the more one sees:* that of what the effect of the great Infusion (call it that) is going to be. *This* particular light on it—this Harvard professor-of-the-future light, this determined high Harvard absence-of-prejudice light. In addition to which I seem to myself to 'hang over' 2 other interwoven strands—my own little personal harking back to the small old superseded Law-

3. The manuscript has "game (Dartmouth) match" with "game" crossed out.
4. See 29 March 1905.
5. James Russell Lowell (1819–91), Henry Wadsworth Longfellow (1807–89), and William Wetmore Story (1819–95), whose biography HJ had published the previous year; see 19 March 1905.
6. Sargent's portrait (1882) of the daughters of the American painter Edward Darly Boit (1840–1915) in the Boston Museum of Fine Arts, his famous portrait (1888) of Isabella Stewart Gardner in Fenway Court, and his decorative freize of the Prophets in the Boston Public Library on Copley Square. HJ had seen Edwin Austin Abbey (1852–1911) paint some of the Grail murals for the Boston Public Library; see reference at the end of this entry.
7. Hugo Münsterberg (1863–1916), German psychologist and philosopher in the United States. WJ was instrumental in bringing him from Freiburg to head the Psychology Laboratory at Harvard, 1892–95. WJ later revised his opinion of Münsterberg downward.

School[8] (in presence of the actual—the big new *modern*); and some sort of glance at one's old vision of Memorial Hall—with something to be gouged out of it—as a ramification of the image and suggestion of the Union. Then the Cambridge fantastication seems to have only too much to 'give'—God help me! It gives and gives; everything seems to give and give as I artfully press it. And what pressure of mine *isn't* artful?—by the divine diabolical law under which I labour!!—Well then, I am thus taking for granted that my bridge across to Boston is represented by the flying leap from the (H.H.) Sargent at the Union to the other Sargent, the Boston one and the Abbeys, etc.—and thereby to the MIDDLE of my Boston business.

x   x   x   x   x

["New England: An Autumn Impression," the *North American Review* April-June 1905, and "Boston," the *North American Review* and the *Fortnightly Review* March 1906; both reprinted in *The American Scene*, London and New York (1907).]

Coronado Beach, Cal., Wednesday, March 29th, 1905.[1]

I needn't take precious time with marking and re-marking here how the above effort to catch up with my 'impressions' of the early winter was condemned to speedy frustration and collapse. I struggled but it all got beyond me—any opportunity for the process of this little precious, this sacred little record and register—but the history is written in my troubled and anxious, my always so strangely more or less aching, doubting, yearning, yet also more or less triumphant, or at least uplifted, heart. *Basta!* I sit here, after long weeks, at any rate, in front of my arrears, with an inward accumulation of material of which I feel the wealth, and as to which I can only invoke my familiar demon of patience, who always comes, doesn't he?, when I call. He is here with me in front of this green Pacific—he sits close and I feel his soft breath, which cools and steadies and inspires, on my cheek. Everything sinks in: nothing is lost; everything abides and fertilizes and renews its golden promise, making me think with closed eyes of deep and grateful longing when, in the full summer days of L[amb] H[ouse], my long dusty adventure over, I shall be able to [plunge] my hand, my arm, *in*, deep and far, and up to the shoulder—into the heavy bag of remembrance—of suggestion—of imagination—of art—and fish out every little figure and felicity, every little fact and fancy that can be to my purpose. These things are all packed away, now, thicker than I can penetrate, deeper than I can fathom, and there let them rest for the present, in their sacred cool darkness, till I shall let in upon them the mild still light of dear old L[amb] H[ouse]—in which they will begin to gleam and glitter and take form like the gold and jewels of a mine. x x x x x

The question, however, is with, is of, what I want now, and how I need to hark back, and hook on, to those very 1st little emotions and agitations and stirred sensibilities of the first Cambridge hours and days and even weeks—though it's really a matter for any *acuteness*, for any quality, of *but* the hours, the very first,

---

8. In Dane Hall, the old Law School, where HJ was briefly enrolled in the academic year 1862–63.

1. At about the midpoint of his lecture tour HJ spent a week in the Hotel del Coronado at Coronado Beach, near San Diego, to work further on *The American Scene*.

during which the charms of the brave handsome autumn (I coax it, stretching a point with soft names) lingered and hung about, and made something of a little medium for the sensibility to act in. That was a good moment, genuine so far as it went, and just enough, no doubt, under an artful economy, to conjure with. What it is a question of at present is the putting together with some blessed little nervous intensity of patience, of a third Part to the *New England: an Autumn Impression* now begun in the *N.A. Review.* I drop out Boston—to come in later (next), into *Three Cities*—the three being B., Philadelphia, and Washington. There is absolutely no room *here* to squeeze in a stinted, starved little Boston picture. Oh, the division is good, I see—the 'three' will do beautifully and so for winding up the little *New England,* will Cambridge and its accessories. I feel as if I could *spread* on C., and that is my danger, as it's my danger everywhere. For *my* poor little personal C. of the far-off unspeakable past years, hangs there behind, like a pale pathetic ghost, hangs there behind, fixing me with tender, pleading eyes, eyes of such exquisite pathetic appeal and holding up the silver mirror, just faintly dim, that is like a sphere peopled with the old ghosts. How can I speak of Cambridge at all, e.g., without speaking of dear J. R. L. and even of the early *Atlantic,* by, oh, such a delicate, ironic implication?—to say nothing of the *old* Shady Hill and the old Quincy St. and those days that bring tears, and the figure for Shady Hill, the figure and presence, of J. N. and of S. N., and even of G. W. C. and the reminiscences of that night of Dickens,[2] and the *emotion,* abiding, that it left with me. How it *did* something for my thought and him and his work—and would have done more without the readings, the hard charmless readings (or *à peu près*) that remained with me. (This is, of course, an impossible side-issue, but one just catches there the tip of the tail of *such* an old emotion of the throbbing prime!) The point for me (for fatal, for impossible expansion) is that I knew there, *had* there, in the ghostly old C. that I sit and write of here by the strange Pacific on the other side of the continent, *l'initiation première* (the divine, the unique), there and in Ashburton Place[3] (which I just came in time to have that October or November glimpse of before seeing its site swept bare a month ago). Ah, the 'epoch-making' weeks of the spring of 1865!—from the 1st days of April or so on to the summer (partly spent at Newport, etc., partly at North Conway)! Something—some fine, superfine, supersubtle mystic breath of that may come in perhaps in the *Three Cities,* in relation to any reference to the remembered Boston of the 'prime.' Ah, that pathetic, heroic little *personal* prime of my own, which stretched over into the following summer at Swampscott—'66—that of the Seven Weeks War, and of the unforgettable gropings and findings and sufferings and strivings and play of sensibility and of inward passion there.[4] The hours, the moments, the

2. James Russell Lowell's Cambridge home, Elmwood, is mentioned below. Shady Hill was the Cambridge home of Charles Eliot Norton (1827–1908), one of HJ's earliest mentors in Cambridge. Jane Norton (1824–77) was the sister, and Sara (1864–1922) the daughter of Charles E. Norton; George William Curtis (1842–1921), an American travel writer and novelist, was a close friend of the Nortons'. HJ had met Dickens briefly at Norton's home in 1867. See *Notes of a Son and Brother* (1914), Chap. VIII.

3. The first James family home, in Boston 1864–66, was at 13 Ashburton Place.

4. Those weeks began with WJ's departure on a scientific expedition to the Amazon; HJ visited the painter John LaFarge (1835–1910) and especially the Edmund Tweedy household—which included his beloved cousin Mary "Minny" Temple (1845–70)—in Newport; in August he was in North Conway,

days, come back to me—on into the early autumn before the move to Cambridge and with the sense, still, after such a lifetime, of particular little thrills and throbs and daydreams there. I can't help, either, just touching with my pen-point (here, here, only here) the recollection of that (probably August) day when I went up to Boston from Swampscott and called in Charles St. for news of O. W. H., then on his 1st flushed and charming visit to England, and saw his mother in the cool dim matted drawingroom of that house (passed, *never*, since, without the *sense*), and got the news, of all his London, his general English, success and felicity, and *vibrated* so with the wonder and romance and curiosity and dim weak tender (oh, tender!) envy of it, that my walk up the hill, afterwards, up Mount Vernon St.[5] and probably to Athenaeum was all coloured and gilded, and humming with it, and the emotion, exquisite of its kind, so remained with me that I always think of that occasion, that hour, as a sovereign contribution to the germ of that inward romantic principle which was to determine, so much later on (ten years!), my own vision-haunted migration. I recall, I can FEEL now, the empty August st., the Mt. Vernon St. of the closed houses and absent 'families' and my slow, upward, sympathetic, excited stroll there, and my sense of the remainder of the day in town—before the old 'cars' for the return home—so innocently to make a small adventure—vision-haunted as I was already even then—linking on to which some-how, moreover, too, is the memory of lying on my bed at Swampscott, later than that, somewhat, and toward the summer's end, and reading, in ever so thrilled a state, George Eliot's *Felix Holt,* just out, and of which I was to write, and *did* write, a review in the *Nation.* (I had just come back from a bad little 'sick' visit to the Temples somewhere—I have forgotten the name of the place—in the White Mountains; and the Gourlays[6] were staying with us at S[wampscott], and I was miserably stricken by my poor broken, all but unbearable, and unsurvivable *back* of those [and still, under fatigue, even of these] years.) To read over the opening pages of *Felix Holt* makes even now the whole time softly and shyly live again. Oh, strange little intensities of history, of ineffaceability; oh, delicate little odd links in the long chain, kept unbroken for the fingers of one's tenderest touch! Sanctities, pieties, treasures, abysses! x x x x x

But these are wanton lapses and impossible excursions;[7] irrelevant strayings of the pen, in defiance of every economy. My subject awaits me, all too charged and too bristling with the most artful economy possible. What I seem to feel is that the Cambridge *tendresse* stands in the path like a waiting lion—or, more con-gruously, like a cooing dove that I shrink from scaring away. I want a little of the

---

New Hampshire, in the White Mountains with Wendell Holmes and John Gray (see end of this entry); Minny Temple was spending the summer there (see *Notes of a Son and Brother,* Chap. XIII). WJ returned from Brazil in March 1866, and HJ alludes here to his back ailment; he spent the summer recovering at Swampscott on Massachusetts Bay, 40 miles north of Boston, where he wrote a review of George Eliot's *Felix Holt,* published (unsigned) in the *Nation* August 1866.

5. The younger Oliver Wendell Holmes. 131 Vernon Street in Boston was the last residence of HJ's father.

6. Cousins of the Jameses'.

7. The lapses and excursions were salvaged in the autobiographical *Notes of a Son and a Brother,* New York and London (1914). See also HJ's memoir of Du Maurier, *LA* II, 876–906.

tendresse, but it trembles away over the whole field—or would if it could. Yet to present these accidents is what it is to be a *master;* that and that only. Isn't the highest deepest note of the whole thing the never-to-be-lost memory of that evening hour at Mount Auburn—at the Cambridge Cemetery when I took my way alone—after much waiting for the favouring hour—to that unspeakable group of graves. It was late, in November; the trees all bare, the dusk to fall early, the air all still (at Cambridge, in general, *so* still), with the western sky more and more turning to that terrible, deadly, pure polar pink that shows behind American winter woods. But I can't go over this—I can only, oh, so gently, so tenderly, brush it and breathe upon it—breathe upon it and brush it. It was the moment; it was the hour, it was the blessed flood of emotion that broke out at the touch of one's sudden *vision* and carried me away. I seemed then to know why I had done this; I seemed then to know why I had *come*—and to feel how not to have come would have been miserably, horribly to miss it. It made everything right—it made everything priceless. The moon was there, early, white and young, and seemed reflected in the white face of the great empty Stadium, forming one of the boundaries of Soldiers' Field, that looked over at me, stared over at me, through the clear twilight, from across the Charles. Everything was there, everything *came;* the recognition, stillness, the strangeness, the pity and the sanctity and the terror, the breath-catching passion and the divine relief of tears. William's inspired transcript, on the exquisite little Florentine urn of Alice's ashes, William's divine gift to us, and to *her,* of the Dantean lines—

> *Dopo lungo exilio e martiro*
> *Viene a questa pàce—*[8]

took me so at the throat by its penetrating *rightness,* that it was as if one sank down on one's knees in a kind of anguish of gratitude before something for which one had waited with a long, deep *ache.* But why do I write of the all unutterable and the all abysmal? Why does my pen not drop from my hand on approaching the infinite pity and tragedy of all the past? It does, poor helpless pen, with what it meets of the ineffable, what it meets of the cold Medusa-face of life, of all the life *lived,* on every side. *Basta, basta!* x x x x x

There remains what one may, what one *must,* not pass without looking at it. But the infinite pity of dear J.R.L.—that is a vision of mine, a vision of all faithful and tender, that both challenges and defies expression in the same troubled tormenting way. I don't know why, but there rises from it, with a rush that is like a sob, a sudden vividness of the old *Whitby* days, Whitby walks and lounges and evenings, with George D[u] M[aurier]—bathed, bathed in a bitter-sweet of ghostliness too.[9] *Basta, basta.* The word about Elmwood—that is all it can, at the very most, come back to; with the word about Longfellow's house, and about poor W. W. Story's early one—and the reminiscence of that evening—late after-

---

8. HJ is recalling inaccurately the lines from Dante's *Paradiso,* X, 128–29: "ed essa da martiro e da essilio venne a questa pace."

9. For HJ's reminiscences of time spent at Whitby on the Yorkshire coast with Lowell and Du Maurier, see *Letters* III, 347.

noon—walk with William, while the earlier autumn still hung on, through all the umbrageous 'new' part of Cambridge; up to where Fresh Pond, where I used to walk on Sunday afternoon with Howells, once *was!* (Give a word if possible, to *that* mild memory—yet without going to smash on the rock of autobiography.) That return, with William, from the Country Club, hangs somehow in my mind, with the sense that one had, at the time, of the quality of this added grace to life—a note in the general concert of the larger *amenity* surrounding this generation. The type of thing, the pleasant type, the large old country ('colonial') house, with its view, its verandahs, its grounds, its sports, its refreshments, its service, its civilization, and what these things give that wasn't there before, in the old thinner New England air and more meagre New England scheme. There is too much—I am piling up matter; but I seem to remember certain reflections, certain images that came to me there in the sense of the more chances, the larger liberality, again, surrounding the young, the generation of today, than in *my* time—I seem to remember vaguely feeling, on the spot, on the wide verandah, among the old trees (the *growth* of all the fine umbrage, everywhere), that there would be some small report, or effect, to be made of it. A mere vignette is enough, but my thing can be *only* all small vignettes throughout. A small vignette for every little item, any little item: keep the thing down to that, and my paper is done. But the thing is to catch just the notes that were IN that country club 'value.' Wasn't the 'sport' image of the young people, the straight brown young men, with strong good figures and homely faces, one of them? I mean as associated with that of the strong, charmless (*work* that 'charmless' right), stalwart, slangy girls, in whom one feels the intimation, the consequence, of the absence of danger, from the men—as one feels throughout, in the N.E., in each sex, the absence of a sense, the absence of the consciousness, of, or of the existence of, danger from the other. Other echoes and trailing lights, too, does one seem to gather in from the kindly after-sense of that afternoon—where, on one of the large overhanging verandahs, we talked, W. and I, with good Scotch Mr. Muirhead—isn't he?—who is the author of the excellent American Baedeker.[10] The sense of the American *club,* which was to be so handsomely confirmed for me, and which certainly has in it to contribute a page—here and there, throughout a paragraph—or two: *that* I probably entertained, in germ, on that occasion. And there must have come to me then too, as we went back, my 1st good vision of the striking symptoms, so new to me, of the admirable Boston 'Park system,' which was to become more emphatic, more vivid, during the time I afterwards spent with Mrs. Gardner (ah, to squeeze a little, a little of what I felt, out of *that,* too!) at Brookline, at her really so quite *picturable* Green Hill—which would yield a 'vignette,' I think, whereof I fully possess all the elements. The way the large, the immense 'Park' roads of the new System unrolled themselves in their high type during 2 or 3 of the drives I took with Mrs. G.—and the way the 'value' of the road, as an earnest and a promise and a portent, stood up and seemed to 'tell.' The *material* civilization—'don't doubt—with these things everything is possible.' But I abound too much, as usual: I waste my art: I do my thing in too costly a way—I damn the expense too

10. J. F. Muirhead was responsible for the 3rd revised edition of the Baedeker in 1904.

consistently, too heroically, too ruinously. Still, I dabble a moment longer in the mild soft afterglow of that little excursion with William, at the end of which we walked home (after alighting from the tram) through the still summerish twilight of the region (of Cambridge) that I used to know as the region *near* the region (about the 'Fayerweather St.,' etc.) where the dear Gurneys[11] anciently lived. Whenever one is with William one receives such an immense accession of suggestion and impression that the memory of the episode remains bathed for one in the very liquidity of extraordinary play of mind; and I seem to recollect, thus, how he gave life and light, as it were, to the truth, the interest, of the change wrought all about there, by the two facts of the immense rise in the type and scope and scale of the American house, as it more and more multiplies, and of the special amenity of the effect, for the 'streets,' of the large tree-culture. The over-arching clustered trees, the way dignity and style were helped by them, the embowered city—cities—of the future. I recall a little *those* vibrating chords. But, ah, all this suffices, surely suffices above all, if I make my point that to an inordinate degree, alas, all this pleasantry of picture and evocation has a truth only as applied to the summer and autumn alone. The way with the winter bareness all one's remarks are falsified and all the meanness and ugliness comes out. The transformation is complete, and even the 2 or 3 elements of winter beauty do little to save the picture, do almost everything to betray it. The snow, the sunshine, light up and pauperize all the wooden surfaces, all the mere paint and pasteboard paltriness. The one fine thing are the winter sunsets, the blood on the snow, the pink crystal of the west, the wild frankness, wild sadness (?)—so to speak—of the surrender.

x   x   x   x   x

I was tackling (when I broke off this at Cambridge so long ago) the question of whether I mightn't let my little current float me into the presence of J.S.S., for the space of ten lines, by the way of his splendid portrait of H.H.[12]—floated into the presence of *that,* as one was, by the impulse to do something with one's 1st impression of the *Union,* and its great high Hall; do it, really, too, as a part of that one *first and only afternoon ramble* there with H., blessed boy,[13] to which the small poetry, the small sharper or intenser sensibility of my renewal of impression really reduces or refers itself. (It was when I came back with him—or rather to him—from Chocorua, the day before I went on to Cotuit and Howard S.)[14] He was alone there, in Irving St., and had come to meet me, all blessedly, in Boston, and it was that same afternoon, I judge, that we made a brief simplified little tour, before dusk—having tea afterwards with Mrs. Gibbens.[15] So I reconstitute it, but

11. The family of Ephraim Whitman Gurney (1829–86), professor of history at Harvard. Mrs. Gurney (née Ellen Hooper) was sister of Mrs. Henry Adams (née Marian "Clover" Hooper).
12. See initial entry for 1904.
13. WJ's eldest, Henry (1879–1947), was usually called "Harry" to distinguish him from his uncle.
14. Howard Overing Sturgis (1854–1920), youngest son of the expatriate banker Russell Sturgis, lived virtually all his life in the family's Georgian villa, Queen's Acre (called Qu'Acre), on the edge of Windsor Great Park with his friend William Haynes Smith (known as "the Babe"). WJ's summer home was at Chocorua, New Hampshire.
15. Mother-in-law of WJ.

what was above all with me at the time was the then feeling that *that,* the quality just simply of that little moment, would be very possibly about all the general Cambridge fact, in short, would have to give me. It was just the last of the 'Long,' as they would say at Oxford,[16] the place was still empty, but everything was furbishing and preparing for Term. He took me to the great new Law School—and I lived back feebly in to my melancholy little years (oh, so heart breaking) at the old, so primitive and archaic; and I saw John Gray, afar off, reading in the great new Library, and I wondered, on the spot, if I mightn't be able to make something of that![17]

Thursday, March 30th, 1905 (Coronado Beach).

So much as the foregoing I scrabbled yesterday, and it has given me a sense of getting on—done for me, in its degree, what the 'process,' the intimate, the sacred, the divine, always does (ah, how it *grew,* in those 'wasted' years!): floated me back into relation with the idea, with the possibility, into relation again with my task and my life. But *voyons, voyons.* The other pieces of my little tapestry hang there before me—the figures and bits I must work in, to eke out the effect of Cam[bridge]. There was Dedham, where I went in a pouring rain, to dine with Sam Warren—went with Mrs. G.,[1] who took me there, from my Brookline visit to her, as she took me to that other strange place, on another day, Blue Hill or wherever, to see Wm. Hunt's daughters. And then there is my day, my 2 different days (but the first the best) with Bob at Concord,[2] and there is my small and adequate scrap of a stop over.

16. The Long Vac, or long vacation between Trinity and Michaelmas Terms at Oxford, i.e., the summer months.

17. John Chipman Gray (1839–1915), a friend from HJ's youth (see note 5 above) and later Royall Professor of Law at Harvard. This episode is recorded, although Gray is not identified, in *The American Scene* 1, vii.

1. Mrs. G. was Isabella Gardner. William Morris Hunt (1824–79), French-influenced American painter in whose Newport studio HJ briefly studied in the early 60s—as had WJ and the painter John LaFarge.

2. The youngest brother Robertson James lived in Concord.

Detached Notes

The Chaperon
(1893)

The following two notes exist in the Houghton manuscript of nine unlined sheets torn from a 7″ x 9″ secretary tablet, written in ink on both sides. Pages are numbered in red ink, and page 18, dated 6 June 1893, is crossed out, although still legible and here reproduced.

Is there a subject for comedy—for a pretty three-act comedy—latent in *The Chaperon?* [1] It seems to shimmer before me that there *is*—but I can't tell till I try. Three questions (exclusive of this matter for E.C.) [2] rise before me in a row, with importunate solicitous faces. One is the question of the play I began so long ago on the subject that, for convenience, I have provisionally labelled *Monte-Carlo;* the other is the question of having something in my hand ready for Daly in the event of there arising between us a question of a second play. [3] The third is this desire to thresh out *The Chaperon* a little and see what's in it. The sense of a margin (absit omen!) makes all the difference. It makes one good-humoured and patient and pliant and impersonal and divinely willing, makes one care only for the process and the prize and not a bit for the subjective accidents. The definitely wise, the concretely practical thing is probably for me to sit down without delay before the Monte-Carlo idea; and I hereby declare myself ready (ready?—ah, passionately eager and impatient!) to begin my siege. I should like, however, *en*

1. Answering HJ's praise of *The Second Mrs. Tanqueray* (27 May 1893), Arthur Wing Pinero wrote: "in *The Chaperon* you have the germ of a fine comedy for the theatre." See 13 July 1891 and *Complete Plays* 455, 607–08; and also HJ's resumption of the idea in the dictated notes, "Rough Statement for *The Chaperon*," 14 November 1907.
2. Edward Compton. HJ had shown Compton the first act and scenario for his three-act *Guy Domville;* see *Letters* III, 410–12. See also 6 June 1893.
3. For the "Monte Carlo" note see *Complete Plays* 54–55 and also 30 August 1893. On the "second play" for Augustin Daly see 24 November 1892.

attendant, to make a note, to make a notch against the question of what may be feasible with *The Chaperon;* to look into it a moment as I pass and have the amusement of having just started my hare! The idea of the play is expressible enough—the idea of a girl who, reversing with courage and compassion, the usual relation, takes out and imposes on society, making sacrifices to do so, her discredited mother. A part of the drama (either of the story or the play), is in the sacrifices in question. In the tale, which is very brief and simple, she stands ready to sacrifice her lover. He doesn't exact it—he comes round to her and she does her work and keeps him as well. But the tale can, essentially, contain only the germ of the play. What presents itself, offhand, as indispensable for the play—without *approfondissement* of more than the results of a mere glance—is an intensification of the element of sacrifice and an intensification of the element of the mother's *milieu,* of the signs and tokens, the associations and appendages, the stamp and colour that are part and parcel of it and offer it to the view. Everything, in a word, must be satirically intensified and dramatically pointed. The struggle must be more arduous than in the tale, the renunciation more heroic, the difficulty greater, the personality and situation of the mother more contrasted, the victory more brilliant. The whole thing must be at once more general, more typical, and more special. All sorts of things, as it were, must depend on the daughter's success. There must be *complications* in the mother's life, and yet a picture—very droll, very satiric—of the whole "desolation of propriety," as the story calls it, in which that life is consciously past. There are the people whom the girl's struggle is with, and who must be intensely *selected,* to make it dramatic. There must be something, someone whom the girl must deal with *in* the mother's past as well as the mother herself. How directly, as one approaches it, one begins to see the drama open out; see it give, *give, give* as one presses! It *always* gives—gives something; the question that remains is whether in the particular case it gives *enough.* The charming thing is that even if it doesn't one is, when one reaches that question, so far—so much the farther—on the general way. The Maresfield interest becomes, in the play, one of the big wheels of the action. May the added someone or something, in the mother's "past," in the problem that the daughter has to deal with, not perhaps be the old lover, the correspondent for whom the mother was divorced. I needn't absolutely have a divorce unless I want to. It may have been only a scandalous separation and thereby serve my purpose; especially if it disposes of some questions—why the mother didn't marry her lover etc. etc. Let us assume then, for the moment, that the lover *is* there, to add to the girl's difficulty and danger. Make the machinery to *capture* her, to prevent her, more important; the Maresfield machinery, I mean—the Maresfield bribe. Make the girl's second lover more dramatically active than Guy Mangler. In this way one gets the bribe, somehow, as well as the loss—what she gives up—at home—and what is held out to her elsewhere. Not what is held out to her to make her drop her mother as Bertram Jay wishes to make her drop her: (he's on the family—her own family side)—but what is held out to make her *sacrifice* her, give up trying to put her through and look out only for herself. The way Rose *works* this, in the tale, is of course a thing to be made intensely dramatic and ironic in the play. Mrs. Vaughan-Vesey becomes—can only become—important in the play. On the other hand the family must be reconstituted—the grandmother doesn't seem to me to be what I can find *de mieux.* Aunt Julia—yes, a representative of property etc.; another sister, yes—a representative of the opposite—the proper course (comedy-character—with secret flirtation of her own verging on scandal)—and then possibly, conceivably, the *father?* No; I think not—the struggle isn't with him, it's with the world. I mean that from the moment it's not a question of making *him* reaccept her mother, he can only be awkwardly placed in the action. Therefore he's out of it, and one gets by that the benefit of his inheritance for Rose—her means, the thing that makes her valuable. She must sacrifice money—yes: that is her *family* prospect. But she must sacrifice a *lover*—or have the question of sacrificing him above all. I seem to see a pretty part that would make a *third* suitor—and perhaps the successful one: the part of a clever *observant,* sincere fellow (the real "hero") who has had no *parti-pris* about her in advance and who is won to help her by the gallantry of her course. The thing assumed here (D.V.) is an action in which he *may* help her—help her, say, with the lover, who constitutes a difficulty. I seem to see all sorts of things—they *swarm* upon me. I see Aunt Julia as an *uncle,* a rich, intolerant bachelor, to diminish the number of women (Rose 1, sister 2, Mrs. Tramore 3, Mrs. Vaughan-Vesey 4, Lady Maresfield 5). In the way of men there would seem to be: The Hero (1), Bertram Jay (2), Guy Mangler (3), the Ex-Lover (4) and the young man whom her sister (Edith) has her flirtation with (5). I must add that Lady Maresfield and Mrs. Vaughan-Vesey may be resolved into one person, and this may also happen to the "hero" and Bertram Jay. (I don't, I confess, just in a glance, at all see *that* duplication.) Nor at the first blush is the role of the lover very apparent to me. Of course at the first blush there is nothing but the germ of the subject: I mean a kind of *faith* in it, enveloped in a mist of confusion. Out of the mist there looms, somehow, a first act—a first act in which the various things (and more) are settled that are settled in the first chapter of the tale. I vaguely see a place in which a meeting of the various people is possible: an hotel in Switzerland, at Aix-les-Bains—or at the Italian lakes. The girl here is *introduced* to her mother, made acquainted with her, has the mother's situation revealed to her. She sees her cold-shouldered etc. She is shocked, pained by it—affected, in a word, as also is in the tale, and is moved to take up the position she takes in the tale. What depends upon it—what she loses by it, made clear to her. The Maresfield-Vesey interest must be, here, the cold-shoulderers, and *their* evolution, their transition is that they see, later, how she draws. The "observant" suitor (the added one) plays, practices, ironizes as I may say, on the situation in conjunction with Mrs. V-V.—or on *her* in conjunction with the situation. *He* believes in the girl, is charmed, has no doubts. By making him so, however, I lose the chance of bringing him over—making him serve her work, as Rose makes Captain Jay in the play. There may be a way of attaching this personage—in some way—to Mrs. Tramore. I see that the difficulty—one of them, and the main one, in what the story gives at least—is the sufficiently unheroic character of Bertram Jay. He doesn't *do*—as he is—for the hero. And yet his being as he is, is important for the comedy interest. Can't I imagine the other fellow, the inserted personage, making Rose's acquaintance for the *first* time on the very occasion of this crisis of the first act. He's an outsider when the curtain rises—but drawn into the action by the very effect of her behaviour. If I keep the ex-lover, discredited, disreputable now [may there not be a question of his *marrying* her (Mrs. Tramore) now that her husband is dead?—marrying her to satisfy the claims of respectability, the standards of the Philistines] if I keep him, I say, and keep him as an annoyance, a mortification to Mrs. Tramore, I get a kind of *lien* for the new hero, a link of introduction or attachment. I am wondering in other words whether an entrance may not be found for him, and after an entrance a strong and valid part, as a kind of relative, a cousin, of the lover, to whom Mrs. Tramore has applied, to whom she has appealed, to interfere, to relieve her of him, to help her to get rid of him. He is on the spot for that purpose, and his situation gives him his vision of Rose. Two alternatives arise (for *me*): the idea of making Mrs. Tramore's lover a perfect *bore* of fidelity, desiring to *marry* Mrs. T; while she now *doesn't* want that, has outlived the phase of desiring it; and the idea of her wanting it and having sent for New Hero, his kinsman, to force it on, and then been moved to a different determination by the entrance into her life of her daughter. The idea would be here that the girl conceives the bold and superior design of acting for mother *without* the marriage—putting her through *herself,* independently, without it; on the basis of disliking so the poor ex-lover. Both she *and* his kinsman dislike him: they *meet* on *that*. Ignominy—satiric treatment—of the social view, the social standard, that makes it the condition—*et encore!*

x x x

One seems, yes, to see, *à peu près,* a first act, of a good deal of life: but not at an hotel abroad, on second thoughts, no. The two sisters have been living abroad— with their father: partly *on account of* their mother, who is in England and whose presence there has been a reason for their keeping away. They only know—Rose only knows, what this father has *bien voulu* tell them about her. The father dies— they have a prim, rich, fussy bachelor uncle to whom they devolve more or less by this circumstance. He goes for them—or they come back, and the first act takes place in his house in London just after their return. It is abroad—during her last year—that Rose has met Bertram Jay. It is the proper, conventional, worldly uncle who has embraced the idea of Mrs. Tramore's now marrying her former lover—regularising her position. He has, fatuously, busy-bodily *sent* for the lover to express to him, thus opportunely, his views on this subject. The lover, for reasons, has sent his kinsman—a cleverer, more creditable, more distinguished person—to treat, to converse, to see *de quoi il s'agit,* etc. This is *his* introduction to Rose, his first encounter with her. Happy thought—that is it seems to twitch my sleeve as one! Keep the ex-lover personally out of the play altogether—make him present, like Mme Benoîton,[4] only by reference and contention. So the kinsman, the new lover, the Hero, is hereby brought. Mrs. Tramore is brought, in the simplest and most natural way in the world, by her own act. She has meditated, planned her visit as a kind of bold, calculated *coup*—she has had in mind its *"effect"* on her daughter—as a means of capturing her, of making a good impres-

4. In Sardou's play *La Famille Benoîton,* the mother of the family, Mme Benoîton, is alluded to but never appears on stage; HJ applied the idea of the absent but influential character to Mrs. Newsome of *The Ambassadors.* See "Project of Novel," 1 September 1900.

sion on her, before a bad one is made by the representations and machinations of others. She is ignorant of Mr. Tramore's (her brother-in-law's,) *ingérance*—and is confronted now for the first time with the machinery set in motion, in the name of the grotesque proprieties, to make her (and *encore* only questionably!) tidy herself up by this tardy union. It is *part* of the ground—this new knowledge, this present pressure, on which she meets her daughter. Mrs. Vaughan-Vesey has come, partly at Mr. Tramore's instance and partly at that of her own speculations—to see what can be done for her brother Guy Maresfield. It is for her, also, perhaps—or doubtless—that Mr. Tramore has sent as a form of feminine support, of chaperonage, to advise about the girls and look in particular after Edith.

x   x   x

I reflect, however, that it may be a mistake to reduce Lady Maresfield and Mrs. Vaughan-Vesey to a common identity. Don't I sacrifice, thereby, lose something indispensable? The number of women needn't disturb me so much—it's a part of the essence of the subject, which represents, for Rose, a struggle with society. I don't get my "society" if I make my women too few. Lady Maresfield and her daughter perform totally different, perform opposed functions. Mrs. V.V. is the intensely modern woman who is with Rose etc. Let me, therefore, to begin with, try to see Lady M. in first act, alone. She needn't even have been "sent for" by Mr. Tramore: she has come, by her own officiousness etc., on speculation. She wants to get Rose for her younger son. Her opposition, her scandalization, when she hears, or divines, what Rose forfeits. This counts as part of the public opinion that the girl has to face and fight. Then *elle se rabat,* for Guy, on Edith—but with the divided mind of watching to see how it turns out for Rose, and if she (Rose) may not perhaps get, somehow, from her mother, *more* than she forfeits from her uncle. The young Edith, meanwhile, flirtatious and hypocritical, which her sister is not, is meanwhile, carrying on surreptitious commerce with some detrimental—some German music-master, or some such person. Make Bertram Jay by no means military—make the hero military if you like. Bertram Jay becomes political and parliamentary. He becomes the timid, the prudent, the shockable lover as contrasted with the brave. He is another of the "social forces" with which the girl has to count. But in this connection, of course, one sees rise before one the question and the difficulty of the "love-interest" and the marriage question from the moment the serious side of this matter is taken from the circumspect lover and attached to another man. In the story the girl *uses* Bertram Jay, as it were—and then, later, marries him. To make her marry the Hero *without* using him offers, of course, infirmities. He *must* be an *agent,* in other words; and we shall manage that. Bertram Jay is a *comedy-agent,* and a reluctant and unwilling one; and the Hero is a sentimental agent—an eager and sympathetic, or at least clever, wise, observant and sustaining one. He must find his activity partly in being the showman of the human spectacle. Bertram Jay drops out by being too cautious, *too* anxious, too tactless, too parliamentary. He must fail her on a crucial occasion, when, instead, she finds the Hero there. This occasion must be the climax of the action, of an action extremely *corvée,* thoroughly overhauled and solidified. In the simplest expression it consists of the effort of the girl to *place* her mother.

The intensity and the interest of this effect depend largely upon the question of *where* she wants to place her. This point, this *where*, must become supremely and admirably concrete in the third act. It must be a great occasion—it must have high importance. It must be something higher than Lady Maresfield—something for which Mrs. V.V. is operative in the spirit she exhibits in the tale. Is it a great party at a Duchess's—is it something more than a party? Is it a charity bazaar?

x   x   x

June 6th, 1893.

I postpone, I drop the above for the hour *pour me recolleter* with the question of the Scenario sketched for Compton and as to which it is tolerably clear that, as regards complexity of action, it can be considerably improved. It can be improved with patience—it can be improved with resolution and devotion and above all it can be improved with *reflection*. The main little mass of it is there but something more is wanted—and I must take some quiet creative hour (ah, quiet creative hours—their very name in this general connection is sweet!) to think that out. Little by little, D.V., the right thing will come. As I in a primary way rest my eyes on it, I seem to see the required, the augmented interest to the . . . [the manuscript breaks off at this point].

The "E. P. D. Subject"
(1893)

The Houghton manuscript consists of fifteen unlined numbered sheets, $6\frac{1}{2}''$ x $7\frac{1}{2}''$, written in ink on one side. A title page (in a hand other than HJ's) reads: "MS. 'Note on beginning of Tale on the "E. P. O.[D.]" Subject' (summer of 1893, June)." It refers to the earlier Edward Parker Deacon notes; see 28 February 1892 and 15 June 1901.

I

"In the first place he has not a particle of sympathy with any of my tastes," said Mrs. Vanneck.

The young man to whom these words were addressed was not instantly ready with a reply to them; he hesitated, feeling that the occasion was serious and having had, as yet, but little experience of unappreciated voices. He was shy, he felt his cleverness to be a faculty less developed than his companion's, and it was the first time she had spoken so freely, so resentfully of her husband. He admired her—it was the reason he came to see her so often; nevertheless her indictment of poor Vanneck struck him as the least bit abrupt, as if it had not been, in the language of the time when he rehearsed plays for private theatricals, sufficiently led up to. He had not been fully aware until this moment that she was so unhappy. At the same time it seemed to him that he now fully took in all the charm of her nature. She had never been so lovely as in crossing this line that separated candor from reticence. It was as if she had stepped out into the free air and taken the freshness with her cheeks and lips. She was perhaps a trifle too short for perfect beauty; but there was no such clear depths in any other gray eyes, no such golden threads in any brown hair. Moreover, she was so young to be so clever, and so unhelped to be so cultivated. On a later occasion Hamilton Dane discovered that she had two or three years less youth than himself; her culture, it is true, remained for him a country unexplored. At the moment they really became intimate she had already written a novel which Vanneck, in spite of his failure to enter into her pursuits, had consented to meet the expense of publishing. Hamilton Dane,[1] however, was not literary, and the first time he had been presented to himself in the light of imagination was when she told him that his natural place was in the House of Commons. He was at the present moment indeed looking for something to do, and if he should first find it and then do it, he might, as a subsequent step, consider the question of proposing himself to an electorate on the strength of it. Meanwhile such an appeal would probably be judged premature. George Damant's[2] only obvious qualification for anything was that he was "six foot three," and there was accordingly a great deal of him to be disposed of. His father was a bewildered country-gentleman, his mother was the daughter of a tarnished peer, his brothers were five in number. He was not thought the stupidest of the young men, and he was not thought the handsomest; but this didn't prevent his being both very simple-minded and very good looking. When Mrs. Vanneck complained to him that her husband fell very short he broke out, after a little—"By Jove, that's not right!"

"Do you know what he did?" asked Mrs. Vanneck. "He married me to get into society."

"Then you've done for him about as much as he could have expected."

"He married me for Papa, don't you know," Mrs. Vanneck continued, filling out the indictment with a liberal hand.

"*I* wouldn't have married you for that!" her companion exclaimed, turning a little red as he laughed. She gave him an instant her pretty stare, and it dawned upon him dimly that his attempt to say something graceful might possibly have had an opposite sound—seemed to convey that such a bribe would have been inadequate. What he meant was that it would have been unneeded. Mrs. Vanneck smiled with indulgence; she had never, from the first, tried to persuade herself that what she liked him for was a promptitude of wit. She could trust him to know at least, however, what her last declaration signified—not to be ignorant that her father, Lord Littlewood, had had a hand, often a heavy one, in public affairs. She had met Henry Vanneck free of the high political world, in which he had taken no place whatever. She felt, it must be added, for what she could *not* trust George Damant when he presently inquired: "But what was it you married *him* for her [then]?"[3]

That was never a question to ask when a woman *had* married for money. She sometimes spoke the truth to Vanneck, but she had never till today uttered it in any great quantity to this particular visitor, and she had reached the furthest point to which she was, as yet, prepared to go in putting him in possession, as it were, of the secret of her soul. When a woman had talked to a gentleman about her hidden misery she had said enough. Therefore she told George Damant, in answer to his question, that she had married because her mother made her. Her mother

1. This name is written above "George Damant himself," which HJ crossed out.
2. This is written above "Hamilton Dane's," which HJ crossed out.
3. The manuscript clearly reads "her" but HJ must have intended the word "then."

was dead now and couldn't contradict her. Besides, George Damant would never have appealed from anything she said—she could see (and she saw with deep joy) that he believed everything. The same causes are far from producing in different cases the same effects; for this limitless credulity was at times exactly what she found most irritating in her husband. Yesterday she had disliked Vanneck more than she had ever done for he had not taken exception to a word of the account she had given him of the circumstances in which, the day before (as it had come to his knowledge), she had met young Damant. There were things she wanted to keep from him, not because she was afraid of him (she flattered herself she was afraid of nobody and of nothing), but because she felt them in this manner more important and more peculiarly her own. She spent the rest of the occasion to which I have alluded in talking of her husband with a frankness which showed her confidence in her visitor's sympathy even if it produced an occasional alarm about his understanding.

"The most tiresome thing of all is that he is so utterly futile."

"Futile?" said George Damant, with his deep vagueness.

"I mean he's such a muff. No one takes him seriously."

"He isn't thought clever?" the young man went on.

"He isn't thought *anything*. He cuts pictures out of the illustrated papers and pastes them in books."

"I know another fellow who does that!" the young man laughed. Then, as his hostess gave another of her pretty stares, he added: "I don't mean *me!*" He didn't add that he meant one of his best friends, and he was glad he had not when Mrs. Vanneck went on:

"Henry's tastes, his occupations, his habits, are all intensely frivolous. He pays calls, he leaves cards, he spends hours in shops, he worries about the flowers at dinner and about the children's clothes."

"I know the sort of fellow you mean," said young Damant, tapping his upper teeth gently with the silver knob of his walking-stick and fixing an uncertain blue eye on the "mystery of things."

"The K. B. Case and Mrs. Max"
[*The Ivory Tower*]
(1909-1910)

The notes which follow—dating from about mid-December 1909 to 14 January 1910—comprise HJ's preliminary sketches for *The Ivory Tower,* undertaken for Harper. They fall between two bouts of illness, the first, early in 1909, to some extent the result of depression at the failure of the New York edition, and the other virtually upon him as he wrote the last of these pages—this too due to mental stress but also to his practice of "Fletcherizing"—the prolonged chewing of his food—which seriously affected his digestive system (see *Letters* IV, 546–58). The Houghton manuscript material is in a variety of forms, from the brief item on a scrap of paper $4\frac{1}{2}'' \times 7''$ to the substantial $8'' \times 10''$ pages of the large manuscript in pencil that concludes the material. There are also two typescripts. See accompanying footnotes for more specific detail; see also the dictated "Notes for *The Ivory Tower*" (1914). K.B. is Katherine De Kay Bronson.

Splendid for the K.B. case that the 'sympathetic American' whom I've been thinking of should come to play the part I want for him in the foreign, in the cosmopolite *milieu,* through this process: that he is brought to see that if he doesn't some other man, *an* other man, will—a particular other dangerous (foreign?—or domestic, *badly* domestic) personage will, and that so it is he decides and, as it were, lends himself to wear the appearance—which is all *she* wants, as an antidote to her humiliations, and yet save her from the absolute peril of accepting the service from the other fellow, who would, to a certainty, take some base advantage of it. I see him as 'put up' to this—I mean see the situation interpreted and lighted and made clear for him by an indispensable personage of the interpretative appreciative yet functional sort, woman or man, but woman probably, friend of my Heroine's, whom the Action must gather in. Yet, ah, *so* functional too must this figure be—in the sense, I mean, of what will depend on it; which is the *only* sense of the functional.[1]

x   x   x   x   x

I just jot down here that I seem to see as *characters* off-hand something like:

My Heroine
Her Mother-in-law
The important Friend—1st in N.Y., then in Florence—(The American Type in Florence).
The young (unmarried) American girl (in love with Other Man) (who beats them so easily both).
The Foreign Woman (Great Person).
The Hero (American).
The Other Man (interested Party) do. (1st 'Danger').
The Foreign Man. 'Danger' (2d).
The American Husband (Type of the Type).
The Young Man (English or other attached to the 'Important friend').

The Hero is the *Cousin* of the Deceased Husband and Young Agent, etc., of the Mother-in-law's Property.

The Mother-in-law, in Book I, gets her *early* impression of Important Friend—they have Heroine's situation a bit 'out'—and I immediately see, here, how young unmarried New York woman is indispensable, functionally, here—to prepare her effect etc. The Interested (Other) Man already wants to marry her. She cares nothing for him, but already dreams of Hero, who, she believes, cares nothing for *her*. The Important friend urges her coming abroad (thinks she's not dangerous and *may* be convenient). The Mother-in-law suspects, fears, alone. Isn't 1st scene between Girl (of 25) and Other Man?[2]

Mrs. Max[3]

Anne Drabney ⎱ I (Nan Drabney) ⎰	Horton Crimper ⎱ 4 (Haughty Crimper) ⎰
Augusta Bradham ⎱ 2 (Gussy Bradham) ⎰	Basil Hunn 5
Cissy Foy ⎱ (Cecelia Foy) ⎰	Davy Bradham ⎱ 6 Bradham ⎰
	Mrs. Drabney 7

1. This entry probably precedes by only a very short time the dated entry which follows it. The Houghton manuscript has a title page with the following written in ink, in a hand other then HJ's: "Preliminary statement for 'Mrs. Max' (unfinished novel which formed the germ of 'The Ivory Tower')." See entry for 10 February 1909 ("some little time ago") on the "K. B. Case"; also see the dictated "Notes for *The Ivory Tower*" (1914).
2. All the foregoing is from a manuscript of four unlined sheets, 8" x 10", written in pencil on one side of the sheet. There is also a typescript of 1½ double-spaced pages, 8" x 10½".
3. The names in the following list are from five different Houghton manuscripts. The group, numbered 1 to 7, are written in pencil on one side of a white unlined sheet, 8" x 10"; under "Davy" (no. 6)

Graham Riser (Gray Riser)

Fielder

Finder

Hincher   *Betterman*

Clencham   Harold Rising

Grabham

          Wrencher   Alan Wrencher

Grey Riser

Grey Fielder

Bright Riser

Shimple—Kate Shimple

Moyra Brandish

Brinting   Kate Crimple

Grey Bradham

Alan Wrencher

Kate Crimple

Mr. Betterman

Wentworth Hench

Wenty Hench

Cantopher

Augerer

Grey Bradham

Kate Augerer

Cornard Cressingham

Cornard Rosemary

Perrot

Romper, Finder, Shimple

Moyra Ruddle

Bruit, Ode

Brasher, Oddsley

Grabham

Mention

Toyt

Bulpit

Peregrine (King) (P. Roy)

December 17th, 1909.[1] The receipt of a letter from Duneka (F.A.)[2] about a serial Fiction for Harpers comes in at an odd psychological moment and with an odd psychological coincidence today—when I have been literally in the very act of sitting down to a statement of the little idea that I have for these few years past carried in my brooding brain as the 'K.B.' (Venice) idea—struck out some longish little time ago now in a talk about K.B. with C.F.,[3] who had had for years a great deal of acute observation of her, and who struck out something, as a little significant truth of her case, the formulation of an aspect of her situation, which immediately began to shine for me, in an appealing ironic light, as a little subject, a particular and interesting case indeed, out of which something might be made. And last winter, when I couldn't do it, it came up for me again—with *more* of its little vivid intensity, with developments and a whole picture, relations and elements and aspects falling into their place and conspiring together; so that at pres-

---

"Devon" is crossed out, and preceding the subsequent "Bradham" are "Conny" and "(Constant)"— both crossed out. The names from "Graham Riser (Gray Riser)" to "Brinting Kate Crimple" are written in pencil on one side of a white unlined sheet, 5″ x 7″. The next nine names are written on one side of a white unlined sheet, 5″ x 7″; the first seven are written in pencil, and between the first two names, "Howard" (in pencil) is crossed out and "Wentworth Henck" is underlined in ink; the last three are written in ink. The single name "Kate Augerer," underlined (with a flourish), is written in ink on a white unlined sheet, 4½″ x 7″. The names from "Cornard Cressingham" to "(P. Roy)" are, with one exception, written in ink on one side of a grey unlined sheet, 6″ x 7″; the exception, "Cornard Rosemary," is written in pencil in a hand other than HJ's.

1. This material is from a 70-page Houghton manuscript written in pencil on one side of unlined sheets, 8″ x 10″, numbered 1 to 60 and then, beginning with "I / Cissy Foy was to see . . . ," numbered 1 to 10. There is also a typescript of this material, 26 double-spaced pages, 8″ x 10½″. See completion of this sketch in 4 January 1910.

2. An editor at Harper's. See *Letters* IV, 453–54.

3. C. F. is probably Constance Fletcher.

ent it seems quite to cry out to me, with touching clearness and confidence and trust, to take pity on it and disengage it from its comparative confused limbo; thresh and worry it out a little, see what is really in it, set it down, in fine, in the old devout sacred way, for appreciation and constructibility, as I haven't hitherto had time or freedom of mind to do. To this small fond prayer and twitching of my sleeve on its part I have been, as I say, on the very edge of responding, when Duneka's letter comes in and seems, I confess, in spite of whatever other hostile preoccupations, rather movingly to force my hand. But I can only consider for the Harpers, at present, the question of a *short* novel—80 to 100 thousand words— and various throbbing possibilities crowd upon me in respect to my working out a plan for the use of this material, and the use of it in the only way in which it seems now pretty clear that I shall henceforth be able, with any vital, or any artistic, economy, to envisage my material at all—that is in the 'dramatic' way. *That* more and more imposes itself, and madness seems to me simply to lie in the direction of the unspeakable running of the '2 hares' at once—by which one means of course alternately. More than ever then, at any rate, does it seem to me worth my while to cipher out the subject of this thing for the possible 'serialised' employment, after the manner of my late so absorbing and endearing plunge into the whole process of the *Outcry* (to say nothing of *tutti quanti,* in the old, the ineffable, the exquisite, the pathetic and tragic 'sacred' days); from the moment, that is, that no *prima facie* presumption of the 'dramatic' value or plasticity of the *donnée* in question doesn't look me at all directly in the face. It doesn't here, thank God; and it doesn't for this reason—that I've seen my stuff—from the moment I began to get at all embracingly nearer to it—as peculiarly (*that's* the point) an Action, and that, for me, now, surely when an Action plants itself before me, it ceases to be a question of whether it '*can*' be Dramatic (in the splendid and whole sense—and in that only—in which I use the word) and becomes a question simply of what other form and *allure* it could conceivably take on. The process of the *Outcry* has been of enormous benefit and interest to me in all this connection—it has cast so large and rich and vivid a light upon my path: the august light, I mean, of the whole matter of method. I don't in the least see thus—beforehand!—how or why my 'K.B.' Case, as I may call it for convenience, should *se soustraire* from the application of that method and not be positively responsive to that treatment. Its having commended itself to me as peculiarly an action from the moment I began really to look at it is an enormous argument in favour of this possibility—and in fact, truly, would seem to settle the question. Of course I myself see *all* my stuff—I mean see it in each case—as an action; but there are degrees and proportions and *kinds* of plasticity—and everything isn't theatrically (using the term scientifically and, ah, so non-vulgarly!) workable to what I call the peculiar and special and ideal tune. At the same time one doesn't know— ideally—till one has got into real close quarters with one's proposition by absolutely ciphering it out, by absolutely putting to the proof and to the test what it will give. What then do I see my K.B. case, under the pressure and the screw, as susceptible of giving? *Any* way I want to see; but *if* the way that has begun to glimmer and flush before me does appear to justify itself, what infinite *concomitant* advantages and blessings and inspirations will then be involved in it! Porphyro grows faint really as he thinks of them.

Just stated, first of all, in its most crude and lumpish, its most *sommaire* form, then, my question is that of a still youngish and still 'living' American woman who is suddenly thrown upon the world, and upon her first real freedom, by the death of a husband with whom she has had a bad time and as to whom she has yet been, by her nature and her conscience, devoted and irreproachable. She has nursed him through ten years of ill-health brought on by his bad habits—his vices; she has given up her young life, very much, all in New York, so that he should be tended and kept going to his very poor tune at best. She is not, it should be said, a woman considered either very pretty or very clever—but she has a personality (or for some few), a charm of her own. She has some oddity of appearance—something that doesn't attract the *plupart*. But she longs for experience and freedom and initiation—in her own way; she has no children; she has some money—just enough; and she somehow takes for granted, after what has happened, some new freedom and some new chance. The question is what she shall *'do'* (I think she must be *35 or 36*)—and she's the sort of person (childless—2 children lost) as to whom it's assumed that she *may*—though not too easily—marry again. She has a little money of her own, but the rest depends on her mother-in-law, a figure of importance, *much* importance, in the scheme; the 'rest' being that lady's own fortune, which the deceased son and husband has only had an allowance—a very good allowance—from, during his lifetime, that has all depended on his Mother's discretions. *She* is a person who may possibly still live a longish time.

x   x   x   x   x

January 4th, 1910.[1] I take this up again after an interruption—I in fact throw myself upon it this a.m. under the *secousse* of its being brought home to me even more than I expected that my urgent material reasons for getting settled at productive work again are of the very most imperative. *Je m'entends*—I have had a discomfiture[2] (through a stupid misapprehension of my own, indeed); and I must now take up projected tasks—this long time *entrevus* and brooded over—with the firmest possible hand. I needn't expatiate on this—on the sharp consciousness of this hour of the dimly-dawning New Year, I mean; I simply invoke and appeal to all the powers and forces and divinities to whom I've ever been loyal and who haven't failed me yet—after all: never, never yet! Infinitely interesting—and yet somehow with a beautiful sharp poignancy in it that makes it strange and rather exquisitely formidable, as with an unspeakable deep agitation, the whole artistic question that comes up for me in the train of this idea of a new short serial for the Harpers, of the *donnée* for a situation that I began here the other day to fumble out. I mean I come back, I come back yet again and again, to my only seeing it in the dramatic way—as I can only see everything and anything now; the way that

1. This lengthy entry, which completes the sketch of the "K. B. Case" begun in the entry for 17 December 1909, covers at least ten days: see the reference, near the end of the entry, to "Jan. 14th, 1910."
2. HJ had suffered a "nervous breakdown": he had been worried about his heart and was examined in February 1909 by the heart specialist Sir James Mackenzie, who pronounced his heart tolerably sound. HJ saw Sir William Osler in March 1910 for a complete examination. See *Life* 665–67.

filled my mind and floated and uplifted me when a fortnight ago I gave my few indications to Duneka. Momentary sidewinds—things of no real authority—break in every now and then to put their inferior little questions to me; but I come back, I come back, as I say, I all throbbingly and yearningly and passionately, oh, *mon bon,* come back to this way that is clearly the only one in which I can do anything now, and that will open out to me more and more and that has overwhelming reasons pleading all beautifully in its breast. What really happens is that the closer I get to the problem of the application of it in any particular case, the more I get *into* that application, so the more doubts and torments fall away from me, the more I know where I am, the more everything spreads and shines and draws me on and I'm justified of my logic and my passion.

x x x x x

What I seem to see then is the drawingroon of Mrs. Bradham's New York house on a Sunday afternoon in April or May—three or [four] weeks after her husband's death, and on the first occasion of her ever 'receiving,' in her bereavement and her mourning, even those immediately near her. I make out a number of them there now, and I see by their means my situation constitute and foreshadow itself. I see in other words my Exposition made perfect—see the thing as almost the Prologue, after the manner in which the first Book is the Prologue in *The Other House.* Oh, blest *Other House,* which gives me thus at every step a precedent, a support, a divine little light to walk by. *Causons, causons, mon bon*—oh celestial, soothing, sanctifying process, with all the high sane forces of the sacred time fighting, through it, on my side! Let me fumble it gently and patiently out—with fever and fidget laid to rest—as in all the old enchanted months! It only looms, it only shines and shimmers, *too* beautiful and too interesting; it only hangs there too rich and too full and with too much to give and to pay; it only presents itself too admirably and too vividly, too straight and square and vivid, as a little organic and effective Action. In consequence of my impulse always to make the 1st step of my situation place itself only and exactly where that situation may be conceived as really beginning to show, I seem to have a sight of my 'young unmarried American woman' and my 'Husband of Important Woman—American Husband—type,' as laying together the first squared stones of my basis; this I mean if I can make them functional—and whether I can make them functional I shall be able to worry out only by patiently and wisely fumbling on. It commends itself to my perception at once that Martha Bradham (Bertha Bradham?) must have an appendage or a belonging of some sort—one absolutely foresees the need of that—and the most *like* sort is embodied for me in this glimmering of the attached and appended Girl, *un peu de ses parents,* whom it's a question of her taking to Europe with her, and whom I see in the forefront on this important, this decisive, Sunday afternoon. It's the What is Nan to do?—it's the How is Nan to live?—it's the Discussion of the Future of Nan, that gives its stamp to the occasion and that I see thus ushered in. I see it, I *have* it so, that I even ask myself—! But *pazienza,* and step by step. The two houses, Mrs. Drabney's and her Daughter's-in-Law, communicate—by a passage along the covered verandah or balcony behind. The two women are at Mrs. Drabney's, looking over

old things, young things, of the dead husband's: we have these facts, as we have
others, given us by Cissy Foy as she gives them to Davy Bradham, who calls
early in the afternoon—rather early—hoping to find his wife, whom he is to pick
up there, by arrangement, to call elsewhere, a call of importance and decency (on
some one of his people, his aunt) with her. She has not come, but Cissy, bored
and unoccupied, waiting, hoping for eventualities of her own, passes the time, the
moments, with him—much to our amusement and his; much to our edification and
information; much to the illustration of the character and situation of each. Well I
lay *dès maintenant* the basis of the question of *de quoi il s'agit,* dramatically and
actionally, in this first Act. I have already to some extent stated it in speaking of
the issue as the question of what Nan Drabney will now 'do'—which comes round
a good deal—and part of the function of the act is to show *how* it comes round—
to that of what her late husband's traditionally predominant and strenuous mother
(with her whole theory of Nan's character, history, situation, liabilities, etc.) takes
her stand on in respect to their relation, their common bereavement, their proper
observance of it—and her own possible intentions. *She* has (the) money; she is
rich; the fortune (hers) being partly her own and partly that left her by her late
husband, Maxwell Drabney's Father; left her outright, wholly to dispose of—with
an allowance made their son, in whom he had no faith, and whose bad habits,
eventuating in the long illness through which Nan has nursed him—ten years of
it, ten deadly years, mainly spent in the country—gave him all-sufficient grounds.
Nan has some means of her own—enough, in strictness, modestly to live on; with
presumptions of a continuation by her mother-in-law of the allowance made to
Maxwell. This, and Mrs. Drabney's further and eventual dispositions, testamentary and other, as well as her general attitude and general employment of her own
life—and even possible bestowal of her own *hand* (?)—depend much (this is one
of the functions of all these preliminary parts to demonstrate) on how Nan—now
for the first time free and at all at ease to display herself, attest and reveal herself,
'pans out.' It comes over me that I may find an indispensable use and value for
(in) making Mrs. Drabney's own possible remarriage a contributive issue: which
demands, however, a bit of looking at. What makes this worth weighing is my
glimmering vision of the final grab of her hand and fortune by Horton Crimper—
on finding that Nan has dished herself and doesn't get the latter—has every appearance of having it withheld from her in consequence of the events in Florence.
But it seems to me that what is determinant—largely—in this connection is Mrs.
Max's age; and my action involves her not being less than 35. Say she has been
older than her husband by 3 years—that is possible and easy—he will have died
at 33. Say they had been married eleven years, and her long sacrifice to him, her
incarceration and sequestration with him, have gone on for about 9—upwards of
10. Say accordingly that he—well, say that Mrs. Drabney is 56 at the beginning,
or even 55; and she needn't be more. Ah no, stay—if he has died at 32, she, his
mother, to have married quite early and had him at 21 or 22, needn't be *more*
than 56. There *is* the resource of my making him her *stepson*—whereby he may
have died older, and Nan's *épreuve* been longer and harsher—a bigger sacrifice;
whereby I can add a valuable year or two—making her 37—to her age. This is
worth thinking of, and the only thing against it is the diminution of pious *motive*

on that basis—though I think I see a sufficiency of that element as presentable. Mrs. Drabney has had no child—Nan has had two and lost them. Her husband *left* her his son to do her best for—and she has been important about the charge; making him thus her own. Say he was ten when she married his Father; she may have had him all for 15 years, he marrying at 25 and dying at forty. If I don't make Max's long illness the result of vice—but I really think I see this, with its advantages. I can at any rate try it and see how it works out. I *posit* Mrs. Drabney's own marriageability and her suspicion, her circumspection, her jealousy, her exaggerated claim of mourning, on the article of Maxwell's widow. If I make him in fact 'innocent'—only infinitely tiresome and selfish and suffering—I put truth into Mrs. Drabney's motive and into her retroactive sentiments of the order I intend. Cissy Foy puts it that she thinks him, poor Max, *now* so much more wonderful and herself so much more devoted, than was really the case;—just as she also passes the sponge over the extent to which she worked poor Nan during the whole dozen years, and the extent to which poor Nan consented to be workable. Well, so I leave this element; except that I seem to see, the more I think, that Maxwell must have been *good*—only impossible. Isn't Mrs. Drabney's idea that they shall mourn him together in a very crapy and conventional way—and that her step-daughter-in-law shall in particular give herself for an indefinite future time to these rites and this attitude? She makes assumptions of this sort; she is full of them—and *what pervades them all is the sense of Nan's dependence on her for the* LARGER *footing of life.*[3] Nan has her own 7 or 8 thousand (dols.) a year, yes; but the allowance from Mrs. Drabney may be stinted or ample, handsomer or more meagre, or definitely *nil,* according to the manner in which Mrs. Max, at this crisis of her career, presents herself. One of Mrs. Drabney's assumptions is that, united as they are by their bereavement and their mourning, whatever Nan does she does it *with* her. She will go abroad with her—yes, in their common crape; but she'll be startled by any pretension on Nan's part to go alone—as it were; to enjoy herself and see the world. This has come up for Nan—this sense of her own yearning and reaching out, and yet sense of her own oppression; and the Function of this Exposition, as it were, the individual Action of this First, is to clear up the whole air of this question—to present the question, give it its development and deal with it. What is here my particular climax? What is my *dénouement d'acte?* Why, as I see it, that Nan decides, selects, takes to her own feet and invokes her adventure. She decides, that is, to break with Mrs. Drabney, and the latter's companionship and surveillance, to the extent of starting off without her—taking Cissy Foy with her as a companion instead. Everything must contribute to my making this an all efficient objective, as it were, a climax of the right emphasis and promise. My act then, its function and interest and entertainment, consists of the course and process I follow to arrive logically and thrillingly at that determination of the elements. I show by and through what and by and through whom the climax in question is brought about. The persons involved are Mrs. Drabney herself and, for women, Mrs. Bradham and Cissy Foy; and for men

---

3. This italicized passage, from "*what pervades*" to "*footing of life*," is underlined in red ink, and "LARGER" is doubly underlined in red ink in the manuscript.

Basil Hunn, Horton Crimper, and Davy Bradham. I see the process pretty vividly; it glimmers before me, but it will glimmer more and more; and let me at any rate, *en attendant,* just dash down here provisionally 2 or 3 elements of the matter of which I thus just catch the tip of the tail. Nan is 'in love' with Basil Hunn—for whom she herself has no attraction of that sort whatever. Free now—ah, she'd marry him in a minute; that would be *her* solution of her future. He is her late husband's relative—cousin, a young New York lawyer (*à la* Harry—or older, more developed and more New York); and has had, from considerably back, charge of her own little fortune. She has not spent that, and he has taken care of it for her while she has lived with her sick husband and nursed him, on the income made them by Mrs. Drabney's allowance. Basil Hunn, kind to her, sorry for her, even liking her and feeling interested in her up to a certain point, but not conscious of any real person[al] charm (that appeals to himself) in her, has so fostered her little interests and resources that they have increased and multiplied. He has come to see her this Sunday afternoon for that purpose—she having sent for him. Her recent bereavement (6 or 8 weeks previous—or I think even less) has kept her, Mrs. Drabney's attitude aiding, a bit inaccessible and barricaded hitherto; and this day is a new day, a date or an epoch, marking her re-communications with the outer world. Seizing things, irrespective of their order here as yet and just as they come to me, I seem to see the *clou* of the act (or one of two *clous*), the *scène à faire,* as it were, in this appeal that she makes to him, as a friend as well as a Trustee, to know just where she is, how she may regard her outlook, what feel herself able to do. She doesn't *know* herself, she looks out upon her future with curiosities and anxieties, uncertainties—she feels that he somehow can tell her things, give her informations, warnings, advice, that will help. She *sounds* him, I say, as it were—but only to feel that, kind as he is, there is nothing intimately personal for her to look to from him, and she turns away with a certain pang of disappointment and humiliation. She is really romantic— deeply and foolishly romantic—though she half knows that it doesn't in the least fit her type, and that, given her type, the show of it will make her, *must* make her, more or less ridiculous. She wonders if she is ridiculous to *him.* But she can't find out—he doesn't let her know or show her anything of that kind; he is only awfully obliging and clear and kind and inspeakable—and she (deep within) is in love with him and desirous of him more than ever. It is thus, however, that he really answers the general question that she puts to him, and that is the question of what she had better 'do.' He answers it in the sense, that is, that she is perfectly free to go away—'for all *him!*' She would be willing to stay—she would ask nothing better than to stay—on the least word or hint received from him to the effect that he would like it. She puts to him the question of whether it is important she should be near him (near him is so what she would give her eyes to be) so as to communicate better about her interests; and he smiling, reassuring her, as a little amused at her simplicity, assures her that everything will go on quite well and easily if she is on the other side of the Atlantic. He even says to her that she'll marry again—says it, without any bad or false note in it, in the key of the seriousness and clearness and kindness and wisdom she has appeared to demand of him. She'll marry again, still young, provided, attractive, interesting as she is:

the only thing he hopes is that she won't marry a foreigner. Save for that it will be natural, inevitable, happy. He quite understands what a long ordeal, what a devil of a life she has had—and his idea is all for her having a change, a relief, a new start, etc. This it is that 'settles' her—his very kindness, the very imagination he is so good as to expend on her behalf and as to what will be good for her, has so little of any quality it would so deeply touch her *by* having. She completely controls herself, observing all the forms of serenity—but the scene is crucial. Don't I therefore all the more want to make something hang in the balance here for her, and with this—the absolute concrete form and dramatic value of the question which it's the function of the Act to present and then push to its solution? To ask this is of course to say immensely, Yes—and what I accordingly want is the most concrete form of my question possible, is the greatest dramatic value the connection will give. Well, pressing gently and firmly in the old ineffable way, I seem to get something like this, which I just note in its main items, the links and *liaisons* of it, and all roughly, first; to catch it.

(1) Nan's quasi-acceptance of her 'fate,' her common mourning, with Mrs. D.—combined with her (romantic) yearning to throw off the oppression of it.

(2) The fact that she would accept anything, any quantity of Mrs. D. now—in order to remain 'near' Basil Hunn, as it were; give up going abroad altogether, or go only with *her* if (through his looking after Mrs. Drabney's affairs too) this might keep her more in touch with him by the chance (Mrs. Drabney's affairs being so much bigger than hers) of its perhaps occasionally bringing him out to her. That they absolutely need have no personal meetings and communions over her own, he has struck her as perfectly emphatic and definite and 'hopeless' about. This is a kind of a blow—and she feels herself then and there, and utterly, give up all hope; and not only this but (since he affects her as absolutely shipping her off) knows, in her bitterness, dissimulated as it is, what moves those women who, slighted, jilted, *dépitées* by the man they have really cared for, respond, by a ricochet, to the advances, to the next one who approaches them. Don't I see her as (tentatively—indirectly and 'delicately,' *vu* her fresh mourning) approached at this juncture or moment by Horton Crimper, who is interested in her 'expectations' and believes in them and wants, as it were, to put down his name, stick in his pin and reserve his place. He approaches her to give her to understand that when they *can* talk of it—well, there is something that he only wants to say. At the same time he feels that her 'expectations' are much bound up in her keeping well with Mrs. Drabney—and what he is really taking upon himself is to guard that interest. His idea is that they shall go abroad together and that he shall go with them—and that practically is what he proposes to Nan. Under the effect and the impression of her scene with Hunn she rather assents to it—she is responsive partly as she would be under the sting of the *spretae injuria formae* in the other quarter. But he asks from her some definite word—so that he may, as he says, act; something that may serve as a sort of pledge. She says she'll think—she'll let him know—as it might, or may be, before he goes, and he says he'll come back to her—come back, that is, from having tea off in another room into which the scene opens: tea served by Cissy Foy, and at which Davy Bradham, also perhaps his wife and two or three other persons who have 'come round' with Mrs. Drab-

ney (to say nothing of Mrs. D. herself—??? disapprovingly studious of the more
or less shocking Cissy—for Cissy is 28) are present. (That tea a great convenience
and resource; that tea, and the approach through the other house, and the coming
to it thence of those wanting it and yet to whom as by reason of her mourning,
Mrs. Drabney doesn't give it—which help the movement of my Act.) *Je dois bien
noter* that Horton Crimper has known Max Drabney from early days, and has seen
something—a little—of his wife, even under their sequestration during the few
previous years, and that he intimates—he shows—that he understands her feeling
Mrs. Drabney, and her tie with Mrs. Drabney, rather a burden. He enters into
that; he's clever and plausible and agreeable and diplomatic; he's everything but
sincere and straight—and everything but in the least *really* cared for by Nan. But
he takes for granted the fact, and the importance, of her union with Mrs. Drabney—if only, a little avowedly even, for the benefit of the way the former lives.
What he assumes is that she will continue her allowance to Nan—a large allowance; making it the same as she made it to Maxwell; and this even if she (Nan)
marries him—an old good friend of her stepson's. What he is really concerned to
do is to see that she doesn't marry a foreigner. And he has, as it were, a rendezvous for this—for her last, her reflective word on the 'abroad' plan—before leaving her. What their scene is terminated by belongs to an order of considerations
that I haven't yet, in this mere scrambling scrabble, even begun to fumble out.
What I at any rate get hold of here is that Mrs. Bradham is now projected upon
her, to make her—again *interestedly,* in great measure—a very different sort of
appeal—and one which so makes all the difference. It's a sort of 'irony of her
fate' that these people—almost every one alike (Basil Hunn and the girl, Cissy
Foy, being the main *exceptions*)—see her, and in one way and another try to
practise on her, to 'work' her, as a Value; which is what she so awfully little sees
herself as being, *really*—though she tries a little, flutteredly, romantically, to take
it from them that she *is*—and it's part of her little drama, in its pathos and its
'poignancy'—also a good bit in its comedy and its irony—that she discovers by
the demonstration of life, by the demonstration of her adventure, that she isn't.
This is what she comes to—what Basil Hunn, at the end, sees her, compassion-
ately, kindly, humanly, sees her come to: this sense, under the discipline of events,
that she *isn't* a Value, a hard, fine firm *worldly* Value, at all—by the real measure
of such calculations and imaginations as Flora Bradham's—and also, in its degree,
Horton Crimper's. *Mrs. Bradham's* motived and interested demonstration to her
in Act I reposes on the fallacy (the *'vulgar'* fallacy on Flora's part) that she is
going to be. Well, *here* it is that I seem to want the effect of Basil Hunn—his
effect as to determining her accessibility to such an influence, an eloquence, a
logic, as Flora Bradham's—give it the additional chance with her of her seeing,
of her directly gathering, of her intimately feeling, that there's nothing for her to
hope from *him.* Roughly speaking, and so far as this first mixed glimmer goes, I
seem to want to put them—her and him—*twice* in presence: once before her scene
with Flora B., and once after. It is her scene with him—and I think her first—
that *settles* for [her] that she'll lend herself to Flora's representations; make up
her mind to see them as attractively determinant. She is to wait to tell her—which
involves a second scene (for Flora B.) with her; this second one, after her first

with Basil (or shall I call him *Conrad*—Conrad Hunn? does it go?) being the one in which she lets him know how she has closed, in a manner, with the Bradhams, and in which, confirmatory, congratulatory, he strikes her as fairly shipping her off. I seem thus to have a second scene with Flora appointed for her, in which she lets the latter know that she has decided—that she will go. I thus seem to get, for the Act, I note, three *pairs* of scenes, at least; three occasions on which the second scene, later on, in the same place, and in respect to matters, to a question, to an aspect of the situation *entamé* in the first, the second is preappointed; after which at its right moment it takes place. So it is for Nan with Horton Crimper; so it is with her for Flora Bradham; so it is with her for Conrad Hunn. And this leaves out the possibility of something of the same sort for her with Cissy Foy— her Confidante really, all through—besides leaving out the element of Cissy's sentiment for and relation with Horton Crimper—to say nothing of Cissy's expositional scene with Davy Bradham. Above all it doesn't as yet take account of the question of Mrs. Drabney's appearances and aspects—of the way in which my case involves the due and vivid presentation of her; the way in which I seem to see for her, as a pair of clean wheels in the action, a scene with Conrad and a scene with Nan. I seem to want her to be present at some exhibition of Mrs. Bradham's tone and life—to be seen, in a manner, seeing and realising what may lurk in all that picture. But above all it's with Conrad on one side and Nan herself on the other that I see her mainly concerned. She has her sense of the *romantic* in Nan—her sense of the frivolous, of latent laxities and dangers. *Si elle le laisse entrevoir,* or *le laisse deviner,* to Hunn, he is however amused—with even a little sceptical compassionate hope for the poor woman (Nan herself) that she *may* be so qualified. And then there is (what I make out I must lay the ground for) the element of Mrs. Drabney's relation with Horton Crimper—whom (Mrs. D.) my denouement involves his marrying in 4th Act—or being made to successfully cause himself to be accepted by! Perhaps—it comes to me as I go—this qualification of Nan by Mrs. Drabney—this exhibition of her view and attitude—must in measure come off between the latter and *Crimper* as part of *their* relation—his and Mrs. D.'s—and as expressible by her to him from the moment that they treat together of Nan at all. And that they do so treat together seems invoked, doesn't it, on the face of the matter, in my situation—he taking the favourable view, he *having,* up to Nan's disconcerting (to *him*) contrary determination, taken it, of the two women's remaining and acting together, going to Europe together, with Nan's consequent retention of advantages: that is of pecuniary ones. This is essentially what he has put before Mrs. Max in his scene of approach, scene of intimation to her, scene, as it were, of *sounding* her (as to his own chances, profit and advantage) early in the Act. Don't I—as it just now strikes me?—want to make this passage between these 2 occur after her, Nan's, 1st scene with Hunn, so that with her soreness, her vague hidden *blessure,* as it were, she may be shown as trying to lend herself to Horton's insidious appeal; after the manner of a wounded woman who, even while she hides her wound, turns almost to any kindness. She does just turn faintly to *his*—enough to show the difference as made by Mrs. Bradham's appeal later on—when she has just a little the air of *going back on* what she has first said to him: going back in the *second* scene I imagine between them. Thus do I get Hunn's 1st scene with her placed by my scheme, so far as it seems to shape, rather *early* in the act—and with that, too, in its degree prepared for. I have my provision of Cissy Foy and Davy Bradham there (rich in expositional power) all this time, I must remember—I have *them* there at any rate; and there glimmers upon me as sequent to them the question of the possibility of Mrs. Drabney before any appearance by Nan herself. I postulate this as prepared for— *mayn't* I just, this way, *mon bon?*—1st by Cissy and Davy Bradham together (ah, I see them a little as preparing for *Everything!*) and then Cissy and Horton Crimble (Davy having *gone,* to come back if I want him).

Thus perhaps I get:

I. Cissy Foy, Davy Bradham.
II. Cissy, Davy, Horton Crimble.
III. Cissy, Horton Crimble.
IV. Cissy, Horton, Mrs. Drabney.
V. Horton, Mrs. Drabney.

Thus just these first little wavings of the oh so tremulously passionate little old want (now!) make for me, I feel, a sort of promise of richness and beauty and variety; a sort of portent of the happy presence of the elements. The good days of last August and even my broken September and my better October come back to me with their gage of divine possibilities, and I welcome these to my arms, I press them with unutterable tenderness. I seem to emerge from these recent bad days—the fruit of blind accident (Jan. 1910)—and the prospect clears and flushes, and my poor blest old Genius pats me so admirably and lovingly on the back that I turn, I screw round, and bend my lips to passionately, in my gratitude, kiss its hand. It somehow comes to me that if I have Mrs. Drabney on early, as it were, the relations of place inevitably so determine themselves—shifting a little from what seemed 1st to flush; determine themselves to her being in her daughter-in-law's house—*having* been there till her entrance, with Nan, upstairs; instead of Nan's being, and having been, upstairs with *her* in the older Drabney house. This seems to me to provide better for her, Mrs. D.'s, exit and return, etc.: she goes *back* to her own—and comes *from* it again as I want her—with the immense resource of Cissy Foy's administration of tea in the other rooms—*dans le fond,* etc., aiding and coming in to my aid for almost everything. (I *see* an immense hostility, let me here just parenthetically—bracketedly—throw off, between Cissy and Mrs. Drab—[Cissy *calls* them Mrs. Max and Mrs. Drab],[4] and it's a sharp little element of the matter that if, or when, the determination of Nan's choice and preference takes place—her virtual rupture with Mrs. Drab on the 'Europe' ground— the alternative presented by her to her mother-in-law is that of *Cissy's* companionship, countenance and comfort; her starting forth, as it were, under Cissy's guidance. Cissy has been a great deal in Europe—Cissy *knows;* above all she *thinks* she knows. Mrs. Drab immensely *se méfie d'elle.* She is archi-modern; she is the Europeanized American girl. She is Julia Tucker—of the *neiges d'antan.* Oh, how *pretty* it seems to me all this can be!) But I, just before I knock off to go out (Jan. 14th, 1910), clutch the tip of the tail of *this,* that I have—*may* have—here my VII as between Mrs. Drab and Conrad Hunn. This makes:

4. HJ's brackets.

VI. Mrs. Drab, Horton, Hunn.

VII. Mrs. Drab, Hunn.

Shan't I—all speculatively!—have provided for Crimper's exit (and return) by an understanding on his part with Cissy that he will join her there at tea? Or even join her *chez* Mrs. Drab (work this out as a convenience).

VIII. Mrs. Drab, Hunn, Nan. Mrs. Drab goes off on *arrangement* with Hunn—previous to Nan's entrance—that she shall see him again. She goes to her own house and own people—and when he has had his scene with Nan *he* goes to Cissy Foy. That is, he has his scene with Nan—and she asks him to wait—to go to tea with Cissy. Yes—that's right. Crimper comes in, comes back with Nan—yes, that's it—*after*—*on*—her scene with Hunn; and then it is that Hunn's exit is determined. He does what both the women have asked of him—he goes to wait. Crimper then has his scene with Nan—unless I can avoid these 2's and 2's—*all* 2's and 2's—run *something* of this together. Let me see at any rate (as I've already seen it) what it makes. It makes VIII, as I say, Mrs. Drab, Hunn, Nan. And then:—

IX. Nan, Hunn, with:—

X. Nan, Hunn, Crimper (Hunn's Exit) and:—

XI. Nan, Crimper.

She arranges for his return. He goes out. *He rejoins Mrs. Drab.* But he doesn't do this till Flora Bradham arrives; and I think I see the Part, the ½ Book, end—that is, the Act reach its mid-moment—with the arrival of Flora Bradham prepared for—*immensely* prepared for—by Cissy and Davy. This determines Horton's exit and leaves Nan and Flora face to face. So the Part terminates, making Scene XII and having XIII started.

I

Cissy Foy was to see afterwards how the whole history, the succession of interesting, if often bewildering, matters to be eventually unfolded to her sense, had exactly taken its start with Davy Bradham's turning up in Madison Avenue that Sunday afternoon of the eventful Spring and finding her more or less in charge of the situation. Mrs. Drab, as she was apt a trifle cynically to call her Cousin Nan's immediate neighbour and ostensible mother-in-law—Mrs. Drabney more properly speaking—had appointed the earlier hours of the day for an 'overhauling' (as Cissy's irreverence again viewed the circumstance) of material memories, intimate properties, sacred relics; the process above stairs and in the adjacent house (from which, on two floors, an aperture had been made, for convenience, within recent years) had apparently dragged itself out, so that Nan wasn't yet back to preside at luncheon for her guest and this young woman had but vaguely nibbled in solitude. The two others, the bereaved wife and the afflicted and deprived stepmother—as Mrs. Drab merely was, after all—were still occupied together in the melancholy rite; in spite of which, let me add, Cissy had begun to flatter herself, with Mr. Bradham's arrival, that the occasion wouldn't hang heavy on her hands. She had her particular view of it—a little project of her own that would be put to the proof—and was sharply interested in this distinctly bold experiment. Though she had been but a fortnight in the house—having joined her distressed relative there a month after Maxwell Drabney's death and when his own people, great ralliers at dreary junctures and at such almost only, had had time to disperse—she had begun to believe that she saw her way, and that her happy thought, one of the happiest she had ever had, was going, as she would have said, to be put through. This conviction quickened and enriched for her the charming gathered light of the end of April, reflected at a hundred points, to an effect of high elegance and cheer, by poor long-suffering dismally dead Max's relinquished 'things'; which he had enjoyed so little in life, but which it was Cissy Foy's private intention that as many of his survivors as possible, and his sacrificed wife most of all, who had profited by them quite as little, and without his so good and so tragic reasons for it, should now proceed to testify to the value of—hideous after all as some of the objects were. Yes, she thought most of them dreadful—as how couldn't things be toward the acquisition of which Mrs. Drab had had a voice?—but their type of ugliness didn't invalidate them as resources, and to the appraisement of resources in general Cissy's own difficult history had been such as to direct her very straight.

Even New York itself, at any rate, was pretty enough for almost anything on such a day and in that quarter; a positively crude atmospheric optimism broke in with the shining afternoon—to the degree even of causing Mr. Bradham to figure fairly as a promise of help. He had never in his life, she felt sure, presented himself under that aspect to anyone, but she had her present reasons for quite clutching at him, and as he appeared she tossed down her lemon-covered French volume (not of fiction, but of criticism: she paid the awful shade of Mrs. Drab, which always loomed there, the tribute of this discrimination) without even sticking in a folder. It was impossible to give less the impression of a weight to apply than this sleek image of social accommodation; but her impulse was none the less to press him on the spot into her service. He immediately explained that he had been expecting to find his wife with Mrs. Max—they were to pay a call together, and his instructions had been definite: he was to pick her up there not later than four, she coming on from some place where she would have lunched. The quarter past four had sounded, but bringing with it of course no Flora; something abject in his surrender to the possible further implications of which fact was noted by Cissy as a fresh example of his inveterate humility as a husband. Whatever her husband should be, poor man, he wasn't to be humble after the conspicuous Bradham fashion, and nothing could prove better that Flora wasn't 'really clever' than that she should so little mind having reduced him to such a state in the eyes of those nations of the earth whose society they frequented. No society worth speaking of could be anything but disagreeably affected by the humble husband—when it didn't feel him, that is, either as preparing his revenge or as doing penance for his crimes. She didn't believe in Davy's crimes, though crimes in general so interested her that she was easily disposed to 'posit' them; the only question left therefore was whether he would ever be capable of revenge. If he would help her to what *she* wanted she would be willing to help him to that. But did he suffer? She doubted it—though there might some day be fun in finding out that he exquisitely did. He took refuge at any rate meanwhile in the appearance of thinking Flora very very nearly as fine as she clearly thought herself.

Notes for
"London Town"

1907–1909

"London Town" notes (Houghton Journal VIII, 22 August 1907 to 1 October 1909), $4\frac{1}{2}'' \times 7''$—and almost indistinguishable in size from HJ's pocket diaries (with which it has been confused)—has red leatherette covers and marbled endpapers. Of 140 marble-edged pages, $36\frac{1}{2}$ are written in black pencil and the remainder are blank. HJ refers to this as the "little red book."

On 22 June 1903 HJ signed an agreement with Macmillan for a book tentatively named "London Town" ("by reason of one's wishing to mark that it isn't a question, exactly, of London *City*," HJ explained). Various demands—especially his tour of the United States and the revision of his fiction for the New York edition—prevented HJ from writing the proposed book. This notebook records some of his preparatory observations; the kind of attention HJ was giving to odd corners and architectural detail suggests the form the book would have taken.

August 22d, 1907 Spring Gardens.[1]

While I linger to look, in front of the great demolitions and temporary hoardings: the old houses, few, very few, that survive, the good old brick fronts, the spoiled

---

1. The two-and-a-half-year hiatus, except for the single entry for 31 August 1906, suggests missing notebooks; it is likely, however, that there was little notebook keeping while HJ prepared the New York edition, *The American Scene*, two series of articles for *Harper's Bazar*—"The Speech of American Women" (November 1906–February 1907) and "The Manners of American Women" (April–July 1907)—and his contribution to the composite novel *The Whole Family* (1908) (his chapter, "The Married Son," appeared in the *Bazar*, June 1908). See HJ's reference to the "sacred years" in his entry for 10 February 1909.

windows; the 2 or 3 with good 18th century doors and door-tops behind the back of the hideous new Admiralty extension. One of these, this late summer afternoon, with such a pretty misty London light, is open into dusty chambers or offices: and a cat lies sleeping in the sun, vague dim pretty sunshine, while the large red glazed door-top—like this[2] but higher—makes little old-world effect as of a homelier time. What has just struck me, *à propos* of the long new Mall is the extraordinary typical charm today of the London August light. The far away blue haze on the *low* palace front (where the monument is not yet) almost as of some 'blue distance,' some hill-horizon, in the country. The *silvery,* watery, misty light—or say misty, water, silvery—*that* order. And my *liking* this time the pleasant high *cossus* (English-opulent) backs of Carlton Terrace. The note of association here—the amusement to me, as I find—and now I catch *on* to it—of the feeling *for,* about, what is being (even so poorly) attempted for the greater greatness of poor dear old London; the kind of affectionate sense of property, the sentimental *stake* in it. Came back to this vista, to the Horseguards, to St. James's Park. Looking at the backs of Carlton Terrace—near the Russell Sturgis's old house[3]—I find I don't know what little 'handsomeness,' little London domestic or 'social' charm, in the way each second floor window, between the Corinthian pillars of its Colonnade, has its own solid little under-bracketed, stuccoed balcony. But the deplorable Boer monument, opposite, in the little garden under the new Admiralty, and the at present so *bête* and common curve of the—bulge of the—face of the Grand Hotel (round into Whitehall). *Passages* in London, however, make vistas, and just at this hour I catch a little specimen of it and of the way that they make a little charm and a little picture. There is an opening at the end of the terrace through into Trafalgar Square at the end of (the shortness of) which just a bit of the Nat[ional] Gall[ery], the ugly cupola itself, sits up and *speaks* to one. Speaks to one, that is, if one have the old London sense, the feeling and the fondness. How *all* one's appreciations here need that: nothing so fine, beautiful or artistic, as to work for much without it. The way the 'mean' little Roman warrior's statue of Jacobus Secundus—iron, lead?—that used to stand behind the Banqueting Hall in Whitehall, has been placed just before the part of the Admiralty Extension that looks on the small garden like some unwelcome household ornament put away at last—though originally expensive, most expensive—in a bad back room. The whole thing, here, the Horseguards back, and the house—old grey-black house, off to the right—identifying—with its HIGH second story and rococo pediment—never so 'precious' for old-times.

August 23d. Good and 'pretty' this noon the *mouth* of Walbrook, beside the Mansion House, with the narrow slightly *grouillant* dusky vista formed by the same with the second-hand book shop let into the base of St. Stephen's (*plaqué* over with a dirty little stucco front) and the rather bad spire above—very bad, rough masonry and *mean* pinnacle. Interior (all alone here this cool summer noon) very much better than poor smothered outside (smothered in passages and by the high

2. HJ sketched a fanlight.
3. At 17 Carlton House Terrace, S. W.

rear of the Mansion House) gives a hint of—very fine *quadrillé*-panelled with old grey plaster rosettes and garlands—Dome—quite far and high, and today, with the florid old oak pulpit and canopy, the high old sallow sacred picture opposite, the 18th century memorial slabs, the place is quite the *retreat*, with the vague city hum outside, as they all get it, of the ghostly sense, the disembodied presences of the old London. There is an old grey print of the interior of the uniform—horizontally uniform—upper windows (not *clerestory* which are higher) before the hideous modern glass; dedicated to C.W., Esq. (Wren's son), as a view of one 'of the noble proofs of his father's superior genius.'[1]

Out of the space beyond the Mansion House, where the (dishonoured) ch. of St. Swithin's (??) stands, opens St. Swithin's[2] x x x x x St. Swithin's, no, is in Cannon St. with London Stone let into it, and the Lane is parallel to Walbrook and runs from the E. side of the Mansion H., as Walbrook from the W., down to Cannon St. Station. Very pretty *enfoncement* of court and front of Salters' Hall in St. Swithin's Lane, on right—which I must visit early in autumn.

x   x   x   x   x

The Tower so *pretty* today from the River, with one's back turned (on the steamboat) to the terrible Tower Bridge. (Yet right and *fine* symbol of our time), the whole low clustered mass so interesting, with its *ruddy* tinges of colour, a sort of suffused human complexion given by the long centuries. The *terrace* open to the public now—so long closed after an 'outrage,' and with many people, the whole thing was (just now, I write this on the boat) pleasant, I mean almost incongruously charming. But the *Pool* of London, all around me now as I write—the little tugs and tenders drawing the flat-bottomed barges—the little steamboats with their noses up as if their shrill whistle came through them, and the churn of the greasy brown flood kicked up by their travel. This whole steamboat thing to be done again—much better than when I did it last. The vast black fuliginous south bank impossible to deal with—but fortunately I am limited by Southwark. Only I don't quite *see* my Southwark—as yet. *Ça viendra.* I am stopping on the boat this amusing afternoon—just to *do* the River to Greenwich now that *j'y suis* (Aug. 23d—saw Bill off to Quebec this a.m.).[3] My only day—at this season—for months to come. Moreover, fortunately, I haven't to deal with it.

x   x   x   x   x

The barges, drawn up—I mean *especially* those drawn up—on the *Verge*, and the hollow flat-boats; such pretty things to *draw*. I have been as far as Greenwich—the grey—silver grey—hospital looking quite superb and archaic and *interesting*, but have caught a boat back, and now, 3:30, am on the return—so as to face toward London, which is the right way. The *blunt* barges—blunt, say: 'blunt' is good. The North shore awfully picturesque—a great *fouillis* of black and brown and russet odds and ends between Limehouse pier—in fact just above it. x x x x x

---

1. Here a page has been cut out of the notebook.
2. "Dishonoured" perhaps because modernized.
3. William James, Jr. (1882–1962), second son of WJ, was studying painting in Paris.

Have tried (4 p.m.) to get into St. Magnus the Martyr, close under London Bridge, and just south of the *Fire* column—but it's closed. The face of the grey stone columnar building at N.W. side of London Bridge—Fishmongers' Hall wharf— rather fine—but the Thames St. squalor here of the worst (base of Fish St. Hill).

August 24th. Have turned this a.m. into St. Clement Danes, the 2d church facing W. at end of Strand and opposite Arundel St. The interior, where I sit writing this, very elegant and charming with its light galleries vaulted—so[1]—on Corinthian capitals of the pillars; its (caved?)[2] 'barrel-roofed' ceiling and elaborate *stucchi,* fruited garlands and cherubs' heads. Also its very long high deep set windows springing continuously from just above pavement to roof and passing behind gallery. But the thing all very much over done up, with stars (gilt) and[3] etc., now. x x x x x

I have come out of it into the big newish public green or garden beside the W. side of the Law-Courts—where you see the rich architecture and whence the tower and spire of St. Clement's in profile are pleasing. But newness—large dull legal newness builds in this little expanse, spaciously, all round. There are highish steps at the end, to which I've climbed, and it's all very enlightened and commodious (reverse order) and the grey stone of the Law-Courts is in a good stage of that dusky-silvering which is the best that London buildings can look for in the so operative, so tormenting (no, find the right kindly, affectionate word) air—which so deals with things (as a [fussy] family tone [no, not fussy]) deals with its members. The steps terminate in big stone and iron screen or *grille* opening into other grave clear Law precincts, into *Serle St.,* with its dear old square windowed, square paned 18th century backs (of old chambers) all dingy red brick—more delectable than the new red (Butterfieldian) priggish (self-conscious—*why* self-conscious?) architecture of New Court all perpendicular round-about, but this a.m. rather charming with vivid green and geraniums at the centre. I have walked on to Lincoln's Inn Fields and am writing this in the large central garden or square, where, this moist summer, the lawns, the turf, are extraordinary and where some of the trees are more magnificent (are they the ash?) than I knew. But Lincoln's Inn Fields and the Soane Museum are a bit by themselves—they will give me something, the right little page, when I want it. x x x x x

I missed a little way back a little *joli motif* on the south side of St. Clement Danes, the note of the New London in the circular, the shallow-curved street where the big statued insurance building (or whatever) is replacing the little old sordidries that were yet the old world where that pleasant bookshop (Buxton Forman's), publisher, some time vanished, used to be. The suggestions of the—in the—change to a London bristling with statued fronts. x x x x x

1. HJ sketched the vault.
2. The manuscript has "(caved?)."
3. An indecipherable word is omitted here.

New Square, Lincoln's Inn, still delightful; *do* New Square. x x x x x

Funny little smothered red brick St. Mary Abchurch—with its crooked yard, one of the myriad 'short cuts' of the City, just out of Cannon St. E. of St. Swithin's. Look it up. (St. M.A. and St. Lawrence Pountney.) I never (before this time) discovered St. Augustine and St. Faith just under the back of St. Paul's, and the queer interview of narrow streets, lanes, Watling St., Old Change, Friday St., Bread St. x x x x x

St. Margaret Pattens is the church in Eastcheap, the way from London Bridge to the Tower—the featureless old brown church standing back on the left, with the fire escape in front of it, etc. x x x x x

Here I come suddenly, this same charming day (Aug. 24th) on delightfully placed old St. Dunstan's in the East (the mate of which, St. D. in West, Fleet St., I tried to get into, under the image of Queen Elizabeth, an hour ago). I never chanced upon this one before—just out of Eastcheap, on the way to the Tower, and beyond (south) the little St. Margaret Pattens. High 'fine' Gothic tower and spire, and built as it is on the steep hill down to the river the little old disused and voided churchyard is raised on deep southward substructions under the south wall of the church and employed as a small sitting-place for the specimens of the grimy public—*such* infinitely miserable specimens—who are dozing and gnawing bones (2 tramps under the south wall together doing *that*) in it now. The noise of drays from riverward, the clang of wheels, etc., harsh in the enclosed, built-in space; but the tall (3 or 4) thin trees (a lime and a locust?) make a green shade—and the clock in the tower, or at least the bell, gives out an immense deep note (2 o'ck.). Come back of course—get in. All these city churches have their *hours* on notices at doors. Make record of these.

October 8th, 1903[1907]. The site of Garroways's Coffee House in Change Alley (rebuilt 1874). The place (C.A.) with its old opening from the traffic (of Lombard St.) looks as if it were going to be 'something' but is only a mere modernized desolation which even its crookedness doesn't save—all big office windows and white-tiled walls for the diffusion of light.

October 8th, 1907. St. Edmund, King and Martyr, and St. Nicholas Acon, little grey old squat-towered church in Lombard St., opposite Clement's Lane and just further than Change Alley. x x x x x

Often passed St. Michael's, Cornhill, without taking it in—I mean the 'importance' of its big square grey Gothic tower. *See* it and make small scrap, if possible, of the effect of tower—good way it rises over interposing lower objects as seen from George Yard (out of Lombard St.) beyond it—poor 'gone' G.Y., leading into Michael's Lane. The little quad or court in the flank of the court, out of Lane, an almost 'gone' thing too. The 2 renewed or scraped marble memorial slabs in side wall of church do—verily—nothing. The little intricacies of tortuous business—lanes and courts and nooks are characteristic—Simpson's tavern and chop-rooms—are a note; but the big grey Cornhill Tower as seen from corner by Bumpus's small, almost hidden, book shop, is the only strong bit. 'Bengal Court (modern)—late White Lion court?' Value of *names* even when all the rest is gone. How one likes *both. Allhallows Church* in Lombard St. open 10–4. Close to Gracechurch St. x x x x x

Look at St. Mary at Hill, out of Love Lane (Eastcheap)—poor little dingy temple—and the idea of the poor little dingy place *being* Love Lane at all! Go round to *Back*—opposite St. Margaret Pattens. The funny long passage—internal corridor all indoors, bearing name 9 Mincing Lane—and going to M.L. from Eastcheap. *The feeling of old London,* through, and in spite of, everything, in the City at night—try and make some good morsel—some passage about it—at night and in the dusk of this October day (6 o'ck.).

September 21st, 1909. Just back from Overstrand[1]—beautiful September day. Turned in to St. Bride's Fleet St.—great ample handsome empty 'Palladian' church, mercilessly modernized, brightened, decorated, painted and gilded—but so still in the roaring City—with the *rumeur* outside all softened and faint—so respectable, so bourgeois—such a denial of any cognizance of passions, remorses, compassions, appeals—anything but mildest contritions and most decorous prostrations. But big and square and clear and reverend—in all its simplicity and with no altar to speak—neither book nor bell nor cross nor candle. It is one of Wren's churches and the little baptismal font was saved from the Fire. Immense and massive tower to great height, with superpositions of stages in spire atop—*diminuendo*—like a tower of cards.

Same day. St. Martin Ludgate—on L. Hill at left, just before or below St. Paul's—small dim dark wainscoted church sideways to street and evidently of poor squeezed site—more of the sound of the city—but with 2 or 3 youngish very middle class men in prolonged and absorbed prayer, as at St. Bride's—and here one young girl, in great prostration. Much more favorable than St. B.'s. Poor charmless architectural effort—or accommodation.

Same afternoon again. Wandered up into St. Paul's—which was very full of trippers—but fine and dim and worthy—something to be done with it; and then off Ludgate hill (westward) past the Old Bailey (the new substitute for old Newgate) to St. Bartholomew's hospital. Into the wide grey court where patients were laid out on beds to take the air and talked with such a nice young fellow with charming face (26) laid up with hip disease.

---

1. On 17 September 1909 HJ spent a long weekend at Meadow Cottage, Overstrand, near Comber, with Frederick Macmillan (1851–1936), long his publisher. During this visit conversation may have taken place about "London Town" and the contract HJ had arranged for W. Morton Fullerton to do an analogous work on Paris. For details of the latter, involving Edith Wharton, see *Life* 661.

In the Crypt of St. Paul's, October 1st, 1909, a.m.

—The homely lowly slab-tomb of C. Wren,[1] the builder of this Cath. Church of St. Paul (*ob.* 1723); also the pretty little florid rococo slab (mural) indicating the resting place of his wife. All about here the pavement-slabs of the painters— Turner, Millais, Leighton, Opic, Fuseli, our Pennsylvanian B. West, P.R.A.; Reynolds, Fuseli, Landseer, and others; and in the wall a rather handsome mural monument to Frk. Hall (*ob.* 1888). Also very charming one to Randolph Caldecott of a child holding a medallion: touching memorials, both of them, in the place, to *young* infelicities. Make something of the spacious, vast *cheerful* effect of this crypt—*admirable* Valhalla in its way—with the great temple above it and the London sounds of only the ghostliest faintness.—The War Correspondents, a mural brass, collective; and then W. H. Russell and Archibald Forbes, identical mural monuments. There is also a 'dog' mural monument to Landseer—all right for the dog—mourning by a coffin (relief). The *tombs* of Wellington and of Nelson are great guarded sarcophagi and funereal urns isolated (guarded) in the dim centre of the great Crypt and looming through the deeper shade impressively enough. Say how the vastness of the Crypt gives the measure of the *area* of the Cathedral more than the Cath. itself. And note the memorial slabs to W. Besant, Charles Reade, Barham, George Smith, George Cruikshank, and the fine Rodin bronze bust to W. E. Henley.[2] The mural things *memorial* (as of Hall, Caldecott, etc.); the pavement slabs only sepulchral.

The Library most interesting and charming in high aloofness in the upper vastness of the church—such space in these vast upper areas; and almost *elegant*—VERY with G. Gibbons's[3] carvings—with the London uproar rising more audibly, and

1. Sir Christopher Wren (1632–1723), British architect.
2. HJ lists a series of memorials clustered in one small area of the crypt of St. Paul's. Joseph M. W. Turner (1775–1851), British painter and precursor of the Impressionists; Sir John Everett Millais (1829– 96), British painter; Frederic Lord Leighton (1830–96), British neoclassical painter. (HJ had described Leighton's funeral in *Harper's Magazine* February 1896.) John Opie (1761–1807), self-taught portraitist and historical painter, professor of painting, sculpture, and architecture to the Royal Academy; Henry Fuseli (1741–1825), Zurich-born painter and author, professor of painting to the Royal Academy; Benjamin West (1738–1820), American painter in England and once President of the Royal Academy; Sir Joshua Reynolds (1732–92), British portrait painter; Sir Edwin Henry Landseer (1802– 73), famous British painter of animals; Frank Hall (d. 1888), portraitist; Randolph Caldecott (1846– 86), British illustrator; Sir Walter Besant (1836–1901), British novelist and critic whose essay "Fiction as One of the Fine Arts" (April 1883) prompted HJ's critical response "The Art of Fiction" (see *LA* II, 44–65); Charles Reade (1814–84), British novelist; Richard Harris Barham (1788–1845), a minor canon of St. Paul's, author of the "Ingoldsby Legends"; George M. Smith (1824–1901), publisher and founder of the *Dictionary of National Biography;* George Cruikshank (1792–1878), British caricaturist; Auguste Rodin (1840–1917), French sculptor; and William Ernest Henley (1849–1903), British poet, critic, and editor. In July 1907 (fourth anniversary of Henley's death), a replica of the bust done in 1886 to express Rodin's gratitude for Henley's articles in the *Magazine of Art* praising Rodin's work was placed in the crypt of St. Paul's. HJ had written about some of these artists: "Ruskin's Collection of Drawings by Turner" (*Nation* April 1878); "Lord Leighton and F. M. Brown" (*Harper's Weekly* February 1897); "London [Millais and Leighton]" (June 1897).
3. Grinling Gibbons (1648–1721), sculptor and famous English wood-carver, also did stone ornamentation at Blenheim, Hampton Court, and St. Paul's.

yet fitful and *estompé,* than as it comes, or *doesn't* come, to the Crypt. Come up if only to see the great copy of Luther's Bible, and to read in the Book of Donations for the rebuilding after the Fire, Charles II's autograph in the pale amber coloured ink: 'I will give one thousand pounds a yeare' and James's: 'I will give two hundred pounds a year to begin from mid-summer.'

Same day. Paul's Alley boring so narrowly into Paternoster Row, and so across into Ivy Lane so queerly named.

The insincere recesses and niches, of Wren's, in the high outer and so beautiful sides of cathedral (*so* in the grand manner as the traveller of old used to see them from top of bus).

2 p.m. In the old churchyard of St. Giles to look at the bastion of the old City Wall—'restored' alas, after fire in 1897, but massive and quaint. The large churchyard, with separated (business) passage through it, in itself interesting: with strong and sturdy aspect of tower from it; with so fresh green of turf and plants that have replaced all the burial-stones, after this wet summer. No city churchyard has held its own better, more amply; with hideous workhouses and offices pressing hard, it seems still to bid them stand off—keep their distance civilly, and respect a little the precious history of things.[4]

4. This entry concludes the notebook (Houghton Journal VIII).

II
The Pocket Diaries
1909-1915

Henry James's seven extant pocket diaries offer details of his last years, reminders of appointments, fleeting notes, perceptions, ideas. Earlier diaries probably were destroyed as soon as they became obsolete. These survived because they contained consultable material, including income-tax data and addresses. They might be considered as having minor interest; but within them we find a vivid cumulative picture of an artist's aging as well as the records of aches, pains, depressions, from gout to shingles, from angina to general despair—those anxieties and illnesses James's friend Turgenev described as "the calling cards of death."

In effect James made of them auxiliary notebooks. They fulfilled the needs of an elderly writer accustomed to putting his life into words and seeking to capture the fleeting moments of his diminished existence. They served perhaps a deeper and more psychological purpose: they were a repository of a lonely celibate's despair which would have found articulation in daily life had he had someone to whom to communicate the loneliness that came to him in Lamb House, or in the limited walks afforded him by Rye during long seasons of bad weather. Setting down personal grief was one way of relieving himself, of siphoning off pent-up frustrations. In his younger years he had cultivated stoicism: age became a test of his fortitude.

The pocket diaries represent the ultimate form of HJ's note-taking habits: we have seen how he began with his composition books and the "working out" of his stories. These become widely spaced in the late Edwardian time. Now he dictates notes to his novels (those he will never complete) but when he is at large in London, without his typist, he allows his old pen-in-hand to take over, squeezing these brief entries and comments into available space. They become mini-notebooks as we read on, and the section from mid-August 1910 to a year later could legitimately be considered an "American Journal III" if added to those given in this book. But we keep it in its pocket diary context. At the same time, in his more cryptic entries, we observe his hunger for society and for talk as well as his generosity and his quest for dining companions. When he jots down (for example) the name *Findlaters* (see p. 295) and an address and tea-hour, we can, with little research, illuminate an interesting friendship of his later years with two Scottish maiden ladies who wrote popular novels. Or see him in his regular visits to Jessie Allen or Lucy Clifford, or his meetings with the younger men, Jocelyn Persse and Hugh Walpole—the first-named a gallant man-about-town who brings HJ the London gossip, and the other an on-the-make young writer of whom HJ is extremely fond. Later there come significant entries about Edith Wharton and hints of her affair with HJ's friend Morton Fullerton. HJ lives through the romance vicariously, like his Lambert Strether in *The Ambassadors.*

We have annotated the pocket diaries selectively. Appointment books often record the casual stranger as well as the enduring friend, and it is impossible for an outsider to know the exact meaning of what seem like peripheral encounters. Some of the unglossed names have to do with HJ's committee work during the war. Sometimes we encounter names not hitherto met in his annals, for example the lunch recorded in 1914 with H. Melville—decidedly no relation to the great Herman. Harry Melville or Melvill was a social gadfly, or as some said a "relentless raconteur," well-known in London since Oscar Wilde's day as "Mr. Chatterbox." He was later satirized by Osbert Sitwell in a short story and by Michael Arlen in *The Green Hat.* It is equally startling to discover that HJ, at the time he was denouncing President Wilson for not bringing America into the war, dined one evening with the celebrated Col. E. M. House, Wilson's "alter ego."

An entire Edwardian and post-Edwardian social and literary history could be derived from these brief and hasty jottings. William James wrote of Henry to his parents (13 July 1880) during a quick visit to London: "The way he worked at paying visits and going to dinners and parties was surprising to me, especially as he was all the time cursing them for so frustrating his work." The pocket diaries testify that HJ went on "working" at his social and literary life almost to the end.

There is one pocket diary for each year of 1909 to 1915. The first three are stamped "Lett's Diary" and measure $4\frac{1}{2}''$ x $7''$. The pocket diary for 1909 has blue covers; 1910 and 1911, wine; and the pages of all three have marbled edges. The 1912 diary is stamped "T. J. Smith's One Day Diary" and measures $4\frac{1}{2}''$ x $5\frac{1}{2}''$; it has a wine cover and marble-edged pages. The final three are stamped "Walker's Society Diary" and measure

$4\frac{1}{2}'' \times 5\frac{1}{2}''$. They have green marbled endpapers and pages with marbled edges; the years 1913 and 1915 have wine covers, 1914 greyish green covers. All seven have space for cash accounts (see Appendices), addresses, and memoranda. Following 31 December, each diary allows space for several entries for the new year.

1909

It might be well to describe in brief HJ's Rye circle. By the summer of 1909, after a decade in the "Antient" Town of Rye, HJ was distinctly one of its citizens. He mockingly characterized himself as a country squire in the eyes of his neighbors. (See *Life* 499ff.) The main actors in HJ's drama still come from outside—his brother WJ and sister-in-law Alice, Edith Wharton, Howard Sturgis, as well as Walpole and Persse—but the novelist has cultivated a number of "locals."

The principal supporting roles at Lamb House were those of two of the staff. They arrived on the scene when HJ took the house in 1898. The athletic Burgess Noakes (1884–1975) from nearby Peasmarsh came in as a houseboy and in time was the indispensable valet; a bantamweight boxer, he accompanied HJ on various journeys and cared for him until the end—except for a brief interval of service in World War I. The other was George Gammon, HJ's original and only gardener who won many prizes at local flower shows. Mrs. Paddington, "a pearl of price," was housekeeper until 1912, when she was replaced by Joan Anderson. HJ's last amanuensis, hired in October 1907, was a literary young Englishwoman, Theodora Bosanquet, who had learned to type expressly to work with HJ. She kept remarkable diaries describing the novelist "at work." He treated her and her companion, Ellen "Nelly" Bradley, like a solicitous uncle.

After the morning stint of dictation, usually in the Garden Room, HJ was free to walk about the town: to see the historian of Rye, Leopold Vidler, who lived in the oldest house in town (Friars of the Sack), just around the corner in Church Square; or to visit the John Symonds Vidler family at Mountsfield. As his habit of therapeutic walking and cycling was confirmed, HJ extended his circle well beyond the perimeter of the once-walled town to embrace not only neighboring Playden, Peasmarsh, and Winchelsea, but Wittersham, Ashford, Hastings, and beyond.

Part-time Ryers, like himself, were the Protheros of Dial Cottage in the High Street (its sundial is still there): George Walter Prothero (1848–1922), Cambridge

historian, editor of the *Quarterly Review,* president of the Royal Society of Lit-
erature, and his vivacious wife, Fanny, were intimates of Lamb House as well as
London friends of HJ's (they had a house in Bedford Square). Similarly, the Jacomb-
Hoods had a summer residence just a step away from Lamb House, as well as a
London house in Tite Street. George Percy Jacomb-Hood M. V. O. (1857–1929)
was an artist and correspondent for the *Graphic.*

Walking about Rye, HJ would encounter Walter Dawes, Town Clerk of Rye
from 1882 and a solicitor to the Cinque Ports from 1909. Or he might lunch with
Mr. Grifred Henry James Tayleur, bachelor of independent means and of benevolent pursuits who later acquired HJ's studio in Watchbell Street and donated it
to the town for a boys' club. HJ might visit (as he would also in London) with
Mrs. Kate Perugini (b. 1839), second daughter of Charles Dickens, widow of
another Charles (Collins), and wife of yet another. He would press her for details
about her famous father, whom he had met in Cambridge in his youth.

HJ would walk to Rye Golf Course on the Channel coast and there encounter
the perennial Secretary of the Club (1898–1925), Capt. Dacre Vincent and his
wife, Margaret—an accomplished pianist, leader of the town's musical life, and
later model for E. F. Benson's fictional heroine Lucia. Walks in the other direction would take HJ across the railway line and strenuously up Rye hill to Playden
and the hillside home of architect Sir Reginal Blomfield (1856–1942) at Point
Hill, in whose house, rented during the summer of 1896, HJ wrote *The Spoils of
Poynton.* A bit further would lead HJ up the flight of stone steps to the home of
gardener, author, and dabbler in psychic phenomena Alice Dew-Smith at her well-
named cottage "The Steps." Here he would also see Lady Pollock, wife of Sir
Frederick (1845–1937), formerly Corpus Professor of Jurisprudence at Oxford,
and mother of Jack Pollock and his sister Alice. HJ was often accompanied in his
walks by Alice Pollock's husband, Sydney Waterlow (1878–1944), a Cambridge
contemporary of Leonard Woolf and other Bloomsbury figures and later ambassador to Greece. At Leasam HJ might dine with the M. P. for East Sussex, Col.
Arthur Montague Brookfield (1853–1940), son of Thackeray's intimate friend Mrs.
Janet Octavia Brookfield, and his American wife, formerly Olive Hamilton (of
Buffalo, New York); or with the Warrenders, friends of Edward VII—perhaps the
most aristocratic of the Rye circle. Maud Warrender, daughter of the Earl of
Shaftesbury and wife of Admiral Sir George Warrender, was not only a beauty
but also possessed of a fine contralto voice. When Sir George was at sea he would
listen to records of Lady Maud for consolation.

In Winchelsea, the other Antient Town of the Cinque Ports, lived Ford Madox
Hueffer—later Ford (1873–1939)—imitator of HJ and sometime collaborator with
Joseph Conrad, another admirer of HJ, who lived near Ashford, as did the Poet
Laureate Alfred Austin—whom HJ and Edith Wharton would visit.

Eight miles from Rye Brede Place was the home of the eccentric Moreton Frewen
(1853–1924), economist and adventurer, and his wife, Clara, née Jerome and
sister of Jennie Churchill (mother of Winston) and Leonie Leslie (wife of Shane).
HJ became "Uncle" to their talented daughter Clare (1885–1970), the sculptress,
who lost her young husband, Capt. Wilfred Sheridan (descendant of the Irish
playwright), in the Battle of Loos, September 1915 (see *Letters* IV, 779–80).

Further afield, another concentric circle included Wittersham, home of the music critic Francis Ford and his wife, who often took HJ motoring and entertained him and nephew Aleck at their home on occasion. In 1908 the Old Rectory House became the home of the Hon. Alfred Lyttelton (1857–1913), once Colonial Secretary, and his second wife, Edith, daughter of Archibald Balfour. There HJ often dined; he would remain a faithful friend to Mrs. Lyttelton in her widowhood. Moon Green, a converted oast house, was the country home of Violet Rosa Markham (1875–1959), a dedicated social reformer interested in the British dominions, especially Canada. She brought to tea at Fanny Prothero's Dial Cottage a young Canadian "statesman" (HJ reports), "one *King*"—William Lyon Mackenzie King (1874–1950), who was to be Canada's longest serving Prime Minister. In 1915 she married Lt.-Col. James Carruthers. (See her autobiographical *Return Passage* [1953] and *Friendship's Harvest* [1956].)

Villa Julia, 1 High Wickham Terrace, perched on the heights of Hastings, was the home of Miss Matilda Betham-Edwards (1837–1919), popular English novelist (and part French—of "de Bethams" ancestry) whose most successful book was *The Lord of the Harvest* (1889). There HJ would climb breathlessly (the cabbies would refuse to drive him to the summit) to chat with her about their friends Rhoda Broughton and Mary Elizabeth Braddon. And so to the rim of the last concentric circle, which enclosed Allington Castle in Maidstone, Kent, and to which HJ was driven one bracing day (among others) in January 1912 by Lady Conway. The castle had belonged to the family of Sir Thomas Wyatt, the sonneteer, and in 1905 her husband, Sir Martin, had bought it and begun its restoration.

Back at the center of Rye was Dr. Ernest Skinner, general practitioner, HJ's physician who became increasingly in focus as HJ's Lamb House years drew to a close.

February 1909

The first entries in the extant pocket diaries place us, in their condensed way, squarely in HJ's busy London and suburban life among his particular circle of friends already documented here and in Leon Edel's biographies of the Master. The three terse entries "Terry's"—where HJ goes apparently with great punctuality at 11 a.m. on February 15 to 17—denote a small London theater used only for rehearsals of HJ's light comedy *The High Bid,* produced on 18 February at His Majesty's, which could accommodate the play's large set. Johnston Forbes-Robertson (1853–1937) had tempted HJ back into the theater after his setbacks of the 1890s: he was a finished actor, with a voice and subtlety that could handle James's delicate dialogue; moreover he wanted the play because it would give his wife, the American actress Gertrude Elliott (Maxine's sister), a major role. But he knew the play wouldn't have a long run. After its Edinburgh try-out he decided *The High Bid* was "far too delicate in fibre and literary elegance." There was another difficulty. Forbes-Robertson had acquired a second play destined to fill theaters for years, a veritable gold mine—Jerome K. Jerome's *The Passing of the*

Third Floor Back. In it, a character called "The Stranger" sorts out the lives of sundry persons in a shabby Bloomsbury lodging house. He possesses a distinct divinity, and audiences visioned him as Christ-like. HJ acknowledged he could hardly compete with a "so much more alluring" play about Christ. But Forbes-Robertson had been attracted to HJ's play because it for once gave his wife a better part than himself. He met his commitment by staging HJ's play for five matinées at His Majesty's Theatre, where it had a *succès d'estime,* especially with such critics as Max Beerbohm, who in one of his most sensitive reviews spoke of HJ's "inalienable magic." And he concluded, "Little though Mr. James can on the stage give us of his great art, even that little has a quality which no other man can give us." Other significant critics concurred.

Apparently, remembering how he had been booed at *Guy Domville* a decade or more earlier, HJ wasn't around when the curtain fell. His datebook tells us "play produced 2.30 (went to tea with L. Clifford afterwards.)" Lucy Clifford was the widow of a great mathematician who had died young. HJ greatly admired her pluck in writing novels and plays and acquiring a popular literary reputation, thus finding the means to take care of her children in her widowhood.

These early entries show a whirl of activity. HJ sees his agent James B. Pinker (15 Feb.) and calls, as he usually does, at 9 p.m. on his aristocratic friend Jessie Allen. It was once thought she would be lady-in-waiting to the queen, but failing this her life had been a progress through the great houses of Britain. She showered Venetian tapers and bearskin rugs on HJ and he named her "Goody Allen," as his inscribed books and letters to her testify. We note he dines with J.P.—Dudley Jocelyn Persse—a nephew of Lady Gregory's who had a shock of golden hair— or as HJ phrased it "his constitutional *aura* of fine gold and rose-colour." Jocelyn was a debonair man of thirty who enjoyed society; Irish and good-looking, good-natured, wholly unliterary, he became an object of uncritical admiration and they had a devoted friendship. HJ remembered him in his will (along with Lucy Clifford and Hugh Walpole).

We note also that HJ motors to Hill Hall, near Epping Forest, with Mrs. Charles Hunter, its chatelaine. Called by some "the Lion Hunter," Mrs. Hunter was a sister of the militant suffragette and composer Dame Ethel Smyth, later an intimate of Virginia Woolf. On February 20 to 22 HJ weekends with the Manton Marbles at Brighton: an old New York friend and bi-metallist, Marble once was editor of the *World.* They communicate in brisk telegrams. On this occasion the novelist imposes himself as "the greatest criminal on earth," but also "greatest penitent," and receives a return wire, "You Beauty Boy, come to your only Twins." Edith Wharton used to say HJ liked weekending with the Marbles because, in addition to enjoying the animation of Brighton, he greatly liked the Marbles' bathroom—which she described as one of the best-appointed in England.

HJ is at his dentist's, February 22, and cardiac specialist Sir James Mackenzie's, 25 February—little aware that he will figure for posterity in Mackenzie's brilliant casebook as Case 97—in which Mackenzie describes how to treat a nervous novelist who believes he has a bad heart condition. Actually it was HJ's brother who had serious cardiac symptoms. After seeing the doctor, HJ gives dinner at the Reform Club to Hugh Walpole: their first meeting. This is the begin-

At work in the garden room of Lamb House, from a snapshot by his nephew Edward Holton James, probably 1906.

1880s, from a portrait by Anna Lea Merritt.

1912 camera portrait by E. O. Hoppé.

James and bicycle, a family snapshot, probably 1903.

By kitchen garden of Lamb
House with pet, circa 1900

Pencilled detached notes
for *The Ivory Tower*, 1910: "I
come back, I come back, as I say,
I all throbbingly and yearningly
and passionately, oh mon bon . . ."
(James's thanks to the "guardian
spirit," *mon bon,* of his writing
desk). *Courtesy of Houghton
Library, Harvard.*

entries in the notebook
...de: James's note (see p. 31)
...s up with an earlier note
...en the other way round for
*...Bostonians. Courtesy of
...ghton Library, Harvard.*

Entrance hall to Lamb House, from a photo by the late Alvin Langdon Coburn.

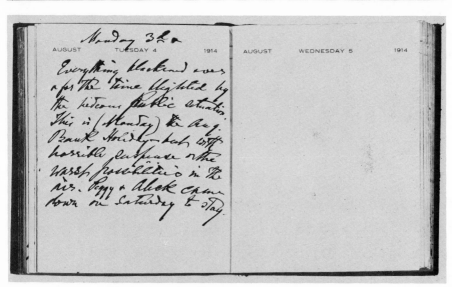

JULY   WEDNESDAY 29   1914   JULY   THURSDAY 30   1914

AUGUST   TUESDAY 4   1914   AUGUST   WEDNESDAY 5   1914

Entries in pocket diary on eve of the 1914 war.

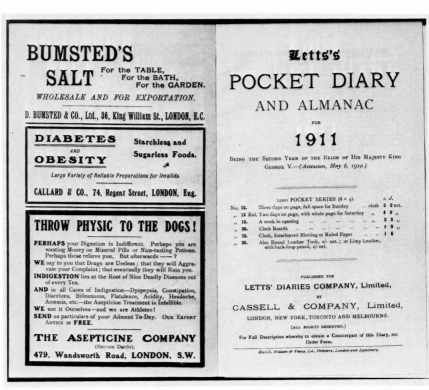

Title page and advertisements from one of James's pocket diaries. *Courtesy of Houghton Library, Harvard.*

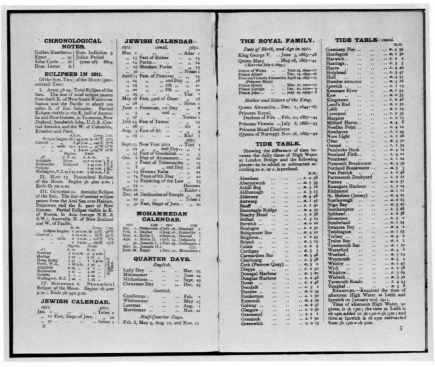

Miscellaneous tables from the 1911 pocket diary. *Courtesy of Houghton Library, Harvard.*

The garden room, Lamb House (destroyed by bombing during World War II). *Courtesy of Houghton Library, Harvard.*

Henry James with Prince Bariatinsky and his wife, the actress Princess Bariatinsky (Lydia Yavorska).

Key entry in notebook (p. 115) of 1895: *"the singular value for a narrative plan too* of the . . . *divine principle of the Scenario." Courtesy of Houghton Library, Harvard.*

ning of an affectionate friendship; the young man, in his early twenties, records in his diary, "by far the greatest man I have ever met." HJ was then in his late sixties. The day before he visits the widow of his old and beloved friend George Du Maurier who describes her son's success with a play, written under a pen name, about a future German invasion of England. The young Guy will lose his life early on the Western front in 1914.

And finally we have signs of HJ's domesticity. He frequents Jaegers, Rimmels, the Haymarket Stores. His surviving servants testified that he bought everything for Lamb House—and shopped with zest: handkerchiefs, gloves and uniforms for the maids, and supplies for his house and for the gardener. As can be seen, a great deal of personal and social history is buried in these early diary notes.

15 February 1909 Monday
    Terry's 11.
    Pinker 3.30
    Clifford 5.
    Allen, 9.

16 February 1909 Tuesday
    Terry's 11
    F. R.'s play

17 February 1909 Wednesday
    Terry's 11.
    J. P. dines, for Gaiety—7.

18 February 1909 Thursday
    Meet Aleck[1] train and lunch him.
    Play produced 2.30 (went to tea with L. Clifford afterwards.)
    Mrs. Hunter 9

19 February 1909 Friday
    C. Fletcher.[2] Prince's 5.

20 February 1909 Saturday
    Went to Brighton 4.30 (Manton Marble's.)

21 February 1909 Sunday
    Exquisite day—long walk on Brighton front with M. M. (B. at its best.)

22 February 1909 Monday
    Returned from Brighton. Walked to Sargent's Fulham Road.[3] Delightful call.
    Queen Alexandra came in with Lady Antrim. Stopped and saw Alice Maude,

1. WJ's youngest son; see 26 December 1908.
2. See 10 February 1909 and May 1909 headnote.
3. Sargent had a large studio in Fulham Road.

Pelham St. Fulham Road (her little shop)—and had tea with her. George Field, dentist 6.

24 February 1909 Wednesday
Motored (on Tuesday) with Mrs. Ch. Hunter out through whole East End (north) of London, Islington, Holloway etc. to Epping Forest and saw and lunched with her at their wonderful and beautiful Hill Hall which they've just acquired and are "doing up." Immense impression.

25 February 1909 Thursday
Called Mrs. Humphry Ward[4] 4 Saw Dr. J. Mackenzie, 17 Bentinck St. 5. Went Windsor (7) and dined with Howard Sturgis.

26 February 1909 Friday
Jager Shop and Haymarket stores (also Rimmels.)
Field 3.30 Theatre 4.15 or so
Sally Norton[5] 5

27 February 1909 Saturday
Called George Ashburner[6] (out.) Then on Mrs. Du Maurier and Lady Jeykll; both at home (the former very interesting about Guy's play.)

28 February 1909 Sunday
Hugh Walpole dines, 8.

March 1909

There are few entries for March. HJ is back at Lamb House and, his amanuensis Theodora Bosanquet records, "much pleased with the success of the play." Amid heavy snow and characteristic coastal gales, HJ continues to socialize. He calls on Lady Pollock, one of his oldest admirers, visiting at The Steps, a familiar cottage at Playden near Rye (2 March). He is back in London for his dentist appointment and another visit to Dr. Mackenzie, still believing he has a heart condition. On March 8th he presides at a lecture given by André Beaunier, French novelist and literary scholar, who talks about Chateaubriand and Madame Réca-mier. The *Times* carries an informative note about this on March 11. The reporter seems to catch HJ's style:

> . . . Mr. James intimated the sphere in which French literature delights, but where Anglo-Saxon literature, not possessing the precious secret, falls heavily. It is the sphere of complex relations between the sexes; of the subtler shades of passion; of the mysterious justice of sensibility in regard to give and take. He deplored the Anglo-Saxon's lack of appetite for the finer and deeper meaning of these things . . . The Frenchman, he said, does not confine his taste for exercise and sport to the physical world. The position of the person called "lady-friend" in Anglo-Saxon was ambiguous—she was

4. See 19 June 1884.
5. Eldest daughter of Charles Eliot Norton.
6. The Ashburners were neighbors of the Jameses in Cambridge, Massachusetts.

either in Byron's company "the unlady" or in Carlyle's "the lady"—but she was not herself.

On 9 March he meets and apparently has a charming chat with Mrs. Everard Cotes, née Sara Jeanette Duncan (1862–1927), a Canadian novelist, and writes her a remarkable letter on writers who "open the door to the Devil himself . . . the sense of beauty, of mystery, of relations, of appearances, of abysses." (See *Letters* IV, 131–32.) The lunch with Mrs. Alfred Sutro, wife of the dramatist (1863–1933) is a part of HJ's renewed activities in the theater. They will introduce him to Maurice Maeterlinck.

1 March 1909 Monday
Returned Rye: 4.25

3 March 1909 Wednesday
Went to see Lady Pollock at the Steps. Great snowstorm began at night and lasted all this day (Wednesday.) Biggest here for years

8 March 1909 Monday
Field 3.
A. Beaunier, 24 Park Lane. 5.15

9 March 1909 Tuesday
Field 3.
Mrs. Cotes, 69 Grosvenor St. 5.

10 March 1909 Wednesday
Dr. Mackenzie 11 a.m.
Mrs. Sutro—lunch 1. (31 Dover St.)
A. Beaunier, 5.15

11 March 1909 Thursday
Field 11.30.
Prothero[7] 1.15 (luncheon)

April 1909

HJ is still staying close to Rye but dashing to London to see his dentist. Aleck James, WJ's youngest, has been with him at Lamb House. For the weekend of 3 April Jack Pollock, son of HJ's old friend Sir Frederick, the professor of jurisprudence at Oxford, arrives for a visit. The younger Pollock is stage-struck (see his memoirs, *Time's Chariot* [1950]) and fits into the novelist's renewed theatrical mood. He is full of the presence in London of the Prince and Princess Bariatinsky: she is the former Lydia Yavorska and has been playing in Ibsen, but having dif-

7. George and Fanny Prothero; see headnote to Pocket Diaries.

ficulty with her English accent. After *A Doll's House* she appears in a version of Henry Becque's *La Parisienne* translated by Pollock, who later will be involved in the production by Gertrude Kingston of HJ's *The Saloon*.

During the next fortnight HJ is ill. Palpitations, depression, general upset, nothing the local doctor, Ernest Skinner, can pinpoint. In a letter HJ speaks of being "anxiously unwell" and having had "a sharp heart-crisis" although reassured by the specialist in London. But he still works and assembles his Italian travelogues in the handsome volume *Italian Hours* and keeps at his late stories for *The Finer Grain*. Hugh Walpole spends his first weekend at Lamb House (April 24) and his diary describes it as "wonderful. He is beyond words." Finally Harley Granville Barker, the gifted director, who found the key to staging Bernard Shaw's talky plays, comes to Lamb House to discuss the proposed season at the Duke of York's Theatre for which HJ is writing his play *The Outcry*.

1 April 1909 Thursday
Go to town with Aleck 4.16.

2 April 1909 Friday
George Field 12.15

3 April 1909 Saturday
Jack Pollock comes 6.30

5 April 1909 Monday
J. Pollock left.

19 April 1909 Monday
Skinner came 10.30

20 April 1909 Tuesday
Skinner came 10.30

22 April 1909 Thursday
Skinner came 10.30

24 April 1909 Saturday
Hugh Walpole comes 6.30

25 April 1909 Sunday
Jack Tennants come to tea 5.

29 April 1909 Thursday
Granville Barker comes 1.30

30 April 1909 Friday
Granville Barker left 1 p.m.

May 1909

Resuming his active life after his brief illness, HJ goes (May 7) to Eastbourne, where his old polio-crippled friend Jonathan Sturges, whom he nicknamed "the little demon," is confined to his room in a hotel and watched by a nurse. Sturges's morale has crumbled in spite of his brave show in the artistic and literary world of London and he is now an alcoholic. HJ speaks of these visits to his valued friend as "a stiff bit of discipline for me . . . my one feeling on the subject of that tragic and terrible little figure is a compassion that makes everything else irrelevant" (1 January 1910 to Gaillard T. Lapsley).

He escorts his Venetian friend, Constance Fletcher, to the Rye cottage called The Steps, where Alice Dew-Smith, the former Alice Lloyd, turns out such books as *The Diary of a Dreamer* and writes about "soul shapes." HJ's secretary, Theodora Bosanquet, describes her as a lady with a plaintive face and weird brown eyes, "an interesting woman." Constance Fletcher lives in Venice with her step-father, HJ's old artist friend of his Roman days, Eugene Benson, in a palazzino in the Rio Marin which is the setting for "The Aspern Papers." Logan Pearsall Smith will have a considerably polished anecdote about the obese Constance, who wrote *Kismet* and other novels under the name of "George Fleming," and once got stuck in HJ's bathtub during a Lamb House visit and had to be frantically rescued by his maids.

HJ's meeting with James M. Barrie (12 May) is related to the impending repertory season at the Duke of York's Theatre, for which Galsworthy, Granville Barker, Shaw, Barrie, and HJ are writing new plays. He and Barrie are also involved in testimony to the Joint Select Committee of the House of Lords and the House of Commons on "Stage Plays (Censorship)" at which Galsworthy reads a letter from HJ attacking the continued existence in England of play-censorship by the Lord Chamberlain. (See *Letters* IV, 532.)

The Findlaters are the two maiden ladies from Scotland who wrote popular novels, Mary (1865–1963) and Jane Helen (1866–1946). HJ met them in New York during his 1905 journey when they were touring. Mary remembered they called on Evelyn Smalley, daughter of the well-known journalist G. W. Smalley, and there found W. D. Howells "very common looking, stout and plain" with his pretty daughter Mildred. HJ walked in in mid-evening, kissed Evelyn Smalley twice, seemed "in a great hurry, passing his hand always over his eyes—all about California, *his* lecture to 900 Ladies of Culture, his princely entertainment in a Hotel where they refused to let him pay the bill." Mary Findlater also describes HJ as "a small rather stout, clean-shaven man, with a sensitive face." After this meeting in the New World, HJ remained a loyal and occasional tea-drinking friend. (See Eileen Mackenzie, *The Findlater Sisters* [1964].)

The "dear great" George Meredith dies on 18 May and we note that HJ, who has known him for many years with great affection, goes to the Westminster Abbey memorial service on 22 May. He dines with Walpole and goes to the "Follies" and then the next day dines with Hugh and Violet Hammersley in Hampstead. They are votaries of painting and friends of Wilson Steer. He continues to see young Walpole and Jocelyn Persse, but an attack of gout confines him to his room at the Reform Club. He pulls himself together and is able to go to Oxford and motor with Howard Sturgis to Ethel Sands's Manor House in the Oxfordshire village of Newington, where Miss Sands has been living since the turn of the century. A square seventeenth century greystone house, set behind a wide forecourt, it has a fine pair of gate posts with griffins mounted on them, a formal garden to the side and at the back a terrace which delights HJ, and formal lawns and meadows stretching away in the distance. Miss Sands was the daughter of a great American beauty admired by HJ during the Victorian years, Mrs. Mahlon Sands, who figured in the circle of the Prince of Wales (see *Letters* IV, 36). Ethel was an accomplished painter, and she moved in "Fitzrovia"—that is, Fitzroy Street, where her artist friends Walter Sickert, Wilson Steer, and the Bloomsbury painters had their studios. A cosmopolitan, widely read, sophisticated woman, she lived at Newington with her painter friend, also an American, Nan Hudson. She belonged in the James circle with ladies like the Parisian Henrietta Reubell, the earlier Lizzie Boott, and the later Edith Wharton—his Anglo-American world. (See Wendy Baron, *Miss Ethel Sands* [1977].) Newington acquired, before Lady Ottoline Morrell's Garsington, an honored name for gathering in the talented and creative Edwardians. There was considerable overlap among the celebrities who came to both these glamor-houses. Lady Ottoline described Newington as "that most lovely and melancholy house." HJ, who arrived later than expected, with his twinging foot enveloped in a gout-boot, talked incessantly, in spite of the twinges. "His words come," Lady Ottoline remembered, "like little hammers and hit every nail they aim at. He has a kind and penetrating spirit." As usual, Ottoline, in spite of her own eccentricities, showed close observation of her fellow mortals. The 1909 Whitsun party at Newington included the Morrells, that is Philip, Lady Ottoline's husband, a Liberal member of parliament, and Lionel Holland, a Conservative M.P. and art collector, a friend of Miss Hudson's; Schuyler Warren and an historian, Una Birch (later Pope-Hennessy); and Howard Sturgis.

HJ was fond of Ottoline. Her version of this party makes a comedy in particular of the lunch at Waddesdon on Whitmonday which she found "more oppressive even than an ordinary museum." She describes how HJ's "basilisk gaze" surveyed Alice de Rothschild's tall footmen, her hothouse flowers, and the heaped white strawberries, and quotes him as murmuring "murder and rapine would be preferable to this." According to Ottoline there was a failure to make the common conveniences accessible in the Victorian manor, "the place which is after all so necessary a provision of even a museum." When Howard Sturgis suggested asking a footman, HJ responded, "Howard dear, what I thought was an Elysian dream you have made into a physiological fact."

But HJ actually enjoyed himself more than Lady O. thought. We note his "wonderful day of beauty and revival of old memories." For he had visited Waddesdon when it was at its height and when his host was Ferdinand de Rothschild— on one occasion with Maupassant and the Napoleonic Count Primoli.

Of others mentioned in these notes, Robert C. Trevelyan (1872–1951) was a writer; Sir George Otto Trevelyan (1838–1928), the British historian; W. E. Norris (1847–1925), a hard-working minor novelist, all gentleness and rigidity, whom

James had visited long before at Torquay and to whom he wrote a New Year's letter faithfully every year; T. Bailey Saunders, a British journalist; and Charles Hagberg Wright (1862–1940), the librarian of the London Library.

6 May 1909 Thursday
9.30 Go to London to vote at Reform, at 5. But call on Pinker: 3.30

7 May 1909 Friday
Went from London to Eastbourne Thursday 6th—to see J.S.

8 May 1909 Saturday
Two days with J.S. etc. Robert Trevelyan there. Returned from Eastbourne to Lamb House 6.30 p.m.

9 May 1909 Sunday
Mrs. Irving at the Steps and at Mrs. Vincent's.[8]

10 May 1909 Monday
Met C[onstance] Fletcher at the Station and drove her to the Steps

11 May 1909 Tuesday
Went up and drove poor C. Fletcher down here to luncheon.
Drove her to Steps again at 5.30

12 May 1909 Wednesday
Go to London 9.30 Go to J.M. Barrie 5.

13 May 1909 Thursday
Findlaters': 39 Harrington Gardens S.W. *5*
Lucy Clifford—9.

14 May 1909 Friday
Lunch Trevelyans 1.30. Walked through park and Kensington Gardens with Sir George. Lovely day. Hugh Walpole dines 7.30 Kingsway Theatre 8.50

15 May 1909 Saturday
Lunch Mrs. Riggs—York Hotel, Albemarle St. *1*.
Go to Queen's Acre p.m.

16 May 1909 Sunday
Queen's Acre. The Bertram Falles [8a]

17 May 1909 Monday
Sally and Lily Norton—5.
C.F. Leyel University Club 3.
Meet C. Fletcher: Victoria 6.53

8. Margaret Dacre Vincent; see headnote to Pocket Diaries.
8a. Howard Sturgis's sister, May, and her husband.

19 May 1909 Wednesday
Lady Pollock: tea. 5 Jack P. walked back across Park with me. Go to J. Allen,
9.

20 May 1909 Thursday
Read proof all day[9]—till dressing to dine Lady Lovelace.[10]
Pick up J.P. 7.40 Walked home by embankment with J.

21 May 1909 Friday
Stores: bath powder etc. Mrs. Gosse 5 Dentist 7 oclk
Norris dines R.C. 8

22 May 1909 Saturday
Abbey—Meredith: noon.
C. Fletcher 20 Dover St. W. 3.30
Hugh Walpole later (Hugh dined and we went to "Follies.")

23 May 1909 Sunday
Hugh Hammersleys. Hampstead 5.30 and dine.

24 May 1909 Monday
Bancroft—Aethenaeum.

25 May 1909 Tuesday
Try on clothes Cook.
Aline Harland's club, 31 Dover St. 5
Dine Granville Barker 6.30

26 May 1909 Wednesday
Tea with Hugh Walpole 5. Lady Lovelace and Miss Lascelles.[11]—Walked
home by embankment—but felt menace of gout (hanging about since 2 or 3
days,) in the evening. When Jocelyn P. came in after dinner (his mother's
death has occurred) and sat with me in gallery.

27 May 1909 Thursday
Attack of gout—

28 May 1909 and 29 May Friday and Saturday
[In this space HJ wrote the following]—in bed Thursday and Friday. Bailey
Saunders and Hagberg Wright came to see me. I had to put off everything,
but got up Saturday noon, spending the rest of the day in room. Weary, dreary
time—and so disappointing.

[Under Saturday's date HJ crosses out: "Go to Newington—Wallingfords.]

30 May 1909 Whitsunday
Went to Oxford 10.30—motored to Newington.

9. For the New York edition.
10. See 5 February 1895 and November 1909.
11. Helen Lascelles, friend of Hugh Walpole, later Mrs. Eric McLagan (see below).

31 May 1909 Whitsun Monday

Bank Holiday. Newington. We all motored over to Waddesdon and lunched with Miss de R. Wonderful day of beauty and revival of old memories of the extraordinary place.

June 1909

HJ played an unwitting Pandarus in the autumn of 1907: the American William Morton Fullerton (1865–1952), Paris correspondent of the London *Times,* presented HJ's letter of introduction to Edith Wharton (1862–1937) at her home in Lenox, Massachusetts. In the spring of 1908, HJ spent two weeks with Edith and Morton in and around Paris; he was unaware that in the interval they had become lovers. In October Edith sent HJ a double confidence from the United States: her marriage to Teddy was unbearable, Morton was her accepted lover. There was a flurried exchange of letters. Early in November Edith and her much older friend Walter Berry arrived at Lamb House.

In June 1909 HJ vicariously enters the world of romance. He assists at a lovers' tryst, a dinner party in the Charing Cross Hotel. The hotel, hard by the railway terminus for travellers up from Rye and Folkestone, is scarcely Edith's sort of hotel (she belongs to the Claridge near Berkeley Square or the Berkeley in Piccadilly); but she and Morton are entertaining HJ at a discreet dinner in Suite 92. HJ finally bids them goodnight and returns to his club. The lovers spend the night: Edith will commemorate it in a Whitmanesque poem for Morton—"Terminus."

The next morning HJ sees Morton off to America at Waterloo Station. That afternoon Edith and HJ take a motor-flight to see their friend Howard Sturgis at Qu'Acre near Windsor. During the next three weeks they pay a round of visits— together and separately—with members of their circle: the young banker of a well-to-do country family, John Hugh Smith (1881–1964); Gaillard Lapsley, the American don at Cambridge; Lady St. Helier; Mary Cadwalader Jones (1850–1935), née Rawle and formerly married to Edith's elder brother; and her daughter Beatrix (1872–1959), already enjoying a reputation as a landscape gardener and soon to become Mrs. Max Farrand. Edith and HJ dine together at Prince's restaurant in London. The month's activities end with a return to Qu'Acre (when they evidently apprise Sturgis of the Edith-Morton affair), a visit to the Humphry Wards' country place, Stocks, and another overnight at Frampton Court. HJ, all the while the supportive and discreet *confidant,* allays her anxieties and comforts her through bouts of psychosomatic hay-fever.

Five weeks after their quiet dinner in Suite 92, Charing Cross Hotel, the three are together again: HJ at Lamb House gives the lovers dinner and a night's lodging. Early next day Edith's motor carries them to the Channel coast for lunch at Eastbourne with the ailing Jonathan Sturges (whose anecdote years ago had given HJ the idea for *The Ambassadors*—see 31 October 1895), and on to Chichester for the night. During the excursion they concoct a plan to free Morton from the blackmailing Parisian Henrietta Mirecourt—his former mistress. Edith will recommend him to Macmillan's to write the book on Paris she had been asked to do (as HJ had been asked to do one on London—see "London Town" notes); Macmillan would offer an advance of £100, Edith to provide HJ with the £100, and he to write Macmillan's that he will stand surety for the sum. (Within a month the plan will have worked and la Mirecourt been silenced; and in September HJ will visit Frederick Macmillan at Meadow Cottage, Overstrand near Comber.) Next morning the three motor to Canterbury for lunch; the lovers then head for Folkestone to spend the night before crossing to France.

Sturgis had written HJ about this latest motor-flight, "Keep it up—run your race—fly your flight—live your romance—drain the cup of pleasure to the dregs." HJ's reply is appropriately full of bird-imagery (Edith is a "Kite" and "the *oiseau de feu* . . . the Fire Bird") and a defensive explanation of his compliance with "her unappeasable summons"; his sympathy, however, was fully with the love-birds.

Furthermore, life was incredibly imitating art. HJ might expect momentarily to hear himself say (making the proper substitution of a name),

> They may say what they like—it's my surrender, it's my tribute to youth. One puts that in where one can—it has to come in somewhere, if only out of the lives, the conditions, the feelings of other persons. [*Morton*] gives me the sense of it, for all his grey hairs. . . . and *she* does the same, for all her being older than he. . . . her separated husband, her agitated history. . . . The point is that they're mine. Yes, they're my youth; since somehow at the right time nothing else ever was.

He had given these words to Lambert Stretcher, awakened in *The Ambassadors* from the romance of the Lambinet by the smudge of mortality on the canvas, and alive in the real world of his Chad and Marie—now become Morton and Edith. Edith will shape her experience into her most Jamesian novel, *The Reef* (1912)— understandably HJ's favorite and declared by him a masterpiece. (See *Letters* IV, 643–46.)

The following March HJ is in London to see the eminent Canadian-born physician Sir William Osler (1849–1919), "the father of psychosomatic medicine," and Edith sees HJ in his rooms at Garlant's Hotel. She writes the fickle and inconstant Fullerton of these visits—in the midst now of considerable *chagrin d'amour*—for associations have reminded her of the night in Suite 92 (see *The Library Chronicle* of the University of Texas at Austin, New Series No. 1, 1985, p. 40). But by the middle of 1910, after HJ has gone to Nauheim with WJ and Alice, the affair has run its course. Walter Berry moves into the guest suite of Edith's Paris home in July; in mid-August he and Edith visit Lamb House and carry HJ with them to Qu'Acre before he sails for the United States. These three will be joined by Morton at the Hotel Belmont in New York for dinner in October, but Berry has become the love—if not the lover—of Edith's life. Teddy Wharton has just left for a world tour.

HJ will offer his support and advice in the remaining crisis to be faced when mad Teddy returns. In July 1911 HJ spends a long weekend at The Mount with Edith, Hugh Smith, and Lapsley. HJ urges her to sell The Mount and to separate from Teddy. Edith accepts the advice but will not be free of Teddy until their divorce in April 1913. She and HJ will continue their warm and intimate friendship until his death, Edith constantly attentive and supportive of the aging and ailing Master.

HJ's brief but amiable response to a New Year's greeting sent him for 1908 by three young admirers at Cambridge led to his paying a weekend visit to the university town. His hosts were Charles Sayle, a librarian at the University Library; A. Theodore Bartholomew, an assistant librarian; and Geoffrey Keynes, an undergraduate in Pembroke College. HJ spent the weekend at Sayle's in Trumpington Street. He also met the poet Rupert Brooke (1887–1915), who took him punting on the Cam. (See Geoffrey Keynes, *Henry James in Cambridge* [1967].) HJ's report of the weekend to Cambridge don Gaillard Lapsley was, "I *liked* it, the whole queer little commerce, and *them,* the queer little all juvenile gaping group."

A week later, June 22, HJ mailed off his preface to *The Golden Bowl* for the New York edition.

Horace Fletcher (1849–1919), American food faddist, recommended chewing one's food until it was reduced to liquid. HJ had adopted the system, "Fletcherizing," in May 1904; he abandoned the practice in February 1910 when he discovered it was probably responsible for digestive difficulties.

Alvin Langdon Coburn (1882–1966) was the experimental American photographer who provided the frontispieces for volumes of the New York edition.

--------‿✽◌‿--------

1 June 1909 Tuesday
Came up to town (4.20 p.m.) with Schuyler Warren and Miss [Una] Birch.

2 June 1909 Wednesday
Lunch Jack Pollock Savile 1.45. Tea 74 Eaton Terrace 5.
Dine Emily Sargent [11a] 8.

3 June 1909 Thursday
Miss Halstan, 31 Dover St. 5. (4–6.)

4 June 1909 Friday
Sesame Club. 29 Dover St. 1.
5.45 from Victoria
Dine with Morton Fullerton and E.W. Charing Cross Hotel.

5 June 1909 Saturday
Saw W.M.F. off to N.Y. at Waterloo 10 a.m.
Went by motor with E.W. to Guilford and thence by beautiful circuit to Windsor and Queen's Acre

6 June 1909 Sunday
Queen's Acre. E.W. Frank Schuster[11b] etc. Wet day

11a Emily (1857–1936), sister of John S. Sargent.
11b. Schuster (1840–1928), wealthy music-lover and social figure.

7 June 1909 Monday
Queen's Acre, morning. E.W. motored me long and beautiful run (to Walling-
ford) in the afternoon. Tea at Virginia Water—and so to Windsor Station,
whence home.

9 June 1909 Wednesday
Lunched Horace Fletcher at Eustace Miles's. Went in evening with Lucy Clif-
ford to see Arnold Bennett's "What the Public Wants," at Hawtrey's Theatre.
Lamentable play and *bête* performance—unspeakably.

10 June 1909 Thursday
Lucy Clifford 2.45
Mrs. Bigelow comes to tea at Prince's 5.

11 June 1909 Friday
Go to 8 Trumpington St. Cambridge
St. Pancras. 5.5.

12 June 1909 Saturday
Cambridge

13 June 1909 Sunday
Cambridge

14 June 1909 Monday
Returned from Cambridge 6'ock.

15 June 1909 Tuesday
Call F. Prothero 5.30.
Dined M.C. Jones (Symonds's) 8.

16 June 1909 Wednesday
Tea M.C. Jones—5.30
Dine with Mrs. Wharton at Lady St. Helier's. 8.

17 June 1909 Thursday
Collier's 3.30 12 Montagu St. M.S.W.
Mrs. Humphry Ward 5.
Dine A.J. Hugh-Smith (Mrs. Wharton)—Carlton 8.15.
(He came back to Reform with me late.)

18 June 1909 Friday
Luncheon with G.T. Lapsley, Ritz's. 1.30
Got to Miss Childers—3.45—14 Embankment Gardens.
Call Mrs. Van Rensselaer[12] 5.30

19 June 1909 Saturday
Holbein exhibition B. Fine Arts Club (afternoon.)
Take Mary Cadwal. and Trix to Theatre—dining with them 1st, 7.15

12. See 25 November 1881.

20 June 1909 Sunday
Howard Sturgis—Windsor—after luncheon.

21 June 1909 Monday
Hugh W.—Eustace Miles 1.45
Coburn. Hammersmith 5
J. Allen 9.*15*

22 June 1909 Tuesday
Mrs. Murray Smith *1.30*.
Dine Mrs. Sullivan B.P. Hotel. 8.

23 June 1909 Wednesday
Mrs. Wharton dines with me Prince's

24 June 1909 Thursday
Phil. Burne Jones[13] 4–7.
Lady St. Helier[14] 8.15

26 June 1909 Saturday
Went down to Queen's Acre. [HJ crosses out the following: "Motor with E.W. to Hurstbourne Saturday Tarrant. Dined and slept at Frampton Court and Dorchester."]

27 June 1909 Sunday
Having slept at Queen's Acre, motored with E.W. to Stocks and lunched. Stopped for tea at Cassidbury and return to Windsor

28 June 1909 Monday
Motored, with E.W. and H.S. to Hurstbourne Tarrant near Andover and lunched with Mrs. Lea Merritt.[15] Had tea at Salisbury and dined and slept at Frampton Court Dorchester. [HJ crosses out the following: "Dolly Stanley 2 Whitehall Court [Lucien] Guitry with M.C.J."]

29 June 1909 Tuesday
Dine Sir Donald Wallace[16] at St. James's Club. 8.15. having come up by train from Dorchester.

30 June 1909 Wednesday
Lunch A. Harland ladies Atheneaeum Dover St. 1.45
Lady Stanley, 2 Whitehall Court 5.
Dined M. Cadwalader [HJ crosses out: "To play with M. Cadwal."]

---

13. Philip, son of Sir Edward; his 1894 portrait of HJ hangs in Lamb House.
14. See 18 March 1889.
15. Anna (Mrs. Henry) Lea Merritt in 1889 did HJ's portrait, which she gave to him in 1905.
16. Sir Donald Wallace (1841–1919), journalist, editor, and author.

July 1909

The first eight entries of the month, starkly brief, reflect HJ's often harried alternation between the Reform Club in London (105 Pall Mall) and the "russet Arcadia" of his retreat at Lamb House in Rye. July proved a particularly busy and full month: he was deeply engrossed in the Wharton–Fullerton affair, the social demands of his wide-ranging Rye circles, the welcome intrusions of various bright young men—Jocelyn Persse and Hugh Walpole—and the relief of cooling motor-flights.

Among others figuring in the pocket diaries at this time are Walter Gay (1856–1937), the American painter, and his wife Matilda, friends of Mrs. Wharton; Archibald Marshall (1866–1934), journalist and minor novelist, who lived during the pre-war years in Winchelsea and Playden and knew HJ and Hueffer. See his autobiography *Out and About, Random Reminiscences* (1933).

Paul Harvey (1862–1948), later Sir Paul, was the son of Edward de Triqueti (a painter) and an English governess, and the nephew of Mrs. Edward Lee Childe (formerly Blanche de Triqueti). HJ knew Paul as a little boy in 1876 when he visited the Childes' home (Château de Varennes, Le Perthuis, in the French Gâtinais). Harvey served in the British diplomatic corps and in 1909 was financial advisor to the Khedive of Egypt; HJ much admired his work and personality. Harvey compiled the Oxford Companions to English and French Literature.

———————e∿ɔ———————

1 July 1909 Thursday
105 Pall Mall

2 July 1909 Friday
Ditto

3 July 1909 Saturday
Ditto

5 July 1909 Monday
Ditto

6 July 1909 Tuesday
Return Lamb House p.m.

7 July 1909 Wednesday
L.H.

8 July 1909 Thursday
L.H.

9 July 1909 Friday
Went up to town a.m. and in afternoon with Clara Frewen etc. to Mrs. G.C. West's play
Tea with Mrs. Jack Leslie
Evening to Stafford House

10 July 1909 Saturday
Return L.H. 11 a.m.
Jocelyn Persse down for weekend 6.30

11 July 1909 Sunday
Tea with Mrs. Dew-Smith (with J.P.)

12 July 1909 Monday
J.P. left. E.W. and Morton Fullerton arrived to dinner and for night.

13 July 1909 Tuesday
Motored with E.W. etc. to Chichester lunching with Jonathan S. at Eastbourne. Slept Chichester, at Dolphin

14 July 1909 Wednesday
Left Chichester 10 a.m. for return—after dash off to Boshan.
Lunched at Petworth (village)—After Arundel etc. Tea at Brighton. Arrived 7.45 L.H.

15 July 1909 Thursday
Motored with E.W. and M.F. to Folkestone and thence Canterbury where we lunched. They returned to Folkestone for France—I returning to L.H. by train

17 July 1909 Saturday
[HJ crosses out: "Hugh Walpole comes down 1.30"]
Garden-party, Mountsfield

19 July 1909 Monday
Walter Gays motor from Folkestone to tea. Had it in Garden. Mrs. Archibald Marshall and her journalist-cousin also came.
Hugh Walpole arrived 6.30.

20 July 1909 Tuesday
Hugh Walpole all day—and Mrs. Lucas Shadwell and her son to tea in garden.
Walked with Hugh to Camber Castle.

21 July 1909 Wednesday
Hugh W. left 9.21.
Go Mallock's Winchelsea. (Mrs. Maclaren motored me back—Mrs. Mallock thither.)

22 July 1909 Thursday
To tea with Harvey Coombes, Seddelscombe. Mrs. Skinner with her motor for 3.45 at foot of street. Came back, beautifully, by roundabout way through Winchelsea, and saw the work at the Friars.

23 July 1909 Friday
Frank Darwin and Bernard D's.
Mrs. Dew-Smith and Mrs. Vincent to tea.

25 *July 1909 Sunday*
Francis Ford comes for me in motor to Wittersham: 3.30

26 *July 1909 Monday*
Paul Harvey, 6.30

27 *July 1909 Tuesday*
Paul Harvey went 9.21.
Protheros arrived Dial Cottage p.m.

29 *July 1909 Thursday*
Go—4.16—to Miss Betham Edwards villa Julia, 1 High Wickham, Hastings
(top of High St.)

August 1909

HJ did a good deal of motoring in August and carried on his usual sociabilities
with Rye neighbors. There was much fraternizing with George and Fanny Prothero whom he found likeable "and loveable and well-bred and utterly easy" but
he added, "though not acutely *interesting* people." Elsewhere he described Fanny
as "a little Irish lady . . . the minutest scrap of a little delicate black Celt that
ever was—full of humour and humanity and curiosity and interrogation—too much
interrogation" (to Grace Norton, 10 August 1909). Mrs. Richard Hennessy (17
August), who motors HJ to Herstmonceaux Castle, "a prodigious romantic ruin"
near Hastings, is a Rye neighbor "of the Brandy family."

William Allen White (1868–1944) from Kansas "from behind Chicago" as HJ
wrote to T. S. Perry (5 August) was "one of the great native fictionists whom
dear W. D. H[owells] perpetually discovers." Howells had just sent him to HJ.
His fiction made little mark, but he became a national figure in journalism by his
editing of the small-town Emporia *Gazette*. He was prominent in the Bull Moose
party and a staunch Republican leader. His editorials were much quoted. This was
apparently his only meeting with HJ.

HJ characterized Matilda Betham Edwards, (20 August) as "a very gallant little
mid-Victorian lady" and he speculated whether she mightn't be decorated by the
French government. For her knowledge of France she had been named an "Offi-
cier de l'instruction publique en France."

———————◌◈◌———————

5 *August 1909 Thursday*
W. Allen White 1.30.

6 *August 1909 Friday*
Motor with Lady Pollock to Hawshurst—at 3.

7 *August 1909 Saturday*
To Mrs. Prentice 4.30
George Ashburner 6.30

9 August 1909 Monday
G. Ashburner went 9.21. Very hot

10 August 1909 Tuesday
Very hot

11 August 1909 Wednesday
Great Heat wonderful weather.

12 August 1909 Thursday
The Walter Campions, Winchelsea 4–6.30
Drove Noel Prentice back. Great Heat and Weather.

14 August 1909 Saturday
Edmund Gosse 6.30

17 August 1909 Tuesday
Motored with Mrs. Hennessy to Herstmonceaux

18 August 1909 Wednesday
Mrs. Ford—cricket-field 5.

20 August 1909 Friday
Go to Hastings: Miss Betham Edwards 4.16.

23 August 1909 Monday
Mrs. Rollo, her husband, Lionel Holland and Mrs. Prothero to tea: 5 o'clk.
She didn't come, however: Master of Rollo did! and the others. Very wet.

24 August 1909 Tuesday
1.30:—Lady Ottoline Morrell to luncheon. She came with Mrs. Kaerner, and
staid till 7.43. We had tea with Protheros. Pouring rain all the while.

26 August 1909 Thursday
Went over to Norman Moore's with the Protheros in his motor, sent for us
3.30, and came back in it; charming interesting place, Hancock's, 3 miles this
side of Battle.

27 August 1909 Friday
Lady Edward Cecil and Mrs. Maxse to tea. (They came early and staying an
hour, left early; after which I walked out to Camber, by the Channel, with F.
Prothero and then back. Lovely day.)

29 August 1909 Sunday
Went with G. Protheros to tea at Point Hill, and afterwards to Mrs. Hennessy's. Beautiful day

30 August 1909 Monday
Go to Mrs. D'Almeida-Cory 4. [HJ crosses out "Go up to see Mrs. Curtis
(?) (or next day.)"]

September 1909

Considerable absence from Rye and a round of visits to country houses, summarized in a letter to Jessie Allen (23 October 1909): "a few little clusters of days in London, where I did some City churches" but before this "I spent four or five days at the Hereford Deanery and the hot and heavy [music] Festival (I can live without that again!) and then conveyed what was left of me to Morgan Hall, Fairford, Goucestershire, my old friends Ned and Gertrude Abbey, R.A. pleasant old house and most interesting and workful big studio; where he is carrying on a vast and most able work of Decoration, all historic and allegoric figure-pieces and compositions for the new Capitol of his native state of Pennsylvania (at Harrisburg) one of those huge American public orders, for scale and cost, which would make the authorities here stare . . . some charming motoring over Cotswolds and things—and away over to Coventry . . . one beautiful day, far off to Tintern Abbey . . . I repaired afterwards to the Fred[erick] Macmillans at Overstrand, a miniature English Newport, with a cluster of London people of sorts, of *one* sort (George Lewises, Edgar Speyers, John Hares, with Lady Battersea and her palace and gardens thrown in) . . . who brunch and tea and dine and Bridge each other all day long and all three months, after having been doing the same all winter in London. But the beauty great, and the luxury and Norfolk oddity and Norfolk character (these two last all new to me—in the land and aspect,) all repaying." He was motored to Norfolk Cathedral, "superlative," and to Ashridge, "where I hadn't been for years and where Lady Brownlow is beautifuller and gentler than ever; and also to Aston Clinton . . . to find old Lady de Rothschild pink and silvery at almost ninety."

The musical festival at Hereford was apparently tedious; HJ found Elgar's "Apostles" hard going; but he went because the Dean of Hereford, the Honorable and Reverend James Wentworth Leigh, was married to the younger daughter of his old friend Fanny Kemble—"old and comfortable friends" who made the "rare and arduous" stay at the Deanery worth while.

During the month HJ welcomed Howells and his daughter to London and gave them dinner with Hugh Walpole in attendance. They went to see *The Importance of Being Earnest,* which HJ had not seen when the original production of the play at the St. James's was removed because of the Oscar Wilde trial for homosexuality.

3 September 1909 Friday
Lunch Lady Kuman, Sevenoaks. Go to Lucy Clifford, London; 9. p.m.

4 September 1909 Saturday
Go to Eastbourne to J. S[turges] a.m. 11.15 from Victoria arr. 12.45

5 September 1909 Sunday
Return from Eastbourne 8.40 p.m. arr. Victoria 10.30

6 September 1909 Monday
Go at 1.40 from Paddington to the Deanery, Hereford.
Arr. 4.55

11 September 1909 Saturday
Abbeys—Fairford (?)

17 September 1909 Friday
Fr. Macmillan, Overstrand.[17] 1.30; Great Eastern
arr. about 4.30

23 September 1909 Thursday
L. Clifford, 31 Dover St. *1.*
Howellses and Hugh Walpole dine with me Prince's, 7.20, for play.

25 September 1909 Saturday
Humphry Wards. Stocks, p.m.

28 September 1909 Tuesday
Miss Tuckerman. Hotel Curzon, *5*

30 September 1909 Thursday
Owen Seaman 1:30, Savile,[18] 'taking' H. W.

October 1909

The few entries reflect another period of gout and prolonged work on the play for the Duke of York's repertory. In a letter of 31 October to Violet Hunt HJ spoke of his "homely and solitary state, my limited resources, my austere conditions . . . I am more and more aged, infirm and unattractive." The Miss Pertz mentioned at the beginning was Florence Pertz, granddaughter of the English Swedenborgian J. J. Garth Wilkinson, who had been a friend of HJ's father. She became a distinguished musicologist.

———⌬———

1 October 1909 Friday
Miss Pertz 5. 72 Prince's Square

2 October 1909 Saturday
Returned Rye 4:25

15 October 1909 Friday
Hugh Walpole came down 6.30

21 October 1909 Thursday
Hugh Walpole left 9.30

17. See "London Town" notes.
18. One of HJ's London clubs.

November 1909

He was still working at his play during November. Rudyard Kipling (1865–1936) lived in his house Burwash about twenty miles from Rye; HJ occasionally lunched there, and the Kiplings sometimes visited him.

For the Ockham visit to see "the unspeakable Byron papers" see entry for 5 February 1895 in the working notebooks. John Buchan (1875–1940), Lord Tweedsmuir, participated in the Byronic episode. He was a popular novelist and later Governor-General of Canada.

———————— ☙ ————————

2 *November 1909 Tuesday*
   Motored over to R. Kipling's to luncheon in their car.
   Returned by train.

3 *November 1909 Wednesday*
   W.E. Norris came down 6.30

4 *November 1909 Thursday*
   W.E. Norris left, 9.30

27 *November 1909 Saturday*
   Went to Ockham (Lady Lovelace's) with Jocelyn Persse.
   John Buchan there—looked with him at old papers.

29 *November 1909 Monday*
   Returned from Ockham to town

December 1909

At lunch (5 December) with Sir Frederick Pollock, at which Jack Pollock probably was present, HJ met the Princess Bariatinsky, the former Lydia Yavorska, who had come to London to play Ibsen and remained with her husband in British exile. HJ went to see her with his old friend Elizabeth Robins (1863–1952) the actress-novelist, who originally came from Kentucky, and who had played major Ibsen roles in London. They were very critical of the Yavorska *Hedda Gabler,* which had been one of Miss Robins's great roles.

The evening of December 9 interested HJ very much for he met Maurice Maeterlinck (1862–1949), the Belgian symbolist playwright, and his wife Georgette LeBlanc, on the occasion of the first performance in London of Maeterlinck's romantic-sentimental *The Blue Bird*. There was supper afterwards at Alfred Sutro's, the dramatist who had translated some of Maeterlinck's works. Many years later the Belgian dramatist remembered the occasion and told Leon Edel that HJ's French was very pure, purer than that spoken by most Frenchmen. In fact on meeting him that night it did not occur to him that HJ was an American. They never dreamed on this occasion that two years later they would be contenders for the Nobel Prize in Literature, which Maeterlinck received in 1911. (See *Letters* IV, 536.)

At the end of December, HJ invited T. Bailey Saunders, the journalist, to spend Christmas with him—mostly out of sympathy because Saunders was having marital troubles. HJ described him to Jessie Allen (26 December 1909) as "a rather dreary lone and lorn and stranded friend." To liven the Christmas HJ invited his typist Theodora Bosanquet and her friend Ellen (Nelly) Bradley to the Yule dinner as he had done the previous year. Miss Bosanquet's unpublished diary puts us into Lamb House for this occasion:

> Dec. 25th. . . . went to dine at Lamb House. Mr. Bailey Saunders staying there. I disliked what I saw of him yesterday, but this evening he was much more pleasant— quite a good talker, and often witty. Mr. James was delightfully genial and nice. Nellie and I each found glove-boxes on our plates! This seems to be his one idea of gifts for ladies! He gave me a glove-box last year. He looked "real lovely" in a cracker mask after dinner—we all did, but he was the best! They were pleasant, benevolent sort of masks only down to the mouth with a hole for the nose. Mr. James's most successful one was a fat old lady with side curls, which made us so hilarious that he had to send for a shaving-glass to see himself in. "Why" he propounded "don't we all wear masks and change them as we do our clothes."

5 December 1909 Sunday
Lunched Frdk. Pollock's: met Russian performers—Bariatinsky.

6 December 1909 Monday
London.

7 December 1909 Tuesday
Went afternoon theatre with Eliz. Robins—in her box: Bariatinsky in Hedda Gabler

8 December 1909 Wednesday
London

9 December 1909 Thursday
Went to tea Lady Lovelace and John Buchan. Stayed dinner, but came away early to go Haymarket to 1st performance *Blue Bird* in Mme Maeterlinck's box. Went with her and Mrs. Sutro afterwards to supper at Sutro's—Maeterlinck there with S.

11 December 1909 Saturday
Returned LH. Friday 1.30

23 December 1909 Thursday
Baily Saunders came p.m.

24 December 1909 Friday
Went to Winchelsea—Mrs. Mallock's—child's afternoon party.

25 December 1909 Saturday
B.S. Miss Bosanquet and Miss Bradley, dined.

1910

January to August 1910

HJ's long illness of 1910, recorded in the ensuing pages, seems to have been the consequence of a severe depression, induced by his aging, his long periods of solitude in Rye, the failure of the New York edition of his novels and tales to earn substantial royalties, and anxieties about his future. It began with an aversion to food; but symptoms soon showed it was more than a digestive upset. The Rye doctor put him to bed and brought in a nurse; however, he found nothing wrong with HJ physically. The novelist began by saying "my illness has no more to do with a 'nervous breakdown' than with Halley's comet"—but he soon talked about being visited by "the black devils of nervousness, direst damndest demons." He spoke too of his "weakness, prostration, depression." In more literary imagery he said "the tunnel is so long and so black."

The William Jameses, alarmed by the news, despatched from Cambridge their oldest son, Harry, a practical man of affairs. He found his uncle a "portentous invalid," in a state at times of hysteria, weeping and sobbing over his fears and loneliness. Harry decided to get him out of Rye to London, and there arranged for a consultation with the eminent Sir William Osler (1849–1919), who confirmed Dr. Skinner's diagnosis. HJ had no heart trouble, no serious digestive disorder, but he was decidedly "melancholic."

Although William James was suffering from a severe heart condition, he decided to come abroad with his wife, to support his brother. Himself a doctor who had never practiced, he called HJ's condition "a nervous breakdown" but found it devoid of delusions or paranoia. He was jaunty about his own condition, and announced he would get his heart "tuned up" at Bad Nauheim near Frankfurt, renowned for its waters and "cures"—he had been there before—and it was agreed HJ would then go back to America with his family. While WJ was at Nauheim, the novelist and his sister-in-law visited Mrs. Charles Hunter's at Hill Hall, in Epping Forest, where she had a perpetual salon. It was a splendid house, ninety minutes from London, sequestered in the woodland. Regular meals, good walks, a great deal of company helped HJ but his depression lingered. He watched his old friend John Singer Sargent decorating a portion of the house, met Sargent's sister Violet (Mrs. Ormond), listened to the Australian virtuoso Percy Grainger play the piano—"a very attractive youth"—encountered George Moore, whom he pronounced "unimportant," and saw other notables, Lord Ribbesdale, the actress Viola Tree, the young Harold Nicolson. He sat for his portrait, during the eighteen days he spent here, to Annie L. Swynnerton, the first woman elected to Britain's Royal Academy.

With passage to America booked by the St. Lawrence route, the two set off to meet WJ in Germany. In spite of WJ's acute symptoms, the ailing brothers and Mrs. WJ decided on a little tour of Switzerland. The journey, as the notes show, was an act of folly. WJ's condition was very serious, and an entry in Mrs. WJ's diary sums up this effort to minister to illness by travel—"William cannot walk and Henry cannot smile." Back in London, HJ was somewhat improved; he began a system of marking his good days and his bad in his diaries: the bad in black, the good in red denoting "red letter days." He awakened one morning feeling as if he had shed his melancholy—and we may speculate that it was at this moment he had the fantastic "dream of the Louvre" described in his autobiography, in which, seriously threatened, he breaks through and vanquishes an evil spirit which flees down the Louvre's great Galérie d'Apollon. In a later entry he alludes to this awakening as a turning point in his illness. There followed the journey home. William James died a week after they reached his country house at Chocorua.

22 January 1910 Saturday
Went to bed very ill. Skinner sent in Nurse Brown at noon.

19 February 1910 Saturday
End of nurse's 4th week. Harry[1] sailed from N.Y. in St. Louis.

27 February 1910 Sunday
Harry arrived via Hastings

11 March 1910 Friday
Nurse Brown left: 7 weeks

12 March 1910 Saturday
Came up to town with Harry—Garlant's Hotel—1 p.m.

14 March 1910 Monday
Saw Dr. Osler with Skinner

19 March 1910 Saturday
Returned Lamb House 4.25 having seen Osler briefly a.m.

---

1. WJ's eldest.

23 March 1910 Wednesday
Harry went to town, bringing down at 6.30 Nurse Barnes

24 March 1910 Thursday
Harry left 1 p.m.

25 March 1910 Friday
Harry sailed Empress of Britain

27 March 1910 Easter Sunday
Edith Wharton and Teddy called—in motor from Folkestone

31 March 1910 Thursday
Harry wires arrival Halifax

1 April 1910 Friday
H. arrives St. John N.B.

6 April 1910 Wednesday
William and Alice arrived Megantic Liverpool. Nurse Barnes leaves 1 p.m.

7 April 1910 Thursday
William and Alice arrived 1.30

10 April 1910 Sunday
Bad day

11 April 1910 Monday
Bad day and night (vertigo from peptonized cocoa.)

12 April 1910 Tuesday
Bad day and night (''grey powder'' from Skinner p.m.)

13 April 1910 Wednesday
Bad—very sick—day etc. from effects of grey powder.
Worse effect on compromised stomach than ever before.

14 April 1910 Thursday
Bad day—bad, very, very bad—night, without bromide etc.

15 April 1910 Friday
Bad day, but visit from Jessie Allen, down from London, in afternoon. Veronal powder at night. No food all day save baked apples 7.30 Good effect of them.

16 April 1910 Saturday
Better day and turn of tide from Skinner's telling me, under William's earnest suggestion, that I wasn't to mind failing of power to eat.

17 April 1910 Sunday
Better day and enormous relief from cessation of *disciplinary* food and beginning of free attitude.

18 April 1910 Monday

Date *real* improvement from free option in regard to taking food—which checks nervousness in face of penalty of not taking it.

19 April 1910 Tuesday

Walk these 3 days (small ones) with W. and A. and return of power to eat. Sense of beneficent difference made by this basis of choice and freedom.

20 April 1910 Wednesday

1st run in car sent from Folkestone by E. W[harton], Morgan chauffeur. Cripps's Corner, Battle, Ose, Winchelsea, home.

21 April 1910 Thursday

Beautiful warm afternoon—2nd run in car. Wittersham, Tenterden, Biddenden, Benenden—both days with W. and A. Took veronal sleeping powder Thursday night; had secondary effects.

22 April 1910 Friday

Went in car to Lydd and N. Romney across the marsh—cold and with menacing rain.

23 April 1910 Saturday

Went again with W. and A. a short and very cold run—Appledore and Stone. Came home overstrained and unwell.

24 April 1910 Sunday

Bad nervous day—very bad, after bad night. W. and A. alone in car to Pennsey. Sad day—bad day.

25 April 1910 Monday

Continued misery—got up in a.m. but went back to bed about 4.

26 April 1910 Tuesday

Remained in bed all day—took Veronal powder at night. Also ate a little dinner with better effect. Mrs. Vincent for 15 minutes about 6.

27 April 1910 Wednesday

Better night last night, got up 10.30. Skinner 11. Ate some food 1 o'ck; and though as weak as after long relapse went out a little with A. and W. Ate fair dinner and had very fair night—2nd after powder.

14 May 1910 Saturday

Came up to Cannon St. with Alice, and motored to Hill Hall, Epping—Mrs. Charles Hunter etc.

18 May 1910 Wednesday

Very bad day—following bad night. Alice unspeakable blessing.

1 June 1910 Wednesday

Left Hill House with Alice—motoring to 105 Pall Mall. We 1st took passage in Empress of Britain, for Quebec etc. August 12th.

2 June 1910 Thursday
Bad day in town following bad night—but got off to Rye with A. at 4.25

3&4 June 1910 Friday/Saturday
Bad but busy days at Rye—able in spite of everything to arrange and prepare some matters. Also Saturday and Sunday saw Skinner both a.m.

6 June 1910 Monday
Started with Alice, 9.30, for Nauheim, to join William. Ashford, Dover, Calais, Brussells.

7 June 1910 Tuesday
Last night Brussells. Great heat and fatigue. Started for Cologne at noon, to spend night.

8 June 1910 Wednesday
Reached Cologne 6.30 Spent last night. Left at noon for Frankfort and Nauheim; arriving latter 5.30

9 June 1910 Thursday
Nauheim Hotel Hohenzollern

23 June 1910 to 1 July 1910 Thursday to Friday
Left Nauheim—beautiful run, almost all day, a lovely one, through Black Forest—Gd. Duchy of Baden—with interval of wait at Frankfort during which Alice and I went to see Goethe House. Arrived afternoon at Insel Hotel, Constance. Here, today Friday—and today Saturday, I am having bad days and nights—but I don't pretend to note the dismal dreadful detail of these. It's all too sad and too bad. Drove Monday (I think) with William and A. to Arenenberg—beautifully perched residence of Queen Hortense and Empress Eugénie. Left Monday for Zurich—H. Baur on Lac. Bad days and bad weather here—charmless stay—with one small lake excursion—threatened overflow and floods, as at Constance and everywhere. We went, I recall, *somewhere,* to big country palace of Grand Duke of Baden—it must have been a drive from Constance, with beautiful gardens and trees and views. Queer dull old villa-palace, like Friedberg (only less picturesque) which Alice and I walked (twice) over to from Nauheim—as well as driving to the queer high-placed sympathetic country house where Goethe wrote (or lodged) Elective Afinities.

2 July 1910 Saturday to 10 July 1910 Sunday
Left Zurich yesterday—beautiful run, by Berne, to Lucerne—Hotel Tivoli, very clean and good. Excursion in boat and electric train all up the valley of the old drive to Engelberg of my far-away young Swiss days. We only went to Wolfenscheissel, or whatever—rare fine day—hot walk up valley with Alice—return from Stanstadt or whatever by boat in the p.m. Very bad day for me Sunday—3d—drive with W in afternoon. We got away from Lucerne to Geneva on the 4th—Hotel Beaurivage. Better days at G.—whole week

spent there; but news of Bob's[2] death—broken to me by Alice (a cable from Harry two nights before) while we were crossing lake a little steam launch to Eaux-vives to make engagements for William with dentist). Dark troubled sad days—one of them in bed with gout stopped mercifully by Dr. Mayar with salicilate (of, I think, soda.) Visit with Alice to the Flournoy young people at Florissant.[3] Visit from Katie Rodgers,[4] on from Lausanne today (Sunday.) Bromide often.

11 July 1910 Monday
Arrived Paris. Used Geneva (Hotel) L.W.

12 July 1910 Tuesday
Crossed to London starting—12 noon—very fair passage.
Left *Nord* at 12.

13 July 1910 Wednesday
Reform Club room—Wm and Alice at Symonds's Hotel. Woke up to bad day.

14 July 1910 Thursday
x x x x x x William very ill—seeing Mackenzie

15 July 1910 Friday
Saw Jocelyn P. for short time—early—4 Park Place
x x x x x x x x

16 July 1910 Saturday
William great source of anxiety. Bromide a help to me.

17 July 1910 Sunday
Took tea with Alice at Mackenzie's. x x x x

18 July 1910 Monday
x x x x x x x x
Saw Mackenzie for myself—3.p.m.

19 July 1910 Tuesday
Acting on M's prescription for bromide: 60 grains a day, if need.
It helps.

20 July 1910 Wednesday
Help from bromide all past week. William sadly down and weak. Forgot to note that Bruce Porter and Hugh Walpole came to see me at Chambers in the a.m. of last week.

---

2. HJ's youngest brother, Robertson.
3. Family of Swiss philosopher Theodore Flournoy; see 11 September 1900.
4. Katharine "Katie" Rodgers was a maternal relative of HJ.

21 July 1910 Thursday
Woke up in great relief—21st. [HJ with red ink then puts down 23 x's] [Hypothesis that HJ may have dreamed the dream of the Louvre on the 21st July 1910 and found relief in it][5]

23 July 1910 Saturday
Lamb House. Brought William down here by the 4.25—very weak, but journey accomplished!

24 July 1910 Sunday
Poor—very bad, nights and days for William. Alice, as always, wonderful and heroic—and Skinner of real help. Difficult days—dreadful gloomy gales—but I feel my own gain in spite of everything. Heaven preserve me.

27 July 1910 Wednesday
Today 27th W. slightly better. Fords called for me in p.m. and took me to Budds—Morton Stephenson and his mother, that is—where we had tea and afterwards drove through Rolvenden and stopping at wondrous *new Maytham* (Jack Tennants') on way back here. William a little better.

29 July 1910 Friday
Settled yesterday with Mrs. Paddington to go. Absolutely necessary, but very painful and unpleasant and sad. Ah these dark days of (temporary, D.V.) farewell to this dear little old place—saturated now with *all* associations! William just a little better.

5 August 1910 Friday
Mrs. Wharton, arriving from France the day before, motored over to LH with Walter Berry and picked me up early. We lunched at Tunbridge Wells and reached Windsor—H.S.'s,[6] before dinner. I went up to town for day on Saturday and spent night. She motored in and took me back to Queen's Acre to lunch, dine and sleep again.

8 August 1910 Monday and 9 August 1910 Tuesday
I came in on Monday 8th with her once more, having things in town to do, and returned to Queen's Acre in afternoon. On Tuesday 9th she started from Windsor to Folkestone, I going with her to boat. Beautiful hot fatiguing day—got back to Lamb House by train. William better, easier, during my absence—and time all occupied with last preparations for my journey to America and long absence.

11 August 1910 Thursday
Left L.H. with W and A by the 1 p.m. to Cannon St. They going, in town, to Garlant's and I to 105 P.M. which has never seemed to me dearer and more precious. Went with Alice on Friday a.m. to 2 shops before taking 12 steamer—train from Euston. Reached Liverpool all comfortably by 3.30—were on board Empress of Britain by 5. The Protheros had come to us most

5. See September to December 1910 headnote and *Life* 668.
6. Howard Sturgis's.

kindly at Euston. Left dock by five or so—for extraordinarily peaceful and beautiful voyage; with no flaw or cloud on it but William's aggravated weakness and suffering—to see which and not to be able to help or relieve is anguish unutterable; now more and more. But the voyage in itself a marvel. We passed the Straits of Belle Isle all lucidly and smoothly—wondrous sight at about 10–11 etc. on Tuesday. Wednesday the sea a great smooth bright river. Entered the St. Lawrence in the p.m.—bad weather (heavy rain only) for the 1st time. Landed Quebec by four o'clock Thursday 18th—six days' voyage. But bad night at horrible vulgar Frontenac Hotel, perched on the eminence as *the* object of interest in the scene. Dismal difficulties over Custom House and luggage, horrible delays and *déceptions*—without the blest Harry's helping us through; he having come to meet us at the dock and made a lodgement in the hotel possible. We left Quebec on Friday a.m. 19th and I write this, Monday 22d, at the peaceful and innocent Chocorua; which we reached by 8 that night, Bill meeting us, all blessedly again, at Intervale with a motor and bringing us over in an hour or so. The dark cloud of William's suffering state hangs over me to the exclusion of all other consciousness—though I am struggling back to work. The weather hot and magnificent; the house ample and easy; the "pathos" of the whole situation, however, wrings my heart.

27 August 1910 Saturday [written late 24 or 25 August]
William much worse and the whole crisis dreadful and unspeakable. Dr. Shedd and his young Dr. son in control—the latter staying here. Alice too wonderful, but *I*—!!´

28 August 1910 Sunday [to 31 August]
William died Friday 26th, 2.20 p.m. Unutterable, unforgettable hour—with those that have followed it to this Monday p.m. Rose at 4.30 today for the dismal journey to Cambridge, Appleton Chapel and Mount Auburn. All unspeakable. Returned here this evening. Harry with us.

September to December 1910

After his period of profound mourning for his beloved brother, HJ began to absorb once more the U.S. life of the Eastern seaboard he had so recently described in *The American Scene*. Aided by Mrs. Wharton and other friends, he motored a great deal and saw much rural scenery and many impressive country homes. It was his last visit to his homeland and it confirmed his old antipathies. American life decidedly was not for him. He continued to react strongly against "the violence of the assault of this appalling country on almost every honourable sense."

However, his change from rural solitude in England to a life of movement and travel, seeing old friends and new places, ministered to improvement, although he still experienced recurrent days of depression. His use in the pocket diaries of the black and red x-marks continued. Their considerable number suggests that the

The Pocket Diaries

symbols were a totality of nervous release either of comfort or despair, and a substitute for words. Certainly the incisiveness of the marks suggest his inner vitality however poorly he might have felt.

During his stay in the United States he consulted doctors in Boston and New York. Perhaps the most important was Jim Putnam, his brother's old friend, now dedicated to psychiatry and a student of Freud: he had attended Freud's Boston colloquia during 1908 and knew Ernest Jones. HJ recorded visits to Dr. Putnam on 21 November and 21 December in 1910, and a consultation on 26 February in 1911. He also summoned him during a very bad day to his Boston bedside on 13 November 1910. A long letter to Putnam of 1912 (*Letters* IV, 594–97) recalls these visits—"I wish I were sitting with you again in Marlborough Street . . . on one of those rather melancholy winter evenings of a year ago." The letter suggests that Putnam offered HJ supportive therapy and enabled him to unburden himself of many of his anxieties. "You tided me over three or four bad bad places during those worst months," HJ wrote. And we may judge this included the loss and mourning for his brother, his sense of aging, his loneliness in spite of his worldly social life, and the isolation of Rye, even though he entered into the life of that little picturesque town to the full.

HJ's life in Boston was facilitated by the presence of his Lamb House valet, Burgess Noakes, whom he had brought with him on the trip; the devotion of his sister-in-law; his affection for his niece and nephews; and the presence of old friends both in Boston and New York—Grace Norton and Mrs. Gardner and various companions of his youth who were now, like himself, aged, among them T.S. Perry. We get a glimpse into the WJ home from an outsider, Somerset Maugham, who recorded that he dined at 95 Irving Street one evening with HJ and Mrs. WJ and learned that the two had tried to follow up WJ's inquiries of many years into psychical research. WJ had talked of trying to "reach over" on his death. Maugham said HJ told him he had promised to stay in Cambridge for a few months "so that if he found himself able to make a communication from beyond the grave there would be two sympathetic witnesses on the spot ready to receive it." No communication was received. HJ later denounced one séance which reported to have had a message from WJ. The language of the message, HJ said, showed the claim to be fraudulent.

Toward the end of the year HJ went on to New York. He found the bright city, at the approach of Christmas, stimulating. To Fanny Prothero he wrote, "I won't pretend to speak to you of New York—a queer mixture of the awful, the amusing, the almost interesting and the utterly impossible." He noted also "great, great amelioration of my condition." He put up at the new splendid Hotel Belmont, where Edith Wharton had arrived and where on one evening she dined with the three significant males in her life—HJ, Morton Fullerton, and Walter Berry. At this time the novelist renewed his warm friendship with Mrs. Cadwalader Jones, again using her home near lower Fifth Avenue as a pied-à-terre. There is an allusion to a "Mrs. Cam" in one of his entries and we may speculate that it refers to Elizabeth Sherman Cameron (1858–1944), wife of Senator James Donald Cameron, the long-established friend and hostess for Henry Adams.

———— ᥫᩢ ————

3 September 1910 Saturday
Owe Burgess $7.0

10 September 1910 Saturday
Owe Burgess $9.0 (Nine dls.)

11 September 1910 Sunday
Long afternoon motor-ride with Mrs. Gibbens,[7] Harry and Peggy[8]

12 September 1910 Monday
x x x x x x x x x x x Woke up with a return of the old trouble of the black time which had dropped, comparatively, yet as markedly on red-letter day July 21st, with that blessed waking in my London room. Bad day, Monday, yet went with Harry a beautiful a.m. walk—to Bowles's Pond. Taking bromide.

15 September 1910 Thursday to 21 September 1910 Wednesday
Signs of improvement and all blessedly by application of my own patience and practise—the precious light of dire experience. I am better and can really make my [HJ here marks 7 x's in red ink again] again as on July 21st last—date never to be forgotten. Motored, Alice Peg and I, with kind rich Mrs. Runnells[9] all Saturday afternoon; getting immense help and cheer from it. Walked with Alice to Hilltop (Salters') and dined (at noon) and rambled there, Aleck driving us back here (Chocorua) with so amiable, sympathetic and touching Leigh Gregor, who supped spent the night. Better and better He left Monday a.m., leaving for Montreal and his McGill work. Also Langdon Warner[9a] left, having been here 3 days.

17 September 1910 Saturday
Owe Burgess $11—plus $1 borrowed from him = $12.

22 September 1910 Thursday
Motored today (Thursday) over to "Brocon Woods" with Mrs. Runnells. Mrs. Runnells her daughter etc.; an all day excursion. Wondrous day for golden weather, and general beauty; even to remarkable scene where we lunched with the R's relatives, the vast hotel at foot of Mt. Washington. Rare American document. Dick Fisher here.

24 September 1910 Saturday
Owe Burgess $14. Harry returned from Boston yesterday, Friday. We went to tea, tennis etc. with Runnells's.

25 September 1910 Sunday
Went up to Boston with Harry by evening train. Reached Irving St. 10—slept there—breakfasted with Mrs. Gibbens. Called on Grace Norton a.m. Took

7. WJ's mother-in-law.
8. Margaret Mary, WJ's daughter.
9. Mother of Alice, whom Billy (WJ's second) would marry early in 1912; see August to December 1911 headnote.
9a. Warner (1881–1955), American orientalist and professor at Harvard.

Taxi-cab into town, and picking up Harry lunched with him North Station. Then went (2 hours 1/2) to Hancock, to T.S. Perry's.[10]

28 September 1910 Wednesday
Yesterday wet and bad; but walked with Thos. in p.m. Today walked to Hancock with him, and in afternoon Lilla[11] drove me (6 miles) to Dublin and Raphael Pumpelly's. Wonderful view, beautiful drive.

29 September 1910 Thursday
Rose 6 a.m. Took train from Hancock, picked up Harry in town; came back to Chocorua. My days successful—feel great gain.

1 October 1910 Saturday
Owe Burgess $16.

2 October 1910 Sunday
Chocorua. Walked with Peg up to Hilltop, lunched (dined) and walked back. In all 8 miles.

3 October 1910 Monday
x x x x Woke up to bad day—bad consciousness of sickness and attributable to reason of diet. But motored both a.m. and p.m. with Runnellses

4 October 1910 Tuesday
x x x x x x x x x x x x x x x x x x Return of heat—bad day—very bad.

5 October 1910 Wednesday
Increase of heat—x x x x x x x x x x x x x x x x x x Miserable day. Most oppressive, dreadful air. The latter accounts, I think, for much. Appetite wholly gone; with the dire consequence.

6 October 1910 Thursday
Bad, in fact most wretched day—spent in bed (the 1st so spent since early part of last May.) But improvement this evening through symptoms (marked) of power to eat. Air still hot and evil.

7 October 1910 Friday
Better today—cold rain. Have begun to eat, with marked effect again. Just lunched; able to do it and to carry my burden a little better. I cannot [explain] my relapse from Tuesday a.m., this will be fair and attack encouragingly short, though yesterday and Wednesday were so bad.

8 October 1910 Saturday
Owe Burgess $18

9 October 1910 Sunday
Better day—up and saw to packing, wrote letters etc. But air here and whole tension, strained and *sense of the place* awfully hostile to recovery.

10. Thomas Sergeant Perry (1845–1928), critic and editor, a friend of HJ's since boyhood.
11. Née Cabot (b. 1848), a painter, married T. S. Perry in 1874.

10 October 1910 Monday
Monday 10th wrote letters a.m. and with Harry came up to Boston p.m., leaving Alice and the others to follow this week. Cold radiant, overtonic weather and sense of air, light, lustre of colour, making so for agitation and nervous pain. Here, at Cambridge, better. Went into Boston a.m., did many things. Here in Irving St. alone with Harry and Aleck; breakfasted, dined, with dear kind Mrs. Gibbens. Feel great benefit of having come away from C.—and such a day as today. Arranged to go on to New York tomorrow.

13 October 1910 Thursday
Came on to New York Wednesday 12th. by the 1 p.m. from South Station— very comfortable journey (*all* Pullman cars) arriving 6. Lunch on car at *12.40* etc. Found Whartons at this Hotel Belmont. Great, very great amelioration of condition; justifying my whole idea. [HJ here again marks in 14 red x's]

15 October 1910 Saturday
Owe Burgess $20—less $1.70—I having given him $2 on last day at Chocorua, and he having lent me 30 cents. Owe him thus $18.70—or call it $19. M. Fullerton arrived this a.m.

16 October 1910 Sunday
Called last night on Mrs. Smalley. Teddy Wharton started on tour round the world today 3.30, with brave charming Johnson Morton

17 October 1910 Monday
E. Wharton, Walter Berry and Morton Fullerton dined with me tonight at Hotel Belmont.

18 October 1910 Tuesday
E.W. sailed for France. W.M.F. and I lunched with W.B. at beautiful University Club. M.F. and I dined together.

19 October 1910 Wednesday
Came to Lawrence Godkin's [12]—much less well again. Alice Lyon [13] dined, and I made shift, however.

20 October 1910 Thursday
Lunched with M.C. Jones—but still unwell. Called on Mrs. Smalley, Mrs. Jones and W.M.F. Dined with Lawrence G.
x x x x x x x x x x x

21 October 1910 Friday
Ill—but had visit from Bay Emmet [14] and went out with Mrs. Cam back in taxi and went to bed—miserably unwell, but had, after 10 o'clk, better night.

---

12. Son of E. L. Godkin of the *Nation;* see 26 November 1892.
13. Friend of the Godkins.
14. Ellen Gertrude Emmet, daughter of Ellen James Temple (1850–1920), Minny's younger sister, and Christopher Temple Emmet (1822–84); in 1900 she painted a portrait of HJ.

22 October 1910 Saturday
Came back to Cambridge by 1 o'clk. Express from N.Y. arriving 6—excellent train, and just pulled through.

23 October 1910 Sunday
Gradual [6 red x's]

24 October 1910 Monday
[15 red x's]

25 October 1910 Tuesday
[27 red x's]

26 October 1910 Wednesday
[14 red x's]

27 October 1910 Thursday
[12 red x's]

28 October 1910 Friday
[15 red x's]

29 October 1910 Saturday
Owe B. $22. [14 red x's]

30 October 1910 Sunday
[8 red x's]

31 October 1910 Monday
[4 black x's]

2 November 1910 Wednesday
[9 black x's]

3 November 1910 Thursday
[12 black x's]
1st bromide today late

4 November 1910 Friday
[5 black x's]

5 November 1910 Saturday
[5 black x's]

6 November 1910 Sunday
[6 black x's]
Went in to see Dr. J. Putnam

7 November 1910 Monday
[5 black x's]

8 November 1910 Tuesday
[5 black x's]

9 November 1910 Wednesday
[9 black x's]

10 November 1910 Thursday
[5 black x's]

11 November 1910 Friday
[A variation is introduced into this ritual; HJ has alternate black and red x's—one black, one red, one black, one red, one black. There are 5 x's: the second and fourth are red.]

12 November 1910 Saturday
[The x-system changes. HJ starts with a red, then a black, then a red, then a black, then a red. First, third, and fifth x's are red.]

13 November 1910 Sunday
Jim Putnam came out to see me [two red x's]

14 November 1910 Monday
[4 red x's]

15 November 1910 Tuesday
[4 red x's] Posted *Saloon*[15] to Pinker.

16 November 1910 Wednesday
[9 red x's]

17 November 1910 Thursday
[4 red x's]

18 November 1910 Friday
[4 red x's]

19 November 1910 Saturday
Owe Burgess Two Dollars. [Black x] (Paid.) [red x]

20 November 1910 Sunday
[1 black x, 2 red x's, 1 black x]

21 November 1910 Monday
[4 black x's]
Drove in to see J. Putnam [3 red x's]

22 November 1910 Tuesday
[11 red x's]

23 November 1910 Wednesday
[16 red x's]

---

15. HJ's dramatization, begun December 1907, of his story "Owen Wingrave"; produced January 1911. See *Complete Plays* 641–49.

24 November 1910 Thursday
[8 red x's]
Thanksgiving Day: Arthur and Theodora Sedgwick[16] dine.

25 November 1910 Friday
[14 red x's]

26 November 1910 Saturday
Owe Burgess $2. Tea Mrs. Brooks Adams[17] 4.45
[17 red x's]

27 November 1910 Sunday
[6 red x's]

28 November 1910 Monday
[8 red x's] Bill's[18] studio—to Mrs Gardner's with Bill.

29 November 1910 Tuesday
[14 red x's]

30 November 1910 Wednesday
[20 red x's]

1 December 1910 Thursday
[14 red x's]
With Peggy to the Henry Higginsons,[19] 5 p.m., seeing only Ida.

2 December 1910 Friday
[15 red x's]
Motored with Jim Crafts—afternoon.

3 December 1910 Saturday
[15 red x's]

4 December 1910 Sunday
[8 red x's]

5 December 1910 Monday
[13 red x's]
Drove in to T.S. Perry's to dine: Music: young Harris, Nina Fletcher etc.

6 December 1910 Tuesday
[12 red x's]

7 December 1910 Wednesday
[18 red x's]

16. Arthur George (1844–1915) and Maria Theodora (1851–1916); Mrs. Charles Eliot Norton was their sister.
17. Née Emily Davis (d. 1927), wife of Peter Chardon Brooks Adams (1848–1927)—brother of Henry Adams.
18. WJ's second son.
19. See December 1904.

8 December 1910 Thursday
[11 red x's]

9 December 1910 Friday
[16 x's red] To Bill's studio—admirable portrait of Peggy. Tavern Club with Bill.

10 December 1910 Saturday
[14 red x's]

11 December 1910 Sunday
[14 red x's]

12 December 1910 Monday
[14 red x's]

13 December 1910 Tuesday
[15 red x's]

14 December 1910 Wednesday
[6 red x's, 10 black x's]

15 December 1910 Thursday
[15 red x's]

16 December 1910 Friday
[7 red x's] [8 red x's]

17 December 1910 Saturday
[13 red x's]

18 December 1910 Sunday
[7 red x's]

19 December 1910 Monday
[11 red x's]

20 December 1910 Tuesday
[HJ has written a number of x's in red; he then proceeds to superimpose blacks—so that he gets 11 black x's; then he has a series of red x, black x, red x, black x—11 x's alternating black and red. Then he has 6 black x's.]

21 December 1910 Wednesday
[13 black x's] Drove in to see James Putnam. [5 black x's and 7 red x's]

22 December 1910 Thursday
[10 red x's]

1911

January to July 1911

There is a decided increase in the social rhythm of HJ's year in the United States with the coming of 1911. He is in New York again in January staying with Lawrence Godkin, son of his former *Nation* editor, and moving on to Mary Cadwalader's in Greenwich Village. We find him attending a business meeting of the recently founded American Academy of Arts and Letters, to which he was elected in 1905. His entry is emphatic—"impression simply sickening." And in a letter he says, "some of the elements frankly appalled me." He would remain critical of this body, in whose existence he distinctly believed but whose structure he found faulty. It consisted of a mix of writers, painters, and composers: the writers knew little about the painters, the painters little about the writers, and the musicians were uninformed about both. HJ's letters to the Academy are a constant complaint; he had never heard of many of the candidates and did not know how to vote.

Still worried about his health, HJ consulted in New York the fashionable socialite doctor Joseph Collins, who later would write a series of books using reminiscences of his famous patients and scrambling them in with his indiscriminate general reading. In *The Doctor Looks at Biography* (1925), Collins tells us that HJ "put himself under my professional care and I saw him at close range nearly every day for two months; and talked with him, or listened to him, on countless subjects." He found HJ had "an enormous amalgam of the feminine in his makeup; he displayed many of the characteristics of adult infantilism." He judged him "solitary hearted." His great defect, said Collins, was that his "amatory coefficient was comparatively low; his gonadal sweep was narrow." But if HJ was thus "a-sexual" he was "out of the ordinary." HJ's verdict on Collins, delivered to Dr. Putnam, was that "beyond being very kind and interested he did nothing for me at all." As for his treatment, HJ described it as "baths, massage and electrocutions." Collins from the first had declared HJ "sound and well" but treated his patient in a cosmetic manner, prescribing among other things an "abdominal support."

In Boston, Isabella Stewart Gardner commissioned a portrait of HJ from the novelist's favorite nephew, Billy, for her Venetian palace in the Fenway where she had made a kind of architectural collage of her art collections. He sat also, we note, for a portrait by the Philadelphia painter Cecilia Beaux (consistently misspelling her name Baux), commissioned by his old friend Mrs. Richard Watson Gilder, the former Helena De Kay, whom he had known in the early Newport time.

We find also in his diary the name of Theodate Pope Riddle, the architect, who had built Avon Old Farm at Farmington, Connecticut. He had met her during 1904–05 and enjoyed her lavish style of life and her collection of Impressionist painters.

George Abbot James, an old New England friend (not a relative) whom he had known long before, came to HJ's rescue during the prostrating heat wave, which terminated his stay in America, and gave him the run of Lowland House, at Nahant, on the coast where the great porch offered breeze and comfort. HJ sailed with Burgess on the Mauretania for one of the briefest journeys of all his crossings. Aboard the ship, the novelist was invited to the table of George Meyer, Secretary of the Navy, and an assortment of business men "whose 'tone' and general *allure* had been illuminating—yet not wholly uplifting to me. The breeding and culture—or cultivation and civilization—the general amenity and lack of finish one may be a prominent New York man and yet lack!" On this voyage, HJ also had some talk with "the street-boy-faced Edison."

———ᘒᔷᘒ———

13 January 1911 Friday
At Lawrence Godkin's 36 W. 10th St. Came to New York at 1 o'clk. (arriving here 6) with Peggy, who has gone elsewhere.

18 January 1911 Wednesday
At M. Jones's 21 East 11th St. Came here today.

25 January 1911 Wednesday
Went to business meeting of Am. Academy at University Club. Small attendance, but impression simply sickening.

29 January 1911 Sunday
Dull and difficult dinner John Cadwalader's.[1] Drove Herkomer,[2] the younger, home.

---

1. A successful lawyer, cousin of Mary Cadwalader Jones; see August to December 1911 headnote.
2. Son of Sir Hubert von Herkomer (1849–1914), painter, Slade Professor of Fine Arts at Oxford 1885–1894.

30 January 1911 Monday
Lunched L. Shipman, Player's Club. Went to 1st night of young E. Sheldon's play[3]—"The Boss." Scant feeding all day.

31 January 1911 Tuesday
Unwell—collapse—and kept bed. Bad day.

1 February 1911 Wednesday
In bed—but much better after 5 p.m.—[In other conditions of light, air, independence—above all of resolute *nutrition—aurais que me ressaisir,* probably, at that stage—even by going straight out. This later reflection—Feb. 7th—confirmed by what Collins says.][4]

2 February 1911 Thursday
In bed—less well again. Sent for Dr. Collins, who blessedly came at once.

3 February 1911 Friday
Dr. Collins came, afternoon. Great help, encouragement, support. Pronounces me as sound and well!

4 February 1911 Saturday
Went out, with M.C.J. in Mrs. Whitridge's motor—fine 2 hours. Saw Dr. Collins here 5:30 Arranged to leave tomorrow.

5 February 1911 Sunday
Left New York 12, noon, with Peg., arrived Back Bay 5.30—met by Bill.

8 February 1911 Wednesday
Wore 1st time Collins's abdominal "supporter."

9 February 1911 Thursday
[5 red x's] Wore today—2nd day—the abdominal belt prescribed by Collins. Called on Miss Longfellow. Walked—walked, in the mild still snow-portending air. *Very auspicious.*

10 February 1911 Friday
Dr. Roberts[5] 10 o'clk.

11 February 1911 Saturday
Roberts, 10 o'clk.

12 February 1911 Sunday
Went to Concord 11.7 (from Somerville.) Lunched with Mary J. Returned here 5.30

13 February 1911 Monday
Went to Roberts a.m. and afternoon. Damnably sore mouth.

---

3. Edward Brewster Sheldon, American dramatist (1886–1946); *The Boss* opened in New York on this date.
4. HJ's brackets.
5. Dentist.

14 February 1911 Tuesday
Went to Roberts briefly afternoon. Extraordinary apparent effect of Collins belt—as general "supporter" all through this very bad strain.

16 February 1911 Thursday
Roberts, 10 a.m.

20 February 1911 Monday
Roberts 10 a.m. Went with Harry to afternoon tea at Charles Eliot's. Crowd of people. Talked, after 40 years, with Eleanor Shattuck (Mrs. Whiteside.)

21 February 1911 Tuesday
Dined Mrs. Field's 7.30 with Bill and Mrs. Bill. Went to Roberts at 10 and at 6.

22 February 1911 Wednesday
Went to Roberts 10 (Universal holiday—Washington's Birthday.) Burgess went to Roberts 2 who took out eleven teeth!—Walked with Harry up North Avenue in afternoon. Lovely winter day with such hints of spring, such a sunset and such melancholy, tragic hauntings and recalls of the old far-off years.

23 February 1911 Thursday
Roberts (Thursday) 1.30. Rec'd. from Jack Pollock news of arrival of O.H. (Feb. 15.)

24 February 1911 Friday
Roberts, 1 o'clk. Mrs. Gardner 6.30

25 February 1911 Saturday
Went in to T.S. Perry's, 5 p.m. to stay till Monday night.

26 February 1911 Sunday
Adorably beautiful day, light, air. At 103 Marlborough St. people to lunch, tea etc. Went a.m. to see J.J. Putnam.

27 February 1911 Monday
Walked with T.S.P. to St. Botolph Club, saw Dr. Camp's very fine portrait; and then walked far up along new Embankment of Back Bay—new quarter.

28 February 1911 Tuesday
Drove back to Irving St. last night. Art Museum yesterday afternoon. Bellamy Storers—56 Fenway—4.45

1 March 1911 Wednesday
Rich'd Dixey's—opera—dinner 6.30 44 Beacon St.

3 March 1911 Friday
Club dinner—Algonquin 7 o'clk.

4 March 1911 Saturday
Sat to Bill[6]

6. Billy James's portrait of his uncle now hangs in the Gardner Museum, Boston.

5 March 1911 Sunday
Sat to Bill

6 March 1911 Monday
Sat to Bill. Dined Mrs. J.W. Elliott[7] 7.30 124 Beacon st.

7 March 1911 Tuesday
Sat to Bill

8 March 1911 Wednesday
Ned Boit,[8] Colchester St. Brookline 7.30. Sat to Bill a.m.

9 March 1911 Thursday
Mrs. Wirt Dexter—opera Sat to Bill.

10 March 1911 Friday
Sat to Bill. Dined Mrs. Gardner and opera.

11 Saturday
Sat to Bill. Lee Warners dined.

12 March 1911 Sunday
Sat to Bill. Lunched T.S. Perry's.

13 March 1911 Monday
George James 7.30. Sat to Bill a.m. Tarbell[9] came to see picture.

14 March 1911 Tuesday
Sat to Bill—and then called on Tarbell with him. George Ashburner and S. Norton dined.

15 March 1911 Wednesday
Go to 21 East Eleventh St.—came on this p.m.—arrving happily 6.

16 March 1911 Thursday
Mrs. Benedict[10] 4.30 37 Madison Avenue. Dine Judge Barlow, 10 Lexington Avenue. 7—for concert

17 March 1911 Friday
Lunch Bay Emmet 1.30. Called Constance Fletcher (129 W. 46th St.)

18 March 1911 Saturday
Dine Theodate Pope, St. Regis. Call Helena Gilder, 24 Grammercy Park

20 March 1911 Monday
Benedicts' 5. Dine Lawrence Godkin, 8. Went for 1st time, 11 a.m., for treatment to Collins—Neurological Institute East 67th St.

21 March 1911 Tuesday
Went to Collins 11. C. Fletcher, and Harrison Rhodes dine here.

7. Maude, daughter of Julia Ward Howe, wife of painter John Elliott.
8. Edward D. Boit; see 11 December 1904.
9. Edmud C. Tarbell (1862–1938), American painter; Professor of Painting at Boston Museum.
10. Widowed Clara, née Woolson, younger sister of Constance Fenimore Woolson.

22 March 1911 Wednesday
Collins 11. Went last night after dinner to Mrs. De Koven's—much music. And today p.m. to Howard Cushing's studio.

23 March 1911 Thursday
Dined S. Olins—Ritz-Carleton. Collins in the a.m.

24 March 1911 Friday
Collins 11. Saw Mrs. Smalley ½ hour. Lunched Century. Benedict 5.15. Dined Winthrop Chanlers[11]—with Cabot Lodges.[12]

25 March 1911 Saturday
Mrs. Smalley 4.45. Collins, 11; lunched Century. Dine Whitridges 8. Went with Arthur Sedgwick to Bar Association.

26 March 1911 Sunday
Call Mrs. S. Van Rensselaer 5. Dine Collins 7.30.

27 March 1911 Monday
Collins 11. Whitridges—dine and theatre

28 March 1911 Tuesday
Collins 11. Mrs. Riggs: 3.30. French reading Benedicts 5. Opera—"Norma."

29 March 1911 Wednesday
Collins. Joe Walshes 5 (525 Madison Ave.) Circus with M.C.J.

[HJ crosses out the following dates]

30 March 1911 Thursday
Collins 11 Lunch Bay and Leslie Mrs. Sullivan 5

31 March 1911 Friday
Minnie Peabody 5 Round table dinner 7.30

[HJ crosses out the following two entries]

1 April 1911
Dined Lawrence Godkin

2 April 1911 Sunday
Dined, with M.C.J. at Douglas Robinson's.

5 April 1911 Wednesday
Let Helena Gilder know about my sitting to Miss B[e]aux—telephone. Write Rosina Sherwood 251 Lexington Ave.

7 April 1911 Friday
Went to tea with Will Emmets[13] 50 East 76 st.

11. Mrs. Chanler, née Margaret "Daisy" Terry (1862–1952), daughter of painter Luther Terry, friend of HJ's since the 70s in Rome.
12. Sen. Henry Cabot Lodge (1850–1924) and the former Anna Cabot Mills Davis.
13. William Temple, son of Katherine "Kitty" (née Temple, elder sister of Minny) and Richard Stockton Emmet; HJ's cousin.

8 April 1911 Saturday
Motor out New Rochelle (the J. Lapsleys) with Pauline Emmet.
University Club—3.

9 April 1911 Sunday
Lunch Fredk. Whitridges 1. Call on Mrs. Chapman 5
Dine John Cadwalader 8

10 April 1911 Monday
Dine Will Emmets 7.30.

11 April 1911 Tuesday
William Archer,[14] Century: 1.30

12 April 1911 Wednesday
Sit to Cecilia B[e]aux, 20 Grammercy Park, 11.

13 April 1911 Thursday
Sat Cecilia B[e]aux
Call Mrs. Scheiffelin
Went to play with C.M.J.[15] "The Concerts."

14 Friday 1911 Good Friday
Went to "Parsifal" with C.M.J. Very long but splendid performance.

15 April 1911 Saturday
Went out to Zoological Garden, Bronx, with M.C.J.

16 April 1911 Easter Sunday
Luncheon party here. Murray Butlers[16] etc.
Saw Howells.
Dined John Cadwalader with F. Millets[17] etc.

17 April 1911 Monday
To dine with Mrs. Frank Barlow

18 April 1911 Tuesday
Dined with Lawrence Godkin.

19 April 1911 Wednesday
Unwell—went to bed in afternoon.
Harry dined with M.C.J.

20 April 1911 Thursday
Return to Cambridge with Harry 5. p.m.

14. William Archer (1856–1924), distinguished drama critic, translator of Ibsen, author of highly successful play, *The Green Goddess*.
15. Slip of the pen for M. C. J.—Mary Cadwalader Jones; again in next entry.
16. Nicholas Murray Butler (1862–1947), President of Columbia University 1901–45.
17. See 15 October 1894.

23 April 1911 Sunday
Dine Frank Higginsons[18] 7.30 274 Beacon St.

24 April 1911 Monday
[6 red x's] Long walk out from Boston by waterside from end of West Boston
Bridge

7 May 1911 Sunday
Called on Isabella Gardner, Fenway Court

8 May 1911 Monday
Dine Mark Howe's[19]—7.30

17 May 1911 Wednesday
M.M.J.[20] operated for appendicitis by Dr. John Elliott.

18 May 1911 Thursday
Went to Needham (the John Elliot's) to dine and sleep.
Great, terrible heat.

19 May 1911 Friday
Dr. Elliot motored me back to Cambridge in the a.m.
(Peggy very ill—going to Farmington doubtful.)

20 May 1911 Saturday
Came to Farmington by 2 train to Hartford. Met by Jacacci[21] in motor—heat
extreme.

21 May 1911 Sunday
Lunched, at Farmington, with Admiral and Mrs. Coles.

22 May 1911 Monday
Much motoring—to Hartford and elsewhere—place delightful, people angels.

23 May 1911 Tuesday
Theodate Pope motored me over to New Haven to lunch with Prof. Day etc.
Very happy impressions of Yale.

24 May 1911 Wednesday
Went yesterday by motor in the p.m. to Middletown—and had long afternoon
run today. Heat broken—cool and wet

25 May 1911 Thursday
Theodate P. nobly motored me, with Burgess and baggage, the 80 miles over
to Salisbury, through Lichfield. Splendid cool day. We stopped at Westover
School—very charming place; and "made a few remarks" to the many girls.

---

18. Brother-in-law of Mrs. George Higginson, née Elizabeth Hazard Barker (d. 1961), daughter of
HJ's aunt, née Jeannette James (1814–42), Mrs. William H. Barker.
19. Mark Antony DeWolf Howe (1864–1960), New England editor, poet, and scholarly antiquary.
20. Niece Peggy.
21. Auguste Jacacci, French-born writer and art historian.

26 May 1911 Friday
Today, Friday, coolish and charming here at Elly Hunter's.[22]

27 May 1911 Saturday
Renewal—embellished—of impression of 7 years ago.
Lunched (yesterday Friday) with Bay[23] and Blanchard.

31 May 1911 Wednesday
Motored to Stockbridge with Leslie[24] from Salisbury, and lunched with Miss Tuckerman—charming day, beautiful impression.

1 June 1911 Thursday
The "ramble" below was this *Thursday;* on Friday Rosina[25] and Grenville motored me beautifully to Farmington.

2 June 1911 Friday
Great good from long ramble—3 hours of afternoon, by myself (though with 2 Emmet dogs,) over the hillsides and lonely "bets" about Borak Matif.
Friday night at the Popes—dinner-party Friday night.
Theodate at 10.15 Saturday motored me the 140 miles to Cambridge via Pomfret

4 June 1911 Sunday
Nahant.
Went by Taxi from Boston in the afternoon to Brookline to see Mrs. Gardner, Greenhill.

5 June 1911 Monday
Came down here to Lowland House, Nahant, by hired motor from Cambridge—afternoon (hour and $\frac{1}{2}$.)

8 June 1911 Thursday
Nahant.
George James, kindest of hosts, motored me yesterday afternoon to Marblehead and Salem—with Mrs. Blake.

10 June 1911 Saturday
Motored with G.A.J. and Mrs. Blake to Newburyport and had tea at "Dur Island" with Mrs. H. Prescott Spofford etc. Dreadfully dreary impression.

11 June 1911 Sunday
Nahant.
Received last night from New York the news of death of Jonathan Sturges at Eastbourne, Friday morning at 11 o'clk.

---

22. Ellen James Temple, widowed in 1884, married George Hunter (1847–1914).
23. Ellen Gertrude Emmet; see 21 October 1910.
24. Bay Emmet's youngest sister.
25. Rosina Hubley Emmet, daughter of Ellen and Christopher Temple Emmet, and her half-brother George Grenville Hunter, son of Ellen and George Hunter.

12 June 1911 Monday
Met Mrs. Gardner (by driving over) at Lynn Station, at noon, (she motoring me over to East Gloucester to lunch with Cecilia B[e]aux). Came back from Lynn by trolley and walk.

14 June 1911 Wednesday
[HJ had written for this date "Sail Mauretania" but crosses it out.]

16 June 1911 Friday
Nahant.
Saw Dr. Winslow, of this place, after luncheon. Then G.A.J. and Mrs. Blake motoring me to far end of Lynn, I walked drastically, heroically back over the beaches and along the west cliff-path etc. some 7 good miles.

18 June 1911 Sunday
Bill came down to us at Nahant to luncheon, I meeting him at Lynn and driving him back.

19 June 1911 Monday
Mrs. Blake departed—to our regret! Mrs. "Bay" Lodge dined Sunday night.

23 June 1911 Friday
Beautiful afternoon run to the "Middlesex Falls" with G.A.J. and "the cherub." Wonderful landscape "Reservations"—great achievement.

24 June 1911 Saturday
Went up to Boston and by boat and met by Ellerton J., was motored again all through the admirable parkways, Blue Hill etc, and lunched with E. and O. at Milton.

25 June 1911 Sunday
Motored back from Milton yesterday, after beautiful impression, and so from Boston by train to Lynn and tram. Saw for the 1st time wondrous starling and flying bi-plane—Atwood Wright machine. Extraordinary thrilling beauty. Nahant. On p. 443 of the copy of Beauchamp's Career, read over here, note noble and beautiful "aside" of G.M.'s—as novelist, frankly, to his readers. Very *important* and suggesting so many reflections. It's in Chapter "Trial Awaiting the Earl."[26]

28 June 1911 Wednesday
Harvard Commencement.[27]

30 June 1911 Friday
Motored in from Nahant and met Alice, Harry, Peg and her nurse at South

26. At the midpoint of Chapter 48, "Of the Trial Awaiting the Earl of Pomfrey," of George Meredith's novel *Beauchamp's Career* (1875) appears the brief passage that begins, "We will make no mystery about it." Meredith's auctorial voice is quite opposite in effect to what HJ lamented in Trollope's fiction.

27. HJ accepted an honorary degree.

Station, I going to Intervale, they to Chocorua; where they left train, I going
on with B.[28]

1 July 1911 Saturday
Intervale, the good Merrimans, since last evening.
Motor-run in afternoon. Great heat.

2 July 1911 Sunday
Intervale in increasing heat. Motored to Chocorua.

3 July 1911 Monday
Intervale—awful heat.

4 July 1911 Thursday
Intervale—heat unsurpassed. But the 2 hours of afternoon motor life-preserving.
Went over today (p.m.) by motor, in undiminished heat, to Chocorua and saw
them all. But the place—where the impression aggravated by the temperature
too pathetic, tragic impossible to me.

6 July 1911 Thursday
Left Intervale in blest afternoon thunderstorm for Boston—Harry coming on
train at West Ossipee.

7 July 1911 Friday
Rain and thunder etc. all the way—cooling reviving. But torrid heat at St.
Botolph Club where I spent night. Came by rail up at 10 to Springfield—
12.30—where E. W[harton] all angelically met me with Cook and the car.
Admirable run to the Mount with luncheon in the shade—at 2.30 or so—by
the way.

9 July 1911 Sunday
The Mount.
Gilliard Lapsley arrived last p.m.

10 July 1911 Monday
The Mount. Great and deadly heat—but immense refreshment from the blest
Car. The beauty of the Country admirable—beyond praise. Dear little John
Hugh Smith[29] also here—arrived an hour after us (on Saturday.)

12 July 1911 Wednesday
John Hugh gone. Heat not gone—but delightful runs with E. and G.L. The
Country all about magnificent—adorable.

13 July 1911 Thursday
Gilliard left this noon. E.W. and I walked—in the greater coolness—about the
place. Teddy W. arrived before dinner. Great sad tension. Cook motored me
this noon to Pittsfield, and I reached Nahant, by Bray's motor at 7.30—the
run to Boston, where I arrived at 6, being admirably cool through rain and

28. Burgess Noakes.
29. See June 1909 headnote.

change (though no rain *here,*) and welcome here admirably kind. Today Saturday hottish—but the sea airs blessèd.

16 July 1911 Sunday
Nahant.
Harry came down from Boston to lunch—went back after tea.

24 July 1911 Monday
Nahant.
Came up from Nahant, for packing in Irving St. and town etc. (George James motored me to town, and I came out thence—he bringing me and leaving me. I write this at Hill Hall—picking up the lost stitches.)[30] Went back to Nahant that evening—and I think that on Tuesday or Wednesday Morton Prince,[31] whom I like so, dined. But *those* facts are already dim.

27 July 1911 Thursday
Nahant.
Milton Bray's motor brought me up to Irving St. for more things to do there— and Burgess being with me I stopped over the night. Dined that evening (Thursday 27) with Grace Norton and Richard N[orton][32] the latter very interesting and able. Dear Grace I probably then saw for the last time! Went to Roberts for last visitation of teeth this Friday a.m. Returned to Nahant by train.

29 July 1911 Saturday
Today Mrs. Bell[33] came to luncheon with her niece Mrs. Burr and the latter's husband. *This* I commemorate—for the sake of Helen B's memory and the last vision of her.

30 July 1911 Sunday
Took leave of dear G.A.J.—motored away at 10 a.m. with Milton Bray, Burgess and my effects. Found Alice in Irving St. who had blessedly come down from Chocorua to be with me at the last; also Harry, out from town. Lunched, dined with Mrs. Gibbens, etc. Went into town for last things on Monday; and on this Tuesday noon drove into Boston and took train to New York—Harry joining us at station. Went to H[otel] Belmont; beautiful cool rooms. Went after dinner to see Mrs. Smalley—*abîme* that impression. Walter Berry called when I got home—10 o'clk. Then a.m. Wednesday motored early (7.30) to Cunard Dock. Harry's company to the last a blessing. A departure easy and beautiful on big and not crowded Mauretania. George Meyer—Sec. American Navy—offered me a place at his table etc.

30. See 19 August 1911.
31. Morton Prince (1854–1929), Vienna-trained American psychiatrist, early explorer of the unconscious and dissociation of personality.
32. See 27 December 1892.
33. Helen Olcott Bell (1835–1918), daughter of Rufus Choate.

August to December 1911

HJ's first reaction on his return to England was one of delight at being restored to Lamb House. He wrote lyrical letters about its rural charm and the beauty of his garden after his overcrowded and "very difficult year" in the United States. An unusual heat wave sends him off to Scotland to the grouse-moor of the New York lawyer, John Cadwalader, at Millden which he rents annually for shooting from Lord Dalhousie during August and September. Cadwalader, "a gallant, unblemished, really *original* gentleman and friend," is a cousin of Mary Cadwalader Jones, who runs the place for him. HJ was never a sportsman, but he finds the moors therapeutic for long walks.

On his return to Rye, and faced with the approach of the rugged coastal winter, HJ recognizes that his old depression is closing in on him. He is happiest, he tells Fanny Prothero, "in dear old London and its ways and works, its walks and conversation." He speaks of "the solitude, confinement and immobilization" of Rye—the dead silence of Lamb House where he is thrown during "hibernation" wholly on himself "with nothing to do and nowhere to go, in the darkening and the muddying." All that was available to him for his walking was a stroll, often in inclement weather, to the end of the High Street, or the little further stretch of its pavement.

These thoughts led him to attempt a reorganization of his life in London where he lived in his room at the Reform Club, the traditional male club of the time, which did not permit him to have his female typist in his room for his work. Discussing the matter with Miss Bosanquet ("I haven't a seat and a temple for the Remington and its priestess") she tells him there are two vacant rooms, with a separate entrance, in the back of her flat at 10 Lawrence Street, Chelsea. They have a fireplace and a bath—a ten-minute taxi ride from the Reform.

With the help of his typist, HJ put in minimal furnishing and all necessary comfort and found the rooms quite large enough for his pacing as he dictated. He set to work eagerly on the first part of his autobiography, which would become *A Small Boy and Others.*

The death of King Edward VII in 1910 had resulted in cancellation of the Duke of York's Repertory for which HJ had written his play *The Outcry.* HJ converted the play into a novel, and it attracted sufficient interest to run into five editions. But he now, with the resolution of his London working arrangements, faced a new problem. He remembered how in the days when he lived in De Vere Gardens, his servants used to take to drink during his long absences on the Continent. What was he to do with his perhaps less bibulous but nevertheless idle servants confined to Lamb House during his winter absence? For the moment he had found a solution. When his nephew Billy became engaged to the daughter of the head of a Pullman car company, Alice Runnells, a gracious and charming woman, HJ threw out the idea that they might have Lamb House for a prolonged honeymoon in England. They would be servanted and could enjoy the conveniences of the house and also find entrée into his own London world. The couple accepted with delight and stayed for a great part of 1912. This gave HJ time to instigate a search for a flat large enough for his elderly needs in London, which would provide enough room during winter for his servants.

Otherwise 1911 provided HJ, once he had resumed his English life, with his usual encounters, dinners, and theater-going with his confirmed friends—Persse, Walpole and the new young man from Eton and Cambridge, Percy Lubbock; he renews his friendship with Edward Warren (1856–1937), the architect, and his wife Margaret, née Morrell, whose daughter Dorothy is his godchild; he meets Gertrude Kingston, the actress who produced his one-act play *The Saloon* while he was traveling, and tries to induce her to take his old play *The Other House* (see *Letters* IV, 586); he meets again Sir Hugh Bell and Lady Florence Bell whom he saw frequently during his earlier theater years, and he becomes friends with the aesthetic Claude Phillips (1846–1924), Keeper of the Wallace Collection and an art critic. We come on other names: A. C. Bradley (1851–1935), the Shakespeare scholar; the Hon. John Collier (1850–1934), also an art critic, and a painter, who had married a Huxley; the prolific essayist Frederic Harrison (1831–1923); J. B. Warner, the lawyer of his sister Alice; and Mrs. Frederic Myers and her husband (1843–1901), old friends of William's, involved in the Society for Psychical Research. He also sees something of Lady Astor; the French society painter Jacques-Émile Blanche (1861–1942); Prince Arthur, Duke of Connaught, the third son of Queen Victoria; the sculptress Clare Frewen Sheridan. There were also other connections, such as the former American beauty who had made an international marriage of the kind HJ celebrated in his fiction: his compatriot, Adela Grant, of Boston, wife of the seventh Earl of Essex and a friend of the American Lady Randolph Churchill. Also George Nathaniel, Lord Curzon (later Earl, and Marquess, 1859–1925), whose wife, the former Mary Leiter of Chicago, had died in 1906; HJ had met her as early as 1891 before she became Curzon's vice-regal consort. He served as Viceroy of India (1899–1905).

7 August 1911 Monday
Mauretania reached Fishguard late in the evening. I went on to Liverpool—and waked to the still ship in the summer dawn.

8 August 1911 Tuesday
Disembarked Liverpool early—and in great heat—and came up to town by luncheon time. Great heat in London. Protheros met me at station.

9 August 1911 Wednesday
Came down to Rye by the 11. train. Hottest day of summer in England—96°.

12 August 1911 Saturday
Bailey Saunders came over from Eastbourne.

13 August 1911 Sunday
Long talk with B.S.—long, very long story *from* him—about his own sad affairs. Alas, alas!

14 August 1911 Monday
B.S. went this a.m.

19 August 1911 Saturday
Came to Hill Hall, the Charles Hunters—through the partial strike on the S. Eastern. Motored out to Hill in car hired 33 Wardour St.

4 September 1911 Monday
Came back from Hill, where I have been since the 19th Aug. Had motor-car from 33 Jermyn St.

5 September 1911 Tuesday
Moorfield Storey[34] lunched with me Prince's. Great heat.

7 September 1911 Thursday
J.B. Warner dined with me at Prince's and I took him to Little Theatre, Fanny's 1st Play (B. Shaw,) and afterwards round to see Granville B.

8 September 1911 Friday
Go to Overstrand 1.30. Arr: 4.25

9 September 1911 Saturday
Lunched with Lady Battersea.[35]
Motored over to Blickling—wonderful without; rather poor within. Phil B. took me in to see Lady Speyer.

10 September 1911 Sunday
Motored over to tea at Gunton—kind Charles Harboards etc.

11 September 1911 Monday
Fredk. Macmillan took Nadal[36] and me to see 3 strange old churches. Dined at the George Lewises.[37] Phil Burne Jones only.

12 September 1911 Tuesday
Came up from Overstrand with Fred. Macmillan—early—breakfasting in train as in September 1909.
Came down to Windsor (Queen's Acre) in time for tea. Edith Fairchild and W. Haynes-Smith alone with Howard. Hot day—all in minor key.
Edith Fairchild went to town for day. Howard and I alone together till dinner—such a ghostish day!

14 September 1911 Thursday
Came up from Windsor a.m. Go to Scotland p.m. Left Euston *8*, with Burgess. Arr. Millden to breakfast.

15 September 1911 Friday
John Cadwalader, kindest host; Mary C. and Beatrix, Tommy Hastingses[38] of

34. Moorfield Storey (1845–1929), an eminent lawyer and reformer, first president of the N.A.A.C.P.
35. Constance, daughter of Sir Anthony de Rothschild (1810–1876), in 1877 married Cyril Flower, Tory M. P., who became Lord Battersea in 1892.
36. Ehrman Syme Nadal, a Virginian attached to the American Legation in London from 1878 to 1884.
37. Sir George (1833–1911) and Lady Lewis—he an eminent solicitor—were old friends of HJ's.
38. American architect (1860–1929) with the firm of McKim, Mead, and White, wrote for *Harper's Monthly;* his wife was Helen R. Benedict of New York.

N.Y., Alex. Newbigging, Tony Navarro,[39] one Kindermann (badly lame, but so active gallant and touching;) Montague Erskine etc. Bad cold, taken from "change." Went for walk with deaf and droll Mrs. Hastings. The country again amirably, adorably, handsome.

18 September 1911 Monday
Hastingses left. My throat-condition etc. trying, but I get some encouraging hill-walks—by myself. Do all I can—and find I can do it. Can walk long, can scale moors—if I do it very deliberately, patiently and slowly.

20 September 1911 Wednesday
Today 20th joined the shooters at luncheon—Mary Cadwal. on pony, I on foot. Fair distance, great success; glorious weather.

21 September 1911 Thursday
Glorious day again. Joined shooters at Black Moss at luncheon *(2.)* Started at 11—grand walk over moors. Mary Cadwal. and Beatrix on ponies. I walked all there and back—7 miles of moor—good feat and proof of condition and resource.

Left Millden (by motor-car for Edzell) at 11.45. Reached Edinburgh, after tiresome waits, changes and crowds, by Forth Bridge, etc, at 5. Sent on Burgess by night train to town and home. Waiting and resting here at Caledonian Hotel till tomorrow.

25 September 1911 Monday
Came up from Edinburgh to 105 Pall Mall: leaving 12 (noon,) and arriving belatedly 9 p.m.

26 September 1911 Tuesday
Fine day, and active, in town; Came back to L.H. by the 4.25

6 October 1911 Friday
G.W. and F. Prothero, left. They had been here since I returned—been at Dial Cottage—I had seen them every afternoon.

7 October 1911 Saturday
Edmund Gosse 6.30

9 October 1911 Monday
Gosse went.

Situation here impossible to health and wellbeing. Light has broken—and I go tomorrow to town.

10 October 1911 Tuesday
Lucy C. after dinner and I came up by the 10 o'clk to Cannon St.

11 October 1911 Wednesday
[HJ here puts ten x's in red ink]
Hoppé Photographer, 59 Baker St. *11 to 1 o'clk.*

39. See 9 October 1899.

Rhoda Broughton 99 Cadogan Gdns. 5.
[9 red x's]
Improvement from conditions here immediate and unspeakable.
Light has so broken!
[9 red x's]

12 October 1911 Thursday
H. Walpole dined today and we went to Coliseum and saw Sarah B: "Procès Jeanne D'Arc." etc.

13 October 1911 Friday
Called on Rhoda Broughton 99. Cadogan Gardens.

14 October 1911 Saturday
Went Queen's Acre—4.30.

15 October 1911 Sunday
Queen's Acre—Percy Lubbock[40] here. Walk with him in Windsor Park, late afternoon.
Returned last night late from Windsor.
Went to see Marriott Watson at Harley St. Doctor's.

17 October 1911 Tuesday
Dined last night Mrs. Mason's.[41] (with S. Abbots)
Went today to see Mrs. Berensi (of Rome etc.) Buckland's Hotel.

18 October 1911 Wednesday
Dramatists' Club, Burlington Hotel, *1.15*.

20 October 1911 Friday
Write to H.G. Ticehurst, Warden Hotel; about typing.
Jocelyn Persse dined with me; we went to Lady Windermere's Fan; and Guy Darracott and Geoffrey Millar[42] supped with us afterwards at Prince's. Had called on Mrs. Du Maurier in afternoon—hence the 2 boys.
Came down to Lamb House by 4.25

22 October 1911 Sunday
Fords called from Wittersham and motored me over to tea and back. Called at 6 on Mrs. Vincent and found charming Mrs. Rollo. Great gale blowing. Today motored with Mrs. Ford (short,) who came back to tea.

24 October 1911 Tuesday
Mrs. Dew-Smith at The Steps; *4.30*

---

40. Percy Lubbock (1879–1966), British critic and biographer, editor of *The Letters of Henry James,* 2 vols. (1920).
41. Alice Mason (1838–1913), a friend of Lizzie Boott's and HJ's since the early 70s; after a brief marriage to Sen. Charles Sumner she resumed her maiden name. See *Letters* I, 327–29 and *Life* 146.
42. Guy Darracott Millar and Geoffrey Millar, grandsons of George Du Maurier; Guy was HJ's godson. See *Letters* IV, 83–84.

25 October 1911 Wednesday
Miss Betham Edwards, Villa Julia, Hastings, by the 4.16. Went there (to Villa Julia) this afternoon—the 3d time I've been these three or four years. Basta!

26 October 1911 Thursday
Mrs. Fredc. Harrison, Ladies' Athenaeum, Dover St. 5.
Return from Rye 12.55 up.

27 October 1911 Friday
Clare and Wilfred Sheridan, Mitchen Hall by the 4.12 from Waterloo to *Guildford.*

30 October 1911 Monday
Returned from Sheridans' noon. Lunched Athenaeum Bailey Saunders. Called on Mrs. Mason—staid an hour. Went to Gosse's after dinner.

31 October 1911 Tuesday
Miss Bosanquet 4.30
Dine A. Sutros ?7 Haymarket Theatre afterwards.

1 November 1911 Wednesday
Lunch Protheros 1.30
Dine John Collier's, North House, 69 Eton Avenue, 7.45.

2 November 1911 Thursday
Lunch Norris, 1.30
Called Mrs. Humphry Ward, 5.
Dine Edward Warrens

3 November 1911 Friday
Tea with Miss Kingston, 24. Vict. Square, 5.
Dine Mrs. Phipps, 8.

4 November 1911 Saturday
Go to Queen's Acre p.m.

6 November 1911 Monday
Call at 5 on Mrs. Van Rensselaer 23 Glebe Place.
Dined Ethel Sands-Jacques Blanches. Went to Covent Garden—to Russian Ballet

8 November 1911 Wednesday
Lady Ottoline M. (44 B. S.) 5[43]
Dine Athenaeum 7.30 (A.C.B.)[44]
Declined today invitation conveyed through A.C. Bradley, to become President of English Association for 1912.

---

43. Lady Ottoline Morrell and her husband, Phillip, M. P., lived at 44 Bedford Square.
44. Andrew Charles Bradley (1851–1935), eminent Shakespeare scholar.

9 November 1911 Thursday
Hugh Walpole (16 Hallam St.) 5.
J. Collins dine, 8.
Lunch H. Ward's—1.30. [D.C.] Lathburys, 23 S. Eaton Place 5.
Hugh Bells, 95 Sloane St. 8.15.

13 November 1911 Monday
Mrs. Hunter, 30 Old B. 8.15

14 November 1911 Tuesday
Dined Fredk. Macmillans, 22 Devonshire Place: 8.15.

15 November 1911 Wednesday
Götterdämmerung, H.W.

16 November 1911 Thursday
Went to Mrs. Hammersley's funeral at Hampstead.
Dined Mrs. Waldorf Astor's, 4 St. James's Square.
Prince Arthur, Lord Curzon, Lady Essex etc.

17 November 1911 Friday
Blanche: St. James's Club 1.30
Dined Lincoln's Inn Hall *6.45 for 7 sharp.*

18 November 1911 Saturday
Lady Jekyll 5.30[45]

19 November 1911 Sunday
Lady D. Nevill: 2[46]
Mrs. Gaskell 5. (14 L.S. St.)

21 November 1911 Tuesday
Lady Mond 5. (35 L.S.)

22 November 1911 Wednesday
Mrs. Macmillan 5.30
Dine Edw. Warren's, 8.

23 November 1911 Thursday
20 Hanover Square: Royal Soc. Lit. 2.45 p.m.
Dine Mrs. Rathbone, 39 Cadogan Gdns. 8.15

24 November 1911 Friday
Ethel Sands, 5 o'clk.

25 November 1911 Saturday
Go to Hill, p.m.

45. See *Letters* IV, 8.
46. Lady Dorothy Nevill (1826–1913), née Walpole (of the family of Sir Robert Walpole). The eccentric authoress Lady "Dolly" was a friend of Edmund Gosse and part of the Overstrand circle—"a Tory of the Tories."

26 November 1911 Sunday
Hill Hall: Helleu and daughter, Sargent, Percy Grainger,[47] etc.

27 November 1911 Monday
Returned from Hill noon.
Lady Jekyll 8.15

28 November 1911 Tuesday
Lady Ritchie 5.
Dined Mary Hunter

29 November 1911 Wednesday
Dine Countess V. Arnim,[48] St. James's Court, 8.15.

30 November 1911 Thursday
Mrs. Fred. Myers 5.15. 2 Rich Terrace
Mrs. McIlvaine[49] 8.15.

1 December 1911 Friday
Yates Thompsons[50] 8.15 19 Portman Sq.

2 December 1911 Saturday
Went 1.15 to Stanley Clarke's memorial service.[51]
Called on Rhoda B.
Went to Bariatinsky play and afterwards to supper with Jocelyn Persse etc.

3 December 1911 Sunday
Lunched Mrs. Pakenham.[52]
Called on Mrs. Rathbone 5.

4 December 1911 Monday
Called on Ethel Sands
Dined Literary Society

5 December 1911 Tuesday
Field 6.30

6 December 1911 Wednesday
Call Gertrude Abbey[53] 5
Dine Mrs. Grau (8) at 36 Grosvenor Road

---

47. Paul Helleu (1859–1927), French painter, and Grainger (1882–1961), Australian pianist and composer.
48. Elizabeth Mary Beauchamp, Gräfin von Arnim, later Countess Russell (d. 1941), author of the novel *Elizabeth and her German Garden* (1898).
49. Wife of Clarence W. McIlvaine of Harper's.
50. Thompson took over the *Pall Mall Gazette* from his father-in-law, George Murray Smith.
51. See 12 January 1887.
52. See 25 November 1881.
53. Née Mary Gertrude Mead, widow of painter Edwin Austin Abbey, who had died during the summer; see also 11 December 1904.

7 December 1911 Thursday
Dine Mrs. Wharton, Berkeley Hotel, 8.

8 December 1911 Friday
E. Gosse 1. Whitehall Gdns. 8.15

9 December 1911 Saturday
Went to Hill with Edith W—motoring there.

11 December 1911 Monday
Motored back from Hill.
Dined Edith Wharton 7.
Went to *Kismet*[54]

12 December 1911 Tuesday
Dined with Robert Norton[55] and Edith W.
Lily Norton 5

13 December 1911 Wednesday
Dine Alf. Lytteltons 16 Gt. College St. 8.15

14 December 1911 Thursday
Hugh Walpole dines with me 8.

15 December 1911 Friday
Lunch Mrs. Murray Smith 1.45
Go to Queen's Acre

16 December 1911 Saturday
Dine Ethel Sands 8.

18 December 1911 Monday
Went to Lady Margaret Levitt's 10.30.

19 December 1911 Tuesday
Allen—9.

20 December 1911 Wednesday
Lady Charles Beresford 8.15 (1 Gt. Cumberland Place.)
Elizabeth Robins 10.30, St. James's Court.

21 December 1911 Thursday
Called Rhoda Broughton 4.
Dine Mrs. Rathbone 8.15

22 December 1911 Friday
Benedicts: 5
Dine Mme Ormond:[56] 94 Cheyne Walk W., at 8

23 December 1911 Saturday
Lucy Clifford 9. p.m.

54. A play derived from a novel by Constance Fletcher, who wrote under the pseudonym George Fleming. See *passim* headnotes.
55. Norton (b. 1868), formerly in the British Foreign Office; an amateur painter and close friend of Edith Wharton.
56. Violet, née Sargent (1870–1955), sister of John S., in 1891 married M. Francis Ormond.

Call Countess Arnim 5.
Clifford, 9.

24 December 1911 Sunday
Dine Gosse 7.45

25 December 1911 Monday
Dine Fredk Macmillans 8.

27 December 1911 Wednesday
Dine Claude Phillips, 8

29 December 1911 Friday
Went to Protheros 9 p.m.

30 December 1911 Saturday
Came down to Lamb House 1.30

1912

The diary notes for 1912 suggest that HJ had a happy and busy time during the first nine months; he then relapsed into illness, this time an attack of "shingles"— *herpes zoster*—a painful visitation that lingered into 1913. In the early months of the year we see him escorting his nephew and his new bride; their being in Lamb House is "a great joy and pacification" to him. They go to the Russian ballet, then in its first revelations of music, color, and fairy-tale, with Nijinsky and Diaghilev's other famous dancers. He takes the bridal pair to Hill Hall where they meet assorted members of Mary Hunter's salon. Billy James is busy looking at pictures, and the couple spend much time buying furniture for their future home in Boston. Their "Uncle Henry" goes on shopping rounds with them.

The dictation arrangement in Chelsea is maintained. The *Small Boy* volume is completed by the year's end. Word of a WJ séance reaches HJ and is pronounced "utterly empty and illiterate." And HJ sees much of his old friends in all this whirl—especially Lucy Clifford whose "great personal sweetness and frankness and niceness, and her heroic and arduous life, her admirable courage and labour and gaiety and independence through it all" HJ has admired for years. She is also, he adds, "thoroughly Londonized and convenient."

The suffragettes are by now militant, and HJ goes with some interest (with the Humphry Wards) to an anti-suffrage rally in Albert Hall. We note that he dines with Mary Cholmondeley, a firm, decisive lady novelist with an upturned nose, who like the Findlaters has her own public and her own special kind of success. Her novel *Red Pottage* (1899) had a wide readership. Percy Lubbock has left an interesting memoir of her (1928) showing her place in the James circle.

In the first week of May HJ reads his paper on Browning's "novel" in *The Ring and the Book*. He is at his old practice of rewriting other writers' works. The reading is a great success—it takes place before the Royal Society of Literature, which is celebrating the Browning centenary, and is enthusiastically reported in the press. HJ's tonal style and his felicity of phrase arouse high admiration.

The honeymooners leave in June for America. HJ is back summering in Rye and unhappy because Miss Bosanquet is on holiday and her substitute typist Lois Barker doesn't have Bosanquet's speed or accuracy. Edith Wharton descends with her motor and takes HJ off to Cliveden, later to be a center of reaction during the Chamberlain-Hitler era. He meets the Astors, reporting favorably on Nancy Langhorne (1881–1969), bride of the second Viscount Astor. In 1919 she will become the first woman Member of Parliament.

Now that his nephew is gone, he takes up seriously the question of a flat in London. Before the end of the year he finds a spacious one at 21 Carlyle Mansions, in Chelsea, its two large rooms—sitting and dining—looking over the river with a long view that Whistler once painted. He has two bedrooms, one for himself and the other for his work, as well as rooms for cook and parlormaid, and a small room for Burgess.

A mysteriously liberal offer from Scribner's for HJ's next novel boosts HJ's morale in the midst of his autumnal visitation of shingles. What he does not know is that Edith Wharton has diverted some of her royalties to him. (See *Letters* IV, Appendix II.)

The laconic diary for the remainder of 1912 reflects the intensity of HJ's uncomfortable illness. HJ has high hopes when an eminent medical man, Sir Henry Head F.R.S. (1861–1940), who has read *The Wings of the Dove* with admiration, visits him in November and prescribes a sedative to which HJ apparently proves allergic. He swears off doctors, but is soon calling them in again, even though he always feels he is himself observing and ministering to his bodily ills. During a spell in London, he poses for a drawing by Sargent, commissioned by Edith Wharton. The result dissatisfies everyone, including Sargent, and he does a second one, which today is in the Queen's collection of portraits of those who have received the Order of Merit.

It is interesting to note that HJ meets at the end of the year "an interesting Frenchman"—André Gide (1869–1951). Gide comes to a Christmas party at Edmund Gosse's which HJ attends. Of others mentioned in the diary for this year, Violet Hunt (1866–1942) was then involved in her affair with Ford Madox Hueffer (later Ford, 1873–1939); there are also the Irish historian Alice Stopford Green (1847–1929), wife of historian John Richard Green; Mary and Julian R. Sturgis (1848–1904), old friends of the novelist's—he was elder brother of Howard (see *Letters* III, 21); Edward Marsh (1872–1953), a friend of poets and painters and a highly esteemed civil servant; Florence Wolseley, the former Louisa Erskine, wife of Field Marshal Viscount Garnet Wolseley, an old friend of HJ's (see notebook entry 11 September 1900). Augusta Lady Gregory, mentioned here, figures also in the notebooks. HJ has a cordial friendship with his admirer Arthur Bingham Walkley (1855–1926), the drama critic of the London *Times,* who from the first discerned a relationship between the work of Proust and of HJ. HJ's brief allusion to Bernard Berenson (1865–1954) does not suggest a particular friendliness: he disapproved of him and his type of art criticism.

———❧———

1 January 1912 Monday
Went to Lady Maud Warrender's Christmas Tree, Leasam 4.30
(I came down to Lamb House on Saturday Dec. 30th, 6.30.)
Extraordinarily mild—warm—days.

2 January 1912 Tuesday
Lamb House

3 January 1912 Wednesday
Lamb House
Fords of Wittersham tea'd here.
Went round to Dacre Vincents' 9 p.m.

4 January 1912 Thursday
Lamb House
Skinner came to tea

5 January 1912 Friday
Lamb House
Arthur Bradley came to tea.

6 January 1912 Saturday
Allington 11.30. a.m. Went to Allington Castle, Maidstone, Lady Conway
and Agnes, coming over for me in their motor-car.

7 January 1912 Sunday
Allington 3 o'ck.
Motored with Lady Conway over to Rochester and saw Cathedral etc., mo-
tored on to Cobham (Ld. Darnley's,) but only round park; came back to tea.

8 January 1912 Monday
2 p.m. Manton Marble motored me back from Allington to Lamb House; in
an easy hour and ½.

13 January 1912 Saturday
Lamb House
Mrs. Alf. P. Lyttelton etc. lunched—*1.30*

14 January 1912 Sunday
Go up to town via Hastings 4.20 (Train leaves Hastings 5—arrs. Victoria
6.55.)

15 January 1912 Monday
Dined Mary Hunter for theatre—"Oedipus Rex" at Covent Garden (with John
Sargent and Holworth Williamson.)

16 January 1912 Tuesday
Dine with Hugh Hammersley 16a Sackville St. 8. Went afterwards with him
and 2 guests, to St. Mays's Hospital, Alms and the Wrights' Laboratory; and
then with him to *his* rooms, for a short time, in St. James's Square.

17 January 1912 Wednesday
Dine with:—Florence Pertz: 72 Prince's Square, Bayswater W., at 8 o'clk.

18 January 1912 Thursday
Called Rangers' Lodge 5.30
Went 74 Eton Terrace, 9

19 January 1912 Friday
Went to: Violet Hunt's South Lodge, Campden Hill 5.
Went after dinner to Mrs. Clifford's.

20 January 1912 Saturday
Write one of *these* days H.M. Walbrook[1]—*to come to tea.*

21 January 1912 Sunday
Send 2 weeks' B.W. to J.A.[2]

22 January 1912 Monday
Dine Arthur Hammersleys' 8. 56 Prince's Gate.

23 January 1912 Tuesday
Dine Mary Cholmondeley 8. 2 Leonard Place Kensington—between High St.
and top of Earl's Court Road.

24 January 1912 Wednesday
Sargent's, Tite St. 11
Dined Hesletines, 196 Queen's Gate. 7.30

25 January 1912 Thursday
Hugh Walpole 4.30

26 January 1912 Friday
[HJ crosses out "Violet Hunt's South Lodge"]

27 January 1912 Saturday
Mrs. Julian Sturgis's; go to Wancote, Compton, Guildford 4.30

28 January 1912 Sunday
Wancote Spent day in bed—arriving very bad with aggravation of cold of past
week.

29 January 1912 Monday
Motored up from Wancote kindness of Mary Sturgis's car, 11.30
Mrs. Green, Tea, 5 o'clock 36 Q.G.
Dine May Gaskell 14 Lower Seymour St. 8.15

30 January 1912 Tuesday
Met Bill and Alice at Paddington, 11.30 p.m.

1 February 1912 Thursday
Sit Sargent 11.
Bill and Alice present, and then Mrs. Hunter, who took us 3 to lunch with
her. Bill and Alice dined with me at Prince's, and went afterward to Olympia.

---

1. Drama critic for the *Pall Mall Gazette* who favorably reviewed HJ's *The Saloon.*
2. Back wages for Joan Anderson, HJ's cook.

2 February 1912 Friday
Tea at Garlant's with Bill—Alice resting
Dine John Baileys[3] 34, Queens Gate Gardens 8.15.

3 February 1912 Saturday
Ranee[4] *5.30*
Peter Harrison Dinner shifted to *8 today.*

4 February 1912 Sunday
Lunch Mrs. Pakenham 1.45
Called Lady Du Cane
Called on (and found) R.H. Benson[5]

5 February 1912 Monday
Called Mrs. Rollo. 5.

6 February 1912 Tuesday
Unwell—went to bed noon

7 February 1912 Wednesday
Lamb House Came down to Rye unwell—after several bad days—by the 4.25.
Went to bed on arrival

8 February 1912 Thursday
Lamb House
Spent day in bed—took medinal at night.

9 February 1912 Friday
Got up at noon.
Walked out with Bill and Alice.

15 February 1912 Thursday
Came up, very unwell, from L.H.—by 12.50 train, and heroically dined Mrs.
Humphry Ward 8.15

18 February 1912 Sunday
Lunch Lady Du Cane

24 February 1912 Saturday
Went (motored with Bill and Alice down to Hill Hall.) Address of W. and G.
driver who took me (with return Monday a.m.) for 50/:—P. A. Treacher *46
Caledonian Road* Telephone 800 Hammersmith.

26 February 1912 Monday
Motored back to town with B. and A., who went down to Rye.
Went at 5 to tea with Mrs. McIlvaine

3. John Baileys (1864–1931), British literary critic.
4. Margaret Brooke, Ranee of Sarawak; see 5 February 1892.
5. Mgr. Robert Hugh (1871–1914), son of Edward White Benson, Archbishop of Canterbury.

28 February 1912 Wednesday
Go to Anti-Female-Suffrage Meeting at Albert Hall in Humphry Ward's box.
Went back to supper with the Wards. 8.

29 February 1912 Thursday
Went to 2 Richmond Terrace.

1 March 1912 Friday
Hugh Walpole lunches 1.45
Go to tea with von Glehn's[6] 5

2 March 1912 Saturday
Go down to Rye 4.25

3 March 1912 Sunday
With Alice at Fuller Maitland's[7] tea

4 March 1912 Monday
Came up by 12.55 to Cannon St.

6 March 1912 Wednesday
Dine 8, O.B.S. for Artists' Ball.

7 March 1912 Thursday
Ballot Reform
Dined Gosse 8.

8 March 1912 Friday
Lunch with Jocelyn P. Conservative Club 1.45
Call for Hugh Walpole for Hampstead (Wells's etc.) 7.30.
Drove H.W. home 10.45

9 March 1912 Saturday
Sidney Colvin's[8] afternoon lecture.
(Went 9 o'clk.) to Empire Theatre with Jocelyn Persse and Mrs. Black

10 March 1912 Sunday
Sidney Waterlow lunches with me 1.45.
Call Mrs. Lecky, 5.

11 March 1912 Monday
Go to Florence Pertz's lecture.

13 March 1912 Wednesday
Sit to Sargent 11.
Lady Macmillan 5.
Mrs. Du Maurier 6
Dine Sutros: 31 Chester Terrace N.W. 7.45

---

6. Jane, née Emmet (a cousin of HJ), and her husband the painter Wilfred von Glehn.
7. J.A. Fuller-Maitland (1856–1936) English music critic, husband of novelist Ella Fuller Maitland.
8. See 21 December 1895 and 15 March 1912

14 March 1912 Thursday
Lunch—1.45—Dilke's[9]: *53*, S.G.
Dine Emily Sargent 8.

15 March 1912 Friday
Mrs. Saxton Noble 5
Colvin's 3d lecture on R.L.S.[10]
Dined Mrs. Green 8. 36 Grosvenor Road S.W.

17 March 1912 Sunday
Pakenhams 1.30
Lady Reay[11] 5.
Mrs. R.H. Benson 6.

18 March 1912 Monday
Clifford, 9 p.m.

20 March 1912 Wednesday
Mrs. Arnold, 4 Carlyle Sq. 5.
Lady Lovelace 8.15

24 March 1912 Sunday
Lunched R.H. Bensons

27 March 1912 Wednesday
Mrs. Ward 4.45

28 March 1912 Thursday
Ranee—tea—5

29 March 1912 Friday
Tea Ethel Sands 5.30
Howard Sturgis dines 7.30 (Play.)

31 March 1912 Sunday
Lunch with Lady Reay 1.30
Lady Bell—*tea*.

1 April 1912 Monday
Hugh Walpole dines 7.30 (Play—Milestones.)

6 April 1912 Saturday
Protheros 5

8 April 1912 Monday
Went Lucy Clifford's 9

9. Lucy Clifford's daughter Ethel had married into the Dilke family. S.G. probably is Sussex Gardens.
10. Robert Louis Stevenson.
11. Wife of Donald James Mackay, eleventh Baron Reay (1839–1921), Governor of Bombay from 1885 to 1890.

9 April 1912 Tuesday
Miss Darragh, 30a Sackville St. 4.30

11 April 1912 Thursday
Called Lady Lovelace 5—found her alone an hour.
Dine Mrs. Curtis, 8.

12 April 1912 Friday
To tea with F. Prothero; after which we had a little Bloomsbury walk.

13 April 1912 Saturday
Called on Colvins, British Museum.
Saw Lady C. only

16 April 1912 Tuesday
Mrs. Prothero 5.
Ralph Latimer[12] dines with me 7.30, and goes to Pinero's play.

17 April 1912 Wednesday
Dramatists' Club lunch 1.30.
Ethel Sands 5.15

18 April 1912 Thursday
Bill, up from L.H. for the day, lunched with me 2.
L. Clifford 5.
Went after lunch, and then again at 6, to Bariatinsky rehearsal[13] at Court Theatre.

19 April 1912 Friday
Went to Stores—beautiful warm day. Then to Alf. Parsons's,[14] Bedford Gardens to ask about Lily Millet[15] since the *Titanic* horror. She is there—but couldn't see me. Met Violet Hunt and F.M. Hueffer and went home with them for $\frac{1}{2}$ an hour.

20 April 1912 Saturday
Went down to Rye 4.25 p.m.

23 April 1912 Tuesday
Came up from Lamb House by 4.16 to Victoria after 2 beautiful days with Bill and Alice; also with the Protheros, who are at Dial Cottage.

25 April 1912 Thursday
Went in afternoon to Court Theatre—Prss. Bariatinsky's *Thérèse Raquin*. Took Miss Bosanquet and we lunched 1st in Sloane Square.

---

12. Friend of Jessie Allen's and Mrs. Daniel Curtis's.
13. Dramatization of Zola's novel *Thérèse Raquin* (1867); see 25 April and 2 May 1912.
14. Alfred William Parsons (1847–1920), landscape gardener and artist.
15. Her husband, HJ's old friend Francis D. Millet (see 15 October 1894), had just gone down with the *Titanic*.

26 April 1912 Friday
Eddie Marsh, Brooks's 1.45. (Telephone 165 Treasury.) Hugh Walpole. 5.

28 April 1912 Sunday
Went at 5 to say good-bye, at 99 Cadogan Gardens to Rhoda Broughton, whom I have seen often this winter and who departs tomorrow.

30 April 1912 Tuesday
Bill and Alice come up to Garlant's today, dine with me (I calling for them at 7.40) and go to see Russian Dancers at Palace.

2 May 1912 Thursday
Hugh Walpole lunches.
H.W., Bill and Alice at the Italian place Sloane Square. We then went to Thérèse Raquin at Court 7.
Dine with B. and A. at Dieudonnés and went to Tivoli with them—Harry Lauder.[16]

3 May 1912 Friday
B. and A. lunched with me in Sloane Square, and I went with them most of the afternoon to see furniture etc.
Dined alone at club—they otherwise engaged.

4 May 1912 Saturday
Went with B. and A. to London Museum at Kensington Palace.
Alfred Parsons lunched with me 2.
Went in afternoon to see Mrs. Mason (an hour with her) after seeing B. and A. off to Rye at 4.25

6 May 1912 Monday
Helen Lascelles 17 Queen's Gate Place 5.
Dine Literary Society 8.

7 May 1912 Tuesday
Deliver Address Browning Centenary Caxton Hall 3.
Jack Pollock dines with me 8.

8 May 1912 Wednesday
Roland Prothero's 3 Cheyne Walk 1.30
F. Prothero 5.
Dine Charles Boyd[17] St. James's Club. 8.15

9 May 1912 Thursday
Miss Lawrences 5.30
Dine Lady Playfair 72 S.A. St. 8.

16. Harry MacLennan Lauder (1870–1950), popular Scottish singer and entertainer.
17. British journalist with W. E. Henley's *National Observer* and later political secretary to Cecil Rhodes.

10 May 1912 Friday
Dine with Jocelyn Persse 4 Park Place and Theatre.[18]

11 May 1912 Saturday
H.M. Walbrook to tea 5.30
Went to Lucy Clifford's, 9.

12 May 1912 Sunday
Lily and Margaret Norton, 4.
Call Lady Lewis, 5.30

14 May 1912 Tuesday
F. Prothero 5.30
Jack Carter dined with me. 8 o'clk.

15 May 1912 Wednesday
Tea with Miss Sinclair[19] Albemarle Club, 37 Dover St. 4.30
Dine John Cross[20] (8) Queen Anne's Mansions S.W.

16 May 1912 Thursday
Lady Ottoline M., 5.30.

17 May 1912 Friday
Call E. Warrens 6.
Dine St. John Mildmays 8.15 31 Gloucester St. Warwick Sq.

19 May 1912 Sunday
Mrs. Pakenham 1.30
Lady Lewis 5.
Dined Lady Ottoline 8.

20 May 1912 Monday
E. Bigelow.[21] Garlant's 5.

21 May 1912 Tuesday
Lady Charnwood 108 Eton Square. 5.
Filson Young[22] dines with me 8 o'clk. His Address: 53 Upper Brook St. W.

22 May 1912 Wednesday
Lady Macmillan 5.

23 May 1912 Thursday
Dine Edw. Warrens 8.

18. They saw Sowerby's *Rutherford and Company;* see *Letters* IV, 619.
19. May Sinclair (1865–1946), British novelist.
20. John Walter Cross (1840–1920), husband and biographer of George Eliot.
21. See Lubbock II, 288–90.
22. A man of letters, Young (1876–1938) had reported very favorably in the *Pall Mall Gazette* on HJ's Browning Centenary paper.

24 May 1912 Friday
Tea 4 Prince's Gate (Frances Wolseley.)[23]
Dined Garlant's with Bill and Alice, who came up this p.m.

25 May 1912 Saturday
Motor B. and A. down to Hill [Hall], Epping Forest.

26 May 1912 Sunday
Hill.
Walk alone. 5.45—7.30

27 May 1912 Monday
Hill
Same walk with Wilfred von Glehn

28 May 1912 Tuesday
Motored home

1 June 1912 Saturday
Lucy Clifford 5. (Phelps of Yale.)[24]
We went (after my dining with her at her club) to Beerbohm Tree's[25] awful, unspeakable *Othello!*

2 June 1912 Sunday
Jocelyn Persse lunched with me.
Called on Mrs. Pakenham, 5
    "   " Mrs. Lawrence, 6.
W.E. Norris dines 8.

3 June 1912 Monday
Went to Robert Gregory's Show[26]
Called on Mary Clarke, Rangers' Lodge. Stayed an hour

4 June 1912 Tuesday
May Sinclair, Edwards Square Studios—5.
Dine Mrs. Hunter, Earl's Court. 8.15.

5 June 1912 Wednesday
Lunched Dramatists' Club.
Dr. Mackenzie 133 Harley St. 5.
Lady Gregory[27], 100 Cheyne Walk 6 o'clk
Roger Quilter[28] (dined) 7 Montague St. P.S. 8

23. Daughter of Viscount Wolseley; see 11 September 1900.
24. William Lyon Phelps (1864–1943).
25. Herbert Beerbohm Tree (1853–1917), popular British actor and theater manager.
26. Robert Gregory (1881–1918), only child of Lady Gregory, who designed sets for the Abbey Theatre; Major in the Royal Flying Corps, he was killed in action on the Italian front, January 1918.
27. Augusta Lady Gregory; see 23 January 1894.
28. Roger Quilter (1877–1953), English composer.

6 June 1912 Thursday
Royal Institute of Painters (Piccadilly.)
Pastel Society. (Mrs. Sutro 10–5.)
Macmillans 8.15.
Ethel Sands, Carfax 10 a.m.
6 p.m. Bill and Alice come up.

7 June 1912 Friday
Lunched with A.B. Walkley Dieudonnés 1. Found there (at Hotel) Henry Higginson, with whom I walked $\frac{1}{2}$ an hour.
10–6 British Museum (Prints and Drawings) Sidney Colvin
Dined with Wilfred and Jane v.G. in company with Bill and Alice and took them all to Irish Players—"Play Boy."[29]

8 June 1912 Saturday
Fredk. Pollocks. Luncheon, 2.
Wolseleys' Hampton Court to tea. Went, and stayed on to dinner.

9 June 1912 Sunday
Went with Bill to see (tea with) Lord and Lady Courtney.
Then alone to Mrs. Roland Prothero.
Dine Mrs. Lawrence 8.15

10 June 1912 Monday
Harrison Rhodes lunches (1.45) Reform.
Palgraves[30] and Carlo Gaskell,[31] 2 Carlyle Square. 5.
Went late (7) to see B. and A. briefly at Garlant's

11 June 1912 Tuesday
Called for B. and A., Garlant's 4.30—went with them to tea at Mme Ormond's
Alice suddenly ill—went with Bill at 10 o'clk. to Almroth Wrights Hospital for advice as to Doctor.

12 June 1912 Wednesday
Pinker 3.45
Mrs. Du Maurier 5
Hugh Walpole lunches, Sloane Square 1.45
Dine Yates Thompson's 8.15 19 Portman Square W.

13 June 1912 Thursday
Alice ill since Tuesday—all engagements for them stopped.
Dined Phil B.J. 8

14 June 1912 Friday
Write M.C.J. at Symonds's she being due tomorrow.
Dine Filson Young, 8. (?) 53 Upper Brook St. W.

29. *The Playboy of the Western World*, 1907 comedy by John Millington Synge (1871–1909).
30. See 23 May 1901.
31. Charles Milnes Gaskell; see 25 November 1881.

15 June 1912 Saturday
Saw M.C.J. for an hour at Symonds's after dinner.

16 June 1912 Sunday
Spent hour with Alice (much better) and Bill.
Went for walk in Park and Kensington Gdns. with M.C.J. and thence with her to tea with Lucy Clifford.

17 June 1912 Monday
Lunched at 47 Prince's Gate, 1.30, with the Charles Milnes Gaskells
Called on Jessie Allen. 5.
Saw Alice (still better) and Bill, before dinner.—Went 10.30 to small and very charming musical party at Lady Agnew's

18 June 1912 Tuesday
Went to Kensington Palace with M.C.J. in afternoon; and then with her to tea with Mrs. Wilton Phipps.
An hour with B. and A. before dinner

19 June 1912 Wednesday
Ralph Barton Perry[32] lunches. 1.45

21 June 1912 Friday
Lunch with Mrs. Murray Smith. 1.30.

22 June 1912 Saturday
Osterley[33]

25 June 1912 Tuesday
Go to Oxford[33a]—to stay with Presdt. of Magdalen

26 June 1912 Wednesday
Mrs. Lamb, 8 Bevington Road. 4.15 p.m.
Dine Christ Church 7.30

27 June 1912 Thursday
Lunch with Somerset Beaumont,[34] Brown's Hotel 1.30.
Dine Miss Tuckerman, Curzon Hotel 8.15

29 June 1912 Saturday
For Car:—H. Westley 24 Broughton Road, West Ealing W.
Go to Hill till Monday

1 July 1912 Monday
Return from Hill
Go to see Ranee (12 B. Hyde Park Mansions) 5.15.
"Coriolanus" (A. Bradley) Burlington House: 8.45 (Took Lucy Clifford)

32. Ralph Barton Perry (1876–1957), professor of philosophy at Harvard.
33. Osterley Park, Osterley, Middlesex, home of Lord and Lady Jersey, "original" of the country house in "The Lesson of the Master" and in the play *Summersoft* (later the short story "Covering End").
33a. To receive an honorary degree.
34. Somerset Beaumont, brother-in-law of Stopford Brooke (see 18 February 1894), was tenant of HJ's De Vere Gardens flat after he moved to Lamb House.

2 July 1912 Tuesday
Lady Herbert, 1 Hill St. Knightsbridge. 5.30
Dine Rathbones 8.15, 39 Cadogan Gdns. S.W.

3 July 1912 Wednesday
Lunch with Countess Arnim 1.30.
Mrs. Arnold 4 C.S. at 5.
Dine Miss Mundella. 8.

4 July 1912 Thursday
Lunch Alice Mason: 1.30.
American Embassy 4–6.
Sir Edward Elgar's.[35] 5. 42 Netherhall Gdns. Hampstead.
Macmillans, Claridges, 10.30.

5 July 1912 Friday
Lunch Lady Carnarvon[36] 20 Hertford St. W. 1.30
Dine Lady Crewe 8.30.

6 July 1912 Saturday
At Holy Trinity Sloane St.
Rachel Phipps etc. 12.
Ockham—July 6th 4.40 from Waterloo.

8 July 1912 Monday
Return from Ockham—Lady Bell motoring me up early.
Mrs. Rochfort Maguire 1.30.
Dine Edward Warrens 8.
Jessie Allen 5.30

9 July 1912 Tuesday
Call for K.O. Rodgers. 1.15—for luncheon at Prince's.
Go to Howard Sturgis's to dine

10 July 1912 Wednesday
B. Berenson lunches with me—1.30
Dined Edmund Gosse's

11 July 1912 Thursday
Came down to Lamb House by morning train. Great and increasing heat.

12 July 1912 Friday
Great heat
Went round after dinner to Dacre Vincents' and sat on terrace (in garden) over cliffs. Archibald Marshalls.

13 July 1912 Saturday
Great heat: 88°, 89° etc.
Went over to T. Bailey Saunders and to Eastbourne by the 4.16 arriving about 6:15.

35. Elgar (1857–1934), British composer.
36. HJ had visited Lord and Lady Carnarvon at Highclere with its immense park in July 1886.

14 July 1912 Sunday
Eastbourne
Attack of gout in right foot—alleviated by aspirin, but keeping all the very hot day still, with my foot up, mostly reading Erskine Childers's very able and curious "Riddle of the Sands." [37]

15 July 1912 Monday
Foot better after renewed aspirin.
Came back from Eastbourne still lame, however, and in great heat, before luncheon.
It was tonight, not last Friday, that I limped round to the Vincents.

16 July 1912 Tuesday
Wrote at much length to dear Harry congratulating him on his admirable news of his appointment to the "business-managership" of the Rockefeller Institute in New York.
Miss Barker, new amanuensis, came and practised on Remington by herself in garden-room.

17 July 1912 Wednesday
Started work again, after long interruption, and under difficulties, with Miss Barker—who seems to be without everything, and especially any degree whatever of speed!
Marked pectoral benefit from slow and sustained walking.
Went up to Steps—then down with Mrs. Dew-Smith.

18 July 1912 Thursday
Worked in forenoon better.
Went out to Camber—walked considerably and favourably
Break of heat—turn of it to quite cold rain.

21 July 1912 Sunday
Edith Wharton arrived by her motor-car from Paris—to stay till Tuesday.

22 July 1912 Monday
Lovely day—motored (3.15 to 8.15) to Crowborough with E.W.

23 July 1912 Tuesday
Edith Wharton left 11 a.m.

25 July 1912 Thursday
Went up to town by the 12.50 train, arriving 3.15.
At 5.30 was called for at Reform by Edith W. and Walter Berry, who motored me out to Windsor, where I dined and slept at H. S.'s, the inexhaustibly patient and kind.

26 July 1912 Friday
Queen's Acre
Gave up the formidable push on to Wemmergill—.

37. Childers (1870–1922) in 1903 published this novel about a German plan to invade England.

Went after lunch into town—in E.W.'s car—with Walter B., who looks very ill and leaves for New York tomorrow.
Returned with Cook[38] to Qu'Acre.

27 July 1912 Saturday
Queen's Acre
Motored to Cliveden with E.W. after lunch; had tea there and promised Mrs. Waldorf to come back on Tuesday till Thursday.

28 July 1912 Sunday
Motored, with E.W., beautifully, in afternoon (lovely day) over to Newbury to see Lady St. Helier, but found her away and her house let. Had tea at Inn— and most wonderful and beautiful run back to Qu'Acre.

29 July 1912 Monday
Miss Barker's wage. (*Dane End, Ware* for telegrams.)
Motored, with E., Howard and Babe[39] over to tea with Ranee at Ascot. Vernon Lee[40] there, with whom I had a good deal of talk.

30 July 1912 Tuesday
Afternoon run to Cliveden. Three New Yorkers (*such* New Yorkers!) staying for night with Nancy A. Beautiful walk on the slopes down to and by river (6–8.) with E.W.

31 July 1912 Wednesday
Cliveden
Americans left—day wet—Spencer Lyttelton arrived.
Wrote long letter to Alice before luncheon etc.
Day better p.m. Walked with E. through grounds, over slopes and by river— into Taplow Woods.
Evening Arthur Ainger[40a], Mrs. John Astor and son Vincent.

1 August 1912 Thursday
Cliveden
Agreed to stay over today Thursday.
Stroll in a.m. with Lyttelton, Ainger, the latter leaving early.
Second stroll with E., but had pectoral attack after lunch—through too much hurry and tension on slopes and staircase.
Quiet till Dinner—but second attack on mounting to room 10.30.
Lord Curzon at dinner.

2 August 1912 Friday to 5 August 1912 Monday
Cliveden
Waldorf Astor arrived in evening after dinner from town and showed me old drawings of Cliveden etc.
Left today at 12, with E. much upset by attack.
Astors most kind.

38. Mrs. Wharton's chauffeur.
39. William Haynes-Smith, Sturgis's companion.
40. See 12 January 1887.
40a. Former tutor of Howard Sturgis's at Eton, then his lifelong friend.

Lunched quietly with Howard at Qu'acre, and then had admirable car and dear Cook lent me by Edith for most beautiful and merciful return, by myself, across country back to Rye, where I write up this. Admirable afternoon; admirable run through so lovely interesting land from about 2 to 6.30. Gave Cook 40/. Went straight to bed on arriving last night. Cook wonderfully returned to Qu'acre. Staid in bed late—till 5.30—yesterday and today. Very light feeding—at dinner-time in green room. Early bed again, but feeling return of need for movement. Read all both days—Autobiography of Sir Wm Butler, and Andrew Lang's Maid of France.

5 August 1912 Monday
Got up after breakfast in bed. Confirmed sense of return of need of movement after very accumulated immobility—this last so bad thing.
Weather blustering and cold.

7 August 1912 Wednesday
Worked again in forenoon, Miss Barker having returned from her absence since 24th

8 August 1912 Thursday
Edith W. arrived at 5 from town—or rather from Ashford and the Alfred Austin's,[41] with Gross[42] and Cook.

9 August 1912 Friday
Claude Phillips and Frank Schuster came in very shortly after luncheon, having motored over from Folkestone. We sat in Garden talking long and animatedly (very amusingly) and then the 2 men departed and shortly afterwards wonderful E. in her car, to go and sleep at Metropole at Folkestone and cross today Saturday from there to Boulogne (F. Schuster also crossing,) and then go on into Normandy to stay with the Jacques Blanches!

25 August 1912 Sunday
Walked slowly up to Point Hill to tea at 5, sat in Blomfield's Garden watching play on his so beautiful lawn-terrace court. Met there Clutton Brocks,[43] who walked down with me to this house and saw garden etc.

26 August 1912 Monday
The quantity of tempest and wet and cold all this month horrible and unprecedented; but have walked when I could—*always* to demonstration of immensely helpful effect. Visit from Skinner this p.m. 6.

28 August 1912 Wednesday
Went out in tram (4.10) to Golf Club and met Skinner by appointment—to walk slowly back with him to Rye.
Beautiful afternoon

41. Austin, Poet Laureate from 1896; see 16 March 1894.
42. Catherine Gross (1853–1933), Mrs. Wharton's housekeeper and companion.
43. Arthur Clutton-Brock (1868–1924), English literary and religious scholar.

29 August 1912 Thursday
Took Clutton Brocks out to tea at Golf Club but had little pectoral bout on leaving it for tram again; by reason of high wind, flurry, worry and, I believe, *strychnine,* prescribed these 3 days by Skinner.

31 August 1912 Saturday
Mrs. Alfred Lyttelton and May Gaskell arrived *à l'improviste* to tea—stayed an hour. Also—George and Fanny Prothero most blessedly arrived this p.m. and came in for hour of evening.

1 September 1912 Sunday
Fanny P. came at 3.15, and I went toward 4 out for slow and most beneficent stroll with her—till 5.30; beneficent by reason of fresh and vivid demonstration (a 1000 times renewed,) of direct *remedial* effect of circulation after blight—blight since the Camber bad turn.
Went to tea at Dial Cottage, where came Violet Markham and one *King,* young Canadian "statesman," whom I brought round to garden here etc.

11 September 1912 Wednesday
Went up to town 1 o'clk. Went at 9 p.m. to Mrs. Clifford.

12 September 1912 Thursday
To Dr. George Field (dentist) 10:30
To Mr. (Walter) Jessop at 12. (73 Harley St. W.) Went from Jessop to Curry and Caxton with prescription for 3 new pairs of glasses
Look at flat—21 Carlyle Mansions.

13 September 1912 Friday
Returned Rye 4.25

14 September 1912 Saturday
To tea at Wittersham with the Protheros, Violet Markham having kindly sent her car. Mrs. Arthur Strong there.

15 September 1912 Sunday
The foregoing entry belongs to today.

16 September 1912 Monday
From 11.30 a.m.—beautiful day's motor tour with Protheros and Violet Markham (in her car.) To Barfrestone (near Canterbury)—wonderful little old church. To Elham, to Lyminge (St. Ethelburga,) and to tea at Beechborough. Home 7.30.

17 September 1912 Tuesday
Miss Bosanquet began work from *yesterday.* Paid her 40/.
Motor run of 2 hours (Seddlescombe, Battle etc.) with Lady Mathew.

18 September 1912 Wednesday
Motored over to tea at Great Wigsill with Lady Edward Cecil—she having kindly sent her car.

19 September 1912 Thursday
Hugh Walpole came—6.30

20 September 1912 Friday
Lady Mathew took us in her car to tea with Mrs. Dew-Smith at her Bungalow.

21 September 1912 Saturday
Hugh Walpole left 4.16.

25 September 1912 Wednesday
The Bariatinskys and Jack Pollock lunched with me.

30 September 1912 Monday
Began to feel bad symptoms of corporeal neuralgia—violent and vicious new and discouraging visitation. Went to bed early and took aspirin, with plan of going to town to see Pinker and take flat if possible.[44]

1 October 1912 Tuesday
Bad night but better this a.m. and determined to come up to town, for urgency. Came up by 4.16 to Victoria. Went to Granville Barker's Winter's Tale—incredibly stupid and hideous.

2 October 1912 Wednesday
Fair night last night save for remainder of nightmare of play: and saw Pinker in a.m.; after which went to 21 Carlyle Mansions. Returned there at 4 again and saw Mrs. Constable.[45] Went after dinner to Voysey Inheritance,[46] but ill and came away.

3 October 1912 Thursday
105 Pall Mall. Very bad—horrible, excruciating night of pain; but better in the a.m.—after tea etc. brought by Kemp at 9. Went to City and saw company and got off home by 4.25. Very unwell—wretched journey

4 October 1912 Friday
Had wired Skinner last p.m. from Ashford and found him at 7. Possibility of *Shingles*—confirmed on going to bed by appearance of body, left side, of vivid red welts—sores—blisters. Unmistakeable shingles—and relief to know it. Wretched night.

13 October 1912 Sunday
Ends 2d week of damnable shingles. Skinner daily—mainly twice a day—and time practically all in bed. Mrs. Prothero most kind—but very miserable week.

14 October 1912 Monday
Begins 3d week of almost intolerable illness.

---

44. With beginning of illness HJ pencils in entries through 25 October 1912.
45. Then occupant of 21 Carlyle Mansions.
46. Play by Granville-Barker.

18 October 1912 Friday
Have been up more—dictating letters to Miss Bosanquet in a.m.—till 1.30.
The Protheros gone. Have signed lease of 21 Carlyle Mansions. Better, but
great pain very obstinate; very poor time.

19 October 1912 Saturday
Miss Bosanquet ill and absent
Called on her at Bradley's

20 October 1912 Sunday
Miss B. ill and absent. Went again in afternoon to ask.

21 October 1912 Monday
Begins 4th week of illness. Continuance of great local pain and bad nights.

25 October 1912 Friday
Miss Bosanquet left for 10 days.
                    [HJ resumes use of ink]

27 October 1912 Sunday
Difficult day. Mrs. Hunter motored over from Sandwich to lunch. The F.
Fords came to tea. Went to bed as soon as they had gone. Visit from Horace
Plunkett 6—whom I saw in my room.

28 October 1912 Monday
Slight sense of very vague amendment or faint turn of the tide.

29 October 1912 Tuesday
Slight continued subsidence of pain—but wretched after-effects of night medicine.

30 October 1912 Wednesday
Very bad day from night-drug.
Judge Mackarness (sitting here at County Court) called 5.30.

31 October 1912 Thursday
Very bad night, through stopping all anodyne, which had become impossible.
But I feel how right to stop—through having very poor day. Yet I went out to
Bank and High St. for a bit in a.m.

2 November 1912 Saturday
Great return of distress—extreme aggravation of pain.
Bad, bad night.

3 November 1912 Sunday
Poor, poor day of settled pain. But saw my old friend Kenneth Campbell from
Wittersham and his niece. (His London address is 23 Wimpole St.)

New Year's Eve, 1912
Dined at Edmund Gosse's with André Gide. Brought him away to his hotel.

1913

At the first of the year, HJ moved from Lamb House into 21 Carlyle Mansions, Chelsea (rent £42.7 quarterly, or about $800 annually). He is recovering from his shingles but still has bad days and is developing angina (he calls these "pectoral attacks") and edema in his lungs, which however is quickly brought under control. The pages of the diaries for the first half of the year are dotted with the names of HJ's doctors: Wheeler, Mackenzie, Stewart, Grove, and Des Voeux (who will be his last). The new apartment, with its river view, is a great success with HJ and his servants, Joan Anderson, the cook, Minnie Kidd, the maid, and Burgess Noakes, his valet. He completes *A Small Boy and Others,* published to splendid reviews in April. By this time he has started work on the sequel, *Notes of a Son and Brother.*

Much activity is going on among HJ's friends during the period of sparse diary entries as the novelist approaches his seventieth birthday—April 15th. A committee of English friends—Hugh Walpole, Edmund Gosse, Lucy Clifford, with Percy Lubbock as secretary—solicits modest contributions (maximum £5) for a suitable gift. HJ hears of the plan, tries to stop it, is reprimanded by Mrs. Clifford for being "cold, callous and ungracious." But he succeeds in stopping Edith Wharton's American plan to gather in a purse for the novelist ($500 per person is asked) which she hopes he will invest in a motor car—without thinking that this would require costly maintenance, including a chauffeur. The English endeavor proves acceptable: Sargent agrees to paint HJ's portrait but refuses to take money and gives the sum to a young sculptor, Derwent Wood, to do a bust of James. In addition, a residue of funds enables the committee to present a silver-gilt porringer and dish—a "golden bowl." HJ spends a frenetic morning with what Mrs. Clifford describes as "his staircase a sort of highway for messenger and telegraph boys carrying messages, wonderful flowers arriving, the telephone bells going like mad; his faithful servants standing on their heads, and a general effect of lunacy." She rescues HJ and take him to lunch at her club. The newspapers take generous editorial notice of HJ's life of achievement and dedication.

During May and June HJ sits to Sargent nine times in his Tite Street studio in Chelsea, with various friends present to keep up the conversation, among them Jocelyn Persse and Ruth Draper (1884–1956), the young American monologuist. Later a private view is held. HJ writes a letter of thanks to his more than 200 friends and puts into the list some of those who had been involved in the aborted Whartonian venture. He announces the portrait will go to the National Portrait Gallery and calls the famous rendering "truly a consummate portrait and living, breathing, thinking, *feeling* man." In his letters he seems gratified that the portrait is compared with Reynolds's Dr. Johnson.

For the rest we note that Amy Lowell is among the luncheon visitors to Lamb House, that HJ is busy with his honeymooning nephew, and in the summer Harry James, his oldest nephew, and niece Peggy, now a young woman (he has known her since her childhood), visit with him. *Notes of a Son and Brother* is completed that autumn. He has a new friend in the gifted critic and conversationalist Desmond MacCarthy (1877–1952) and meets during the year Georg Brandes (1842–1927), the eminent Danish critic.

1 January 1913 Wednesday
Put down Gide at Athenaeum.

2 January 1913 Thursday
Servants came up from Rye

3 January 1913 Friday
Entry of servants and effects from Lamb House to 21 Carlyle Mansions Cheyne Walk S.W.

4 January 1913 Saturday
Left, after luncheon, Garlant's Hotel with Burgess for Carlyle Mansions
Telephone to Christopher Wheeler.[1] 1st visit from him 8:30 p.m.

10 February 1913 Monday
Went 11.30 to see Dr. James Mackenzie, 133 Harley St.
Excellent Report.
Walked thence down to Reform Club and lunched.
Went to tea with Hugh Walpole (and Helen Lascelles.)
Returned here 7.

11 February 1913 Tuesday
Rose with bad pectoral pain—of new type. Couldn't work or eat. Stayed indoors. Wheeler came in evening. *Very* bad night.

12 February 1913 Wednesday
Very, very bad morning. Wheeler came back and gave me opium: slow to give relief. Wheeler returned to Meet Dr. Kenneth Stewart. Saw him and left

---

1. Homeopathic physician (1868–1949) active in Incorporated Stage Society.

me with him. Stewart very carefully examined me and diagnosed source of new pain.

13 *February 1913 Thursday*

Stewart returned yesterday p.m. Nurse (Harding) had meanwhile come; and I spent night sitting upright, or nearly, in bed, with pillows—to my great relief from pain. The pain practically went—but the opium helped. Stewart again today.

14 *February 1913 Friday*

Stewart found me better yesterday p.m.—and doesn't come again till Monday. Kidd at Rye with her demented mother and Nurse in her room—here. All that most worrying.[2]

17 *February 1913 Monday*

Stewart came.

20 *February 1913 Thursday*

Stewart came.

25 *February 1913 Tuesday*

Great little superfluity of Nurse left this afternoon.
Kidd returned.

28 *February 1913 Friday*

Went out—11.30—in Bath Chair.
Sidney Colvin in afternoon.
Wheeler in evening

1 *March 1913 Saturday*

Went out in Bath Chair. Many—too many—afternoon visitors all fortnight.

24 *March 1913 Monday*

Went to see Mrs. Perugini who told me very particular and interesting things about Charles Dickens her father.
Richard Norton was there at first.

5 *April 1913 Saturday*

Mrs. Ward's, Temple 4.30

15 *April 1913 Tuesday*

10 Downing St. 8.15 (???)[3]

17 *April 1913 Thursday*

Macmillans, 8: (???)

19 *April 1913 Tuesday*

Benedicts come at 3.

2. Mrs. Wharton secretly provided a nurse for Kidd's mother, and Kidd was free to continue her service in Carlyle Mansions.
3. HJ's 70th birthday; apparently invited to the Prime Minister's.

15 May 1913 Thursday
Dined Mrs. Lee Mathews,[4] Gordon Square, C. Wheeler coming to fetch me, and went afterward to Chiswick Theatre to see *Lolotte*—Bariatinsky.

18 May 1913 Sunday
Sit to Sargent Tite St. 11
Lunch Fredk Macmillan 1.30

19 May 1913 Monday
Lady Colvin 5.

22 May 1913 Thursday
Sit Sargent: 11
Lunch Gertrude Abbey 1.30
Mrs. Jopling Rowe.[5] 32 Dover St. 5 o'clk.

23 May 1913 Friday
Lady Bell, 6.
Christopher Wheeler comes 8.30

25 May 1913 Sunday
Sit Sargent 11
Lady Elgar 5 Severn House, Nether Hall Gardens, Hampstead.

27 May 1913 Tuesday
Mrs. Clifford at New Theatre 3.20.
Try on at Cook's[6]
Ruth Draper comes 9.30

28 May 1913 Wednesday
J. and W. V. Glehn. 148 New Bond St.
Mrs. McIlvaine 5.30

29 May 1913 Thursday
Sargent 11.
Mrs. Sutro: 3.30 (?)
[HJ had written "Ranee, 5 Hyde park Mansions 8" but crosses this out.]
C. Wheeler comes.

30 May 1913 Friday
Gosse's Lecture 5
[HJ erased the words "Queen's Acre p.m."]

1 June 1913 Sunday
Sit Sargent 11
To Queen's Acre, 3.30

---

4. Wife of Lee Matthews, closely connected with the theater.
5. Louise Jopling (Mrs. George Rowe), painter in London's art-bohemia. See her *Twenty Years of My Life* (1925)
6. Apparently HJ's tailor.

2 June 1913 Monday
C. Wheeler (??)

3 June 1913 Tuesday
Holt lunches 1.45.
Called on Mrs. Paul Draper 5.30
Hugh W. dines 8.

4 June 1913 Wednesday
Mrs. Sutro motored me to Hampton Court: from 3.15. Lovely day and impression.
Dine Ranee 5 Hyde Park Mansions W.

5 June 1913 Thursday
Sit Sargent *11*.
Mrs. McIlvaine 1.45
Called on Miss Hogarth
[HJ crosses out "Mrs. Rathbone 5.15"]

6 June 1913 Friday
Dine Mrs. Hunter 30 O.B. S. 8.15

7 June 1913 Saturday
[HJ crosses out "Mrs. Trower 9 Bryanston Square 5.15."]
Dick Norton The Grange. 5.

8 June 1913 Sunday
Sargent 11.

9 June 1913 Monday
Mrs. Rathbone 5.15

10 June 1913 Tuesday
Dine with Claude Phillips 8.
[HJ crosses out "Mrs. Lee Mathews for *Great* Adventure"]

11 June 1913 Wednesday
Tea Price Collier's 5.
57 Seymour St.

12 June 1913 Thursday
Mrs. Ward. 4.45 o'clk
Mrs. Van Rensselaer 6 (Tel. Kensington 3146)

13 June 1913 Friday
Sargent 11.
Helen Lascelles 5. 15 Queen's Gate Place,
Telephone: Western 4560

14 June 1913 Saturday
74 Eaton Terrace 5.30[7]

7. Jessie Allen's.

15 June 1913 Sunday
Sit Sargent 11.
Lunch Christopher W's 1.40
Go to *Alvin*[8] afterwards if necessary. [HJ drew a box around that] or else Eric
Barrington
    " " Lady Lyttelton, Chelsea H.

16 June 1913 Monday
Dine Vicarina 7.45[9]

18 June 1913 Wednesday
Wm Richmonds: 3.30
Lady Colvin, 5
Dine Mrs. Green. 8.

19 June 1913 Thursday
H.E.E.Laughlin lunches. 1.45

20 June 1913 Friday
Mrs. Lee Mathews—play. (32 Gordon Square 7 o'clk. for Arnold Bennett
play.)[10]

21 June 1913 Saturday
Osterley, afternoon.
Dine Gosses, 8.

22 June 1913 Sunday
Langdon Warners *lunched.*
Went to Gertrude Abbey's 5. Kept till 7.30
Dined at Reform with Hagberg Wright

23 June 1913 Monday
Percy Lubbock after lunch
Dined Von Glehns 8.

24 June 1913 Tuesday
Sat to Sargent for last time.
French play—taking Jessie Allen.

25 June 1913 Wednesday
Lady Macmillan tea. 5
Mrs. Hunter 7.30 (Russian Ballet.)

26 June 1913 Thursday
Mrs. Woods, Temple Gardens, 5. [10a]

27 June 1913 Friday
Dined Mrs. Curtis 8

8. The photographer A. L. Coburn.
9. HJ returns to his old habit of feminizing and Italianizing certain English words, in this case "vicar."
He is apparently alluding to Fanny Kemble's daughter, the former Frances Butler, who married the
Honorable and Rev. James Leigh, later Dean of Hereford.
10. The Bennett play was *Milestones*.
10a. Margaret Louisa née Bradley (1856–1945), poet and novelist.

Lunch Jacomb Hoods 26 Tite St. S.W. One o'clk.
Hugh Walpole 5.
H. Gilchrist 27 Danvers St. 4

28 June 1913 Saturday
Lunch Emily Sargent 1.30
Alvin L[angdon] C[oburn], tea, 5.
Take Daguerreotype.

29 June 1913 Sunday
Mrs. Pakenham 5.
Dine club and go to 7 Chilworth St. 9

30 June 1913 Monday
Go at 4 to Derwent Wood's (?) with Sargent
To Williams about furniture 5
Jack Carters, 6 Great Cumberland Place.

1 July 1913 Tuesday
Mrs. Woods 5. (Temple.)

2 July 1913 Wednesday
Dined with E.W[harton] at Cavendish Hotel

3 July 1913 Thursday
Dined with Robert Norton (Argyll House) with E.W.

4 July 1913 Friday
Lunched with Robert Norton.
American Ambassador[11] Claridge's 4–6. Talked only with W.P. Cresson 2d
Sec. (of 71 Jermyn St.)

5 July 1913 Saturday
Beautiful (exceedingly) motor-run into Sussex with E.W. and R.N. to latter's
villa in Ashdown Forest; where we had tea. We lunched at East Grinsted, and
I returned with E[dith] alone—arriving 7 o'clk.

8 July 1913 Tuesday
Helen Lascelles's wedding[12]
Francis Wharton lunched.
Went Russian Opera, Mrs. Hunter's Box.

9 July 1913 Wednesday
Sat Derwent Wood 11–1
Took O.W.H. to see portrait[13]
Dine E.W. 8.15
Hester Adlercron came to tea, 5.

11. Walter Hines Page (1855–1918).
12. She married Eric McLagan.
13. Justice Oliver Wendell Holmes.

10 July 1913 Thursday
Sit D.W. 11

11 July 1913 Friday
Sit D.W. 11
Servants leave for Rye.
Lunch Price Colliers' 57 Seymour St. 1.30
Dine Emily Sargent 8.

12 July 1913 Saturday
Sit D.W. 11
Lunch at Ed. Warrens's 1.15.
Go to Mrs. Prothero's 6

13 July 1913 Sunday
Sat Derwent W. 11–1.
Tea with Mrs. Rathbone
Dined Reform and L.C. after dinner

14 July 1913 Monday
Sat D.W. 11–1
Wilfred and Jane E. [von Glehn] came in.
Lunched Reform
74 Eaton Terrace 5.30–7
Dined Edward Warrens

15 July 1913 Tuesday
Sit D.W. 11
At 1. 75 Upper Berkeley St. Lunch with Mrs. Crawstay.
Hugh Walpole comes to tea: 5.
Took rooms for H[arry] and P[eggy James] at B. P. Hotel

16 July 1913 Wednesday
Harry and Peg arrived and I dined with them at Buck. palace Hotel.

17 July 1913 Thursday
Took Harry and Peg to Palace Theatre (Pavlowa), they dining with me 1st at Princes.

18 July 1913 Friday
Went to Pinker, noon; taken ill there, pectorally; came home in great pain, went to bed and fainted away. Burgess call-in Dr. Groves (?) of Oakley St. Had already sent for Des Voeux who sent in by 10 o'clk Nurse Blackboro. He had come at 5.

19 July 1913 Saturday
In bed—very wretched; D.V., but better. Better as day progressed
D.V. evening

20 July 1913 Sunday
D.V.

21 *July 1913 Monday*
D.V.
Harry lunched.
Nurse (Blackborow) left p.m.
Harry again and Peg. before dinner.
Mrs. Prothero also briefly.

22 *July 1913 Tuesday*
Lamb House
Last day at Carlyle Mansions for the present.
Harry has left for the Continent.
Des Voeux came noon—very reassuring and interesting
(*"Very* great powers of recuperation.")
At 4.25 I left town with Peggy, whom I had met at Charing Cross—Burgess
in attendance. Journey rather a strain but arrival propitious!

23 *July 1913 Wednesday*
Difficult night. Great nervousness, but better as day went on. Went out with
Peg to Delves's etc, before luncheon and afterwards, at 5, walked her for 2
hours most beneficently. Went to bed early after dinner, but with great encouragement.

24 *July 1913 Thursday*
At work again with Miss B[osanquet] from 11.15.
Walked "under the hill" with Peg after dinner.
Lamb House again dear and delightful and helpful to me.
Walk of 2 hours and ½—all most restorative.

25 *July 1913 Friday*
Slightly gouty foot.
Worked 2 hrs. and ½ before noon, and after luncheon (that is at 4.10) took
tram out to Camber with Peg; gave her tea at Golf Club and walked there for
some time. Beauty of the golf-links, wh. we had all to ourselves and of the
delicate exquisite grassy surface.

[The following undated entry appears at the end of the list of Addresses at the
back of the diary for 1913. It must be from July or August of that year. See
entry for 6 November 1913.]

FOR *NOTES OF A SON AND BROTHER*

Up to the point of my ceasing to quote from Father's letters (Babolain) [sic]
I have done about 360 pages; what I am at is *about* 600

Send next Vol. to:—Émile Boutroux [14]

[HJ then adds Boutroux's Paris address.]

2 *August 1913 Saturday*
Mary Cadwal came down from town (belatedly—6:30) with Murkell.

14. Boutroux (1845–1921), French philosopher.

3 August 1913 Sunday
Peg and I walked back from golf-club, after tea there, with M.C.J. Lovely afternoon.

4 August 1913 Monday
Took M.C.J., Peg and Mrs. Vincent drive to Lydd and Romney the New. Looked at the 2 fine old churches and had tea at Romney.

5 August 1913 Tuesday
M.C.J. left by the 9.25. Visit delightful, I think, all round.

8 August 1913 Friday
3.30. Motored—too briefly—Peg and I—with Lady Mathew, by appointment—Udimore, Seddlescombe etc., and came back with her to tea at the Steps, walking home thence.

10 August 1913
Went with Peg by 4 o'clk train out to Camber, and at "Golf View" picked up Lady Mathew's 2 little grandsons and took them to tea with us at Golf Club. Delightful little boys, Charles and James—great success. We restored them to Golf View, walking home by the Channel in most exquisite conditions of weather and beauty of all aspects. Home 8.

14 August 1913 Thursday
Harry blessedly arrived from Paris.

19 August 1913 Tuesday
Peg went up to town to go down to Stratford and stay with Howellses. Harry accompanied and saw her off from Paddington, coming back to dinner.

21 August 1913 Thursday
Harry took me beautiful motor-run over to Hythe etc., and back by Lyme. (2 other beautiful runs—on to Canterbury etc.—not noted at time.)

23 August 1913 Saturday
Peggy returned from Stratford and Howellses.

29 August 1913 Friday
Harry went up to town to sail tomorrow in the New York.

31 August 1913 Sunday
Howells and Mildred came down from town to luncheon and left, after early tea, again. Poor wet day. They sail for Boston on Tuesday. [HJ then crossed all this out. Then having done so he wrote underneath "The above *is* right."]

2 September 1913 Tuesday
Peggy went up to town to go on to visit to Wessons and Banwell Abbey Somerset.

7 September 1913 Sunday
Motored over to Hastings (with Fanny Prothero) to meet Peggy on return from visit to Banwell Abbey.

8 September 1913 Monday
Cable from Harry from N.Y.

15 September 1913 Monday
Peggy went up to town for last things. Returned 6.30

17 September 1913 Wednesday
Desmond MacCarthy lunched—one of these days; and was at tea the day before.

18 September 1913 Thursday
Lady Maud Warrender lunched—unless it was the *previous* Thursday!

19 September 1913 Friday
Peggy went up to town to sail tomorrow—met by Mrs. Wesson etc. and spending
night with them at Savoy

20 September 1913 Saturday
Peggy sailed in Mauretania

21 September 1913 Sunday
Edith Wharton and Mrs. Bay Lodge arrived by motor from Folkestone (France
etc.) to luncheon, and went on to town after early tea.

23 September 1913 Tuesday
Sydney Waterlow came down 8 p.m. (Mrs. Wharton and Mrs. Lodge back to
tea, from town, and off again, to Folkestone and France before 4 and 6.30.)

25 September 1913 Thursday
Sydney Waterlow left a.m.

26 September 1913 Friday
Cable from Peggy of arrival at Quarantine N.Y.—3.30

27 September 1913 Saturday
Walked up to tea at Steps with Lady Mathew—F[anny] P[rothero] accompany-
ing.
Sydney Waterlow married today [15]

28 September 1913 Sunday
Francis Ford motored me over to Wittersham to tea; and kindly brought me
back.

29 September 1913 Monday
Lady Edward Cecil and Mrs. Maxse motored over to tea here. We had it in
garden.

1 October 1913 Wednesday
Visit—so unfortunate and superfluous from young Ehrmann of the wine mer-
chants. Ordered 2 doz. port.

15. He had divorced Alice Pollock and married a Miss Eckhardt.

Lady Mathew and Kathleen to tea here—with Protheros and Fords. Lady M leaves tomorrow.
Kidd went up to town a.m. and brought me back objects in Carlyle Mansions in p.m.

20 October 1913 Monday
Logan Smith[16] arrived 6 o'clk.

21 October 1913 Tuesday
Dismal wet day—remained in doors entirely. Much talk with Logan S.

22 October 1913 Wednesday
Logan Smith left this a.m.

27 October 1913 Monday
J.B. Pinker arrived 6.30 to dine and sleep

28 October 1913 Tuesday
Pinker left 9.25.
Miss Bosanquet returned to work after several weeks absence

31 October 1913 Friday
Mrs. Wharton and Percy Lubbock motored over from Folkestone to tea.
Edith du Cane and her brother Copley came afterwards.

6 November 1913 Thursday
Mrs. Alfred Lyttelton[17] at 3—quite extraordinarily interesting and touching.
The Elie Halévys to tea at 4.30.
At 6 o'clk. I took down and posted to the Macmillans complete copy of Notes of a Son and Brother.[18]

13 November 1913 Thursday
War and Peace II 301 [19]

15 November 1913 Saturday
Letter from Harry under date of Nov. 4th. Cabled him return of Brazil Letters.[20]

x x x x x x x x x x x
Walk with Tayleure in bright sharp afternoon

16 November 1913 Sunday
Francis Fords came to tea—from 4.

17 November 1913 Monday
F. Dunster: 4

16. Logan Pearsall Smith (1865–1946), noted for his aphorisms and ardent gossip.
17. The former Edith Sophy Balfour (1865–1948).
18. Published May 1914.
19. See *Letters* IV, 619, 681.
20. WJ's letters of 1865 from Brazil when he was a member of the Agassiz expedition, not included by HJ in his autobiography. They were published by Carleton Sprague Smith in "William James in Brazil" in *Four Studies,* Nashville: Vanderbilt University Press (1951), pp. 97–138.

18 November 1913 Tuesday
Posted long letter to Harry.
More letters—to bed very late indeed.

19 November 1913 Wednesday
Joan and Kidd left for town 1.6. I came away with Burgess by the 4.16 via
Hastings and reached Carlyle Mansions very tired (7.30) but with joy.

20 November 1913 Thursday
Went in afternoon to see Mrs. Prothero.

21 November 1913 Friday
Lunched with the George Maquays to meet Laura Wagnière.[21]
Very charming. Took her to 31 Tite St. to see my portrait afterwards.
Dined with Mme Ormond, her children and J.S.S[argent]. Great social day for
me.

22 November 1913 Saturday
Went to see Mrs. Phipps

23 November 1913 Sunday
Called Rhoda Broughton

24 November 1913 Monday
Visit from Wm Darwin and Lily Norton.

25 November 1913 Tuesday
Hugh Walpole came 4 o'clk for an hour.
Went at 8.45 to Georg Brandes's lecture on Shakespeare[22]

26 November 1913 Wednesday
Went out at 3.30 with Mrs. Sutro in motor-car—we looked for a bookcase for
me.

27 November 1913 Thursday
Called on Rhoda B.

28 November 1913 Friday
Mrs. Van Rensselaer 5.

29 November 1913 Saturday
Hugh Walpole lunches 1.45

30 November 1913 Sunday
Lady Butler, St. Petersburg Hotel. 5.

1 December 1913 Monday
Aline Harland lunches.

21. The former Laura Huntington had married into a Swiss banking family. Her mother, Ellen Greenough, had married into the Huntington family, which owned the Villa Castellani on Bellosguardo; it
figures in *Roderick Hudson* and *The Portrait of a Lady*. See her memoirs, *From Dawn to Dusk*,
privately printed in Switzerland.

2 December 1913 Tuesday
I lunch with E. Gosse at House of Lords.[23] 1.30
Mrs. Hunter dined, 8.

3 December 1913 Wednesday
Pinker lunches, 1.45
Dine Alfred Sutros Went with them to *The Wild Duck*

4 December 1913 Thursday
Mrs. Sutro's car 3.30
Dine Macmillans 8.15

5 December 1913 Friday
Saw H.W. at Reform about the Portrait view.
Went to Edward Warrens 5.30, and stayed on to dinner.
Took Dorothy [Warren] on return home to stage door of her theatre.
Returned 9.—
Lefanu came down 9.30.

6 December 1913 Saturday
Went to see Rhoda Broughton.
Then hour with Hagberg Wright at Reform Club.
Dismal day of rain.

7 December 1913 Sunday
Went at 5 to Richard and Lily Norton at the Grange

8 December 1913 Monday
Lunch Countess Arnim 1.30
Hugh W. calls for me at Reform at 3.15.
Call at Heinemann's.

9 December 1913 Tuesday
Lady Jekyll lunches 1.45

10 December 1913 Wednesday
Posted Scribners last p.m. Copy pp. 305–400 post them today:
To Hugh Walpole; tea, 5.

11 December 1913 Thursday
Dine Ranee. 8.15 Hyde Park Mansions

12 December 1913 Friday
Go to Mrs. Jordan Mott, 30 Gt. Cumberland Place: 6.

13 December 1913 Saturday
Ethel Sands lunches, 1.45

14 December 1913 Sunday
Called on Mrs. Rathbone [crosses out "Lady Bell 5.30"]

22. Gosse had been appointed librarian of the House of Lords in 1904.

15 December 1913 Monday
Richard Norton lunches 1.45 [''Hugh Walpole'' is crossed out and Norton's name is substituted]

16 December 1913 Tuesday
33 Tite St. a.m. and p.m.
Hugh Walpole lunches 1.45
Went 5.30 to Mrs. Jordan Mott's

17 December 1913 Wednesday
33 Tite St. a.m. and p.m. [crosses out ''Dick Norton lunches (?)'']

18 December 1913 Thursday
33 Tite St. a.m.
Agnes Conway lunches 1.45.
33 Tite St. 3–4.
Went 5.30 to Miss Cholmondeley

19 December 1913 Friday
Bailey Saunders lunches.
Mrs. Willie Arnold, 6.

20 December 1913 Saturday
Dine with R.H. Benson, alone, and went with him to the Alhambra.

21 December 1913 Sunday
Lunched at Reform Club alone
Went to see Mrs. Charles Lawrence
Wilfred and Jane von Glehn and Roger Quilter dined here, 8.

22 December 1913 Monday
Called on Mrs. Earle 5.30. (14 Sloane Gardens.)
(Markedly successful and encouraging walk there and back.)

23 December 1913 Tuesday
Called on Mrs. Winslow and Eleanor, Rutland Court (14.)

24 December 1913 Wednesday
Go to George Prothero, convalescent.—5.45

25 December 1913 Thursday
Dined with Emily Sargent

26 December 1913 Friday
Dorothy Warren lunches here, and I drove her home; after which I walked with great benefit for 2 hours exactly, and then went to 74 Eaton Terrace.

27 December 1913 Saturday
Called Rhoda Broughton

28 December 1913 Sunday
Called on Emily Sargent and Lady Du Cane.

29 December 1913 Monday
  Bruce Richmond's[24] 5.30

30 December 1913 Tuesday
  Called on Lady Gregory and Sir Hugh Louis
  Dined Edmund Gosses *en famille*

31 December 1913 Wednesday
  Richard Norton lunched.
  Called on May Sturges, 6

23. Bruce Richmond (1871–1964), editor of the *Times Literary Supplement.*

1914

The ominous year of the war dawns quietly enough for HJ. Life in his Carlyle Mansions apartment is orderly and organized. He has friendly neighbors in the building and dines regularly with John Singer Sargent's sister Emily, of whom he is fond. But the inroads of aging and disability continue. The entry for 2 February offers an example: HJ records a "momentous interview" with his dentist George Field. What was "momentous" was that Field decided his health might be improved by extracting all his much-dentisted teeth.

He is preoccupied early in the year with his two-installment article on "The Younger Generation" of novelists but he is no longer in touch with that generation; and he is unable to deal with the new D. H. Lawrence. Otherwise he writes of the older and middle-aged Conrad, whom he praises but with reservations that offend the Polish writer, and he makes public those reservations about H. G. Wells he had hitherto recorded in their private correspondence. He also attacks Arnold Bennett, pats Hugh Walpole on the back, praises Compton Mackenzie, and admires Edith Wharton. The articles are reprinted in his last volume of criticism of that year, as "The New Novel." The volume, *Notes on Novelists*, appears as the war breaks out.

Notes of a Son and Brother, like its predecessor, is published to high praise, and HJ sends a copy to Henry Adams. Adams's response is evidently along the line of "was that our life?" HJ answers "I still find my consciousness interesting—under *cultivation* of the interest . . . It's I suppose because I am that queer monster the artist, an obstinate finality, an inexhaustible sensibility" (*Letters* IV, 705–06).

As during the previous summer, his niece Peggy comes to England to visit; she brings an American friend, Margaret Payson, whom HJ finds the embodiment of all the negative qualities he had incorporated in his old tales about innocent and ignorant little American girls like Daisy Miller or Pandora Day. In one of his letters to America he speaks of Miss Payson's "curiously aggressive and assertive insignificance." But he makes her an honorary niece out of deference to Peggy, feeling that she is not a worthy companion for a daughter of William James. He has the same feelings for a school chum of his 23-year-old nephew, Aleck. But in spite of his strictures he introduces his young Americans into various social scenes while maintaining his own social life. The diary entries contain many familiar names.

The 1914 diary reaches its dramatic moment with HJ's exclamation on the eve of the war "Everything blackened over and for a time blighted by the hideous Public situation." There follows a three-month silence in the diary. Before HJ leaves Lamb House the echoes of the cataclysm reach his doorstep when refugees from Belgium shuffle wearily up West Street to HJ's studio in Watchbell Street which he had offered as a shelter.

Soon the younger members of HJ's acquaintance are in the service—Jocelyn Persse in the Royal Welsh Fusiliers, Desmond MacCarthy in the Red Cross as an ambulance driver. Hugh Walpole, rejected because of bad eyesight, leaves for the Russian front as a war correspondent. Emulating Walt Whitman (as he remarks) HJ starts visiting the wounded soldiers, particularly those from the Continent. In St. Bartholomew's Hospital he speaks French to some Belgians but they are Flemish and do not understand him. However he communicates with them in his own way. Ill and tormented he continues into 1915 with his war work.

1 January 1914 Thursday
Charles Boyd lunched
Christopher Wheeler came in evening.

2 January 1914 Friday
Distinct and most distressing, and all but *very* bad, attack of pectoral flatulence (pressing on heart), as result of long recent use of Purgen aperient. The cumulative effect if unmistakeable quite damnable. Kept the house all day. Just escaped really bad attack.

3 January 1914 Saturday
Again bad day in-doors, with strong evidence of the particular pectoral pressure being caused by after action of double dose (2 tablets) of Purgen aggravated by (proffered) remedy of Wheeler; which I most mistakenly took. But went to Mrs. Perugini in afternoon. (There were 3 or 4 others.)

4 January 1914 Sunday
For 1,2,3 and 4 see 1913[1]

5 January 1914 Monday
Bad day again, but worked, 2 hrs. a.m. as I had done Friday, Saturday and Sunday, and went out to Tailor's (trying on) and 2 or 3 small jobs; returning home to meet W. and J. von Glehn, coming to take leave before going to America. *Very* bad and marked wrong effect of Wheeler's homeopathy. Took Bromide—bad too.

---

1. Entries for 1–4 January appear under those dates in closing pages of 1913 diary.

6 January 1914 Tuesday
Went to see Rhoda *Broughton*. [Crosses out "Mrs. Sutro in car, 3"]

7 January 1914 Wednesday
Mrs. Sutro in car, 3.
Went to British Museum, to tea with Mrs. S.,[2] and then joined with her, Lucy Clifford (6 o'clk) at Marble Arch "Cinema".

8 January 1914 Thursday
To 74 Eaton Terrace to meet John Carters, 5. Very pleasant meeting after so long, with the J. C's. Walked from here to Eaton Terrace—and walked back to my great advantage. Mild soft p.m. J.C. really interesting.

9 January 1914 Friday
To theatre with Lucy Clifford (Savoy.) Dine with her at 32 Dover St. 7.

10 January 1914 Saturday
Laura Wagnière lunches 1.45 [Crosses out "H. Dunster lunches."] Took her afterwards to Bond St. picture exhibition and New Gallery Cinema.

11 January 1914 Sunday
H. Dunster lunches. 1.45
Dine Mrs. Gaskell, 8.15, 14 Lower Seymour St. W.—*Dined in company* of Lord Milner only.[3]

12 January 1914 Monday
Dined with Emily Sargent

13 January 1914 Tuesday
Guy Millar lunched, and his brother Gerald Arthur and May Coles came in afterwards.
Called on Rhoda Broughton. Walked home in great cold.

14 January 1914 Wednesday
Jocelyn Persse lunches 1.45.
Go to Maquays' 5.30
Gilliard L[apsley] dines, 8.

15 January 1914 Thursday
L. Meteyard lunches 1.45 Went with him to Sargent's Fulham Road Studio 3.30 [crosses out "(Or about.)"]
Went to American Embassy. Thursday Mrs. Page's "day."

16 January 1914 Friday
Went to see Lathburys and walked home from Albert Hall Mansions. Christopher Wheeler came in for hour after dinner.

2. Probably Mrs. Frances Sitwell (Lady Colvin). See *Life* 573.
3. Milner, first Viscount (1854–1925), former high commissioner for South Africa.

17 January 1914 Saturday
Send Week-End Cable Tavern Club "Forbear" Boston.
Called on Rhoda B.—walked considerably.

18 January 1914 Sunday
Lunch Maquays 1.30. 22 Nottingham Place.
Called on Mrs. McIlvaine and Mrs. Jacomb-Hood.

19 January 1914 Monday
Howard Sturgis lunches 1.45. (He is at 26 Chester Terrace, Regent's Park N.W.)
Called on Jessie Allen.

20 January 1914 Tuesday
Miss Heymman [Heynemann][4] comes with photog. of Sargent's Portrait at 3.
Drove Miss H. home, and then went to Maple's for a purchase, and afterwards to the Protheros.

21 January 1914 Wednesday
Mrs. Sutro calls in car 3.

22 January 1914 Thursday
Kenneth Campbell lunches 1:45.
Dine with Mrs. Sutro for theatre.

24 January 1914 Saturday
Called 74 Eaton Terrace and then went to Paul Harvey's, 5, by arrangement.

25 January 1914 Sunday
Lunch with Jack Carters 1:45
Tea with John Carters.
To Claude Phillips 10.30 H. Ainley read Enoch Arden to music.

26 January 1914 Monday
Claude Phillips dines, 8.

27 January 1914 Tuesday
With C. Wheeler to Poël's *Hamlet*.
Go to Edward Compton's, 1 Nevern Square, S.W. 5.30.

28 January 1914 Wednesday
Went to see Des Voeux at 1—for bad throat of these last days. Then lunched at Reform—talked ½ an hour with Robert Ross,[5] we lunched together. Also with Hagberg W[right]. Dined Emily Sargent 8.

---

4. Julie H. Heynemann, American painter studying with Sargent. The photograph of the 70th-birthday portrait, signed both by James and Sargent, was sent to the friends and admirers who contributed to the birthday fund.
5. Robert Baldwin Ross (1869–1918), art critic and Oscar Wilde's executor.

29 January 1914 Thursday
Miss Tomlinson lunches—1.45. Drove her to see my Portrait in Tite St., and then to her Queen's Gate house. Came home early and have sprayed and sprayed poor sad throat.
[Crosses out "With C. Wheeler to an afternoon Poel performance."]

30 January 1914 Friday
Tea with Pennells[6] 4.30 (3 Adelphi Terrace House.)
Dine Jocelyn P.

31 January 1914 Saturday
Sydney Waterlow came at 5—staid to near 7.
Findlaters lunch here—1.45
Dine Lady Courtney, 8.
Bad throat—stayed in all afternoon.
Met Mervyn O'Gorman at dinner.

1 February 1914 Sunday
Lunch Miss Maves 1.30
Dine 20 Bedford Sq. 8.
Bad throat; staid in all afternoon.

2 February 1914 Monday
Called on Fred. Macmillan.
Sent Edition to Jocelyn Persse
Cabled to Peggy about Flat here.
Went to see Dr. Geo. Field about my teeth p.m.—momentous interview

3 February 1914 Tuesday
Eliz. Robins lunches here 1.30
Go to Geo Field at 6.30
Christopher Wheeler comes 8.45.
[Crosses out "Dined Edward Warrens, 8."]

4 February 1914 Wednesday
Lunched with Lady Lewis 1.45. Went thence with Max Beerbohm to Savile Club for an hour, and then to George Prothero's

5 February 1914 Thursday
Called on Rhoda Broughton

6 February 1914 Friday
Tea Mrs. Colefax[7] 5. 85 Onslow Square S.W.
Mrs. Hunter comes to dinner, 8.

7 February 1914 Saturday
George Field 1.30
Cabled Peggy about flat.

---

6. Joseph Pennell (1857–1921), American illustrator, and his wife Elizabeth.
7. Sybil Halsey (d. 1950), wife since 1901 of Arthur Colefax (d. 1936), was a famous hostess in London.

Joined Mrs. Hunter in her box at *Parsifal* 5. Dined with her at Savoy (Mrs. Swinton and Colonel Hippesley then went back to opera for 1 hour.) [Crosses out "Mrs. Trower 5, tea. 9 Bryanston, Sq."]

8 February 1914 Sunday
Called on Emily Sargent
Erskine Childers came in.
Dine Mrs. Black's, 103 Sloane St. 8.

9 February 1914 Monday
Lunched with A.B. Walkley at Dieudonné's, 1.30. Met there Henry Bernstein[8]
Go to George Field for teeth, 4.

10 February 1914 Tuesday
Raffalovich[9] and friend lunch 1.45.
Called on Lathburys (*walked* thence most of the way home.)

11 February 1914 Wednesday
Went to see William Darwin and then to 74 Eaton Terrace
[Crosses out "Miss Heymman [Heynemann] with photographs at 3."]

12 February 1914 Thursday
Hugh Walpole lunches 1.45
Dine Rathbones 8.15.

13 February 1914 Friday
George Field at 4. and went back again at 7 for big extraction. Took less oxygen—with result of less sickness.

14 February 1914 Saturday
Hugh Bells 5.30

15 February 1914 Sunday
Basil de Selincourts lunch. 1.45
Called on Mrs. Pakenham; on Eric Barrington, whom I missed, and on Mrs. Phipps, with whom I found Lord George Hamilton[10] talking of Mr. Thornton. Interesting talk

16 February 1914 Monday
Walked with great advantage from Hereford Gardens to Athenaeum
George Field 2
Hugo Bell—
Vote at Athenaeum afternoon.
Alma Harrison 8.
Athenaeum after dentist's.
·Dine Harrisons' 8.

8. Henry Bernstein (1876–1953), popular French dramatist.
9. André Raffalovich (1864–1934), affluent cosmopolitan who wrote on homosexuality and edited the letters of Aubrey Beardsley, of which he had lately sent a copy to HJ.
10. George Francis Hamilton (1845–1927), former under-secretary for India.

17 February 1914 Tuesday
Tea with Hugh Walpole 5. Walked afterwards with great advantage from Hallam St. to Pall Mall.

18 February 1914 Wednesday
Vide next page but one.[11] Short visit after luncheon from Mrs. Reginald Blunt.

19 February 1914 Thursday
Pinker lunches 1:45. Go to George Field 5:30.
Called at 74 Eaton Terrace—after having been at A. and N. Stores;[12] where my balance today is £7.0.0.

20 February 1914 Friday
This entry belongs to 18th. Called on Rhoda Broughton 5; and walked back thence with Lady Ritchie to 9 St. Leonard's Terrace—after which I walked home by back streets.

21 February 1914 Saturday
George Field 2:30. Went to see Mrs. Du Maurier.
Dine Violet Ormond, 8.

22 February 1914 Sunday
Call Courtenays [Courtneys]. (the Courtenays absent[13]), I went to see Rhoda Broughton and walked home.

23 February 1914 Monday
Mrs. Colefax 8.15 (85 Onslow Square.)

24 February 1914 Tuesday
George Field 3.45
Met Mrs. Sutro and Lady Jekyll and went in former's car to tea with latter—remaining in conversation after Mrs. S's departure.

25 February 1914 Wednesday
Lucy Clifford lunches 1.45. Went with her afterwards to her dressmaker and to the "West End" Cinema.
[Crosses out "Call on Mrs. Cuyler at Grosvenor Crescent—5:30."]

26 February 1914 Thursday
[Crosses out "Lucy Clifford lunches 1.45."]

27 February 1914 Friday
Lady Jekyll calls for me in her car 3 o'clk. We went to Richmond Park.
Dined American Embassy 8.15
(6. G.S.)
[Crosses out "Hugh Walpole lunches 1.45."]

11. See entry below for 20 February 1914.
12. Army and Navy Stores.
13. The variously spelled Courtenays allude apparently to William Leonard Courtney (1850–1928). editor of the *Fortnightly Review* and a former theater critic for the *Daily Telegraph*.

28 February 1914 Saturday

Out at 12.20 and went to Bank and Reform Club for light food.
Then to George Field. 2 o'clk. He gave me relief to upper jaw, and I walked afterwards from there down to Athenaeum, where I had cup of tea at 4.45 and then drove to call on Mrs. Cuyler, 1 Grosvenor Crescent. I then walked from Belgrave Square back home—to my very great profit.

1 March 1914 Sunday

Dr. Munro Anderson lunches 1.45 Drove him home and then walked thence part of the way (from Hanover Square W.) and to Eric Barringtons, 5.15

2 March 1914 Monday

Hugh Walpole lunched, and I drove him afterward as far with me as to George Field's 4, where I got 2d machinery. Went afterwards to club for hour and walked partly home.

3 March 1914 Tuesday

[Crosses out "Hugh Walpole lunches 1.45"]

4 March 1914 Wednesday

Mrs. Earle 5.15.
Dine Jack Carters 8.30 3 Gt. C. Place.

5 March 1914 Thursday

Miss Mond—1.30.
Edward Warren lunches 1.45.
Drove E.P.W[arren] home; went for an hour to the Athenaeum; voted at the Reform Club ballot; and then went to see Rhoda B. Walked home from there— *very well.*

8 March 1914 Sunday

H. Dunster lunches 1.45
Young Mme André Michel[14] called.
Went at 4.45 to The Humphry Wards—and afterwards, about 6 to Rhoda Broughton, carrying Bernard Mallet to his house.

12 March 1914 Thursday

Send article[15] to Bruce *Richmond*.
George Field 3.30
Called on Mrs. Lathbury, 5.
Dined with Alfred Sutro's and went afterwards with her to his play.

13 March 1914 Friday

Notes of a Son and Brother *appears*.[16]
The Scott Cinematograph—Lucy Clifford comes. 3.

14. Rose Marie Ormond (b. 1893), niece of Sargent, married Robert André Michel. He would be killed in action on 13 October of this year and four years later his wife would die (29 March 1918) in a German bombardment of Paris.
15. "The Younger Generation" for the *Times Literary Supplement.*
16. The autobiography had come out on 7 March in New York.

14 March 1914 Saturday
George Field, 3.
74 Eaton Terrace, 6.
Dine Emily Sargent 8 o'clk.

15 March 1914 Sunday
Richard Norton lunches 1.45
Mrs. Bernard Mallet 5.
Dine Edmund Gosses' 8 o'clk.

16 March 1914 Monday
Ballot at Athenaeum 4.
Rhoda Broughton (with Mrs. Belloc-L.) [17] 4.15
Dressing and Food at Reform, and go to Anna Karénine afterwards. Went to supper, briefly afterwards, with J. Pollock and Princess [Bariatinsky].

17 March 1914 Tuesday
Ring up L.C[lifford] 8.30

18 March 1914 Wednesday
Logan Smith lunches 1.45
Go to tea with Mrs. W. Arnold (4 Carlyle Square) at 5.
[Crosses out "Arthur Benson at 2.—Hanover Square 5 o'clk."]

19 March 1914 Thursday
Hugh Walpole 1.45
Mrs. Eric Maclagan [McLagan] 5, 15 Queen's Gate Place.
[Crosses out "Article for Bruce Richmond appears."]

20 March 1914 Friday
Eddie Marsh 1.45.
[Crosses out "Dine Protheros 8.15"]

21 March 1914 Saturday
Percy Lubbock lunches 1.30
Mrs. Comyns Carr 5, 64 Ebury St.
J. Allen: 6.15
Lady Bryce came to see me 4, staid till 4.50

22 March 1914 Sunday
Mrs. Ford and Morton Stephenson come 3.15
Courtneys', 4.30–5.
Dine with Ch. Stuart Wortleys. 8.15 7 C.W.

23 March 1914 Monday
Went to Mrs. Colefaxe's 5.

24 March 1914 Tuesday
Went out, in town, on errands, in car with Gertrude Abbey.

17. Marie Belloc-Lowndes (1868–1947), sister of Hilaire Belloc and a novelist.

Went by taxi, at 9, up to young dance at Wells's—Hampstead. Back here by 11.

25 March 1914 Wednesday
Mrs. Sutro calls in car, 3.15. Went to Zoo, where we walked about a long time to my great benefit; then to tea at Mrs. S's.
Go to Protheros—6.

26 March 1914 Thursday
Mrs. de Selincourt lunches 1.45.
Go to see Anne Ritchie, 6.

27 March 1914 Friday
Called on Rhoda Broughton

28 March 1914 Saturday
Joined Lucy Clifford and Ethel D[ilke] in box at Vaudeville Theatre (3 o'ck.) for deplorably platitudinous performance—dramatization of Arnold Bennett; drove her home, and then came by appt. and had tea (5.30) with Emily Sargent.
Dined with Lady Lovelace 8.15

29 March 1914 Sunday
Lunch Owen Lankester. 5 Upper Wimpole St. 2
Went to John Collier's view of pictures. Came back—called on Lady Courtenay.

30 March 1914 Monday
Dorothy Warren lunches 1.45.

1 April 1914 Wednesday
Lady Macmillan 5
With Mervyn O'Gorman's ticket to R. United Service Institute—8.30

3 April 1914 Friday
Bad days: climax of the long effect of privation of exercise—a more intense demonstration of imperative need of sacrificing *everything* to this boon I couldn't possibly have had. Long resolute walk from Piccadilly Circus down to Westminster and thence all along the Embankment to the corner of Chelsea Barracks and Hospital Road. I was more than 3 hours—nearer 4—on foot—the length of the effort was the effective benefit—and this benefit was signal. I broke the hideous spell of settled *sickness,* which had become too cruel for words—and if I haven't now learned the lesson—! I worked in consequence well again yesterday (Friday) forenoon; but renewed my locomotion in due measure again in the afternoon. That is I called on Rhoda B., but walked both there and back—with better and better effect.

5 April 1914 Sunday
Lunch today (5th) with Jacomb-Hoods. Went to tea yesterday with George

and Janet Trevelyan.[18] Today lunched with Jacomb-Hoods; and went to tea with Lady Lyttelton at Chelsea Hospital.

6 April 1914 Monday
Went to tea at the Ladies Athenaeum, 32 Dover St., with Elizabeth Robins—long and interesting talk.

7 April 1914 Tuesday
Mrs. Humphry Ward lunched with me, 1.45.
Went to tea, 4.30, with Logan Smith and Mrs. Berenson,[19] then to welcome Wilfred and Jane Von Glehn back from America (6.15.) Roger Quilter there.

8 April 1914 Wednesday
H. Melville[20] lunches 1.45.
Mrs. Sutro came for me in car 3.15. Went with Mrs. S. out to the Burnham Beaches and had tea at Beaconsfield.

9 April 1914 Thursday
Margaret Warren lunched today—1.40, bringing with her Mlle. Saint-René Taillandier[21]
Called 5.30 at 74 Eaton Terrace.

10 April 1914 Friday
Charles Boyd lunched and staid to 3.45.
I called, 4.45, on Mrs. Pakenham, had tea with her, and walked from Hartford St. home—or nearly: through the Park, Prince's Gardens etc.

11 April 1914 Saturday
Peggy arrives either tonight or tomorrow a.m.
The G.W. Protheros lunch, 1.45.
Went to see Rhoda Broughton

12 April 1914 Sunday
Met Peggy and Margaret Payson at Euston 1.30, and went with them to Garlant's. Went afterwards out with P. and sat a little in St. James's Park. They both dined here.

13 April 1914 Monday
Went out with Peggy in afternoon, from Garlant's, and they both again dined here.

14 April 1914 Tuesday
Desmond Macarthy lunched.
Called on the Miss Lawrences and had tea with them; and then walked from 4 Prince's Gate home.
Peg and M.P. again dined here.

18. George Macaulay Trevelyan (1876–1962), Regius professor of modern history at Cambridge.
19. Logan Pearsall Smith's sister Mary, the former Mrs. Frank Costelloe, now married to Bernard Berenson.
20. Harry Melvill (1861–1936); see p. 284.
21. Margot née Morrell, wife of architect Edward P. Warren; Madeleine St. Renée Taillandier, sister of André Chevrillon. See notebook entry for 22 May 1892.

15 April 1914 Wednesday
Logan Smith lunched.
Peg and M.P. moved from Garlant's into Flat no. 3 in these Mansions and I met and welcomed them there, and afterwards called on Rhoda Broughton.

16 April 1914 Thursday
Dine Emily Sargent 8.

17 April 1914 Friday
Pinker lunches 1.45
Go to see J.M. Dent 4. (10 Bedford St., Covent Garden.)
Took Nieces to see Rhoda Broughton, 5.

18 April 1914 Saturday
Morton Prince lunches 1.45.
Lady Ottoline 5.

19 April 1914 Sunday
Tea Emily Sargent, with Nieces.

20 April 1914 Monday
Went to see Rhoda B. 5.

21 April 1914 Tuesday
Mrs. Sutro's car 2.30 Wonderful warm day—exquisitely vernal; foretaste of summer. Run out to Box Hill and up and over it; then down the more gradual and beautiful way, over the downs, to Epsom, where we had tea. A.B. Walkley with us.

22 April 1914 Wednesday
Went to Miss Cholmondeley's with Peg.
Bernard Shaw's play with Mrs. Sutro.

23 April 1914 Thursday
Lunch with Franco Thomas at 2. (2 Mulberry Walk,)
Call at 74 E.T. at 1.50. Drove J.A[llen] home after his luncheon, and then joined Peg at 4 Culford Mansions. Afterwards walked home with her, and further. [Crosses out "Gilliard lunches, 1:45."]

24 April 1914 Friday
Lunch Raffalovich Claridge's 1.45
Went with Peg to her dressmaker's—rather a long affair; then to bid Rhoda B. goodbye; after which I walked home with Peg—and further awhile by myself.

25 April 1914 Saturday
Bad day, but went out in afternoon and walked along Embankment to Westminster. Went to bed on return

26 April 1914 Sunday
In bed all day, but kind visit from Mrs. Hunter in afternoon.

27 April 1914 Monday
Emerged into light again after much mystification; as I always *do,* I hold,
thank the powers, emerge.
Went to the Meteyards picture-view after luncheon—and did a good deal of
walking home.
[Crosses out "Ranee lunches 1.45."]

28 April 1914 Tuesday
Still better today—with more confirmatory light. Had to go to Bankers,
Stores etc, and then Tea at Athenaeum, with Bailey Saunders and Luke
Fildes.[22] After which I did again much walking home via Westminster.

29 April 1914 Wednesday
Ranee lunches, 1.45.
Dine Macmillans 8.15
Bad day—again—remained helpless and unwell; but pulled myself together
sufficiently for effort of dining at the M's, where I got better. Sat between
Lady Hare and Mrs. Barry Pain, and Mrs. Playfair motored me home.

30 April 1914 Thursday
Better today—worked well, and went in the afternoon to 74 Eaton Terrace.
Before that I had tea with Peggy and one or two others.

1 May 1914 Friday
Peggy and Margaret P. lunched with me at Prince's after their forenoon at
Academy Private view. Then we went to Mrs. Woods at Temple, 3:45 sharp.
She showed us church and Hall etc.—and we had tea with her afterwards.
Nieces came home in cab—I walked as much as the time before dinner al-
lowed.

2 May 1914 Saturday
Lunch Lady Courtenay[23] 1:30. Went to see Mrs. Perugini.

3 May 1914 Sunday
Miss Heynemann, 2:45. To Lucy Clifford to tea.

4 May 1914 Monday
Went out with Peg and M. P. and left cards at 1 or 2 houses, then took them
to call at 4 Prince's Gate, very successfully, whence I walked home with
them here—good long walk with 2 companions and conversing all the way:
marked measure of my improvement and benefit in that way. Dined with
them and young American painter seeing Sargent 1st at Emily's on the "outrage" to Portrait.[24]

5 May 1914 Tuesday
Mrs. MarKae lunches 1:45.
Mrs. Trevilian at York Hotel, Albemarle St. 5.

22. Sir Samuel Luke Fildes (1844–1927), painter.
23. This Courtney would probably be Kate (one of Beatrice Webb's sisters), wife of Leonard Courtney, first Baron, a journalist who became a professor.
24. A suffragette had damaged the HJ portrait using a meat-cleaver; Sargent was able to repair it.

6 May 1914 Wednesday
Gosse lunches 1:45. Mrs. Sutro's car—3:30.
Out with Nieces to St. Alban's where had tea, Mrs. S. kindly bringing us back here.

7 May 1914 Thursday
Took Peggy to Lawrence Binyon's show[25] at British Museum, and then came back and picked up Margaret P. and Jane V.G.
Dined Lady Ottoline 8.15
American Embassy with Nieces at 5. Took them to Embassy. The Prime Minister etc. were at dinner at the Morrells'.

8 May 1914 Friday
Wilfred and Jane lunch 1.45.
Called 5.30 at 74 Eaton Terrace—and was kept too long to be able to get more than scrap of walk home. Bad.

9 May 1914 Saturday
Wm Darwin lunches with me, 1.45 Went with him to the Royal Academy afterwards and thence home with him to tea. I walked from there (Egerton Place) back here.

10 May 1914 Sunday
The George Trevelyans 4.30

11 May 1914 Monday
Lady Wolseley comes to tea 4–4:30 Lady W's visit charming; after which, 5.15, I went in taxi on urgent errand to Gt. Portland St; and then walked thence, by Portland Rd. etc, over to top of Tottenham Ct. Rd. and so down the same to Shaftesbury Ave. to Pall Mall and the Reform, where I dined and afterwards read in the Gallery.

12 May 1914 Tuesday
Take Nieces to Scott Cinema: 3.
Call 95 Sloane St. 5.30. Walked back after call, by the pleasant way.

13 May 1914 Wednesday
Lunched 4 Prince's Gate (taking the two Margarets) at 2.
Sesame Club, Francis Fords, 4.30
With Mrs. S to Alfred's comedy.

14 May 1914 Thursday
Christopher Wheeler lunches, 2.
Owen Wister[26] dines here 8.
[Crosses out "Thursday (today) tea at Sesame Club with the Francis Fords. (29 Dover St.)"]

25. Robert Lawrence Binyon (1869–1943), poet and art historian, then in charge of prints at the British Museum.
26. Owen Wister (1860–1938), son of HJ's old friend Mrs. Wister of Philadelphia who had been writing "westerns" since the nineties. His *The Virginian* (1902) is regarded as the classic of the genre.

15 May 1914 Friday
Ray Lankester's 4.30. 331 Upper Richmond Road. Putney

16 May 1914 Saturday
Took long turn in Battersea Park—from 3.45 to 7.

17 May 1914 Sunday
Took Peggy to lunch with Mrs. Rowlinson 1.45 Hill Lodge, Hillsleigh Road
C.H.
Went to 74 Eaton Terrace.

18 May 1914 Monday
Hagberg Wright dines with me here 8.

19 May 1914 Tuesday
Went to tea with the Pennells—Adelphi Terrace.

20 May 1914 Wednesday
Had tea with Gertrude Abbey.
Dine Emily Sargent's 8.

21 May 1914 Thursday
Lunch Mrs. Playfair 1.45 (26 Cheyne Walk.)
Dine Fritz Jackson's 8.30. 64 Rutland Gate. S.W.

22 May 1914 Friday
Angela MacInnes, 5. 102 Church St. Kensington.
Dine *à l'improviste* with Nieces.

23 May 1914 Saturday
Went to tea with W.E. Darwin (and Sara Norton.)

24 May 1914 Sunday
Called on Emily Sargent and on Mrs. Pakenham
Dine (almost alone and so drearily!) at the Athenaeum!

25 May 1914 Monday
Had tea, accompanied by Nieces, at House of Commons with Phillip Morrells.
While there the division on 3d reading of Home [Rule] Bill took place—Gov't
majority 77. Took Lady Ottoline home. Rather historic occasion. [HJ crossed
out everything from "3d reading" to end.]

26 May 1914 Tuesday
Mrs. J. R. Green lunches 1:45.
Mrs. Sutro comes to take me to Academy 3.30. Went to tea with her at her
club, and walked thence (from Dover St.) back home here—in 2 hours.

27 May 1914 Wednesday
Went to 24 Bedford Sq: at 4; and then to Mrs. Colefax, 5. (85 O.S.) then got
home and dressed and returned to B.S. to dine with the Phillip Morrells, 7;
and go afterwards to Drury Lane Opera—The Magic Flute.

28 May 1914 Thursday
Lunched with Nieces 1.45.
Went at 5 to 74 Eaton Terrace.—Walked home.

29 May 1914 Friday
Lunch Paul Draper's 2
Called on Mrs. Du Maurier with Nieces
Dined with Emily Sargent (with Nieces)

30 May 1914 Saturday
Went after to dinner to meet Mary Cadwal at Waterloo by Oceanic, and drove her to Symonds's.

31 May 1914 Sunday
Katie Rodgers lunched with me here (1.45) with the Nieces.
Go to see Flora Priestley,[27] 5.
Dine at hotel with Mary Cadwal, 8.15.

1 June 1914 Monday
Drove down to Hill in M[ary] H[unter]'s blest car with Nieces—to luncheon and tea. Drove back thence in same way at 6.30. Great Bank Holiday crowds, but very beautiful and fortunate day, admirable impression of Hill—and more than ever of M.H.

2 June 1914 Tuesday
Went to 74 Eaton Terrace; and then, having had tea there, to see Katie Rodgers at Belgrave Mansions.

3 June 1914 Wednesday
With Mrs. Sutro to Witley.

4 June 1914 Thursday
Mary Cadwal and Ruther [sic] Draper and Nieces lunched; and I drove M.C. afterwards to Kensington Gdns., where we strolled etc.
Mrs. Hunter's Opera Box (G.G)? Took Nieces there to Rosencavalier [sic], and left them with Mrs. H. from 3d act on.

5 June 1914 Friday
Dine with Edith Playfair, 8. (72 S. A. St.)

6 June 1914 Saturday
Went with Nieces to tea at Chelsea Lodge.

7 June 1914 Sunday
1.45 K. Rodgers lunches here again with Nieces. Also M. Cadwal and the Grenville Hunters lunched.

I called with Nieces on Emily Sargent at 5, and at 6.15 or so drove Peg to Queen's Hall to hear Mrs. Besant. I came thence, leaving her there, in motorbus to Victoria, and from there walked home very desirably.

27. Flora Priestley (1859–1941), British painter who lived on the Continent and a friend of Sargent's.

8 June 1914 Monday
Got to see Mrs. Ford at 33 Beaumont Street
Dine Edward Poynter[28] (?) 70 Addison Road

9 June 1914 Tuesday
Hugh Walpole lunches, 2.
Went at 3.45 to M. Cadwal's at Symonds's—and took stroll with her before
she had to return for interview with H.W. on behalf of E[dith]W[harton]. Then
drove to tea at Athenaeum where I talked with Townsend of Queen's Gate,
who did me good by telling me of friend of his, of 78, who had lived with
bad *angina pect.* for 25 years, and is now much better than formerly, having
swallowed enough "dynamite" (mine) to blow up St. Paul's. Returned to
M.C. for ¼ hour; and then from there walked by Brook St. and through Hyde
Park to Prince's Gate.

10 June 1914 Wednesday
With Peggy to Ranee's 5
Dine Emily Sargent: 8.

11 June 1914 Thursday
Barrett Wendell lunches 1.45
Stores (or Harrod's and Miss Lawrences) Harrod's for wall-paper dado for
L.H. or Hines'. (Failure at Harrod's today to find what I wanted but benefit
great of walking from 4 Prince's Gate by Ennismore Gdns and Fulham Road
home.) *I do,* oh I *do* walk better! and make out that the art of developing this
further is open to me.

12 June 1914 Friday
K.P. and L. Loring lunch[29] 1.45
Picked up Clive Bell and took him in my taxi today to Berners St.
Went after luncheon to Saunderson, Berners St., and found papers for Lamb
House green room.
Carried Ruther [sic] Draper to:—Dine, with Peggy, at Mrs. Yates Thomp-
son's; 19 Portman Square: 8.15 (?)

13 June 1914 Saturday
Lunch with American Ambassador 1.30, to meet Mr. Roosevelt.[30]
Lady Wolseley's car here at 3.30. Beautiful day—beautiful visit with Nieces
at Hampton Court and tea with Lady W.

14 June 1914 Sunday
Lunched with Nieces *chez elles*
[Crosses out "Mrs. J. R. Green lunches 1.45"]
To Automobile Club 6.45; for Lee Mathews and Christ.
Wheeler's Stage Society play.

---

28. Sir Edward Poynter (1836–1919), President of the Royal Academy.
29. Katharine Peabody Loring, Alice James's friend and companion, and her sister Louisa.
30. Probably Franklin Delano Roosevelt, then assistant secretary of the Navy.

16 June 1914 Tuesday
Chiropodist 9.30
W.E. Norris lunches 1.45.
To the Rawlinson's, Campden Hill to tea with Peggy and M.P.
[Crosses out "Tea L. Clifford, 4.30."]

17 June 1914 Wednesday
Ruth Draper lunches 1.45.
Dine with Nieces and bring Hugh Walpole, 8.15.

18 June 1914 Thursday
Lunch Lady Charles Beresford's 1.40
Mrs. Belloc Lowndes with Peggy.—4.30—Went with Nieces afterwards to
Mrs. Philip Lee Warner's

19 June 1914 Friday
Dine with W.E. Norris, Wyndham's; 8.15
[Crosses out "National Club"]

20 June 1914 Saturday
Mrs. Charles Hunter and her car for Lord D. at Cobham 2. Wonderful beau-
tiful day; incomparable old house and park; charmingest hospitality of Lord
D.; altogether unforgettable impression.

21 June 1914 Sunday
Christopher Wheeler's 24 Upper Mall, 5

22 June 1914 Monday
To the Bruce Richmonds' with Nieces, 10. (Ruth Draper.)

23 June 1914 Tuesday
Mrs. Rawlinson 5. With Nieces. Garden teaparty—very pretty and pleasant.
Walked home by (from) Prince's Gate etc.

24 June 1914 Wednesday
Lady Macmillans' with Nieces 5 o'clk.
Academy soiree 10 o'clk.

25 June 1914 Thursday
Mrs. Green lunches 1.45
Went with Peggy to Mrs. F.W.H. Myer's and walked back westward with her
through St. James's Park etc.
Dine F. Macmillans 8.15
Talked happily with John Morley, and went afterwards to admirable music at
Sargent's studio.

26 June 1914 Friday
Aleck due Glasgow today (if not yesterday).
Lunched with Mrs. Jordan Mott—early afternoon: went with her to Lady Randolph C's play: *The Bill. Fort mauvais.* Tea with Hugh Walpole at *Carleton,*
taking Nieces: five. Drove Hugh home to Strand Hotel after putting Nieces

into taxi; and then walked myself home (to Chelsea Barracks corner) through great beauty of St. J. Park, and sense of so blissfully improved power of motion.

27 *June 1914 Saturday*
To Stocks, by train, with Nieces.
[Crosses out "Osterley Park, afternoon."]

28 *June 1914 Sunday*
Edward Poynter 5. (70 A.R.)
Dine Lady Battersea 10 Connaught Place 8.15
The 2 Troubetzkoys drove me home.

29 *June 1914 Monday*
Spent hour with Cabot Lodges at the Coburg Hotel.

30 *June 1914 Tuesday*
Lunch with Peggy 1.45
To Christopher Wheeler's 4.30
Take Nieces to Lady Macmillan's party at Claridge's 10.30

1 *July 1914 Wednesday*
Cabot Lodges and Ruth Draper lunch 1.45.
Mrs. Colefax's, 5.
Lady Bell's (Cabot Lodges) 10.

2 *July 1914 Thursday*
To Bramshill with Mrs. Hunter—by 2. or 2.30. Too wondrous impression to write of. Got back by 8.30 and took Aleck to the Paul Drapers' at 11.
[Crosses out "Mrs. Eric Maclagan [sic] 5." and "Dine Emily Sargent 8.15."]

3 *July 1914 Friday*
Miss Bosanquet at Cheltenham till Monday—3 days out.
Peggy and M.P. left 10.30 for Cornwall.
Hugh Walpole lunches 1.45. Drove him back to Garrick Club; then called on Mrs. Curtis in Cork St.
Aleck and Demmler[31] dined 8.

4 *July 1914 Saturday*
Aleck up to see me this a.m. to talk over the D[emmler] situation.
Gilliard Lapsley lunches 1.45.
Osterley Park with Mrs. Jordan Mott 4.30.
Aleck dines 8.15

5 *July 1914 Sunday*
Aleck and Demmler lunch—1.45.
74 Eaton Terrace: 5.45
Dine Mrs. Lee Mathews 32 Gordon Square 8.15.

---

31. A school friend of Alex James's of whom HJ disapproved as unworthy of his nephew's company. See next entry.

6 July 1914 Monday

Went for 1st time to Bain's new shop 14 K. William St. Strand. Went to tea with Lady Charnwood—Mrs. Thorpe there. Walked home by S. Eaton Place, Commercial Road and the Embankment. Walter Berry, just from Paris, dined with me *à l'improviste.*

7 July 1914 Tuesday

Harry Melvill lunches 1.45

Sidney Colvins; 4.30 35 P.G.T. Walked partly home—Charles Boyd with me. The party a crowded one to hear Muriel Foster sing.

8 July 1914 Wednesday

Phil B.-J. lunches 1.45.

Dine Emily Sargent 8.

Mrs. Curtis, Vernon Lee, etc.

9 July 1914 Thursday

Go to N.Y. Life Assurance today *3.15.*

Pinker lunches, 1.45.

Sally Norton 5.45

Go to American Embassy 4.45

10 July 1914 Friday

Women-servants went to Rye for rest of summer etc.

Lunched with Peggy. 1.45, bringing Eddie Marsh and Rupert Brooke.

At 5. Mrs. Fletcher, 9 Stanhope St. Hyde Park Gdns. W.J. Collins dined with me Reform Club 8.15

11 July 1914 Saturday

Miss Bosanquet unwell.

Went out early—to New York Life Assurance etc.

Lunched with Nieces.

Went with Jessie Allen to tea with Franco Thomas.

Dined with Peggy at the Protheros.

12 July 1914 Sunday

Lunched with Peggy etc. Aleck there.

Went to tea with Emily Sargent. She and Violet alone. Dined with Nieces.

13 July 1914 Monday

Great heat

Lunched with Nieces and Aleck. Mrs. Prothero and others there.

Came down to Rye with Burgess by 4.30.

Kenneth Campbell joined me at Ashford.

14 July 1914 Tuesday

Great heat

Blessed impression again of Lamb House and of escape from the torrid, horrid town.

16 July 1914 Thursday
Owen Wister arrived before luncheon. Walk with him in p.m. very illustrative of my improved state.

17 July 1914 Friday
Afternoon walk with O.W. Still more testifying by its comparative ease and freedom to my better condition. Laus Deo!

18 July 1914 Saturday
At 4.15 saw O.W. over to Hastings on his departure thence by the 5 express to Victoria (due there at 5.44) Had tea afterwards at H. and walked lengthily and easily. Ret: 7.16

19 July 1914 Sunday
G.W. and F. Prothero, at Rye for weekend, dined here last night.
(Went out to Golf-Club with her in p.m.)

22 July 1914 Wednesday
Lawrence Godkin came down by the 6.30 to dine and sleep.

23 July 1914 Thursday
Lawrence G. left by the 9.20
Walked out to Golf-Club with Tayleure [sic], who had tea with me there.

25 July 1914 Saturday
Peggy, Aleck and Margaret Payson arrived for luncheon.
Logan Piersall [sic] Smith and Harold Worthington came to tea and a walk. Logan's yacht at Rye Harbour.

26 July 1914 Sunday
Logan S. and H.W. with us pretty well all day—to luncheon, to tea at Camber, with walk back, and to dinner.

27 July 1914 Monday
Peggy, Aleck and M.P. left by the 9.20

28 July 1914 Tuesday
Young Edward Sheldon, of New York, came to luncheon.
At 3.30 Francis Ford called for me to motor over to Budds to tea. Lionel Ford there. So struck afresh with the beauty of the place—in the beauty of the day. Morton Stephenson brought me home.

29 July 1914 Wednesday
Walked over to Winchelsea (Station) by the fields (middle way). Exquisite beauty of pastoral scene and afternoon. Came back by 6.52 (motor) train.

30 July 1914 Thursday to 3 August 1914 Monday

Rye

Identified yesterday the date of sending Ellen Terry the little one-act play (afterwards The High Bid)[32] from Osborne Crescent Torquay as August (toward end of) 1895—nearly 19 years ago. This gives me all the sequences:—

The note from Edward Warren from Point Hill, here, asking me to come to them—that Aug: (when it was impossible). The visit of Jon. Sturges to me at the Osborne in September and the return with him ill, gravely ill, to town (toward end of month or early in October I seem to make out). It was while there *then* that I conceived, under the effect of something he told me, the subject afterwards treated in *The Ambassadors*[33]; what he said being indeed the mere germ. In that winter of 95–96 I saw at the Warrens' in Cowley St. the little drawing in watercolours of the Lamb House gazebo-front that is down in the drawingroom here—Edward's gift to me afterwards. Went that autumn a great deal to see Jonathan at his nursing-home in Upper Wimpole Street; made him in fact my constant attention. (Oh the old full De Vere Gardens days of those years!)

In (and for) July 1896 went down to Bournemouth to escape the uproar in town.[34] Had engaged W. MacAlpine as amanuensis that winter-spring and begun the practise of dictating. Went on with it over "In the Cage" and "What Maisie Knew." MacAlpine joined me at Bournemouth for a little—I gave him, I remember, his 1st bicycle and lessons, and he at once became a great adept (I had myself begun the summer before at Torquay). Went down that August to be near Elly Hunter and her daughters at Dunwich in Suffolk (she had been the previous winter at Harrow, where I had been several times out to see her).[35] Spent August at Dunwich save for coming up to town and going down thence to Torquay for short visit to W.E. Norris at Underbank. I have forgotten to note that the Paul Bourgets came to Osborne Crescent there (at Torquay) the previous summer, Aug.–Sept. 1895, and made some stay— in great *late* (September) heat. Jon. S. came then *after* they had gone. Sept. 1896 I came back from Underbank to Dunwich, and went thence to spend 3 days with . . .

3 August 1914 Monday and 4 August 1914 Tuesday
Everything blackened over and for the time blighted by the hideous Public situation. This is (Monday) the Aug. Bank Holiday—but with horrible sus-

32. See notebooks 24 November 1892.
33. See notebooks 31 October 1895.
34. HJ went to Bournemouth in July 1897 (he was at Point Hill, Playden, Rye, during the summer of 1896) to escape the London celebrations of Queen Victoria's Diamond Jubilee. In February 1897 William MacAlpine became his first typist. He was then working on *What Maisie Knew* (1897) and "In the Cage" (1898).
35. In August 1897 HJ had gone to Dunwich in Suffolk to be near his cousin Ellen Temple and her daughters; see 6 January 1897 for Harrow visit. He interrupted the Dunwich stay to spend two weeks at Underbank in Devonshire.

pense and the worst possibilities in the air. Peggy and Aleck came down on
Saturday to stay.

[There are no entries for the next three months.]

2 November 1914 Monday
Mrs. Sutro's (Club) 31 Dover St. 4.45

3 November 1914 Tuesday
Lunch Prothero's 1.30

5 November 1914 Thursday
Lunch Norris. Wyndham. 1.30
Go to American Embassy 5.

6 November 1914 Friday
Received from Walter Berry £5.0.0 for Belgians, and from Mrs. Wharton, through
W.B., another cheque for £10.0.0

17 November 1914
Paid to Crosby Hall Fund W.B.'s £5 and ½ of Mrs. W's £10.

7 November 1914 Saturday
Constance Gardner lunches 1:30

8 November 1914 Sunday
F. Pertz lunches

9 November 1914 Monday
Jordan Mott's 5.30 G.C. Place

12 November 1914 Thursday
Phil B.J. lunches
Mrs. Pakenham, 5.
Dine Bernard Mallet's 8 43 C. Gdns.
[HJ crosses out "Wilfred Sheridans 5.30"]

13 November 1914 Friday
Lunch Mrs. Jordan Mott. 1.30

14 November 1914 Saturday
Ethel Dilke 5.30 (No. 53 S[ussex] G[ardens])

15 November 1914 Sunday
John Borie lunches 1.30.
Wilfred Sheridans 5.
Sutros 7.30

16 November 1914 Monday
Franco Thomas lunches 1.30

17 November 1914 Tuesday
Lunch with Emily Sargent 1.15

Tea C. Gardner, Claridge's.
Dine Evan Charteris[36] and E. Gosse, Carlton 8.15

18 November 1914 Wednesday
Mrs. Belloc-Lowndes lunches 1.30

19 November 1914 Thursday
Mrs. Green lunches 1.30
American Embassy 5

20 November 1914 Friday
Go to St. Barthol's.[37]
Dine Reform, Hagberg Wright

24 November 1914 Tuesday
Percy Lubbock lunches 1.45

26 November 1914 Thursday
Lunch Protheros 1.30
American Embassy 5

27 November 1914 Friday
Jessup, St. Bart's. Spent 2 hours in the two wards. (J.?) Donston Wain. [Crosses
out "Pinker lunches, 1:45"]

28 November 1914 Saturday
Went to see Harry [James] at the Ritz—back a few hours before from Paris
and leaving tonight for Holland. Spent hour with him till he had to go to
Victoria. Dined with Emily Sargent—John[38] just returned and very interesting.

30 November 1914 Monday
George Protheros and Nephew 1.30.
Dined Mrs. Astor 8.15

1 December 1914 Tuesday
Pinker lunches 1.45
Mrs. Sutro 31 Dover St. 5
[Crosses out "Lady Ritchie and Hester lunch 1.30"]

2 December 1914 Wednesday
Lunch Lady DuCane 1.45
St. Barts, 5 etc.

3 December 1914 Thursday
This afternoon at 4.30 The Belgian Tea, Crosby Hall
Lunch Lady Hamilton 1.30 1 Hyde Park Gdns. W.
Dine with Haldanes 8.15 28 G.A.G.

---

36. Charteris (1864–1940), son of the 6th. Earl of Wemyss; barrister and biographer of Sargent and Gosse.
37. St. Bartholomew's hospital, where HJ visited the wounded.
38. Sargent, ignoring the war, had continued his summer's painting in the Austrian Tyrol.

4 December 1914 Friday
Lunch with G. Protheros 1.30
Dine with Evan Charteris, Carlton, 8.15

8 December 1914 Tuesday
E. Bigelow 1.30
To Mrs. Yates Thompson 5.40
Dine Edmund Gosse, 8. 1 Whitehall Gdns.

9 December 1914 Wednesday
3.30 Order dinner at Reform Club
Call for Evan Charteris 4.15 to: go to Reception of E. Boutroux at British Academy
Col. A.J. Barry and H. de G. Glazebrook dine with me Reform 8.

10 December 1914 Thursday
Lunch with James Bryce Athenaeum, 1.30.
Go to Lady Elgar's concert 3.30
Attend meeting of Motor Ambulance Committee[40]—11 Waterloo place 5 o'clk.

11 December 1914 Friday
Lunch Claude Phillips 1.30
Go to St. Bart's

12 December 1914 Saturday
Clare Sheridan lunches 1.45.

13 December 1914 Sunday
Logan Smith lunches 1.45

14 December 1914 Monday
Mrs. Sutro lunches

15 December 1914 Tuesday
Meeting of Tadema Fund, Royal Academy 5

16 December 1914 Wednesday
Lunch J.S.S[argent] 1.30
Dine Peter Harrison's 7.45.
Tea L. Clifford ¼ to 5.

17 December 1914 Thursday
May Coles lunches 1.45

18 December 1914 Friday
The Irvings lunch 1.45
St. Bart's—4.30

39. HJ became honorary president of the American Volunteer Ambulance organization.

19 December 1914 Saturday
The Ranee lunches 2

20 December 1914 Sunday
Logan Smith and Arthur King lunch 1.45
Robin Bensons 5.
Dine H. de G. Glazebrook (76 Eden Park Rd.) 7.30

21 December 1914 Monday
Lunch 4 Prince's Gate 2.
Tea with Mrs. Colefax 5. (85 Onslow Square)
De Glehns (6.30?)[40]

22 December 1914 Tuesday
E.G. Lowry lunches 1.45
Margaret Clifford 5 o'clk.

23 December 1914 Wednesday
Roger Quilter lunches 1.45
Go to Mrs. Maguire's (3 Cleveland Square) 5

24 December 1914 Thursday
Motor to Hill—11.

25 December 1914 Friday
Went to see Arthur King.
Dine Emily Sargent

26 December 1914 Saturday
Go to Protheros 4.30

27 December 1914 Sunday
Lunch Mrs. McIlvaine 1.45.

29 December 1914 Tuesday
Margaret Clifford lunches 1.45.
Went to St. Bart's afternoon. Taking tobacco evening.
Heard, with horror and despair from George [Gammon] of the fall in great
gale of the dear old L.H. Mulberry tree.[41]

30 December 1914 Wednesday
Tea Mrs. J.G. Butcher 5. 32 Elvaston Place.
Dine Alfred Sutros 8.

31 December 1914 Thursday
Dick Norton lunches 1.45.
Go to Arthur King by 4.

40. The Von Glehns changed their name to De Glehn at the war's outbreak.
41. See *Life* 705.

1915

The war is at the forefront of the last months of Henry James's life. He takes his duties seriously as continuing chairman of the American Volunteer Motor Ambulance Corps led by Richard Norton, the son of his old friend Charles Eliot Norton. An entry such as that of 16 January marks one of his last social occasions, his visit to an old fortress located near Deal, Kent, some five miles up the Channel coast from Dover. It was used in 1914–15 by Prime Minister Asquith as an informal conference site for government and military leaders. On weekends Asquith's wife, Margot, enlivened the gatherings by inviting such figures as HJ. On this occasion Winston Churchill, then first Lord of the Admiralty, is present and out-talks HJ. (See *Letters* IV, 734–35.)

He continues to go to St. Bartholomew's, and his pocket diary becomes a roster of soldier acquaintances. A virtual "Saga of Sapper Williams" begins with the entry for 1 February and HJ's seeing to Williams's proper dental care. But Williams is no exception: HJ sees to the same care for Private Percy Stone. And he gives various thoughtful assistance to enlisted men. His sympathies are deeply engaged with the maimed. The brief outburst of August 31st—when he has met the one-armed young officer—is revealing: "They kill me!" He aches at the death, 23 April, of the poet Rupert Brooke—the beautiful youth who took him punting during a Cambridge weekend in 1909—and of the handsome young Wilfred Sheridan, 9 September, husband of Clare Frewen. Burgess Noakes is wounded, but soon demobilized and returned to HJ by mid-year.

HJ continues to write and to manage a still active professional career—seeing through the press a uniform edition of his major tales, fourteen volumes (1915–20) using, with one exception, the New York edition. He continues work on the resumed *Sense of the Past,* writes two memorial essays, the one on "Mr. and Mrs. Fields" and another on the origin of the *Nation.* Interviewed on his war work by a *New York Times* reporter, he takes his copy and rewrites it into a feature article about himself. His article on his hospital visits, "The Long Wards," is published in Edith Wharton's anthology *The Book of the Homeless* (1916). In mid-year he reads with chagrin H. G. Wells's parody of him, "Of Art, of Literature, of Mr. Henry James"—a lampoon provoked perhaps by HJ's unfavorable critique of 1913. (See Leon Edel and Gordon N. Ray, *Henry James and H. G. Wells,* [1958]).

Six months before his first stroke, he decides to become a British subject: "Hadn't it been for the War I should certainly have gone on as I was." He had kept his American citizenship in England for forty years. In mid-October, anxious about stray papers and records, he goes to Rye and empties cupboards and drawers, but there is no total destruction. An angina attack forces his return to London. His final piece of writing is an introduction to Rupert Brooke's posthumous *Letters from America* (1916). The first stroke comes December 2. Others follow. But he insists on dictating from his deathbed and fights off death until the end of February, with, however, considerable loss of coherence and mental function.

1 January 1915 Friday
Martin Secker[1] lunches 1.45

2 January 1915 Saturday
Lady Ritchie and Hester lunch 1.45

6 January 1915 Wednesday
Kenneth Campbell lunches.

7 January 1915 Thursday
Dine with Emily Sargent 8.

8 January 1915 Friday
Adlercrons lunch 1:45.

9 January 1915 Saturday
Go to Rhoda Broughton 5.

10 January 1915 Sunday
Col. Irving and Logan P.S. lunch 1.45.
Went to see Mrs. Chamberlain

12 January 1915 Tuesday
Tea with Mrs. Cuyler, 5. 1 Grosvenor Crescent W.
Dine with Emily S. 8.

13 January 1915 Wednesday
Elizabeth Asquith[2] lunches 1.45
Mrs. Sutro, 31 Dover St. W. 4.30

1. Entries for 1–2 January are on pages so dated at the end of the 1914 diary. Secker was publishing a uniform edition of HJ's selected tales, a pocket-size volume for each tale.
2. Elizabeth Asquith (1898–1945), daughter of Prime Minister Herbert H. Asquith (1852–1928).

16 January 1915 Saturday
Went to Walmer Castle[3]

18 January 1915 Monday
Returned from Walmer a.m.
Dined with Florence Pertz, 8. 72 Princes Square S.W.

19 January 1915 Tuesday
Glazebrook and R. Borie lunched.

20 January 1915 Wednesday
Mrs. Napier lunches 1.45

21 January 1915 Thursday
Jocelyn P. lunches 1.45.

22 January 1915 Friday
A. Dew Smith lunches 1.45.

23 January 1915 Saturday
Lunch Emily Sargent 1.30.
Go to see L. C.

24 January 1915 Sunday
H. Ritchie at 3.30.
Rhoda B. afterwards.

25 January 1915 Monday
St. Bart's 4.30 (W.D. Wein) also Sapper T. J. Williams 1st London Division,
R.E. about whom and his teeth I write to George Field.

26 January 1915 Tuesday
Glazebrook Committee, at office, 4.

27 January 1915 Wednesday
Mrs. Sutro 32 Dover St. 4.30

29 January 1915 Friday
G. E. Lowry lunches 1.45.
Call 10 Downing St.
Dine Mrs. Hunter, 8.15

30 January 1915 Saturday
Went to 3 to see E. Ritchie 13 Tite St.
Also Rhoda Broughton, 5.

31 January 1915 Sunday
W. Donston Wain lunches 1.30
Lady Bell, 5.15

3. See headnote to this year.

1 February 1915 Monday
Write to Sapper Williams about dentist. 113a Tolworth Park
Road Surbiton
Protheros' 4.30

2 February 1915 Tuesday
Tea with Agnes Conway 16 Buckingham Palace Gdns. S.W.
Dine Jacomb Hoods 7.45 21 Tite St.

4 February 1915 Thursday
Go to Waterloo to meet 11.30 in from Surbiton.

5 February 1915 Friday
Lunch with Rhoda Broughton 1.30

6 February 1915 Saturday
May Coles lunches 1.45
Protheros: 4.15

8 February 1915 Monday
Monday 4: to Glazebrook at office for "interview."

9 February 1915 Tuesday
Helen Lascelles (McClagan) [McLagan] at tea, 5. 15 Queens Gate Place.
Dine Emily Sargent 8.

10 February 1915 Wednesday
Pinker lunches 1.45.
Rhoda B. 5.

11 February 1915 Thursday
To Rhoda B. 4.30

12 February 1915 Friday
Marie Belloc Lowndes lunches 1.45, 74 Eaton Terrace at 4.10.

13 February 1915 Saturday
Lunch with G. E. Lowry, 1.30, at 51 Lower Belgrave St.
Protheros 4.30 (J. Barnes.)

14 February 1915 Sunday
Lunch with Mrs. Falles 2. 95 Piccadilly
Go to Fritz Jackson. 4.
Mrs. Pakenham 5.30

15 February 1915 Monday
Sapper Williams at Dr. Field's 5.15

16 February 1915 Tuesday
Miss Tomlinson lunches. 1.45. [HJ crosses out "Roland Prothero 4:30"]
Mrs. Wolcott: Ritz Hotel, Room 518, Tea 5 o'clk.
Comte de Grune, 37 Sloane Gardens, 6.15

17 February 1915 Wednesday
Tea with (Royall?) Tylers[4] 4.30. 26 Egerton Crescent S.W.
Jim Barnes dines.

18 February 1915 Thursday
[HJ crosses out "Morton Stephenson lunches 1.45."]
Mrs. Napier. 4.30.
Mrs. Earle 6.

19 February 1915 Friday
John Bailey lunches 1.45.
See Williams at Dr. F's 5.15.
St. Thomas's Hospital, 6

20 February 1915 Saturday
Lunch Mrs. Lindsey and Clare Sheridan, 1 Gore St. Queen's Gate, S.W.
Go to Garlant's 4.
  "   "   74 Eaton Terrace 5.30

21 February 1915 Sunday
Roland Protheros 4.30
Lady Bell. 5.45

22 February 1915 Monday
Sapper Williams lunches. 1.45
Go to Bryce Lecture, King's College 4.30

23 February 1915 Tuesday
Geo. Protheros—4.15.

24 February 1915 Wednesday
Bailey Saunders lunches. 1.45
Rhoda Broughton.

25 February 1915 Thursday
Morton Stephenson lunches 1.45
Dine Bucklers 8.15 28 Hans Place S.W.

26 February 1915 Friday
Lunch with Lady Essex 1.30 Bourdon House. Davies St.
Went to St. Bart's.

27 February 1915 Saturday
Dine Edmund Gosse 8

28 February 1915 Sunday
Logan Smith lunches
Mrs. de Selincourt lunches 1.45.
Charles Boyd lunches also.
Maisie Lee Warner 6 Marloes Road. 4.30

4. Elisina Royall Tyler and her husband William were close friends of Edith Wharton's.

1 March 1915 Monday
Cleary Bisset etc. Civil Service Stores
Tea with Rhoda B. 5.

2 March 1915 Tuesday
Emily Sargent 8

3 March 1915 Wednesday
Mrs. Van Rensselaer 4.
Call for Dick Borie, 89 G.R. at 5.30

4 March 1915 Thursday
Went to Athenaeum and met John Cross and Augustine Fitzgerald.
Dine Lady Lewis. 8.15 [HJ crosses out "Crosby Hall: 1:30. Embassy at 5."]

5 March 1915 Friday
Moreton Frewen lunches 1.45.
Emily Sargent, 8.

6 March 1915 Saturday
Protheros with J. Cleary 4.

7 March 1915 Sunday
Lunch with Peter Harrison's

8 March 1915 Monday
Lunch Protheros 1.30

9 March 1915 Tuesday
Dine O'Gormans 8. 21 Embankment Gdns.

11 March 1915 Thursday
Went to American Embassy 5.
Dined at Chelsea Lodge.

13 March 1915 Saturday
Lunch with Rhoda Broughton 1.30.
Take Cleary to Protheros, tea (4.15) for wounded.
Gilliard L. dines 8.

14 March 1915 Sunday
Mrs. Chamberlain 4.45

15 March 1915 Monday
M. Hunter lunches, 2.
L. Clifford 5

16 March 1915 Tuesday
M. Vincent lunches 1.30
Sir James Frazer's Lecture Royal Institution 3 o'clk.
Went to E. Sands to tea: 5.30

17 March 1915 Wednesday
Harry arrived London this a.m.[5]
Lunch with M. Hunter 1 (Prince and Press. Victor-Napoleon, Réjane, Primoli, Arthur Balfour, Duc d'Albe etc.!)
Dined with Harry at hotel.

18 March 1915 Thursday
Dined with Harry at Hotel (Ritz)

19 March 1915 Friday
Harry dined with me here

20 March 1915 Saturday
Harry sailed this a.m.
Went to 24 Bedford Square to tea with wounded. Walked homeward thence (and across Green Park) with Charles Boyd—as far as Victoria.

21 March 1915 Sunday
P. Lockwood lunches
Tea with Lady Charnwood 4.30, 108 Eaton Square
20 Bedford Square 6.45 for Tea.

22 March 1915 Monday
Ethel Sands lunches 1.45
Go to be at *Bain's* (3.45) about Montaigne, etc.

Tea, 4 Culford Gdns, 4.30
Hugh Bells' 6.20

23 March 1915 Tuesday
Lunch Rochfort Maguires 1.30
To the J.G. Butchers—to tea with wounded—4. 74 Eaton Terrace: 5:45. [HJ crosses out "Sir James Frazer's lecture, 3 o'clk Royal Institution."]

24 March 1915 Wednesday
Call for Mrs. S. at 32 Dover St., 4.

25 March 1915 Thursday
Edmund Gosse lunches 1.45.
Richard Norton comes to tea at Reform 4.30
Go to Mrs. Guy Du M. 6 o'clk.

26 March 1915 Friday
Lunch 10 Downing St. 1.45
Mrs. Van Rensselaer 4.
Mrs. Colefax 5:25–5:30 (85 O. S.)
Went in to Emily Sargent's work-room 6.15

27 March 1915 Saturday
Call St. George's Hospital, 24 Bedford Square, 4.
Dine, alone, Charnwood 8 (108 E.S.)

5. HJ's nephew was in Europe on a mission for the Hoover Commission for Relief in Belgium.

28 March 1915 Sunday
R.H. Bensons 5. *Tea.*
(Call on the Courtneys 4.30 Call O'Gormans 5.45.)

29 March 1915 Monday
Logan Smith's 5.

30 March 1915 Tuesday
Lunch 51 Lower Belgrave St. 91.30.)
J.G. Butchers' 4.
Mrs. Lee Mathews, 9

31 March 1915 Wednesday
To luncheon 1.45.
Private Patrick Clark. Leinster Reg't. King William Ward. Westminster Hospital.
Jocelyn P. at Reform to tea; 4.30. Went afterwards to 4 Culford Gdns. S.W.

1 April 1915 Thursday
George and Janet Trevelyan at lunch 1.45.
Went to see Frederick Langford, Private, Liverpool Scottish, at St. George's Hospital (King Ward.) [HJ crosses out "A. Donston to tea at Reform, 5 o'clk."]

3 April 1915 Saturday
Prof. Gayley lunches 1.45
Miss Heynemann 3.30.

4 April 1915 Sunday
Lunched at Reform
Called on Rathbones.

6 April 1915 Tuesday
Anne de Selincourt lunches 1.45
To Rhoda B's
Went to tea with wounded soldiers at J.G.B's—and thence to R.B.'s. [HJ crosses out "Go to J. G. Butcher's, 4."]

7 April 1915 Wednesday
Lunch Emily Sargent 1.30
Royall Tylers, 26 Egerton Crescent 4.30

8 April 1915 Thursday
E.G. Lowry lunches with me Reform 1.45
St. George's Hospital—C. Fdk. Langford
Rhoda B. 5.45 [HJ crosses out "Hunter's House Temple."]

10 April 1915 Saturday
Prothero's 4.15

11 April 1915 Sunday
The Findlaters lunch.
Went to Humphry Wards

12 April 1915 Monday
Lunch at Reform with Sir J. Wolfe Barry, 1.30.
Dine with Evan Charteris

13 April 1915 Tuesday
Dined at Bath Club 8.15 with Phil B-J. and Lily Norton

14 April 1915 Wednesday
Mrs. Adlercron lunches 1.45.
Dine Emily Sargent's 8 o'clk.

15 April 1915 Thursday
L. Clifford lunches 1.45
Glazebrook's meeting, 4.
Dine 10 Downing St.

17 April 1915 Saturday
Lunch E.G. Lowry 1.30 26 Milner St. Cadogan Square.
Took 3 convalescent wounded soldiers from St. Bart's to tea 24 Bedford Sq.
and delivered them home again. Stopped there a little to see W.J. Vince of
Grenadier Guards.

18 April 1915 Sunday
Mrs. Curtis, Miss Allen and Violet Ormond lunch 1.45
Go to Humphry Wards' 4.30
Go to Hugh Bells' 6.

19 April 1915 Monday
Telephone Dr. Field inquiry about his attending to Private Percy Stone (who
has practically lost one eye.)
Telephone to C.M. Gayley about Athenaeum this afternoon.
Go to Athenaeum ballot: 4.30
Go to Humphry Wards' 6.
Dined with W.E. Norris, Wyndham Club, 8. o'clk.

20 April 1915 Tuesday
Mrs. Ward, 6.16. [HJ crosses out "Meeting at Glazebrook's office, 4 p.m."]

21 April 1915 Wednesday
Arthur Benson, Athenaeum 1.40
Gailliard, Reform Club, 8. (?)

22 April 1915 Thursday
G.W. Protheros lunch 1.45.
American Embassy 5. [HJ crosses out "Glazebrook's?"]

23 April 1915 Friday
Lunch Francis Horner 1.30 16 Lower Berkeley St. W.
Meeting at Glazebrook's office 4

25 April 1915 Sunday
To Lady Courtney 4.30
To Mr. Galbraith Horn. 5.45 Campden House Court. 42

26 April 1915 Monday
Lunch with G. W. Protheros 1.30
Go to Mudie's about H. Dunster and send chocolate from stores to St. Bart's.
Mrs. O'Gorman. 5.30. [HJ crosses out "Call Mrs. E. G. Lowry.]

27 April 1915 Tuesday
St. Bart's and 24 Bedford Sq: 4.
The deaf soldier in Harley Ward: John Willey. The other in same ward with
wounded arm:—Bard.

28 April 1915 Wednesday
Mrs. Sutro lunches, 1.45.
Dine with Edmund Gosses, 8.15

29 April 1915 Thursday
William M. Roughead[6] lunches 1.45
Ethel Sands 5.

30 April 1915 Friday
St. Bart's.—Paid a long visit. Extraordinarily beautiful weather—sudden burst
almost of summer.

1 May 1915 Saturday
Lily Norton lunches 1.30.
Go to Windsor to tea; but come back to dine (at 8) with Charles Gayley at
Athenaeum.

2 May 1915 Sunday
Tea with Mrs. E. G. Lowry 4.45. [HJ crosses out "Mrs. Lawrence, 5."]

3 May 1915 Monday
Send shaving things to W.J. Vince, St. Bart's.
To Dr. Field's to see P. Stone. 5.

5 May 1915 Wednesday
Lunch with Pinker, Arts Club 1.45.
Eddie Marsh dines 8.30

7 May 1915 Friday
have had a poor week—unwell ever since Monday, though with some better-
ness yesterday, and even some small ability to work (I sent off morsel to the
N.Y. Nation today.)[7]

6. Scottish jurist (1870–1952) who had been sending HJ his chronicles of famous murder trails in
Scotland. See *Tales of the Criminous* (ed. W. N. Roughead 1956), which contains HJ's letters to
Roughead.
7. HJ's article on the founding of the *Nation* by E. L. Godkin was published in that journal 8 July
1915.

Went to St. Bart's this afternoon—till near 7 o'clk.
Send *pocket-comb* to Private Alfred Conmitty, Henry Ward!

9 May 1915 Sunday
Went to tea (19 Ashburn Place), with Mrs. Stillman and afterwards to see Stopford Brooke (the younger) at nursing home near by.

10 May 1915 Monday
Go to Glazebrook's office 12.30.
Went to tea with Lady Du Cane, and walked home thence by the Embankment.

11 May 1915 Tuesday
John Bailey and Dr. Kennedy lunched.
Went to tea with E. Sands and Nan Hudson—in their garden etc.

13 May 1915 Thursday
Dined with Mrs. Rochfort Maguire. 8.30.

14 May 1915 Friday
Lunched with 2 Findlaters, 6, Glebe Place
Tea with L. Clifford and then went to Sidney Colvin's English Association lecture 5.30. Drove Mrs. C. home afterwards.

15 May 1915 Saturday
Lunch with Protheros 1.30.
St. Bart's Hospital

17 May 1915 Monday
Send p.o. 5/ to W.J. Vince
Roger Quilter lunches 1.45
Send cigarettes to Pvte. A. Tucker, Kenton Ward, St. Bart's.
E.G. Lowry comes to tea: 4.45
Dine with Lady Battersea 8.15 (10 Connaught Place: W.)

18 May 1915 Tuesday
Dine Macmillans 8.15 22 Devonshire Place. W.

19 May 1915 Wednesday
Marie Belloc failed, through illness, to lunch; and I went early (2.15) to Imperial Meeting at Guildhall. Thence to tea at 32 Dover St. and walked with Mrs. Sutro and Hedworth Williamson down thence, to Westminster Cathedral—very noble impression there.

20 May 1915 Thursday
To Glazebrook, 4.
Went to Embassy, and afterwards to Geo. Protheros.

21 May 1915 Friday
S. Colvins lunch 1.45
Go to tea with Theodate Pope, Hyde park Hotel, 5.
Dine with Emily Sargent 8.

22 May 1915 Saturday
Lunch with Col and Mrs. House,[8] 18 Bolton St. 1.30
Call on Hugh Bell at nursing home—5.30. 3 Devonshire Terrace Marylebone

23 May 1915 Sunday
Charles Millar lunches 1.45.
Was called for by Theodate Pope in car and went out to Richmond Park Hampton Court (Bushey Pk.) in wonderful beauty of day and park chestnut blooms.

24 May 1915 Monday
Motored at 10.30 down to Hill with J.S. Sargent R.A. in car kindly sent by Mrs. Charles Hunter; lunched, tea'd and dined and came back after dinner in same car, with J.S.S. and Lord Headfort. Extraordinary beauty of day—weather, season, 1st bloom of foliage and blossom. Never saw Hill so lovely.

25 May 1915 Tuesday
Went to see Mrs. Sutro, and sat a while in Regent's Park; then came back with her to tea; and at 6.20 called on Theodate Pope.

26 May 1915 Wednesday
Lunch Edward Warrens: 1.40.
André Chevrillon there.

27 May 1915 Thursday
Poor day, but lunched with the Lawrences, 4 P.G.
Frances Wolseley and Sir Coleridge Crane being there.
Went then to Storys, High St. Kensington.
Call on Hugh Bell.
Call (6.15) 74 Eaton Terrace but instead of those calls came home and went to bed.

28 May 1915 Friday
In bed.
Logan Smith, John Bailey, Theodate Pope and Dr. Kennedy all came to see me. Had visit, in my room, the p.m. before (after dinner hour,) from the Carlino Perkinses.

29 May 1915 Saturday
Motored to St. Albans with Theodate Pope

30 May 1915 Sunday
Went to see Glazebrook
at home unwell, a.m.

1 June 1915 Tuesday
Luncheon with Emily Sargent 1.30
To Mrs. Playfair's Garden—tea with the wounded, 4–6
26 Cheyne Walk W.
Went to Theodate Pope 6.15.

---

8. Texas-born Col. E. M. House, who would acquire fame as a high figure during the later stages of the war as President Wilson's "other self."

2 June 1915 Wednesday
Day lunches with me at Reform 1.45.
Barber, Reform. Bain's
Jocelyn P. comes to tea Reform 5
Theodate P.; H.P.H. 6.30.

3 June 1915 Thursday
Lunch with Lowry 26 Milner St. 1.45.
I give tea to the Belgians at Crosby Hall: 4.
Dine with Mrs. Eliot Yorke. 8.15. 17 Curzon St.

5 June 1915 Saturday
The Carlino Perkinses lunch 1.45
Go to St. Bart's

6 June 1915 Sunday
Miss Heynemann and Ch. Boyd lunch, 1.45
Go to Royal Hospital.

7 June 1915 Monday
Meet C.M. Gayley, Athenaeum, 2.

8 June 1915 Tuesday
Lunch Mrs. Astor, 1.30
Went to tea with M. Cadwal. to Mrs. Whitridge, Almonds' Hotel 5.30 [HJ
crosses out "To tea with wounded at Lady Playfair's, 4."]

9 June 1915 Wednesday
Lady Randolph's[9] (committee.) 5.30 72 Brook St. W.
[HJ crosses out "Lunch with Mrs. Astor, 1:30."]

10 June 1915 Thursday
Lunch with Claude Phillips 1.40
American Embassy, 4.30.
Dine Emily Sargent; 8.

11 June 1915 Friday
Tea with Mrs. Prothero and "Charley". 4.30
Eddie Marsh dines, 8.15

12 June 1915 Saturday
St. Bart's, afternoon.

13 June 1915 Sunday
Went to see Rex Benson at Military Hospital 17 Park Lane—admirable
impression—and then went to Mrs. Pakenham.
Walked home thence; i.e. from Hertford St., Park Lane

14 June 1915 Monday
Geoffrey Millar dines 8

9. Lady Randolph Churchill.

15 June 1915 Tuesday
Lunch Claude Phillips 1.30. Then went, 4.30, to Symonds's Hotel and "took out" M. Cadwal. We took taxi to Kensington Gdns. Bayswater side, then walked through Gdns. to tea-place on Kensington side. Very decent tea there, and then walk with her down to Brompton Oratory where she took taxi. I walked home.

16 June 1915 Wednesday
Went to tea with Hugh Glazebrook.

17 June 1915 Thursday
Call for Jessie Allen 4.15 to go to tea in Franco Thomas's Garden.
Gilliard L. dines, 8.15.

18 June 1915 Friday
Mrs. Bliss lunches, 1.45.
Mrs. MacDonald 59 Harrington Gdns. 5.
Dine American Embassy, picking up M. Cadwal, 8.15.

19 June 1915 Saturday
The Carlino Perkinses lunch (3) at 1.45.
Went to Saint. Bart's.

20 June 1915 Sunday
Lunched at Athenaeum with C.M. Gayley.
Went to tea with Mrs. Chamberlain

22 June 1915 Tuesday
Mrs. Playfair, wounded soldiers, 4.
Mrs. Colefax at 62 Cadogan Place, 6.

23 June 1915 Wednesday
Edmund Gosse lunches 1.45.
Went to tea with Glazebrook

24 June 1915 Thursday
Went to 6 Raymond Buildings, Gray's Inn, to see Nelson Ward. (3.30.) Go to Embassy (Picked up at Symonds's Hotel and went.)

25 June 1915 Friday
Lunched at Reform with William White [10] and John Sargent
Tea at 74 Eaton Terrace. Walked home thence by Embankment. (7 to 8.)

27 June 1915 Sunday
Ethel Arnold's car at 3.30.
M. Cadwal. lunched with me, and we went together to the Old Manor House, Whitton, Middlesex. An exquisite adventure!

---

10. J. William White, the Philadelphia physician HJ met in the United States in 1905. See Lubbock II, 91–93.

28 June 1915 Monday
Go to Glazebrook as preliminary to meeting at 2.30.
Go to 24 Bedford Square. 5.30
Dine with Emily Sargent, 8

29 June 1915 Tuesday
Go (early) to American Embassy, 4 Grosvenor Gardens, about Passport.

30 June 1915 Wednesday
St. Bartholomew the Great, Burghelere Marriage, at 2.
Tea with Mrs. Woods, the Temple, 5. [HJ crosses out "taking Mary Cadwal."]

1 July 1915 Thursday
Tea in Mrs. Playfair's Garden with wounded, 4.
Dine with Mrs. Bliss, Ritz: 8.15 Room 218.

2 July 1915 Friday
Irwin Loughlin lunches here 1.45
Hugo Bell comes to Reform 4 o'clk; to tea.

3 July 1915 Saturday
Great heat.
Lunched with Jocelyn Persse, Conservative Club, 1.45.
Went to St. Bart's

4 July 1915 Sunday
Great heat.
Lunched at Reform, alone.
Went at 5 to tea with Mrs. Lawrence

5 July 1915 Monday
Lunch with J.B. Pinker, 1.45, at Arts Club. Went with him to Nelson Ward's.

6 July 1915 Tuesday
Took Lucy Clifford to tea in Kensington Gardens. Walked home with her, and thence most of the way back here.

7 July 1915 Wednesday
Dine 24 Bedford Square (without dressing,) 8.

9 July 1915 Friday
Mrs. Lawrence calls at 4.
Ran out to Hampton Court. Sat in gardens—extraordinarily beautiful; and had tea in garden of hotel by the bridge.

10 July 1915 Saturday
Dine Charnwoods 8. [HJ crosses out "Mrs. Charles Lawrence came for me in car, 4 o'clk."]

11 July 1915 Sunday
Go to Hill 10.30 [HJ crosses out "W.M Richmonds' Beavor Lodge, Hammersmith, 4.30."]

12 July 1915 Monday
Mrs. Lee Mathews comes at 9.

13 July 1915 Tuesday
The Wounded in Mrs. Playfair's garden, 4.
Mrs. Green 5. (36 G.R.)
Dine Sir William Lawrence 8.15 Elm Pk. Gardens, 68.
[HJ crosses out "2 Queen Anne's Gate, 11:30. Glazebrook's meeting."]

14 July 1915 Wednesday
Lunch Herbert Stablers 1.30. 32 Lower Belgrave St.
A.V.M.A.C.[11] 3 o'clk. 2 Queen Anne's Gate. [HJ crosses out "74 Eaton Terrace."] Ralph Curtis, Reform 5.30

15 July 1915 Thursday
Ralph C. (??)

16 July 1915 Friday
Lunch with the Lowrys 1.45 (26 Milner St. S.W.)
Mrs. Lawrence 4. Motored with her out to St. Albans—in bad wet. Visited the Abbey—assisted at service in choir. Only persons present.

17 July 1915 Saturday
Maud Story and Daughter lunch 1.45
Christopher Wheeler came 9. [HJ crosses out "Called Richmond, Beavor Lodge, 4:30"]

18 July 1915 Sunday
Lunched with M. C. J. at Symonds's Hotel, and went afterwards to Kensington Gardens, where we walked and had tea. Dined alone at Reform.

19 July 1915 Monday
Dick Borie lunches with me here, bringing Captain Middleton, 1.45. [HJ crosses out "at Reform."]

20 July 1915 Tuesday
To Glazebrooks at 5.

21 July 1915 Wednesday
Tea Mrs. Tyler, Burlington Hotel, 5.

22 July 1915 Thursday
Logan Smith; Crosby Hall 3.

23 July 1915 Friday
Glazebrook (E.P.R.) at 4. [HJ crosses out "Lady Lyttelton, Royal Hospital, 2."]

24 July 1915 Saturday
Lunch with Willie Buckler at Cafe Royal. 1.45

---

11. American Volunteer Motor Ambulance Corps.

25 July 1915 Sunday

Went at 11 a.m. and worked 3 hours with Glazebrook—on terrace in his Garden—over R.N[orton]'s A.V.M.A.C. Report. Lunched with M.C.J. at Symonds's, and went with her later on to tea at Mrs. Wilton Phipps's. Walked back with her thence to hotel, and dined at Reform Club.

26 July 1915 Monday

Received my Certificate today and took Oath of Allegiance[12] at Nelson Ward's: 4.45

Go to Bain for wedding-present book to send Miss Page.

Go to Nelson Ward 4.45.

Go to 24 Bedford Square 6.

27 July 1915 Tuesday

Lunched with Miss Mundella 1.30

Called for Lyttelton Tuesday 3. Went with her to Belgian Hosp. in Ledworth Square and then back to Chelsea H., which she showed me all over as never before. Most charming and interesting. Went to tea at Club (Reform) alone etc. and walked home thence.

28 July 1915 Wednesday

Go to Crosby Hall about 3.30

30 July 1915 Friday

Lunch with Logan S. 1.30.

Go down to Lady Wolseley's H.C.

Came home from Lady W's in chartered car, very unwell and went to Bed. Date from that day the beginning, with intermissions, very brief, of all this late and present (Sept 12th) crisis.

2 August 1915 Monday

To Barley End with M.C.J.—in Whitridge's car sent up at 11 a.m. Return by Bank Holiday train less agreeable—in late afternoon

3 August 1915 Tuesday

Tea M.C.J.

5 August 1915 Thursday

Dine Edmund Gosse 7.45

6 August 1915 Friday

Dine Emily Sargent, 8.

7 August 1915 Saturday

Mrs. Chas. Lawrence, 3.30.

Went by car to tea, at Virginia Water with her, and stopped at Howard Sturgis on return—reaching home at 9.

---

12. On this day HJ became a British subject and swore allegiance to King George V. See *Letters* 772–73 and *Life* 702–04.

8 August 1915 Sunday
Lunch with M.C.J. 2
Went with M.C.J. to tea at Mrs. Phipps's

9 August 1915 Monday
Eddie Marsh lunches here 1.45
I go to B.S. and Co. by 3.30 and await Axel Munthe[3] at Reform from 4.30

10 August 1915 Tuesday
Mrs. C. N. L. lends me car to go out to tea at Queen's Acre with M.C.J. whom I call for at 3

11 August 1915 Wednesday
Lunch H. Stablers' 1.30 32 Lower Belgrave St. (Too ill to go—went to bed instead.)

13 August 1915 Friday
Went to tea with L. Clifford, 32 Dover St. 4.30

14 August 1915 Saturday
Go to Grand Guignol with M.C.J. picking her up at Symonds's at 2.15 sharp.

15 August 1915 Sunday
Lunch Emily Sargent 1.30
J. W. White and M.C.J. (with J. S.S.) only there.
Went afterwards with M.C.J. for prowl in city—even as far tower; and after carrying her home went at 6, to see Violet Asquith.[14] Dined at R.C.

16 August 1915 Monday
Eddie Marsh lunches 1.45
Went, 4 o'clk. to see Nelson Ward about my will—and his becoming my English executor.

17 August 1915 Tuesday
Mrs. Lawrence's car calls for me, 3. We went down to Guildford and Great Langley Manor, where we missed the Laughlins, and got back to this door 7.20

18 August 1915 Wednesday
Dine with Evan Charteris and Arthur Balfour, 96a Mount St. W., 8.30

19 August 1915 Thursday
Went to tea at 74 Eaton Terrace.
Walked to Reform and dined there

21 August 1915 Saturday
Dine with Emily Sargent 8

---

13. Dr. Axel Munthe (1857–1949), Swedish-born doctor whose memoirs, *The Story of San Michele* (1929), were an international best-seller. HJ had met him at his villa on Capri.
14. Daughter of the Prime Minister who later married Sir Maurice Bonham-Carter.

25 August 1915 Wednesday
Nelson Ward, 4.

28 August 1915 Saturday
Unwell, dismally unwell and helpless, for many past days; almost, or quite, unprecedented and illuminated, or at least illuminating, stomachic and digestive crisis; with, suddenly, gout as climax.

29 August 1915 Sunday
Gout—but yielding to my blest remedy. Indoors all day and in afternoon, at tea, visit from Gunther of the Am. Embassy, whom I made very welcome; he sat some time and was most interesting and pleasant. Very good type.

30 August 1915 Monday
Got out in afternoon, and went to tea, as member of the Athenaeum, at the United Service Club—which I like in its pompous pictured vastness and void— it recalls to me so old Augusts and Septembers of the Past!

31 August 1915 Tuesday
Lunched at Ritz with Mrs. Hall Walker to say good-bye to her brother, Wilfred Sheridan[15] back to front after week's leave; he splendid and beautiful and occasion somehow such a pang—all unspeakable: 8 or 10 persons: sat between Mrs. Frewen and Lady Poltimore. Afterwards at tea at Lady C's—very interesting (splendid) young *manchot*[16] officer, Sutton. They kill me!

1 September 1915 Wednesday
Lunch 1.30 with Aline Harland etc. Berkeley.
Read and Aitkin at office 3.30. 24 Bedford Square, 5.

2 September 1915 Thursday
After very bad—horribly "panting"—day had to send, in great distress, for Dr. Harrison, 6 Swan Walk, whom I like and who gave some information etc. that lights—or will light—my poor old path, I think. I had a much better night.

3 September 1915 Friday
Better day, indoors; Dr. Harrison, who is very sympathetic, intelligent and non-medicating, came again—at 6.

4 September 1915 Saturday
Wrote to Richd. Norton Hotel de la Haute Mère Dieu, Châlons sur Marne, on question of correcting R.C.'s wrong use of our A.V.M.A.C. title—as "Anglo-American" Corps.
Mary Hunter calls for me in her car at 2.30. Went out to Enfield and to Waltham Abbey, which she helps to find, in the YMCA huts, the Munition Workers.

15. Wilfrid Sheridan was killed in action ten days later.
16. One who has lost his arm.

5 September 1915 Sunday
Went out early, to try forenoon walk; got into Battersea Park. Crawled back and lunched with Emily Sargent, at 1.30—and go to Lucy Clifford, to meet Henri Davray, at 5. Went to L. C's and met Davray, but came home unwell; wretched.

6 September 1915 Monday
[HJ crosses out "Sent tonight, lateish in evening for Dr. Harrison."]

7 September 1915 Tuesday
At 4 today the E.G. Lowrys came up from Lamb House to look at No. 73, which they decided at once to *take* of the Glehns—all at my instance; they coming afterwards here to tea, and I rejoicing in the good stroke for Wilfred and Jane.

8 September 1915 Wednesday
Sent again in evening for Harrison.

9 September 1915 Thursday
Dr. Harrison a.m.
Meeting at 11 W.P. of Council, 4 o'clk.
Go to see Aitkin at 3.15 (Impossible). Didn't go.
Harrison p.m.

10 September 1915 Friday
Harrison a.m.
Harrison p.m. [HJ crosses out "30 Old Burlington St. to dine: 8.15."]

11 September 1915 Saturday
Harrison away till Monday.
Went out by bold push with Mrs. Hunter in car to Enfield and Waltham Cross YMCA Munitions. Man motored me home alone.

12 September 1915 Sunday
Very bad, quite dreadful, panting night. Very bad a.m. hours—foodless; but more and more convinced, of vital, life-saving necessity of getting able to walk again and recovering precious help from it that has again and again so affirmed its value in the long and ravaged past! Such a consecrated confidence!

21 September 1915 Tuesday
Lowry at office.

27 September 1915 Monday
Went for Electric Light treatment to Miss Van Becker, 31 Eaton Terrace, 5. oclk.

28 September 1915 Tuesday
Van Becker, 3 o'clk. 34 Eaton Terrace, 4.

29 September 1915 Wednesday
Michaelmas—Autumn Quarter Day
Tea with Lily Norton, 35 Dover St., 5 o'clk.

23 October 1915 Saturday
Dr. Des Voeux came. 1st

24 October 1915 Sunday
Dr. Des Voeux came 2nd

25 October 1915 Monday
Des Voeux came 3d

26 October 1915 Tuesday
Des Voeux [17] fourth and fifth—and Nurse.

17. HJ continued in the care of Dr. Des Voeux and on 2 December had the first of a series of strokes. See the Deathbed Dictation.

III
Dictated Notes

Dictated Notes
1900–1915

The Turning Point of My Life
(1900–1901)

The Houghton typescript consists of four double-spaced, unnumbered pages, 8″ x 10″; the fourth page has only two lines.

When a distinguished friend,[1] whose sympathy I have a pampered sense of almost inveterately enjoying, lately remarked to me that every man's life had had its "turning-point," and that there were cases, particular lives, as to which some account of what had turned on it, and how and why the turn had come, couldn't fail to be interesting, I glanced back at my own career in the light of this generalisation—only perhaps, however, to look too blank and unrecognising. This made the light, thanks to the source of it, glow more brightly—that is with an even more than customary kindness; my own case and my own life were in other words a matter into which my friend could sufficiently enter to remind me of their having had upon a time at least the appearance of one of the momentous junctures in question; occasions of the taking of the ply that is never again to be lost, occasions of the true vocation or the right opportunity recognised more or less in a flash, determinations in short of character and purpose, and above all of a sharper and finer consciousness. It so happened that I had in the deepest depths of the past spent a year at that admirable institution the Harvard Law School,[2] and that, with-drawing from it prematurely—though under no precipitation that I may not now comfortably enough refer to;—I brought away with me certain rolls of manuscript that were quite shamelessly not so many bundles of notes on the perusal of so many calfskin volumes. These were notes of quite another sort, small sickly seed

1. At this point in the typescript some hand other than HJ's has inserted, in ink, "[Mark Twain]''; the distinguished friend, however, was probably William Dean Howells. See the reference below to "the first literary nosegays": HJ's first signed stories appeared in the *Atlantic Monthly,* of which Howells was sub-editor under J. T. Fields. See *Life* 72–73, 88–91.

2. HJ was enrolled during the academic year 1862–63.

enough, no doubt, but to be sown and to sprout up into such flowers as they might, in a much less trimmed and ordered garden than that of the law. My friend had reason enough to remember two or three of the first literary nosegays they were to enable me to gather—boldly disposed on his own editorial table as he was one day to find them; and he now suggested to me the inference that, since the tribute with which I was so promptly to affront him had, in principle, forced its way up through a soil that so little favored it, I must there, in the cold shade of queer little old Dane Hall,[3] have stood at the parting of my ways, recognised the false steps, even though few enough, already taken, and consciously committed myself to my particular divergence. Let me say at once that I welcomed the suggestion—for the kindly grace of it, the element of antique charm and bedimmed romance that it placed, straight away, at the disposal of my memory; by which I mean that I wondered whether I mightn't find, on ingenious reflection, that my youth *had* in fact enjoyed that amount of drama. I couldn't, I felt, be sure; but the question itself, and its accompaniments, appealed to me; giving me, the ancient, the classic thrill known to all those who have felt the ground made firm for talking about themselves. So at any rate seems to stand before me, wreathed with flowers, smiling Opportunity; with the reminder in her eyes of the numberless men and women who, on smaller provocation, have leaped to her embrace. It is well enough to talk, overflowingly, of the things one had thrown off and that seem so to have ceased to be part of oneself; but real bliss of publication, I make out, must be for those one has kept in—that is if they have at all richly accumulated and are too tightly packed to be gouged out (or, to put it more delicately, too shy or too proud to consent to be touched).

3. Dane Hall housed the Harvard Law School.

Rough Statement for *The Chaperon* (November 1907)

The Houghton manuscript bears the title "Rough MS and Scenario for the first act and beginning of Second of a proposed 3 act comedy, founded on 'The Chaperon' about 1909 [?]." It consists of fifty-three typed pages.

The varied history of this literary item—sometime story and would-be play—is told in *Complete Plays*, 607–608. See the notebook entries of 13 and 21 July 1891 for HJ's initial idea for the short story "The Chaperon," and the detached notes for *The Chaperon* for its preliminary development as a play.

Irresistible the pressure of inducement just to break ground, if nothing more, for a first go at the elements involved in this application of my idea; as nothing is done till one begins actively to grope, till one makes something in the nature of a start, however false, and with no matter how many steps to retrace and how many merely experimental *percées* into the vague or into the impossible one may make. This is the only way the possible comes; one must explore the country right and left, leaving no square foot of it untrodden or unsearched.

What I seem then to have got hold of, essentially, for the basis of my Exposition is the Occasion of the girl's—that is of Rose Tramore's—keeping for convenience the little names, provisionally, of the Tale—Birthday, or coming of age, or whatever; I mean the date at which, under the terms of her Father's will, her freedom of action practically begins. This seems to me very arrangeable, quite without difficulty; she simply comes of age, comes into her little money, which isn't very much, at twenty-one, quite as if she were a boy. The fact that an entertainment of some sort, of however mild an order, should commemorate this circumstance, may not on the face of it appear extraordinarily natural, but may be made so, quite easily, with moderate tact and ingenuity. It has only to be sufficiently *constaté* that the young Tramores, the three of them, have always, ever

439

since their domiciliation with their Grandmother, enjoyed this little institution of the birthday-party, by an amiable family tradition, and by the epicurean humour in especial of their late Father, whose habit it has been to make up for a good deal of light and easy neglect of them (leaving them altogether to his Mother and Miss Tramore) by these three little commemorations or recreations in the year, one for each, for which he has provided conjurors, or fiddlers, or birthday cakes, or whatever, in the past; and for which he would now presumably do the thing more handsomely, were he alive to adorn with his presence this important date for his eldest child. What I am supposing is that he has been dead for rather more than a year, and that to-day is precisely a sign of the coming out of mourning, as it were, of the two Girls, who have practically stayed at home, so to speak, ever since; with the first appearances in the "world" of each of them, the first small social launching of the elder in particular, prematurely overdarkened by their bereavement, and above all by their highly sincere and decorous observance of it: an observance that has in Rose's case seemed rather excessive and overdone even to old Mrs. Tramore and to Julia T.; whom I see as somehow a bit irritated and ruffled in advance of this first symptom of the Girl's capacity for her own view and system and little private idea and conviction, firmly grasped and quietly, persistently applied, about everything. The boy is at his crammer's or wherever, and though probably present to-day, I make out no urgent use for him; the two others have then been living, in their old way, with their Grandmother, though of course, I must be careful to note, not absolutely buried; Rose having necessarily had to form the few social relations that immediately come into play: which, as this must be perfectly clear, I conceive her having formed during the year of her first "coming out"; the brief time between that event and her Father's death, during which she went about more or less under his easy and highly adequate protection, making the acquaintance of the sort of people he knew, "good" society, the best, essentially; into which her prettiness, cleverness, all the attributes it is necessary she should have, have made him quite happy and proud to be able to introduce her. It is from that time, for instance, that her acquaintance with Lady Maresfield dates, and the marking her for her own, then and there, by that lady, who has seen how beautifully she will probably do for the young up-growing, up-climbing, Guy. In connection with which remember that the little share of her patrimony that she comes into must be something of a respectable thing; the figure of it, with a thousand other items and values, to be fixed at closer quarters; as well as the very important matter of her further, though her wholly contingent, expectations from Old Mrs. Tramore; who can give or withhold quite according to her own pleasure and to the attitude taken by each of these young beneficiaries. It is highly conspicuous, of course, that she can "cut off" Rose at her discretion, if sufficiently displeased with her, and can divide everything between her unmarried middle-aged Daughter and her Son's two other children; who are such quite other affairs than Rose, and so comparatively plastic and, as it were, abject. But meanwhile, at any rate, Rose has enough of her own not only to "go on" with, but to make Lady Maresfield, not to speak of others, regard it as a "factor," a potential one, in an appreciable prospective income for Guy. It mustn't be presented as imperceptible to the other young man either, the young man who figures in the

Tale as the rather priggish and precautionary, but really decent and sincere and loyal, Captain of Engineers, Bertram Jay; but whose profession, situation etc., I must now visibly alter to something more Contributive. I postulate that he will have met her first, and got his impression and so forth, during the year of her so distinctly successful little going-about before the subsequent sequestration; the continuity and consistency of which, *par parenthèse,* it would be admirable to be able to make salient as one of the many sharp, effective Notes of Character and Design, of intelligent choice and the Long View, on the part of my young woman. She has seen him since, but only three or four times, as she has seen also the youth presented in the Tale as Guy Manger; but has seen nothing much of anyone, as we definitely make out, and has really spent her time in nursing the conscious purpose and storing up the precious courage, to which it is the function of Act First to represent her as giving effect to in the most conspicuous and interesting and "dramatic" manner possible. Bertram Jay has had contact with old Mrs. Tramore, who approves and favours him and on whom—this being an Element of almost the first Value—she exactly counts to throw his weight, with Rose, on *her,* the old woman's side, in the conflict of judgment, opinion, in fine sharp and decisive action, which she has begun, though within a very short time, to see brewing and looming and darkening the domestic prospect, between herself and her Granddaughter. I make it out that Jay's function in this act is essentially to represent, to Rose, in common with Julia Tramore, the old woman's high and passionate, at any rate absolutely rigid and final view of the situation: I see him as yet, so far as I grope my way, for the time lucidly confined to that function. Her break with him is thus part and parcel of her break with her Grandmother, her Aunt, her Brother, and her Sister; her ultimatum to him part and parcel of her ultimatum to *them;* her making up of her mind, luminously, insurmountably, to do without him so far as any further Discussion is concerned, but the other face of her preparedness, which I should like, I seem to make out, to be the subject of a little separate scene with each (save that here, at this stage, are of course abysses for further sounding) to do without most of the things that have made up her life hitherto. Salient, moreover, before I go further—and it bears on the question of her actual "means"—the high value of her definite "forfeit," as the price of her perversity: it being important for my purpose that she should forfeit something still more tangible than her place "in the Family" and the sympathy and esteem, the very intercourse, as it were, of the other members of it. She must forfeit money in some marked and eminent degree; she must bring money, in some degree or other, to her Mother—it is even one of her motives; yet I must reconcile this with her still having that which may still keep her in question for Lady Maresfield and such-like, during the period of her sacrifice and her ostracism. Apropos of which, at the same time, I recall that these designs of the Importunate are precisely to get her to give her Mother up, to renounce her missionary work, her quixotic campaign, as the bad job it is one of the Functions of Act Second to make it superficially appear; and so go back to the loaves and fishes, to the recovery and realisation of her possible prospects, that is, if she makes it up with the scandalised old woman before the latter dies disinheriting her. To put it simply and provisionally, just to get it down, Mrs. Tramore, the elder, has resources her share of which, conditioned on "good terms," may accrue to her; and Miss Tramore has the same—the latter and Bertram Jay being, with the Brother and Sister, indeed, if I "drag *them* in," (all, as yet here, however, preliminary darkness) the immediate expository mouth-piece of these stern realities. By which I probably mean, in fact, by which I still more prettily and interestingly mean, I daresay, that, after having had all the needful home-truths about her Step from the three others, it is she herself who is the most, who charmingly becomes the most, authoritative exponent of them to the more or less deputed and delegated, the earnest, the anxious, the remonstrant, the supplicating, but the altogether baffled and discomfited, Jay. It in fact rises before me Interesting that, face to face with this question of Who the presented Agents here are limited or multiplied to; face to face with the question of keeping them down in First only to such as may be Agents and Values again in Second and Third; it glimmers beautifully, I say, that the young man, here through may, more effectively than not, do the whole business of old Mrs. Tramore, by his acting, speaking, comporting himself, in her name and at her behest; she having adopted him thus as her candidate and solemnly laid it on him to do what he can. I see this is an Artful Simplification, an accretion of value and interest for him; and as ministering, in fine, to my in every way sublime Economy. The Brother and Sister, Eric and Edith, say, have very conceivable uses wrapped up in them for Third; and Julia Tramore not less, she being presumably of the first degree of Designation for First; on the basis of involved sequences, later, finally, catastrophically, of all due vividness. Thus I get for the present Opposition the four persons thus named, with the further Social Adjuncts to be gone into. Step by step, inch by inch, one silver thread of the tangle handled at a time.

Old Mrs. Tramore, then, must be, I descry, conveniently, yet rather amply and "handsomely" suburban; this the most workable basis, I piously, if not presumptuously, judge, for my fundamental dispositions in Act First. What I thus sketchily see, to begin with, is the bright and beautiful afternoon, early in June, on which Rose's birthday-party is taking place, with people out from town in carriages, in motors even, *supposons*, and by train, a number of people sufficient to show the effort the fine old hostess has made to have a bright and copious muster of old friends—on the basis of cards sent out three weeks before and the further little fact that the high pitch of the Crisis (between herself and Rose) has come only after the invitations have been issued: so that things have been left as they are rather than cancelled—all the more that the old woman doesn't really know the "length" to which Rose has, all the while, really been going: the length, that is, of communication with her Mother already entered into, though she has obeyed the letter of her Father's wishes and impositions, by not yet having been to see her. She has only let her know, definitely, that she comes, and comes to stay, the Hour she is Free. Technically speaking, perhaps, she is not free till the day has wholly elapsed; so that, giving her plan the benefit of this doubt, she has determined to take her flight, to begin this new relation, only on the morrow. A part of the Function of Act First is to show this patience as more or less violently modified, to show her Departure, to show the Step in short, as dramatically precipitated. Wherewith, one promptly discerns, one of one's first cares is to establish and set forth, as an almost prime preliminary, how much of a shadow, in the form of a shock, a scandal, a general and particular flurry and chatter, this Coming Event has cast before it. Here spreads itself precisely, therefore, one of those Visions of Beauty which consist of the right, the felicitous and triumphant Determination of the March of the exhibited Case; the creation of the process or picture by which Clearness and Interest become complete; stage adding itself to stage, suspense to suspense, appearance to appearance, and the whole thing logically and dramatically developing. It is of the essence, in other words, that the ground is first thoroughly laid, up to the last point of excited expectation and curiosity, for our view of the particular thing that is happening, as to which our knowledge grows minute by minute; and that then from a given moment Rose's advent takes it all up, where artful Preparation has left it off, simply stationing itself at the right point to hand it over to her; and that *with* this appearance or irruption she takes it completely in charge to climax. But the Preparation here will have to be of the most consummate; which is but a reason, an inspiration and a value the more.

Roughly speaking, then, old Mrs. Tramore is out in the grounds, where the beautiful day permits all the best of everything to go forward; and we have the sufficient image of her reported, reflected, and borne in to us by a pointed reference and echo, while our own immediate picture is constituted in the Drawing-room of the house, open to the terrace, verandah, lawn and whatever, and serving as a partial place of transit and arrest; also rendered comparatively private and proper for my uses by the fact that everyone instinctively goes further, has been "shown through," as it were; no one pausing, lingering, or making use of it without such good reasons as our action brings into play and makes them conform to. Admirably interesting and appealing, always, this question of one's first "struck" note; the determination, really mathematical in its logic, of the point furthest back and yet at the same time nearest to, at which one's March must visibly, audibly, fruitfully begin; as with the concentrated germ of the Whole of the Rest folded up in it. There is always question of the sufficiently Far Back for Clearness, and the sufficiently Near To for Straightness and Immediacy. Well, I seem, till the contrary is proved, to clutch that point here with the production of the two Young Men, as I call them, the youths who figure, so very slightly, in the Tale as Eric Tramore and Guy Manger, but who here immediately acquire an appreciable value. I seem to make out, for experiment, that, at rise of Curtain, the young Eric, coming in from the Grounds, meets the Butler just introducing the young Manger, to whom he says—the Butler does—that everyone is outside, but that he can pass through this way. Important, evidently, that there must be the appearance of two Ways out to where everyone is gathered; a way, and especially a course of Egress and Departure (always from the Grounds) more directly connected with the Entrance to the House; so that there is the presumption, the indication, of coming and going, but in particular of going, independently of this passage through the Drawingroom; it being marked that the latter becomes thus the scene of such passages, encounters and contacts as are specially motivated and conditioned there. Another point to make here instantly, further reflection shows me, is that the Occasion, at rise of Curtain, is already waning to its close, though the long June afternoon still is bright; and that the main movement is the ebb of the tide, the stream of departure so that the latter part of the act, the whole Climax, finds the principal Agents free and unencumbered. Putting aside the three other persons I have here next to deal with (I mean after Eric and Guy), there can be no entrance, of any outsider, save for the purpose of getting away. What glimmers to me now, at any rate, is that the butler *first* shows young Manger in, with an "Oh yes, sir, you can as *well* go this way: the Ladies receive in the Grounds" and that is just as the visitor is about to pass across and out to the visible Terrace or whatever, that the young Eric comes in from the quarter, greeting him with an: "Oh yes, you're very late, but you can get *through;* though if you'll wait a moment I'll take you." This note of the youth's lateness is emphasised, with some reference to the fact that people are moving off; and with some occasion for Guy to ask if his Mother is still there; with the answer on the other's part as to Lady Maresfield's—Oh yes!—"sticking"; and perhaps even to the presence of the sister, Mrs. Vaughan-Vesey of the Tale, a Value, I assume, for later on; and part of the sign of the way the family have rallied. What is instant, at any rate, here, is Eric's motive for hurrying in, indicated by an immediate sign to the Butler to wait, even while he receives the other youth, with whom I conceive for him considerable identity of futile type, age, occupation, and vague state of preparation of some "smart" profession; presumably, on the whole, not military. Eric sends the Butler up to his room for a certain box of precious cigarettes—those Granny provides being (for younger Manger) so beastly; producing ring of keys from his pocket and giving him instructions where to look, so that some minutes are provided thus for the Butler's absence while the two young men wait; Guy indicating, for that matter, his preference and purpose to wait; with a good little touch of reinforcement in fact thus glimmering upon me. He carries in his hand a small, or indeed a rather ridiculously large, box done up in white paper and pink ribbon, a tribute in the form of chocolate-creams, marrons glacés, or whatever that he has brought in the form of a birthday offering to the young Rose; but that he has immediately become shy, self-conscious, and awkward about, on finding it a question of his sallying forth with it across the lawn and presenting it before a lot of people. I am not sure even—since one must thresh out every alternative—that he may not have an initial passage with the Butler before Eric appears; the Butler having relieved him of his parcel and, having, also, as we learn and see, introduced him into Drawingroom at his rather flurried and preoccupied request, and standing there with the beribboned object delicately held to await his indications.

All outside, sir: Mrs. Tramore receives in the Grounds.

Then could you—ah—carry that out for me?

(Very grave.) Leaving you to—a—follow sir?

Oh no, I'd go with you. But I don't like to take it myself.

Nothing to—a—go off, sir?

Oh dear no—*(then rueful)* unless chocolate-creams, in large masses, *do* explode.

(On which the BUTLER, *who naturally has his business at the Door to attend to, availing himself impenetrably of this pretext.)* I had better perhaps place them here, sir—according to your first Idea.

(The young MANGER, *swayed by every breath, is constitutionally flurried, and agitatedly embraces this amendment.)* It *was* my Idea—where she'll see them; and perhaps wonder—!

In which case should I mention, sir—?

Oh yes, *do* mention; or *(as he sees* ERIC *come in)* perhaps, my dear chap, *you* kindly would! *(Then as* ERIC *takes in with surprise the very large beribboned box, with very big bows, that the* BUTLER *has now set down.)* Chocolate-creams—for Miss Rose!

ERIC. *(Who, entering from Terrace, has signed to* BUTLER *to wait, but is also amused at size of box.)* Half a Ton?

GUY. *(Complacent though flushed.)* For her Birthday!

ERIC. I'm afraid I should have to mention the Number as fatal. But do it yourself—they're all out there.

GUY. *(Who, by large open glass doors, has looked out, pulling himself up, rather, apparently, at what he sees; while the* BUTLER *approaches* ERIC, *who unhooks from left-hand pocket-button of his trousers a silver key-chain, with rings and several keys attached.)* I should like you to *take* me out!

ERIC. I *will*—with my Cigarettes. *(To* BUTLER, *who takes the keys from him.)* The *best* tin box in one of my locked drawers: search 'em *all* till you find it! I'll wait. *(After which, while* BUTLER *goes out and he turns to* GUY.) Granny's are too beastly!

GUY. *(Coming away from window; simple, surprised.)* Is Mrs. Tramore smoking?

ERIC. *(With fine youthful impatience and importance.)* For all I know—she has so lost her head!

GUY. *(Wondering, interested, but never anything if not simple.)* Through having such a Crowd?

ERIC. *(Prompt, sharp.)* Through having such a Grand-daughter.

GUY. *(As thinking quite to seize the point.)* Do you mean your so awfully successful Sister?

ERIC. *(Emphatic, resentful.)* I mean my Sister Rose, whose Success strikes me as mainly in setting us All—I mean all of us who have lived together here with Granny since Papa's Death: Aunt Julia and Edith and Me, you know—most awkwardly by the Ears; and in availing herself, for the purpose of this handsome Celebration—though I do say it!—of her Twenty First Birthday.

GUY. *(Anxious, alarmed.)* You don't mean to say she has gone and got Engaged?

ERIC. *(Youthfully superior; his thumbs in his waistcoat armholes; his eyes on the other a moment.)* There are more ways than that, old Chap, of making a Fool of yourself!

GUY. *(Gloomy, vague.)* And that's what she's doing—?

ERIC. *(Distinct, definite.)* What she's doing is to make some such Exhibitions of all of *us*—and above all such an Exhibition, as one may say, of the Character and Conduct of our late admirable Father who, in a most important particular, took pains to lay down the Right Line for us. From that Line Rose has just proclaimed it her intention to Deviate.

GUY. *(At sea, imperfectly following.)* "Proclaimed" it—before the Crowd?

ERIC. *(In his own manner.)* Before the Crowd assembled—but not in time, most unfortunately, to *prevent* its assembling.

GUY. *(Mystified but impressed.)* She's up to something, you mean, to put off a Party for?

ERIC. *(Like an approved man of character, and above all of action.)* I'd have put it off—if we had known it in Time. But she spoke but this Morning.

GUY. *(More and more anxious.)* What then did she speak of?

ERIC. *(Bringing it out with gravest effect.)* She spoke of Mamma.

GUY. *(Enlightened, relieved, even a little amused.)* Oh—I see!

ERIC. *(With the same high gravity.)* We *don't* speak of Mamma. *(Then for return of* BUTLER.*)* So *hush!* *(To* BUTLER.*)* Put them down.

GUY. *(While* BUTLER *places cigarette-box and goes out.)* But do you mean it affects *my* Chance?

ERIC. *(Who has gone to the table and taken out a cigarette; sniffing it.)* I didn't know you *had* a "chance"! *(Then as he passes him one.)* Will you have a Cigarette?

GUY. *(Distressed, though taking the cigarette.)* You haven't known about it all this Time?

ERIC. *(Impatient, lighting his cigarette, but, in his preoccupation, offering the other no light.)* Known about what?

GUY. *(Almost touchingly simple.)* Why, that—more than fifteen months ago— she Refused me.

ERIC. *(Smoking.)* Ah, fifteen months ago she Refused fifty fellows! That was before Papa's Death.

GUY. *(Definite.)* The year she came out—so tremendously Out! *(Ingenuous.)* She refused me twice.

ERIC. *(Dry.)* Do you want her to do it again?

GUY. *(Embarrassed, rueful, even slightly boobyish; scratching his thigh and looking askance at the big box.)* That wasn't what I brought those Sweets for!

ERIC. Hadn't you then better eat them yourself? I don't think it a particularly good moment for you to try again.

GUY. *(Then his eyes still a bit sheepishly and shamefacedly askance on his massive tribute.)* My Mother, you know, supposed that—with the Day and all, the charming Celebration and the happy Occasion it rather *would* be; and she directed me herself therefore to bring with me some nice little thing that would *please.*

ERIC. *(Amused.)* Ah, so that's your idea—? Well, you quite sufficiently "please"—yourself, my dear fellow,—however you come; please all of us together, I mean, so that I'm sure we're very glad to see you. But *(after an instant, with decision)* I think there's something you ought to know.

GUY. *(With a slight awkward hesitation, as from delicacy.)* Well, there are a lot of things that my Mother has told me!

ERIC. *(With a return of his dryness.)* It's your Mother then that takes the principal interest—?

GUY. *(All candidly.)* Why, isn't she here now—what she calls preparing the ground for me?

ERIC. She is here, I believe, and has been for the last couple of hours: I've encountered Lady Maresfield, I confess, at every turn of the Garden. But I doubt that she can have told you what she can't possibly *know;* and what I think, *(after further consideration, then with emphasis and importance)* I had better mention to you, without delay; to clear your mind—or at least to clear your Mother's!— of any fond hopes for which we might, later on, be held responsible!

GUY. *(Plaintively, conscientiously.)* Ah, but my Mother's mind *is* so terribly clear!

ERIC. *(Turning on him with a certain superior pity.)* Not, I take it, about the terms of my Father's Will—which have hitherto been nobody's business but our own, but which I think, from to-day, should really be, like Lost Articles, advertised to "Whom it may Concern."

GUY. *(With a foolish, awkward, yet amiable, laugh.)* It's at least her notion— if you press me!—that you're not, you know, half badly off!

ERIC. *(Throwing up his hands in sharp impatience, breaking off, taking a turn, but then facing round again as with importance and resolution.)* Do you know anything about Mamma?

GUY. *(Much of the space of the room between them; looking at him an instant and speaking not without a certain mild "point.")* You *do* speak of her then?

ERIC. *(Unperturbed.)* I never *have,* in the whole Course of my Days—but *(as justifying it to him completely)* Rose has now made it necessary we should do so One for All.

GUY. I've at least always heard that Mrs. Tramore is lovely.

ERIC. *(Very straight, grave and* digne.) So lovely that my Father was—at an early stage—forced to take Action.

GUY. *(Half confessing, half wondering.)* You mean there was a Row?

ERIC. *(Superior; not faltering.)* In the Divorce-Court—yes: when—by Papa's Decree, to say nothing of that of the Court itself *we* were too young to know. Since when we've never so much as seen her.

GUY. *(Artlessly but irrepressibly pleased at this advantage.)* I have—at the Opera.

ERIC. *(With high propriety.)* We've never—in view of that Danger so much as *been* to the Opera. *(Reconstituting, presenting, their young Annals, their past History.)* We made Papa that sacrifice—as we made him all those of which, as I'm free to confess to you I think with all justice, he made, to the day of his Death, such an absolute point. We remained *his*—and I—for it sharply marks my Position—consider that we're His still; that we're in fact now His more than ever.

GUY. *(Impressed, interested, but slightly abashed and a good deal mystified.)* Do you mean that Mrs. Tramore—a—thinks—

ERIC. *(Breaking straight in.)* We've not the least idea what Mrs. Tramore thinks: it was settled in our Infancy that that was the *last* thing that was good for us. It was Papa's Arrangement that we were to live in Ignorance; and the Arrangement has perfectly *worked.* So we *have* lived—save for losing Him; "immune," as they say—till Rose takes this extraordinary occasion to start up and spoil All!

GUY. *(Following, but at a loss.)* But what does she want to do?

ERIC. *(As if it's so much more than enough.)* She wants to See her.

GUY. *(Wondering.)* And you consider that she *mayn't—?*

ERIC. Not if I can possibly prevent it!

GUY. *(After an instant; watching, as in suspense, his movements.) Can* you possibly prevent it?

ERIC. *(Arrested; his hands in his pockets, his shoulders up; after reflection.)* No. *(Then to explain.)* Rose is a Case.

GUY. *(As with, after all, his own opinion.)* She's a Brick—that's what I think, you know, she is!

ERIC. *(Dry, unmoved, ironic.)* You strike me as exactly expressing the Degree of her Sensibility! I mean, to the weight of Papa's high Example and Authority.

GUY. *(Yielding, conceding.)* Oh, of course she ought to mind—!

ERIC. *(Distinct, definite.)* She ought to mind her younger Sister, she ought to mind her elder Brother, she ought to mind her fine—and, I recognise, *firm*—old Granny, who has harboured us here from far back, and who remains the previous Vessel, as it were, of Papa's beautiful Influence. She ought, above all, to mind Public Propriety—and *(with significance)* a Lot more Things besides.

GUY. *(Who has taken this in as rather portentous; turning it over.)* Do you suppose my Mother's Appeal—

ERIC. *(Curt; sceptical; having quite, by his exhibition of his case, worked himself up to exasperation; so that he speaks, for the instant, indifferently and impatiently.)* You had better ask her!

GUY. *(Vague.)* Ask Miss Tramore—?

ERIC. Ask Lady Maresfield—if she thinks she can do any good. Only there are things that, in that case, she ought to know.

GUY. *(Interested.)* Things I may tell her?

ERIC. *(With a gesture, an impatience of assent.)* That Either of us who, under his Will, breaks its grand Provision—

GUY. *(As* ERIC *has paused as for positive pomp of effect.)* Loses a lot?

ERIC. *(With his effect.)* Loses Everything.

GUY. *(Impressed indeed.)* Everything?

ERIC. *(Making it unmistakable.)* Everything. But come out. I am conceiving at this point the Entrance, from the Terrace, of the personage not appearing at all in the Tale, but whom I make out as of high importance here—an importance I shall presently develop all the ground of; and whom I simply dub, to begin with, for convenience, the Colonel. In connection with which Entrance, as the two young men are about to leave, I immediately, suspending further detail, jot down roughly for benefit of memory the Concatenation of Sequences of the whole Act, the fine frame or mere osseous skeleton of it, as I from here experimentally view it. The Colonel arrives from the Grounds with of course, his abundant and vivid Motive; and I won't now tackle detail of the passage immediately taking place—the simple getting him in and getting the others out—beyond seeming to see that Eric shall have rung, just sharply pressed the bell, as he finally moved about, for Butler, and that on the latter's arriving he says to him, indicating the box of cigarettes on table, "Bring these." It is the Colonel who checks the Butler with his inquiry before the latter's Exit to Grounds and I thus promptly see that he mustn't have met the young men or crossed with them—a needless awkwardness—and that to this end, and probably certain other ends, though this alone would be enough, there must be a third easy Entrance to the Room. I have seen to the Left the Entrance from the Hall and main Passage of the House; which supposes the Diningroom where indoor Refreshments are liberally going on off in that quarter; which becomes a quarter of Reference. There is thus easily besides the Connection with Terrace and Grounds another Door or Passage to Right, as to a couple of other Rooms, smaller Sitting-room, Library, etc., upon which the Terrace also opens; so that they likewise may be entered from Garden. This is the way then the Colonel has come in, just as the young men go out and as the Butler, under orders, is about to follow them. He is instantly checked by the Colonel with the latter's question as to whether Lady Maud is there, whether he has seen her come or go, in fact whether the Colonel, who has passed through the other parts in search of her, is in time to get at her before she goes further. This is the Motive with which I bring him on; which he makes immediately vivid; and which gains further significance from the Butler's saying, that is becoming able to say, at sight of the person in question, just after the inquiry: "Here *is* her Ladyship";—and he may even announce her, true to his automatic habit, by her full name, as she appears at Entrance to Left. She and the Colonel thus instantly meet; the Butler goes out to Grounds, and they have their scene together. (Worth noting here, for remembrance, the small matter of a touch before the exit of the two young men. Eric has touched the button of the bell at the moment he says his second Everything; then he adds to his companion his "But we must go out." The Butler instantly appears, to whom he addresses his order to bring out the cigarettes, and makes his exit, while the Butler speaks to Guy. *"And* the chocolate-creams, sir?" On which I give a little the effect of the confidence about the girl's forfeiture of means just made him, by his hesitating, debating, while he just scratches his chin, and after a rueful glance at his massive tribute, decides and says "No!" He goes out after his friend, and then it is the Colonel arrives from Right in time to arrest the Butler. The moment there is of the briefest; the Colonel simply saying "Have you seen Lady M.?" and the man, one easily sees, on reflection, not uttering the superfluous word or two I imputed above, but simply with his look to the door Left as she appears there, announcing her by name; though indeed on reflection I see that as this is her first visit to the House he won't know her. Never mind; she has come in the moment before, while he was still outside, and he has heard her name herself to a footman. He simply hands it on, after the very momentary interruption caused by Eric's ring for him.) But I go into too many details that can wait so well till after I have finished, fully and simply stated, straight off, my present concatenation, as I have called it, of sequences. I shall come back, exhaustively, to the Function of the Scene between the Colonel and Lady Maud, as well as to the Function of each of these two individuals; though I can't forbear just noting here even now that he tells her he has come to stop her off, as it were, and why—because, in three words, he thinks it's better, given something that clearly has happened to the House, though, mind you, he doesn't at all know yet *really* what this is, she shouldn't, so to speak, make so bold. She promptly replies that she has come by reason of an invitation straight from Rose herself—the nicest little note in the world that the Girl has been so good as to write her. The Colonel retorts to this that he knows, precisely, all about the nice little note—Rose having mentioned to him, out there in the Grounds just now, that she had taken this step and is hoping for the practical response. But none the less, the Colonel feels, it won't do—it won't at all do. And pray why won't it do?

Well, it will make a difficulty for her. There's thunder in the air—or there's powder—and I've been enough in the House, as an old soldier, to smell it. Something has happened—I don't quite know what; but Mrs. Tramore is as grim as a Death's head, and I don't advise you to go near her. He suggests, or appears to suggest, that he won't answer for it that in such an event there mightn't be a scene—out there before everyone; so that "My dear woman, just nip away again unobserved, and forgive me the crudity of my warning, for which I feel that you'll live to thank me. You see I know her, and you don't." Then for clearness: "I'm not talking of Rose herself, poor child—but who, you know, is a most interesting creature; I'm talking, my dear, and entirely for your benefit, of the terrible old woman."

LADY MAUD. *(Who has taken this with immediate interest and good humour, though with my idea of her listening to him and watching him quite amusedly and ironically while he speaks, as if she knows, as indeed she does, more than he of the very thing he is talking about, and has thus her card up her sleeve.)* You say my "showing" may make a difficulty for Rose. But mayn't it perhaps make, rather, a facility?

COLONEL. It will scarce make a "facility" for anyone that the Old Woman shall be rude to you.

LADY MAUD. *(With her smile and her air.)* People are never rude to me.

COLONEL. *(With his own similar resource.)* That, my dear, is because you always choose the right ones. With these people here you'd choose the wrong.

LADY MAUD. I haven't chosen—I'm called. Don't you understand, if you've talked with Rose, why she has sent for me?

COLONEL. *(A bit annoyed, as she looks so knowing.)* Why, because it's her coming of age, as she calls it,—and because, as she says, she has cast, for the occasion, a very wide net.

LADY MAUD. *(Amused.)* Is that the way she puts it?

COLONEL. I make use of her own sweet metaphor.

LADY MAUD. She's very clever.

COLONEL. Of course she's very clever. Too clever for any of them here.

LADY MAUD. *(Full of her knowledge.)* She's too clever for you, my dear—if you haven't guessed then, on the spot, what she's up to.

COLONEL. *(Struck, and even as with a sense of his own odd density, clapping his finger-tips to his forehead.)* She's going to her Mother?

LADY MAUD. *(As playing her card.)* She has practically sent for me—as Flora's best friend—to bring her.

COLONEL. *(Immensely startled.)* Lord o'mercy! *(Yet amused too and wondering.)* To snatch her up and run with her?

LADY MAUD. I mean that she three days ago let Flora know she may count on her.

COLONEL. *(Immensely interested, but vague.)* But count for What?

LADY MAUD. For Society.

COLONEL. *(Throwing up his hands.)* But—how and where?

LADY MAUD. At Home. She can come to her.

COLONEL. *(Still mixed.)* Flora can come here?

LADY MAUD. *(Enjoying it.)* Rose can come to us. She announces, my dear, that she Will.

COLONEL. *(Not even yet wholly catching on.)* Come to see her?

LADY MAUD. *(For her climax.)* Come to Stay. Come to Live. *(Highly serene.)* Always.

COLONEL. *(Now really astounded.)* You don't mean to tell me she's going to Chuck—

LADY MAUD. *(Taking him up, laying her hand straight on his arm and holding him an instant with her eyes on him.)* What *does* she in fact Chuck?

COLONEL. Why, by the rigour with which Tramore settled it, Everything.

LADY MAUD. *(Assured.)* Then she'll do it. She wants to chuck all she can.

COLONEL. *(Facing it, taking it in.)* I say, I say, I say!

LADY MAUD. *(Smiling, but with a certain reflection on his tone.)* Don't you like it?

COLONEL. *(Rubbing the back of his head with something of a grimace.)* We'll say I *admire* it!

LADY MAUD. *(Good humouredly.)* I admit it's Heroic.

COLONEL. *(Emphatic.)* It's Sublime! She gives up, poor dear, so much more than she Knows!

LADY MAUD. *(After an instant; as having, a little awkwardly for herself, to recognise this, but passing it off as with a slight sarcastic dig at him.)* Well, so long as she hasn't to give up You—!

COLONEL. *(As in possession, more and more, of what it means.)* Ah, Maud, I feel that—as the one old Friend of her Father's who, whether by the wisdom of the serpent or by the sweetness of the dove, whether for a sign of my constitutional "cheek" or only for a proof of my constitutional insignificance, has managed to remain, miraculously, with a foot in either Camp, has contrived the trick of still seeing Them Here while being known or suspected yet to see You, and above all *Her,* Elsewhere, of being loyal to my poor stiff old Friend and his Memory, in short, without undue prejudice to Sympathies less arduous, even though of course, as you'll allow, less Exemplary—I feel, I say, that as such a monstrous master of social Equilibrium, it will be a question not nearly so much of her giving me up as of her taking me quite systematically and comfortably *on.*

LADY MAUD. *(Impatiently.)* If what you want is to make me again remark to you that I don't know what, for so many years, we should have done without you, I decline to be dragged again through the Dust of that Abjection. I call your attention moreover to the fact that the Day of Deliverance for Flora has come, as it were, in spite of you.

COLONEL. *(Interested in this view.)* She regards it then, poor dear, *as* her Day of Deliverance?

LADY MAUD. *(Her shoulders up as for all there is, vainly, to say of it.)* Did you ever see Flora—

COLONEL. *(Instantly, comprehendingly taking her up.)* Depart from her glassy, her inimitable calm? I'm bound to say that, to the best of my recollection, and for the particular Charm we most value in her—Never!

LADY MAUD. Well then you'll see her Now! *(After an instant, almost with unction.)* It's Beautiful to see her!

COLONEL. *(Appreciative, as with the vision.)* You make me *want* to!—if her Ecstasy has gone the length of really deputing you—!

LADY MAUD. *(Prompt.)* "Deputing," my dear? She brought me every inch of the way.

COLONEL. *(Astonished, again, even alarmed.)* To this Door? *(Anxious.)* Then where *is* she?

LADY MAUD. *(Again enjoying her effect.)* In the victoria.

COLONEL. *(Quite aghast.)* And where's the victoria?

LADY MAUD. *(Serene.)* I told it to drive up and down.

COLONEL. *(As for the lurid vision.)* With May[1] Tramore *in* it?

LADY MAUD. *(Amused.)* If she hasn't—in her Ecstasy—tumbled out!

At which moment it is, I think, that the Butler, who of course has had time to do everything outside and get round and back into the House, effectively intervenes; appears at Left and announces to the two others "Mrs. Charles Tramore!" She is there upon them, upon the Colonel in particular—though I mark Lady M. as not prepared either for the *coup de tête* of this sudden portentous and dangerous irruption: I see her there upon them, as I say, with the most characteristic Entrance and Aspect possible; her extreme prettiness and extravagant elegance of preserved youth, of immense care of herself, not really betraying the least departure from the glassy calm and the charming candid serenity that the Colonel has just appraised in her, and with the note, from the first and always, which is the prime note and value of her personality and effect through the whole play that though she expresses herself at moments with a certain innocent intensity of the superlative, and makes funny little statements about her emotions, opinions, conditions, her visible glossy, dainty, perfectly arranged and unperturbed state betrays at each moment, in the drollest way, the account she gives of herself. She stands there like a lovely large-eyed expensive doll: she says something like: "I felt I *had* to come up—don't you think?" It's her note also that she's always placidly, tenderly, weakly—and one feels at bottom all indifferently—appealing. She proceeds with the sweetest, most fixed, least fluttered stare and smile: "I'm too awfully agitated to sit!" Meanwhile they're both upon her; talking together. "But, my dear May,[2] you really oughtn't, you know. But, my dear, this is dreadful! But, my dear May, how reckless! But, my dear May, You'll spoil all!"

I think this last will probably prove a good cue for her—for something in the way of: "Then she *will* come!"

LADY MAUD. *(In despair, with movements of precaution, while the* COLONEL *has gone to the window upon the Terrace, to the door Right etc.)* She won't come if you dish us!

---

1. HJ has forgotten, in dictating, that his character's name is Flora and is now calling her May.
2. See preceding note.

COLONEL. *(Talking together with* LADY MAUD.*)* She won't come if you make a scandal!

MRS. TRAMORE. *(Absolutely unagitated by every sign, only looking about her with interest, as if taking in, in a perfectly detached way, the place, and its signs and tokens, her Daughter's habitation.)* She couldn't come to me here?

BOTH OF THEM TOGETHER. My dear woman, it's Madness!

MRS. TRAMORE. *(Smiling at them with her beautifully gloved and folded hands.)* But you don't know what it is to Wait!

COLONEL. *(Impatient, moving about, shrugging his shoulders, throwing up his hands.)* If you'd but take it from me what it may be for you *not* to Wait.

MRS. TRAMORE. *(Centre, looking straight before her with her beautiful fixed doll-like eyes.)* I've waited, you know, for Eighteen Years.

LADY MAUD. *(As ready to throw herself upon her to get her out.)* Then you might wait eighteen minutes.

Something is said, by her like Can't you let her know? which he echoes with: "Go out to her in the Grounds before everyone?"

Is she in the Grounds?

With all the rest of them?

With my other children?

With twenty Tramores!

Can I see her from there?

They both, as climax of short sharp scene get possession of her for retreat; the Colonel saying to Lady M.: "Take her, take her, take her—before anyone sees."

LADY MAUD. And not come back?

COLONEL. But don't you see? and, Lady M. then disappointedly assenting, Mrs. T., submitting, has yet an appeal to him:

MRS. TRAMORE. You don't back her? He throws up his arms: "I back her!"

LADY MAUD says: then come to us! He replies: "to-night!" and hustles them off.

I see meanwhile, that I didn't jot down, in the above rough adumbration of possibilities, the Colonel's question to Lady M. as to "Why" it is that Rose wants to go to her Mother; the thing that brings Lady M.'s reply: "To do her good"; with, possibly, the Colonel's demand then of "What good?" and her retort, to this, of some contributive Value or other. She may only say perhaps: "Ah, you must ask *her!*"—that is ask Rose herself; which has the value and merit of putting in element of preparation for the so potentially interesting passage, the Climax of the Act between Rose and the Colonel. It drives in the little silver-headed nail for that. Also, there is no hint in the foregoing—as how should there be?—of what is almost the major indispensable of the scene, the provision required, so absolutely, so intensely, for the *placing*, the identification, in relation to the Girl and to her Mother, of each of these two. The passage required, for Value and Effect, that the vision of who and what each of the parties is, who it is, on one side and the other, that is talking thus, that some such perfectly definite little brief basis shall have been made firm and sharp. Exquisitely manageable, however, this; and by my making Lady M. "do" it about the Colonel, to himself; and making the Colonel "do" it, in the same degree, to Lady M., about *herself. C'est la moindre*

des choses, as Difficulties go. So merely smeared a pictorial note, at any rate,
does, I think, vividly justify my sense of this enormous importance of putting in
the brief sharp vision, apparition, of Mrs. T., without a moment's more delay.
No further reference to her has, or can have, required Value or Effect without the
momentary *production* of her. Then the ground becomes firm, the spectator knows
where he is; nothing, in other words, need, or can, prevent the March from being
straight and strong. But I've tumbled into delay again as to memorising just here,
before anything else, the order of my little successions. Let me parenthesise, all
importantly, first, what I just above stupidly overlooked, that there is no reason
for the Colonel's not himself immediately hustling off the two women, not himself
departing with them in order to get them away, unless I give him his explicit
motive for remaining; which is there, fortunately, in perfectly precious little form,
and has only to be plucked in the manner of a full-blown rose from its stem. It
comes his reason, his urgent ground for remaining, and his liveliest interest in
doing so, exactly from the fact, about Rose's intention, that Lady M. has imparted
to him—exactly from this fact in general, and above all from Mrs. Tramore's last
word, her appeal about his "backing" the Girl in particular. "I'll back her," he
says, and he *gives* it, with all due point and force, that this is exactly why he
doesn't go away; why he remains there, waiting, wanting immediately to see Rose
again, all eager to do so—both so that he shall serve Mrs. Tramore's anxiety and
his own lively interest. So here is abundance of Provision; the carpet more and
more smoothly laid and tightly drawn.

The two women then have no sooner gone than, at Right, the door to what I
have called Library and so forth, the one by which the Colonel has himself come
in, if I mistake not, Lady Maresfield appears; having passed in, by the same
verisimilitude as the Colonel from the Grounds, and been ready, immediately, to
explain her entrance. One would have liked to make her arrive from Left, for a
particular reason; but this is impossible without the appearance of her crossing in
that manner with Mrs. T. and Lady M.—a fatal stupidity; and the only thing I
lose is my not being able to give her a word about her having come from the
quarter that one postulates as the Tea-room. Her reason of presence is immediate—she is looking for Rose; with whom her business, she intimates, is urgent—
just as the Colonel's is, we know, on his side; and since she is apparently by the
line of Lady Maresfield's quest, not now in the Grounds, where at any rate the
latter has missed her, it would have been mildly convenient for the Colonel to be
able to say, with his own impatient interest, "Isn't she then in the Tea-room?"
This, however, is nothing to waste words on—I mean for myself thus—and if I
give him, immediately, "Won't she be—if she isn't outside—in the Tea-room?"
it comes practically to the same thing. What is fundamental, and of the first importance here, is some formulation of the terms of acquaintance, of intercourse,
of preliminary reciprocity, between these two—just to match, as it were, the perfectly constituted formulations of the preceding scene; but with the pressure of
Time, of Space, going of course all the while crescendo; every inch, every instant
and fraction of such, being, I needn't say, a precious stinted quantity before Rose's
Entrance. Existing acquaintance, of a vague London order—but I won't go into
that now; it is exactly what trips me up in this would-be mere bald statement of

Sequences: I finish my statement first; then come back for real, consummate goug-ing everything out of everything. The passage between these two—suffice it—is constitutive according to its Function; and I may just note that it surely needn't draw itself out much, in fact can't do so, by reason of its thus discounting the scene that follows: all of Lady Mare.'s business being intensely reservable of course for the latter; with no clumsy leak in advance. Exquisite, really, for the Form this measure, this perfect sanctity and purity of the Passage or Part true consummately, ideally, to its Function, and keeping its edges as clear and sharp as steel from other muddlements and communities. So much, I say, for what awaits us between Lady Mare.'s and Rose; which we arrive at in its order. There is, however, valuably, importantly, or—to say the only word—constitutively— which I see the Colonel handling with her—beyond the mere little fact that they both "want" Rose. I can't help just worrying this Value here for a moment, in order to formulate it. What I do see, certainly, first of all, is that the very flurry and commotion, in either breast, which, on mention of Rose, betrays itself straightway by the holding back of neither, by their breaking ground on the Re-markable Matter or Startling News, they have just learnt, he from the women who have just left him, she from her Son, in the Grounds, on his going out there with his friend—I do descry this, I say, as a pictorial contributive Value. It gives the note of the consternation created; and really gives it the more strongly in propor-tion as the pair have not really had anything more (as they may so well, after all, not have been likely to have) than a mere sketchy, scrappy, casual London ac-quaintance. But more than this is wanted; and indeed, stupid that I am, I get it on the instant—it having been at the back of my head all the while; Lady M. becom-ing straightway for the Colonel, the sharp, high, vivid expression of the intensely shocked "worldly, conventional, social view," of Rose's projected action. She *gives* him this, of course; whereby I take it as figuring for him as a Determinant, in his own predisposed sense—that is as the sketch for the large formidable pic-ture, to be hung up now in Chester Square, say, of the arrayed, the inimical, ignoring, cold-shouldering, dropping and cutting scandalised proper world. More-over, as I instantly see, on exerting the smallest squeeze, I obtain here other Values, other little sharp, crisp Values, that neither of the two previous passages could give me, and that, though here just within the limit, are essentially of the sort that can't brook another moment's holding over. Not sharply, not possible "formulated" yet, one immediately grasps, the Truth of the Peculiar Horror and Scandal, the Unprecedented Degree of the Commotion, surrounding poor Mrs. Tramore's Case 18 years before: the most important point in the world this, as I need scarcely state. The whole thing rests, as my little Tale in its way set forth, on the fact that all this *histoire* was prodigiously Exceptional—in the supposed Displeasingness of its features, an affair standing altogether by its dreadful, unef-faceable, unforgivable Self; so that the Attitude of Society has ever been in the same degree Exceptional, with not a muscle of its rigour relaxed, nor a symptom of the common inevitable eventual Condonation yet beginning to peep. Of the essence that this vital truth shall be established at the earliest juncture—whereby I had been taking for granted that it might just a little be dealt with between the Colonel and Lady Maud. There is, indubitably, some little place for it there; but it has to reckon there—being of course moreover wholly out of the question in the previous scene, which needfully stretches the nature of Eric's allusion to his Mother to the utmost length—with the sharp celerity of that encounter, which loses truth, on the spot, if it loses a certain breathlessness; accordingly these moments of this Scene Fourth *is* obviously my first moment of the golden opportunity; in conjunction with which it figures to me further, by the blessed law that the *squeezed* material, once it is real material, always gives out, as it were, the precious phosphorescent glimmer of what one needs—that here exactly pops in my germ of what I need the Colonel most particularly to "give" about the actual present facts of Mrs. T.'s position and existence (for herself) and, coincidently with this, of the form and habit of his own sustained Countenance of her, his continued, in short, friendship for her. He must make his little vivid statement with a sharp, effective radiation of rather droll, pitiful Picture in it, of what the current fact and features literally and familiarly (to him) are; not "discounting" even this, however, in view of what I reserve for him, at Climax, with Rose. He has facts to give her about her Mother; though, after all, as by that time her Determination will have been *wholly* taken, I seem to make out the case for their being most predominantly, quite most, administered to Lady Maresfield. She brings them on, as it were; promptly "voicing," as the newspapers say, the reprobation of the world, and forecasting it, though again, remember well, without discounting what I reserve for her with Rose. Her tone, her attitude, affect and aggravate the Colonel, who, given his idiosyncracies, is driven into sharper opposition by them; so that he positively "draws" her a little, into portrayal of the particular consistency and duration of the terms of the poor lady's outlawry—under the ban (pile this up) as London has never really seen a woman once well-connected before: all of which promotes what I want, for Clearness and Sharpness from the moment Rose comes on on the part of the Colonel. It is at the Climax then of Lady Maresfield's own "statement," as it were, in which her allusion to Mrs. T. as "that horrible woman," or something of that sort, rings out—it is at this juncture, I say, and quite as if she may have caught the expression as she stands there, that Rose appears: the Colonel seeing her first and raising a sharp hand of caution, an imperative "Hush!" as he becomes aware of her. She arrives up at Back from the Grounds and stands there a moment, in her birthday array, framed by the window-space and gravely looking from one to the other in a manner to suggest her guessing without difficulty to what this appearance of a somewhat heated passage between them refers itself, and who it is Lady Maresfield is in the act of denouncing. With which I immediately remember the stupid omission, in the immediately foregoing, of what I had in view definitely to note: the circumstance of Lady Mare.'s mentioning to the C., on her own entrance, not only that she has thought Rose might be in the room, but has thought she might be awaiting her, in consequence of her having mentioned to her, in the Grounds five minutes before—that is the older woman's having mentioned to the younger—that she would like so immensely a few minutes privately, as might be, with her. Yes, she has said this to the C., directly, for presentation of a motive; and she seems to convey that it is her habit to assume that when she has made such intimations of her desires, she mostly finds them promptly taking effect. This by itself is a note, for that matter, that just perceptibly aggravates the Colonel; he puts it quite forth, on his side, that he is staying on purpose for a word with the Girl; in connection with which I really seem to see the "fat on the fire," as it were, a little between them. To which, still further, let me note, just here, that it has glimmered before me as a little elementary effect that Lady Mare.'s denunciation, representation, misrepresentation, indignant evocation in fine, of Mrs. T., the parcel of monstrous colours, in fine, in which she brushes her off, gains for us, gains for irony and comedy, by the fact that we have just had Mrs. T. in our eye, in her habit as she so remarkably lives, survives and blooms; and that I also *constater* that Lady Mare. has never at all seen her, I mean in the multitude of London chances, which Guy has profited by; and that this marks the particular circle of revolution in which Lady M. goes round—all such chances being really out of her ken. She is really the dry hard kind of grim dragon of a British Matron; with the attenuation or aggravation of her characteristic desire to push her advantages and provide for her young. Rose, at any rate, is meanwhile there, as much "led up to" as can possibly be perpetrated; and with Lady M.'s instantly checking and recovering herself enough to greet her all eagerly with an "Oh, it's so sweet of you to have come!" Which Rose slowly advancing, after having completed at her ease, as it were, her look from the Colonel to the lady, and from the lady to the Colonel, receives with a reserve, or even with a vague protest that appears to indicate that she hasn't come for *this* formidable Visitor at all. In fact—I seize the conviction— she makes it clear, for my presently-to-be-realised advantage, that this is particularly not the case: she simply looks, keeps looking, like a sort of beautiful young Fate at the elder woman quite hard for a minute, and even disconcerting the latter's own fine hardness perceptibly by doing so, and by making no acknowledgement of the speech just addressed to her. I seem to want her to convey that the phrase, the tone "that horrible woman!" or whatever it is, continues to ring in her ears. Then, when her attitude has sufficiently conduced to this rather striking image, it is to the Colonel she speaks, and quite, for him, as an old and interesting, a valued and charming family friend.

ROSE. I'm so glad to find you—for three words. (*Then as she comes down, brushing past, as it were,* LADY MARESFIELD; *speaking only to the* COLONEL.) I was afraid you had gone without speaking to me. Lady Mare. instantly breaks in, before he has had time to do more than make a gesture, as with her prior claim: which bits only await treatment. The Colonel does the graceful thing, gives way, and there is an exchange or two during which Rose says nothing to their companion; only says to him that he must then come back to her—and that he had better meanwhile go and have his tea properly. He promises his return, and his exit to Left leaves her with Lady Maresfield; toward whom her attitude, not a little inscrutable, is that of not breaking silence till she is forced, as it were, of leaving the burden of approach, the inevitable floundering and embarrassment—if Lady M., has any delicacy—all on the other hands. Lady M., hasn't, in point of fact, any delicacy and immediately shows it: she straightway mentions to Rose that her Son Guy has just told her, just repeated to her—as it was his duty—what Eric Tramore has told him: viz. of her entertained, of her nourished, of her domestically imparted intention of "seeing" her Mother. I go on, with my Concatenation, straight from here; but again can't help just parenthetically noting, memorising, that this must quite definitely "give" that Lady Mare. knows it *only* from her Son; so that we have it definite that, as the Colonel has just been shown as knowing it only from Lady Maud, so, evidently and definitely, the thing hasn't as yet spread abroad. It is precisely in order to speak before it has had time to do so— and this exactly is the manner in which she puts it—that Lady Mare. now presents, announces, describes and images herself as rising there as the remonstrant, the warning Voice of Society. I give her this Function—the grand gist and essence of which is that if she does carry out her perversity Rose will simply find that she can't decently marry. Or she puts this at least for Climax, luridly presents first, the other things she forfeits; showing moreover that she hasn't needed to have, as yet, from old Mrs. Tramore the family view of her wicked course: she has gathered that sufficiently from her Son's echo of Eric's tone. A truce, however, to this immediately lingering; everything has to be come back to in such abysmal detail, and with such exhaustive thoroughness. Suffice it that the scene terminates with Bertram Jay's advent: he being announced by the Butler, Left, at exactly the right psychological moment. He is discomforting too, in his degree and manner to Lady Maresfield, thanks to the possibilities or presumptions as to his "carrying off" Rose, that cluster about him and some foretaste of which she has already had—as may well be involved, moreover, in the fact that if I don't get my "Preparation" for this Entrance between the two women in some way or other I don't get it at all. This highly vital fact, with its lesson to be extracted to the last drop; while I for the moment just now jot down that the Young Man determines Lady M.'s exit, that after this scene between the Others then, that is with its sequel, the "shank" of the Act, his exit is determined by the entrance of Julia Tramore, the aunt, from Grounds with request from her Mother, the old woman, still grimly encamped under her tree, that he will come out to see her. He goes, by Back after appealing to Rose for prospect of his seeing her again before leaving. Julia observes on this, conceivably if not monstrously, that perhaps after he has seen her Mother he won't want to see her niece, and then, on his exit, has her own highly important passage with the Girl. Into all the Values of this I don't pretend to go at this moment; suffice it that her exit is determined by Jay's return from Grounds, after his Interview with the old woman, and with his request to her Daughter that she will immediately go to her. Exit Miss Tramore; on which I get Jay's second and contrasted scene, his transformed attitude and appeal, to the Girl. He of course on his first entrance had arrived, late, straight from town; having heard nothing, knowing nothing. I get, I say, my Big Value for this encounter, which culminates then in the Colonel's return, as by his previous agreement; producing Jay's exit and departure. Then my Grand Climax, as it were, of the Situation of Rose and Colonel, culminating—well, in what I make it culminate in; and Curtain.

I am much moved to strain on to a preliminary rough ciphering-out of Second; but such a cloud of considerations still hangs about what I have here in hand that I must just worry with it a moment longer. All sorts of things come up; as for instance, in the light of future needs and opportunities, the whole of the future Situation, the question of the best Value for the Maresfield Young Man, as to whom my indication at the beginning of this Act is of course a mere vague hint, the survival of what was in the Tale; a form that will clearly take great bettering, in respect to what one may wish to get out of him, to do with him and use him for, in the further complexity. I see of course that the Tale really gives me nothing for him that is of special value here; and as one wants of course but to go in for Interest at any price, he must be conceived in the light of that interest; as to which I find myself just catching a considerable Glimmer, to be further caught, to be exhaustively worked out, further on. And then, as regards the foregoing, there are all sorts of things to be said about all my Values and possible, or rather and inevitable, Developments and Intensifications, from Rose's entrance on, she remaining on to Curtain, as the extremely interesting Agent and Centre of them all: to say nothing, for that matter, of those that precede her entrance—though I mustn't even accidentally speak as if the Whole thing were not one Intense and Continuous Fusion. On the degree to which the matter of the relation of my Young Woman and principal Young Man has to be, and will be, can't help, in my hands, becoming, richly and charmingly Interesting, I needn't Discant: there are so many things *in* it—*as,* for that matter, there are such innumerable workable and desirable things, right and left at every turn, in all the rest. But this is my Horse-of-Battle, my High Ridge of Interest and to keep it so, vividly, from beginning to end, is of course the golden key to—well, to what I want. All this, however, goes so without saying. What I wanted particularly to note is that, as my rough adumbration stands, I get the Family Opposition to the Girl directly embodied only in her Situation with Julia Tramore, who represents thus, of course, represents officially and portentously, as it were, the Family, speaks for Them, for her august old Mother, the suggested Image of whom, invisible, but intense, and ruling the scene in spite of her absence from it, one wishes somehow to make felt, to make felt, to make appreciable, to cause, as it were, effectively and, I say, portentously, to play through. Miss Tramore represents, above all, and "voices" the dead Father and the view he would take of the case were he there; speaks for this, urges this, makes it definite, gives it all its Value; gives their Value, above all, to the facts, the sharp material facts that represent, collectively, the consequences and penalties, the losses and forfeitures, entailed by Rose's act. We must know with the most perfect clearness what these are, with what clearness they are present to herself, and with what clearness present to Bertram Jay, after his interview with old Mrs. Tramore has made them so. I want them present also—by which I mean *represented as* present to the Brother, and Sister; for whom, with these things, as I even thus roughly thresh them out, and therefore, evidently, still more, as I shall consummately cipher them in detail; for whom, I say, the Climax of Act I strikes me, even under this light pressure, and as a consequence of this vague squeeze, as having more use and play than the foregoing scratches glance at. Yes, I want, all naturally, my Climax here *enriched* and, as it were, amplified as much as possible; and there are uses for the Brother and Sister in conducing to such enrichment and amplification. In the jottings, or as I say, the scratches, for they are no more, just perpetrated, *from* them, I say, this would result, that each of my Situations or cumulative passages, from Rose's Entrance to End would consist of two persons, practically; since the overlapping two or three times of a third doesn't count to speak of. This is very well, but I needn't in the least accept it as final; and I have my Brother and Sister all convenient, all contributive, all logically, and in fact indispensably, involved, for some small creation of the relief of Number. There Glimmer upon me the ways, the lights, in which They may fill out, animate and curiously, amusingly, ironically, illustrate, in the interest of fine Comedy, the Family Attitude exemplified by Miss Tramore—to which they give further body and colour. The simplest way to put it, and it immediately and dramatically imposes them, is that, as they profit handsomely by everything Rose relinquishes and forfeits, I must have them there to *do* so; have them there for the representation and picture of their doing it; with whatever features and illustrations of their partly priggish, partly rueful, in any case pictured and presented state of Conformity, of disciplined submission, of interested calculation (though not in the least heinous, or really ugly, of course) may be achievable for them. Beautiful and exquisite problems the very keeping of all this is the Tone, the right and bright and light, and always interesting, but never ugly, not overdone, nor in any way miscarrying or deviating, or, I needn't say, blundering, Ironic. The working in of Eric and Edith, or whatever their names may confoundedly be, is a part of the little goldmine that awaits me again to dig in; suffice it for the moment that I see them as presently reinforcing their Aunt in her Supreme Appeal, as, after a bit, associated with her in it; or perhaps even as kept in abeyance then, to be associated and admirably involved in my Climax Proper, as I must call it, the Situation of Rose and her invaluable old Family Friend and Man of the World, her old contributive Chorus and Critic and Precious General Agent, the Colonel. So many things crowd upon one in these widenings and intensifyings of Vision, that one scarce knows which first to clutch at, and one, for the moment, pushes in and overlies the next, driving it, driving them, out of one's head. Thus, for instance, the vital little truth of one's definitely seeing the Course of Action in the Girl *develope,* before one's eyes, under dramatic Determinations, from moment to moment and point to point: which is but a little way, precisely, of stating the very principle and meaning and beauty of Drama. It is a Concatenation of things visibly, appreciably, terribly or comically, at any rate logically and traceably determined within the frame of the picture before one's eyes; of every golden grain of applicable sense and force in which axiom I neither more nor less than propose that every inch of my March, and every touch of said Picture shall be a proof and an example. What I cling to is the Vision of her being *precipitated,* on the spot, and before us, to her Step; with everything that happens to her—and the whole of the Show, from her Entrance, is describable as a close succession of things happening to her—promoting the necessity, creating the inevitability, of her (so to speak) Deed. It grows there before us; all the others, that is, all save the Colonel, whose Function is a thing entirely apart, minister to its growth by the Fatuity (blest word—*that's* the comprehensive, vivid Idea I want) of their attempting just the opposite; so that really a lovely description of her line, of her situation and little history, is that it's a struggle, direct and intimate, with surrounding and appealing and would-be smothering Fatuity. Fatuous everyone, fatuous with the exception, all and always, the precious Colonel,—with whom the interest and charm of her tie is that *they* have in common *their* not being Fatuous. Fatuous in their respective ways the figures of 2nd and 3rd, fatuous Lady Maud, fatuous the young Maresfield scion, whose elder Brother, decidedly, dies, is killed by some hunting accident or something, between 1st and 2nd., so that his social and matrimonial value have gone straight up; and so that when in II I confront him, in the midst of Rose's Desolation, as I must call it, before Bertram Jay has played round and up, vulgarly speaking, I may confront him with the Girl as a temporarily thinkable Relief or Alternative or Solvent or Issue, or even slight Bribe; for I gather it to be a part of the complexity here that he really does care for her. The making right of his type entails of course a thorough and interesting working-out of his Mother's and his curious and "amusing" relation with her. Fatuous, above all,—and this is just really, for irony and comedy and charm and grace and interest and pathos and Everything—fatuous above all is Bertram Jay himself; so that the drama of their relation, his and Rose's, the full extraction of meaning and picture from it is in the process of her reduction, conversion, transformation, clarification, illumination, of this element in him till his fine high-toned priggishness, with all sorts of good things beneath and behind it, becomes under her conscious and intelligent pressure, a "finer humanity"; a wider and kinder and brighter and more detached and amused sense of things, and of her situation and mission in particular; as to which I keep thinking of sidelights beautiful and valuable and helpful and droll, all the while on the part of the Colonel. The conversion of Jay, as well as the Bringing Out of her Mother, becomes thus the very description of what we see her actively and subtly and charmingly about, as consciously and fondly, even, capable of till she brings it to full Fruition; which full Fruition is the vague and remote and most embracingly general label for my Climax of Second—I come back to this just to note my sense, strong as one turns the matter over, that, very presumably, the Climax of the brief and rapid situation of the Colonel and the two women should be, over and beyond his vow to "back" Rose, her demanding of him this, that he let her Daughter know of her having been there, of his having waved her away, and of her having yielded on condition of his thus immediately telling Rose. She makes it [her] condition of going. He promises—then she goes.

Act Second

I have to break ground here, I feel, from very far off indeed, to approach my place of Siege, by rather wide circumvallations, beginning with considerations quite general, and drawing closer drawing in, from these to the more particular and to the Centre. On the face of it one's subject here has the air of presenting rather more the aspect or category of the Difficult—as if, however, really, any thing appreciably worth doing, in these conditions were more Difficult than any other thing. What I mean is that, speaking, as I say most Generally, the Act, is, by its nature, in a large degree, or at all events in an appreciable one, the picture of a State or Status: full of character, full of colour, full of comedy, full in a word of *things*, including lively Interest (as I see and feel it all); but with the March and the Movement to be, doubtless, by due need, a little more artfully and ingeniously and scientifically extracted from it than in the case of what has preceded. What I most rudimentarily get, at any rate, is that I think, to begin with, a term of not much less than two years, in fact even a little more, has elapsed since the beginning of the last interval; two years that have run their course for Rose's Domestication with her Mother. Speaking again in an elementary fashion, all the warnings and vaticinations addressed to her in First bore on what she would be "in for," and in the most lurid, or at least intensely deterrent symbols: in spite of which she went her way. Well, now we have as first conditioned the picture of what she really *was* "in for"; what she has been, all this time, and still is, "in for." The time seems considerable, but I somehow don't make it out as less: it has to be considerable to present its meaning and bear its fruit. It becomes thus indeed a little longer than a term of two years, since I seem experimentally to disengage that they, the persons the thing gives me, are all together, toward the summer's end, gathered at some little foreign place to which Rose, now completely managing her Mother's life ("She believes in you," the Colonel says to the Girl with whom he is now an immense chum, "as she believes in the Preservation of her Figure, the Understanding of that Figure by her Paris Dressmaker"—or, experimentally, something of that sort; some shibboleth or superstition or sign and token, that passes with poor Mrs. Tramore for a rule of life, a Working Faith), has conducted her, in the absolute and unperturbed inveteracy of their ever being invited anywhere; anywhere, that is, that they will go—by which I mean that Rose, with her plan of campaign, her pious demonic subtlety, will consent to their going. Potentially exquisite, it gleams upon me here, the exhibition for their present situation, of this Generalship of exclusion, selection, discretion, precaution, high and delicate fastidiousness, as to their contacts and doings; even though it happens that, till something really worth while comes, the effect of it is to leave them all high and dry, utterly isolated, frequented, haunted, encompassed, for the nearer circle with no one but the Colonel and Lady Maud and young Maresfield and One Other Man, I seem speculatively to grope toward, a compromising man, a dreadful man, a man with amusement to give, a floating spar of Mrs. Tramore's great faraway shipwreck or crisis, who keeps imaging and symbolising and recording it, as for that matter Lady Maud does too, in her somewhat different way; though all under Rose's superior Control and Conduct and Compression: a part of the state of things that have ended in the absolute collective, grateful, plastic, comic, devout submission to her as their eventual Guide and Redeemer out of Bondage, if they will only be utterly good, and take the Law from her in every particular. There float before me Patches, as this most preliminary Process *is* but a floating before one of Patches—as of awfully characteristic and "comico-ironic" Exhibition of this high prudent system of vigilance, exclusion, selection, and all that sort of thing, on Rose's part, as for the organisation of her eventual victory: though just let me note here before I break off, that as each of my Acts essentially embodies a Crisis, and is, organically, the picture of the Crisis, so this one is partially, and for its start and beginning, a Crisis of Discouragement—presenting first the high bleak table-land, as it were, of the very Desolation of their general Propriety; which as yet has led to nothing at all—so that the March, here, can only be, all designated and indicated, as that of what it *begins,* under visible, vivid Determination, to lead to. It begins, I say; we see it so begin, as soon as the Desolation is duly and adequately presented and *constatée;* then the March is that of its further logical, and awfully dramatic and interesting, Development to a Climax.

The way I seem to see them is, as it were, at some last gasp of their high and dry state, their dreadful, desperate, fruitless propriety and respectability, reaching the vividest, drollest, blankest neutrality, as it were, in every direction and relation, on the part of Mrs. Tramore, and with the apparent failure of Rose's sacrifice, her devotion, her diplomacy, her wonderful behavior generally, to do anything for them—for I keep lumping Lady Maud *with* them, for the sake of the illustrative possibilities of "quaintness" of her,—in a worldly and social way, the particular way for which she has laboured. She has laboured, she has calculated and plotted, to float her Mother back into the innermost waters of the Harbour of Safety, and Mrs. Tramore, blandly and prayerfully passive, with her indefeasible superficiality and frivolity and amiability and juvenility, her utterly shallow, and serene passivity has sat, arrayed and hatted and gloved, ready to the last twist of a ribbon, to disembark, as it were, on the sacred strand; but with no summons whatever, no faint symptom of a call, an opportunity, a possibility, yet looming into sight. In short the situation depicted with all its foreshortened vividness in the Tale. My cue for Mrs. T.'s aspect and image throughout Act II is just the little figure that I think I used in the Tale; that of her sitting, as in the most temporary manner possible, on the edge of her chair, with "her things on," as waiting for the carriage which is to come and take her and drive her to some happy place to which she has not the faintest chance of going. Well, so things are—only with the faithful Colonel, always hovering, always revolving, always returning, and above all, always interested, intensely interested in Rose, always amused, amusing and tremendously Contributive. The particular Hour, as I feel it, is one at which the situation seems to "kind of" threaten to crack and give way as by excess of tension; as by having got, though to an extent they all loyally dissimulate, on all their nerves—especially of course on Rose's, whose wound-up and overdone state, smilingly as she masks it, is in a manner the key of what we see happen. The Colonel comes and goes with *his* protected and privileged contacts and communities—he brings in reports of the outer life; he is, by function and character, their medium of communication and knowledge. If Rose has learned a short time before of the death of her Grandmother, and of what has happened at home since, as it were, that is of her own disinherited and further proscribed and condemned and branded state, it is all and only through the Colonel; as to which bereavement, moreover, I seem to see that she, as for perfect decorum, has put on light, perfunctory, though highly becoming, technically respectful and decorous mourning. Such is the image, that of very charming and simple qualified mourning, a summer array of "tasteful" black and white, that she presents in this Act. Say we take her at the moment when it has really come up for her, under some Determination, quite supremely, whether she *can* "stand" it, any longer, the dreary *impasse* of her situation; whether she can stand it for another month, week, day or hour. Say they have gone to the little place, which I think of somehow as a pleasant, a beautiful and, as *might* have been propitious quiet resort in the Austrian or Bavarian Tyrol, on some calculation of her's, Rose's very own, worked out entirely by herself, that some "good," of a vague, sweet, blessed sort, would thereby come to them; say that they have taken rooms in a sort of chalet or Dependance of the main little hotel, which has its garden in common with the latter; the ladies being lodged together in the Dependance and the Colonel just a little way off at the hotel. Say, further, in conformity with this, that their presence has been somehow blighting, measurably detrimental, in regard to a small circle, as it were, of English habitués, on whom the landlord largely counts, *has* counted, from year to year, for his month of September or whatever; and say some effect, some consciousness, distinctly depressing and menacing, of this kind, is in the air on rise of Curtain, with our attestations of it and of the other elements of the Case and Crisis rendered salient, amusing, interesting. Say we get it not only that they have Broken Down, but that this has somehow to-day got to be Recognised: say it comes up for them too unmistakably, and that the brunt of it is what Rose, trustedly, really quite unchallengedly, but all discouragedly, deject-edly, even all sceptically now at last, has to meet. They *have* it there, somehow— they have it before them that they can't "go on," as it were, unless something happens, since none of the things originally dreamed of have as yet in the least done so; and I want to give the note of Rose's Temptation, as it were, which she feels might become sharp on this, were it only to take the form of lurid Opportu-nity—the temptation, in other words, to throw up her sorry game, to "chuck" her vain speculation and clear out, saving at least her own skirts or skin. For she, above all, is Bored, poor Rose, to within an inch of her life; the society of the outlawed, of the supposedly "unspeakable," has come at last to excruciate her— that is her Mother's which is the real crux, has—by its desperate vapidity, vacuity and propriety. What I seem to clutch, as Constatations, in their order, or at any rate in their cluster (since the order requires, obviously, full threshing out) is that, perhaps first, of their appreciable Detrimentalism as to the little place they occupy; their having prevented this, that and the other annual visitor from coming, or having determined this, that or the other annual visitor, and his wife and daugh-ters, prematurely to depart; their having, in fine, in some appreciable way exer-cised an uncanny and disquieting influence—which makes the landlord say, though appreciating *them* too, for the expense they are at, fidget and wonder and appear moved to bring the so odd matter to a head. *Mettons* that they have been there from rather early, having come on purpose, and with all their leisure—no late engagements or complications to keep *them* in town!—and so are encamped; with, after all, the Effect of their Presence, I hint to myself, a matter of Appreciation more by themselves, as an acute consciousness of their Detrimentalism, than a ground for the landlord's worriment—an element that, I see, wouldn't plausibly work, and that I don't really need. It's all a question with and for and roundabout Themselves; this, properly dealt with, making it quite a sufficient little silver-mine for all my Values. Their vision becomes thus a consciousness of everything as Negative; they haven't even the thrill or incident of shocking people and driving them away; they so create the desert about Them that, in the oddest, uncanniest, as well as drollest, way in the world, there *are* no People, to *be,* in any manner affected; all of which is a part of what is thrown up, appreciably diffused in the air, by the Break-down. I somehow seem to want to make some of the wrong people come, and I see thus that I do perfectly descry reason to be grateful for my Second Man, as I call him, the representative of the true Detrimental as distinguished from Themselves; the one whom they have never been able to get rid of, and whom in London, with whatever sneaking fondness for him still, they constantly have to try to suppress and relegate. I seem to see, as a happy value that, given their desperation now, they are only all too glad to have him again, with what he may have brought them from outside, from elsewhere, to relieve them of the burden of Themselves. I catch the tip of the tail of the idea that the three women are at the very first alone on the ground, at the place, together, and have been so for some little time, and that this ministers, in due course, to desperation—that is to desperation for Rose; who is the one for whom it most matters—matters, that is, to Us. The tip of this tail would seem to give me the successive arrivals, from elsewhere, of the four or five men: that is of my Second Man, as I call him, of the Colonel, of the Maresfield Scion, and of Bertram Jay. Each of these Contributive, each of these sharp Determinants. Besides, or rather *with* which, with everything to be disengaged from the richness, there flare at me the two images, as I thus parenthetically clutch at them, of what I call Lady Maud's Case, the case of her Demoralisation, for Rose to deal with; the case of her not Playing the Game (awfully precious this clue or note, for presentation of Rose, of her vigilance as to their Playing the Game;) and the case of the Awful Person, probably Impossible Woman, previously known and "shed," bearing down on them, and who must be as wildly waved away as the Colonel had to wave Mrs. Tramore at Wimbledon. Discussion, Discussion, the acute Discussion of their state, even as might be among Survivors on a Raft, casting about and differing as to what it is best to do. The waves of Discussion breaking against Rose's mask or armour of fortitude, but with such possible ironic amusement and interest in the presentation of it all. Everyone, that is each, is *shown* as demoralised, except Mrs. Tramore whose glassy surface of exquisite Ignorance never for an instant belies itself—though ah, the possibilities of all this crowd upon me almost too thick for discrimination. But steady and easy, step upon step: what I disengage for the instant, stated with the last crudity, is these differences in the two or three Demoralisations of which I see the Colonel as more or less the confidant. What I meant just now by Lady Maud's Case is her aspect and share in what I have called the frank Break-down. She does, all cynically give it up as a vain job; and though she makes Rose no "scene" (I see that as all inferior), Rose has it out with her, just as she would have it out with Rose if she dared, that Opportunity is all that is wanted for each of them somehow to collapse. Say Lady Maud wants, positively, cynically and admittedly, the Impossible Woman, their old pal—wants her for the simple change and relief and diversion and vulgarity she'll bring. "My dear, she's so delightfully vulgar—and we're just dying for want of that; with our perfect Distinction that has landed us on this sand-bank. Do let us have her, before we all become idiots!"—or something of that sort. Rose is "Disappointed" in her, and has to be austere and explicit about it; catching her, however—for I seem really to require it—in some *act,* some covert fact, of the course of subterfuge that I have called not playing Fair. And yet with, all the while, this hauntedness of her own by the sense . . . [the manuscript breaks off at this point.]

Notes for *The Ivory Tower*
(Summer 1914)

One of the two novels HJ left unfinished at the end of his life, *The Ivory Tower* remains a fragment of three Books and one chapter of a fourth out of a proposed ten Books. Along with HJ's notes for the novel, it was published in 1917 by W. Collins Sons in London and Scribner's Sons in New York. Percy Lubbock wrote a brief preface for the volume; Scribner's curiously added this edition as volume XXV to the Selective New York Edition in 1918. See *Life* 690–92 for the story of HJ's abandoning this novel at the outbreak of World War I.

HJ's notes for *The Ivory Tower,* which he dictated to Theodora Bosanquet in the summer of 1914, resume and develop the idea sketched as "The K. B. Case and Mrs. Max" during December 1909 and January 1910; HJ retained many items from the pool of names for characters in that earlier sketch. Two typescript versions of the notes remain in the Houghton Library. The earlier, TSa (73 pp.), is entitled "Preliminary Remarks about the Novel" and preceded by a page of explanatory introduction by Percy Lubbock. The second, TSb (110 pp.), is entitled "Remarks about Novel" and preceded by a slightly different page of introduction by Lubbock, at the bottom of which is written (in pencil): "In this, the original copy, I have now corrected the names in pencil. P. L. April 1917."

Lubbock's published text follows TSb except in a few instances, which are noted. The "corrections" in that typescript have mainly to do with characters' names:

> Basil Hunn (or B. H.) becomes Graham "Gray" Fielder
> Chowne (occasionally Chown) becomes Gaw
> Moyra becomes Rosanna
> Crimper becomes Vint

Gregg becomes Betterman
Cecilia "Cissy" Foy becomes (variously) Heroine, the Heroine,
my Heroine, our Heroine, the Girl, Miss X
"Gussy" Bradham becomes "Gussie" Bradham.

TSb changes 'Number" or "No." (or on one occasion "Act") to "Book"
and usually substitutes a word for a Roman numeral—i.e., "Number IX"
or "IX" becomes "Book Nine"—but Lubbock's published text is quite
inconsistent in this matter. The "Lennox" of TSa becomes "Lenox" in
TSb and in the published text. Where TSb has "H." or G." Lubbock's
text has frequently spelled out "Horton" or "Gussie." Other "corrections" are indicated in the footnotes.

Augusta Bradham, "Gussie" Bradham, for the big social woman. Basil Hunn
I think on the whole for Hero. Graham Rising, which becomes familiarly Gray
Rising, I have considered but incline to keep for another occasion.

Horton Crimper, among his friends Haughty Crimper, seems to me right and
best, on the whole, for my second young man. I don't want for him a surname
intrinsically pleasing; and this seems to me of about the good nuance. My third
Man hereby becomes, I seem to see, Davey Bradham; on which, I think, for the
purpose and association, I can't improve.

My Girl, in the relinquished thing, was Cissy Foy; and this was all right for the
figure there intended, but the girl here is a very different one, and everything is
altered. I want her name moreover, her Christian one, to be Moyra, and must
have some bright combination with that; the essence of which is a surname of two
syllables and ending in a consonant—also beginning with one. I am thinking of
Moyra Grabham, the latter excellent thing was in the Times of two or three days
ago; its only fault is a little too much meaning, but the sense here wouldn't be
thrown into undue relief, and I don't want anything pretty or conventionally
"pleasing." Everything of the shade of the real. Remain thus important the big,
the heavy Daughter of the billionaire, with her father; in connection with whom I
think I give up Betterman. That must stand over, and I want, above all, a single
syllable. All the other names have two or three; and this makes an objection to
the Shimple, which I originally thought of as about odd and ugly enough without
being more so than I want it. But that also will keep, while I see that I have the
monosyllable Hench put down; only put down for another connection. I see I
thought of "Wenty" Hench, short for Wentworth, as originally good for Second
Young Man. If I balance that against Haughty Crimper, I incline still to the latter,
for the small amusement of the Haughty. On the other hand I am not content with
Hench, though a monosyllable, for the dear Billionaire girl, in the light of whom
it is alone important to consider the question, her Father so little mattering after
she becomes by his death the great Heiress of the time. And I kind of want to
make *her* Moyra; with which I just spy in the Times a wonderful and admirable

"Chown"; which makes me think that Moyra Chown may do. Besides which if I keep Grabham for my "heroine" I feel the Christian name should there be of one syllable. All my others are of two; and I shall presently make the case right for this, finding the good thing. The above provides for the time for the essential. Yet suddenly I am pulled up—Grabham, after all, won't at all do if I keep Bradham for the other connection; which I distinctly prefer: I want nothing with any shade of a special sense there. Accordingly, I don't know but what I may go in for a different note altogether and lavish on her the fine Cantupher; which I don't want however really to waste. When Cantupher is used there ought to be several of it, and above all men: no, I see it won't do, and besides I don't want anything positively fine. I like Wither, and I like Augurer, and I like, in another note, Damper, and I even see a little Bessie as a combination with it, though I don't on the whole want a Bessie. At any rate I now get on.

[1] What I want the first Book to do is to present the Gaws, the Bradhams and Cissy Foy, in Three Chapters or Scenes, call them Scenes of the Acts, in such a way that I thus present with them the first immediate facts involved; or in other words present the first essence of the Situation. What I see is, as I further reflect, that it is better to get Graham Fielder there within the Act, to have him on the premises already, and learnt so to be, before it has progressed beyond the first Scene; though he be not seen till the Second Book. When Rosanna goes over to her Father it befals before she has had more than twenty words with him that one of the Nurses who is most sympathetic to her appears in the long window that opens from the house on to the verandah, and it is thus at once disclosed that he has come. Rosanna has taken for granted from the quiet air of the place that this event hasn't yet occurred; but Gray has in fact arrived with the early morning, has come on the boat from New York, the night one, and is there above with, or ready to be with, the dying man. Perfectly natural and plausible I make it that he doesn't begin at once to pervade the place; delicacy, discretion, anxiety naturally operating with him; so that we know only he is there, and that matters are more or less taking place above, during the rest of the Book. But the fact in question immediately determines, for proprieties' and discretions' sake, the withdrawal of Rosanna and her Father; they return to their own abode; and I see the rest of the business of the act as taking place partly there and partly, by what I make out, on the Bradhams' own premises, the field of the Third Scene. Here is the passage between the two young women that I require, and my Heroine, I think, must be on a visit of a number of days to Gussie. I want Davey first with Rosanna, and think I get something like his having walked over, along the cliff, to their house, to bring her, at his wife's request, over to tea. Yes, I have Davey's walk back with Rosanna, and her Father's declining to come, or saying that he will follow afterward; his real design being to sneak over again, as I may call it, to the other house, in the exercise of his intense curiosity. That special founded and motivated condition is what we sufficiently know him by and what he is for the time (which

---

1. [Lubbock's note:] From this point the names of the characters, most of which were still uncertain, are given in accordance with Henry James' final choice; though it may be noted that he was to the end dissatisfied with the name of Cissy Foy and meant to choose another.

is all the time we have of him) identified by. I get thus for Book 2 that Gray, latish in the afternoon, coming down from his uncle's quarter, finds him, has a passage or scene with him, above all an impression of him; and this before he has had any other: we learn that he hasn't seen his uncle yet; the judgment of the doctors about this being operative and they wishing a further wait. I want Rosanna's Father for his first very sharp impression; this really making, I think, Scene First of Book 2. It gives me Scene 2 for what I shall then want without further delay of his first introduction to his Uncle's room and his half hour, or whatever, there; with the fact determined of the non-collapse of the latter, his good effect from the meeting quite rather, and the duration of him determined to end of Book 2. After Book 2 he is no more. Scene 3 of Book 2 then can only be, for Gray, with Rosanna; that scene having functions to be exercised with no more delay at all, by what I make out, and being put in, straight, then and there, that we may have the support of it. I by the same token see Book 3 now as functional entirely for the encounter of Gray with the two other women and, for the first time, with Davey; and also as preparing the appearance of Horton Vint, though not producing it. I see *him,* in fact, I think, as introduced independently of his first appearance to Gray, see it as a matter of his relation with Cissy, and as lighting up what I immediately want of *their* situation. In fact don't I see this as Horton's "Act" altogether, as I shall have seen and treated Book 1 as Rosanna's, and Book 2 as Gray's. By the blest operation this time of my Dramatic principle, my law of successive Aspects, each treated from its own centre, as, though with qualifications, The Awkward Age, I have the great help of flexibility and variety; my persons in turn, or at least the three or four foremost, having control, as it were, of the Act and Aspect, and so making it *his* or making it *hers.* This of course with the great inevitable and desirable preponderance, in the Series, of Gray's particular weight. But I seem to make out, to a certainty, at least another "Act" for Rosanna and probably another for Horton; though perhaps not more than one, all to herself, for Cissy. I say at least another for Horton on account of my desire to give Gray as affecting Horton, only less than I want to give Horton as affecting Gray. It is true that I get Gray as affecting Horton more or less in Book 3, but as the situation developes it will make new needs, determinations and possibilities. All this for feeling my way and making things come, more and more come. I want an Aspect under control of Davey, at all events—this I seem pretty definitely to feel; but things will only come too much. At all events, to retreat, remount, a little there are my 3 first Books sufficiently started without my having as yet exactly noted the absolutely fundamental antecedents. But before I do this, even, I memorise that Gray's Scene with Rosanna for 3 of Book 2 shall be by her coming over to Mr. Betterman's house herself that evening, all frankly and directly, to see him there; not by his going over to her. And I seem to want it evening; the summer night outside, with their moving about on the Terrace and above the sea etc. Withal, by the same token, I want such interesting things between them from immediately after the promulgation of Mr. Betterman's Will; I want that, but of course can easily get it, so far as anything is easy, in Book 4, the function of which is to present Gray as face to face with the situation so created for him. This is obviously, of course, one of Gray's Aspects, and the next will desirably be, I dare say too; can only be, so far as I can now tell, when I consider that the Book being my Fourth, only Six of the Ten which I most devoutly desire to limit the thing to then remain for my full evolution on the momentum by that time imparted. Certainly, at all events, the Situation leaves Newport, to come to life, its full life, in New York, where I seem to see it as going on to the end, unless I manage to treat myself to some happy and helpful mise-en-scène or exploitation of my memory of (say) California. The action entirely of American localisation, as goes without saying, yet making me thus kind of hanker, for dear "amusement's" sake, to decorate the thing with a bit of a picture of some American Somewhere that is not either Newport or N.Y. I even ask myself whether Boston wouldn't serve for this garniture, serve with a narrower economy than "dragging in" California. I kind of want to drag in Boston a little, feeling it as naturally and thriftily workable. But these are details which will only too much come; and I seem to see already how my action, however tightly packed down, will strain my Ten Books, most blessedly, to cracking. That is exactly what I want, the tight packing *and* the beautifully audible cracking; the most magnificent masterly little vivid economy, with a beauty of its own equal to the beauty of the donnée itself, that ever was.

However, what the devil *are,* exactly, the little fundamentals in the past? Fix them, focus them hard; they need only be perfectly conceivable, but they must be of the most lucid sharpness. I want to have it that for Gray, and essentially for Rosanna, it's a *renewal* of an early, almost, or even quite positively, childish beginning; and for Gray it's the same with Horton Vint—the impression of Horton already existing in him, a very strong and "dazzled" one, made in the quite young time, though in a short compass of days, weeks, possibly months, or whatever, and having lasted on (always for Gray) after a fashion that makes virtually a sort of relation already established, small as it ostensibly is. Such his relation with Rosanna, such his relation with Horton—but for his relation with Cissy——? Do I want that to be also a renewal, the residuum of an old impression, or a fresh thing altogether? What strikes me prima facie is that it's better to have two such pre-established origins for the affair than three; the only question is does that sort of connection more complicate or more simplify for that with Cissy? It more simplifies if I see myself wanting to give, by my plan, the full effect of a revolution in her, a revolution marked the more by the germ of the relation being thrown back, marked the more, that is, in the sense of the shade of perfidy, treachery, the shade of the particular element and image that is of the essence, so far as she is concerned, of my action. How this exactly works I must in a moment go into—hammer it out clear; but meanwhile there are these other fundamentals. Gray then is the son of his uncle's half-sister, not sister (on the whole, I think); whose dissociation from her rich brother, before he was anything like *so* rich, must have followed upon her marrying a man with whom he, Mr. Betterman, was on some peculiarly bad terms resulting from a business difference or quarrel of one of those rancorous kinds that such lives (as Mr. Betterman's) are plentifully bestrown with. The husband has been his victim, and he hasn't hated him, or objected to him for a brother-in-law, any the less for that. The objected-to brother-in-law has at all events died early, and the young wife, with her boy, her scant means, her disconnection from any advantage to her represented by her half-brother, has betaken herself to Europe; where the rest of *that* history has been enacted. I see the young husband, Gray's father, himself Graham Fielder the elder or whatever, as dying early, but probably dying in Europe, through some catastrophe to be determined, two or three years after their going there. This is better than his dying at home, for removal of everything from nearness to Mr. Betterman. Betterman has been married and has had children, a son and a daughter, this is indispensable, for diminution of the fact of paucity of children; but he has lost successively these belongings—there is nothing over strange in it; the death of his son, at 16 or 18 or thereabouts, having occurred a few years, neither too few nor too many, before my beginning, and having been the sorest fact of his life. Well then, young Mrs. Fielder or whoever, becomes thus in Europe an early widow, with her little boy, and there, after no long time, marries again, marries an alien, a European of some nationality to be determined, but probably an Englishman; which completes the effect of alienation from her brother—easily conceivable and representable as "in his way," disliking this union; and indeed as having made known to her, across the sea, that if she will forbear from it (this when he first hears of it and before it has taken place) and will come back to America with her boy, he will "forgive" her and do for her over there what he can. The great fact is that she declines this condition, the giving up of her new fiancé, and thereby declines an advantage that may, or might have, become great for her boy. Not so great then—Betterman not *then* so rich. But in fine— With which I cry Eureka, eureka; I have found what I want for Rosanna's connection, though it will have to make Rosanna a little older than Gray, 2 or 3 or 3 or 4 years, instead of same age. I see Gray's mother at any rate, with her small means, in one of the smaller foreign cities, Florence or Dresden, probably the latter, and also see there Rosanna and her mother, this preceding by no long time the latter's death. Mrs. Gaw has come abroad with her daughter, for advantages, in the American way, while the husband and father is immersed in business cares at home; and when the two couples, mother and son, and mother and daughter, meet in a natural way, a connection is more or less prepared by the fact of Mr. Gaw having had the business association with Mrs. Fielder's half-brother, Mr. Betterman, at home, even though the considerably violent rupture or split between the two men will have already taken place. Mrs. Gaw is a very good simple, a bewildered and pathetic rich woman, in delicate health, and is sympathetic to Gray's mother, on whom she more or less throws herself for comfort and support, and Gray and Rosanna, Rosanna with a governess and all the facilities and accessories natural to wealth, while the boy's conditions are much leaner and plainer—the two, I say, fraternise and are good friends; he figuring to Rosanna (say he is about 13, while she is 16) as a tremendously initiated and informed little polyglot European, knowing France, Germany, Italy etc. from the first. It is at this juncture that Mrs. Fielder's second marriage has come into view, or the question and the appearance of it; and that, very simultaneously, the proposal has come over from her half-brother on some rumour of it reaching him. As already mentioned, Betterman proposes to her that if she will come back to America with her boy, and not enter upon the union that threatens, and which must have particular elements in it of a nature to displease and irritate him, he will look after them both, educate the boy at home, do something substantial for them. Mrs. Fielder takes her American friend into her confidence in every way, introduces to her the man who desires to marry her, whom Rosanna sees and with whom the boy himself has made great friends, so that the dilemma of the poor lady becomes a great and lively interest to them all; the prétendant himself forming also a very good relation with the American mother and daughter, the friends of his friend, and putting to Mrs. Gaw very eagerly the possibility of her throwing her weight into the scale in his favour. Her meeting, that is Mrs. Fielder's meeting, the proposition from New York involves absolutely her breaking off with him; and he is very much in love with her, likes the boy, and, though he doesn't want to stand in the latter's light, has hopes that he won't be quite thrown over. The engagement in fact, with the marriage near at hand, must be an existing reality. It is for Mrs. Fielder something of a dilemma; but she is very fond of her honourable suitor, and her inclinations go strongly to sticking to him. She takes the boy himself into her confidence, young as he is,—perhaps I can afford him a year or two more—makes him 15, say; in which case Rosanna becomes 18, and the subsequent chronology is thereby affected. It isn't, I must remember, as a young man in his very first youth, at all, that I want Gray, or see him, with the opening of the story at Newport. On the contrary all the proprieties, elements of interest, convenience etc., are promoted by his being not less than 30. I don't see why I shouldn't make him 33, with Rosanna thus *two* years older, not three. If he is 15 in Dresden and she 17, it will be old enough for each, without being too old, I think, for Gray. 18 years will thus have elapsed from the crisis at Florence or wherever to the arrival at Newport. I want that time, I think, I can do with it very well for what I see of elements operative for him; and a period of some length moreover is required for bringing the two old men at Newport to a proper pitch of antiquity. Mr. Betterman dies very much in the fulness of years, and as Rosanna's parent is to pass away soon after I want him to have come to the end. If Gray is 15, however, I mustn't make his mother too mature to inspire the devotion of her friend; at the same time that there must have been years enough for her to have lived awhile with her first husband and lost him. Of course this first episode may have been very brief—there is nothing to prevent that. If she had married at 20 she will then be, say, about 36 or so at the time of the crisis, and this will be quite all right for the question of her second marriage. Say she lives a considerable number of years after this, in great happiness, her marriage having taken place; I in fact require her to do so, for I want Gray to have had reasons fairly strong for his not having been back to America in the interval. I may put it that he *has,* even, been back for a very short time, on some matter connected with his mother's interests, or his own, or whatever; but I complicate the case thereby and have to deal somehow with the question of whether or no he has then seen Mr. Betterman. No, I don't want him to have been back, and can't do with it; keep this simple and workable. All I am doing here is just to fix a little his chronology. Say he has been intending to go over at about 25, when his mother's death takes place, about 10 years after her second marriage. Say then, as is very conceivable, that his stepfather, with whom he has become great friends, then requires and appeals to his care and interest in a way that keeps

him on and on till the latter's death takes place just previous to Mr. Betterman's
sending for him. This gives me quite sufficiently what I want of the previous order
of things; but doesn't give me yet the fact about Rosanna's connection in her
young history which I require. I see accordingly what has happened in Florence
or Dresden as something of this kind: that Mrs. Fielder, having put it to her boy
that he shall decide, if he can, about what they shall do, she lets Mrs. Gaw, who
was at this juncture in constant intercourse with her, know that she has done so—
Mrs. Gaw and Rosanna being, together, exceedingly interested about her, and
Rosanna extremely interested, in a young dim friendly way, about Gray; very
much as if he were the younger brother she hasn't got, and whom, or an older,
she would have given anything to have. Rosanna hates Mr. Betterman, who has,
as she understands and believes, in some iniquitous business way, wronged or
swindled her father; and isn't at all for what he has proposed to the Fielders. In
addition she is infatuated with Europe, makes everything of being there, dreams,
or would dream, of staying on if she could, and has already in germ, in her mind,
those feelings about the dreadful American money-world of which she figures as
the embodiment or expression in the eventual situation. She knows thus that the
boy has had, practically, the decision laid upon him, and with the whole case with
all its elements and possibilities before her she takes upon herself to act upon him,
influence and determine him. She wouldn't have him accept Mr. Betterman's cruel
proposition, as she declares she sees it, for the world. She proceeds with him as
she would in fact with a younger brother: there is a passage to be alluded to with
a later actuality, which figures for her in memory as her creation of a responsibility; her very considerably passionate, and thereby meddlesome, intervention. I see
some long beautiful walk or stroll, some visit to some charming old place or
things—and Florence is here indicated—during which she puts it all to him, and
from which he, much inspired and affected by her, comes back to say to his
mother that he doesn't want what is offered—at any such price as she will have
to pay. I see this occasion as really having settled it—and Rosanna's having always felt and known that it did. She and her mother separate then from the others;
Mrs. Fielder communicates her refusal, sticks to her friend, marries him shortly
afterwards, and her subsequent years take the form I have noted. The American
mother and daughter go back across the sea; the mother in time dies etc. I see
also how much better it is to have sufficient time for these various deaths to
happen. But the point is that the sense of responsibility, begetting gradually a
considerable, a deepening force of reflection, and even somewhat of remorse, as
to all that it has meant, is what has taken place for Rosanna in proportion as, by
the sequence of events and the happening of many things, Mr. Betterman has
grown into an apparently very rich old man with no natural heir. His losses, his
bereavements, I have already alluded to, and a considerable relaxation of her
original feeling about him in the light of more knowledge and of other things that
have happened. In the light, for instance, of her now mature sense of what her
father's career has been and of all that his great ferocious fortune, as she believes
it to be, represents of rapacity, of financial cruelty, of consummate special ability
etc. She has kept to some extent in touch with Gray, so far that is as knowing
about his life and general situation are concerned; but the element of compunction

in her itself, and the sense of what she may perhaps have deprived him of in the way of a great material advantage, may be very well seen, I think, as keeping her shy and backward in respect to following him up or remaining in intercourse. It isn't likely, for the American truth of things, that she hasn't been back to Europe again, more than once, whether before or after her mother's death; but what I can easily and even interestingly see is that on whatever occasion of being there she has yet not tried to meet him again. She knows that neither he nor his stepfather are at all well off, she has a good many general impressions and has tried to get knowledge of them, without directly appealing for it to themselves, whenever she can. Thus it is, to state things very simply, that, on hearing of the stepfather's death, during the Newport summer, she has got at Mr. Betterman and spoken to him about Gray; she has found him accessible to what she wants to say, and has perceived above all what a pull it gives her to be able to work, in her appeal, the fact, quite vivid in the fulness of time to the old man himself indeed, that the young man, so nearly, after all, related to him, and over there in Europe all these years, is about the only person, who could get at him in any way, who hasn't ever asked anything of him or tried to get something out of him. Not only this, but he and his mother, in the time, are the only ones who ever refused a proffered advantage. I think I must make it that Rosanna finds that she can really tell her story to Mr. Betterman, can make a confidant of him and so interest him only the more. She feels that he likes her, and this a good deal on account of her enormous difference from her father. But I need only put it here quite simply: she does interest him, she does move him, and it is as a consequence of her appeal that he sends for Gray and that Gray comes. What I must above all take care of is the fact that she has represented him to the old man as probably knowing less about money, having had less to do with it, having moved in a world entirely outside of it, in a degree utterly unlike anyone and everyone whom Mr. Betterman has ever seen.

But I have got it all, I needn't develop; what I want now independently is the beginning, quite back in the early years, of some relation on Gray's part with Horton Vint, and some effect, which I think I really *must* find right, of Horton's having *done* something for him, in their boyish time, something important and gallant, rather showy, but at all events really of moment, which has always been present to Gray. This I must find—it need present no difficulty; with something in the general way of their having been at school together—in Switzerland, with the service rendered in Switzerland, say on a holiday cours among the mountains, when Horty has fished Gray out of a hole, I don't mean quite a crevasse, but something like, or come to his aid in a tight place of some sort, and at his own no small risk, to bring him to safety. In fine it's something like having saved his life, though that has a tiresome little old romantic and conventional note. However I will make the thing right and give it the right nuance; remember that it is all allusional only now and a matter of reference on Gray's part. What must have further happened, I think, is that Horty has been in Europe again, in much later years, after College, indeed only a very few years previous, and has met Gray again and they have renewed together; to the effect of his apprehension of Gray's (to him) utterly queer and helpless and unbusinesslike, unfinancial, type; and of

Gray's great admiration of everything of the opposite sort in him—combined, that is, with other very attractive (as they appear) qualities. He has made Gray think a lot about the wonderful American world that he himself long ago cut so loose from, and of which Horty is all redolent and reverberant; and I think must have told him, most naturally told him, of what happened in the far off time in Florence. Only when, then, was the passage of their being at school, or better still, with the Swiss pasteur, or private tutor, together? If it was before the episode in Florence they were rather younger than I seem to see them; if it was after they were rather older. Yet I don't at all see why it should not have been just after— this perfectly natural at 16 for Gray, at 17 for Horty; both thoroughly natural ages for being with the pasteur, and for the incident afterwards; Gray going very naturally to the pasteur, whom in fact he may have been with already before, during the first year of his mother's new marriage. That provides for the matter well enough, and I've only to see it to possess it; and gives a basis for their taking up together somehow when they meet, wherever I may put it, in the aftertime. There are forms of life for Gray and his stepfather to be focussed as the right ones— Horty sees this pair *together* somewhere; and nothing is more arrangeable, though I don't think I want to show the latter as having dangled and dawdled about Italy only; and on the other hand do see that Gray's occupation and main interest, other than that of looking after his elder companions, must be conceived and presented for him. Again no difficulty, however, with the right imagination of it. Horty goes back to America; the 3 or 4, or at the most 4 or 5, years elapse, so that it is with that comparative freshness of mutual remembrance that the two men meet again. What I do see as definite is that Horty has had up to the time of Gray's return no sort of relation whatever with Mr. Betterman or his affairs, or any point of the question with which the action begins at Newport. He *is* on the other hand in relation with Cissy; and there are things I have got to account for in his actual situation. Why is he without money, with his interest in the getting of it etc.? But that is a question exactly *of* interest—I mean to which the answer may afford the greatest. And settle about the degree of his apprehension of, relation to, designs on, or general lively consciousness of Rosanna. Important the fact that the enormous extent of her father's fortune is known only after his death, and is larger even than was supposed; though it is to be remembered that in American financial conditions, with the immense public activity of money there taking place, these things are gauged in advance and by the general knowledge, or speculative measure, as the oldfashioned private fortune couldn't be. But I am here up against the very nodus of my history, the fact of Horty's connection with the affairs that come into being for Gray under his uncle's Will; the whole mechanism, in fine, of this part of the action, the situation so created and its consequences. Enormous difficulty of pretending to show various things here as with a business vision, in my total absence of business initiation; so that of course my idea has been from the first *not* to show them with a business vision, but in some other way altogether; this will take much threshing out, but it is the very basis of the matter, the core of the subject, and I shall worry it through with patience. But I must get it, plan it utterly right in advance, and this is what takes the doing. The other doing, the use of it when schemed, is comparatively easy. What strikes me first of all is that the amount of money that Gray comes in for must, for reasons I needn't waste time in stating, so obvious are they, be no such huge one, but the New York measure, as in many another case: it's a tremendous lot of money for Gray, from his point of view and in relation to his needs or experience. Thus the case is that if Mr. Gaw's accumulations or whatever have distinctly surpassed expectation, the other old man's have fallen much below it—or at least have been known to be no such great affair anyhow. Various questions come up for me here, though there is no impossibility of settling them if taken one by one. The whole point is of course that Mr. Betterman *has* been a ruthless operator or whatever, and with doings Davey Bradham is able to give Gray so dark an account of; therefore if the mass of money of the acquisition of which such a picture can be made is not pretty big, the force of the picture falls a good deal to the ground. The difficulty in that event, in view of the bigness, is that the conception of any act on Horton's part that amounts to a swindle practised on Gray to such a tremendous tune is neither a desirable nor a possible one. As one presses and presses light breaks— there are so many ways in which one begins little by little to wonder if one may not turn it about. There is the way in the first place of lowering the pitch alto- gether of the *quantities* concerned for either men. I see that from the moment ill- gotten money is concerned the essence of my subject stands firm whatever the amount of the same—whatever the amounts in either case. I haven't proposed from the first at all to be definite, in the least, about financial details or myster- ies—I need hardly say; and have even seen myself absolutely not stating or for- mulating at all the figure of the property accruing to Gray. I haven't the least need of that, and can make the absence of it in fact a positively good and happy effect. That is an immense gain for my freedom of conduct; and in fine there glimmers upon me, there glimmers upon me——! The idea, which was vaguely my first, of the absolute theft practised upon Gray by Horty, and which Gray's large appeal to his cleverness and knowledge, and large trust in his competence, his own being nil—this theft accepted and condoned by Gray as a manner of washing his own hands of the use of the damnosa hereditas—this thinkable enough in respect to some limited, even if considerable, amount etc., but losing its virtue of conceiv- ability if applied to larger and more complicated things. Vulgar theft I don't want, but I want something to which Horty is led on and encouraged by Gray's whole attitude and state of mind face to face with the impression which he gets over there of so many of the black and merciless things that are behind the great pos- sessions. I want Gray absolutely to inherit the money, to have it, to have had it, and to let it go; and it seems to me that a whole element of awkwardness will be greatly minimised for me if I never exactly express, or anything like it, what the money is. The difficulty is in seeing any one particular stroke by which Horty can do what he wants; it will have to be much rather a whole train of behaviour, a whole process of depredation and misrepresentation, which constitutes his delin- quency. This, however, would be and *could* be only an affair of time; and my whole intention, a straight and compact action, would suffer from this. What I originally saw was the fact of Gray's detection of Horty in a piece of extremely ingenious and able malversation of his funds, the care of which he has made over to him, and the then determination on his part simply to show the other in silence that he understands, and on consideration will do nothing; this being, he feels in his wrought-up condition after what he has learnt about the history of the money, the most congruous way of his ceasing himself to be concerned with it and of resigning it to its natural associations. That was the essence of my subject, and I see as much in it as ever; only I see too that it is imaginable about a comparatively small pecuniary interest much more than about a great. It has to depend upon the *kind* of malpractice involved; and I am partly tempted to ask myself whether Horty's connection with the situation may not be thinkable as having begun somewhat further back. One thing is certain, however; I don't want any hocus-pocus about the Will itself—which an anterior connection for H. would more or less amount to: I want it just as I have planned it up to the edge of the circle in which his misdeed is perpetrated. What glimmers upon me, as I said just now, is the conception of an extreme frankness of understanding between the two young men on the question of Gray's inaptitudes, which at first are not at all disgusts—because he doesn't *know;* but which makes them, the two, have it out together at an early stage. Yes, there glimmers, there glimmers; something really more interesting, I think, than the mere nefarious act; something like profoundly nefarious attitude, or even genius: I see, I really think I see, the real fine truth of the matter in *that*. With which I keep present to me the whole significance and high dramatic value of the part played in the action by Cissy Foy;[2] have distinct to me her active function as a wheel in the machine. How it isn't simply Gray and Horty at all, but Gray and Horty and *her;* how it isn't She and Gray, any more than it's She and Horty, simply, but is for her too herself and the *two* men: in which I see possibilities of the most interesting. But I must put her on her feet perfectly in order to see as I should. Without at all overstraining the point of previous contacts for Gray with these three or four others—than which even at the worst there is nothing in the world more verisimilitudinous—I want some sort of relation for him with her *started;* this being a distinct economy, purchased by no extravagance, and seeing me, to begin with, so much further on my way. And who, when I bethink myself, have his contacts been with, after all, over there, but Horty and Rosanna—the relation to Mr. Betterman being but of the mere essence. Of the people who matter the Bradhams are new to him, and that is all right; Cissy may have been seen of him on some occasion over there that is quite recent, as recent as I like; all the more that I must remember how if I want her truly a Girl I must mind what I'm about with the age I'm attributing to Gray. I want a disparity, but not too great, at the same time that though I want her a Girl, I want her not too young a one either. Everything about her, her intelligence, character, sense of life and knowledge of it, imply a certain experience and a certain time for that. The great fact is that she is the poor Girl, and the "exceptionally clever" in a society of the rich, living her life with them, and more or less by their bounty; being, I seem to see, already a friend and protégée of Rosanna's, though it isn't Rosanna but the Bradhams who put her in relation with Gray, whether designedly or not. I seem to run here the risk a bit of exposure to the charge of more or less repeating the figure of Charlotte in The Golden Bowl, with the Bradhams repeat-

2. The name replaces "my Heroine, for whom decidedly I must arrive at a name, if but provisional."

ing even a little the Assinghams in that fiction; but I shake this reflection off, as having no weight beyond duly warning; the situation being such another affair and the real characteristics and exhibited proceedings of these three persons being likewise so other. Say something shall have passed between Cissy at a *then* 25, or 24 at most, and Gray "on the other side"; this a matter of but two or three occasions, interesting to him, shortly before his stepfather's death—a person with whom she has then professed herself greatly struck, to whom she has been somehow very "nice": a circumstance pleasing and touching at the time to Gray, given his great attachment to that charming, or at any rate to Gray very attaching, though for us slightly mysterious, character. Say even if it doesn't take, or didn't, too much exhibition or insistence, that the meeting has been with the stepfather only, who has talked with her about Gray, made a point of Gray, wished she could know Gray, excited her interest and prepared her encounter for Gray, in some conditions in which Gray has been temporarily absent from him. Say this little intercourse has taken place at some "health resort", some sanatorium or other like scene of possibilities, where the stepfather, for whom I haven't even yet a name, is established, making his cure, staving off the affection of which he dies, while this interesting young American creature is also there in attendance on some relative whom she also has since lost. I multiply my orphans rather, Charlotte too having been an orphan; but I can keep this girl only a half-orphan perhaps if I like. I kind of want her, for the sake of the characteristic, to have a mother, without a father; in which case her mother, who hasn't died, but got better, will have been her companion at the health resort; though it breaks a little into my view of the girl's dependence, her isolation etc., her living so much with these other people, if her mother is about. On the other hand the mother may be as gently but a charge the more for her, and so in a manner conducive; though it's a detail, at any rate, settling itself as I get in close—and she would be at the worst the only mother in the business. What I seem to like to have at all events is that Gray and Cissy, have *not* met, yet have been in this indirect relation—complicated further by the fact of her existing "friendship", say, as a temporary name for it, with Horton Vint. She arrives thus with her curiosity, her recollections, her intelligence—for, there's no doubt about it, I am, rather as usual, offering a group of the personally remarkable, in a high degree, all around. Augusta Bradham, really, is about the only stupid one, the only approach to a fool, though she too in her way is a force, a driving one—that is the whole point; which happens to mark a difference also, so far good, from the Assinghams, where it was the wife who had the intelligence and the husband who was in a manner the fool. The fact of the personal values, so to call them, thus clustered, I of course not only accept, but cherish; that they are each the particular individual of the particular weight being of course of the essence of my donnée. They are interesting that way—I have no use for them here in any other.

Horton has meanwhile become in a sort tied up with Cissy, as she has with him; through the particular conditions of their sentiment for each other—she in love with him, so far as she, by her conviction and theory, has allowed herself to go in that direction for a man without money, though destined somehow to have it, as she feels; and he in love with her under the interdict of a parity of attitude on the whole "interested" question. The woman whom he would give truly one of his limbs to commend himself to is Rosanna, who perfectly knows it and for whom he serves as the very compendium and symbol of that danger of her being approached only on that ground, the ground of her wealth, which is, by all the mistrusts and terrors it creates, the deep note of her character and situation; that he serves to her as the very type of what she most dreads, not only the victory, but the very approach of it, almost constituting thus a kind of frank relation, a kind of closeness of contact between them, that involves for her almost a sinister (or whatever) fascination. It is between him and my ambitious young woman (I call her ambitious to simplify) that they are in a manner allies in what may be called their "attitude to society"; the frankness of the recognition, on either side, that in a world of money they can't *not* go in for it, and that accordingly so long as neither has it, they can't go in for each other: though how each would—each makes the other feel—if it could all be only on a different basis![3] Horty's attitude is that he's going to have it somehow, and he to a certain extent infects her with this conviction—but that he doesn't wholly do so is exactly part of the evidence as to that latent limitation of the *general* trust in him which I must a good deal depend on to explain how it is that, with his ability, or the impression of this that he also produces, he hasn't come on further. Deep down in the girl[4] is her element of participation in this mistrust too—which is part of the reason why she hangs back, in spite of the kind of attraction he has for her, from any consent to, say, marry him. He, for that matter, hasn't in the least urged the case either—it hasn't been in him up to now, in spite of a failure or two, in spite of the failure notably with Rosanna, to close by a positive act the always possibly open door to his marrying money. I see the recognition of all this between them as of well-nigh the crudest and the most typical, the most "modern"; in fact I see their relation as of a highly exhibitional value and interest. What the Girl indeed doesn't, and doesn't want to (up to now) express, is exactly that limit, and the ground of it, of her faith in him as a financial conqueror. She is willing more or less to believe, to confide, in his own confidence—she sees him indeed as more probably than not marked for triumphant acquisition; but the latent, "deep down" thing is her wonderment as to the character of his methods—if the so-called straight ones won't have served or sufficed. She sees him as a fine adventurer—which is a good deal too how she sees herself; but almost crude though I have called their terms of mutual understanding it hasn't come up for them, and I think it is absolutely never to come up for them, that she so far faces this question of his "honour", or of any capacity in him for deviation from it, as even to conjure it away. There are depths within depths between them—and I think I understand what I mean if I say there are also shallows beside shallows. They give each other rope and yet at the same time remain tied; that for the moment is a sufficient formula—once I keep the case lucid as to what their tie is.

What accordingly does her situation in respect to Gray come to, and how do I see it work out? The answer to that involves of course the question of what *his,*

3. The exclamation point replaces a full stop.
4. Substitution for "Girl."

in respect to *her*, comes to, and what it gives me for interest. She has got her original impression about him over there as of the man without means to speak of; but it is as the heir to a fortune that she now first sees him, and as the person coming in virtue of that into the world she lives in, where her power to guide, introduce and generally help and aid and comfort him, shows from the first as considerable. She strikes him at once as the creature, in all this world, the most European and the most capable of, as it were, understanding him intellectually, entering into his tastes etc. He recognizes quickly that, putting Davey Bradham perhaps somewhat aside, she is the being, up and down the place, with whom he is going to be able most to *communicate*. With Rosanna he isn't going to communicate "intellectually", æsthetically, and all the rest, the least little bit: Rosanna has no more taste than an elephant; Rosanna is only *morally* elephantine, or whatever it is that is morally most massive and magnificent. What I want is to get my right firm *joints,* each working on its own hinge, and forming together the play of my machine: they *are* the machine, and when each of them is settled and determined it will work as I want it. The first of these, definitely, is that Gray does inherit, has inherited. The next is that he is face to face with what it means to have inherited. The next to that is that one of the things it means—though this isn't the light in which he first sees the fact—is that the world immensely opens to him, and that one of the things it seems most to give him, to offer and present to him, is this brilliant, or whatever, and interesting young woman. He doesn't at first at all see her in the light of her making up to him on account of his money; she is too little of a crudely interested specimen for that, and too sincere in fact to herself—feeling very much about him that she would certainly have been drawn to him, after this making of acquaintance, even if no such advantages attached to him and he had remained what he had been up to then. But all the same it is a Joint, and we see that it is by seeing *her* as we shall; I mean I make it and keep it one by showing "what goes on" between herself and Horton. I have blessedly that view, that alternation of view, for my process throughout the action. The determination of her interest towards him—that then is a Joint. And let me make the point just here that at first he has nothing but terror, but horror, of seeing himself affected as Rosanna has been by her own situation—from the moment, that is, he begins to take in that she is so affected. He takes this in betimes from various signs—before that passes between them which gives him her case in the full and lucid way in which he comes to have it. *She* gives it to him presently— but at first as her own simply, holding her hand entirely from intimating that his need be at all like it; as she must do, for that matter, given the fact that it is really through her action that he was brought over to see his uncle. She thinks her feelings about her own case right and inevitable for herself; but I want to make it an interesting and touching inconsistency in her that she desires not to inspire him, in respect to his circumstances, with any correspondingly justified scene. Definite is it that what he learns, he learns not the least mite from herself, though after a while he comes quite to challenge her on it, but from Davey Bradham, so far as he learns it, for the most part, concretely and directly—as many other impressions as I can suggest helping besides. I want him at all events to have a full large clear moment or season of exhilaration, of something like intoxication, over the change in his conditions, before questions begin to come up. An essential Joint is constituted *by* their beginning to come up, and the difference that this begins to make. What I want of Davey Bradham is that he is a determinant in this shift of Gray's point of view, though I want also (and my scenario[5] has practically provided for that) that the immediate amusement of his contact with Davey shall be quite compatible with his *not* yet waking up, *not* yet seeing questions loom. I must keep it well before me too that his whole enlarged vision of the money-world, so much more than any other sort of world, that all these people constitute, operate inevitably by itself, promotes infinite reflection, makes a hundred queer and ugly things, a thousand, ten thousand, glare at him right and left. A Joint again is constituted by Gray's first consciousness of malaise, first determination of malaise, in the presence of more of a vision, and more and more impression of everything; which determination, as I call it, I want to proceed from some sense in him of Cissy's attitude as affected by his own reactions, exhibition of questions, wonderments and, to put it simply and strongly, rising disgusts. She has appealed to him at the outset, on his first apprehension of her, exactly as a poor girl who wasn't meant to be one, who has been formed by her nature and her experience to rise to big brilliant conditions, carry them, take them splendidly, in fine do all justice to them; this under all the first flush of what I have called his own exhilaration. He hasn't then committed himself, in the vulgar sense, at all— had only committed himself, that is, to the appearance of being interested and charmed: his imaginative expansion for that matter being naturally too great to permit for the moment of particular concentration or limitations. But isn't his incipient fear of beginning to be, of becoming, such another example, to put it comprehensively, as Rosanna, doesn't this proceed precisely from the stir in him of certain disconcerting, complicating, in fact if they go a little further quite blighting, wonderments in respect to Cissy's possibilities? She throws her weight with him into the *happy* view of his own; which is what he likes her, wants her, at first encourages her to do, lending himself to it while he feels himself, as it were, all over. Mrs. Bradham, all the while, backs her up and backs *him* up, and is in general as crude and hard and blatant, as vulgar is what it essentially comes to, in her exhibited desire to bring about their engagement, as is exactly required for producing on him just the wrong effect. Gray's tone to the girl becomes, again to simplify: "Oh yes, it's all right that you should be rich, should have all the splendid things of this world; but I don't see, I'm not sure, of its being in the least right that *I* should—while I seem to be making out more and more, round me, how so many of them are come by." It is the insistence on them, the way everyone, among that lot at any rate, appears aware of no values *but* those, that sets up more and more its effect on his nerves, his moral nerves as it were, and his reflective imagination. The girl[6] counters to this of course—she isn't so crude a case as not to; she denies that she's the sort of existence that he thus imputes— all the while that she only sees in his attitude and his position a kind of distinction that would simply add to their situation, simply gild and after a fashion decorate

5. Substitution for "Scenario."
6. Substitution for "Girl."

it, were she to marry him. I want to make another Joint with her beginning, all the same, to doubt of him, to think him really perhaps capable of strange and unnatural things, which she doesn't yet see at all clearly; but which take the form for her of his possibly handing over great chunks of his money to public services and interests, deciding to be munificent with it, after the fashion of Rockefellers and their like: though with the enormous difference that his resources are not in the slightest degree of that calibre. He's rich, yes, but not rich enough to remain rich if he goes in for that sort of overdone idealism. Some passage bearing on this takes place, I can see, about at the time when he has the so to call it momentous season, or scene, or whatever, of confidence or exchange with Rosanna in which she goes the whole "figure", as they say, and puts to him that exactly her misery is in having come in for resources that should enable her to do immense things, but that are so dishonoured and stained and blackened at their very roots, that it seems to her that they carry their curse with them, and that she asks herself what application to "benevolence" as commonly understood, can purge them, can make them anything but continuators, somehow or other, of the wrongs in which they had their origin. This, dramatically speaking, *is* momentous for Gray, and it makes a sort of clearing up to realities between him and Rosanna which offers itself in *its* turn, distinctly, as a Joint. It makes its mark for value, has an effect, leaves things not as they were.

But meanwhile what do I see about Horton, about the situation between them, so part and parcel of the situation between Gray and Cissy and between Horton and Cissy. Absolute the importance, I of course recognise, of such a presentation of matters between her and Horton, and Horton and her, as shall stand behind and under everything that takes place from this point. In my adumbration of a scenario[7] for these earlier aspects I have provided, I think, for this; at any rate I do hereby provide. I want to give the effect, for all it's worth, of their being constantly, chronically, naturally and, for my drama, determinatively, in communication; with which it more and more comes to me that when the great *coup* of the action effects itself Gray shall have been brought to it as much by the forces determining it on *her* behalf, in relation to her, in a word, as by those determining it in connection with Horton. She helps him to his solution about as much as Horton does, and, lucidly, logically, ever so interestingly, everything between them up to the verge is but a preparation for that. Enormous meanwhile the relation with Horton constituted by his making over to this dazzling person (by whom moreover he wants to be, consents to be, dazzled) the care or administration of his fortune; for which highly characteristic, but almost, in its freehandedness, abnormally, there must have been preparation, absolutely, and oh, as I can see, ever so interestingly, in Book 2, the section[8] containing his face to face parts with Mr. Betterman. It comes to me as awfully fine, given the way in which I represent the old dying man as affected and determined, to sweep away everything in the matter of precautions and usualisms, provisions for trusteeships and suchlike, and lump the whole thing straight on to the young man, without his having a condition or a

7. Substitution for "Scenario."
8. Substitution for "Section."

proviso to consider. What I have wanted is that he should at a stroke, as it were, in those last enshrouded, but perfectly possessed hours, make over his testament utterly and entirely, in the most simplified way possible; in short by a sweeping codicil[9] that annihilates what he has done before and puts Gray in what I want practically to count as unconditioned possession. Thank the Lord I have only to give the effect of this, for which I can trust myself, without going into the ghost of a technicality, any specialising demonstration. I need scarcely tell myself that I don't by this mean that Gray makes over matters definitely and explicitly to Horton at once, with attention called to the tightness with which his eyes are shut and all his senses stopped or averted; but that naturally and inevitably, also interestingly, this result proceeds, in fact very directly and promptly springs, from his viewing and treating his friend as his best and cleverest and vividest adviser— whom he only doesn't rather abjectly beg to take complete and irresponsible charge because he is ashamed of doing so. Two things very definite here; one being that Gray isn't in the least blatant or glorious about his want, absolutely phenomenal in that world, of any faint shade of business comprehension or imagination, but is on the contrary so rather helplessly ashamed of it that he keeps any attitude imputable to him as much as possible out of the question—and in fact proceeds in the way I know. He has moments of confidence—he tells Rosanna, makes a clean breast to *her* and with Horton doesn't need to be explicit, beyond a point, since all his conduct expresses it. What happens is that little by little, inevitably, as a consequence of first doing this for him and then doing that and then the other, Horton more and more gets control, gets a kind of unlimited play of hand in the matter which practically amounts to a sort of general power of attorney; as Gray falls into the position, under a feeling insurmountably directing him, of signing anything, everything, that Horton brings to him for the purpose—but only what Horton brings. The state of mind and vision and feeling, the state of dazzlement with reserves and reflections, the play of reserves and reflections with dazzlement (which is my convenient word covering here all that I intend and prefigure) is a part of the very essence of my subject—which in fine I perfectly possess. What happens is, further, that, even with the rapidity which is of the remarkable nature of the case, Horton shows for a more and more monied, or call it at first a less and less nonmonied individual; with an undisguisedness in this respect which of itself imposes and, vulgarly speaking, succeeds. I express these things here crudely and summarily, by rude signs and hints, in order to express them at all; but what is of so high an interest, and so bright and characteristic, is that Horton is "splendid", plausible, delightful, *because* exactly so logical and happily suggestive, about all this; he puts it to Gray that *of course* he is helping himself by helping Gray, that *of course* his connection with Gray does him good in the business world and gives him such help to do things for himself as he has never before had. I needn't abound in this sense here, I am too well possessed of what I see— as I find myself in general more and more. A tremendous Joint is formed, in all this connection, when the first definite question begins to glimmer upon Gray, under some intimation, suggestion, impression, springing up as dramatically as I

9. Substitution for "Codicil."

can make it, as to what Horton is really doing with him, and as to whether or not he shall really try to find out. That question of whether or no he *shall becomes* the question; just as the way he answers it, not all at once, but under further impressions invoked, becomes a thing of the liveliest interest for us; becomes a consideration the climax of which represents exactly the Joint that is in a sense the climax of the Joints. He sees—well what I see him see, and it is of course not at all this act of vision in itself, but what takes place in consequences of it, and the process of confrontation, reflection, resolution, that ensues—it is this that brings me up to my high point of beautiful difficulty and clarity. An exquisite quality of representation here of course comes in, with everything that is involved to make it rich and interesting. A Joint here, a Joint of the Joint, for perfect flexible working, is Horton's vision of his vision, and Horton's exhibited mental, moral audacity of certainty as to what that may mean for himself. There is a scene of course in which, between them, this is what it can only be provisionally gross and approximate to call settled: as to which I needn't insist further, it's *there;* what I want is there; I've only to pull it out: it's *all* there, heaped up and pressed together and awaiting the properest hand. So much just now for *that*.

As to Cissy Foy meanwhile, the case seems to me to clear up and clear up to the last perfection; or to be destined and committed so to do, at any rate, as one presses it with the right pressure. How shall I put it for the moment, *her* case, in the very simplest and most rudimentary terms? She sees the improvement in Horton's situation, she assists at it, it gives her pleasure, it even to a certain extent causes her wonder, but a wonder which the pleasure only perches on, so to speak, and converts to its use; so does the vision appeal to her and hold her of the exercise on his part, the more vivid exercise than any she has yet been able to enjoy an exhibition of, of the ability and force, the *doing* and man-of-action quality, as to the show of which he has up to now been so hampered. She likes his success at last, plainly, and he has it from her that she likes it; she likes to let him know that she likes it, and we have her for the time in contemplation, as it were, of these two beautiful cases of possession and acquisition, out of which indeed poor little impecunious she gets as yet no direct advantage, but which are somehow together there *for* her with a kind of glimmering looming option well before her as to how they shall *come* yet to concern her. Awfully interesting and attractive, as one says, to mark the point (such a Joint *this!*) at which the case begins to glimmer for Gray about *her,* as it has begun to glimmer for him about Horton. I make out here, so far as I catch the tip of the tail of it, such an interesting connection and dependence, for what I may roughly call Gray's state of mind, as to[10] what is taking place within Cissy, so to speak. Since I speak of the most primitive statement of it possible he catches the moment at which she begins to say to herself "But if Horton, if *he,* is going to be rich——?" as a positive arrest, say significant warning or omen, in his own nearer approach to her; which takes on thereby a portentous, a kind of ominous and yet enjoyable air of evidence as to his own likelihood, at this rate, of getting poor. He catches her not asking herself withal, at least *then, "How* is Horton going to be rich, *how,* at such a

---

10. Both typescripts have "for." In TSb Lubbock has crossed out "for" and pencilled in "as to."

rate, has it come on, and what does it mean?''—it is only the "*If* Horton, oh *if*———?'' that he comes up against; it's as if he comes up against, as well, some wondrous implication in it of "If, if, *if* Mr. Gray is, 'in such a funny way,' going to be poor———?'' He sees her *there,* seeing at the same time that it's as near as she yet gets; as near perhaps ever—for this splendid apprehension sort of begins to take place in him—as[11] she's going to allow herself to get; and after the first chill of it, shock of it, pain of it (because I want him to be at the point at which he has *that*) fades a little away for him, he emerging or shaking himself out of it, the beautiful way in which it falls into the general ironic apprehension, imagination, appropriation, of the Whole, becomes for him *the* fact about it. She has them, each on his side, there in her balance—and this is between them, between him and her; I must have prepared everything right for its being oh such a fine moment. What I want to do of course is to get out of *this* particular situation all it can give; what it most gives being, to the last point, the dramatic quality, intensity, force, current or whatever, of Gray's apprehension of it, once this is determined, and of course wondering interest in it—as a light, so to speak, on both of the persons concerned. What I see is that she gives him measure, as it were, of Horton's successful proceeding—and does so, in a sort, without positively having it herself, or truly wanting to have it beyond the fact that it is success, is promise and prospect of acquisition on a big scale. What it comes to is that he finds her believing in Horton just at the time and in proportion as he has found himself ceasing to believe, so far as the latter's disinterestedness is concerned. No better, no more vivid illustration of the force of the money-power and money-prestige rises there before him, innumerably as other examples assault him from all round. The effect on her is there for him to "study," even, if he will; and in fact he does study it, studies it in a way that (as he also sees) makes her think that this closer consideration of her, approach to her, as it were, is the expression of an increased sympathy, faith and good will, increased desire, in fine, to make her like him. All the while it is, for Gray himself, something other; yet something at the same time wellnigh as absorbing as if it were what she takes it for. The fascination of seeing what will come of it—that is of the situation, the state of vigilance, the wavering equilibrium, at work, or at play, in the young woman—this "fascination" very "amusing" to show, with everything that clusters about it. He really enjoys getting so detached from it as to be able to have it before him for observation and wonder as he does, and I must make the point very much of how this fairly soothes and relieves him, begins to glimmer upon him exactly *through* that a consciousness as something like the sort of issue he has been worrying about and longing for. Just so something that he makes out as distinguishable there in Horton, a confidence more or less dissimulated but also, deeply within, more or less determined, operates in its way as a measure for him of Horton's intimate sense of how things will go for him; the confidence referring, I mustn't omit, to his possibility of Cissy, after all, whom his sentiment for makes his most disinterested interest, so to call it: all this in a manner corresponding to that apprehension in Gray of *her* confidence, which I have just been sketchily

11. After the dash TSa has "that it's as near. . . .''

noting. The one disinterested thing in Horton, that is, consists of his being so attached to her that he really cares for her freedom, cares for her doing what on the whole she most wants to, if it will but come *as* she wants it, by the operation, the evolution, so to say, of her clear preference. He has somehow within him a sense that anyway, whatever happens, they shall not fail of being "friends" after all. I see myself wanting to have Gray come up against some conclusive sign of how things *are* at last between them—though I say "at last" as if he has had *much* other light as to how such things *have* been, precedently. I don't want him to have had much other light, though he needs of course to have had *some;* there being people enough to tell him, he being so in the circle of talk, reference, gossip; but with his own estimate of the truth of ever so much of the chatter in general, and of that chatter in particular, taking its course. What I seem to see just in this connection is that he has "believed" so far as to take it that she *has* "cared" for his friend in the previous time, but that Horton hasn't really at all cared for her, keeping himself in reserve as it is of his essence to do, and in particular (this absolutely *known* to Gray) never having wholly given up his view on Rosanna. Gray believes that he hasn't, at any rate, and this helps him not to fit the fact of the younger girl's renounced, quenched, outlived, passion, or whatever one may call it, to any game of patience or calculation, rooted in a like state of feeling, on Horton's part. I want the full effect of what I can only call for convenience Gray's Discovery, his full discovery of them "together", in some situation, and its illuminating and signifying, its in a high degree, to repeat again my cherished word, determinant character. This effect requires exactly what I have been roughly marking—the line of argument in which appearances, as interpreted for himself, have been supporting Gray. "She has been in love with him, yes—but nothing has come of it—nothing could come of it; because, though he has been aware, and has been nice and kind to her, he isn't affected in the same way—is, in these matters, too cool and calculating a bird. He likes women, yes; and has had lots to do with them; but in the way of what a real relation with *her* would have meant—not! She has given him up, she has given *it* up—whereby one is free not to worry, not to have scruples, not to fear to cut across the possibility of one's friend." That's a little compendium of what I see. But it comes to me that I also want something more—for the full effect and the exact particular and most pointed bearing of what I dub Gray's discovery. He must have put it to Horton, as their relations have permitted at some suggested hour, or in some relevant connection: "Do you mind telling me if it's true—what I've heard a good deal affirmed—that there has been a question of an engagement between you and Miss Foy?—or that you are so interested in her that to see somebody else making up to her would be to you as a pang, an afront, a ground of contention or challenge or whatever?" I seem to see that, very much indeed; and by the same token to see Horton's straight denegation.[12] I see Horton say emphatically No—and this for reasons quite conceivable in him, once one apprehends their connection with his wishing above all, beyond anything else that he at this moment wishes, to keep well with Gray. His denegation is plausible; Gray believes it and accepts

12. Substitution for "Denegation."

it—all the more that at the moment in question he *wants* to, in the interest of his own freedom of action. Accordingly the point I make is that when he in particular conditions finds them all unexpectedly and unmistakably "together", the discovery becomes for him *doubly* illuminating. I might even better say trebly; showing him in the very first place that Horton has lied to him, and thereby that Horton *can* lie. This very interesting and important—but also, in a strange way, "fascinating" to him. It shows in the second way how much Cissy is "thinking" of Horton, as well as he of her; and it shows in the last place, which makes it triple, how well Horton must think of the way his affairs are getting on that he can now consider the possibility of a marriage—that he can feel, I mean, he can *afford* to marry; not having need of one of the Rosannas to make up for his own destitution. This clinches enormously, as by a flash of vision, Gray's perception of what he is about; and is thus intensely a Joint of the first water! What I want to be carried on to is the point at which all that he sees and feels and puts together in this connection eventuates in a decision or attitude, in a clearing-up of all the troubled questions, obscurities and difficulties that have hung for him about what I call his Solution, about what he shall be most at ease, most clear and consistent for himself, in making up his mind to. The process here and the position on his part, with all the implications and consequences of the same in which it results, is difficult and delicate to formulate, but I see with the last intensity the sense of it, and feel how it will all come and come as I get nearer to it. What is a big and beautiful challenge to a whole fine handling of these connections in particular is the making conceivable and clear, or in other words credible, consistent, vivid and interesting, the particular extraordinary relation thus constituted between the two men. That one may make it these things for Gray is more or less calculable, and, as I seem to make out, workable; but the greatest beauty of the difficulty is in getting it and keeping it in the right note and at the right pitch for Horton. Horton's "acceptance"—on what prodigious basis save the straight and practical view of Gray's exalted queerness and constitutional, or whatever, perversity, can *that* be shown as resting? Two fine things—that is one of them strikes me as very fine—here come to me; one of these my seeing (*don't* I see it?) how it will fall in, not to say fall out, as of the essence of the true workability, that the extent to which i's are not dotted between them, are left consciously undotted, to which, to the most extraordinary tune, and yet with the logic of it all straight, they stand off, or rather Gray does, the other all demonstrably thus taking his cue—the way, I say, in which the standing-off from sharp or supreme clearances is, and confirms itself as being, a note of my hero's action in the matter, throws upon one the most interesting work. Horton accepts it as exactly part of the prodigious queerness which he humours and humours in proportion as Gray will have it that he shall; the "fine thing", the second of the two, just spoken of, being that Horton never flinches from his perfectly splendid theory that he is "taking care", consummately, of his friend, and that he is arranging, by my exhibition of him, just as consummately to *show* for so doing. No end, I think, to be got out of this wondrous fact of Gray's sparing Horton, or saving him, the putting of anything to a real and direct Test; such a Test as would reside in his asking straight for a large sum of money, a big amount, really consonant with his theoretically intact resources and such as he with the highest propriety in the world might simply say that he has a immediate use for, or can make some important application of. No end, no end, as I say, to what I see as given me by this—this huge constituted and accepted eccentricity of Gray's holdings-off. I have the image of the relation between them made by it in my vision thus of the way, or the ways, they look at each other even while talking together to a tune which would logically or consistently make these ways *other;* the sort of education of the look that it breeds in Horton on the whole ground of "how far he may go." The things that pass between them after this fashion quite beautiful to do if kept from an overdoing; with Horton's formula of his "looking after" Gray completely interwoven with his whole ostensibility. It is with this formula that Horton meets the world all the while—the world that at a given moment can only find itself so full of wonderment and comment. It is with it above all that he meets Cissy, who takes it from him in a way that absolutely helps him to keep it up; and it *would* be with it that he should meet Rosanna if, after a given day or season, he might find it in him to dare, as it were, to "meet" Rosanna at all. It is with Horton's formula, which I think I finally show him as quite publicly delighting in, that Gray himself meets Rosanna, whom he meets a great deal all this time; with such passages between them as are only matched in another sense, and with all the other values with which they swell, so to speak, but his passages with the consummate Horton. Charming, by which I mean such interesting, things resident in what I *there* touch on; with the way *they* look at each other, Rosanna and Gray, if one is talking about looks. Gray keeps it in comedy, so far as he can—making a tone, a spell, that Rosanna doesn't break into, as she breaks, anything to call *really* breaks, into nothing as yet: I seem to see the final, from-far-back-prepared moment when she does, for the first and last time, break as of big and beautiful value. *That* will be a Joint of Joints; but meanwhile what is between them is the sombre confidence, tenderness, fascination, anxiety, a dozen admirable things, with which she waits on Gray's tone, not playing up to it at all (playings-up and suchlike not being verily *in* her) but taking it from him, accommodating herself to it with all her anxiety and her confidence somehow mixed together, as if to see how far it will carry her. Such a lot to be done with Gussie Bradham, portentous woman, even to the very cracking or bursting of the mould meanwhile—so functional do I see her, in spite of the crowding and pressing together of functions, as to the production of those (after all early-determined) reactions in Gray by the simple complete exhibition of her type and pressure and aggressive mass. She is really worth a book by herself, or would be should I look that way; and I just here squeeze what I most want about her into a sort of nutshell by saying that it marks for Gray just where and how his Solution, or at any rate some of its significant and attendant aspects, swims into his ken, with the very first scene she makes him about the meanness then of his conception of his opportunity. Then it is he feels he must be getting a bit into the truth of things—if that's the way he strikes her. His very measure of taste and delicacy and the sympathetic and the nice and the what he wants becomes after a fashion what she will want most to make him a scene about. I have it at first that he lends himself, that her great driving tone and pressure, her would-be act of possession of him, Cissy and the question of Cissy being the link, have amounted to a sort of trouble-saving thing which he has let himself "go to", which he has suffered as his convenient push or handy determinant, for the hour (sceptical even then as to its lasting)—but which has inordinately overdosed him, overhustled him, almost, as he feels in his old habit of financial contraction, overspent and overruined him. He does the things, the social things, for the moment, that she prescribes, that she foists upon him as the least ones he can decently do; does them even with a certain bewildered amusement—while Rosanna, brooding apart, so to speak, out of the circle and on her own ground, but ever so attentive, draws his eye to the effect of what one might almost call the intelligent, the patience-inviting, wink! Oh for the pity of scant space for specific illustration of Mrs. Bradham; wherewith indeed of course I reflect on the degree to which my planned compactness, absolutely precious and not to be compromised with, must restrict altogether the larger illustrational play. Intensities of foreshortening, with alternative vividnesses of extension: that is the rough label of the process. I keep it before me how mixed Cissy is with certain of the consequences of this hustlement of Mrs. Bradham, and how bullyingly, so to call it almost, she has put the whole matter of what he ought to "do for them all," on the ground in particular of what it is so open to him, so indicated for him, to do for that poor dear exquisite thing in especial. Illustrational, illustrational, yes; but oh how every inch of it will have to count. I seem to want her to have made him do some one rather gross big thing above all as against his own sense of fineness in these matters; and to have this thing count somehow very much in the matter of his relation with Cissy. I seem to want something like his having consented to be "put up" by her to the idea of offering Cissy something very handsome by way of a "kind" tribute to her mingled poverty and charm—jolly, jolly, I think I've exactly got it! I keep in mind that Mrs. Bradham wants him to marry her— this amount of "disinterestedness" giving the measure of Mrs. B. at her most exalted "best". Wherewith, to consolidate this, her delicacy being capable—well, of what we shall see, she works of course to exaggeration the idea of his "recognising" how nice Cissy was, over there in the other time, to his poor sick stepfather, who himself so recognised it, who wrote to her so charmingly a couple of times "about it", after her return to America and quite shortly before his death. Gray "knows about this", and of course will quite see what she means. Therefore wouldn't it be nice for Gray to give her, Cissy, something really beautiful and valuable and socially helpful to her—as of course he can't give her money, which is what would be most helpful. Under this hustlement, in fine, and with a sense, born of his goodnature, his imagination, and his own delicacy, such a very different affair, of what Gussie Bradham has done for him, by her showing, he finds himself in for having bought a very rare single row of pearls, such as a girl, in New York at least, may happily wear, and presenting it to our young person as the token of recognition that Mrs. Bradham has imagined for them. The beauty in which, I see, is that it may be illustrational in more ways than one—illustrational of the hustle, of the length Gray has "appreciatively" let himself go, and, above all, of Cissy's[13] really interesting intelligence and "subtlety". She refuses the

13. TSb here repeats "the Girl's" from TSa.

gift, very gently and pleadingly, but as it seems to him really pretty well finally—refuses it as not relevant or proportionate or congruous to any relation in which they yet stand to each other, and as oh ever so much overexpressing any niceness she may have shown in Europe. She does, in doing this, exactly what he has felt at the back of his head that she would really do, and what he likes her for doing—the effect of which is that she has furthered her interest with him decidedly more (as she of course says to herself) than if she had taken it. He is left with it for the moment on his hands, and what I want is that he shall the next thing find himself, in revulsion, in reaction, there being for him no question of selling it again etc., finds himself, I say, offering it to Mrs. Bradham herself, who swallows it without winking. Yet, in a way, this little history of the pearls, of her not having had them, and of his after a fashion owing her a certain compensation for that, owing her something she *can* accept, is there *between* him and my young person. They figure again between them, humorously, freely, ironically—the girl[14] being of an irony!—in their appearances on Mrs. Bradham's person, to whose huge possession of ornament they none the less conspicuously add.

But my point here is above all that Gray exactly *doesn't* put the question of what is becoming of his funds under Horty's care of them to the test by any cultivation of that courage for large drafts and big hauls, that nerve for believing in the fairy-tale of his sudden fact of possession, which was briefly and in a manner amusingly possible to him at the first go off of his situation. He forbears, abstains, stands off, and finds himself, or in particular is found by others, to the extent of their observing, wondering and presently challenging him, to be living, to be drawing on his supposed income, with what might pass for the most extraordinarily timorous and limited imagination. He *likes* this arrest, enjoys it and feels a sort of wondrous refreshing decency, at any rate above all a refreshing interest and curiosity about it, or rather, for it; but what his position involves is his explaining it to others, his making up his mind, his *having* to, for a line to take about it, without his thereby giving Horton away. He isn't to give Horton away the least scrap from this point on; but at the same time he is to have to deal with the world, with society, with the entourage consisting for him, in its most pressing form, of, say, three representative persons—he has to deal with this challenge, as I have called it, in some way that will sort of meet it *without* givings-away. These three persons are in especial Rosanna and the two Bradhams; and it is before me definitely, I think, that I want to express, and in the very vividest way, his sense of his situation here, of what it means, and of what *he* means, *in* it, through what takes place for him about it with Rosanna and with the Bradhams. It is by what he "says" to the Bradhams and to Rosanna (in the way, that is largely, of *not* saying) that I seem to see my values here as best got, and the presentation of their different states most vivified and dramatised. These are scenes, and the function of them to serve up for us exactly, and ever so lucidly, what I desire them to represent. If the greatest interest of them, of sorts, belongs to them in so far as they are "with" Rosanna, there are yet particular values that belong to the relation with Davey,[15] and the three relations, at any rate, work the thing for me. They

14. Substitution for "Girl."
15. After "Davy" TSa has "—decidedly I *keep* Davey Bradham, the one name I find myself up to now quite sure of—. . . ."

are perfectly different, on this lively ground, though the "point" involved is the same in each; and the having each of them to do it with should enable me to do it beautifully; I mean to squeeze *all* the dramatic sense from it. The great beauty is of course for the aspects with Rosanna, between whom and him everything passes—and there is so much basis already in what has been between them—without his "explaining", as I have called it, anything. Even without explanations—or all the more by reason of their very absence—there is so much of it all; of the question and the dramatic illumination. With Gussie Bradham—*that* aspect I needn't linger or insist on, here, so much as a scrap. I have that, see it all, it's *there*. But with Davey I want something very good, that is in other words very functional; and I think I even wonder if I don't want to see Davey as attempting to borrow money of him. This—if I do see it—will take much putting on the right basis; and it seems to kind of glimmer upon me richly what the right basis is. My idea has been from the first that the Bradham money is all Gussie's; I have seen Davey, but the very type and aspect, by all his detached irony and humour and indiscretion and general value as the unmonied young man who has married the heiress, as Horton would have been had he been able to marry Rosanna. But no interfering analogy need trouble me here; Horton's not having done that, and the essential difference between the men, eases off any such question. Only don't I seem to want it that Gussie's fortune, besides not having been even remotely comparable to Rosanna's, is, though with a fair outward face, a dilapidated and undermined quantity, much ravaged by Gussie's violent strain upon it, and representing thus, through her general enormous habit and attitude, an association and connection with the money world, but all the more characteristically so, for Gray as he begins to see, that almost everything but the pitch of Gussie's wants and arrangements and ideals has been chucked, as it were, out of its windows and doors. Don't I really see the Bradhams thus as *predatory?* Predatory on the very rich, that is; with Gussie's insistence that Gray shall *be* and shall proceed as quite one of the *very*, oh the very, very, exactly in order that she *may* so prey? Yes and so it is that Gray learns—so it is that a part of Davey's abysses of New York financial history, is his own, their own, but his in particular, abyss of inconvenience, abyss of inability to keep it up combined with all the social impossibility of not doing so. I somehow want such values of the supporting and functional and illustrative sort in Davey that I really think I kind of want him to be the person, *the* person, to whom Gray *gives*—as a kind of recognition of the remarkable part, the precious part, don't I feel it as being? that Davey plays for him. He likes so the illuminating Davey, whom I'm quite sure I want to show in no malignant or vicious light, but just as a regular rag or sponge of saturation in the surrounding medium. He is beyond, he is outside of, all moral judgments, all scandalised states; he is amused at what he himself does, at his general and particular effect and effects on Gray, who is his luxury of a relation, as it were, and whom I somehow seem to want to show him feel as the only person in the whole medium appreciating his genius; in other words his detached play of mind and the deep "American humour" of it. Don't I seem to want him even as asking for something rather big?—a kind of a lump of a sum which Gray, always with amusement, answers that he will have to see about. Gray's seeing about anything of this sort means, all notedly, absolutely *all*, as I think I have it, asking Horton whether he can, whether he may, whether Horton will give it to him, whether in short the thing will suit Horton; even without any disposition of the sum, any account of what he wants to do, indicated or reported or confessed to Horton? Don't I see something like this?—that Gray, having put it to Horton, has precisely determined, for his vision, on Horton's part, just that first important plea of "Really you can't, you know, at this rate"—even after Gray has been for some time so "ascetic"—"It won't be convenient for you just now; and I must ask you really, you know, to take my word for it that you'd much better not distract from what I am in the act of doing for you such a sum"—by which I mean, for I am probably using here not the terms Horton *would* use—"much better not make such a call (call is the word) when I am exactly doing for you etc." What I seem to see is that Davey does have money from him, but has it only on a scale that falls short, considerably, of his appeal or proposal or whatever; in other words that Gray accommodates him to the third, or some other fraction, of the whole extent; and that this involves for him practically the need of his saying that Horton won't let him have more. I want that, I see it as a value; I see Davey's aspect on it as a value, I see what is determined thus between them as a value; and I seem to see most this *covering* by Gray of Horton in answer to the insinuations, not indignant but amused, in answer to the humorously fantastic picture, on Davey's lips, of the rate at which Horton is cleaning him out or whatever, this taking of the line of so doing and of piling up plausibilities of defence, excuse etc., so far as poor Gray can be plausible in these difficult "technical" connections, as the vivid image, the vividest, I am concerned to give of what I show him as doing. The covering of Horton, the covering of Horton—this is much more than not giving him away; this active and positive protection of him seems to me really what my subject logically asks. What then is that *is* it, *is* what it most of all, for the dramatic value, asks, how can this be consistently less than Gray's act of going all the way indeed? I don't know why—as it has been hovering before me—I don't want the complete vivid sense of it to take the form of an awful, a horrible or hideous, crisis on Horton's part which, under the stress of it, he "suddenly" discloses to Gray, throwing himself upon him in the most fevered, the most desperate appeal for relief. What then constitutes the nature of the crisis, what then *can*, or constitute the urgency of the relief, unless the fact of his having something altogether dreadful to confess; so dreadful that it can only involve the very essence of his reputation, honour and decency, his safety in short before the law? He has been guilty of some huge irregularity, say—but which yet is a different thing from whatever irregularities he has been guilty of in respect to Gray himself; and which up to now, at the worst, have left a certain substantial part of Gray's funds intact. Say that, say that; turn it over, that is, to see if it's really wanted. I think of it as wanted because I feel the need of the effect of some *acute* determination play up as I consider all this—and yet also see objections; which probably will multiply as I look a little closer. I throw this off, at all events, for the moment, as I go, to be looked at straighter, to return to presently—after I've got away from it a bit, I mean from this special aspect a little, in order to come back to it fresher; picking up meanwhile two or three [16] different matters.

-16. Substitution for "2 or 3."

The whole question of what my young man has been positively interested in, been all the while more or less definitely occupied with, I have found myself leaving, or at any rate have left, in abeyance, by reason of a certain sense of its comparative unimportance. That is I have felt my instinct to make him definitely and frankly as complete a case as possible of the sort of thing that will make him an anomaly and an outsider alike in the New York world of business, the N.Y. world of ferocious acquisition, and the world there of enormities of expenditure and extravagance, so that the real suppression for him of anything that shall count in the American air as a money-making, or even as a wage-earning, or as a pecuniarily picking-up character, strikes me as wanted for my emphasis of his entire difference of sensibility and of association. I have always wanted to do an out and out non-producer, in the ordinary sense of non-accumulator of material gain, from the moment one should be able to give him a positively interested aspect on another side or in another sense, or even definitely a *generally* responsive intelligence. I see my figure then in this case as an absolutely frank example of the tradition and superstition, the habit and rule so inveterate there, frankly and serenely deviated from—these things meaning there essentially some mode of sharp reaching out for money over a counter or sucking it up through a thousand contorted channels. Yet I want something as different as possible, no less different, I mean, from the people who are "idle" there than from the people who are what is called active; in sort, as I say, an out and out case, and of course, an avowedly, an exceptionally fine and special one, which antecedents and past history up to then may more or less vividly help to account for. A very special case indeed *is* of course our Young Man—without his being which my donnée wouldn't come off at all; his being so is just of the very core of the subject. It's a question therefore of the way to make him *most* special—but I so distinctly see this that I need scarce here waste words——! There are three or four[17] definite facts and considerations, however; conditions to be seen clear. I want to steer clear of the tiresome "artistic" associations hanging about the usual type of young Anglo-Saxon "brought up abroad"; though only indeed so far as they *are* tiresome. My idea involves absolutely Gray's taking his stand, a bit ruefully at first, but quite boldly when he more and more sees what the opposite of it over there is so much an implication of, on the acknowledgement that, no, absolutely, he hasn't anything at all to show in the way or work achieved—with *such* work as he has seen achieved, whether apologetically or pretentiously, as he has lived about; and yet has up to now not had at all the sense of a vacuous consciousness or a so-called wasted life. This however by reason of course of certain things, certain ideas, possibilities, inclinations and dispositions, that he *has* cared about and felt, in his way, the fermentation of. Of course the trouble with him is a sort of excess of "culture", so far as the form taken by his existence up to then has represented the growth of that article. Again, however, I see that I really am in complete possession of him, and that no plotting of it as to any but one or two material particulars need here detain me. He isn't, N.B., big, personally, by which I mean physically; I see that I want him rather below than above the middling stature, and light and nervous and restless; extremely restless above all in presence of

17. Substitution for "3 or 4."

swarming new and more or less aggressive, in fact quite assaulting phenomena. Of course he has had *some* means—that he and his stepfather were able to live in a quiet "European" way and on an income of an extreme New York deplorability, is of course of the basis of what has been before; with which he must have come in for whatever his late companion has had to leave. So with what there was from his mother, very modest, and what there is from this other source, not less so, he *can,* he could, go back to Europe on a sufficient basis: this fact to be kept in mind both as mitigating the prodigy of his climax in N.Y., and yet at the same time as making whatever there is of "appeal" to him over there conceivable enough. Note that the statement he makes, when we first know him, to his dying uncle, the completeness of the picture of detachment then and there drawn for him, and which, precisely, by such an extraordinary and interesting turn, is what most "refreshes" and works upon Mr. Betterman—note, I say, that I absolutely require the utterness of his difference to *be* a sort of virtual determinant in this relation. He puts it so to Rosanna, tells her how extraordinarily he feels that this is what it *has* been. Heaven forbid he should "paint"—but there glimmers before me the sense of the connection in which I can see him as more or less covertly and waitingly, fastidiously and often too sceptically, conscious of possibilities of "writing". Quite frankly accept for him the complication or whatever of his fastidiousness, yet of his recognition withal of what makes for sterility; but again and again I have all this, I have it. His "culture", his initiations of intelligence and experience, his possibilities of imagination, if one will, to say nothing of other things, make for me a sort of figure of a floating island on which he drifts and bumps and coasts about, wanting to get alongside as much as possible, yet always with the gap of water, the little island *fact,* to be somehow bridged over. All of which makes him, I of course desperately recognise, another of the "intelligent", another exposed and assaulted, active and passive "mind" engaged in an adventure and interesting in *itself* by so being; but I rejoice in that aspect of my material as dramatically and determinantly *general.* It isn't *centrally* a drama of fools or vulgarians; it's only circumferentially and surroundedly so—these being enormously implied and with the effect of their hovering and pressing upon the whole business from without, but seen and felt by us only with that rich indirectness. So far so good; but I come back for a moment to an issue left standing yesterday—and beyond which, for that matter, two or three other points raise their heads. Why did it appear to come up for me again—I having had it present to me before and then rather waved it away—that one might see Horton in the *kind* of crisis that I glanced at as throwing him upon Gray with what I called violence? Is it because I feel "something more" is wanted for the process by which my Young Man works off the distaste, his distaste, for the ugliness of his inheritance— something more than his just *generally* playing into Horton's hands? I am in presence there of a beautiful difficulty, beautiful to solve, yet which one must be to the last point crystal-clear about; and this difficulty is certainly added to if Gray sees Horton as "dishonest" in relation to others over and above his being "queer" in the condoned way I have so to picture for his relation to Gray. Here are complexities not quite easily unravelled, yet manageable by getting sufficiently close to them; complexities, I mean, of the question of whether——? Horton is abysmal, yes—but with the mixture in it that Gray sees. Ergo I want the mixture, and if I adopt what I threw off speculatively yesterday I strike myself as letting the mixture more or less go and having the non-mixture, that is the "bad" in him, preponderate. It has been my idea that this "bad" figures in a degree to Gray as after a fashion his own creation; the creation, that is, of the enormous and fantastic opportunity and temptation he has held out—even though these wouldn't have operated in the least, or couldn't, without predispositions in Horton's very genius. If Gray saw him as a mere vulgar practiser of what he does practise, the interest would by that fact exceedingly drop; there would be no interest indeed, and the beauty of my "psychological" picture wouldn't come off, would have no foot to stand on. The beauty is in the complexity of the question—which, stated in the simplest terms possible, reduces itself to Horton's practically saying to Gray, or seeing himself as saying to Gray should it come to the absolute touch: "You *mind,* in your extraordinary way, how this money was accumulated and hankypankied,[18] you suffer, and cultivate a suffering, from the perpetrated wrong of which you feel it the embodied evidence, and with which the possession of it is thereby poisoned for you. But I don't mind one little scrap—and there is a great deal more to be said than you seem so much as able to understand, or so much as able to want to, about the whole question of how money comes to those who know *how* to make it. Here you are then, if it's so disagreeable to you—and what can one really say, with the chances you give me to say it, but that if you are so burdened and afflicted, there are ways of relieving you which, upon my honour, I should perfectly undertake to work—given the facilities that you so morbidly, so fantastically, so all but incredibly save for the testimony of my senses, permit me to enjoy." *That,* yes; but that is very different from the wider range of application of the aptitudes concerned. The confession, and the delinquency preceding it, that played a bit up for me yesterday—what do they do but make Horton just as vulgar as I *don't* want him, and, as I immediately recognise, Gray wouldn't in the least be able to stomach seeing him under any continuance of relations. I have it, I have it, and it comes as an answer to *why I worried?* Because of felt want of a way of providing for some Big Haul, really big; which my situation absolutely requires. There must be at a given moment a big haul in order to produce the big sacrifice; the latter being of the absolute essence. I say I have it when I ask myself why the Big Haul shouldn't simply consist of the consequence of a confession made by Horton to Gray, yes; but made not about what he has lost, whether dishonestly or not, for somebody else, but what he has lost for Gray. Solutions here bristle, positively, for the case seems to clear up from the moment I make Horton put his matter as a mere disastrous loss, of unwisdom, of having been "done" by others and not as a thing involving his own obliquity. What I want is that he *pleads the loss*—whether loss to Gray, loss to another party, or loss to both, is a detail. I incline to think loss to Gray sufficient—loss that Gray accepts, which is different from his meeting the disaster inflicted on another by Horton. What I want a bit is all contained in Gray's question, afterwards determined, not absolutely present at the moment, of whether this fact has not been a feigned or

18. TSa and TSb both have the unhyphenated "hankypankied."

simulated one, not a genuine gulf of accident, but an appeal for relinquishment practised on Gray by the latter's liability to believe that the cause is genuine. I clutch the idea of this determinant of rightness of suspicion being one with the circumstance that Cissy in a sort of *thereupon* manner "takes up" with Horton, instead of not doing so, as figures to Gray as discernible if Horton were merely minus. Is it cleared up for Gray that the cause is *not* genuine?—does he get, or does he seek, any definite light on this? Does he tell any one, that is does he tell Rosanna of the incident (though I want the thing or proportions bigger than those of a mere incident)—does he put it to her, in short does he take[19] her into his confidence about it? I think I see that he does to this extent, that she is the only person to whom he speaks, but that he then speaks with a kind of transparent and, as it were, (as it is in her sight) "sublime" dissimulation. Yes, I think that's the way I want it—that he tells her what has happened, tells it to her as *having* happened, as a statement of what he has done or means to do—perhaps his mind isn't even yet made up to it; whereby I seem to get a very interesting passage of drama and another very fine "Joint." He doesn't, no, decidedly, communicate anything to Davey Bradham—his instinct has been against that—and I feel herewith how much I want this D.B. relation for him to have all its possibility of irony, "comedy", humorous colour, so to speak. I want awfully to do D.B. to the full and give him all his value. However, it's of the situation here with Rosanna that the question is, and I seem to feel that still further clear up for me. There has been the passage, the big circumstance, with Horton—as to which, as to the sense of which and of what it involves for him, don't I after all see him as taking *time?* after all see him as a bit staggered quand même, and, as it were, *asking* for time, though without any betrayal of "suspicion", any expression tantamount to "What a queer story!" Yes, yes, it seems to come to me that I want the *determination of suspicion* not to come at once; I want it to hang back and wait for a big "crystallisation," a falling together of many things, which now takes place,[20] as it were, in Rosanna's presence and under her extraordinary tacit action, in that atmosphere of their relation which has already given me, or *will* have given, not to speak presumptuously, so much. It kind of comes over me even that I don't want *any* articulation to *himself* of the "integrity" question in respect to Horton to have taken place at all—till it very momentously takes place all at once in the air, as I say, and on the ground, and in the course, of this present scene. Immensely interesting to have made Everything precedent to have consisted but in preparation for this momentousness, so that the whole effect has been gathered there ready to break. At the same time, if I make it break not in the right way, unless I so rightly condition its breaking, I do what I was moved just above to bar, the giving away of Horton to Rosanna in the sense that fixing his behaviour upon him, or inviting or allowing her to fix it, is a thing I see my finer alternative to. The great thing, the great find, I really think, for the moment, is this fact of his having gone to her in a sort of still preserved uncertainty of light that amounts virtually to darkness, and then after a time with her coming away

19. TSa has "in short, that he takes . . . ." TSb has "in short that he take. . . ." Lubbock has pencilled in "does" for "that" in TSb.
20. After "place" both TSa and TSb have "as, as it were, ..."

with the uncertainty dispelled and the remarkable light instead taking its place. That gives me my very form and climax—in respect to the "way" that has most perplexed me, and gathers my action up to the fulness so proposed and desired; to the point after which I want to make it workable that there shall be but two Books left. In other words the ideal will be that this whole passage, using the word in the largest sense, with all the accompanying aspects, shall constitute Book 8, "Act" 8, as I call it, of my drama, with the dénoûment occupying the space to the end—for the foregoing is of course not in the least the dénoûment,[21] but only prepares it, just as what is thus involved is the occupancy of Book 7 by the history with Horton. Of course I can but reflect that to bring this splendid economy off it must have been practised up *to* VII with the most intense and immense art: the scheme I have already sketched for I and II leaving me therewith but III, IV, V, and VI to arrive at the completeness of preparation for VII, which carries in its bosom the completeness of preparation for VIII—this last, by a like grand law, carrying in *its* pocket the completeness of preparation for IX and X. But why not? Who's afraid? and what has the very essence of my design been but the most magnificent packed and calculated closeness? Keep this closeness up to the notch while admirably *animating* it, and I do what I should simply be sickened to death not to! Of course it means the absolute exclusively *economic* existence and situation of every sentence and every letter; but again what is that but the most desirable of beauties in *itself?* The chapters of history with Rosanna leave me then to show, speaking simply, its effect with regard to (I assume I put first) Gray and Horton, to Gray and Cissy, to Cissy and Horton, to Gray and Mrs. Bradham on the one hand and to Gray and Davey on the other and finally and supremely to Gray and Rosanna herself. It is of course definitely on that note the thing closes— but wait a little before I come to it. Let me state as "plainly" as may be what "happens" as the next step in my drama, the next Joint in the action after the climax of the "scene" with Rosanna. Obviously the first thing is a passage with Horton, the passage *after,* which shall be a pendant to the passage before. But don't I want some episode[22] to interpose here on the momentous ground of the Girl? These sequences to be absolutely planned and fitted together, of course, up to their last point of relation; to work such complexity into such compass can only be a difficulty of the most inspiring—the prize being, naturally, to achieve the lucidity *with* the complexity. What then is the lucidity for us about my heroine, and exactly what is it that I want and don't want to show? I want something to take place here between Gray and her that *crowns* his vision and his action in respect to Horton. As I of course want every point and comma to be "functional", so there's nothing I want that more for than for this aspect of my crisis— which does, yes, decidedly, present itself before Gray has again seen Horton. I seem even to want this aspect, as I call it, to be *the* decisive thing in respect to his "decision". I want something to have still depended for him on the question of how she is, what she does, what she makes him see, however little intending it, of her sensibility to the crisis, as it were—knowing as I do what I mean by

21. TSa and TSb have "dénouement" on both occasions in this sentence.
22. TSa and TSb have "episode, or, as I call it always, using Passage in the most comprehensive sense, to interpose. . . ."

this. But what does come up for me, and has to be faced, is all the appearance that all this later development that I have sketched and am sketching, rather directly involves a deviation from that *help by alternations* which I originally counted on, and which I began by drawing upon in the first three or four Books. What becomes after the first three or four[23] then of that variation—if I make my march between IV and VIII inclusive all a matter of what appears to Gray? Perhaps on closer view I can for the "finer amusement" escape that frustration—though it would take some doing; and the fact remains that I don't really want, and can't, any other exhibition than Gray's own *except* in the case of Horton and the Young Woman. I should like *more* variation than just that will yield me withal—so at least it strikes me; but if I press a bit a possibility perhaps will rise. Two things strike me: one of these being that instead of making Book 9 Gray's "act" I may make it in a manner Cissy's own; save that a terrific little question here comes up as involved in the very essence of my cherished symmetry and "unity". The absolute prime compositional idea ruling me is thus the unity of each Act, and I get unity with the Girl for IX only if I keep it *to* her and whoever else. To her and Horton, yes, to her and Gray (Gray first) yes; only how then comes in the "passage" of Gray and Horton without her, and which I don't want to push over to X. It would be an "æsthetic" ravishment to make Book 10[24] balance with Book 1 as Rosanna's affair; which I glimmeringly see as interestingly possible if I can wind up somehow as I want to do between Gray and Horton. In connection with which, however, something again glimmers—the possibility of making Book 9[25] quand même Cissy and Horton and Gray; twisting out, that is, some admirable way of her being participant in, "present at", what here happens between them as to their own affair. I say these things after all with the sense, so founded on past experience, that, in closer quarters and the intimacy of composition, prenoted arrangements, proportions and relations, do most uncommonly insist on making themselves different by shifts and variations, always improving, which impose themselves as one goes and keep the door open always to something *more* right and *more* related. It is subject to that constant possibility, all the while, that one does pre-note and tentatively sketch; a fact so constantly before one as to make too idle any waste of words on it. At the same time I do absolutely and utterly want to stick, even to the very depth, to the *general* distribution here imagined as I have groped on; and I am at least now taking a certain rightness and conclusiveness of parts and items for granted until the intimate tussle, as I say, happens, if it does happen, to dislocate or modify them. Such an assumption for instance I find myself quite loving to make in presence of the vision quite colouring up for me yesterday of Book 9[26] as given to Gray and Horton and Cissy Together, as I may rudely express it, and Book 10, to repeat, given, with a splendid richness and comprehensiveness, to Rosanna, as I hope to have shown Book 1 as so given.[27] Variety, variety—I want to go in for that for all the possibilities of my case may

23. TSa has "three or four" in this and the preceding sentence; TSb has "3 or 4" in both instances. .
24. In place of "Book 10" TSa has "No. X" and TSb has "Book No. 10."
25. For "Book 9" TSa has "No. IX" and TSb also has "Book 9."
26. For "Book 9" TSa has "IX" and TSb has "nine."
27. TSa ends this sentence "shown I so given"; TSb ends it "shown One as so given."

be worth; and I see, I feel, how a sort of fond fancy of it is met by the distribution, the little cluster of determinations, or, so to speak, for the pleasure of putting it, determinatenesses, so noted. It gives me the central mass of the thing for my hero's own embrace and makes beginning and end sort of confront each other over it.

Is it vain to do anything but say, that is but feel, that this situation of the Three in Book 9 [28] absolutely demands the intimate grip for clearing itself up, working itself out? Yes, perfectly vain, I reflect, as at all precluding the high urgency and decency of my seeing in advance just how and where I plant my feet and direct my steps. Express absolutely, to this end, the conclusive sense, the clear firm function, of Book 9 [29]—out of which the rest bristles. I want it, as for that matter I want each Book, with the last longing and fullest intention, to be what it is "amusing" and regaling to think of as "complete in itself"; otherwise a thoroughly expressed Occasion, or as I have kept calling it Aspect, such as one can go at, thanks to the flow of the current in it, in the firmest possible little narrative way. The form of the Occasion is the form that I somehow see as here very *particularly* presenting itself and contributing its aid to that impression of the Three Together which I try to focus. Where, exactly, and exactly how, are they thus vividly and workably together?—what is the most "amusing" way of making them so? It is fundamental for me to note that my action represents and embraces the sequences of a Year, not going beyond this and not falling short of it. I can't get my Unity, can't keep it, on the basis of more than a year, and can't get my complexity, don't want to, in anything a bit less. I see a Year right, in fine, and it brings me round therefore to the early summer from the time of my original Exposition. With which it comes to me of course that one of the things accruing to Gray under his Uncle's Will is the house at Newport, which belonged to the old man, and which I have no desire to go into any reason whatever for his heir's having got rid of. There is the house at Newport—as to which it comes over me that I kind of see him in it once or twice during the progress of the autumn's, the winter's, the spring's events. Isn't it also a part of my affair that I see the Bradhams with a Newport place, and am more or less encouraged herewith to make out the Scene of Book 9,[30] the embracing Occasion, of the three,[31] as a "staying" of them, in the natural way, the inevitable, the illustrative, under some roof that places them vividly in relation to each other. Of *course* Mrs. Bradham has her great characteristic house away from N.Y., where anything and everything may characteristically find their background—the whole case being compatible with that lively shakiness of fortune that I have glanced at; only I want to keep the whole thing, so far as my poor little "documented" state permits, on the lines of absolutely current New York practice, as I further reflect I probably don't want to move Gray an inch out of N.Y. "during the winter", this probably a quite unnecessarily bad economy. Having what I have of New York isn't the question of

28. TSa has "Three in IX"; TSb has "Three in Nine."

29. For "Book 9" TSa has "IX"; TSb has "Nine."

30. For "Book 9" TSa has "IX"; TSb has "Nine."

31. In both TSa and TSb "time" has been crossed out; typed in above it TSa has "Three" while TSb has "three."

using *it,* and it only, as entirely adequate from Book 4 to 8[32] inclusive? To keep everything as like these actualities of N.Y. as possible, for the sake of my "atmosphere", I must be wary and wise; in the sense for instance that said actualities don't at all comprise people's being at Newport *early* in the summer. How then, however, came the Bradhams to be there at the time noted in my Book 1?[33] I reflect happily àpropos of this that my there positing the early summer (in Book 1)[34] is a stroke that I needn't at all now take account of; it having been but an accident of my small vague plan as it glimmered to me from the very first go-off. No, definitely, the time-scheme must a bit move on, and give help thereby to the place-scheme; if I want Gray to arrive en plein Newport, as I do for immediate control of the assault of his impressions, it must be a matter of August rather than of June; and nothing is simpler than to shift. Let me indeed so far modify as to conceive that 15 or 16 months will be as workable as a Year—practically they will count as the period both short enough and long enough; and will bring me for Nine and Ten round to the Newport or whatever of August, and to the whatever else of some moment of beauty and harmony in the American autumn. Let me wind up on a kind of strong October or perhaps even better still—yes, better still—latish November, in other words admirable Indian Summer note. That brings me round and makes the circle whole. Well then I don't seem to want a repetition of Newport—as if it were, poor old dear, the only place known to me in the country!—for the images that this last suggestion causes more or less to swarm. By the blessing of heaven I am possessed, sufficiently to say so, of Lenox, and Lenox for the autumn is much more characteristic too. What do I seem to see then?—as I don't at all want, or imagine myself wanting at the scratch, to make a local jump between Nine and Ten. These things come—I see them coming now. Of course it's perfectly conceivable, and entirely characteristic, that Mrs. Bradham should have a place at Lenox as well as at Newport; if it's necessary to posit her for the previous summer in her own house at the latter place. It's perfectly in order that she may have taken one there for the summer—and that having let the Lenox place at that time may figure as a sort of note of the crack in her financial aspect that is part, to *call* it part, of my concern. All of which are considerations entirely meetable at the short range—save that I do really seem to kind of want Book 10[35] at Lenox and to want Nine there by the same stroke. I should like to stick Rosanna at the beautiful Dublin, if it weren't for the grotesque anomaly of the name; and after all what need serve my purpose better than what I already have? It's provided for in Book 1[36] that she and her father had only taken the house at Newport for a couple of months or whatever; so that is all to the good. Oh yes, all that New England mountain-land that I thus get by radiation, and thus welcome the idea of for values surging after a fashion upon Gray, appeals to one to "do" a bit, even in a measure beyond one's hope of space to do it. Well before me surely too the fact that my whole action does, can only, take place in the air

---

32. For "Book 4 to 8" TSa has "IV to VIII"; TSb has "Four to Eight."
33. For "Book I" TSa has "No. I" and TSb has "Number One."
34. For "Book I" TSa has "I" and TSb has "One."
35. For "Book 10" TSa has "X" and TSb has "Ten."
36. For "Book I" TSa has "I" and TSb has "One."

of the last actuality; which supports so, and plays into, its sense and its portée. Therefore it's a question of all the intensest modernity of every American description; cars and telephones and facilities and machineries and resources of certain sorts not to be exaggerated; which I can't not take account of. Assume then, in fine, the Bradhams this second autumn at Lenox, assume Gussie blazing away as if at the very sincerest and validest top of her push; assume Rosanna as naturally there in the "summer home" which has been her and her father's only possessional alternative to N.Y. I violate verisimilitude in not brushing them all, all of the N.Y. "social magnates", off to Paris as soon as Lent sets in, by their prescribed oscillation; but who knows but what it will be convenient quite exactly to shift Gussie across for the time, as nothing then would be more in the line of truth than to have her bustle expensively back for her Lenox proceedings of the autumn. These things, however, are trifles. All I have wanted to thresh out a bit has been the "placing" of Nine and Ten; and for this I have more than enough provided.

What it seems to come to then is the "positing" of Cissy at Lenox with the Bradhams at the time the circumstances of Book Eight[37] have occurred; it's coming to me with which that I seem exactly to want them to occur in the empty town, the New York of a more or less torrid mid-August—this I feel so "possessed of"; to which Gray has "come back" (say from Newport where he has been for a bit alone in his own house there, to think, as it were, with concentration); come back precisely for the passage with Horton. So at any rate for the moment I seem to see *that;* my actual point being, however, that Cissy is posited at Lenox, that the Book "opens" with her, and that it is in the sense I mean "her" Book. She is there waiting as it were on what Horton does, so far as I allow her intelligence of this; and it is there that Gray finds her on his going on to Lenox whether under constraint (by what has gone before) of a visit to the Bradhams, a stay of some days with them, or under the interest of a conceivable stay with Rosanna; a sort of thing that I represent, or at any rate "posit", as perfectly in the line of Rosanna's present freedom and attributes. Would I rather have him with Rosanna and "going over" to the Bradhams? would I rather have him with the Bradhams and going over to Rosanna?—or would I rather have him at neither place and staying by himself at an hotel, which seems to leave me the right margin? There has been no staying up to this point for him with either party, and I have as free a hand as could be. With which there glimmer upon me advantages—oh yes—in placing him in his own independence; especially for Book 10:[38] in short it seems to come. Don't I see Cissy as having obtained from Gussie Bradham that Horton shall be invited—which fact in itself I here provisionally throw off as giving me perhaps a sort of starting value.

37. For "Book Eight" TSa has "VIII" and TSb has "Eight."
38. For "Book 10" TSa has "X" and TSb has "Ten."

First Statement for *The Sense of the Past* (November 1914)

The Houghton manuscript of this "statement" consists of thirteen typed pages. HJ here resumes a theme that had haunted him since the beginning of his career, when he published the short story "A Passionate Pilgrim" in 1871. He turned to it again in a note for 9 August 1900 and developed it fully in his "Notes for *The Sense of the Past*," December 1914 to May 1915.

First Statement: (Preliminary)

The idea of trying if something won't still be done with it has come back to me within a few days, under pressure of our present disconcerting conditions,[1] and yet the desire, combined with that pressure, and forming indeed part of it, to try and get back to some form of work adjustable in a manner to one's present state of consciousness. I put the old beginning away,[2] under frustration at the time, with a sense that there was something in it, a good deal in fact, of its kind, and it now rises a bit confusedly, and even dimly before me, as matter for possible experiment. I remember both the interest with which it inspired me and the sense of an intimate difficulty connected with it, which it would be yet splendid, however, to overcome, and how I just groped my way into it, a certain number of steps over the threshold, as it were, after a somewhat loose and speculative, perhaps also somewhat sceptical, fashion. When I get my old MS. beginning back[3] I must try to recapture some sort of little grasp of my specific idea. It was complicated—I remember that I felt that, which however more inspired than discour-

1. HJ refers to World War I, then but three months old.
2. See entry for 9 August 1900.
3. Theodora Bosanquet went down to Lamb House on 3 November 1914 and recovered the original typescript.

aged: the beauty of it was just that it was complicated, if it shouldn't prove too much so to become splendidly clear, that is to give out all its value of intention. With the somewhat treacherous, or at least considerate, failure of further backing from Rottingdean, I remember suddenly coming to a stop—the thing was too difficult to try on a mere chance, and it appeared to be only in the name of a mere chance, after all, that I had been set in motion. So I put my beginning piously away—though as I seem to find now with a fine, fine little silver thread of association serving to let it dangle in the chamber of the mind. To jump straight to where I seem to recollect having got to and stopped, I see my young man, the hero of the thing, the young American primarily conceived and presented, coming to tell his story to the American Minister (of the period of Ministers, though I had dear J.R.L.[4] in mind as his suppositious listener and critic); *there* it was, about in the middle of that interview, as I remember, that the pen dropped, so to speak, from my hand—partly because of my hearing, stupidly and vulgarly, as I thought, from the Doubleday man, and partly, no doubt, by reason of the rather sharp incidence there of a projected hard knot or two that would have to be as sharply faced and untied. I saw, so far as I remember, the young man's call at the Legation, his extraordinary closeting with J.R.L., as the end and climax of what was to figure as my Introduction or Prologue; which presented itself as of not inconsiderable length, and the jump from which to the far off time, from the present period to the 'Past,' involved in the title, was going to have to be somehow bridged. I don't think I quite saw the bridge; I was groping my way to it with difficulty—and there it was at any rate, as I say, that I gave up insisting. The recovery and reperusal of my MS., and above all the re-writing of it, if in face of the test of renewed acquaintance this seems worth while, will doubtless bring back some of my intentions to me—to which I have during all these years lost the clue. I ask myself for instance what the purpose, the conscious ground or necessity, of the visit to J.R.L., the particular reason for it in a word, may have very exactly been. I recollect thinking it at the time a happy dodge, a very good way of providing for, or, so to speak, against, what was immediately next to come; yet only dimly, dimly now, while I thus vaguely recur to it, does the workable connection seem to come. The scene occurs after what has taken place a night or two before in the empty house in the old London Square: the phenomenon on which the whole thing hinges: namely, the sight by my hero of the young man of the portrait, the full length portrait he has so fondly and intently studied—the sight of him one night that he goes back and lets himself in quietly, and passes upstairs, the sight of him in the room, the other room, with a door and a vista open between them, standing there as in life and looking at him and then moving toward him. I seem to remember that I ended my chapter, or dropped my curtain, with that effect—beyond which nothing directly or, so to speak, crudely related could go; and resorted for the sequel to what my young man comes to the Minister to relate, as his prodigious and unprecedented case. It's all difficult to recover; too far from me and not without the aid of what I at the time wrote to be brought really nearer. Still I like just to play with it and sniff or hover about it a little, just to see what

4. James Russell Lowell, who had been U. S. Minister to the Court of St. James's.

may, under a fond pleading invitation, come back a little of itself. My idea of course—and that's what seems to me really so fine—that of the exchange of identity between my young American of today and his relative of upwards of a hundred years ago, or whatever, on the ground of the latter's reviving for the former under the prodigy of the actual man's so intense and so invoked and so fostered historic faculty, clumsily so to dub it, or in other words his sense of the past, the thing he has always wanted to have still more than historic records can give it, the thing forming the title, as the early part of the Introduction gives it, of the remarkable Essay or Study that he has published, a distinguished and striking little effort, and which we have learnt about to begin with. Yes, it glimmers back to me that at sight of the picture in the London house—all his comings back to see which, to come in for which, have also from the first been dealt with—he has had the extraordinary emotion of recognizing himself, his very self in the person of an ancestor, as if nothing but his clothes had been altered, to the dress of the time, and it is himself who looks out recognizingly *at* himself, just as the so interestingly painted image looks out recognizingly at *him.* My fantastic idea deals then with the phenomenon of the conscious and understood fusion, or exchange, that takes place between them; in connection with which I seize again the tip of the tail of the notion which seemed, which *must* have seemed to me a superior find, and which makes the basis, the mechanism or the logic, so to speak, of the prodigy. My actual young man, my young yearning and budding historian, who in the first chapter of all has been rejected by the young woman in New York (was she a young widow?—I forget!) because her heart is set all on a man of action and adventure, some sort of a type like that, and not on a sedentary student or whatever, my young man, I briefly note again, has been galled and humiliated by this attitude in her and I kind of make out that he has parted with her on a sort of understanding that she may be open to conquest, or to another appeal, if he succeeds in having about as great an adventure, and coming through with it, as any man ever had—or rather a much greater. I see he can't have known of course at all at that moment what this was going to be; the chapter with the young woman serves at any rate in my MS. as the introduction to the Introduction. Well, the sublime idea thrown up by the passage in the London house comes back to me as *this:* that there, face to face with my tremendously engaged and interest hero is this *alter ego* of a past generation of his 'race,' the inward passion of whose also yearning mind and imagination was the sense of the future—he having so nursed and cherished that, wanted so to project himself into it, that it makes him the very counterpart of his eventual descendant. It may be that they are not ascendant and descendant, but only collaterals, so to speak—that's a detail of no importance now. The strain of blood may be none the less effective in producing the relation—a minor question, as I say. What is involved in my prodigy, and makes the real drama, story or situation of it, is that one or the other of the young men in consequence of what so supernaturally passes between them, steps back or steps forward, into the life of the other exactly as that life is at that moment constituted, at that moment going on and being enacted, representing each the other for the persons, the society about him, concerned but with the double consciousness the representation of which makes the thrill and the curiosity of the affair, the consciousness of being the other and yet himself also, of being himself and yet the other also. What appealed to me as of an intensely effective note of the supernatural and sinister kind was this secret within his breast, that is within the hero's breast (for the two, in the 'situation,' are reduced to one) of his abnormal nature and of the effect on others that a dim, vague, attached and yet rather dreadful and distressful sense of it produces on *them*. I might be a little handicapped if I chose to think so by the fact of my having made use of a scrap of that fantasy in *The Jolly Corner*—distinctly do I remember saying to myself in writing that thing that I was filching in a small way this present put-away one and might conceivably afterwards regret it. But I don't mean to regret it if I prove not to want to, or to consider my idea at all compromised by the *J.C.*: the whole thing is so different and so much more ample, and precautions in short can be taken. Let the above rough indication of the core of the thing serve for the moment: the point is that it brings me at once of course to the action, its very self, of my drama: that is, takes up my hero in the alien, the borrowed, the 'past,' as I at first took it for granted, situation, and shows what he makes of it. The situation has of course to be intensely concrete, intensely exhibitional, compact and rounded, the exact right case. *But* here I am nose to nose with *the* difficulty, the crucial, the one I felt awaiting me, and that I seemed to hold off from, in imagination, as if for very dread. The production of the 'old world' atmosphere, the constitution of the precise milieu and tone I wanted, that seemed so difficult in anything of a short compass, and the book in question oughtn't at the very biggest stretch to exceed a hundred thousand words. Eighty thousand would be better—but that's again a detail. Now I remember beating about for the possible apprehension of an alternative—not the showing of the modern young man in the other world, to put it bravely, but the showing of the ancient young man in the actual; this because it would seem easier to do. The other on the other hand was what I first took for granted—and contains much more, probably, the true fruits of one's idea. In fact it stands out, from the moment one gets at all nearer and nearer, as the only form or aspect that *can* give what I want; and I have a sort of feeling already even, on taking up the old faded fancy again, that the intrinsic difficulties *must* probably yield to soft persistent and penetrating pressure, if this be but rightly applied. I think my passage from what I figure as the meeting of the two young men, each the *alter ego* of the other, as I conceive it, to the report of that matter by the living one, so to discriminate, to the extremely bewildered and confounded, yet extremely interested Minister, a really admirable *coup*, for my getting on, and not to be feared, the more it hovers before me, as putting too formidably the question of a transition in itself. If I can but do it as I seem to see it, it will need no transition but the 'jump,' as I figure the matter; its own effective climax, *if* perfectly effective, furnishing all the preparation, all the bridge over, that I shall require. What does he come to see the Minister *for?* I ask above: why, he comes to see him as a man on the eve of a great adventure, from which he perhaps may and perhaps mayn't return, takes certain precautions in advance, gives as it were, in some responsible or possibly in the event helpful quarter, some account of what he may intend or incur; so that in a word there may be some record or clue. In short I have this perfectly present; and I see as immediately sequent and making a new Book, as I suppose I should call it, our vision of him as transported a hundred years back and engaged in the 'then,' the then living and playing complexity of the particular case, the case of his *alter ego* of 1820, say. Turning it over I don't see why 1820 shouldn't respond to my need without the complication of my going further back. I want the moment of time to be far enough off for the complete old-world sense, and yet not so far as to be worrying from the point of view of aspects, appearances, details of tone, of life in general; accordingly if I see my 'present' hour, as really recent, as of 1910, say, I get upwards of a century of 'difference,' which is in all conscience enough—with the comparative nearness so simplifying certain apprehended difficulties.

Well then, what *is* the personal and then existing situation or predicament into which my young man emerges as from below, after the fashion of a swimmer who has dived or sunk or been dragged down for the minute and who comes up to the surface, recovering breath with difficulty at first and then gets by a few strokes more onto the fact of terra firma, where he feels his feet and can stand erect and look about and know where he is? Without my absent MS. I feel I lack a helpful hint or two as to this—though I must remember also how little, up to where my sketchiness had got, I had in the least consistently worked that question out. Roughly, roughly I now recover it, it seemed to come, though very unponderedly, to something like *this:* in connection with which my approach to which, however, I must at once mention, what I think I haven't hereabove, that my notion must have been quite that the 1820 young man, the real one, had anticipated more or less exactly the act or the fact of the 1910; that is, had done just what the latter is doing; which at once, I have to keep straight before me, has to make him a young American too. There immediately crops up a vision of 'difficulty'—which I am not however going for a moment to allow to worry me. They are easily settled from the moment I have so rigidly to respect my limits of space, and thereby my absolute, which I may call also admirable, need to generalise and foreshorten, to take all helpful leaps and jumps. The 'romantic' of course has essentially to be allowed for, but what on earth is the whole thing but the pure essence of the romantic and to be bravely faced and exploited as such? *Romantically* therefore I face the music, as I say, and get over any obstacle by simply working that note or grasping, so to speak, squeezing as hard as I can, that nettle. If asked what sort of young American it could be who in 1820 would come over to make the acquaintance of English relations, come over, that is, so comparatively soon after the wars and animosities between the two countries, I either make up my mind that 1820 isn't, or wasn't, too soon, or that my young man was, like so many, many thousands of his countrymen and above all townsmen, for he comes indispensably from New York, of Tory or Loyalist brood, and therefore never really effectively dissevered. The trouble, in a manner, with this would be that the Loyalists were all ruined, banished or scattered, and that his therefore coming from the States in anything like that character at that period, 'swears' somewhat with the public and historic facts. However, the question is *la moindre des choses;* the merest flicker of ingenuity can settle it. In 1820, after all, more than thirty-five years had elapsed since the end of the Revolution, and even if the 'family,' the people in question, had been gravely incommoded and dispersed

Loyalists, they may within the term of years have come back to the country and recovered themselves, various possibilities aiding; or otherwise a different footing is conceivable and arrangeable. What the footing was is a part, that is a touch or two, of what my modern young man communicated to the American Minister. I put it in there as I may, I put it in enough—as part of what he has entered into possession of at the nocturnal meeting in the London house—the London house in which, with the aid probably of a villa out of town, near town by our measure now, but quite rurally out of it then, the action of my affair takes place. Let me at any rate get at once to the point that I want most of all to express to myself, to make my little statement of as the very central beauty of the thing—this not to postpone it for the moment to anything else, everything else being so placeable and arrangeable, as I hope I don't too fatuously think, in relation to it. What his miraculous excursion into the past, his escapade into the world of that Sense of it that he has so yearned for, what it does to him most of all, he speedily becomes aware with sick dismay, is to make him feel far more off and lost, far more scared, as it were, and terrified, far more *horribly,* that is, painfully and nostalgically misplaced and disconnected, than had ever entered into the play of his imagination about the matter. His whole preconception has been that it would, that it should, be an excursion and nothing more, from which as by the pressure of a spring or a stop, the use of some effective password or charm, he might get out and away again, get back to his own proper consciousness, his own time and place and relation to things. What is terrible, he perceives after a bit, is that he feels immersed and shut in, lost and damned, as it were, beyond all rescue; and that in proportion as this is the case his relation to the other actors in the drama into the centre of which he, as I have said, crops or pops up, becomes of the last difficulty and dreadfulness, of something that I like to figure him thinking of as the most appalling danger. Just *with* which it is that I put my finger on what originally struck me as the very centre of my subject, and the element in it that I spoke hereabove of my having a bit discounted in the stuff of the *Jolly Corner.* The most intimate idea of *that* is that my hero's adventure there takes the form so to speak of his turning the tables, as I think I called it, on a 'ghost' or whatever, a visiting or haunting apparition otherwise qualified to appal *him;* and thereby winning a sort of victory by the appearance, and the evidence, that this personage or presence was more overwhelmingly affected by him than he by *it*. That is what the analogy amounts to—but let me dismiss any sense of inconvenience from it once for all. I have free use of everything I originally caught at in that connection on behalf of my present youth. He feels, after he has a bit taken things in, the particular things about him, he feels *cut off,* as I say, and lost: he is only too much immersed and associated and identified, and that—he couldn't 'realise' it till he should know how it felt—fills him with an anguish that it seems to him he can neither betray nor suppress. If he betrays it and thereby, so to speak, who and what he really is, he is in danger of passing for a madman, or some unspeakable kind of supernatural traitor, to others, and if he accepts the situation, that is, accepts the terror of his consciousness, he becomes the same sort of thing to himself. But what I seem to myself to have wanted most of all is to represent the drama of the whole outward effect (merely outward up to a certain point) of his 'success'; its effect in making him, for all his precautions, his successful ones, seem different and strange, at first attractively strange, to the others and then this in a degree and to a tune that becomes sinister to them, as who should say, even while he wants, for dear life, also, as who should say, to keep it from doing so; intensely wanting as he does to keep things consonant to his safety, his recovery, so to speak, his escape, that is, his return to his own age. His homesickness, as it were, becomes, as I say, appalling, and to fall short of escape identical for him, as it seems, with damnation. In short I see all there is and may be made to be in this; or shall, that is, when I have disposed of a question still hanging about it, but which indeed the only way probably to dispose of is by bringing to the concrete, absolutely, the relation with him, or the inter-relations, of the 'others,' the persons, the three or four, the four or five at most, for I can't afford space for many, in whom my 'rounded' action is embodied. Well then, roughly and roughly enough, what I seemed to see was his intermixture with two sisters, his relatives, though distant, as it were—meaning when I say 'his' those of the real young man of 1820; for whom, to put it platitudinously, they so completely, and yet so more and more worriedly, take him. What I saw without working it out was that he must somehow from the first have found himself in question as the suitor, as the pretended and predestined, of one of the sisters, but not of the one he finds himself caring for most. I haven't got at all at the machinery of this—that must come, and will, being but a matter of ingenuity, but what my *donnée* seemed to be giving me when I left it so many years ago was that they both fall in love with him, that the one designed for him is the wrong one by his measure, that she expresses her state of feeling, that the other, the 'sacrificed' one, doesn't and hasn't and can't, and is thereby but the more sacrificed—she however being contracted by her family to another young man, whom she doesn't like, whom she likes still less from the moment she has seen *ours* and who forms one of my 4 or 5 figures. I see a mother, a hard, pretty awful, and awful to the tune of 1820, mother—the father being dead; and I see, provisionally, such two or three other subsidiary figures. Above all I see—

Notes for *The Sense of the Past*
(December 1914 to May 1915)

On 7 June 1916 Theodora Bosanquet wrote to HJ's agent, James B. Pinker:

> I am leaving at your office today the copy of "The Sense of the Past" and the accompanying "Statements". . . . The first Statement was dictated in the absence of the manuscript (many years old) of the first two books, and half of the third. . . . At the point where it breaks off Mr. James sent me down to Rye to fetch this old manuscript, from which he redictated the first part. The second "Statement" begins at the point where the old original MS left off. . . .

By the beginning of December 1914 HJ's revision had taken him through all of Book Third except for the final six paragraphs. At that point, following Ralph Pendrel's comment about having no intention of committing suicide, HJ began dictating these notes—the "second Statement." He then returned to the conclusion of Book Third and continued through four chapters of Book Fourth. Miss Bosanquet's diaries make no further reference to HJ's dictation of *The Sense of the Past* after the entry for 16 May 1915. See the initial note for this idea, 9 August 1900, and the "First Statement for *The Sense of the Past*," 1–2 November 1914.

The Ambassador *does* of course think him a curious and interesting case of dementia, feels a kind of superior responsibility about him accordingly, is really in a manner "fascinated" and mystified too; and in short quite naturally and inevitably stretches a point to see him, as it were, safely home. This he has it on his mind and his nerves, on his sense of responsibility, effectively to do. But, as naturally, he mustn't acknowledge his conviction, even though Ralph invites him to; and I get I think what I want by making him come down to the street in the cab as from curiosity to test his visitor's extraordinary statement, and then plausibly propose or insist on getting in with him and tracking him, as it were, to his lair: so as to be able to have first-hand evidence of his material situation in the event of whatever further occupation. It's in the street and at the cab door that he makes the point of "seeing home," as if then and there merely extemporised; and with the advantage that I thus seem to get what I remember originally groping for, *having* groped for, when I broke this off just here so many years ago. I gave up taking time to excogitate my missing link, my jump or transition from this last appearance of my young man's in the modern world, so to speak, and his coming up again, where we next find him, after the dive, in the "old." I think I now have quite sufficiently got that transition—I have it perfectly before me. It passes between them; Ralph himself, on their way, in the cab, or probably better still, outside, on the pavement in Mansfield Square and before the house, expresses all I want; puts it, that is, to his benevolent friend, that he *knows* now perfectly that on opening the door of the house with his latchkey he lets himself into the Past. He disappears into the Past, and what he has wanted is that his companion shall know he is there; shall be able to give that account of him if he is missed or wanted; shall also perhaps be able to take in all, whatever it is to be, that may yet happen, and believe in his experience if he ever rises to the surface again with it. This of course but clinches the Ambassador's sense of the refined beauty of his mania; though at the same time the very law of my procedure here is to show what is passing in his Excellency's mind only through Ralph's detection and interpretation, Ralph's own expression of it—so leaving my own exhibition of it to stand over for my final chapter, my supreme dénoûment, when Aurora What's-her-name, under a tremendous "psychic" anxiety and distress of her own, which has been growing and growing within her commensurately with Ralph's own culmination of distress and anguish in *his* drama, which we so centrally and interestingly assist at, comes out to London for relief and throws herself upon the Ambassador with the strange story of her condition, matching and balancing so remarkably poor Ralph's own story of the number of months before. An essential point is that the time of duration of Ralph's plunge or dive is exactly the real time that has elapsed for those on the surface—some six months being about what I provisionally see. The horrid little old conceit of the dream that has only taken half an hour, or whatever, any analogy with that, I mean, to be utterly avoided. The duration is in short the real duration, and I know what I mean when I say that everything altogether corresponds. Then it is, in the final situation, that we get, by a backward reference or action, the real logic and process of the Ambassador's view of how it has seemed best to take the thing, and what it has seemed best to "do" in connection with his strange visitor's exhibition. He gives, he states, what has then determined and guided him; and I see that he states it to Aurora all sufficiently and vividly, so that we don't have any clumsiness of his going back to it, I mean to his account of his own procedure, with Ralph himself when we have Ralph at last restored and, as what all that has gone on in the interval makes it, saved: saved from all the horror of the growing fear of *not* being saved, of being lost, of being *in* the past to stay, heart-breakingly to stay and never know his own original precious Present again; that horror which his conception of his adventure had never reckoned with, and his manner of *getting* saved from which, saved by the sacrifice, the self-sacrifice of the creature to whom he confesses, in his anguish of fear, the secret of who and what and how etc. he *is,* constitutes the clou and crisis and climax of my action as I see it. It will take more working out, which will come but too abundantly, I seem to apprehend, as I go; but I have the substance of it, I have that still, as I had it of old, in my vision, even if a trifle rough, of the two sisters, the mother, Mrs. So-and-so of Drydown, the brother of that period, and whoever or whatever else I may subordinately need—even to the point very possibly of a second young man, the third, that is, in all, who is a wooer or suitor of the younger sister and, for my full kind of quasi-Turn-of-Screw effect, is of a type, a type of the period, entirely opposed to that of the brother. I see him, I have him and *his* affair, too thoroughly to have to waste words on him here. The more I get into my drama itself the more magnificent, upon my word, I seem to see it and feel it; with such a tremendous lot of possibilities in it that I positively quake in dread of the muchness with which they threaten me. The slow growth on the part of the others of their fear of Ralph, even in the midst of their making much of him, as abnormal, as uncanny, as not *like* those they know of their own kind etc., etc.; and his fear just *of* theirs, with his double consciousness, alas, his being *almost* as right as possible for the ''period,'' and yet so intimately and secretly wrong; with his desire to mitigate so far as he can the malaise that he feels himself, do what he will, more and more produce. There must be an *importance* for him, I mean about him, in the view of the others; and this must be definite and consist of some two or three very strong and vivid facts—vivid that is to the imagination of people of 1820. Rather beautiful does it seem to me to have two or three of his actual modern facts stick to him and operate in this sense that I try to project: notably his ''refinement,'' though he tries to conceal it, to dissimulate it; notably his being in 1820 as ''rich'' as he is, or was, in 1910—which counts for an immense well-offness at the earlier period. And then his whole true modern attribute and quality, with a distinguished appearance to match it, and certain things dont il ne peut pas se défaire, that are of the modern pitch of material civilisation, like his perfect and soignées teeth, for example; which that undentisted age can't have known the like of, and which constitute a part of his troubled consciousness of complication. He dissimulates, he succeeds, he fits in above all because he pleases, pleases at the same time that he creates malaise, by not being *like* them all; which it is that gives me what I just above threw out this question for, his ''importance.'' Without the importance I don't see the situation for him at all as I want it, and yet I must bring it in on lines of sufficient verisimilitude—even though while I *say* this the element so visualised fills me with the effect to be got out of it: I mean the charm and interest and fineness of that. In short once I have the importance, as I say, I have everything: the rest all clusters round it. Yes, the more I think of the little man (he must be little) who circles about the younger sister, and of whom she has an intimate horror—*he* rich, by the way, too, and thereby desired by the mother, and with a small sort of raffiné (of that time) Horace Walpole atmosphere about him— but in short I needn't talk of him thus; I possess him too entirely. I keep missing, at the same time, all the while, my fact of putting the essence of what I see straight enough thus—the postulate of the young man from America arriving, coming upon the scene, somehow designated or arranged for in advance as to one or other of the sisters (I leave it rough and a little in the air, so to speak, for the moment. The just how and just why I can dispose of in a page when in closer quarters). The point is that the wrong sister, abetted by the mother, pounces on him, as it were—it's the elder one I see doing this; and it so befalls that he is booked, as we say, to marry her, before, with all the precautions he has to keep, he can, as we also say, turn round. So it is that after a little, after the flush of the amusement of his extraordinary consciousness having begun a bit to abate in the light of the brutalities etc., what I call to myself most conveniently his dawning anguish glimmers and glimmers; what it means to see himself married to the elder sister and locked up with her there in *that* form of the Past. He conceals, he successfully does so, his growing malaise, all the effort and unrest of which, by the by, makes him, he sees, appear to them "clever" beyond anything they have ever dreamed of (they, also, by the way, must pass for clever, as 1820 understood it;) and I watch also, parenthetically, at my need for their not being, with all their pride of gentility, at all as conveniently well-off as they would like, or must require, this fact helping greatly the importance for them that he *is* possessed of means that seem to them quite blessedly large. The note of their thrift, a certain hardness of meanness, the nature of their economies, the brutality (I keep coming back to that) of their various expedients—this and that and the other Ralph has to take in. Meanwhile he is committed to the elder sister—and we have the effect on her of his importance, his means, his cleverness, mixed up with that in him which is mystifying to all of them, but which the elder sister at first at least sets down to the action and the play of a cleverness, a strange cleverness from over the sea, such as she has never before conceived. She holds on and on to him even after the malaise, and his sense of it in them, with his still greater sense of it in himself, has quite begun, as it were, to rage; with which: oh I see somehow such beautiful things that I can hardly keep step with myself to expatiate and adumbrate coherently enough. Let me just nail 2 or 3 things, by 2 or 3 of the roughest simplest strokes, in order to catch and hold them fast before I go on. All the while, all the while, the younger sister, who is ever so touching, charming, really appealing for him—all the while, all the while. I know what I mean by this sufficiently just to see and note here that the elder does after a while break off under the action of the malaise, which Ralph is in the extraordinary position of having in a way to work against and being also, as a means of release to him, grateful to. I can't take time to catch at this moment, but keep it till the next chance, my notation of how and where the younger sister, the one who *really* would have been meant for him, the one for the sake of whom he would almost really swing off backward—my notation, I say (after a break of dictation) of the origin and growth of the special relation between Ralph and herself; she being of course the nearest approach— and in fact it's very much of an approach—that I have in the whole thing to a Heroine. I seem to myself now to have intended somehow, in my original view, an accident, a complication, a catastrophic perversity or fatality, as it were, through which Ralph has addressed himself from the first to the elder, the wrong, sister instead of the younger, the right—and when I try to recover what I so long ago had in my head about this there glimmers out, there floats shyly back to me from afar, the sense of something like *this,* a bit difficult to put, though entirely expressible with patience, and that as I catch hold of the tip of the tail of it yet again strikes me as adding to my action but another admirable twist. Of course I am afraid of twists, I mean of their multiplying on my hands to the effect of too much lengthening and enlarging and sprawling; but the bit that I speak of now is surely of the very essence of the situation. It connects itself with something so interesting and effective, so strong and fine, to express—from the moment one successfully tackles it. "This," then, what I mentioned above, is that Ralph has "taken over" from the other party to his extraordinary arrangement certain indications that have been needed for starting the thing, and which I think of him as having, under the operation of the whole prodigy, very considerably, very enormously, assimilated. Enormous, however, as the assimilation may be, it is not absolutely perfect, and don't I exactly get out of this wavering margin, this occurrence of spots and moments, so to speak, where it falls short, just one of those effects of underlying distress, of sense of danger, as I comprehensively call it, which are of the very finest essence of one's general intention? He knows his way so much and so far, knows it wonderfully, finds his identity, the one he wears for the occasion, extraordinarily easy considering the miracle of it all; but the very beauty of the subject is in the fact of his at the same time watching himself, watching his success, criticising his failure, being both the other man and not the other man, being just sufficiently the other, his prior, his own, self, not to be able to help living in that a bit too. Isn't it a part of what I call the beauty that this concomitant, this watchful and critical, living in his "own" self inevitably grows and grows from a certain moment on?—and isn't it for instance quite magnificent that one sees this growth of it as inevitably promoted more and more by his sense of what I have noted as the malaise on the part of the others? Don't I see his divination and perception of *that* so affect and act upon him that little by little he begins to live more, to live most, and most uneasily, in what I refer to as his own, his prior self, and less, uneasily less, in his borrowed, his adventurous, that of his tremendous speculation, so to speak—rather than the other way round as has been the case at first. When his own, his original, conquers so much of the ground of that, then it is that what I have called his anguish gets fuller possession of it—it being so one thing to "live in the Past" *with* the whole spirit, the whole candour of confidence and confidence of candour, that he would then have naturally had—and a totally different thing to find himself living in it without those helps to possibility, those determinations of relation, those preponderant right instincts and, say, saving divinations. Don't I put it at first that he is excited and amused and exhilarated by the presence of these latter, by the freedom with which he lives and enjoys and sees and knows: the exhilaration proceeding during the "at first" time, as I put it, by the sense, the fairly intoxicating and spell-casting consciousness of how the inordinate business is going. His sense of success, which there is just enough of his critical margin or edge to appreciate, to estimate, and thus relate to his former consciousness and his whole starting-point, this *creates* for him a part of the success, the success with the others, by the very spirit and glamour (to *them*) that it gives him and that keeps up till the change I visualise, the inevitable difference, to phrase it roughly, begins—begins by something that *happens,* something that springs out of the very situation itself for portent, for determination, and which I must work out, or work into, exactly the right dramatic identity for. This I guarantee; but meanwhile I am ahead of my argument, and must hark back for a few minutes to what I left standing and waiting above— that "this" which I was there about to follow up. At once, withal, I see it in images, which I must put as they come, and which make for me thus, don't I seem to feel? one of the first, if not *the* very first passages of my action. An action, an action, an action must it thus insuperably be—as it has moreover so well started with being—from the first pulse to the last. Ralph, taking leave of the Ambassador, the depositary of his extraordinary truth and the (as he hopes) secured connection with the world he cuts himself loose from, dropping as from a balloon thousands of feet up in the air, and not really knowing what smash or what magically *soft* concussion awaits him—Ralph, I say, in entering the house then walks at a step straight into 1820 and, closing the door behind him, shuts out everything to which he has hitherto belonged. His is from that minute, to his own eyes and all his own faculties, the young man in the portrait, the young man we have seen advance to him that night of his vigil in the drawing-room. This bridge or effective transition from the visit at the Embassy to the central drama is thus *found* and is as good as another for my purpose—swift and straight and simple and direct; as I have on a foregoing page, however, sufficiently stated. Well then, I want to make it, *within,* his arrival, practically, from America to the London family: as to which, however, on consideration don't I see myself catch a bright betterment by not at all making him use a latch-key?—to the fact of which an awkwardness and a difficulty would, I seem to make out, or *do,* rather, immediately attach. No, no—no latch-key—but a rat-tat-tat, on his own part, at the big brass knocker; having effected which he stands there a moment, I think, his head very triumphantly high and confident, looking from the steps down at the Ambassador on the pavement; this latter isolated now, by Ralph's having paid and discharged the cab, which has driven away, the moment they got out. What I glanced at as happening between them just thereafter takes place on the pavement, as I have noted, but with this difference, I see with a minute's further intensity of focussing, that he does—well, what I have just stated. Only I seem to want a dumb passage between the two men while the Ambassador just stands, just lingers, as if now at last verily spellbound. (I mustn't forget, by the way, that I have spoken of the rain, or that Ralph has, at the Embassy, and that his Excellency can't be represented as standing there without a vehicle and under his umbrella. So it has been constaté on their coming out of the Embassy that the rain has stopped during Ralph's visit, so that it's all the more quite over when they reach the square.) The Ambassador has said, in reference to the cab, "Oh I won't keep it—I'll walk home; you've really made me need to shake myself!" Thereby I get him held there for the minute seeing the last of Ralph after the latter has knocked and before the door is opened. Ralph turns on its opening—it is held open wide for the moment, and as I seem to see this altogether in latish daylight of a spring, say of a March or April, season, it is no lighted interior that is for a moment exhibited, but just such a Bloomsbury entrance hall as may very well meet the eye to-day. Within then, Ralph arrives; and what for the moment I want summarily to mark is simply that the elder sister is the first person in the "drama" that he sees. She must be handsome, very—handsomer in an obvious way than the younger; not yet at all in sight—not in sight, I think, till after the three others have been, the mother and the two young men, who a little announce and prepare her. It even may be a little, I think, that she is for the time away from home and doesn't return till after the situation is otherwise started. Well then, here it is that what Ralph *knows,* what he is in possession of and has the general preparation for, is so far precarious and, so to speak, treacherous, that—well, all I want to say now is, before I break off, that he takes her, takes the elder one, for the right young woman. This seems easy—so right, in her way, does she appear to be. He knows, he has "had it," from the 1820 young man, what is expected of him in regard to one of the young women; how, in what manner and on what terms and by what understanding it has come to be expected, remaining questions that I shall adequately, not to say brilliantly, dispose of. What I seem to want is to get the relation between these two started on the spot, before any other relation whatever takes place for my young man; feeling as I do that once it is started I can abundantly take care of it. I even ask myself whether I mayn't have my hero's very first impression, the very first of all, of my second man, as I call him, the one other than the brother, who is there for the second sister and whom he should perhaps do well to find alone in the room when he is introduced, waiting there for the others, the objects of his call, and constituting Ralph's immediate impression. It is to *them,* say, that the first sister enters—so indefeasibly and luminously, as it were, do I see my procedure ruled by the drama, the quasi-scenic movement, or essential march and logic and consistency, at any rate. However, I am not pretending in these words, in this rough scenario, to go into any but the most provisional and general particulars. What I want is that my young man should inevitably and naturally *dazzle,* and become aware of it, by the very force of his feeling the distinction and privilege of the prodigious element that has launched him. The others don't in the least know what it is in him, but what I want to make ressortir from it is that he "does" the other fellow, his ancient prototype, the expected cousin from America, with no end of gentility etc. There must be at the same time, of course I see, enormous foreshortenings, great compression and presentation of picture: I want something of this sort to show before the second daughter turns up. Of course such questions as whether it was of the period that the elder one, bred as girls of that time were bred, would "come down" to a couple of "gentlemen visitors" alone, and as by a kind of anticipation of our current modernity—of course such a detail as that is a perfectly easy thing to handle and make right. At the same time withal, in respect to what I said just above about the scenic, let me keep before me how the very essence of all this is to stick as fast as possible to the precedent of the "Screw," in which foreshortening abounded and I didn't, and couldn't, at all hand my subject over to the scenic. The present is of course a much larger and more complicated affair, lending itself much more to the scenic, even in a manner insisting on it a little, or a good bit; but I must guard, and guard, all the while intensely guard, myself, none the less— or I shall sprawl out over ever so much more ground than I shall want, or at all need, for my best effect, to cover. If I may but look it well in the face that the thing can only afford in a very minor degree, not in the least in a preponderant one, to express itself scenically, it takes very little further thinking to see how vital that is, and that the particular effect I want most to catch, that of the crescendo of the malaise, really demands and depends upon the nonscenic for its full triumph. I grasp this entirely; I see how "narrative representation" most permits, most effectively prepares and accompanies, my turning of my present screw, and what a part picture and image and evoked aspect and sense can play for me in that connection.

I catch, it seems to me, with a certain amount of vision already two or three, not to say three or four, of my essential hinges or, as I have called 'em, *clous,* that mark the turns or steps of the action. The first of these is the appearance on the scene of the second daughter after things have got well under way in respect to the first. The first is the fullblown flower—she mustn't be at all too young, by the way; must be going on to thirty, say—and very little trumpet-blow takes place about her, on the part of the others, in advance: all pointing to the fact that she's a sort of neglected quantity—whom nevertheless the little Horace Walpole man does appreciate and pretend to; under all encouragement from the others who think him quite *more* than good enough for her, though not good enough, no, for the elder sister. Beware, by the way, of any little false step here: don't make the pretender in question too eligible or, in the modern lingo, smart; since if this were so Ralph wouldn't pass for more desirable. I must keep him a bit down, in the right sort of way and degree, in comparison with Ralph; bearing in mind at the same time that a sort of leading note in it all is his, ours, sense of the hard old class rigour governing the life about him and of which he sees the salience at every turn. The reappearance at home of the second girl, from wherever she has been (expressible in 10 words) at any rate is, as it were, my first clou or hinge; a fact, an impression, an apprehension, that immediately makes such a difference for Ralph. I forget already whether I said just above that the H.W. man talks to him, takes him into his confidence about her, even to the point of recognising to R. that she doesn't care for his suit and has much incurred her mother's, sister's and even brother's reprobation by that attitude. Vividness to R. of the reign of authority at that time, the much harder rule and discipline; and how half terrified at what she is doing by hanging back, by resisting, the poor girl herself is all the while. Her first relation to him is that of her appealing exactly from this rigour; her first impression of him and emotion about him, he sees, he gives us to see, is that of a sudden this fine young American relation is a person who may side with her, may help her, may intervene and back her up in not accepting addresses from a person she can't get over her dislike of. Yes, that's their first basis, and for this appeal Ralph must have been prepared by his own sense of the kind of uncanny, to put it in a simplified way, little personage her aspirant is. They come nearer together on that, they meet on that, they talk, they begin to understand each other on that—very great though Ralph's responsibility in the matter, the matter of backing up her refusal, may be. It's at any rate the way the real relation with them, with him—his sense of the ancient brutality of the others to her, her mother, her brother, her sister, stirring finely within him. She hasn't dreamed herself, he sees, of any real equality of transaction, of relation with him at all; for if the others are under the dazzle, so much the more under it is she. She sees—that is *he* sees *that* she sees; he likes her to like him—which is what gives her the sense of a privilege she trembles up into the enjoyment of, astonished at herself in her exquisite humility (this *so* touching to R.) even while doing so. The great thing is that he gets into relation with them, and that by the time he has done so the sense of how he needs it, the dim vagueness as yet of how she may perhaps help him, has begun to work in him. He sees, he feels, I make out, that she, as it were, understands him—though how and why she does demands full specification; that in fine what affects the others as his secret, as his queerness, as what they don't know what to make of in him, does the reverse of putting *her* off—it makes her somehow feel that beneath or within all his dazzle he is an object for pity, for pity "about which" she could perhaps do something. The ideal thing for dramatic interest and sharpness would be that there is just one matter in which, just one point at which, just one link with his other identity by which he betrays himself, gives himself away, testifies supremely to his alienism, abnormalism, the nature of his identity in fine; the ideal thing would be that, I say, and that it should be definite and visible, absolutely catchable-in-the-act, enough for her to seize it, come into possession of it, and yet not merely terrify or horrify her: affect her in short, on the contrary, with but a finer yearningness of interest. The ideal, as I say, would be that this fact or circumstance should be tremendously right from the tone of the "Screw" point of view, should be intensely in the note of that tone, should be a concrete and definite thing. Find it, find it; get it right and it will be the making of the story. It must consist of something he has to do, some condition he has to execute, some moment he has to traverse, or rite or sacrifice he has to perform—say even some liability he has to face and the occurrence of which depends somehow on the state in which he keeps himself. I seem to see it, it glimmers upon me; though I didn't think of it at first—I hadn't originally got as far as it—it hovers before me though in the form of the only thing it *can* be. When I call it a liability I seem to catch it by the tip of the tail; seem to get a sort of sense of what it *may* in a manner be. Let me figure it out a bit, and under gentle, or rather patiently firm, direct pressure it will come out. He is liable then say to glimpses of vision of the other man, the one portrayed in the picture and whom he had had the portentous passage with before going to the Ambassador; he is liable, put it, to recurrences of a sense of that presence—which thus, instead of being off in the boundless vast of the modern, that is of the Future, as he has described its being to the Ambassador, *does* seem to him at times to hover and to menace: only not to the appearance or effect of reassuring or relieving him, but only to that of really quite mocking and not pitying him, of showing him to himself as "sold," horribly sold. Say it's as if the man of 1820, the Pendrel of that age, is having so much better a time in the modern, that is in the Future, than he is having in the present, *his* Present, which is the Past, that a chill and a fear, the growth of a despair and a terror, drop upon him from it and signify somehow that he must begin to feel himself lost. That's it, that's it, that may be admirable, if I can get the right hinge or play for it—which of course I can. He hasn't expected it, I think—unless I represent something of it as coming back to him, while he wonders, from that passage between him and the other fellow which we know, so far as we do know, only by his projection of it to the Ambassador— after our having seen the other fellow approach, that is, at the climax of the first, or the critical, night spent by Ralph in the house. We have come to know something of this later on by our sight of his own mental references to it; so that these relations may quite sufficiently hang together for us. Well, what I want is that once he has the extraordinary experience (the experience *within* the experience) of his being under observation by his alter ego, once he has had it in an acute form and connected it wonderingly with some cause, he feels liable to it again if the same kind of cause shall recur; which by the time the phenomenon takes place has for him much more, as I have said above, a suggestion of menace than a suggestion of relief. That's it—it's as if the other fellow feels, knows, has some incalculable divination, of his, Ralph's *weakening,* while nothing is further from himself *than* to weaken; whereby Ralph connects, as I quite grasp, the consequence with the cause. There must be sequences here of the strongest, I make out—the successive driving in of the successive silver-headed nails at the very points and under the very taps that I reserve for them. That's it, the silver nail, the recurrence of it in the right place, the perfection and salience of each, and the trick is played. I seem to see it thus a silver nail that my young man recognises— well—what he does recognise—when the younger girl (for whom, as for them all, I should do well to provide a name without more delay) swims into his ken, and it's another one, another clou d'argent, when the wave of his confidence seems to have begun to spend itself, doing this, however, in face of something that has taken place. Just what this thing is must constitute another silver nail, and I see it thereby as some symptom given, on the part of the others, of a change of attitude, a change of sensibility, as I must call it, or at least may, for want of a better word. I think it of superior force that they, the others, all except my young heroine, shall begin on *their* side the betrayal of malaise, which Ralph is then affected by; rather than that he should begin it, making it thus that they are by the operation, the outward betrayal, of that condition of his own. Here I have the action of the little H.W., who, moved thereto (I express myself thus roughly) by the situation determined for his own interest through the terms appearing destined to develop between R. and the girl, and this though R. isn't at all free for the girl, opens himself on the subject to the three others and so calls their attention to certain things that they before long find themselves, and confess it to him and to each other, affected too in the sense he communicates. To be perfectly definite it seems to me I must have it that the marriage of Ralph and the elder daughter is definitely arranged and fixed for a tolerably near date; since I want the elder girl, "under the effect," to break off something, and there is nothing so good for her to break off as their engagement. The rupture of that, with R's apprehension of how and why it is coming and has come, is of course a silver nail of perfect salience; just as it is another, I see, that this catastrophe, or whatever one may call it, places Ralph and the younger girl face to face as they have not yet been placed. Their recognition of that, his at least, which is also a perception and a comprehension of hers, what is *this,* in its concreteness, but one more silver nail? What I see myself, at the same time, here concerned with is the question of the outward footing Ralph remains on, finds or makes possible, with the two other women etc. when the rupture develops and after it has occurred. I can't have it end the relation, everything so collapsing—so that there must be still grounds for the relation, and they must be strong and positive, or at least definite and presentable. I get something by the provision that the engagement has not been given out nor the marriage announced as to take place; which, meanwhile, is not at all natural unless some advantage not to be too lightly sacrificed is involved with their still superficially keeping on. This requires thinking of, but doesn't in the least defy handling; and indeed I think I get it at a stroke by the fact that they all cling to him, in a sort, even in spite of the malaise, by reason of the convenience proceeding from his means. Decidedly, yes, they must be, through disorders, extravagances, turpitudes or whatever, of the late head of the family, and vraisemblablement through like actualities on the part of the son who has succeeded him in the proprietorship of Drydown, they must be on a hollow and quaking pecuniary basis—which makes Ralph have to have money, even though this wasn't in the least a *common* felicity or luxury in the American world of that period. None the less were there *some* fortunes, without overstrain of the point, and in short I have only to make Ralph all disposed, very peculiarly disposed indeed and very particularly inspired and inwardly needing and wanting, to pay his way handsomely, to be the free-handed-from-over-the-sea relative of the house, in order to pick up whatever link might have seemed missing here, and make it serve my turn. He pays his way, he regales and "treats," right and left; and nothing can be more in the note of the time I give him the sense of than the extraordinary readiness he finds in everyone to profit by this, the want of delicacy and dignity, by our modern measure, in the general attitude toward pecuniary favours. The smaller still lives on the greater, the minor folk on the great, and Ralph literally sees himself, feels himself, enjoys in a manner feeling himself, figure verily as one of the great by his taste of this play of money-patronage that is open to him. There it is: if I get a clou d'argent by the rupture, in short, I get another, still another, by some dramatic demonstration of the fashion after which they are going in spite of their malaise to hold on to him as beneficiaries of a sort. Yes, yes, yes, I have it, I have it: the brother has borrowed money, borrowed it of him bravely, from the first; and the brother opposes the rupture of the marriage for fear that, a complete rupture thus also involved, he will have to pay up to his creditor, his so probably indignant creditor, in consequence of the changed situation. The other two women know this, and what it means for him; and then thereafter see that it needn't mean what they fear, what *he* fears, and isn't going to—for here I just get a sublime little silver nail in the fact that Ralph, comprehending this, beautifully seeing the way it may help him, quite seems to show on the contrary that he won't push his hand, won't expose their private gêne; seeing what he can get for himself by not doing so. Doesn't he in fact even "lend" the brother *more* money, lend it after the very rupture, in order to reassure them and keep on with them and show he doesn't "mind" the breach on the part of the elder girl?—this all because it keeps him along and on the footing of his still possible relation with the younger. In plain terms mayn't one put it that he buys, pays for, in hard cash, the pursuance of his opportunity?—as well as put it that his "dramatic" assurance of this, with its readjustment of his footing, constitutes again a silver nail. (There's nothing, I think, that one must so keep before one as that at first he is made ever so much of—much more of than he could at all have hoped.)

Well then, there he is with the question of the marriage ended—as to which, let me catch myself up to remember, I shall have to give *her* a motive, a presentable ground, since it's ended by her act, which won't make it too anomalous on his part that relations with the house are kept up. I must have him, by the way, not "stay" with them—I see advantages and naturalnesses, facilitations of several sorts, in his not doing that, but, much rather, putting up at one of the inns of the day, or better still in a lodging in one of the old West-end streets. Why not let the young woman make it quite frank and outspoken—happy thought!—and say in so many words that she can't marry him because, heaven help her, she's afraid of him; just that, simply afraid of him, even if he (with his own malaise at this note) can't get out of her any *why,* when he challenges her, as in dignity and decency he must, for a reason. This much affects and impresses him—for there isn't in it, mind, the smallest hint or implication of its being through any jealousy of her sister, whom she doesn't so much as honour with a suspicion. (The sort of Cinderella quality, so to call it, of the younger one, to be shown as more or less felt by him.) The position thus taken with practical suddenness by his prospective bride is the first definite note, at all really sharp one, that he has to reckon with on the subject of the queerness that hangs, that may so well hang, about him; and its sets up thereby the beginnings of the great feeling that I want to impute to him. He thinks all the same, at first, he expects and apprehends, not with pleasure, however, that this attitude of hers won't be supported by her mother and her brother; the thing having taken place between themselves only, and quite abruptly; she striking him as acting by her own sudden impulse alone, and in a manner not at all to suit the others. They will overbear her, he imagines; her mother in particular will bring her round again and into line. He positively fears this even—so that his surprise is great, and his malaise even greater, when the mother, with a full opportunity, by this time, doesn't so much as speak to him on the subject. There must be a passage between them, him and the Mother, in which he wonderingly and observantly, watching now all symptoms and portents, as it were, waits for Mrs. So-and-So to speak, to broach the matter herself, to show him her knowledge of what her daughter has done. He must know, or must believe, that she has now the knowledge—this point having been treated between him and the daughter, as it were, in the scene of the rupture. He *has* of course to ask her if she throws him over with her mother's privity and approval, to which she replies that she doesn't, up to then, that she has broken down but then and there, but that now at once of course she will report herself, so to speak, to her mother. I see it must be the case that she is plain and honest, not at all tortuous or perfidious, and so far as calculating, why calculating quite boldly and confessedly, as to the material advantages accruing; and thereby the more eloquent as to the inward feeling she can't surmount when she renounces these advantages so flatly. Well, the point is, from all this, that our young man is waiting for the mother to express to him that he mustn't on his side take advantage of the girl's backing out, but insistently claim his right not to be so trifled with (the attitude of the family being that they are, for all their straitened means, great people themselves, greater truly than he, and with a greatness for him in the connection,) and is going on as if nothing has happened. He has expected from her, as in character, the information that she has dealt herself, and with the high maternal rigour that then prevailed, *with* the ridiculous child, whom she has thus reduced again to reason and docility. But nothing of that sort comes—the lady of Drydown not only doesn't break ground to him herself in that sense, but betrays to his now considerably excited imagination a fear that *he* will: which will be, truly, awkward, embarrassing and even "scaring" to her; so that what I seem to see happening is verily that when he thus watches her not speak, notes her as forbearing to for reasons of her own, he doesn't take her up on it, decides in fact not to, decides that the question is really had out between them without either of them so speaking, and only by his looking her very hard in the eye, and her so looking at him, and his keeping it up on this and her keeping it up on that. It simply drops thus, by its own force, the question of the marriage, and the fact that he doesn't have it out, and that she allows him, as by taking care, no opportunity to, constitutes another silver nail, likewise, of as good a salience as I could desire. There it is then, so far as that goes; and after I have dealt for an instant now with the question of what the brother's attitude also is in the connection, I see I shall have got what I was reaching out for considerably above, *the particular thing taking, or having taken, place* which must serve for me as the determinant of the phenomenon, the factor, I have settled to tackle. The "other fellow" "appears" to Ralph, and makes him ask himself why, contrary to all consistency or logic, the laws of the game, this extraordinary occurrence should take place. He feels it as portentous—feels it, I see, in a way altogether different from the way in which he felt it on the first great occasion; when it only uplifted and thrilled him, making him conscious of all his force—whereas it now disquiets and alarms him, makes him sound it for its logic and its reason; which he clearly enough interprets to himself. A difficult and intricate thread of exhibition here, but as fine and sharp as I require it if I only keep it so. It comes back to him, it comes over him, that he has freedom, and that his acting in independence, or at least acting with inevitability, has laid this trap for him—that he has deviated, and of necessity, from what would have happened in the other fellow's place and time. What would have happened is that *he wouldn't* have feared his prospective bride, he being the other fellow; and that thus he, Ralph, has done the other fellow a violence, has wronged the personality of the other fellow *in him,* in himself, Ralph, by depriving him of the indicated, the consonant union with the fine handsome desirable girl whom the 1820 man would perfectly and successfully have been in love with, and whom he would have kept all unalarmedly and unsuspiciously in love with him. Deviation, violation, practical treachery, in fact—that is what Ralph's production and his effect on the two women (the mother sharing so in the "off"-ness of her daughter) amounts to and represents for him, aggravated moreover by the interest taken in, the community of feeling enjoyed with, the younger girl—for whom, putting it in rough summary fashion, the other fellow wouldn't have cared a jot. I cling thus to, I work thus admirably, what I have called Ralph's insuperable and ineffaceable margin of independence, clinging taint of modernity—it being by his fine modern sense that the exquisite, the delicate, the worthy-herself-to-be-modern younger girl has affected him, in utter defiance of any capacity on the other fellow's part to appreciate or conceive any such value in her. Off in his inscrutable fact of being and of action the other fellow then has had too *his* insuperable margin of antiquity, as opposed to modernity, his independent sensibility, though of a simpler and ruder, a harsher and heavier sort; and it is as a hovering messenger of this that my young man has, so to put it, drawn him down upon him. There it is—I get so my cause of my effect; I get my fact that the other party to the agreed-to experience turns up, all unexpectedly, all "alarmingly" to *my* party after a fashion to show that violence, that injury, as above formulated, has been done him, and as a protest against its being done further. I mustn't have this fact, I see, as repetitive, mustn't cheapen it with recurrence; must only have it, I seem to grasp, take place three times, each time with its own weight of meaning for *that* time, and then not take place again. It becomes thus each time a clou d'argent of the very sharpest salience. I see the first time as what one may call a warning. I see the second— taking place after Ralph has told the younger girl of what has happened, and what must take place between them on it *has* taken place—I see that as a retribution, or in other words as a thumping, a tremendous aggravator of malaise; and I see the third as having something which I will state in a minute after having said a word more about the second. The second constitutes—by which I mean the occasion of it does—a reflection of the intimacy, or at least the beautifully good understanding, with the younger girl, determined for Ralph by his opening himself to her after the sensation, just above formulated, proceeding from the rupture and the way the two other women have acted about it. It's only at this moment, and from this moment, that she becomes his *confidante,* all the difference being made by that; and don't I see it as an enormous little fact that whereas he goes on in silence, as it were, with the others (putting the two men out of the question, which is a point to be treated separately,) he finds her in no ignorance, either real or pretended, but welling up, virtually, with readiness to let him see that she knows. She *knows*—and I think he doesn't even quite understand why or how she knows; her possession of what she does know striking him as a matter beyond, in its "quality," any communication of it that the others may have been capable of making her. The passage between them representing all this becomes then the determinant of what I have called the retributive, as distinguished from the merely warning, reappearance of the other party. I just want to tuck in here provisionally, and before breaking off for the day, that I hold tight the "motive," the dramatic value, of the third reappearance; which resides in my heroine's relation to it—that is not, definitely *not,* in her having it at all herself, that is not at all directly, but in her becoming aware of *his* having it and, as it were, catching him in the act of the same. Work this out, express this better, or at least entirely, in my next go: I perfectly see it—it only wants clear statement.

I want the business just glanced at, in the four or five foregoing lines, to be as ideally right of course as it can possibly be made; want to squeeze all the effective virtue out of it, in the sense of my generally intended colour and tone, generally intended production of the "new" frisson, as artfully as can be managed. Focussing on it a bit I seem to catch the tip of the tail of the right possibility—though on further thought indeed I am pulled up a little, not being sure it can't be bettered. For I was thinking a moment that she *should,* after all, have herself the direct apprehension, perception or, speaking plainly, vision; have it in the sense that she exhibits herself to R. at a given moment as plunged in stupefaction or confusion by having apparently seen him in double, that is seen him, been sure of him, in a place where, in the conditions gone into or examined and discussed between them, he couldn't possibly have been. In other words she has it to tell him—that to her perception as well, by her experience of it the hour ago or whatever, he rose before her for certain moments in a reality with which everything proves in conflict. That, I say, was what a minute since glimmered upon me— Ralph's having it from *her* as the form of what I call in this connection my third big determinant. But no, but no: what is immeasurably better than that he should have anything of the sort through herself is that she shall have it all absolutely through him. Pressing harder and more intelligently, I come back to the image, the so obviously finest, of her *catching* him under the squeeze, under the dire apprehension, of this third occasion—which I seem to see I can make adequate and operative by her recognising him, just that, after the right fashion, as doing his damnedest *not* to show her, not to betray to her, his intelligence of what he has to infer from, to read into, seeing it in an awful light, something that has just befallen him. It seems to me that I get it and give it, for my best interest, by our having it *all* in the form in which her taxing him with being in a state, a state that she divines, yet but only half understands, determines his at last more or less abjectly confessing to. He breaks down under the beautiful pity of her divination, the wonder of her so feeling for him that she virtually knows, or knows enough; and the question is here of course, isn't it? whether for full lucidity of interest, full logic of movement, he doesn't let her know all or, in vulgar fictional parlance, reveal his secret. That's what it comes to, what it *has* to come to, very much indeed it would seem; that's what the situation would seem to mean, would appear to have to give, as who should say, of finest: their being face to face over all the prodigious truth—which I think there ought to be a magnificent scène à faire in illustration of. The beauty, the pathos, the terror of it dwells thus in his throwing himself upon her for help—for help to "get out," literally, help which she can somehow give him. The logic, the exquisite, of this to be kept tight hold of, with one's finger on every successive link of the chain. But voyons un peu the logic; which, expressed in the plainest, the most mathematical terms possible, is that what this "retributive" admonition signifies for him is, he feels, that he is going to be *left,* handed over to the conditions of where and what and above all *when* he is; never saved, never rescued, never restored again, by the termination of his adventure and his experience, to his native temporal conditions, which he yearns for with an unutterable yearning. He has come to have his actual ones, the benighted, the dreadful ones, in horror—and he just lets her know *how* horrible everything that surrounds her, everything that she herself is surrounded with and makes part of, have become for him, and under what a weight of despair he sinks if what has just again for the third time happened to him means that his fate is sealed. He breaks down to her, has the one outward, the one communicated de-

spair that I see for him in the course of the affair; his throwing himself upon her
for what she can do to avert that doom, his beseeching her, all selfishly, to help
him. I say *all selfishly* for the dramatic, clumsily so to call it, value, working
value, of this; connected, identical, as it is with his readiness, in fact his intense
hope of being able to, profit by the idea of a liberation for him purchased on her
part by some sacrifice—sacrifice, by no means sufficiently, of any hope of *him*,
but of the very stuff of herself, and this up to the hilt. The more I look into this,
the more I see in it; but with proportionately much therefore to be stated about it
with a supreme lucidity. Reduced to its simplest expression, the case stands that
he has fallen in love with her—done so in absolute rebound from the distress that
her sister's, her mother's, breach has brought to an end for him; leaving him
originally to throw himself so much on *her* reaction, by already acquired and
assimilated sense that with her, too blessedly, almost *any* ease for him, whether
but comparatively or absolutely, is possible. Thus had he given way to his having,
as who would say, fallen in love with her; and thus does that fact work, to his
perception, both toward his prime relief and toward his understanding of what he
has to fear. Here I come to something pretty intricate and difficult, yet full of life
and force, say frankly of beauty, if I can get it straight; which is what I must
proceed to. *Why* has what passes, what has passed up to then, between this pair,
why does it bring on or draw down the third, the "retributive" recurrence? Well,
let us see if we don't make out, and thereby but store up still more beauty and
intensity. Put it simply for the moment that the Predecessor has been in love with
the elder sister *while,* all unknowably (at the time) the younger has been in love
with him. That condition on her part, it appears to me, gives the link I want, the
exact one, for what Ralph finds of prepared, as it were, of reciprocal, of ground
laid, for his first understandings with her *when once he has begun to feel* the
interfering malaise of the others. I am here, I quite recognise, brought up against
the question of why if the Predecessor has been so in love, then and there, in the
old time, he should have had this impulse to swing off into conditions so remote
from those of the object of this sentiment. I get partly in answer to this the fact
that Ralph, shown as so much in love in the first Book, has all the same embraced
his opportunity to swing off into where we now have him; but I want something
more than this, and I don't get it by simply leaning strongly on the attachment
inspired in the man of 1820; inasmuch as the more he has been attached the more
explaining will the matter take, the matter flowering into that inordinate phenomenon of the original nocturnal meeting of the two men. If I give full value to the
idea that the present Pendrel's pressure, his hovering, penetrating force has had
much the most to do with what has taken place, that though the man of 1820 has
drawn the man of 1910, exact, (though as to this I must make no modern date
explicit of that) back into his own age, while the latter has drawn the former
forward into *his,* though I do this, I take care, I soigner the effect that Ralph has
begun it, has exerted the original force, has been the determinant for the other and
thrust at him his opportunity. This in a general way clears up a little the particular
aspect of the case that I am turning over; but don't I still nevertheless want something more than that? I want something that the predecessor may affect Ralph as
definitely uttering to him and direfully reproaching him with; and perhaps as I dig

into my material and insist on gouging what I want out of it I meet *this* ground of resentment and reprobation for the predecessor that he feels, or rather that Ralph feels him to feel—for it can all only be *imputation* on R's part—that he isn't, as it were, playing the game; ceases quite to play it from the moment that he inspires the elder girl, whom one had hit it off so with dans le temps, with the alarm of distress and dislike that has operated for her rupture. I find something in that, I find I think enough in that—find it enough that Ralph recognises himself as under displeasure, under vindictive displeasure for not, as it were, playing the game. Let me make him put it for himself that the other man doesn't play the game either, from the moment that he thus "comes in," reappears, as it were, as with the conscious purpose so to "brouiller" things. Have it clear that Ralph has no theory at all of what his double's situation is off in *his* sphere; put it that he is by way of having no sort of constructive or inferential or divinatory notion of that at all: which it would make an extraordinary complication to undertake to give him— by which I mean an impossible one, an unspeakable tangle, within the limits, altogether. Yes, yes; the more I think the more I seem to see this conception of Ralph's to be that the other fellow is endangered and incommoded in his sphere by what strikes him as R's practical perfidy and non-accomplishment. What makes this is that the two women, the two other men etc., and the object of his prefer- ence above all, are thereby handed over to their intensity of malaise—I give Ralph as seeing and feeling and understanding him as *rendered* thereby vindictive, as convicting him accordingly of "perfidy," and of decreeing the punishment which shall consist of not coming to his help: as I must show it as having figured in their original entente that each shall come au besoin to the help of the other. Out of this little store of indications, at any rate, I shall be able surely to help myself to whatever in the connection, and in closer quarters, I find my best interest in.

Definite it is then that, caught by his young friend in the fact of his *intelligent* alarm he makes a clean breast to her of what he feels and understands, of what his intelligence most helps him to, of what, in a word, it is necessary that she shall know—know in order to assist and relieve him, do the particular thing that *will* so act for him: and so bring the whole situation to the point of its dénoûment. What is then this particular thing?—what can it be when I bring it down to a finer point, that is bring the question down, than my general first notion brought it to? Here the very closest and finest logic must govern all one's sequences. Altogether important and indispensable is it that he doesn't "confess to her," really appeal and throw himself upon her, till she has so "caught," as I say, and cornered him, that under the pity and perception and beauty of this he absolutely can't but give in. I have provided above, or sought to, for the motive force establishing in her this capacity—I have sought to do so, I repeat, though I'm not sure I don't still feel a little uncomfortable at being able to do nothing better for her, as would appear, than simply recognise his woe. The beautiful thing would be for her to be able to *refer this woe* to some particular, some portentous observation or consta- tation already made by him: which question I examined and turned over above without breaking down my objection to her directly sharing his vision: I at that point stated that I wished her but indirectly, but derivatively, to do that—through her apprehension of the state into which it has put him. I seem to feel that this then isn't quite ideally adequate or good without I know not what *more* for her: the ability in her, say, to *challenge him first* on some entirely concrete matter which has told her something for herself, something strange and prodigious, or at least deeply mystifying, in advance of the pressure brought to bear by her on him as an indicated, approved, a revealed sufferer, the pressure in fine that makes him break down. The trouble is that so I swing back again this way to too near the objectionability, and thereby ask myself if there isn't a way out, a happy thought, in making her, instead of seeing something more than the normal, making her, as I have used the term, "catch," catch in the fact, something in excess of it, see something *less,* have the queerness of *missing* something—her miss of which needs to be explained. The miss, as I call it, corresponds and matches with his exposure to the retributive visitation, as I have called it; and something glimmers out for me in the way of the very occurrence itself, the fact of the visitation for him, being marked, marked startlingly and mystifyingly to her, not by his experience as in any degree detected by her, discernible to her, but by his apparent exclusion from *any* experience; or in other words by an inexplicable lapse or suspension of his state of being at all. I think that if I can arrange that—her not finding him present when by all the laws and the logic of life he should *be* present, and so having to challenge him for an explanation—in short I believe I do so see something. He is extinguished for her senses by being in the grip of his face-to-faceness with the other man; and don't I make it out as arrangeable that this takes place in the very fact of his having appointed a tryst or rendezvous with her, at which she has found him, but in the midst of which he then astoundingly fails and, as it were, evaporates? I seem to see something like her having gone out to him by appointment, at dusk of evening, in the Square, the enclosed square itself; where as she approaches she has recognised him within, has even spoken to him through the rails, while he awaits her, and there has had an exchanged word or two with her, directing her round to the gate: which she reaches and enters the enclosure by only to become sure, after moments and moments and moments of surprise and stupefaction, that he is definitely *not there.* I think I have it, it is then; it is at these moments, I mean during them, and under the "influence" exactly, upon the other man, of the appointment given her, that the "retributive visitation" takes place. So I get it, get it enough, get in fact all I need. The visitation over he *is* in the place again: he is there before her and what more natural "challenge" can I have for her than her alarmed question, that is her stupefied one, as to what in the world had during those moments, which I can make as long or as short, for intensity, as I like, what in the name of unanswerable wonder had become of him. He is there before her again, but before her with what has happened to him overwhelmingly marked upon him.

I see what then takes place between them as a virtual counterpart, in the way of his telling his story, to his scene with the Ambassador, the whole contents of Book III; only all in the note of his depression, his unspeakable homesickness for his own time and place—whereas the other whole passage had been in the note of his elation, eagerness and confidence. He makes, as I say, a clean breast to her— as he had made it under the then essential restriction to the Ambassador; with the immense difference, however, that whereas the effect in the latter case was to impress his then confidant with his being out of his mind, the present effect is, marvellously, prodigiously, to make our heroine believe in the truth of his extraordinary case, recognise how he puts it to her so because he *is,* because he has remained, exactly so sane, and that it is (prodigiously, marvellously as the force in her to do so may be on her part) to his sanity, exactly, to his convincing consistency, that she rallies. This rallying of hers is of course *the* very point, for interest and beauty, for the climax of the romantic hocuspocus, on my sought total effect; the very flower, so to speak, of what I noted a little back as my scène a faire. As I have already said repeatedly enough, he tells her all, tells her all, all, all; which involves of course his telling her what he feels, has come to feel, in his being so "cut off," so now conclusively and hopelessly cut off, from the life, from the whole magnificent world from which he is truant, unless something, something *she* perhaps can think of, may yet save him. His whole position becomes thus the plea to be saved, to be liberated—with his waiting on her devotion, her affection, her ingenuity, in a word her inspiration, somehow to let him off. All sorts of things to be done with this, in the beautiful and curious and interesting way, especially with the idea that she is sole among those of his actual life whom contact with him, the relation with him, doesn't now make "afraid." Of course this absence of fear on her part has to be *based,* has to have its own logic in order to have all its beauty; and when one asks oneself *why she,* why she only, thus extraordinarily, one seems both at once to be reduced for support, for illumination of it to the fact that she loves him, and that her affection can do it, and to the concomitant recognition that it will, that it *must,* serve. For it is what exactly and immediately supplies to the situation between them the idea of her being able to operate somehow or other by sacrifice, *her* sacrifice, and of herself and her affection and her interest, somehow or other; so far as one doesn't make her interest, her interest in *how* to do it, by its very intensity and, so to speak, curiosity, an inspiring motive. I must have had him put it to her straight, How, how, *how* can you get me off, can you release me from this apprehension of having really lost all I feel and fear I've lost?—so that thus she has to throw herself back *upon* herself under pressure of this dire appeal which involves, obviously, her using everything. For it would seem to me kind of sublime that he now, at last now, opening up, opening out, everything that he has had before to keep back, tells her such things about those fruitions of the Future which have constituted his state, tells her of how poor a world she is stuck fast in compared with all the wonders and splendours that he is straining back to, and of which he now sees only the ripeness, richness, attraction and civilisation, the virtual perfection without a flaw, that she stands dazzled before it and can only be shut up in the heartbreak of remaining so far back behind it, so dismally and excludedly out of it, while he, with her assistance, shaking her off after he has, as it were, used her, wins his way back to it and out of her sight and sense for ever. Immense and interesting to show him as profiting by her assistance without his being thereby mean or abject or heartless; in which light my affair can't afford, given the whole romantic note of it, to place him. Besides the "psychological" truth and consistency here may back me to any extent. The great question is then *of* her "assistance," how it's rendered, what it consists of, how he can take it from her and

how she can give it. I feel that my subject contains the exact, the exquisite rightness for this deep in its breast, if only I watch hard enough to see said rightness
emerge—emerge as it were of itself and as from the operation of what surrounds
it. It dwells somehow deep in the fact, the great dramatic fact of the whole business, that she alone hasn't had the mistrust, the malaise and the fear; in connection
with which I seem to see something of no small, in fact of the greatest, pop out
at me. If he has made her his full "confession" don't I make out that, to balance
this, she also tells him about herself something of the last intimacy—not merely
how she loves him, but something better still than that?—don't I in fact find
myself just leaping and snatching at the idea which answers all my questions of
procedure and has my perfect solution just locked up and waiting within it? What
is more than her confessing to him that she loves *him,* what gives the exhibitional
further twist I was groping for, is that she tells him she has loved the man he is a
substitute for, the man of 1820, the *real* one of that actual year, and that in loving
himself she has but obeyed the irresistible continuity and consistency involved in
his force of representation. I seem to see really my ideal rightness in this—but
must keep my head to state here what I see, for my perfect use, roundabout it. I
have already spoken, far above, of her having loved the other man, the "real"
one, and done so as by the implication that Ralph knows it, is in possession of it,
and has seen for himself what an identity and what a connection reside in it. By
what means, however, has he originally known it, learnt it, got into possession of
it?—unless by one of the others' having stated it to him. I ask myself which then
of the others—but only at once to recognise the matter as already determined for
me by what I have threshed out. He gets the knowledge effectively and, as I call
it, dramatically, to all intents and purposes scenically, by the fact that the little
H.W. man, as I call him, betrays the wanted jealousy of him from the moment
the elder girl breaks off from him. Up to that moment not, but after it, and on his
turning to the younger, with whom the little H.W. man is, as I have shown,
himself in love, *then* entirely. This jealousy is practically what leads to his profession of the truth; so that there can be no question of his needing it from her—he
so reads it in her manière d'être—up to the time of, and the great revolution
constituted by, the scène à faire. What we get thus is her manière d'être for him,
all sufficient, all infinitely touching, before that *scène,* and her condition and her
action *after* the same; which are two quite different things. *Then,* I mean in this
latter case, her avowal, the only entire and direct one, is quite a different thing;
out of which I have to pull, as I say, quite what I want. She has loved the man
of 1820 *all in himself*—keep every shade of discrimination here flawlessly clear.
She has loved him wholly without reward of course, and even under his more
than indifference, his degree of contempt; entirely addressed as he was, and has
been, to her elder sister. Yet I pull up too here, in the midst of my elation—
though after a little I shall straighten everything out—to see that I introduce an
element of confusion in trying to work the matter out as if anything can have
preceded Ralph's own, Ralph's "conscious" arrival. Awfully important, and not
a little difficult, here, not to let any tangle or any embroilment lay its insidious
trap. Doesn't Ralph know by his own experience, if he takes up the action from
the moment, and the moment only, of "arriving," arriving for the first time, all

that has happened for his predecessor and exactly what hasn't? There, however, I gasp with relief, is a question that would be embarrassing to me only if, on intenser reflection, I didn't see that I exactly haven't pretended that he doesn't *repeat,* repeat up to a certain point, the experience of the young man of the portrait? Just now, a page or two back, I lost my presence of mind, I let myself be scared, by a momentarily-confused appearance or assumption that he doesn't repeat it. I see, on recovery of my wits, not to say of my wit, that he very exactly does; without which where is definitely that Past, that made and achieved, that once living and enacted Past which is the field of his business? He deflects in the midst of it, yes, by the uncontrollability of his modernism—that is, at least, by what was incalculable beforehand, the exhibition of the way in which "they" were going to take it. The whole effect of my story is exactly his disconcerted and practically defeated face-to-faceness with the way in which they do take it—a matter, a fact, an appearance, that gives me all I want for accounting for his deflection. Thus is our having, his having, everything *en double* regulated and exhibited: he is doing over what the other fellow has done (though it acts for the other persons in it as if it were the first time—this quite all right, though not looking so at first)—and that accordingly hangs together and stands firm. Therefore accordingly my start, a little above, at being what I there for a moment called disconcerted and defeated was groundless: I was going on perfectly straight and right—and am now doing so again. To repeat, accordingly, I get my full right to deal as by a free hand with that little historic truth of the girl's concealed sentiment for the other fellow, accompanied with her equal consciousness that he doesn't and can't and won't care for her a bit: at least in the same way. This revolution that has taken place for her—and well before the scène—of Ralph's differing so from the 1820 man— in short, in short. Note what occurs to me as to the question or no of whether the portrait, the portrait *in* the house in 1910, is done from Ralph in 1820 or not, done from Ralph himself, or accounted for, as coming into existence afterwards. *The* thing, at this ragged edge, is to keep hold of the clue, as tight as possible, that I have grabbed for my solution in the line of her *making* the sacrifice; making it all with a sublime intelligence *for* him, on account of what he has told her of his own epoch—which she stares at in her deprivation.

To clear up a little the page preceding this, instead of doing it over, I was making a statement, a bit arrested, as to the revolution that has taken place in the girl, previous, well previous, to the scene of the great crisis, as to the attitude toward her of her sister's fiancé, from the moment she feels, exquisitely and almost incredulously feels, that difference in *him* (toward her) which has been more completely defined since her sister's dismissal of him, and which gives her, as well as it gives him, a liberty never yet enjoyed by her. I shall presently come back to the rest of this, the enormous value to be got out of it; but I want not simply to brush by the small hare started yesterday by that sudden remembrance of the question of the portrait, the portrait figuring, or having figured, so extraordinarily to Ralph upwards of a century after its being painted; and which it would seem I must do something about. I see a chance to play with it, with the 1820 production of it, for illustration and intensification of my most-sought effect. It's an excrescence perhaps upon the surface I have already in this rough fashion plotted out; which remark, however, is nonsence, as nothing is an excrescence that I may interestingly, that I may contributively, work in. It gives me moreover, the idea I begin to clutch the tip of the tail of, it gives me another person whom I suddenly see as a great enhancement for my action; the painter-man who gets, doesn't one fancy? into a much straighter and closer "psychologic" and perceptive and mystified and mixed relation with his remarkable subject than any of the others in *their* way do. I get the painter-man as affected in his way too with the famous malaise, and the more affected with his proportionately greater opportunities, as it were, if not of observation at least of a kind of wondering and penetrating consideration. It "kind of" glimmers upon me that there would be something good, something much to the purpose, in having the painter-man *begin* to prepare the turn the situation takes, having him start the question of *what the matter is* (crudely speaking) with the genial young man, after all, and below and outside of his geniality; so that his wonderment, his felt queerness and queernesses, are inevitably communicated by him and sow the seed of the rest of what I want. They sow above all, don't they, or mayn't they be made to? the seed of Ralph's *suspicion of his being suspected,* putting him on his guard against this latter, rendering him uneasy, and whatever else, under the painter's study of him. Wouldn't it be then to the little H.W. man that the artist speaks of his strange impression, in complete confidence and secrecy at first, but sowing what I have called the seed so in the most favourable ground? I recognise that one doesn't quite see how we *know* he does this, as we don't of course see or hear him do it; yet that needn't find itself so ill provided for by Ralph's himself making it out and concluding upon it—which is after all the only way we really know anything. I don't want to repeat what I have done at least a couple of times, I seem to remember, and notably in The Liar—the "discovery," or the tell-tale representation of an element in the sitter written clear by the artist's projection of it on canvas. At the same time I am not afraid; I see its office well enough and needn't trouble if once the idea appeals, as I think it really does. In this case it's worked in early; the notion of my young man having his portrait as a matter of course done in London coming in with perfect naturalness. He has it done for his prospective bride; she takes an interest in it of the very greatest at first; and it is the little H.W. man who recommends, who selects, the artist. I see all sorts of curious things in this—it perfectly bristles with them, and with one's chance, above all, of making the personage in question (and I do want another figure, to people the canvas a little more) a real vision to Ralph, a character of the time, intensely typical for Ralph; through whose sense of all which, however, I tread the delicate ground of imputations to him, of perceptions, discriminations, estimates more or less at variance with his 1820 identity. That delicate ground, I have only to remind myself, is absolutely the very most attaching ground of my process; solvitur ambulando—I have only to find myself in close quarters with it to get from it force and felicity. I present then the painter-man, I make him, do him, see him and use him; use him to very good purpose. Don't I kind of see Ralph's suspicion of being suspected come to a head in the sight of something produced on the little H.W. man's part, on his nerves and in his fancy, in fine, through an active correspondence with the malaise the artist has caused in him through divinably feeling it himself? The foregoing difficult to state, but one is quite possessed of it; there's a great lot in it—only too much, alas, given my faculty for amplifying and going far. However, a rigorous tight hand on the excess of that is my very law of life here. I do feel how an effective further twist or two hangs about the question of the portrait. We get it surely as painted full face on—with the rendered face, in other words, that is turned away from Ralph's 1910 vision of him on that night in the house. Yes, he sits for it in 1820; he sees it grow, he sees and feels what grows out of it—I really don't see why the fact of it, the high conceit of it, mayn't do for me a good deal of my work. It plays a part in the situation—though I must square the difficulty of the artist "feeling about his sitter" as he more and more does and yet being able to keep his method and process, his application of his ability, well in hand, in order to put the thing through. It's a *fine* thing, a very fine one—I need it as that; for the finer it is the more it plays its part in the state of sensibility, all round, at which we increasingly assist. The thing is done for the prospective bride—though she would have been much more likely to have been treated to a fine miniature (alas, but no matter!) And don't I see that the first stroke in the reaction, on her part, as I may conveniently call it, is her abrupt, her sudden inconsequent refusal of the gift? in which she is backed by her mother. Perhaps she refuses it even before it is quite finished—for I want the artist to have spoken about it to the little H.W. man, so to put it, while the work is still in progress; which is also the time of the latter's opening himself about it (as Ralph "makes out") to the two women. Here I have something—the picture's having been destined for the big panel over the principal drawingroom—whereas the place in which my hero finds it in 1910 is the small inner retreat which I have handled in Book II. The mother and daughter startle Ralph, in 1820, by their expression of unwillingness to its hanging where it was intended; but as I want it still on the premises, want some compromise or right thing done about it, so that it shall be there for 1910, I see as arrangeable the business, the tension, the whole significant passage, of its being relegated to the place where everyone concerned will least see it—short of its being turned out of the house; a circumstance I *don't* invoke. I have it there for the other man, as his own portrait, when he is restored to his time by Ralph's liberation from it; I have it there because I want him *in* it, don't you see? for that wonder over it in which Ralph is held during his night of 1910. The other man comes back, the other man is *in* it, in order to carry out his part— well, of what I have recorded.

The "sacrifice," the indispensable, unspeakable sacrifice, on the girl's part, is involved in her relation to Ralph *as she now knows him,* and the quintessential "drama" of it, so to speak, is by the same token involved in *his knowing her* as she knows him, and as, above all, she is known *by* him. There hovers before me a something-or-other in this, a finer twist still, a deeper depth or higher flight of the situation, which seems worth looking into, and which in fact already appears to open out a good bit before me as I consider it. Isn't there something, isn't there even much, in the idea that when once these two have arrived, so to speak, at their understanding, at their mutual disclosures, or at least, that is, at his disclosure and her avowal, he becomes capable of a sort of sublimity in presence, as who should say, of her own? so that there is a kind of struggle between them as to who shall give up most—if I may put it in such a way without excess of the kind of romanticism that I don't want; wanting as I do above all, constantly kept hold of and economised, never let go of nor perverted in the least, the unfailing presence, drawing in everything to itself, of that force of "tone" which makes the thing of the parenté of the "Screw." So much is true and absolute; but doesn't prevent that I am wanting to put my finger on the very centre of the point from which my young man's "liberation" is worked. What hovers before me at this pitch, as I just said, is the *concetto* that, sincerely affected by her sublimity, he is moved to match it—and in all sincerely as I say—by offering to remain with her, as who should say, give up everything *for* her—from the moment he thus takes in that she gives him up for what is to herself utterly nothing, nothing but the exaltation of sacrifice—in short what I see! I have it all, I possess it here, and now must give pause to this long out-ciphering. It seems to give me after all a fourth recurrence of the man of 1820, called back, as it were, by what takes place. I possess it, I hold it fast; simply noting the prime point in regard to my last Book. Rather good and fine, I think, to make it that as the man of 1820 is "called" (since I think I do definitely give him his re-intervention here, though probably at the cost of still keeping these down to three in number, and so running two of the others, as who should say, into one,) so the woman of 1910 is likewise called; so my fundamental idea that the solution of the solution comes about through Aurora's "coming out, coming over," takes effect as I had planned it. The penultimate book ends on the climax I have in mind, as the "Ambassador" Book ended and broke off with the two at the door of the House; and so the ultimate one puts Ralph, always in London, and after the lapse of the real six months or whatever, face to face with his friend of Book I, to whom exactly what was foreshadowed in that Book for my dénoûment had happened. Things, things for her consciousness, her imagination, her growing unrest, her own New York malaise, have happened to *her* too; just how we are to know about them giving me, however, a little knot rightly to untie. I hate its being a "little" knot, savouring so of the perfunctory and the abbreviated; yet how can I want it in the nature of things to do more than adequately balance with the dimensions, or whatever, of Book First? The question is how, with the right sort of beauty of effect, to work in together the Ambassador's re-participation *and* her own, or rather, better put, hers and the Ambassador's own; since I of course, under penalty of the last infamy, stick here still, as everywhere, to our knowing these things but through Ralph's knowing them. It's a bit awkward that I seem to want Aurora's arrival in London and her appeal to the Ambassador for assuagement of her literal climax of trouble, I seem to want that passage to precede my young man's reappearance, re-emergence, so to speak—and yet can't possibly have anything so artistically base. I want the "rescue," on this side of time, by Aurora, as the liberation, *for* rescue on the other side of time, has been by the girl of 1820; I want it to be, on our actual ground, by something that Aurora *does;* I want his restoration and recovery to take place actually and literally through her having got into such a "psychic" state, passed through such a psychic evolution, over there, that she takes action at last, takes the very action that she sort of defied Ralph to make her take in that full, and would-be at least so rich, "scene" of the most preliminary order. What there took place essentially was, as he formulated it, that she would look at none but a man of, as it were, tremendous action and adventure, not being appealed to (however she might attenuate or sophisticate her arrangement of her case) by the "mere" person, the mere leader, of the intellectual life, the mere liver in a cultivated corner, that Ralph has admitted himself to be to her—with a frankness, an abjection, say, that his whole subsequent adventure represents his reaction against. The immense scope his reaction has found then, once he has got over into the "old world," this has developed to the point that no prodigious adventure of any such figure as she may have had in mind comes within millions of miles of the prodigy of his adventure; whereby my conceit is that all the while he is "having" this, all the while she, left to the aftersense of what has passed between them, gradually feels her "state of mind," state of feeling, state of fancy, say, state of nerves in fine, grow and grow (in a sort of way that is corresponding all the while to the stages of his experience) till the pitch of unsupportable anxiety and wonder is reached for her, and being able no longer to stand it, she comes out to London. I make her come to London through considerations, references or whatever, plausible enough; and I make her by the same token want to see the Ambassador— whom she approaches, after the very fashion of Ralph's approach six months or whenever, before, and as if he were almost, so to say, a father-confessor. All this is feasible and "amusing," rather beautiful to do being what I mean; only it must come *after* and by reference backward, so to call it—as I can only make the Ambassador precede her in these renewals, for Ralph, of contact and apprehension. It isn't so much making him aware of the Ambassador first, so to speak, that is the trouble, and making him then aware of Aurora *by* that personage and what comes of reference on his part to the beautiful uneasy and inquiring creature of New York; it isn't so much the scene *with* that young woman herself then taking place: it isn't these that put their question to me, but the terms and conditions on and in which I have his Excellency and his young friend of the previous season confronted. What a blessing thus to find, accordingly, how the old gentle firmness of pressure, piously applied, doesn't fail to supply me. Our young friend is in the house again as he was in it in Book II—the only little hitch being that I didn't show him as *living* there, for the Ambassador, in Book II. He goes to live there, goes *with* that escort to do so on the last page of the Book, but by that very fact to pass into—well everything that we have seen him in and which represents the rupture of continuity with the Ambassador's period. So in short, perfectly, I see that, for consummate reasons, he can't receive this visitor on that exhausted scene at all, but must have the case otherwise—have it in fact just as it comes to me now. The Ambassador, after his visit from Aurora (which we don't know about yet, don't know about till Ralph has *his* knowledge of it from him,) goes then, *walks* then, the day and the season being fine and he walking with the largeness with which dear J.R.L. used to walk—he goes then, I say, to the place where he has last had sight of his so interestingly demented young man of said previous season: he goes there but to have the sensation, by which I mean of course the actual experience, of seeing the very conditions in which he then parted with him practically renewed. The last thing he had stood there on the pavement before the house to see was Ralph's going in with that last look at him and with the open door duly again closing on him. So accordingly the first thing he now sees is Ralph's coming out again with the door closing on him from *behind* and the *first* look the young man addresses to the world of 1910 resting exactly upon the confidant of his former embroilment. I like that—like Ralph's coming straight out of everything we have been having, everything up to the very last sharp edge of it, straight back into this friend's hands. Well, how do I take up, that is how does Ralph take up, and how does the Ambassador, this fresh situation and relation? The Ambassador, after his passage with the so handsome and so distracted young woman from New York, may well have some doubt and some question as to how, and be in some predicament about it; but I grant at once that Ralph has emerged from all trouble and now is, for the whole situation, supreme master and controller. *He* is "all right" at least, and he *re-connects,* on the spot, with all the lucidity and authority we can desire of him. His distinguished friend has come, clearly, on a visit to him—and he embraces that as well as he embraces their not going back into the house. At the previous season, as I have called it, he wasn't yet living in the house, he was only visiting it from his hotel or his lodgings; yet it isn't to these, none the less, that I see him invite his caller to adjourn with him, but, under the happiest inspiration, straight into the Square itself, very pleasant now to sit in (I must rightly and neatly adjust together the times of the year) and in which, under its ancient form, by which I mean of course its earlier, he has been through the scène à faire of 1820. It strikes me as positively "pretty" that they go into the Square together on the leafy June afternoon and that there it is, while they sit down, that the Ambassador reports to him of the visit received at the Embassy from Aurora. He has those things to *tell*—to tell to the young man who had those others to do the like with as presented in Book III; whereby it is very much he, or entirely he, who is the relator, reporter, exhibitor, with Ralph also for cross-questioner, as the Ambassador himself was on the other occasion— I myself having of course too my free hand for showing the elder man as really confessing to his genial bewilderment of interest. However, the extent to which I am possessed of this requires no dotting of "i's"; and the great point simply is that thus we get all we require, as a preliminary to the last pages of all of what has happened to or in, what has happened for and by, Aurora. I scarcely need state that the upshot or conclusion of the two men's talk is that Ralph must of course at once see that young woman; which is the understanding on which the Ambassador leaves him. But I am almost capable of wondering whether I had best give this meeting, this reunion of theirs, in the facts and in the flesh, as it were— so aloof do I feel from the possibility of a kind of graceless literality. I shall see, I shall make up my mind: it will come, in true rightness, it *can* come but so, when I get in close nearness to it. I do seem to conceive that I can beautifully get all my needed value for final climax from taking it all out, or putting it all in, between the two men—especially after they have come out of the Square together for the Ambassador to go, and they stand on the opposite pavement, the bit round the Square, with the house over there in view. Ralph of course has *told* his Excellency nothing; not a syllable of repetition of all that we've been having, of course, issues from him for his friend's illumination. He has only cross-questioned, only extracted everything about Aurora; only taken in *how* his triumph is complete and how that young woman has come down and round. It is thus a question then of his sending her a message, and of his sending it by the Ambassador for whom he sees her (justified thereto very vividly by the latter) simply and all so wonderingly wait. Yes, the message he sends is that he shall be glad to see her. He summons her to him—doesn't offer to go to her. He has said to his companion at first and for their going into the Square that he is not staying at the House, and that his lodgings are elsewhere. The Ambassador, taking the message, has the question, virtually: "She's to come then to you at your hotel?" On which, after an hesitation and resting his eyes a moment over on the house, Ralph says: "No, no. Over there." But I should say I needn't here and now draw this out, and that I have it all and more than all, were it not that I just want to note more emphatically that I provide for everything, provide against the need of any "small" scene with the young woman from New York as a sequence to this full passage with the Ambassador, and as a wind up to the whole thing, together with the balance of such a chapter against the preliminary Book First—I provide for everything, I say, by putting *into* this *finale* between the two men in the Square, by making Ralph acquaint his visitor with, so to speak, *all* the requisite meaning resident in the appeal, from their young woman, that his Excellency has called to report on. I said above that Ralph "tells" the Ambassador nothing—but only receives his own statement and cross-questions him on it; but that qualification refers only to what has been happening to R., in his prodigious alternate character, during the previous six months or whatever. Not a word about all that; but on the other hand every word required to enable us to dispense with another scene for the young woman from N.Y. On that subject Ralph is fully informing, and what I mean and want is that this action in him, holding his interlocutor extraordinarily interested, shall so suffice for our own interest and satisfaction, shall so vividly take the place of it, that we simply shan't in the least miss, but shall find ourselves admirably do without, any bringing "on" again of Aurora. The present and conclusive scene in the Square all sufficiently brings her on, all sufficiently prefigures Ralph's reunion, not to say union, with her, and in short acquits me of everything. A far more ingenious stroke, surely, and to be made more ministrant to effect and to the kind of note of the strange that I want than the comparatively platitudinous direct *duo* between the parties! He has only to give us in advance all that the duo must and will consist of in order to leave us just where, or at least just *as* we want!

Notes for "Mr. and Mrs. Fields"
(Spring 1915)

In the Houghton rough-copy typescript of this essay HJ lapses, in two passages, from dictated "composition" into a discussion of how to handle his reminiscences. The first is in the middle of the seventh paragraph; the second follows a discussion of Christine Nilssen and Charles Fletcher, in the ninth paragraph. Those two passages are reproduced here. The essay appeared in the *Cornhill Magazine* and, with minor corrections and the title "Mr. and Mrs. James T. Fields," in the *Atlantic Monthly* July 1915; see *LA* II, 160–76.

What was to follow made for itself other connections, many of which indeed had already begun; but what I think of in particular as a veracious historian, or at any rate as a beguiled memoriser, or say memorialist, straightening out a little, though not for the world overmuch, the confusion of old and doubtless in some cases rather faded importances, what I especially think of is how there were forms of increase that the "original" magazine[1] grew it might have seemed, rather weak in the knee for carrying. I pin my reference however only to the Fieldses, discriminating for *him* and getting back to the something more I wanted to say about O.W.H.[2] and working in the vision of *his* waterside windows too, with some pleasant little justice to his beautiful abundance in the way of occasional bursts, and how that was essentially one of the *Atlantic* assets. Round off some decent little image of him. Catch with this connection of Mrs. Beecher Stowe[3] and her mixture in it all, with reminiscence of my meeting her that time at the Holmes's

1. The *Atlantic Monthly*.
2. Dr. Oliver Wendell Holmes.
3. Harriet Beecher Stowe (1811–96), author of *Uncle Tom's Cabin* (1852).

and taking her for a great celebrity, as well as noting her extraordinary little vaguely observant, slightly wool-gathering, letting her eyes wander all over the place kind of little way. Pin on to Fields the various other associations of memory, Hawthorne in fact and Hawthorne in his story or two about him—about going down to Salem the winter day and seeing him, in his poor abode, sitting by the stove with his head bound up for toothache, or something of the sort and sadly and shyly producing the *Scarlet Letter* for Fields to take back home and see if it would do. Fields's account of reading it that night, and how I thought this more wonderful than words etc. What there may be about Fields—with mention of his hospitality to my small first things—Howells[4] too aiding; and what he said to H. about my infant pessimism—"his mother's milk scarce dry on his lips," etc. Then what may be, if anything, about Aldrich,[5] but this very questionable; and a get back to Mrs. Fields, who really will serve a little more than I thought; with a stretch to the later time, Julia Ward Howe,[6] Miss. Jewett[7] and her early things, I mean her so very charming things something very nice about *her,* and their visit to me at L.H. quite in the later time. Don't drop out of the Fields himself part the something or other about George Eliot; and don't drop above all the Matthew Arnold reference, and how he gave me the English pages of *Essays in Criticism,*[8] then just out, and these having served for his compositors, to read in Ashburton Place, and with what intense emotion I read 'em. There is plenty, only too much, to straighten out and compress, doing it well over, and giving to it for title perhaps just "Mr. and Mrs. Fields."

. . . . . .

This right enough to develop but with getting on to Christine Nilsson,[9] Trollope,[10] the note of the returns from England again, with the waft of George Eliot, etc. and some such foreshortened image of the mixture as will fetch in the bit about M. Arnold already noted. Don't leave out Leslie Stephen's[11] having been there, and my first sight of him so, first moment of what was to be such a relation; and the lugging in possibly of Aldrich, in the *Atlantic* connection, or the other thing, the weekly publication connection, of which I have forgotten the very name, but in which one read first some of the Trollopes, and it seems to come back to me that certainly *Middlemarch.* Apropos of which if there could be a word about the Fields effort at *arrangement* with these two or three English authors; arrange-

4. William Dean Howells was Fields's assistant on the *Atlantic.*
5. Thomas Bailey Aldrich (1836–1907), fiction writer and poet, in 1881 succeeded Howells as editor of the *Atlantic.*
6. Julia Ward Howe's "Battle Hymn of the Republic" appeared in the *Atlantic* for February 1862.
7. Sarah Orne Jewett, the fiction writer, was a close friend of Mrs. Fields's (who would edit Jewett's letters); the two women visited Lamb House in September 1898.
8. HJ's unsigned review of Arnold's *Essays in Criticism* appeared in the *North American Review,* July 1865.
9. HJ met Christine Nilssen (b. 1843), the Swedish opera singer, at the Fieldses' during her visit to Boston in 1870.
10. Anthony Trollope (1815–82), British novelist.
11. Leslie Stephen (1832–1904), British biographer, father of Virginia Woolf, met HJ at the Fieldses' in the 1860s.

ment with Browning, arrangement with M. A. etc. etc. just touched. Then when I have gouged out of all that the modicum that will more than suffice to my purpose, get on to Mrs. F. again for climax, up to the very "end"; with Mrs. Howe and the "Battle Hymn," her reciting of it, for titivation, and for very last the note of the much later Mrs. F., with Sarah Jewett and a good word about *her* for the very last of all.

Notes for Publishers

Project of Novel [*The Ambassadors*]
(1 September 1900)

HJ sent the ninety-page typescript of the Project—more than 20,000 words—to Harper & Brothers in New York in the autumn of 1900 (after his agent, Pinker, had seen it). He wrote to H. G. Wells on 15 November 1902: "there it remained and has probably been destroyed." It survived at Harper's, however, and is now in the Morgan Library. Parts of it were initially published in *Hound and Horn* April–June 1934, edited by Edna Kenton.

It occurs to me that it may conduce to interest to begin with a mention of the comparatively small matter that gave me, in this case, the germ of my subject—as it is very often comparatively small matters that do this; and as, at any rate, the little incident in question formed, for my convenience, my starting-point, on my first sketching the whole idea for myself.[1]

A friend (of perceptions almost as profound as my own!) had spoken to me, then—and really not measuring how much it would strike me or I should see in it—something that had come under his observation at short time before, in Paris. He had found himself, one Sunday afternoon, with various other people, in the charming old garden attached to the house of a friend (also a friend of mine) in a particularly old-fashioned and pleasantly quiet part of the town; a garden that, with two or three others of the same sort near it, I myself knew, so that I could easily focus the setting. The old houses of the Faubourg St.-Germain close round their gardens and shut them in, so that you don't see them from the street—only overlook them from all sorts of picturesque excrescences in the rear. I had a marked recollection of one of these wondrous concealed corners in especial, which was contiguous to the one mentioned by my friend: I used to know, many years

1. See entry for 31 October 1895.

ago, an ancient lady, long since dead, who lived in the house to which it belonged
and whom, also on Sunday afternoons, I used to go to see. On one side of that
one was another, visible from my old lady's windows, which was attached to a
great convent of which I have forgotten the name, and which I think was one of
the places of training for young missionary priests, whom we used to look down
on as they strolled, always with a book in hand, in the straight alleys. It endeared
to me, I recall, the house in question—the one where I used to call—that Madame
Récamier had finally lived and died in an apartment of the *rez-de-chaussée;* that
my ancient friend had known her and waited on her last days; and that the latter
gave me a strange and touching image of her as she lay there dying, blind, and
bereft of Chateaubriand, who was already dead.[2] But I mention these slightly
irrelevant things only to show that I *saw* the scene of my young friend's anecdote.

This anecdote then—to come to it—was simply in something said to him, on
the spot and on the occasion, by a person who had joined the little party in his
company and who was still another acquaintance of my own: an American, distinguished and mature, who had been in Europe before, but comparatively little and
very 'quietly,' and to whom, at all events, the note of everything that actually
surrounded them in the charming place was practically as new, as up-to-that-time-
unrevealed (as one may say) as it was picturesque and agreeable. This rather
fatigued and alien compatriot, whose wholly, exclusively professional career had
been a long, hard strain, and who could only be—given the place, people, tone,
talk, circumstances—extremely 'out of it' all, struck my reporter as at first watching the situation in rather a brooding, depressed and uneasy way; which my reporter, moreover, quite followed, allowed for and understood. He understood and
followed still better when our preoccupied friend happened at last, under some
determining impression, some accumulation of suggestions, to lay his hand on his
shoulder and make him the small speech from the echo of which my subject took
its flight. But think of the place itself again first—the charming June afternoon in
Paris, the tea under the trees, the 'intimate' nook, consecrated to 'artistic and
literary' talk, types, freedoms of (for the *désorienté* elderly American) an unprecedented sort; think above all of the so-possible presence of a charming woman or
two, of peculiarly 'European' tradition, such as it had never yet been given him
to encounter. Well, this is what the whole thing, as with a slow rush the sense of
it came over him, made him say:—'Oh, *you're* young, you're blessedly young—
be glad of it; be glad of it and *live*. Live all you can: it's a mistake not to. It
doesn't so much matter what you do—but live. This place and these impressions,
as well as many of those, for so many days, of So-and-So's and So-and-So's life,
that I've been receiving and that have had their abundant message, make it all

2. The garden was that of the American painter Whistler, who lived then in the rue du Bac. The
ancient lady was Mme Jules Mohl (1793–1883), widow of the famous German orientalist who taught
at the Collège de France; HJ used to visit her at 120 rue du Bac during the winter of 1875–76. The
convent is the Séminaire des Missions Etrangères at 128 rue du Bac. Mme Jeanne Françoise Julie
Adelaïde Bernard Récamier (1777–1849) had a celebrated literary and political salon in Paris and was
an intimate friend of François-René de Chateaubriand (1768–1848), romantic writer and politician. It
was actually Chateaubriand who spent the last years of his life in the building HJ visited: Mme Réca-
mier had in 1814 retired to one of the buildings of the adjoining Abbaye-aux-Bois in the rue du Bac.

come over me. I see it now. I haven't done so enough before—and now I'm old; I'm, at any rate, too old for what I see. Oh, I *do* see, at least—I see a lot. It's too late. It has gone past me. I've lost it. It couldn't, no doubt, have been different for me—for one's life takes a form and holds one: one lives as one can. But the point is that *you* have time. That's the great thing. You're, as I say, damn you, so luckily, so happily, so hatefully young. Don't be stupid. Of course I don't dream you *are,* or I shouldn't be saying these awful things to you. Don't, at any rate, make *my* mistake. Live!'

I amplify and improve a little, but that was the essence and the tone. They immediately put before me, with the communicative force, the real magic of the *right* things (those things the novelist worth his salt knows and responds to when he sees them), an interesting situation, a vivid and workable theme. To *prove* it workable, indeed, I had to work it out; which is what I have done and what I now give the results of. But I thought it might amuse you to take in also the dropped seed from which they were to spring.

I

My subject may be most simply described, then, as the picture of a certain momentous and interesting period, of some six months or so, in the history of a man no longer in the prime of life, yet still able to live with sufficient intensity to be a source of what may be called excitement to himself, not less than to the reader of his record. Lambert Strether (to give him, for our purpose here, a name, even if it be not final) has behind him so much past that I perforce accept him, and undertake to create on his behalf all the romantic sympathy necessary, just as his fifty-fifth year has struck. He is an American, of the present hour and of sufficiently typical New England origin, who has, at the point of his career that he has reached, the consciousness of a good deal of prolonged effort and tension, the memory of a good many earnest and anxious experiments—professional, practical, intellectual, moral, personal—to look back upon, without, for himself, any very proportionate sense of acknowledged or achieved success. However, he is, in the rather provincial, the somewhat contracted world in which he lives, a highly esteemed figure and influence. Educated, with excellent gifts, intelligent, having passed, for the most part, as exceptionally 'clever,' he has had a life by no means wasted, but not happily concentrated; and rather makes on himself the impression of having come in for many of the drawbacks, even perhaps for the little of the discredit, of an incoherent existence, without, unfortunately, any of the accompanying entertainment of 'fun.' He feels tired, in other words, without having a great deal to show for it; disenchanted without having known any great enchantments, enchanters, or, above all, enchantresses; and even before the action in which he is engaged launches him, is vaguely haunted by the feeling of what he has missed, though this is a quantity, and a quality, that he would be rather at a loss to name. His traditions, associations, sympathies, have all been the liberal and instructed sort, on a due basis of culture and curiosity; he has not been too much mixed up with vulgar things; he has always been occupied, and preoccupied, in one way and another, but has always, in all relations and connections, been ridden by his 'New England conscience.' He has known no extremes of fortune; has never been very poor, yet still less had any but the most limited enjoyment of money; has had always rather urgently to 'do something,' yet has never been without the thing—in a decently remunerative way—to do.

So much for him in a very general way, for everything that further concerns us about his conditions and antecedents is given, immediately, by the unfolding of the action itself—the action of which my story essentially consists and which of itself involves and achieves all presentation and explanation. This action takes him up at the moment of his arrival, one evening of early spring, in England—arrival in connection with a matter, and as the final note of a situation, with everything that has prepared and led up to which we become *dramatically,* so to speak, acquainted. My first Part or two are expository, presentative (on these lines of present picture and movement); and are primar[il]y concerned with his encounter and relation with two persons his portrayed intercourse with whom throws up to the surface what it concerns us to learn. One of these persons is an old friend, also an American, a college-mate, much lost sight of, through separations and interruptions, in recent years, but between whom and Strether the tradition of an old-time alliance, an approach to an intimacy, still exists. The men are of the same age, and with similarities of history and situation, and Waymark, the friend, has been abroad, already, some two or three months—fatigued, overworked, threatened with nervous prostration and taking, somewhat against the grain, a fidgety, discomfortable rest. In communication with Strether, and hearing before-hand of *his* destined arrival, Waymark has thus fidgeted back from the Continent to be in England to meet him, with intentions of rather forlornly clinging and cleaving somewhat marked from the first. They come together, by my notion, at the picturesque old town of Chester, where they spend a Sunday—a Sunday pre-arranged by Strether's having wired from Queenstown: 'No—not Liverpool; wait for me at Chester—like awfully to be with you there a day or two.' The latter has been in Europe once or twice, briefly, with a sense of insufficiency, in earlier years, and has a recollection, very pleasant and charming, of a summer evening spent at Chester—a sweet, melancholy summer afternoon caught there the last thing, then, before re-embarking from Liverpool. It has come back to him as an impression he should like to renew.

Well, they have it there, the two men together; and a due quantity of preparation, explication, implication, comes up between them. They walk through the old 'Rows' and on the old town-walls together; they talk, talk, talk, as they have scarce had a chance of doing for years; they have fallen happily on an early foretaste of a beautiful season; Strether at least surrenders himself freely, quite gaily—for *him*—to a charming renewal of acquaintance with the English spring at its best, as well as with various other impressions. He has not known till now what a sense of holiday he was to have, and is only a little pulled up, or pulled down, by something backward and out of tune in his companion, whose way of taking things he finds to resemble his own rather less than he has been taking for granted. He somehow feels from the first that he is, after long years, after a great deal of grind and not much free play of anything, on the verge of an experience that (in spite of troublous things—prospectively, possibly so—latent and lurking within it) will be rather a fraud if it fails of enabling him also to forget, a little, and merely lounge, break awhile with the actual. I strike here the note that it's 'borne in' upon Strether that his differences with his old friend have come out a good deal in separation, and that if they are to be more or less together for the duration of his stay in Europe, they may yet find themselves not quite perfectly in step. This, in fine, is but part of a slight and comparatively subordinate feature of my business; a minor current, I may call it; the exhibition of the two men as affected in wholly different ways by an experience considerably identical. It's 'too late,'[3] in a manner, for each alike; but one, my hero, has, with imagination, perception, humour, melancholy, the interesting and interested sense of this— sense of what he has lost, or only caught the last whisk of the tip of the tail of; while the other, unamenable, unadjustable, to a new and disarranging adventure (Waymark's never having, previous to this, been out of his lifelong setting at all), fails to react, fails of elasticity, of 'amusement,' throws himself back on suspicion, depreciation, resentment really; the sense of exteriority, the cultivation of dissent, the surrender to unbridgeable difference. Waymark's office in the subject is, in other words, that of a contrast and foil to Strether—of an aid to the illustration and exhibition of many things; but it is also, at junctures, and precisely at the present, the initial, that of an active aid to what, in these opening passages, with the future course of our affair all before them, comes out, under the impressions, in the old town, on the old walls and from the new talks, between the two men.

But another agent, operative on this expository ground, as well as throughout the remainder, promptly comes into play in the person of a lady met by them on the rampart—strolling and looking, as they stroll and look; only unaccompanied, detached, with no one to talk of it to, and coming back to Strether as soon as he sees her, as a person already noticed by him, though with no great intensity, at the hotel at Liverpool, where she was occupied with a companion, another lady, whom she seemed to have come to 'see off' by the outgoing American steamer. She evidently, as they pass, knows Strether's face again; but she takes in at the same moment that of the gentleman he is with, and this—after she has gone on a few steps—determines her, with her uncertainty vanishing, to pull up, while Strether remarks to Waymark that he, Waymark, is evidently known to her. The two men, with this turn round, and a recognition—of Waymark—is what has in fact, on the lady's part, occurred. Waymark doesn't at first recognize her, but she recalls herself, and he places her; so that she presently has joined them and, in the course of a short time, become, as it were, for the moment, their travelling-companion. Waymark's contact with her proves, however, not to have been previously at all close; they have met on occasion, but superficially, and the connection is sufficiently explained. Waymark is an overworked lawyer in an American business community also, like Strether's, not of the first magnitude, but flourishing and important, and his situation in which has been such as to engender for him many responsibilities and much tension. He is a 'prominent man,' there, in his own way; and it is as a prominent man that Miss Gostrey has known him during some

---

3. HJ pondered the theme of "too late" in his notebook entry for 5 February 1895.

family visit or otherwise-determined frequentation. This young woman—young as a slightly battered unmarried woman of five-and-thirty can be—is a study, as it were, of a highly contemporary and quasi-cosmopolite feminine type, and has her high utility in my little drama. The more immediate phase of that utility is that, the three being now together for several days, first at Chester, then in London (before Strether goes on to Paris, which is his specially-constituted objective), she is drawn into a relation with her new acquaintance—that is, with Strether, that makes, in its order, for our illumination. It is the accident of her knowing Waymark that has brought about their combination; but Waymark speedily drops out of it, and the congruity, the amusing affinity, that establishes itself for her, is altogether with Strether. They hit it off, in their degree—especially in Strether's limited one—from the first; they strike up a comradeship which proves full of profit for future lucidity. An American spinster left by the accidents of life free to wander, and having wandered and re-wandered from an early time, Miss Gostrey, clever, independent, humorous, shrewd, a little battered, a little hard, both highly unshockable and highly incorruptible, and many other things besides, is above all full of initiations and familiarities, full of Europe, full of ways and means, full of everything and everywhere. Active and energetic, interested in the human predicament and full of divination of it and semi-cynical helpfulness *about* it, she has no one directly dependent on her, and so finds a happy exercise of her temperament in cultivating a protective attitude when she sees a chance for one. She is inordinately modern, the fruit of actual, international conditions, of the growing polyglot Babel. She calls herself the universal American agent. She calls herself the general amateur-courier. She comes over with girls. She goes back with girls. She meets girls at Liverpool, at Genoa, at Bremen—she has even been known to meet boys. She sees people through. She shops with them in Paris. She shops with them in London, where she has a tailor of her 'very own.' She knows all the trains. She meets a want. In short she is a very especial and, in her way, wonderful person. She takes an extraordinary fancy to Strether from the first; and the fancy that she takes to him is a secondary thread in the web, a little palpable gold thread that plays through all the pattern. She tries, after she has little by little got hold of his situation and entered into it, to help him, to 'do' for him in all sorts of ways, and he much appreciates it, responds to it, and likes her for it, so that with all she positively (mere lone, lean, migratory spinster as she is, but living in her world of reverberations) *shows* him and puts him up to, she is really, for him, quite one of the phenomena of his episode; he remaining for herself, as I say, still more, the job, of all she has ever undertaken, to which she has most zest to offer. He is better than any of the girls, better even than any of the boys, she has yet 'met'; better than the most bloated and benighted of the California billionairesses she has ever seen through the great round of the Paris purchases. What comes of this relation is for later on; at this point it is but the preliminary of the preliminary; definitely functional, as I say, in the way of eliciting for us luminously the conditions in which Strether is involved.

　　This cluster of circumstances has two faces, the more immediate, the less private of which has already bared itself, from the first as between himself and Waymark. He has had to give the latter some explanation of why and how he is directed so straight upon Paris; so that we have, betimes, that thread in our hand. He has come out on a friendly mission—to render, that is, a service, doubtless rather delicate and difficult, to a friend at home, a friend who couldn't come. He has come out to take a look at 'Chad' (Chadwick) Newsome, Mrs. Newsome's son, her only one, these several years in Europe and recalcitrant to every appeal to return: Waymark will not be wholly ignorant of who Mrs. Newsome is. Who she is comes up, at any rate, lucidly, for ourselves; and with it, in brief, the full evocation of Strether's background and setting. These things put before us, by their implications, an American city of the second order—not such a place either as New York, as Boston or as Chicago, but a New England 'important local centre' like Providence, R.I., like Worcester, Mass., or like Hartford, Conn.; an old and enlightened Eastern community, in short, which is yet not the seat of one of the bigger colleges (which for special reasons I don't want). The place of course to be designated with sufficient intensity. Mrs. Newsome is the widow, there domiciled and dominant, of one of the local rich men, a man known to Strether in his time—and not all too agreeably or handsomely; the late Mr. Newsome, hard, sharp and the reverse of overscrupulous, not having left a name (for those who *know*—and Strether is abundantly one of them) of a savour ideally sweet. Mrs. Newsome herself, however, is a very different affair and a really remarkable woman: high, strenuous, nervous, 'intense' (oh, a type!)—full of ideals and activities, many of them really, in respect to her husband's career, of a decidedly fine expiatory or compensatory nature. She is many other things besides; invalidical, exalted, depressed, at once shrill and muffled, at once extremely abounding and extremely narrow, and of an especial austerity (in spite of herself almost, as it were, and of some of her imaginations), an especial refined hardness and dryness of grain and strain. She is old enough to have had by her early marriage, a marriage when she was barely twenty, two children, a son now of about twenty-eight, the one who remains in Europe, and predominantly in Paris, where she can't, for reasons, get at him; and a daughter of thirty, Mrs. Pocock, who lives in the same place as her mother and near her, in close communion with her, being married, to a man somewhat older than herself, actually a partner in the considerable family business, a business, the manufacture of some small, convenient, homely, in fact distinctly vulgar article of domestic use (to be duly specified), to which the late Newsome gave in his time such an impulse that his family derive a large income from it and will continue to do so if their interests are sharply guarded and the working of the thing thoroughly kept up. This charge he, before his death, has laid, by testamentary and other injunction, very strenuously, on his son—who, practically, however, has not shown himself, as yet, as at all adequately responding to it. There are special conditions as to the son's share in the concern, contingencies as to forfeiture of the same in case of non-compliance, and other similar circumstances helping to constitute, with what he may gain and what he may lose, a special situation for the young man. The young man has none the less, however, as it happens, his considerable measure of financial independence through the possession of means inherited from his maternal grandfather; another sharp old local worthy as to whom Strether has also not been without his lights. Mrs. Newsome has thus likewise means of *her* own, coming to her from the same shrewd source and forming a property distinct from her anxious, responsible share in her husband's concern. It is this fact of having been benefited by his grandfather that has placed young Newsome on the footing of being able to act in considerable defiance of everyone and everything.

This practical defiance has been, for his mother, the greatest source of anxiety, for some time, in a life of which strenuous anxiety and responsibility, restless, nervous, and at the same time imperious, conscientiousness, has been the leading note. She has had her ideas and her fears, her suspicions and worries, and indeed, more than all these, her certitudes and convictions. She doesn't approve of Chad's long absence—purposeless, idle, selfish and worse than frivolous. She has all the more ground for regarding it as positively immoral as she is definitely aware of some of the facts of his career and has a horror of the company he keeps. There is a dreadful woman in particular—a woman with whom she knows him to have been living, and as to whom she is divided between the dread that he will marry her—which will be awful—and the dread that he will go on living with her without marrying her—which will be more awful still. She regards him as under a spell, a blight, a dark and baffling influence. He writes, he is kind, he is in ways of his own even reassuring; but she can really get nothing out of him, and she feels that he is not only elusive, but already all but veritably *lost*. She has her theory of the *why*—it's all the dreadful woman. The dreadful woman looms large to her, is a perpetual monstrous haunting image in her thoughts, grotesquely enlarged and fantastically coloured. Details, particular circumstances have come to her—they form, about the whole connection, a mass of portentous lurid fable, in which the poor lady's own real ignorance of life and of the world infinitely embroiders and revolves. The person in Paris is above all a *low* person, a mere mercenary and ravening adventuress of the basest stamp. She would have gone out herself long since were it not that the same highly nervous conditions that prompt and urge also dissuade, deter, detain. She is a particularly intense and energetic invalid, moreover, but still an invalid, never sure of herself in advance, and with recollections of Europe gathered from an early infelicitous round or two with her late husband, memories not of an order to leave traditions of ease. In short, for two or three years past she has, from year to year and from month to month, failed to achieve the move; in connection with which there has been another deterrent still. This deterrent has been the part more and more played in her life by Lambert Strether (full name Lewis Lambert Strether), and to which we catch on wholly through the lights given us by Strether himself. What we have is his depicted, betrayed, communicated consciousness and picture of it. We see Mrs. Newsome, in fine, altogether in this reflected manner, as she figures in our hero's relation to her and in his virtual projection, for us, *of* her. I may as well say at once, that, lively element as she is in the action, we deal with her presence and personality only as an affirmed influence, only in their deputed, represented form; and nothing, of course, can be more artistically interesting than such a little problem as to make her always out of it, yet always *of* it, always absent, yet always felt.[4] But the realities, the circumstances—as they are evoked by Strether

---

4. In Sardou's play *La Famille Benoîton* the mother of the family is like Mrs. Newsome: while her presence is constantly felt she never appears on stage. HJ had long been interested in Sardou's drama; see the detached notes for *The Chaperon* (1893).

first for Waymark—are not the less distinctly before us. Waymark doesn't learn all—it's Miss Gostrey who presently makes all *out;* but Waymark elicits a good deal. Mrs. Newsome has begun by being immensely indebted to Strether, but Strether has also ended by contacting a sense of no small obligation to herself. He has helped her originally with her charities, her reforms, her good works—twenty manifestations of that restless conscience which I have called in a measure unwittingly expiatory; he has been advisory, sympathetic, suggestive, been an influence, for her, making in fact altogether for sanity and success. He has controlled and moderated her, been, in short, in these connections, exactly the clever, competent man needed by a peculiarly high-strung woman. Cleverness, competence, soundness, the thing to do and the thing not to, the way and the way not—these have been, by a happy constitution in our interesting friend, matters easy and natural to him; so that he has played, without great inconvenience to himself, and with an interest too in her subjects and ideals, straight into the current of his earnest neighbour's activity.

What we further learn about him helps to explain it. He himself has, in the New England way, married young, married, at an age not much greater than Mrs. Newsome's (who at present, I've omitted to note, is in her fifty-first year), emphatically for love, married happily for all save the fact of the death of his wife, in a second confinement, at the end of some five years. Left with a little boy of less than that age, Strether has then known such a period of helpless and discomfortable paternity as has deepened the bitterness of his bereavement; a period at once unrelieved and unspoiled by a second marriage, but brought to a term by the death—through an accident (while swimming)—of his boy at the age of about sixteen, an age sufficient to have unfortunately marked the fact that they (the boy and he) had not wholly hit it off together. There have been special facts about the boy, his nature, temperament, tendencies, that Strether has subsequently accused himself, with bitter compunction, of not having understood and allowed for, not handled with sufficient tenderness and tact. Deep and silent penance has he privately performed ever since; and the loss of his son, and the particular conditions and particular consequent feelings, are things that have constituted one of the sharpest elements of his life. It's all a history as to which Mrs. Newsome has repeatedly accused him of being morbid—as if, it is true, in a measure to make up as she can for all the occasions on which he has called *her* the same. He has thought her a little so—or in fact a good deal so—about her son, though holding a good deal himself the impression that Chad, whom he has known a bit as a boy, and in earlier youth, is not a little, really, alas, of an egotist and even a brute. He has *his* theory about Chad, which differs from the mother's, and is, as he considers, the theory of a man of the world as distinguished from such a person as Mrs. Newsome of Hartford, Conn. His own boy, at all events, *wasn't* a brute; he has ached, at times, with the sense that he himself was, in the doomed relation, the brute—unconscious of tender and sensitive things in the lad, stupidly, harshly blundering about them.

And there have been other things in his career—but things of labour and effort mainly, things in which he has tried to steep his disappointments, disillusionments, depressions. It has been his idea of himself, above all, that he has been fundamentally indifferent and detached, fatally unable really to care for anything.

What more proof of it has he needed, to his own mind, than that he has tried half-a-dozen things and successively, rather as he calls it to himself, sneakingly given them up? He tutored at college, after graduating, for a while, and gave that up. He studied law, and was admitted, and provincially, drearily practiced for a time, but made little of that, had hankerings for 'study,' for serious literature, for serious journalism, and threw himself, with characteristic intensity, into experiments in that direction. They failed, in a manner, yet left him still with his yearnings, so that even after accepting and exercising, with a good deal of continuity, a salaried, an authoritative post in connection with the control of a large 'Home,' or some such other beneficent or economic institution founded, patronized, promoted by Mrs. Newsome these aspirations have again, a few years previous to our opening, . . . in the form of an expensive Review, devoted to serious questions and inquiries, economic, social, sanitary, humanitary, Strether carries with some financial ruefulness and Mrs. Newsome subsidises with much public pride.[5] She gave him his chance, at a given moment, and he accepted it from her. Between them they keep the thing going. It has been an alliance, a united superior effort. What they both feel about it is that the thing is of course too good, too enlightened to succeed, but not, uncontestably, to *do* good. It's a great beneficent endeavour, equally honourable to both. It has, moreover, a few hundred subscribers, and all the colleges, all the cultivated groups scattered about the country, take it in and esteem it. It goes to Europe—where they believe it to have attracted attention in high quarters. Strether's name, as the editor, is on the cover, where it has been one of the few frank pleasures of his somewhat straightened life to have liked to see it. He is known by that pale, costly cover—it has become his principal identity. A man of moods and of a very variable imagination, he has sometimes thought this identity small, poor, miserable; while at others thinking it as good as most of the others around him. It's on the cover, at any rate, that Mrs. Newsome has liked to see him—this has been a greater joy to her than she has ever even betrayed; and the common interest, the most especial of many, has done much to bind them together. The feelings connected for her with this intimacy form precisely the subject of my reference just above to her practically deterred condition in respect to breaking in and going off. She has been under a spell from poor fine melancholy, missing, striving Strether. To be plain (though we are not plain at first), she's in love with him. She's fifty, and he's fifty-five, but he's the secret romance—secret, that is, up to a given point; then sufficiently public—that she has never otherwise had. To say that she plays a similar part very exactly for himself would be to say too much; but he likes, admires and esteems her; she is much the most remarkable woman, in her way the most distinguished, the highest, keenest spirit, within his social range; and in their sufficiently 'awake' community she passes for very remarkable indeed. She is *the* personage, almost the great lady, certainly the 'prominent woman' of that community. Indeed her name is in the local papers much more than he, secretly, can like. However, *she* likes it, and the upshot of everything (for I am expatiating here, for you, far too much) is that,

---

5. This sentence is printed as it appears in the original typescript, although some words seem to be missing after the phrase "previous to our opening"; the ellipsis has been inserted.

certain things having, at home, happened in certain ways, certain symptoms in regard to Chad, in Paris, having multiplied—in regard to Chad and in regard to other matters besides—the situation has taken the form of Strether's having offered Mrs. Newsome the service, as a loyal and grateful friend, of coming out to Paris to see what, in the premises, he can do. There has been a plan of *her* coming, but many personal and other things, complications, of sorts, indisposition, nervousness, moral and other apprehensions, have interposed and again checked her; a particular consideration which presently comes out for us has in fact above all interfered. There had been a question, if she *had* come, of Strether's coming with her; then there had been a question of her coming, as it were, with *him*. But the particular consideration I speak of has interposed especially as to *that;* and in the event Strether, tired, overstrained, chronically deficient in holidays and in 'a little change,' has taken his course by himself. It fits in, in short, with a kind of crisis in his personal history, which it may, in a manner, contribute to ease off, to produce an interruption, a suspension, a possible practical evaporation of. He comes on a kind of moral and sentimental mission, but committed to nothing more than to get hold of Chad tactfully, kindly, to try to fish him out of his deep waters. He is to act only within his full discretion, and he is to report on the situation and enlighten Mrs. Newsome's darkness. In particular, at any rate, they have both fully felt, and in almost equal good faith, that it will have been, on the possible bad issue, but a small honour to them if the boy be lost without some earnest, some practical, personal effort to save him. The case has been virtually as simple for them as that. Perdition on one side, salvation on the other.

But I am suffering this sketch already to reach such proportions that I must bear more lightly, must more sternly foreshorten. There is a situation between the three persons thus introduced—Strether, Waymark and Miss Gostrey—which floats us through the episode at Chester and carries us with them up to London, where my Prologue, as it were, culminates. Before it is over I have marked the development of the curious and interesting relation between Strether and Miss Gostrey—a development of which the rapidity is amusing in a high degree to themselves, proceeding as it has done by the liveliest bounds, by a kind of mutual half-tender, half-ironic recognition, and which makes them spectators, commentators, critics together, of those already-marked signs and symptoms in their companion's state which are to result in that demonstration of his case (his case 'in Europe') as a case sharply opposed, representing the opposite pole of possibility, to Strether's own, which I have somewhere above glanced at. Things have, in London, on the eve of the separation of the two men from Miss Gostrey (they going on to Paris together, and she destined to turn up there after a brief interval) that she extracts from Strether (it's the proof of her success with him) the communication of a very private fact of which he has said nothing, even in their mutual expansion, to Waymark.[6] She is by this time, of course, completely *au courant* of what his 'mission' in Paris amounts to; and after a fashion that would be rather pushing, or have struck him as such, if it hadn't struck him as rather pleasant, she has put to him many questions: all of which have vividly illustrated for him her general

---

6. This sentence is printed as it appears in the original typescript.

human awareness and competence. If they haven't, by the same token, fully illustrated for him the kind of turn her interest in himself may be apprehended as capable of taking, that is because he doesn't in general jump rapidly to such conclusions. He only finds in talking with her the special note of a kind of entertainment—almost a vague excitement—that really, yes, quite literally, he doesn't remember ever having known. Full, at all events, of quickened shrewdness and sympathy, full of perceptions and divinations that have given her the courage of her curiosity, she ultimately elicits from him that his relation with Mrs. Newsome has practically become, on the eve of his departure from Worcester (or wherever) Mass., an 'engagement.' She has in fact—she, Miss Gostrey, I mean—pointed the pistol at him; having already elicited so much that it amounts to an implication of the supreme fact. 'If you do it—if you come out all right—she'll marry you?' And then, before they have gone many steps further, leaping from peak to peak, she brings out the rest. 'It's *she* who proposed it to you. *You* didn't—you wouldn't have thought of it. But since she *has*—well, you're flattered. Oh, you needn't deny—and you needn't confess either. It doesn't matter how, if you only do it; for she'll be awfully good to you. She'll take a lot of things off you—personal worries of your own, I mean; which is exactly what ought to be.'

He is really touched at the way Miss Gostrey has entered into his life—at the feeling [s]he has about certain things in it. He does deny—deny the offer as directly made by Mrs. Newsome, but his new friend makes what she likes of that. She has the whole thing—she reconstructs and fairly illumines it. She puts it all there to him—almost as if speaking of others. She even urges with exaggeration, almost with extravagance, his not disappointing a person who has made such an effort for him. Of course she's in love with him, Mrs. Newsome; but for many women that wouldn't have availed—the proceeding would have been too unusual. She herself, she, Miss Gostrey, would really like to know the person capable of it: she must be quite too wonderful. She will be, at all events, clearly, this heroic lady, his providence. Rich, clever, powerful, she will look after him in all sorts of charming ways, and guarantee and protect his future. Therefore he mustn't let her back out. He must *do* the thing he came out for. He must carry the young man home in triumph and be led to the altar as his reward. She gives the whole thing a humourous turn but we get from it all we need. Strether disclaims, deprecates, but really shows himself as so bewildered—that is, so affected both with dazzlement and doubt—over this particular element of his situation, that his condition constitutes of itself a kind of testimony. Yet, superficially, he refuses to recognize in Miss Gostrey's picture anything but a free joke; and to make his disclaimer appear the more sincere, he abounds in her sense and jokes *with* her. 'She won't then, you feel, if I *don't*?'

'Won't, you mean, stick to her offer if you don't capture the child? Surely not, no song no supper. So you *must* capture him. Oh, I see what you're thinking— that Paris is an awful place, and that it may be awfully difficult. But it will be all the more fun.'

'Fun?' poor Strether rather ruefully echoes.

'It's just the sort of job,' she replies, 'that's really, I assure you, in my line and that I should be quite ready to hand in an estimate for. Upon my word, I'd take the order.'

'I wish to goodness then you would!' her companion laughs. 'It would save me a lot of trouble!'

'Well, I'll save you,' she responds, 'all the trouble I can.' And the little scene, with its climax, marks the culmination, as I have indicated, of my Preliminary.

II

In Paris, after his arrival, he has at first such a rush, such an increase of the sense of rest, refreshment, change, long-deferred amusement and ease, without something immediately to do and some responsibility to meet, that he for the moment abandons himself to a certain regret, which he at the same time rebukes as pusillanimous, at his not having come with a wholly free hand, at his really being committed to a responsibility and having very presently a duty to take up and an effort to make. It has all come over him since his disembarkment at Liverpool that he responds to his holiday more even than he had expected, and that he is now responding—after the first few days—to a still quicker tune. He immediately informs himself about Chad, to whom he is of course not wholly without a clue, and learns with a certain relief that the young man is out of town. He sees, immediately, however, meets by an accident, a young man, a young artist-man, a young American art-student, who is his friend and who has a certain amount of perhaps rather visibly reserved news to give about him; a youth who, moreover, immediately rather interests Strether on his own account. This youth—Burbage by name and who is, by the way, three or four years older than Chad—constitutes the first note struck for Strether in a direction destined much to open out to him; being, the young man, a very Parisianised—in respect to the art-world—product, the product, in fact, altogether of an air of which Strether has never yet, directly, tasted a mouthful. Glenn likes him—in fact I'm afraid I shall represent everyone, rather monotonously, as liking Strether (which is a bad note for his intensity of identity, though we must risk it); is communicative, talkative, sociable, immensely 'modern,' and he takes him—takes the two men, Waymark and our hero, about together while they wait for what next happens. They are affected in different ways, as we know, the two men; but it is Strether who so predominantly concerns us that I drop here the notation (drop it, I mean, out of my synopsis) of what refers to Waymark, as it puts on my hands too many things for your patience, and even, perhaps, with all respect, for your intelligence. Burbage is, in short, one of the several agents in Strether's fermentation (besides being a marked type in himself)—and these are an essential part of our drama. Our hero sees Paris a little, accordingly, before Chad turns up, before Miss Gostrey again turns up, before anything particular happens save that he, in a general way, takes the somewhat uneasy measure—a little more fact to fact—of his deputed duty. He makes out things from Burbage, whom he yet is scrupulous not to seem to invite or to expect to bear witness; but it only adds to his vague sense as of something that looms; they bewilder, these impressions, and only seem, as he soon finds, originally to mislead—they carry him on further than his feet feel sure. The result is a sense that Chad must be 'in' pretty deep—in below all possible immediate sounding. Strether is a little shy with his new young artist-man friend—literally a trifle indisposed to betray ignorances and mistakes too marked; so he half the time feels that he absolutely doesn't understand him. It's a good little moment however—a sort of lull at cafés, at restaurants, at theatres, even at the Folies-Bergère, at the wondrous Louvre and at old bookstalls by the Seine, before the too-probable struggle.

After a little, however, Chad comes on the scene; with which Strether is immediately more or less in the presence of his business and his problem. He has grown, by reason of indications gathered, inductions made, during the few days, a little nervous about them beforehand; seems to make out that the image of the actual Chad doesn't fit with the image preconceived by themselves at home, or with that remembered in regard to the boy's earlier time. He has felt that there will probably be differences—marked ones, as is indeed only natural; but the differences when he *sees* the young man and has spent half an hour with him, are such as to give him the sense of really not having known what in the least to expect. What Chad seems to be has the effect, as it were, of so imposing itself, that any previous mistake about it, any mere sense of miscalculation, fades away as irrelevant. There he is, *with* more differences than Strether can at first at all catalogue, and really presenting himself as a positive prodigy in the sphere of transformation. Strether at first so feels that he's 'transformed,' that it must take time to find out *what* he's transformed to. He has vaguely expected, at any rate, to find him coarsened—that would have been mainly the word he would use; brutalized, perverted, poisoned—all in some rather obvious and distressing way; he has braced himself for being distressed about him—and on somehow, surprisingly, becoming conscious that he's *not* distressed, doesn't quite know what to do *with* the 'bracing.' It's as if a good deal of rather fine and serious preparation for the event had been wasted; though indeed he plucks up courage and tries to say to himself that if the corruption, as it were, is so extremely insidious, so therefore the salvation must be supersubtle to match it. For of one thing he *has* satisfied himself—that there has been a horrible woman, *the* horrible woman, that Chad has been quite helpless in her clutches, and, for all he knows, may be as much so as ever. All the same there are inscrutabilities, mysteries, things shading off into the vague. The young man is 'easy' for him and with him to a degree which in itself is a surprise; his manners at least have extraordinarily improved; and altogether the question of tackling him has to adjust itself, feels grounds for finding itself a more complex one. Literally, for a little, Strether rather lets it drop, on the theory of just playing a waiting game till he is so possessed of more of the facts as not to be in danger of making a grave mistake. He has told the young man at first, frankly, amicably, handsomely, that he has come out to represent to him his mother's earnest wish that he shall come home, and to put the whole issue seriously before him; but Chad has been charming about *this* even, goodnaturedly indifferent, cheerfully postponing and adjourning discussion, granting that it's quite worth talking about, but really talking about anything, everything else. Chad is, of course, like everyone else in the whole business a special figure—difficult to do, but to be unmistakeably done; and I don't pretend here to construct him for you. For that you must wait for the book. I repeat that for Strether, at first, the note of the *changed* creature is so strong in the youth that, by itself, it overlies everything else. He feels himself, in the presence of it, to be in the presence of one of the most striking and curious phenomena—in the human and personal order—that he has ever met or had to reckon with.

Meanwhile, at all events, Miss Gostrey reappears—coming back to Paris, where she has quite given Strether rendezvous, looking him up, with frank comradeship, as soon as she arrives, and so presenting herself in short as to become again, inevitably, the receptacle of some of his overflow. She is placed, by this connection, in the presence of Chad, and Strether promptly enough derives a sensible relief, a kind of convenience, from her share of his hopes and fears, contemplations, hesitations, speculations. They continue, the two, more or less, to have some of these things out together, and it's an especial convenience to him that, in Chad's presence, as I say, she catches on still more to *that* particular situation. Some of Strether's views of it amuse her, some of hers amuse him; they hold sundry theories diametrically opposed about it, and Miss Gostrey, certainly, is soon ready to assert that she has sounded it to the bottom. With characteristic acuteness, she has immediately found the true word. It affects Strether himself as the true one—and rather disconcertingly even, before they either of them really know more. 'Save him, my dear man? Why, what are you talking about? There's nothing more about him *to* save. He *is* saved.'

'Ah, but I'm not a bit less convinced than ever,' Strether returns, 'that some woman, playing a great part in his life, and more or less feeding on him, hasn't still hold on him.'

'Exactly then; it *would* be some woman; it's only they who do that sort of thing.' Miss Gostrey, as she goes on, is immensely struck with it. 'It's *she* who has saved him.'

This discomposes Strether's theory of a rescue, precisely, *from* such a person; and the thing is at any rate the first note, is a view of the matter with which he has more and more to count. Miss Gostrey has, by a miracle, not happened to know Chad, to have met him before; a fact that by itself speaks a good deal for his having lived out of the eye of the light. But she now sees him for herself and feels sure that she understands him; and a combination of the three briefly takes place. Chad has meanwhile, after an hesitation, a measurable delay, spoken to Strether of some good friends of his own, awfully charming people, a mother and a young daughter—the mother almost herself *as* young—whom he wants him to know. They are the people he himself likes best in Paris and, as it were, sees most of; and the motive of his recent absence has precisely been a period spent near them in the south of France. He has quitted them, to come up to Paris on purpose to see Strether; but they are soon also to arrive, and he will then speedily arrange a meeting for his visitor, who will be as sure to like them as they will be to like *him*. Strether sees, in fact, several things in this programme—some of which he submits to his friendly Egeria: among them, in any case, is the circumstance, distinguishable to him, that Chad has waited to report (after seeing him, after renewing a blurred young impression of him)—waited to communicate with the ladies in the south, giving his judgement on him and not speaking without their assent. This Strether mentions to Miss Gostrey, who thinks it highly probable and who immediately leaps, in consequence, at the perception of two facts.

One of these is that Chad finds Strether awfully 'possible,' much more possible than he had dreamed; and that if he does mean to show him to his friends Strether may take that quite as a tribute. Strether looks at it—or tries to—accordingly, at her direction, in this light, and somehow feels that, at any rate, it may be—this 'possibility' of his—but a mixture the more. For through a hundred channels the 'mixture' in poor Strether's consciousness has already begun to threaten to become tolerably thick. Sensations, impressions, a whole inert or dormant world of feeling or side of life, find themselves awake and sitting up around him; and so, in short, he goes on. But the second of these conclusions, embraced at a glance—on her interpretations of the symptoms—by Miss Gostrey, is that the lady of whom Chad has spoken has put her hand on him for her daughter, is arranging, as fast as possible, a marriage for the girl with the rich, the flattered, the manageable young American.

'Then it's she,' says Strether rather struck, 'who has saved him.'

But his friend doesn't seem so sure. 'Who? The mother?'

Strether wonders, but without quite seeing *that*. 'Well—the girl. The beautiful pure maiden.' And he wonders again. 'Suppose *that's* what one has come upon. Won't it be possibly a little awkward?'

'Oh,' says Miss Gostrey, 'don't be too sure, in advance, of the shade of your awkwardness. There are many kinds; of every colour and every price. But perhaps!'

Chad meanwhile introduces Strether to other friends; Miss Gostrey, on her side produces a type or two out of her own store; and the business of our hero's enjoying himself—to a degree almost scandalous indeed to Waymark who doesn't enjoy himself at all, but really not in the least, goes an apace. And yet the enjoyment is singularly imperfect, for our friend is haunted with an inward *malaise;* the whole question of his regular report to Mrs. Newsome being, on the evidence before him, more and more difficult to meet. He is fairly ashamed—for it comes to that—of the case of coarseness Mrs. Newsome and he together had made out so luridly, over there, the palpable grossness that they had, as it were, fairly mapped out as the young man's necessary state, the presumable depravity they had (as now seems to him) positively hugged the conception of as the colour of his connection. Poor Strether almost feels as if these things had been the fault of his own mind; the discomfort arises from his having, as he turns things over, to say to himself that they do him little honour. But he tries at least to tell his friend at home, to whom he profusely writes, as much as he can; secretly a little disappointed that he has nothing for her as yet quite bad enough. Sometimes he brushes away the vision of her fine, cold strenuous face and general high-pitched essence. He feels, he scarce knows why, a little false to her; feels even a little afraid of himself. The little spectacle that Chad has meanwhile amiably and thoughtfully evoked for him is largely that of some of the young man's own 'artistic' ramifications. He knows painters, sculptors, studios; knows a celebrity or two; puts Strether in relation—superficial, momentary, but very interesting to Strether—with them; brings about in particular an occasion of contact with a prime celebrity, of a very special note: all of which results in a Sunday-afternoon visit of the type of the one alluded to in my few preliminary pages. There is in other words a particular occasion on which everything—by which I mean a lot of accumulated perception and emotion—seems to culminate for Strether. I 'do' the occasion and the picture, evoke the place and influences, multiply so far as may be, the different sources of impression for our poor fermenting friend—the persons, figures, strangenesses, newnesses there present; give, above all, the wonderful intensity, oddity, amenity of the general intellectual, colloquial air. It's a real date for Strether. Chad's two friends, Mme de Vionnet and her daughter, are, happily, at last there; and there it is, very much in the same beautiful old garden that my original anecdote gives me, that our hero's introduction to them takes place. But this is an occasion on which, through relations already existing for her, Miss Gostrey is also on the ground; whereupon, lo and behold, once in presence, it turns out that Mme de Vionnet is a person she has already known, an acquaintance of a previous time—a time both previous to Mme de Vionnet's marriage and subsequent to it— whom she has lost sight of. The identity of this lady—through Strether's not having got her name right in speaking of her, or having forgotten it or not pronounced it—has not, antecedently to this encounter, come up between them sharply enough for Miss Gostrey to have been guided; so that when she does meet, in Strether's company, Chad's vaunted ladies, she finds it a surprise to be able to fit them in to facts actually known to her. These facts she produces afterwards for Strether, and they are indeed all to Mme de Vionnet's credit—in spite of the circumstance that she is living apart from her husband. By the time, at any rate, they are known in this measure to Strether, the impression, as it were, has been made upon him by the charming woman herself: inasmuch as it now becomes of the essence of the business, becomes vividly and importantly so, that Mme de Vionnet *is* charming, and that he fully recognizes her as such. She is young (that is, she is thirty-eight), bright, graceful, kind, sympathetic, interesting—and doesn't alarm him by being dazzlingly clever (which is the cleverest thing *in* her!). Without having anything that he immediately feels to be positive beauty, she has a face, and a general air and aspect, that singularly speak to him. He likes no less, also, the way she receives him, lends herself to the reference made to him by Chad for her, and to the reference made to *her* by Chad for Strether himself. She lends herself to everything, in short, with the friendliest ease, and strikes our hero from the first—which is the most particular note of all—as a kind of person he has absolutely never seen, nor ever, with any distinctness, dreamed of.

And yet it's not in the least that he has fallen in love with her, or is at all likely to do so. Her charm is independent of that for him and gratifies some more distinctively disinterested aesthetic, intellectual, social even, so to speak, historic sense in him, which has never yet been *à pareille fête,* never found itself so called to the front. She shows him her daughter, a girl of seventeen, who strikes him as almost as much of a revelation; a little tender flower of shy and exquisite good-breeding; different again, in her way and degree, from pretty little girls of seventeen as hitherto known to him. Above all she speaks to him of Chad after a fashion that intensifies his consciousness, his suspicion, as it were, of differences. Chad's being in confirmed relation with her at all, her being interested in Chad and at all socially bound up with him: these things have for Strether—and with all due deference, with all allowance made, for the young man's improved and transformed state—an element of mystification, of slight perplexity, even from the first hour: such an odd sort of personal, or social promotion or transposition do they seem to represent for the boy as known to him in other lights. However, this whole occasion puts so many new meanings into things, does its little part toward shifting so many landmarks and confounding so many small assumptions, that perhaps one case of ambiguity doesn't count much more than another. His judgments, conclusions, discriminations are more or less in solution—in the pot, on the fire, stewing and simmering again, waiting to come up in what will be doubtless new combinations. This whole occasion, I repeat, is a picture and an admonition for him; and among the things it does, it throws him again with the young artist-man, Chad's friend, whom he likes, who is cuter, more 'intellectual' and aesthetic, than Chad, and with whom he has some amusing and suggestive moments. With his enlarged and intensified vision of a life containing—though indeed, by what he makes out, also more or less lacking—ingredients and influences closed to him and, at his actual age, forfeited and foregone, the 'too late' comes immensely home to him, yet only to stir in him the impulse to do the whole thing at least an imaginative justice. He can't, at such a time of day, begin to live—for he feels, besides, with all the rush of the reaction against his past, that he *hasn't* lived: yet there stirs in him a dumb passion of desire, of rebellion, of God knows what, in respect to his still snatching a little super-sensual hour, a kind of vicarious joy, in that *freedom of another* which he has found himself, by an extraordinary turn of the wheel, committed to weigh in the balance: a connection not, however, on the spot, so much taking in Chad's case as that of young Burbage before-mentioned, whose own sense of his opportunities strikes him as perhaps not quite adequate. It's to young Burbage, at any rate, that he indulges in some such little outburst as the one retailed in my preliminary pages—the conditions and effect of which my story more or less reproduces. I leave nothing untouched in fine, that may make of this Sunday afternoon in the old Paris garden, in a circle profuse in intimations, the kind of moral 'dishing' for Strether that I have already glanced at.

When they separate he feels that a relation, a link, of a sort, that will have both more to give him and to ask of him, has formed itself for him with Mme de Vionnet. She asks him to come and see her; she wants to see him again; she is gracious, encouraging, benevolent: and yet all for what? Mysteries, mysteries: he stands in a world of mystery. He doesn't at all know her really—he feels that; but queerer yet is it that he feels he doesn't at all really, at this time of day, know even himself. Has she addressed herself to some conception of him purely delusive and erroneous?—or to some element in him of which he has himself been unconscious, but which she has, with prodigious penetration, made out, in half an hour, as a possibility? Well, he will see.

He walks away, through the grave and impressive old streets of the Faubourg Saint-Germain, with Miss Gostrey, and as soon as they have got, after a spell of silence at first, to a certain distance, he puts her, stopping short, the abrupt question, full of tacit references: '*Isn't* it for her daughter . . . ?'

'That she's nursing your young friend?' They have stopped on a quiet corner of the Rue de l'Université; the day and the hour are tranquil there, and the straight, narrow vista of the austere, aristocratic street stretches before them. For a moment they look at each other, and Strether's companion just visibly hesitates. 'Yes,' she then brings out with decision; and after their eyes have again met they resume their walk; in the course of which—for he sees her home—she is very interesting about Mme de Vionnet, whom she also particularly rejoices to have encountered again. Their acquaintance goes back to old days of school at Geneva, where this charming woman was a *pensionnaire* slightly older, but not much, than herself; a rather isolated young thing, the daughter of a French father and an English mother who, left a widow, had married again—married some second foreigner. The girl was then clever, already charming, polyglot, speaking French and English, and even German, equally well, doing everything, in fact, well that she touched. Afterwards, however, it appeared that she had not had a happy hand at marrying. Miss Gostrey, after a considerable interval, had again met her; by which time her mother, otherwise engaged and entangled, impatient, preoccupied, precipitate, had made for her a summary match, assisted by her possession of a certain sufficient *dot,* with a Frenchman of supposedly the best condition, who yet, in spite of it, had not at all turned out well. Miss Gostrey has lights on the Comte de Vionnet, with whom his young wife was still living at the moment of this second period of observation. But things had even then been ominous, and the tolerably prompt separation, of which she had also heard, was not a thing to surprise her. She believes the husband still to be living and the pair to be on irreconcileable terms; but she also knows how little there can be a question for them of divorce, each of them belonging to the kind of *monde* that, in France, doesn't practise it. Of the kind of *monde* they do belong to she gives Strether all due, all manageable or communicable, notion, putting the presumptions before him vividly and interestingly enough. She particularises, makes him understand it—all of which, however, are processes rather concerning the author than the reader. Strether's acquaintance with Mme de Vionnet, and the conditions of the lady's identity and existence, are, in fine, ushered in—as to which it is sufficient that Miss Gostrey is helpful. Strether, at all events, on the occasion I speak of, sees her home, but doesn't go in, having at the moment another engagement. So, before her door, reverting, taking things up again, they have another word: 'Yes, you *do* see,' he asks, 'don't you? that charming little girl as having done it?'

But she is not, for the instant, all there. 'Done what?'

'Why, saved Chad.'

'Oh yes—as we said. One sees it. The charming little girl has done it. It's *she* who has saved Chad.' And on this they separate.

Strether forms a theory which more or less fits the case—the theory that Chad is more or less in love with Mlle de Vionnet, that her mother has much fostered it, that the young man is a good deal—and not unnaturally—under that charming person's influence, and that he wants to make an end of past complications and mistakes. He wants to marry, thinks it the best thing for himself, and sees in this young girl so highly civilized and so perfectly brought up, so amiable, so pretty, so attractive, an opportunity with much in its favour. But he is afraid, a little; hangs off, is waiting to have quite made up his mind and thereby be strong: all on account of his mother. He has his instinct, his conviction, that his mother will be inimically affected toward such a marriage, as mixing him up exactly with elements—the elements of absence, preparation, 'Europe'—against which she has so much been pleading; and he doesn't want to have the inevitable battle with her before his mind is wholly made up. Strether puts him indeed the question, and he meets it with a negative; denies that he is either in love with the young lady or intending to marry her. But meanwhile Strether has had to report to his mother— finding it more and more difficult to do so with lucidity; and meanwhile, further, he has been to see Mme de Vionnet. From this latter moment his own attitude, mission, simplicity and cogency of position on the whole question in which his presence in Paris has originated—from this latter moment these things undergo inevitable modification. A whole process begins to take form in him which is of the core of the subject, and the steps and shades in the representation of which I cannot pretend here to adumbrate. Chad's case becomes for him a concrete case in a kind of big general question that his actual experience keeps more and more putting to him; so that he finds himself each day more in the presence of a re-sponsibility much less simple than the one he had braced himself to incur. And Mme de Vionnet becomes the most determinant cause of this revolution, this interesting process—becomes so simply by being, and by showing herself, exactly what she is. Though there are always, and more than enough, round about Strether, mysteries, ambiguities and things equivocal, yet one or two convictions and impressions thicken for him, stiffen, harden—and one of these is the estimate of the value of such a relation, for any young man, as such a woman as Mme de Vionnet represents. The value of this relation grows clear and high, to his eyes; and almost grotesque becomes the kind of revision he has to make of the bundle of notions with which he started from home. They all cluster about a woman, and there *is* a woman, most unmistakeably and strikingly. But it's a different thing from what he has mapped out to come to plead, to come to pull, against *her*. The person of most personal charm, indisputably, that poor Strether has ever met, arrays herself on one side, and the group of interests and associations on behalf of which he has proposed to carry Chad off arrays itself on the other. The bustling business at home, the mercantile mandate, the counter, the ledger, the bank, the 'advertising interest,' embody mainly the special phase of civilization to which he must recall his charge—and a totally other cluster of forces weave the ad-verse tangle. Singularly, admirably Mme de Vionnet comes after a little to stand, with Strether, for most of the things that make the *charm* of civilization as he now revises and imaginatively reconstructs, morally reconsiders, so to speak, civilization.

This is a summary sketch of what takes place in my hero's spirit in consequence of this new contact—and I needn't insist on the necessity weighing on the author to paint the contact in a manner to justify it. The whole thing must more or less stand or fall by the way in which both Strether and Mme de Vionnet are done. The latter, of course, is a magnificent little subject, and the artist must be left alone with her. There is much in her—alas, for the artist's ease, *too* much. But the thing none the less works out. One of its workings is that, even to Streth-er's consciousness, she *knows* what she wishes and tries for. She isn't spoiled for him by his analysis of the situation. What is spoiled for him, on the other hand, is his freedom of communication with Mrs. Newsome, which he has sought to make possible by making it really candid, by throwing his whole vision of the matter upon her intelligence and her sympathy. He tells her what he sees. He tells her what he does. He tells her what he thinks. He tells her what he feels. The more, at this point, everything grows, the more he tries, by letter, to keep her in touch with it. Of course he reflects that, after all, what he is doing isn't the very definite thing he came out to do—which was to bring Chad home. Instead of there being representable for her in his life a detachment, a removal, from the female element, there can only strike her as being a greater and stranger abundance of it, and in forms difficult to give her, really, a just notion of. As things go, none the less, Strether has by this time been in a manner frank with Chad as well—only, by the time that hour is able to strike, the young man is shrewd enough himself to make out that, for consistency on his friend's part, the assault is made, the charge sounded, too late. Chad has had a kind of happy instinct in making things play on to the juncture at which poor Strether has become sceptical—at which, accordingly, consequently, he can only do his business at a sore disadvantage. The young man declines to meet any of the propositions with which his visitor is charged—and yet has the covert triumph of seeing that visitor not throw up the game. Strether doesn't break off and go home—Strether stays on and fairly consecrates the situation by his anxious presence. This is what Chad sees, and what Mme de Vionnet sees, and what Strether himself sees, and sees that they see, and sees above all that the lady at home sees. He isn't straight, as it may be called, and he knows it; isn't at all straight after he finds himself not only consenting, but liking, to discuss the question with Mme de Vionnet herself—or even with Miss Gostrey. It isn't a question he came out to discuss at all. He came out to do what he could, but everything is altered for him by the fact that nothing, damn it, is as simple as his scheme. Chad was to have been simple, for instance; but even Chad isn't. Least of all is he now himself. What would have been straight would have been so almost equally, as it were, in either case. If it would have been simple to be able to 'write back': 'It's all right; he consents to come; I come with him, I bring him, only just taking a little turn off with him—perhaps to Norway and Sweden; in which case we sail about the middle of next month': so likewise it would have been comparatively plain-going to have to say: 'He absolutely won't come at all—and you'll have to come out yourself; so that, so far as I'm concerned, it's a failure, and I shall just look about me a bit on my own hook and take ship to rejoin you three or four weeks hence'—so likewise, I repeat, *that* would have been, though disappointing, yet manageable, natural and final. But somehow, on what *does* take place everything is different. Nothing is manageable, nothing final—nothing, above all, for poor Strether, natural. I repeat that he has almost a sense of the uncanny. I repeat, as a good little note of his fallacious forecast, that he has really thought, as a 'resource,' as a clever stroke, of the way it might have eased difficulties off just to *coax* Chad aside for some small sanitary and, as it were, disinfecting jaunt through some one of those regions vaguely figuring to Strether as the more marked homes and haunts of earnestness. If there are smiles for this *naïveté* later, the first smiles are yet all his very own. There is a passage of irony for him, in the connection, with Miss Gostrey. Well, he finds himself sinking, as I say, up to his middle in the Difference—difference from what he expected, difference in Chad, difference in everything; and the Difference, I also again say, is what I give.

'No: Chad won't come'—he has, accordingly, presented to communicate that. But what he has *not* to communicate with it is that he will therefore reappear without him. He won't reappear without him—that is practically what he has very soon to let Mrs. Newsome see; and as he can't reappear *with* him the complication is one that takes, so far as she is concerned, a good deal of explaining. Candid and explicit as he meanwhile tries to be, there are things he *can't* explain. It has been part of his characteristic understanding with the lady at home, and part of her own with him, that if Chad is really, as may be so well on the cards, painfully unamenable, he himself is not—out of any excessive conscience in respect to service or duty owing, to remain too long mixed up, too long in a state of contact that was originally at best rather to be deprecated. That last is a distinct note, one of a great many even, in the relation of Strether and Mrs. Newsome—the feeling she has so much had *for* him, the anxious, scrupulous feeling; which is not wholly unlike, moreover, the state of mind he has really, beforehand, rather been in about himself. They have between them—they had it, at least, to begin with almost equally—a sense that he can't morally, or even personally, cheapen himself too much in the business, can't too long hang about it, rub against it, give himself away for it. *She,* in fact, is very high and fine in all this view of it; is very high and fine indeed altogether—to the point even of being ready rather to let Chad go than to regard with any complacency the prostitution, so to speak, of poor Strether. Reflections and reverberations of all this play over the scene. Chad has meanwhile continued to deny, however, to our friend that he has his eye on Mlle de Vionnet, that her mother has, to any such end, hers on him, and that the question of his marrying the girl has come up between them. They are simply all three the best of friends, and they have made for him a kind of charming second home. Isn't that enough? He puts the case to Strether with every appearance of frankness—pleads quite explicitly for the kind of privilege it is to be *as* he is with *ces dames,* who weren't at all likely to have taken up with one of his type, and who have been, simply, incredibly nice and charming to him. He speaks of the matter as really quite a recognized anomaly—but that doesn't diminish the value he sets on it. His effect on Strether is, curiously, that of moving him without really quite convincing him; the latter assents, in a word, without quite believing. He throws himself moreover again, as it were, on Miss Gostrey; and she again tells him to let her shrewdness answer for it that the question of the marriage is really—though disavowed for whatever reasons of prudence and diplomacy, whatever precautions required by the possible interference of the obnoxious Monsieur de Vionnet—the tie. Strether takes this from her, fitting it fairly into impressions of his own; though there is one thing that does stick in his crop: the question, namely, of why Chad won't at least go home for long enough to see his mother herself and have things out with her at Worcester. Chad promises of course to do this—admits the propriety of it; yet evidently has no intention of doing it at all soon. His perpetual postponement has therefore a motive—is the result of some obscure coercion; and Strether of course connects Mme de Vionnet with it. Yet at the same time he doesn't see her own reasons, or why she should have so peculiarly much to fear. In fine he goes on from day to day and from week to week; only, when he has done so a certain time, he finds himself landed in the *volte-face* in which the process I have described as taking place in him is practically to culminate. Various special things, a business-chance of importance in particular, depend for Chad upon an immediate change of life, a general radical rupture; and yet one fine day, in the presence of news from home that has brought everything immensely to a head, Strether's emphatic word to him is suddenly: 'No then—don't. I seem to see my "mission" differently. Stay as you are.'

'And will you then,' says the young man, wonderfully pleased and impressed, 'see me through?'

Strether has to think another moment; then he takes his jump. 'I'll see you through.'

But immediately afterwards, to make up for this grave inconsequence, he cables to his friend at home that his recommendation to her is, if she at all conveniently can, to come straight out. He more than half then, for a day or two, expects her; but two or three things may happen, and he holds himself in suspense—as also in readiness. She will either cable that she starts, or she will cable to him, more or less emphatically, and rather more than less, to come straight back to *her*. He has thought it over, and if she does so, believes that he will do it: though now really seeing how little he wants to. However, at the expectant word from her he *will*— yes, positively, he will. He gets no answer for three or four days, during which he is awfully restless, and yet with it all has a queer sense of freedom hitherto unknown to him. He *will* go—yes, again, if she calls; but even if he does go things will be somehow, and rather strangely, different: and his sense of freedom is partly just in *that*. Then at the end of the waiting a reply comes. But it proves to be neither a summons to Strether nor an announcement of Mrs. Newsome's embarkation. It is different—something he hadn't thought of. It announces the immediate departure of the Pococks—which is a surprise. But Strether sees a good deal in it—sees more the more he thinks.

III

Mrs. Pocock, as has been mentioned, is the daughter of Mrs. Newsome, Chad's elder sister, married to a partner in the family business, whose own young sister, a girl of about the same age as Mlle de Vionnet, accompanies them. They promptly arrive—a young couple of extremely marked attributes—as little Mamie Pocock is, in her way, the same: a lively (in their way) young American pair, who have been to Europe once before—immediately after their marriage; and consider (so far at least as Mrs. Pocock is concerned) that they know it very well. I can't 'do' this trio for you here—and they will take all proper doing in the book, where they will be adequately attended to; I limit myself to designating their office, which is in a manner that of rather tacitly, coldly and austerely superseding and suspending Strether in *his* function; that at all events of representing Mrs. Newsome on the spot and putting in their plea on behalf of the business, on behalf of the family,

on behalf of propriety, on behalf of his country, on behalf of all the claims that
Strether appears to have handled so ineffectually. As Mrs. Newsome remains personally out of the action, so now she is represented in it by these fresh emissaries.
But Mrs. Pocock herself is the one who principally, or exclusively, counts in this
respect; Mrs. Pocock is a sharp type and *(D.V.)* a vivid picture; Mrs. Pocock
makes for interest and entertainment. She brings, as it were, her mother's ultimatum—which is that if Chad doesn't come home immediately he needn't, so far
as his material advantage is concerned, ever come home at all; Mrs. Newsome
being in possession of options and having command of alternatives upon which
she is actually free to close. Strether is confronted thus with the whole crisis and,
most sharply of all, with what it means for himself. This latter element is more
or less implied—or even, doubtless, I shall make it explicit; the remarkable young
woman, who has nothing in common with her brother, being fully *au courant* of
the state of affairs between her mother and their friend, and empowered to speak
and act, conscientiously, lucidly, indignantly, if necessary, *for* that lady. Mrs.
Pocock arrives, in other words, with a great deal of accumulated resentment,
disapproval, virtue, surprise. Her husband, in truth, is on quite another foot; her
husband is an example, in characteristically vulgar form, and with all due humourous effect, of the same 'fatal' effect of European opportunities on characters
giving way too freely, which Strether more subtly embodies. Pocock, a traitor in
the camp, a humorous, surreptitious backer of his brother-in-law and their friend
does, in short, all he can to amuse us. He has his personal function, in a word—
for which he must be trusted. All the complexities of the drama deepen here;
things grow closer and more tense. Poor Waymark, thrown off from Strether,
whose strange laxities and perversities he deplores, whose general sensibility and
surrender, as he can't help thinking them, he regards as the reverse of edifying,
rebounds to Mrs. Pocock, who strikes up with him an alliance that they both
regard as rather a fine, free intimacy—almost a 'European' affair. They stand
together, they confer together, they exult and lament together, go about together
generally, hold the same opinions and invoke the same conclusions, cheer and
comfort and sustain each other. The whole comedy, or tragedy, the drama, whatever we call it, of Strether's and Chad's encounter of the new complications and
relations springing from the Pococks' presence, from the necessity, for instance,
bravely to confront them with Mme de Vionnet and her daughter, and to confront
Mme de Vionnet and her daughter with *them*—this is a thing, I need scarcely say,
I am not trying thus, *currente calamo,* to formulate. Mme de Vionnet, in it all, is
magnificent; Mme de Vionnet is wonderful; but these things are no more than
what she is throughout. I repeat that, little as I project her here—for the smallest
development of that attempt would take me too far—I must be trusted with her.
Mrs. Newsome and Mrs. Pocock have hatched it between them that *one* aid to the
recovery of Chad may be possibly just this putting in his path of the little Pocock
girl. Strange and ignorant complacencies, fathomless fallacies, have attended this
idea. She is thus produced in Paris for the young man's benefit, and is thus seen
to figure face to face with and in opposition to the little Vionnet girl—who is as
wonderful, in her way, about this introduced representative of a different type of
manners, as her mother. Contrasts and oppositions naturally here play straight up.

The Vionnets and the Pococks, Chad and his sister, Pocock and his brother-in-law, Chad and Pocock's sister, Strether and Pocock, Pocock and Strether, Strether and everyone and everything, but Strether and Mrs. Pocock in especial, with everything brought to a head by *her*—there is no lack of stuff; above all as, on the very eve of the last-named lady's arrival, a sharp thing has happened for Strether.

It has suddenly then come out—suddenly to *his* mind—that Mlle de Vionnet is engaged to be married, only not a bit to Chad. To a very different person, a Frenchman of 'position'—a match markedly congruous and suitable, a candidate presented by her father, unexpectedly insistent, and in whom the proper conditions meet. Strether's theory has therefore sharply broken down—the theory, moreover, which Miss Gostrey has so backed up. The last thing that has happened before the apparition of the Pococks has been precisely a scene with that lady on the question of this so unexpected issue. It takes place, as happens, also on the eve of a departure of her own for a temporary absence. Strether, rather annoyed and disconcerted, charges her with the grossness of her mistake. But the way she meets the charge surprises him the more. She is astonishing. 'It was no mistake. I didn't believe it.'

'Didn't really believe what you said, what you made *me* believe—and therefore consciously misled me?'

She faces it—has to brace herself to confess. 'Yes, my poor dear man—monster as you must think me. I saw that what was gong on for Chad wasn't at all, whatever it might be, *that*. And yet I thought it best to make *you* think otherwise.'

'To make a fool of me?'

'Oh, you know—for your good.'

'But I don't know at all. 'What "good" are you talking about? Why did you do such a thing?' He is troubled—having quite, in the teeth of some difficulties, cherished the theory in question, which has given him another leg to stand on.

Challenged thus, then, she has one of her odd hesitations, evasions, embarrassements. 'Well, I'll tell you when I come back.'

But he insists. 'What the deuce then *is* going on?'

It is, however, for the moment, all he can get from her. 'I'll tell you when I come back.'

She has gone, but meanwhile the fact of Chad's definite *non*-engagement, and with it the breakdown of the most presentable of the grounds for promoting, for condoning, his recalcitrance has had to be produced, has had inevitably to come straight up, for Mrs. Pocock. It facilitates, of course, her position, puts an arm in her hand. What motive that can conceivably remain *is* then presentable? She is moreover more fully armed now—or by so much the less obstructed—in respect to her putting forward her little sister-in-law. But we see what comes of that. *She* sees, and has to make her mother see—constantly, as she is, communicating and cabling (nothing having ever been known like the cabling that goes on—alarming even to Chad, immensely amusing to Pocock, fraught with strange possibilities for Strether and prodigious to Mme de Vionnet). Precipitated thus is the kind of *crux* in his position that Mrs. Pocock's manner of acting for her mother has already prepared. More than she has yet done, as it were, she has it out with Strether why they have come. She puts it in its light, and she gives him the warning that she herself believes to be admirably disinterested and magnanimous, purely conscientious and solicitous. I should premise that her brother has put it to her on her having to recognize the humiliating futility of her attempt to catch him with any such bait as Miss Pocock, that, in respect to his consenting to do what appears to them all so imperative at home, he will stand or fall then by what Strether now says, will let the latter absolutely answer for him, determine his line, determine, quite, as it practically is, his fate. This is a special and superior stroke of Chad's—this inspiration of throwing himself, at the psychological moment, thus completely on our friend. But the inspiration has come, he has taken the measure of the dependence that, for backing him up, he can really place on Strether; and now, acting *on* that dependence, he passes to his sister his word of honour. The scene between them moreover has had other elements—elements rather confounding to some of Mrs. Pocock's complacencies: he really lets fly at her, that is, for the folly of her supposing him amenable to her ridiculous view of the little Pocock. He is fairly angry with her—in respect to what she has thus taken *him* for; and, though he has, to do him justice, tried not to be rude, he has raised for her a sufficiently startling and bewildering curtain, revealed to her, in a manner that she feels to be quite lurid and that makes her shudder off across the sea, the intimate difference now existing in their standards of value. She is *proud* of the little Pocock. *Why* the inspiration just mentioned—the inspiration of standing or falling by Strether's final word—has thus operated in Chad, we also interestingly know. The reason is partly the result of definite passages between them—at one of which I have already glanced; passages from which Chad had eagerly snatched Strether's general sense that, really, the young man has succeeded in growing, by whatever obscure, whatever nefarious process, comparatively too civilized for *him,* Strether, to find it in his responsible conscience to urge as a substitute for that process a mere relapse to the precious place—beautiful business-place, with a big chance for any, for every, new assertion of the paternal smartness, though it may be—which has, at much inconvenience to the family interest, been kept, or rather been all but lost, for him at home. That vision of Strether's attitude is part of the ground, I say, on which Chad's stand to Mrs. Pocock is made; but he has also been confirmed and illuminated by the so considerable acute judgment and observation of Mme de Vionnet, who has not lost, not wasted her time with Strether, and has answered to Chad for the degree to which they can count on him. She has worked, in fine, and the necessary effect has been produced. What takes place accordingly is, as I have indicated, Mrs. Pocock's supreme appeal to their good friend, in which she gives her point, all her deputed meaning, its full value.

We know what this full value is, what Strether 'stands to lose' by any perversity or, as Mrs. Newsome's daughter really takes upon herself to brand it, disloyalty. 'If he doesn't look out, doesn't take care, etc., etc.'—why, he need scarcely, she supposes, dot the i's for him in respect to the natural consequences. If he doesn't, in a word, look out and take care, he forfeits everything comfortable and pleasant that his prospect of marriage with Mrs. Newsome has caused to cluster so richly about his future: the confidence, the esteem, the affection of a noble woman, the good opinion, frankly, for that matter, of a noble community; and at any rate the promise of ease and security, a refined, and even a luxurious, home for the rest of his days. Mrs. Pocock goes so far as to be even a trifle vulgar—in her emphasis and impressiveness—on this article of the luxury, on that of poor Strether's exposed time of life, and, in fine, on that of his having perhaps never yet, by any marked success made, in the course of his variegated career, of anything, created the presumption that he will be able to retire on honours, still less on more substantial accumulations, due to his own abilities. She goes further still—glances for him at her own and her brother's different, but natural, view of the marked favour shown him, conspicuous benefits showered on him, by their mother; and makes the point that he surely owes her—*her*, Mrs. Pocock—something for that indulgence of his interests to which she has lent herself even at the expense of her sense of her own. She also makes the point that, if he were only himself really awake to the former, he would perhaps make out that the game played by Chad is, after all, in essence, but a game calculated to produce such an embroilment, and thereby such a consequent rupture (rupture between their mother and the object of her infatuation) as he himself may pecuniarily profit by. She draws Strether's attention, in other words, both to the way she has—in deference to him— kept her hands off Mrs. Newsome's strange, slightly ridiculous (as many people would, and do, think it) project, at such an age, of a second marriage; and to the perfectly discernible circumstance that if Chad had been acting precisely from a masked hostility to such a consummation, such an admission of an outsider to the privilege of 'pickings,' he couldn't have acted—well, a bit differently. She leaves him, finally, to pronounce as to which of them strikes him as having—to a truly discriminating view—the more fortunate effect upon his personal opportunity. He is accordingly so left then, Strether, and he takes these arguments in, looks them completely in the face, and is, by the turn of that screw, moved so much the nearer to the *crux* of his case. There is even at this point one definitely simple thing for him to do; which is to place himself immediately on Mrs. Pocock's side, signify to her that he can do nothing more in Paris, and that he believes *she* can do nothing, and so, accelerating, determining, her renouncement and her retreat, confess to their common failure and return with her to America. The failure will not, over there, positively have helped him, helped the Review, helped his other employments and emoluments, with Mrs. Newsome; but, at least, with earnest effort earnestly shown, with proper patience properly recorded, with final impatience, not to say moral disgust, inevitably triumphant and determinant, his prospects need not be found to be irrecoverably dished. Chad will be thrown overboard, practically, by such a course; but Strether will at any rate himself have testified to a zeal in Mrs. Newsome's service sufficient to enable him to count on her appointing, as his reward, the too-long delayed day of their nuptials. These things, as I say, he can only turn well over—which we assist (as we assist at everything) at the process of his doing. The upshot is, none the less, only the intenser impossibility, to his spirit, of the step just defined. He *can't* go home with Mrs. Pocock, he *won't* go home with Mrs. Pocock; above all it's impossible to him to throw Chad over. He has given him his word that he will see him through—though, at the same time, Chad has given Mrs. Pocock *his* word that he will surrender, once his summons is distinctly pronounced, to Strether's decision.

Strether has, in this tighter squeeze of his crisis, to take again a little time, to put every question to himself once again, and clear up, so far as he can, his ambiguities. There are one or two that won't clear up: the fact that the supposition of Chad's designs on Mlle de Vionnet has been dispelled leaves, for instance, a vague residuum of the discomfortable, the equivocal, that he doesn't quite know what to do with. What does anything, what does everything, in the intimacy of a youth after all comparatively crude and a woman after all much older and admirably fine and subtle, mean if it doesn't mean—well, what it might at the worst? There is one thing indeed that it *may* signify, and to this explanation Strether sufficiently clings. It *is,* in the light of it, the mother, not the daughter, that Chad has all the while been in love with, and it's in respect to the mother that he is hanging on and on. He has the inextinguishable hope of some turn of the situation that may render their marriage possible. She may consent to a divorce, or M. de Vionnet may, by a kind and just Providence, suddenly and happily be snuffed out. Such are conceivably, to Chad's mind, by Strether's interpretation, the possibilities; and others, that match them, may prevail in that of Mme de Vionnet herself: though *her* 'hanging on' is, at the best, a phenomenon requiring at once more analysis and more elucidation. What requires very little of either, however, and what thereby has most to contribute to our friend's growing stiffness of back, is that—confound the whole thing—he has by this time *seen* too much, felt too much, to retrace his steps to his old standpoint. The distance that separates him from it is, measured by mere dates, of the slightest, but it is virtually ground that he has got for ever behind him. He is conscious of his evolution; he likes it—wouldn't for the world not have had it; albeit that he fully sees how fatal, in a manner, it has been for him. But if he's dished, he *is,* and all that is left for him is to say what he can as mere interesting, inconvenient experience. He is out of pocket by it, clearly, materially; but he has a handful of gold-pieces for imagination and memory. Mrs. Pocock has signified to him that she awaits his supreme reply, awaits his final beneficent interposition with Chad; and, for congruity, he conforms by appearing to take three days for the benefit of the doubt. His intention is to cultivate, during this period, such detachment as he may; to get off somewhere by himself; to see, for a little, nothing of Chad, of Mme de Vionnet, or of Mrs. Newsome's representative—and then come back with his reply. He's rather bored with them all, *en fin de compte,* as the people about him say; he is even a little overdone with other people's adventures, and wouldn't mind a trifling one on his own account, which should yield him a little less worry. Miss Gostrey, after the absence on the eve of which he took leave of her, has, to his knowledge, returned; but he doesn't want particularly to see even *her.* Still less does he wish to see Waymark, who, for that matter, has ended, as a result of the spectacle of his behaviour, by cultivating an estrangement from him that makes Strether half melancholy (so almost insanely odd, or madly morbid, it is) and half merry.

What does in fact befall during this little interval is that he tumbles for two or three days, in spite of himself, into the arms of poor solitary-prowling Pocock, whom the preoccupations of the latter's wife, her earnest exchange of impressions and convictions with Waymark in especial, have left at the mercy of a good deal of more or less con[s]oled leisure. Strether is kind to him, easy with him, amused at him, and, above all, abundantly conscious of *his* reactions and 'game.' Pocock doesn't at all really want Chad brought back—doesn't believe in him as an active element in the business, and doesn't require him as an additional participant in what has been roughly denominated the general and particular 'pickings.' But this is one side, and Pocock has his mixture. He is amused at his mother-in-law's baffled state—a state rare for her and which he has never known the joy, so much as he would have liked it, of directly promoting. All his instinct is to promote it now by acting on his rather coarse divination of the nature of Strether's independence, and above all on his still livelier perception of the character of Chad's own. For Strether, at all events, he performs the present function, while they go about together and Strether shows him bits of Paris, things in it that he mightn't otherwise see—though not always the very things he wants; performs the function of representing as vulgarly as possible the whole particular mass of interests at home on behalf of which the long arm has reached itself out for Chad. Strether, as I have noted, has known the late Newsome and been well aware of what he didn't like about him and what he hasn't, since then, liked to think of and to remember in him and of him; but Pocock, in their walks and talks—Pocock will do nothing but talk of matters at home—happens to bring to his acquaintance two or three facts, illustrative of the deceased's character and practices, of which he has been unwitting and that excite in him a still more marked approach to disgust. They complete his vision, his memory, his theory of the late Newsome. It's the voice of the late Newsome that, as it were from beyond the tomb, makes the demand of Chad, reaches out the arm to draw him back to the supervision of the 'advertising department.' It's as if there were two elements in the youth (as to whom I should take this occasion, hitherto neglected, to parenthesise that my situation requires in him, more perhaps than I have adequately noted, a certain element of the plastic and the wavering, a rigour of attitude not wholly unqualified, so that the drop of the balance for him may, after all, just be a matter of a push, administered with due force, from another hand). One of these elements is discernibly of the none-too-edifying paternal strain, while it is the other, singularly different, that his recent, his actual, situation happens, however deleteriously from some points of view, the point of view in especial of the home-circle, to have fostered on lines not, at any rate, prevailingly vulgar. Pocock, the contact of Pocock, the mind, the manners, the conversation, allusions, ideals, general atmosphere of Pocock, rub into Strether afresh the discomfortable truth that it is in the name of the paternal heritage that he has been launched upon his own errand. At the risk of seeming here to repeat what I may have already repeated, I note further Strether's consciousness, so unwittingly stimulated by Pocock, that the general heritage of the late Newsome is what has above all enabled his widow to render *him* her signal services as well as to diffuse her conspicuous general benefits; so that if he does marry a rich woman, it will be a woman rich in just these connections that have now begun somehow to change their look, to grow ugly and smell badly, for him. These things are all aggravations, attenuations, features and forms of his 'responsibility.' The thing presents itself to him anew in the hardness and clearness of its essential simplicity, and, hammering away for you thus for lucidity's sake, I once more re-formulate his intenser impression of it.

Chad is to 'take up' something, and if he doesn't take it up, there is something, something important, a chance, a share, a haul, that he thereby loses. If he does take it up he takes it under Strether's influence; and this favourable exercise of Strether's influence confirms and consecrates the latter's own personal chance and tie at Worcester. I reiterate these things here on Strether's behalf, in order to intensify the fact that, as he acts now, he does so on full reflection. What this reflection, roughly stated, amounts to then is: 'No, I'll be hanged if I purchase the certainty of being coddled for the rest of my days by going straight against the way in which all these impressions and suggestions of the last three months have made me feel, and like to feel, and want to feel. Whatever is the matter with Chad, it strikes me as having done more for him as a man and a gentleman than would have been done, or than will yet be done, by his having remained in, or being again introduced and compressed into, the box that we have flattered ourselves can be once more made to contain him. It has really made him quite over. As between Mme de Vionnet and the advertising department, then, I decide for Mme de Vionnet, and if my expression, my action *is* to tip down the scale, why, let it tip, and I'll take the consequences. They will really, whatever they may be, immensely interest, and in their way, doubtless, even amuse me. They will represent something—meagre and belated and indirect and absurd as it may be—that I shall have done for my poor old infatuated and imaginative self. I didn't know I had it in me, and it's worth all the journey and all the worry to have found out. It will have cost me—I feel sure, it's in my bones. I forecast the whole thing—everything that my engagement to that wonderful woman at home, so full of high qualities too, represents and promises; but I'm not going to let such a circumstance prevent me. I'll keep my promise to Chad; I'll say to him: "Do as the interest of your situation *here* most prescribes—and say frankly and freely that it's the sense in which I've positively advised you." I stand by that—and *vogue la galère!'*

He breaks away from Pocock, not being able to 'stand,' in the state of his nerves, much more of him; breaks away on the third or fourth day of this little episode, and it's in the course of a day—a day 'off'—that he does succeed in getting by himself, that another incident, full of further significance, of a very complicating kind, presents itself. The situation in now, I recall, that the question of Chad's engagement to Mlle de Vionnet is quite disposed of by the latter's otherwise-appointed nuptials; and that Mme de Vionnet knows—with Chad solicited, restless, precarious in her hands—that Strether has really, in effect, the casting vote for him, and for *her* so far as her fate is (so oddly, so mystifyingly) bound up with the young man's. Strether has made up his mind, and he is to see Mrs. Pocock, in accordance with it, so to speak, on the morrow; he is to give her that answer to her ultimatum on behalf of her mother, as it were, that she has signified to him that she awaits. Strether has it then, as I say, all ready, and in this condition he has taken the train to one of the suburbs of Paris quite at random, scarce knowing, and not much caring, where he is. The effect of his complete decision is a queer sense of freedom and almost of amusement. It's a lovely day of early summer; the aspect of things is such as to charm and beguile him—the air full of pictures and felicities and hints for future memory. Suddenly, with these predispositions, in a suburban village by the river, a place where people come out from Paris to boat, to dine, to dance, to make love, to do anything they like, he comes upon Mme de Vionnet and Chad together—Mme de Vionnet and Chad presented somehow in a light that, in spite of all preparation and previous perplexity, of all embarrassing questions and satisfactory and unsatisfactory answers, considerably startles and pulls him up. The case shows them, somehow, as they have not yet been shown; it represents them as positively and indubitably intimate with the last intimacy; it is, in a word, full, for Strether, of informing and convincing things. He meets it then and there as he can—which is the way they also, conscious, inconvenienced, but carrying the whole thing bravely off, deal, on their side, with the encounter. Each side acquits itself with such discretion and ease as it can command; and the passage between them is in fine full of interest. Of course I am not attempting in any degree whatever to represent or render it here, or to do more than thus glance at it and pass. They separate, on pretexts, and Strether goes back to Paris alone. But he goes back with a deeper and stranger sense, a sense that his responsibility is verily deep and sharp. It staggers him a little, and he has to brace himself afresh; he doesn't back down from his decision, but he rather wishes the incident hadn't occurred. At the same time he feels rather ashamed—ashamed, I mean, of his regret; for the essence of his attitude to himself on the whole business has been that what he *is* moved to he wants not to shirk. Here is a beautiful chance then not to shirk. He looks what he has seen in the face; he passes a discomfortable night on it; that is one way not to shirk. There are other ways too, and he vigorously cultivates them, for the next twenty-four hours, all. He shakes himself, snubs and scolds himself, brings himself sternly and rigidly into line. Why should he pusillanimously wish he mightn't so sharply have *known,* since all the value of his total episode, and all the enjoyment of it, has precisely been that 'knowing' was the effect of it? He is, all the same, rather inconsequently disposed not to go to Mrs. Pocock that very day with his answer; and while, exactly, he is hesitating as to the positively final immediacy and urgency of this step, another incident, not, superficially, at least, more simplifying than the previous, somewhat surprisingly overtakes him. He receives a visit from Mme de Vionnet, and Mme de Vionnet's visit is a wonderful affair, but which, again, I can, beyond naming it, really give you here no more than I have given you anything else. It gives her away to him—which is the last thing he had expected anything to do; and gives her away as the consequence of her fears. It's her fears, her weakness now, her surprising spilling of her cards, that definitely tell him, face to face, what he had previously neither really made out for himself, nor really dismissed: the strange fact—of an order both so obscure and so recorded—of the passion of this accomplished woman of almost forty for their so imperfectly accomplished young friend of a dozen years less. Strether is in the presence of more things than he has yet had to count with, things by no means, doubtless, explicitly, in his book; but with which, pitying the remarkable woman all the more that her present proceeding reduces her, for the hour, in some respects, to a tolerably common category, he does his best to get, as it were, into relation. He sees and understands, and such is the force in him of his alien and awkward tradition, that he has, almost like a gasping spectator at a thrilling play, to *see* himself see and understand. Mme de Vionnet is, precisely like some woman less clever and less rare, in a 'funk' about the possible loss of Chad. He has become a cherished necessity to her. Her passion simplifies and abases her; ranges her in a category; presents her as a case; does, in short, more things than I can now enumerate. Infinite tact and delicacy of *presentation* of course lavished on all this. But the upshot of it, after all, is but to confirm Strether's vision of the influence and the benefit the situation has represented for Chad. If he has found him transformed, that effect ceases to be wonderful in the presence, so vividly, of the forces making for it. Mme de Vionnet's visit is at any rate a frightened appeal. She comes to entreat him to *keep* Chad for her. They have both got scared the day before, but she in particular, and the more, all night, her fears and her imagination have dwelt on it, as to the way their friend may be practically affected by the impression they were conscious of making on him. She beseeches him not to be practically affected. She tells him, shows him, proves to him, how good she is for Chad. He is rueful as to assenting to that, but he is helpless as to denying it, and, not to multiply my words here, he at all events dismisses her with the reassurance that his view is his view, that he doesn't mean to take back any word he has given, that his mind was in fact, the day before, all made up to confirm it; and that, in fine, no 'impression' of anything or anybody now will have made any difference. Besides, for that matter, what has she supposed he had supposed? He has, really and truly, in his 'secret heart,' not known what he has supposed—and hence his sharp emotion, the upset to his nerves, on the previous day. But he doesn't tell Mme de Vionnet that.

She leaves him, and he does nothing that day—Chad, meanwhile, 'lying low' very markedly; but on the morrow he goes and reports himself to Mrs. Pocock. If his responsibility has been complicated and thickened it proves, none the less, after all, too much for him. He tells her—and the announcement is practically made to Mrs. Newsome—that he has thought over everything he has owed it to her to think over since their last interview, but that his attitude remains just what he was then obliged to let her fear it to be. He 'sides,' so to speak, with Chad; he holds that Chad, by meeting his mother's views, will give up more than he gains, and he has frankly expressed himself to him in that sense. He recognizes the effect his words, of which he has counted the cost, will probably have; but he has not been able to act in any other way. I pass briefly, for you, over this juncture, and over the effect of it on the Pocock party, who, with Waymark, shocked and scandalised—approximately or vulgarly speaking—in their train, are quickly determined by it to departure and disappearance. They withdraw from the scene, they return straightway home, with all the proper circumstances and concomitants. Strether has immediately afterwards gone to Chad and told him what he has done; his sentiment about him being that he can't quite, all the same, wash his hands of him. On the other hand, what can he do more for him than he has already done? He lingers in Paris a little—he has wanted to see the situation 'through.' But with the direction events have taken from him, it sufficiently comes over him that they *are* through. His imagination of them drops, and if he rather glosses over for the pair the quantity they have cost him, the last tribute strikes him, at last, as the very most he can manage. He does gloss it over—with Chad at least; he carries out, to his utmost, the spirit of his promise to 'make it all right.' That is a pious misrepresentation, in the interest of Chad's stability, absolutely precious, now, to Strether's imagination: but it is a part of the amusement and the harmless *panache* of his proceeding. He measures exactly, himself, the situation. He knows he won't make it all right. He knows he can't make it all right. He knows that, for Mrs. Newsome, it's all hideously wrong and must remain so. But he only (that is as with Chad) knows this; and he misrepresents, as I say, the question with what he believes to be a certain success—making the matter, at all events, and without much difficulty, none of Chad's business. It's the last thing moreover, naturally, that he conceives Chad as being touched by, or conceives, with any intensity, Mme de Vionnet.

After these things have happened, however, and especially after the departure of the Pococks, he has a kind of moral and intellectual drop or arrest—of the whole range of feeling that has kept him up hitherto—which makes him feel that his work is done, that his so strange, half-bitter, half-sweet experience is at an end, that what has happened, through him, has really happened *for* him, for his own spirit, for his own queer sense of things, more than for anyone or anything else, and that now he has no reason for stopping any longer. Now he *will* go back, and he gathers himself up, and he's ready. He has waited till the moment he wished—he couldn't have gone before; the whole affair had become a thing of his own that he had to watch and accompany, as it were, out of a deep inward necessity, sympathy, curiosity, perversity, if need were, to its conclusion; but he recognizes the conclusion, so far as *he* is concerned with it, when he sees it—recognizes that his hour has sounded. The sound is like the bell of the steamer calling him, from its place at the dock, aboard again, and by the same act ringing down the curtain on the play. He goes back to all the big Difference, over there, that he foresees—the big Difference of his having spoiled himself for any future favour from Mrs. Newsome, and spoiled the poor fatuous Review, as an implication and a consequence, for any future subsidy. These things, and many more things, are before him—evoked, projected, made vivid, made certain. But before he goes, on the eve of his departure, two other things happen which mark, to the extent of their interest and importance, that the curtain has *not* yet quite dropped, the play is not *yet* quite over. The first of these is an interview that he has with Mme de Vionnet, who either comes to see him again or addresses him an earnest request, which he complies with, to come to *her* (I've not yet determined which) after that last scene with Chad to which I have just referred. Of what has passed between them on this occasion she has, of course, immediately received from Chad all tidings, and, affected by it in more than one interesting manner, and moved, in particular, to the deepest gratitude, she has placed herself, in what she feels to be for the last time, in relation with him. On what Chad has told her, repeated to her, of his making everything 'all right,' as regards himself, his personal situation and responsibility, at home, she has her own impressions, suspicions, divinations, and, though she can do nothing *for* poor Strether, as it were, though she sees in him and in his behaviour more things than she can even be explicit about with him, she obeys an irresistible instinct in desiring once more to see him and, however poorly, to thank him. He has not, frankly, from a feeling quite absolute, though difficult to justify or—in this place, for instance—explain, wanted any further vision of Chad or contact with him, and he seeks none, and practically makes any, for the young man himself, impossible, after the just-above-mentioned passage. He has done with *him,* or at any rate feels that Chad has done, and that Chad (immensely, though perhaps after all a trifle ruefully, just a shade regretfully and anxiously, obliged) is ready, on his side, to let him pass away. But as to Mme de Vionnet, it's another affair, and to just a last sight of everything in her that he has found wonderful and abysmal, strange and charming, beautiful and rather dreadful, he thus finally adjusts and treats himself. The meeting, the scene, then, takes place, and is the happy and harmonious *pendant* (from the point of view, I mean, of interest and effect) of the previous one, the one referred to a moment ago, the scene of 'appeal' after Strether's encounter with the pair in the country and her consequent apprehension and commotion. But don't imagine I pretend to give it to you here. I merely mark it with this little cross as probably the most beautiful and interesting morsel in the book, and I would say most handsomely 'done'—say so did I admit that there can be any *difference* of morsels in any self-respecting work-of-art, where the morsel *not* handsomely done simply incurs one's own pity long before the critic—if there *were* a critic!—has cut the eye-teeth of any knowledge of *how* competently to kick it. You must leave me accordingly with this passage and with my treatment of it. It is really the climax—for all it can be made to give and to do, for the force with which it may illustrate and illuminate the subject—toward which the action marches straight from the first. So there it is.

The second of the two situations of which the one just noted is the first deals scarcely less handsomely with Strether's relation with poor Maria Gostrey, and with hers with him—taking it up again effectively, I should say, if it were correct to speak of it as having really at all dropped. But it hasn't really at all dropped; it has only seemed, here, to fall into the background through my not wanting to risk too much to confuse and complicate my statement by insistence, at every point, on its quite continuous function. I have not named Miss Gostrey in sketching the stages of the business after the arrival of the Pococks, but it is, from step to step, with the aid of her confirmed relation to Strether that I show what I need to show. It's a relation the fortunate friction of which projects light, the light of interpretation and illustration, upon all that passes before them, upon all causes and effects. After his question is settled, after the Pococks have gone and Waymark, as a sequel to a final brush with Strether and a presumably-not-at-all final sign from Mrs. Pocock, has gone with them; after Strether has seen Chad for the wind-up I have noted and then, as it were, washed his hands of him; after he has seen Mme de Vionnet on corresponding lines, there are two things he is left face to face with. One of these is what I have already so much more than sufficiently evoked, his end, the end of his play, of his stay, and his domestic penalty and consequences—all another business, all for him, on the spot, only taken for granted and accepted; the other is the presence, the personality, the general form and pressure of Maria Gostrey. *She* is his residuum—that of the three or four months' experience and drama after everything else has come and gone. He is there with her in Paris now alone, as it were; and I see a particular moment of the place and season: the midsummer emptiness reached, the flight of everyone, the rather stale hot, empty city—but with the sense of freedom and of a now strangely full initiation interfusing it all, which the pair seem, as it were, to have quite to themselves. Miss Gostrey, poor dear, but vivid and all herself to the last, is informed with the principle of standing by her friend, so to speak, to the end, and the meaning and moral of what she has done for him, the play of the circumstance that, all the while, she has just purely and simply fallen in love with him—these things gild with their declining rays this last of his complications. Here again I have something that I can't fully trot out for you; here again I can only put in the picture with a single touch of the brush. It will be brushed in another fashion in its order and proper light. Fate gives poor Strether, before she has done with him, just this other chance; and we see him see it and look it in the face and hold out his hand to it with half a kindness and half a renouncement; we see him all touched and intelligent about it, but we don't do anything so vulgar as to make him 'take up,' save for a friendship that he quite sincerely hopes may last, with poor convenient, amusing, unforgettable, impossible Gostrey. Very pretty, very charming and pleasant and droll and sad all this concluding but I don't want to represent every woman in the book, beginning with Mrs. Newsome, as having, of herself, 'made up' to my hero; for vivid and concrete and interesting as I desire to make him, the mark of the real never ceases to show in him, and with the real only the real—of verisimilitude, of consistency—consorts. But it's none the less a fact that Mrs. Newsome, Miss Gostrey, and poor magnificent Mme de Vionnet herself (though this last is a secret of secrets) have been, in the degree involved, agreeably and favourably affected by him. Mrs. Newsome has—as we fairly figure to ourselves—'proposed.' Mme de Vionnet has been, only, exquisite over what *might* have been! Miss Gostrey, at all events, doesn't repeat Mrs. Newsome by proposing, but Strether has as clear a vision of his opportunity as if she did— and he has even his moment of hesitation. This moment of hesitation is what we get—what I give. He shows her that he has it—that is, that he sees he can marry her on the morrow if he will—at all events on the morrow of his return to America, or (since she in that case will follow) on the morrow of *that;* is, as I say, everything that is pleasant and appreciative about it—everything but what he would be if he assented or accepted. He *can't* accept or assent. He won't. He doesn't. It's too late. It mightn't have been, sooner—but it is, yes, distinctly, now. He has come so far through his total little experience that he has come out on the other side—on the other side, even, of a union with Miss Gostrey. He must go back as he came—or rather, really, so quite other that, in comparison, marrying Miss Gostrey would be almost of the old order. Yes, he goes back other—and to other things. We see him on the eve of departure, with whatever awaits him *là-bas,* and their lingering, ripe separation is the last note.

P.S.—I should mention that I see the foregoing in a tolerable certitude of Ten Parts, each of 10,000 words, making thus a total of 100,000. But I should very much like my option of stretching to 120,000 if necessary—that is, adding an Eleventh and Twelfth Parts. Each Part I rather definitely see in Two Chapters, and each very full, as it were, and charged—like a rounded medallion, in a series of a dozen, hung, with its effect of high relief, on a wall. Such are my general lines. Of course there's a lot to say about the matter that I haven't said—but I have doubtless said a great deal more than it may seem to you at first easy to find your way about in. The way is really, however, very straight. Only the difficulty with one's having made so very full a Statement as the present is that one seems to have gone far toward saying *all*: which I needn't add that I haven't in the least pretended to do. Reading these pages over, for instance, I find I haven't at all placed in a light what I make of the nature of Strether's feeling—his affianced, indebted, and other, consciousness—about Mrs. Newsome. But I need scarcely add, after this, that everything will in fact be in its place and of its kind.

September 1st, 1900. [signed] Henry James

Description of *The Finer Grain*
(May ? 1910)

The description was published in E. V. Lucas, *Reading, Writing and Remembering: A Literary Record* (New York and London: Harper and Brothers, 1932), p. 184. Lucas explains: "The following description of one of his [HJ's] collections of short stories, *The Finer Grain,* which he prepared for the publishers, but which I imagine was not used and has come inexplicably into my possession, will illustrate his desire not to be misunderstood. It is far indeed from the 'jacket' style of today."

The Finer Grain consists of a series of five Tales [1] representing in each case a central figure (by which Mr. Henry James is apt to mean a central and a lively *consciousness*) involved in one of those greater or less tangles of circumstance of which the measure and from which the issue is in the vivacity and the active play of the victim's or the victor's sensibility. Each situation is thereby more particularly a moral drama, an experience of the special soul and intelligence presented (the sentient, perceptive, reflective part of the protagonist, in short), but with high emphasis clearly intended on its wearing for the hero or the heroine the quality of the agitating, the challenging personal *adventure*. In point of fact, indeed, it happens in each case to be the hero who exhibits this finer grain of accessibility to suspense or curiosity, to mystification or attraction—in other words, to moving experience: it is by his connection with its interest in the "grain" woman that his predicament, with its difficult solution, is incurred. And the series of illustrations of how such predicaments *may* spring up, and even be really characteristic, considerably ranges: from Paris to London and New York, and then back again, to ambiguous yet at the same time unmistakable English, and ultra-English, ground.

---

1. "The Velvet Glove," "Mora Montravers," "A Round of Visits," "Crapy Cornelia," and "The Bench of Desolation." "The Velvet Glove" had appeared in the *English Review* March 1909, and "Crapy Cornelia" in *Harper's Magazine* October 1909; for the other three see Index.

Description of *The Outcry*
(July ? 1911)

This description appeared on the dust jacket of the novel, published by Methuen, London, in October 1911; it was taken, apparently without revision, from HJ's prospectus for the book written for the publisher.

"The Outcry" deals with a question sharply brought home of late to the conscience of English Society—that of the degree in which the fortunate owners of precious and hitherto transmitted works of art hold them in trust, as it were, for the nation, and may themselves, as lax guardians, be held to account by public opinion. Mr. Henry James's study of the larger morality of the matter, if we may so call it, and which is the case of a lax rather than a jealous guardian, becomes conspicuous and acute. Hence springs the drama, almost a national as well as a personal crisis—a rapid, precipitated action, moving through difficulties and dangers to a happy issue.

The Deathbed Dictation

December 1915

Following his first and second strokes, in December 1915, HJ summoned Theodora Bosanquet, his typist, to take dictation. The text reproduced here is from the copy of the original document recording that dictation, made by Leon Edel in the autumn of 1937 when he was given access to the James papers then on deposit in the Widener Library at Harvard by WJ's son Harry (see *Letters* IV, Appendix V).

HJ's profound anguish over World War I and his involvement with refugees and the wounded seem to have become associated in his mind with Napoleonic memoirs such as those of Gen. Marcelin Marbot (see 26 March 1892). Another stimulus may have been his having seen during recent months his old Roman acquaintance, the Bonaparte Count Giuseppe Primoli, and also the Prince Victor Napoléon and Princess Clémentine of Belgium. Furthermore, his autobiographical volumes were of recent date—and the unfinished third volume still awaiting completion. One of the most fascinating accounts in *A Small Boy and Others* (1913) describes HJ's visit to the Gallerie d'Apollon of the Louvre—"the local present fact, to my small imagination, of the Second Empire." In the Paris of that Second Empire the name of Napoleon was still to be found everywhere; he represented the glory of a recent and heroic French past. The Napoleonic-Jamesian sense of power is clearly enough connected in this dictation with the sense of artistic achievement—especially in the touching first paragraph of 11 December 1915.

This is an artist's final gropings apparently for a project, dictated at the threshold of the future. Few such exist in the annals of literature. HJ unconsciously underlined the significance of these notes in a late exchange recorded by WJ's widow. She spoke of her son Billy and his friends and said that HJ was their connection with England and Europe. "Yes, I know," HJ replied, "and I should say, without being fatuous, with the future."

It is to be noted (Mrs. WJ reported) that even after HJ lapsed into a coma, his hands continued to move across the bedsheet as if he were writing.

8 December 1915

I find the business of coming round about as important and glorious as any circumstance I have had occasion to record, by which I mean that I find them as damnable and as boring. It is not much better to discover within one's carcase new resources for application than to discover the absence of them; their being new doesn't somehow add at all to their interest but makes them stale and flat, as if one had long ago exhausted them. Such is my sketch state of mind, but I feel sure I shall discover plenty of fresh worlds to conquer, even if I am to be cheated of the amusement of them.

11 December 1915

Wondrous enough certainly to have a finger in such a concert and to feel ourselves[1] touch the large old phrase into the right amplitude. It had shrunken and we add to its line—all we can scarce say how, save that we couldn't have left it. We simply shift the sweet nursling of genius from one maternal breast to the other and the trick is played, the false note averted. Astounding little stepchild of God's astounding young stepmother!

. . . on this occasion moreover that having been difficult to keep step, we hear of the march of history, what is remaining to that essence of tragedy, the limp? We scarce avoid rolling, with all these famished and frustrate women in the wayside dust . . . mere patchwork transcription becomes of itself the high brave art. We [word missing—the typist apparently could not make out what he said] five miles off at the renewed affronts that we see coming for the great, and that we know they will accept. The fault is that they had found themselves too easily great, and the effect of that, definitely, had been, within them, the want of long provision for it. It wasn't why *they* [were] to have been so thrust into the limelight and the uproar, but why they [were] to have known as by inspiration the trade most smothered in experience. They go about shivering in the absence of the holy protocol as in the—they dodder sketchily about—as in the betrayal of the lack of early advantages; and it is upon *that* they seem most to depend to give them distinction—it is upon that, and upon the *crânerie* and the *rouerie* that they seem most to depend for the grand air of gallantry. They pluck in their terror handfuls

---

1. The plural pronoun may be the "royal we" anticipating the Napoleonic stance that begins to manifest itself in the battle scene and the image of the imperial eagle later in this passage. On the other hand it might refer to HJ and his *mon bon*—for he elsewhere addresses the guardian angel of his work in this kind of language.

of plumes from the imperial eagle, and with no greater credit in consequence than that they face, keeping their equipoise, the awful bloody beak that he turns round upon them. We see the beak sufficiently directed in that vindictive intention, during these days of cold grey Switzerland weather, on the huddled and hustled campaigns of the first omens of defeat. Everyone looks haggard and our only wonder is that they still succeed in "looking" at all. It renews for us the assurance of the part played by that element in the famous assurance [divinity] that doth hedge a king.

12 December 1915

We[2] squeeze together into some motorcar or other and we so talk and talk that what comes of it.—Yes, that is the turn of public affairs. Next statement is for all the world as if we had brought it on and had given our push and our touch to great events. The Bonapartes have a kind of bronze distinction that extends to their finger-tips and is a great source of charm in the women. Therefore they don't have to swagger after the fact; fortune has placed them too high and anything less would be trivial. You can believe anything of the Queen of Naples or of the Princess Caroline Murat. There have been great families of tricksters and conjurors; so why not this one, and so pleasant withal? Our admirable father keeps up the pitch.[3] He is the dearest of men. I should have liked above all things seeing our sister pulling her head through the crown; one has that confident—and I should have had it most on the day when most would have been asked. But we jog on very well. Up to the point of the staircase where the officers do stand it couldn't be better, though I wonder at the *souffle* which so often enables me to pass. We are back from [word lost] but we breathe at least together and I am, devotedly yours

12 December 1915, P.M.

Dear and most esteemed brother and sister,[4]

I call your attention to the precious enclosed transcripts of plans and designs for the decoration of certain apartments of the palaces, here, of the Louvre and the Tuileries, which you will find addressed in detail to artists and workmen who are to take them in hand. I commit them to your earnest care till the questions relating to this important work are fully settled. When that is the case I shall require of you further zeal and further taste. For the present the course is definitely

2. The plural pronoun here clearly enough refers to HJ and whatever friends used to take him motoring, Edith Wharton in particular. HJ may subconsciously have associated the imperial eagle of the preceding passage with the figure of the "Firebird" and her "eagle-pounce"—Mrs. Wharton's typical arrival in her "Chariot of Fire." (See *Letters* IV, 620-21.)

3. HJ seems to be confusing the Bonaparte and James families—as he will more explicitly in the following letters.

4. Miss Bosanquet's diary records: "Resumed dictation at 2:10 p.m. on the same day. The letter following began 'Dear and highly considered Brother and Sister' but after its conclusion HJ reconsidered the opening words and changed them."

marked out, and I beg you to let me know from stage to stage definitely how the scheme promises, and what results it may be held to inspire. It is, you will see, of a great scope, a majesty unsurpassed by any work of the kind yet undertaken in France. Please understand I regard these plans as fully developed and as having had my last consideration and look forward to no patchings nor perversions, and with no question of modifications either economic or aesthetic. This will be the case with all further projects of your affectionate

Napoléone[5]

My dear brother and sister,

I offer you great opportunities in the exchange for the exercise of great zeal. Your position as residents of our young but so highly considered Republic at one of the most interesting minor capitals is a piece of luck which may be turned to account in the measure of your acuteness and experience. A brilliant fortune may come to crown it and your personal merit will not diminish that harmony. But you must rise to each occasion—the one I now offer you is of no common cast, and please remember that any failure to push your advantage to the utmost will be severely judged. I have displayed you as persons of great taste and great judgment. Don't leave me a sorry figure in consequence but present me rather as your very fond but not infatuated relation able and ready to back you up, your faithful brother and brother-in-law

Henry James

Undated

across the border[6]
all the pieces

Individual souls, great . . . of [word lost] on which great perfections are If one does . . . in the fulfillment with the neat and pure and perfect—to the success or as he or she moves through life, following admiration unfailing [word lost] in the highway—Problems are very sordid.

One of the earliest of the consumers of the great globe in the interest of the attraction exercised by the great R.L.S. [Robert Louis Stevenson] of those days, comes in, afterwards, a visitor at Vailima[7] and [word lost] there and pious antiquuities to his domestic annals.

These final and faded remarks all have some interest and some character—but this should be extracted by a highly competent person only—some such, whom I don't presume to name, will furnish such last offices. In fact I do without names not wish to exaggerate the defect of their absence. Invoke more than one kind presence, several could help, and many would—but it all better too much left than too much done. I never dreamed of such duties as laid upon me. This sore throaty condition is the last I ever invoked for the purpose.

5. The merging of identities is explicit. HJ uses the original Corsican spelling of the Emperor's name— he would have spelled it out for Miss Bosanquet, as he always did with difficult or unusual words.
6. Some of these fragments, dictated during the last two weeks of December, were taken down in longhand by HJ's niece Peggy while Miss Bosanquet was temporarily absent.
7. HJ may have been thinking of Henry Adams, who with John LaFarge had visited Robert Louis Stevenson at Vailima, Samoa, three years before Stevenson's death in 1894.

Appendices

"Hugh Merrow": An Unfinished Story

This unfinished story exists in a Houghton typescript of twenty-three pages, 8″ × 10″, double-spaced and with numerous corrections, some forty-seven of them written in in ink. It is difficult to date this fragment with accuracy, but it derives from an idea recorded in the notebook entry for 7 May 1898 and developed on 11 September 1900.

It was only for a moment that Merrow failed to place them, aware as he was, as soon as they were introduced, of having already seen them. That was all they at first showed, except that they were shy, agitated, almost frightened: they had been present to him, and within a few days, though unwittingly, in some connection that had made them interesting. He had recovered the connection even before the lady spoke—spoke, he could see, out of the depths of their diffidence, and making the effort, he could also see, that the woman, in the delicate case, is always left by the man to make. "We admire so very much your portrait at the Academy—the one of the beautiful little boy. We've had no one to introduce us to you, but we thought you'd perhaps just let us call. We've—a—been wondering. We were so struck."

"We were most awfully struck," said the young husband, who was as "nice-looking" in his way as she in hers—and indeed their ways were much the same. He had gained confidence from his wife's attack.

"Oh, I'm sure I'm happy to see you. You've—a—been wondering?" Yet he hardly liked, Hugh Merrow, to take the words out of their mouth. "Struck" he had seen they were, struck with his picture of happy little Reggie Blyth, six years old, erect in a sailor-suit, so struck that their attitude in front of it, three days before, was what had made him remember them—he having been really as much impressed with it as they, poor dears, had been with his work. He had gone back to the exhibition, just open, to look at a couple of things by friends to which he had apparently not done justice on varnishing day or at the private view, admonished thereto by an apparent perception of the failure in the friends themselves, whom he had since met and to whom, with an amenity altogether characteristic of him, he wished to make it up. Moving through the rooms on his way out he had not denied himself the pleasure, nor avoided the imprudence, of passing within eyeshot of his own principal performance, partly for the joy of again seeing himself so luckily hung. If either of the two friends to whom he wished to make it up had chanced to be there with a different motive—they were hung so much worse— they might easily have had their revenge by accusing him of hovering greedily where he could catch compliments. They would indeed have been justified in the sense that he *had,* indubitably, slackened pace at the sight of the pleasant—oh, the peerless!—young couple who were so evidently lost in admiration. Their attention had affected him, at a glance, as so serious and so sweet that instinctively, with the artist's well-known "need" of appreciation, he had treated himself to the bare opportunity of picking up some word that would further express it. And he had been to that extent repaid that a remarkable expression, on the young woman's lips, had reached his ear. "Oh, it kills me!"—that was what she had strangely sighed; yet without turning off and rather as if she liked to be killed. Merrow had himself turned off—he had got rather more than he wanted. He winced for compunction, as if he had pushed too far, and it served him right that what she had said needn't in the least have been a tribute to the painter. He guessed in fact on the spot the situation: it was a case of a young husband and a young wife deprived by death of a little boy of whom Reggie Blyth, extraordinarily handsome, blooming with life and promise—under a master-hand certainly—too poignantly reminded them. Reggie, clearly, resembled their child, brought him back, opened their wound; in spite of which they were still fascinated—they had seemed fairly to devour him. But their interest had been in *him,* not in Hugh Merrow; so that on their thus reappearing their proper motive immediately presented itself. What they had been "wondering," as the wife said, was, inevitably, whether they mightn't perhaps persuade him to paint their little dead boy. They would have photographs, perhaps some other portrait, some domestic drawing, or even some fatuous baby bust, and their appeal to him—from which it *was* natural they should hang back— would be on behalf of these objects and of such suggestions and contributions as they might otherwise make.

That, as I say, had quickly come to him—with the one contradictory note indeed that mourning was not their wear; whereby the death of the child would not have been recent. He saw it all, at any rate—and partly from habit, for he had been approached repeatedly for a like purpose, such being the penalty of a signal gift; but he saw it disappointedly, as he had seen it before and the qualification of his welcome to the errand of these visitors cost him the greater effort as the visitors themselves were unmistakeably amiable. They were visibly such a pair as would always be spoken of in the same way—"Oh yes, the young Archdeans; charming people." He was in possession of their name through the presentation of their card before their entrance. They were charming people because in the first place they could *feel*—which was an aptitude one seemed, in the world, to encounter less and less; and because in the second, as husband and wife, they felt so together—were so touchingly, so prettily, as he might call it, united in their impulse. The tall young man, all shapely straitness of feature and limb, erectness that was not stiffness, with his simple but sensitive face, his rich colour, his pleasant clothes, his lapse of assurance, had been as much taken by their idea, Merrow knew, as the bereaved mother herself, whose type, equally fortunate, equally a thing of achieved fineness, though not on the present occasion a thing of better balance, added the light that made the painter inwardly exclaim as he read their story and looked from one to the other; "What a beautiful child it must have been!" That stuck out for him, awake as he was to the charm of beauty, harmony, felicity, of everything that made for "race"—what beautiful children they ought to have! He had seen so many of the mismatched and misbegotten that his eyes rested with a sudden surrender on this appearance of forces—if they could be called forces—really helpful; by which he was in fact so held that while Mrs. Archdean continued to explain, he quite lost, for the instant, the sense of her words. He was thinking that she was ever so delicately and dimly pretty, that her mouth was as sweet as her eyes, and her nose as handsome as her hair; and he was thinking other things besides. They were charming people partly because happy conditions had produced them, easy, goodly, generous English conditions, current London plenitudes, such as would operate, in turn, by the fact of their own happiness, which couldn't fail to be always decorative, always at least enhancing to the general scene, by mere casual presence.

But what distinguished them for Merrow, of a truth, still more than these comparatively commonplace elements of good luck and good humour, was the way they made him think of them as above all exquisitely at one with each other. He was single, he was, behind everything, lonely, and it had been given him so little to taste of any joy of perfect union, that he was, as to many matters, not even at one with himself. The joy of perfect union, nevertheless, had hovered before him as a dream—in consequence of which he was now insidiously moved by this presentation of a case of it. These handsome, tender, bereaved young persons were acting in entire concert. They had plenty of pleasures, but none would be so great for them as for him to attempt what they proposed. The wife, moreover, would care for it in the measure in which it would touch the husband; the husband would care for it in the measure in which it would touch the wife. This it was that made them beautiful, and from this it was that his disturbing thought sprang. Even as Mrs. Archdean proceeded, helplessly, with her errand, he said to himself that it was *them* he should like to paint, and to paint intensely together. He already saw how he should express in it the truth that, in their world where so much had been loosened, they *were* intensely together. It was an association free, in fine, from worldly, from vulgar disagreements. So at least our friend had judged it till it threw out a surprise for him. He found himself presently with something else to think of; having meanwhile met the inquiry of his visitors as nearly half way as was permitted by his small eagerness to work from photographs and conversations.

"It's not a little boy we should like—or at least *I* should," said Mrs. Archdean. "It's a little girl."

Her husband, at this, as Hugh looked vague, laughed out his awkwardness.

"We don't, we should tell you, feel quite the same about it. My own idea's the boy—all the more after seeing how you do them. But of course it's for you to say."

Our young man was amused, but he tried not to show it. "Which you had better have?"

"Which you think you could do best," said Mrs. Archdean.

He met her eyes, and he was afterwards to remember that what he had then seen in them was the very beginning, the first faint glimmer—yet with a golden light, however dim—of a relation. She intensely appealed to him; she privately approached him; she attempted an understanding with him apart from her husband—and this although her affection for her husband was complete. Of course moreover it was open to that personage to attempt another understanding. All this was much for Hugh to see in a few seconds; but he had not painted portraits ten years for nothing. "Ah then, you've both a boy and a girl?"

"No—unfortunately not," said Captain Archdean with a queer face.

"Oh, you've had the grief of losing them?" Merrow considerately suggested.

It produced, oddly, a silence, as if each of his companions waited for the other to speak. It was the wife again who had to clear it up. "We have no children. We've never had any."

"Oh!" said her host in vagueness.

"That's our bad case"—and Captain Archdean, for relief, still treated it with a measure of gaiety. "We should have liked awfully to. But here we are."

"Do you mean—a—?" But Hugh could scarce imagine what they meant.

"We shall never have any," the young wife went on. "We've hoped, we've waited. But now we're sure."

"Oh!" said Hugh Merrow again.

"From the moment we come we have to tell you all this, and perhaps you'll only think us ridiculous. But we've talked it over long—it has taken all our courage. We gained a great deal—so you see it's partly your own doing—from the sight of *your* child."

She had so sounded her possessive that Merrow was for the moment at a loss. "Mine? Ah," he said cheeringly, "if I could only have one either!"

"I mean the one at the Academy—the dear little sailor-man. You can have as many as you like—when you can paint them that way!"

"Ah, I don't paint them for myself," our young man laughed. "I paint them—with a great deal of difficulty, and not always all as I want—for others."

"That's just it," Captain Archdean observed more lucidly than before. "We're just such a pair of others—only we shouldn't make you any sort of difficulty. Not *any*," he added with a spasm of earnestness that showed Merrow both what he meant and how he felt. His desire was so great that it overcame his reluctance to mention the subject of price. He was ready to pay the highest the artist could be conceived as asking. "All we want is that he should be such a one as we *might* have had."

"Oh, better than that," the young woman interposed. "We might have had one with some blot, some defect, some affliction. We want her perfect—without a flaw. *Your* little boy"—and she again, for her host, incontrollably intensified the pronoun—"is the absolute ideal of everything."

"So that to make ours the same," said her husband, "Mr. Merrow will have to make him a boy."

She looked again at the painter. "I think you'll have to tell us first that we don't appear to you crazy."

Merrow, while he, as before, met her look, found himself aware of a drop of his first disappointment. There *was* something in her that made—and made, in effect, quite insistently—for a relation; that positively forced it on him as, for his own part, a charity or an act of good manners. And it made the difference that he didn't much care if they were crazy or not, or even if he himself were. Their funny errand had begun to appear to him, but it would be part of the fun that they should fully state their case. Merrow desired this moreover in no spirit of derision; he already saw that, pleasant as they were, no fun, for anyone concerned in the transaction, would be obstreperous. "What exactly is it then that you ask of me?"

"Well, absurd as it may seem, to *give* us what we're not so happy as to have otherwise, to create for us a sort of imitation of the little source of pleasure of which we're deprived. That—as you know you may do it—will be something."

Merrow considered. "Haven't you thought of adoption?"

Captain Archdean now promptly answered. "Very much. We've looked at a hundred children. But they won't do."

"They're not *it*," said his wife.

"They're not *him*," he explained.

"They're not *her*," she continued. "You see we know what we would like."

"Oh, but you don't quite seem to!" Merrow laughed. "*Is* it a boy or a girl?"

"Which would you rather do?" Mrs. Archdean inquired. "Which would most naturally come to you, for ease, for reality?"

"Ah, reality!" Merrow goodhumouredly groaned. "Reality's hard to arrive at with so little to go upon. You offer me, you see, no data, no documents. It's worse even than if she were dead."

"Oh, thank God she's not *dead!*" Mrs. Archdean oddly exclaimed. "We give you a free hand, but we trust you."

Again Merrow paused. "Have you tried anyone else?"

She looked about the room, at studies, heads, figures placed, a little at random, on the walls, and at two or three things on easels, started, unfinished, but taking more or less the form of life. One of these last was, as happened, another portrait of a child, precisely of a little girl, pretty and interesting, eminently paintable, in whom our young man had found an inspiration. The thing but foreshadowed his intention, yet the essence of the face seemed the more to look out from it; and Mrs. Archdean, who had approached it, turned from it, after a long gaze, to answer. "No—it's something we've never imagined till now."

"Not," said her husband, "till we had seen your little Reggie. It all comes from that—he put it into our heads. It came to us—to both of us at the same moment—that if you could do him you could do what we want." The poor gentleman, making every concession for the absurd sound of their story, yet the more assured, or the more indifferent, for having broken, as he evidently felt, an inordinate amount of ice, paused again, pressingly, and again struck out. "It's the idea, you see, of something that would live with us. He'll be *there*—he'll be in the house. It won't be as it is now."

"With nothing!" the young mother, as she wished to be, strangely sighed.

"When we look up we shall see him," her companion said. "And when we talk we shall mention him. He'll have his name."

"Oh, he'll have everything!"—Mrs. Archdean repeated her murmur. "Your little boy," she went on, "has everything. How," she asked, "could you part with him?"

"Oh," said Merrow, "I've lost so many that I'm used to it."

She looked at him as if studying in his face the signs—deep and delicate as they would be—of so much experience. "And you can have as many more as you like."

Merrow didn't deny it; he was thinking of something else. "Have you seen little Reggie himself?"

"Oh dear, no!"

"We don't want to," Captain Archdean explained. "We wouldn't for the world." He had arrived at stating the facts of their odd attitude very much as a patient consulting a doctor enumerates aches and pains.

And his wife added her touch. "We don't *like* children—that is other people's. We can't bear them—when they're beautiful. They make us too unhappy. It's only when they're not nice that we can look at them. Yours is the only nice one we've for a long time been able to think of. It's something in the way you've done him." With which she looked again at the little girl on the easel. "You're doing it again—it's something in yourself. That's what we felt." She had said all, and she wound up with an intimate glance at her husband. "There you have us."

And Merrow felt indeed that he did; he was in possession; he knew, about their charming caprice, all that was to be known, though perhaps not quite whether the drollery or the poetry of it were what most touched him. It was almost puerile, yet it was rather noble. "Of course," he presently said, "I feel the beauty and the rarity of your idea. It's highly original—it quite takes hold of me."

"It isn't that we don't see it ourselves as wildly fantastic!" one of them hastened to concede; to which he found himself replying, with a sound of attenuation, that this was not necessarily against it. But it was, just then, by a word of the young wife's that he was most arrested. "The worst we shall have done will be after all but to make you refuse."

"And what will you do if I refuse?"

"Well, we shan't go to anyone else."

"We shall go on as we have done," said Captain Archdean with a slight dryness of decency.

"Oh well," Merrow answered, more and more determined, he was conscious, in the sense of good humour, of an indulgence as whimsical even as their own proposal—"oh well, I don't want you to take me as stupidly unaccommodating, as having too little imagination, even if you yourselves have perhaps too much. It's just the intrinsic difficulty that makes me hesitate. It's the question of doing a thing so much in the air. There's such a drawback as having *too* free a hand. For little Reggie, you see, I had my model. He was exquisite, but he was definite—he lighted my steps. The question is what will light them in such a case as you propose. You know, as you say, what you want, but how exactly am *I* to know it?"

This inquiry, he could see, was not one that Captain Archdean could easily meet; and it was to be singular for him later on that he had entertained at the moment itself a small but sharp prevision, involving absolutely a slight degree of suspense, that their companion would, after an instant, be less at a loss. He really almost decided to let the matter depend on what she might say; according to which it depended with some intensity. He was not unaware that in spite of the scant response of the painter in him, who could but judge the invitation as to a wild-goose-chase, he had been already moved, to rather a lively tune, by curiosity. It was as if something might come to him if he did consent, though what might come indeed might not be a thing that he himself should call a picture. Whatever it was to be, at any rate, it affected him at the end of another minute as having begun to come; for by that time Mrs. Archdean had spoken, his suspense was relieved, his prevision was justified as to her not being so simple a person as her husband. "Won't your steps really be lighted by your interest?"

He wondered. "My interest in what, dear madam? In you and your husband?"

"Oh dear, no. In the artistic question itself—which we only suggest to you. In forming a conception which shall be, as you say of little Reggie, definite. In *making* it definite. In inventing, in finding, in doing—won't it be?—what the artist does. I mean when he tries. For we do," she added with a smile, "want you to try hard."

It was the same light note as her husband's some minutes before, a hint of great remuneration, should remuneration help the matter. But her smile corrected the slight impatience of the previous words and warranted Merrow's responding with the pleasantest pliancy. " 'First catch your hare'—! Do you mean I should be at liberty to reproduce some existing little person?"

The young woman, as with kindled hope, looked at him ever so gently. "That's your affair. We should ask no questions."

"We should only like the little person," Captain Archdean intervened, "to be somebody quite unknown to us and whom we should be likely never to see."

His wife reassured him with a look. "He'd change her, disguise her, improve her." And she turned again to their host. "You'd make her *right*. It's what we trust you for. We'd take her so, with our eyes closed, from your hands."

Her face as she said this became somehow, for Hugh Merrow, more beautiful than before; and the impression had to do with his still more lending himself, even while he kept judging technically the vanity of the task. "I should naturally have the resource of making her as much as possible like her supposed mother."

"Oh," Mrs. Archdean returned with her eyes on her husband, "I should wish her as much as possible like her supposed father. If that counts as a condition you must be merciful to it, for it's my only one."

Captain Archdean faced the speakers in an attempt to combine the air of confessed and cheerful eccentricity with the fact of something more inward, a real anxiety for the fate of the image he had projected, or perhaps, still more, his wife had; then he made a point that served as a refuge for his modesty. "It's not a little girl, you know, who *would* naturally look like me."

Merrow conscientiously demurred. "I beg your pardon—there's nothing she might more easily do. But Mrs. Archdean, I judge," he continued, "dreams of a little girl in your likeness, while you dream of a little boy in hers."

"That's it," the Captain genially granted. "One *sees* little boys like their mother."

"Well, the thing is so fundamental," said our friend, "that you really must settle it between you."

The remark produced a pause, slightly awkward, to which Mrs. Archdean, again a little impatiently, made an end. "Oh, I *could* of course do with such a possession as little Reggie."

"There it is!" her husband exclaimed. "It's of that picture that one can't not think."

"I see—yes," Merrow returned. "But I'm afraid I myself can't think of it much more. When once I've done a thing—!"

Captain Archdean looked at him harder. "You prefer something different?"

Merrow waited a moment, during which their companion again spoke. "Is it really quite impossible for *you* to decide?"

He still wondered. "Why, you see you're both so handsome—!"

"Well then," the Captain laughed, "make him resemble us both!"

"You'll at any rate really think of it?" said his wife. "I mean think of which will be best."

Her fine young face quite terribly pleaded, and there was no use his pretending to ignore the fact of the recognition of feeling in her that he felt her to know him, to have seen him, gather from it. He again answered her inwardly and for himself before speaking—and speaking differently—to her ear and to her husband's. He found himself trying to see in her what she must have been as a child, and he so far made it out that he held for a moment the vision of something too tenderly fair. Yes, he had painted children, but he had never painted the thing that—say at eight years old—she would have been. "It will take much thought, but I'll give it all I can."

"And about what will be the age—?"

"Well, say about eight."

This made them at once eager. "Then you'll readily try?" They spoke in the same breath.

"I'll try my very hardest!"

They looked at each other in joy, too grateful even to speak. It was wonderful how he pleased them, and he felt that he liked it. If he could only keep it up!

————— e☙ɔ —————

Cash Accounts and Addresses

HJ's records of income and expenditure are contained mainly in his seven surviving pocket diaries (1909–15), usually in the sections marked "Financial Records" or "Memoranda," but occasionally among the dated diary entries. Some of the latter have been left in place in the text because of their special nature: HJ's account of extending an allowance to Burgess Noakes during visits to the United States or of borrowing small sums from him, and of the disposition of funds donated for war relief by Mrs. Wharton and others. Two of the extant notebooks contain brief financial statements on the flyleaf; see initial footnotes. The picture of HJ's financial situation is augmented by the data in *Life,* passim. The appearance of lists of addresses are similarly accommodated by the diaries; some few addresses are found, like his financial statements, among the diary entries proper and on one occasion on the flyleaf of a notebook. All of these have been arranged chronologically according to their appearance.

Cash Accounts

1881

Club Subscription[1]
Reform
   To Imprs. Coles & Biddulphs. Charing Cross, every 1st Jan.
   £10.0.0

1. This item is written on the flyleaf of the first American Journal.

Athenaeum—to Imprs. Drummond, 4
    Charing X every 1st Jan. £8.8.0

Savile

1893

My weekly bill at Hotel National Lucerne
(May 1893—room 59, 1st floor with balcony
            —and table d'hôte—was about 200 frs. £8.0.0)

15000
25000
30000
───────
75000 [1]

Income 1909

Jan. 5:   From Pinker Scribner Royalties £10.0.0.

Jan 13:   Syracuse [1] £82.0.0.

Jan 15:   Macmillan Co. Royalties (less vols. of Edition charged for) £10.10.0.

Feb. 11:   from Syracuse 51.4.7

Mar. 11:   Syracuse 51.4.6
              Pinker Royalties etc. with ("Velvet Glove") 56.4.4

Mar. 15:   From Heinemann (on 2 Pennell [2] books) £100.0.0

Mar. 25:   From Heinemann other royalties £15.0.0

April 1:   Received from Pinker—small promiscuous royalties £7.0.0

April 13:   Recd. from Syracuse 51.3.7

May 11:   From Syracuse 51.4.7

May 20:   From Houghton Mifflin and Co. (royalties) 36.8.0

May 25:   From Pinker and Forbes Robertson 90.0.0

1. This item is on the last page of the second notebook (Houghton Journal III). The arithmetic sum is in pencil. HJ had "35000" originally: it is overwritten with "30000." The addition was correct before the change.

1. Income from real estate in Syracuse, New York, inherited by HJ and WJ from HJ Sr. WJ's son Harry reorganized the property to increase the yield.

2. The American illustrator Joseph Pennell (1860–1926) illustrated the first English edition of *A Little Tour in France* (1900), the first edition of *English Hours* (1905), and the first edition of *Italian Hours*, which would appear in October 1909.

June 14:   From Syracuse 51.3.7

June 17:   From Harper and Bros for "Crapy Cornelia" less J.B.P.'s[3] commission 92.3.6

June 25:   From Pinker and Herbert Trench[4] on acct of royalties on *The Other House* 90.0.0

July 10:   (Pinker from Houghton Mifflin and Co. small royalties) 10.0.0

July 13:   from Syracuse 81.17.8

Aug. 11:   from Syracuse 51.6.8

Aug. 19:   From Pinker, for Mora Montravers 37.16.0

Sept. 13:   From Syracuse 51.6.8

Oct. 11:   From Syracuse 51.7.9

Oct. 20:   From Pinker, for Harpers Bazaar etc. 57.18.1

Nov. 4:   From Pinker as the Harper's advance on *Julia Bride* 180.0.0

Nov. 10:   From Houghton Mifflin and Co. through A. Constable and Co: on semi-annual royalties 33.18.6

Nov. 13:   From Syracuse 51.4.7

Dec. 4:   From the New York Macmillan Co. royalties: 6.2.2

Dec. 13:   From B. S. and Co.[5] from Syracuse 51.4.7

Disbursements 1909

Jan 12:   Paid Ashmead Jan 12th 1909:—£47.18.9 Income Tax.

June 23:   Returned my income to F. A. Ashmead Assessor of Taxes 27 Charles St. Regent St. S. W. on June 23rd for 1909–1910 (ending April 5th) as £.1020 (£600 "foreign possessions") 400 literary earnings.

x   x   x   x   x   x   x   x   x   x   x   x

Returned 1907–1908 £850

"   1908–1909 £1096

"   1909–1910 £1020   £1000

Aug. 2:   Aug. 2d Paid Premium on my Policy to New York Life Insurance due tomorrow £129.12.0. *Policy 1108535.*

---

3. Pinker, HJ's literary agent.
4. Herbert Trench (1865–1923), Anglo-Irish poet and scholar, was planning a repertory season at the Haymarket Theatre. The play was not produced; see *Complete Plays*, 67–68, 679.
5. Brown, Shipley and Co., 123 Pall Mall S. W.

Income 1910

Jan. 4:   From Pinker, for the Scribners (Edition) for "Bench of Desolation" (Putnam) and for *Question Speech* (H. M. and Co.) 164.13.5

Jan. 12:   From Syracuse 82.1.0

Feb. 2:   From Pinker for Macmillan royalties on Edition

> 84.17.
> 45

Ditto for *Round of Visits;* both sums making less his commission £*116.17.4.*

Feb. 14:   From Syracuse 51.6.8

Feb. 17:   (Feb. 17th my balance with B. S. and Co. is today (or was yesterday) £*646.15.5.*)

March 12:   Balance at Lloyd's Bank today: £43.16.9

March 15:   From Syr's[1] £51.5.8

April 5:   From Pinker—odd royalties (cashed cheque at Lloyds bank.) 16.7.0

April 6:   Heinemann royalties 50.14.

April 15:   Syracuse 51.3.7.

May: From Pinker £18 in ½ payment by the English Review for *A Round of Visits*

May 13:   From Syracuse including an extra from "Sinking Fund" 102.9.2

June 4:   From Pinker, royalties on 2d fee for Round of Visits 29.16.0

June 13:   From Syracuse 51.5.8

July 4:   From Pinker for Scribner royalty 114.9.9
          From Pinker forfeit from Frohman[2] £180

Aug. 4:   From Pinker on account of Methuen's vol. of stories 90.0.0

Aug. 10:   William owes me Aug. 10th £90.14.0
          My balance at Lloyds Bank Rye: Aug. 10th 1910 £89.8.9

Aug. 11:   Syracuse: 51.8.9

---

1. Syracuse.
2. Charles Frohman (1860–1915), American producer, began early in 1909 to plan a repertory season at the Duke of York's Theatre; HJ's three-act comedy *The Outcry,* completed in January 1910, was to be included. The death of Edward VII in May 1910 and the closing of the theaters during the period of mourning scotched those plans. Frohman forfeited, as had been agreed, the advance of $1000—or £200; Pinker's commission was the usual 10%.

Sept. 7:   From Syracuse $250

Sept. 8:   Houghton Mifflin and Co. "Italian Hours." $1075

Sept. 20:   I have with Brown Bros: $2089.

Oct. 4:   From Syracuse $150

Oct. 16:   New York. Hear from Pinker that Scribners are to pay me $432.78 on Edition in December.

Oct. 25:   From A. J. (repaid loan £85) $420

Nov.:   Received fr. Syracuse $250
           "   Houghton Mifflin and Co. (autumn royalties) $216
Rec'd from Pinker: balance of Methuen's payment for Finer Grain, and Scribner's ditto $654.75

Dec. 4:   From Syracuse Dec. 4th $250
From Pinker (Tauchnitz etc;) paid in to Lloyds Bank Rye, Dec. 1st 1910 27.13.5
Paid by Pinker into Lloyds Bank (for Scribners from Edition.) £80

Disbursements 1910

Feb. 17:   Paid income tax for 1909–1910 to F. A. Ashmead, Charles St. Haymarket: £59.10.0

June ?:   Returned income for *1910,* through Bernard Mallet, as property income £713; as Literary Income, at g d tax on *earned* income, £596. Total £1309

June 18:   Nauheim. Returned my income for 1910–11, under Bernard Mallet's blessed instructions, to H. S. Bateman Esq., Surveyor of Taxes, 48 Dover St. W. as £988.
And I noted on it that I have for 11 years been paying £132 a year as Life Insurance Premium. £988 becomes thus *3d year's* income for the average of 3 years forming the figure of my next (June 1911) return; the return for 1911–1912. The 2 other years will accordingly be:—1908–09—£1096. 1909–1910—1020. To which add this £988 and divide by 3.

June 22:   Sent cheque ½ Reform Club
       "   "   Cheyne to Whiteman.

Aug. 3:   Due Aug. 3d to New York Life Insurance Company on my policy 1108535 £129.12.0: which will make my 13th payment out of 15. Fuller's Rye Rate due October and April. Fletcher's due July and December; each of a little less than £8. In all about £32 a year.

Sept. 15:   Sent to Lloyd's Bank through Brown Bros., Boston, £100 (487 dollars) to be paid into my deposit account there.

Sept. 19:   Sent £7.10 by cheque on L. B. for rent of cottages.

Oct. 26:   Paid Paine Furniture Co. $22 for shaving stand—by cheque.

Oct.:   Drew $100

Nov. 1:   Drew $100 from Brown Brothers. Paid Burgess $26—thus advancing him $4.

Nov. 3:   Drew $102 (Cook's bill) From Brown Bros. and Co.

Dec. 16:   Sent £50.10 to Reform Club Draught ($255.15/100) from Brown Bros.

[Dec]. 29:   Paid Reform, Athenaeum and Lit. Soc. annual dues by by cheques on Lloyd's Bank. Also cheque to Eleanor Meares: total £31.13
             Paid Otto Kahn. Eight. 68th St. New York $150 for Mrs. S[malley] fund: by cheque on Brown Bros. Also Boring House dues—£2.2.0 making Total drawn on Lloyds Bank £33.15.0

Income 1911

Jan. 1:   From Syracuse: Four hundred dollars. $400

Feb. 2:   From Syracuse Two hundred and fifty dollars. $250

Feb. 7:   By Pinker, from Macmillan Co., to Brown Bros.—$368. the equivalent of £65.19.8.
             Hear from Lloyds Bank Rye under date of Jan. 11th that my Bal. there was then £150.10
             From Macmillan and Co., royalties, paid into Lloyds Bank Rye—£14.10.11

Feb. 23:   From Pinker that he has paid into Lloyds from *Saloon* Feb. 14th £18.18.1

March 2:   From Syracuse $250.

March 3:   (Balance with Brown Bros. March 3d $3,635.)

March 7:   Hear from Pinker that he has paid into Lloyds Bank £8.0.0 more from the Saloon. Say—$40

April 2:   From Syracuse *$250.*

April 18:   Sent to Lloyds Bank Rye Draft for £75.

May 3:   Received from Syracuse and paid into Brown Bros. $250.
             Received from Houghton Mifflin and Co. with semi-annual acct. of royalties for *all* books:—$140.35

May 6: Hear today from Lloyds Bank that my Balance there by reason of House-rate (£7.14.5) acknowledged same date from Rye, April 25th was: £156.6.1—really, however, £148

June 15: Received from William Heinemann £17.18.9 and paid it into Lloyds Bank Rye

July 3: $650 *Dols.*

July 15: Hear from Pinker that he has paid into Lloyds Bank for me £104.4.5. Of the list of paid-in royalties accompanying, Scribner's semi-annual payment on Edition was £104.18.5. The whole sum (£115.16.5) docked by his commission (£11.11.7).[1] Also from said Bank that they have received it, (the £104.4.5); and that my total balance there on July 4th was: *£217.8.9.* This makes my present (July 16th) total in the 2 Banks about £932 equals $4,657.

Aug: Brown and Shipley advise me under date of 8th that my Balance with them, transferred from Brown Bros. Boston, is *£513.17.6.*

Oct. 8: From Edgar Stoneham 9.0.0

Oct. 12: From Syracuse for 3 months 184.19.11

Oct. 18: From J. B. Pinker, as Methuen's royalty on *Outcry,* less diminution, £262.18.11

Nov. 1: From Pinker from Scribner's sum "down" on The Outcry, less commission etc. *£180.0.0*

Nov. 3: From G. H. Eldridge Rye, from stock in Literary Society—£0.18.0

Nov. 15: From Constable and Co. for Houghton Mifflin and Co. £33.17.9 Balance with Lloyds Bank that day is £146.13.3

Dec. 5: From Pinker, H. M. and Co. and Harpers. *Question of Our Speech* and royalties on *Ambassadors* £4.7.1

Dec. 20: Received from Pinker (£52.8.8) royalties on my New York Edition.

Disbursements 1911

January: My annual subscription of £1.1.0 due January 1912.[2]

Feb. 15: Sent draft yesterday (the semi-annual £25) to Dawes Son and Prentice

March 14: Post cheque to A. Whiteman

March 25: Cheque due to Albert Whiteman

---

1. Arithmetic problems here: £11.11.7 is indeed 10% (Pinker's usual commission) of the "whole sum" (£115.16.5); but the remainder should be £104.4.10.
2. Subscription to Salisbury Branch, Royal National Lifeboat Institution.

April 17:   Posted £7.14.5 to C. A. Gaffard, *Rye House Tax.*

April 18:   Posted yesterday £5.15 to Reform Club for Procession tickets: June 23d.

May 9:   At B. B. and Co's, this noon, learnt my balance to be $4,000, after my paying for 2 Drafts on London of £9 and £6.

June 10:   My income to be returned for 1911–1912 as £1000—either to H. S. Bateman Surveyor of Taxes, 48 Dover St. W. or the Charles St. Haymarket Assessor.

June 13:   Write for 2 Drafts to Brown Brothers.

June 15:   Post Drafts to Reform Club and to A. Whiteman, Rye.

Dec. 10:   Sent Joan A.[3] £9.0.0—including her wages, and the board wages up to Friday 15th

Income 1912

Jan. 18:   My balance at Lloyds Bank Rye on Saturday p.m. Dec. 30th 1911 was £130. Paid in there Jan. 18 £14.12.5.

Feb. 9:   Balance Lloyds Bank today:—£153.3.0

Mar. 4:   Balance Lloyds Bank, March 2 £140.5.0

May 22:   Paid into Lloyds, Rye £24.17.8

July 26:   Balance at Lloyds £180

Sept. 28:   Balance at Lloyds £156

Nov. 1:   £144.8.7 balance at Lloyds yesterday

Nov. 2:   Received cheque from Pinker on behalf of Nelson and Sons *(The American)*[1] £9.19.2

Disbursements 1912

Jan. 15:   Paid my Income-Tax, of £45.2.10 on £1000 income, to F. A. Ashmead, 27 Charles St. Regent St. W.

Feb. 5:   Paid J. Adams Rye £5.5.0 subscription to East Sussex Hospital.

Feb. 9:   *Paid Milson £60*

---

3. Joan Anderson succeeded Mrs. Paddington as HJ's cook just before he moved into Carlyle Mansions.

1. With Macmillan's permission, HJ gave Nelson & Sons the revised version of *The American* (volume II of the New York edition) to include in their series of cheap editions.

Mar. 25: Cheque due to Whiteman and to Dawes, Son and Prentice, Rye

May 20: Paid Richmd. Milson yesterday £40. Balance of his Bill (for everything save new Range) £18.16.7

June 2: Paid Rye Rates to C. J. Fletcher.

June 13: Drew £5.0.0 Cash (R. C.)[2]

Aug. 2: My Insurance Premium—£129.12.0 on Policy 1108.535—due tomorrow.

Income 1913

Jan. 31: Rec'd from Pinker and Macmillan, £18.15.3 (Edition de Luxe).[1]

Feb. 18: Received from Harry (Syracuse) £204.

Mar. 15: Received from Pinker Scribner's payment of 1st Half of sum down for Novel (less commission): £738.6.3.[2]

Mar. 25: Received from W. Heinemann £8.13.1—royalties on 5 books! (March 25th 1913).

Begin return for 1914–15 *here*.

Apr. 12: From Syracuse £184.12.4.
From Pinker on behalf of Scribner's, Macmillans and Nelson (April 26th.) £592.15.

End of May: From Houghton and Mifflin through Constable £21.0.0

July 1: From Scribner's royalties on New York Edition, through Pinker £36.18.5.

July 12: From Syracuse £184.16.1.

July 15: From *The Times* (Balzac)[3] £13.0.0.

Oct. 12: Received from B. S. and Co. advice of Oct. 1st remittance from Syracuse £223.13.0.

Oct. 15: My (inclusive) Balance with Brown Shipley and Co.—900.0.0

Oct. 23: From Edgar Stoneham, for rent of garden £6.0.0.

2. Reform Club.

1. The first issue, English edition (1908–09), of *The Novels and Tales* (New York edition): sheets of the ordinary issue of the American edition by Scribner's with a new title-page, "Macmillan and Co." Advertised as "Edition de Luxe."

2. The result of Mrs. Wharton's arrangement with Scribner's to divert $8000 from her royalties and offer the sum to HJ as an advance for *The Ivory Tower*.

3. "Balzac" appeared in the *Times Literary Supplement* 19 June 1913; see *LA* III, 139–51.

Nov. 13:   From Houghton Mifflin and Co. Draft for $153 for semi-annual roy-
            alties £31.14.0.
            Small royalties from Nelson, Harpers and H. M. and Co. through
            Pinker. Dec. 1st 1913 £12.14.9.

Dec. 5:   Small royalties from George Brett, N. Y. £4.10.6.

Dec. 6:   Balance with B. S. and Co. £743.2.10

Disbursements 1913

March 24:   Paid 1st quarter's rent Carlyle Mansions £42.7.0
            Paid Albert Whiteman £7.6.0
            Paid Income tax for 1912–13. £49.10.0

June 24:   Made Return of Income £1300.

Aug. 3:   Paid my New York Life Insurance premium (Policy 1108535)—
            £129.12.0

Sept. 30:   Paid rent for my Flat by cheque—£42.7.0—yesterday, Michaelmas
            quarter-day. (To City West End Properties Ld.; Bush Lane House,
            Bush Lane, E.; and cheques crossed "Lloyds Bank Ld., a/c Pay-
            ees.")

Dec. 7:   Paid House tax, to C. A. Gafford, Rye—£7.14.5.
            Also pd. for my coming year's Telephone (due Dec. 25.)—£6.10.0

Dec. 26:   Paid quarter's rent to "Properties": £42.7.0

Dec. 27:   Paid Quarter's Rent to Properties Dec. 25th £42.7.0[4]
            Paid C. J. Fletcher, Collector of Rates and Taxes Rye: £15.15.4
            Paid Albert Whiteman £7.10.0.

Income 1914

Jan. 2:   Received from J. B. Pinker £25.5.8 Scribner's ½ yearly royalties on
            sale of Edition. Lowest figure, alas, yet! (Without Pinker's commish.
            £28.1.10)

Jan. 3:   Balance at Lloyds Bank Rye today £56.3.6

Jan. 12:   Received through B. S. and Co. from Syracuse £224.0.0
            Received from Macmillan and Co. cheque on annual royalties—
            £11.4.0. Paid the above into my credit at Lloyds Bank, Rye

Feb. 3:   From Pinker, the Macmillan royalties on Edition £25.9.6

---

4. An inadvertent repetition of the entry for 26 December.

April 1:   From Pinker, Macmillan's cheque "down" for Notes of a Son etc. £135.0.0
            From F. Heinemann on some few royalties £4.0.0

Apr. 23:   From Quarterly Review for my George Sand.[1] £25.0.0

Apr. 30:   From Pinker, on small royalties—Nelson and Duffield and Co. £15.2.1.

May 15:   From Houghton Mifflin and Co. £34.14.6

June 30:   From Pinker representing royalties from H. M. and Co. (Question of Our Speech) £6.10 (Harpers Ambassadors) £8.1 and Scribners (both Collect. Ed. and others, £43.18.3) making in all, minus commission: £47.16.7.[2]

July 2:   I have paid this into Lloyds Bank (Total of the foregoing with amt of P's commission not extracted, was £52.6.2.)

July 20:   Balance at Lloyds Bk. today, £100

Aug. 6:   Sent my 2 New York Life Insurance papers for collecting my Dividend to Brown Shipley and Co. Policy 1108535 Dividend £597 and fraction.

Aug. 12:   Paid into B. S. and Co. to me (£597.12.5) 597.12.5
            Dividend from N.Y. Life Insurance Company

Sept. 2:   Advice from New York Life Insurance Co. (this Sept. 2d 1914) of their augmentation of paid-up insurance due my Estate to £1153.10.0

Sept. 11:   From Harry, arrears of Syracuse remittance £115.11.9

Sept. 12:   Wrote to Harry telling him to "hold" the October Syracuse remittance

Sept. 23:   Received from Mrs. Wharton her cheque for Ten Pounds to spend for Belgian refugees or in any other war donations. Sent £2 to Miss Sedley for those at Rye. Balance of £8. (Oct. 9th still intact.)
            Oct. 15: Paid to Mrs. Ch. Wheeler for Hammersmith Refugees £3.0.0 of the above balance of £8.0.0; leaving thus £5.0.0 of Mrs. Wharton's cheque.
            Oct. 30: Paid the above £5.0.0 to Mrs. Wheeler for the Hammersmith Belgian Refugees.

Sept. 26:   Balance at Lloyds tomorrow after G.G.'s[3] Draft £82.

Oct. 3:   £80.4.0[4]

---

1. Review of Wladimir Karénine's *George Sand, sa vie et ses oeuvres, vol. III*, the *Quarterly Review*, April 1914; see *LA* III, 775–99.
2. Puzzling arithmetic; see next entry.
3. George Gammon, HJ's gardner at Lamb House.
4. This and the following entry evidently indicate HJ's balance at Lloyds Bank, Rye.

Oct. 10:   £78.8.0

Oct. 17:   Lloyds: Balance £77.12.0

Oct. 24:   Lloyds Bank: Bal. £76.6.0

Oct. 31:   Lloyds Balance at today £75.0.0

Nov. 3:   Balance deposit Stores £6.7.10

Nov. 15:   From Houghton Mifflin and Company semi-annual royalties £18.10

Nov. 22:   From Pinker Dent's cheque for advance on *Notes on Novelists* £180.0.0

Dec. 3:   Cheque from Pinker for Nelson's ("American") and H. M. and Co. (Question of Our Speech) £5.16.4

Disbursements 1914

Jan. 6:   Subscribed to Mudie's for H. Dunster, for 6 months (£1.4.0)

Made my Return of Income to A. G. Michels, Assessor 117 Beaufort St. S. W. as: £1300. This is based on:—

> Apr. 5 1912 to Do. 1913 £1880
> Apr. 5 1911 to Do. 1912 £1100
> Apr. 5 1910 to Do. 1911 £1000
> Division by 3—£1326

Return to be made in June 1914 from £ 1300 (1913–14) £1100 (1912–13) added to the return for that fiscal year (1914–15) and divided by 3.

Here ends return of income for 1914–1915
Here begins return of income for fiscal year 1915–16

June 24:   Payment of Premium of Fire Policy due to Alliance Assurance Co. Ld., Bartholomew Lane E. C. on Midsummer Day £1.10.0 (Policy 3662034). Also on Policy 3662035 (for £300) Premium £0.4.6. The larger policy is for £2000; and the whole sum to be paid for the two is £1.14.6 (Dawes Son and Prentice) (Richard Milsom). Annual payment of assurances due on *Midsummer* (quarter-day) June 24th. Premium on Fire Policy to London Assurance Corporation (2388604) £2.0.0. (address Fire Dept. of Royal Exchange, E. C.) Also same company, on Policy W. 12961, under Workman's Compensation Act 1906 (against claims by Servt's etc.) £1.5.9.

July 15:   Returned my Income for the fiscal year 1914–15 to Arthur G. Michels, 117 Beaufort St. as £1300. This results from the addition of £1625, all moneys received from April 15th 1913 to April 5th 1914 and £1300, income returned for 1913–14, and £1100, income returned for 1912–13. My return for 1915–16 to be made therefore from £1300 (1913–14) and £1300 (1914–15) *plus* the moneys received from April 5th 1914 to April 5th 1915: the whole divided by 3.

Sept. 29:   £7.10.0 to Albert Whiteman, 76 Brayebrook Road, Hastings.
To the "Properties"—£42.7.0

Dec. 14:   Paid to C. J. Fletcher Collector etc. rates and taxes on Lamb House Rye to the extent of £18.0.0.

Income 1915

Jan. 5:   From Scribner Sons through J. B. Pinker £27.18.9 on royalties for Edition

Jan. 7:   My Balance at Lloyds Bank Rye is £102.2.0.

Jan. 19:   Received through B. S. and Co. from Syracuse £206.1.0.

Jan. 27:   From Macmillans (Jan. 27th 1915) £14.13.7—annual royalties on old volumes.

Feb. 1:   From Ch. Scribner's Sons, through Pinker as advance on royalties from Notes on Novelists £232.6.4.

Feb. 5:   Cheque from Pinker for royalties from Macmillans on the Edition de Luxe—marking increase! £36.9.10.

Mar. 1:   Cheque from Pinker, representing remittance from Harpers on The Ambassadors £4.18.8.

Mar. 27:   From Wm. Heinemann £5.4.1.

Apr. 13:   From Syracuse—£286.9.2.

Apr. 30:   From Pinker Secker's remittance on 1st 4 vols. of Tales:[1] £20.18.6.

May 4:   Pinker from Nelson on *The American* £4.3.11.

May 18:   (17th really) from the Houghton Mifflin Co. semi-annual acct. £42.0.0.

June 25:   From Reginald Smith, for Cornhill and Atlantic[2] £45.15 (paid into Lloyds Bank Rye).

June 26:   Balance at Lloyds £101.1.10.

July 17:   Should have noted the receipt on June 20th from Pinker of royalties from Scribner on Collected Edition: £26.16.6.

Oct. 16:   Syracuse remittance: £251.11.9.

Nov. 15:   From Houghton Mifflin and Co. semi-annual royalties £20.0.0.
No. Miss Tuckermann's Draft, 304149.

---

1. *The Uniform Tales of Henry James,* issued by Martin Secker, London, in 14 volumes; the first four, issued 15 April 1915, were "The Turn of the Screw," "The Lesson of the Master," "The Aspern Papers," and "Daisy Miller."
2. For "Mr. and Mrs. Fields," the *Cornhill Magazine* and, with minor corrections and the title "Mr. and Mrs. James T. Fields," the *Atlantic Monthly* July 1914; see "Notes for 'Mr. and Mrs. Fields.' "

Disbursements 1915

Feb. 2:   Paid my Income Tax on "Possessions": £60.16.8.

Mar. 27:   Here including the £286 etc. of Apr. 13th, ends report of income for fiscal year 1915–1916.

Apr. 13:   Here begins my return for 1916–1917.

July 17:   Paid July 17th for Rye rates and taxes to C. J. Fletcher £17.12.7.

Nov. 15:   Returned my income to Arthur G. Michels for 1915–16 (year ending 5th April 1916) as £1450. This results from: (1913–14) £1300 (1914–1915) £1300 (1915–1916) £1750 swollen, in Aug 1914 by Life Insurance dividend of £597 and the division by 3) 4350 = £1450. My return for 1916–17 will therefore be arrived at by the addition of:— (1914–15): £1300 (1915–16): £1450 and the amounts received between April 30th 1915 (inclusive) and April 5th 1916; the three figures being then divided by 3.

Addresses

1889–94[1]

Smiths
5 Prospect Place
Melton Road, W.
Woodbridge, Suffolk

V. P.[2]
12 Chelsea Gdns
S. W.

W. M. Fullerton
5 Rue Vignon
Paris

Mrs. Comfort
12 Wellington Crescent
Ramsgate (lodgings)

Lloyd Bruce
N. A. Review
3 East 14th St.
New York City

1909

W. Rothenstein[1]
11 Oakhill Park
Frognal. Hampstead N. W.

Mrs. Bigelow (Edith)
Bay Tree Cottage
Aylesbury

Charles du Bos[2]
48 rue de la Tour
Paris

Evelyn Smalley
Box 175
White Plains, New York

Mrs. G. W. Smalley
328 W. 57 St.
New York

---

1. This list is written on the last page of the second notebook (Houghton Journal III).
2. Probably Violet Paget (Vernon Lee).

1. William Rothenstein (1872–1945), British artist, sketched HJ in 1897.
2. Du Bos (1882–1939), bilingual French translator and critic, was a friend of Edith Wharton and a follower of Paul Bourget.

Eleanor Meares
Killinure
Boundary Road
Hove

Owen Wister
913 Pine St.
Philadelphia

Gaillard Thomas Lapsley
12 W. 37th St.
New York City

Percy Lubbock
Emmet's Ide Hill
Sevenoaks

W. D. Howells
130 West 57th St.
New York City

Bruce Porter[3]
3234 Pacific Avenue
Presidio Gate
San Francisco

H. G. Wells
17 Church Row
Hampstead N. W.

Henry Adams
23 Avenue du Bois de Boulogne
Paris

Mrs. G. W. James[4]
191 Prospect Avenue
Milwaukee, Wis

Bay Emmet
62 Washington Square South
New York City

Antonio Avignone[5]
Villino Castagnola Sori.
Riviera di Genoa
Italy

Ned and Louisa J.
22 rue St. Dominique
Paris

Miss Gregory
29 Dennington Park Road
West Hampstead N. W.

1910

Giuseppe Primoli
29 Avenue Trocadero
Paris

Otto Kahn (Banker)
8 East 68th St.
New York City

Miss Bosanquet
7 King's Cross Mansions
W. C.

Miss Esme Hubbard (Cora Prodmore)
5 Southwell Gardens
S. W.

Ethel Sands
42 Lowndes St.
S. W.

Lady Colin Campbell
67 Carlisle Mansions
S. W.

Richard G. Badger
194 Boylston St.
Boston

Alexander Robertson's, my great-grandfather's native place and Kirk,
Polmont near Edinburgh

Eliza Ripley
987 Madison Avenue

3. Porter was an amateur of the arts whom HJ met in San Francisco during his lecture tour of 1904 to 1905. He married WJ's daughter, Peggy, after HJ's death.
4. Caroline, "Carrie," widow of HJ's younger brother Garth Wilkinson, "Wilky."
5. Captain Antonio Marcello Avignone, an old friend of HJ's, formerly attached to the Arsenal in Venice, and a member of the Bronson-Curtis circle there.

Wilfred von Glehn
73 Cheyne Walk
Chelsea S. W.

Mrs. Wharton
c/o H. R. L. Edgar Esq.
81 Nassau St.
New York City

Carrie James
191 Prospect Avenue
Milwaukee Wis.

Bruce Porter
3234 Pacific Avenue
Presidio Gate
San Francisco

1911

Dr. Joseph Collins
37 West 54th St.
New York

Mary (Wilkinson) Matthews
Bradbourne Park House
Sevenoaks

Helena Gilder
24 Grammercy Park
New York

Susan (Joe) Walsh
525 Madison Avenue

James Ford Rhodes
392 Beacon St.
Boston

Owen Wister
1004 West End Trust Building
Philadelphia, Pa.

J. S.
58 Hopedale St.
Allston, Mass

Sibyl Childers
12 Sloane Terrace Mansions
S. W.

Miss Bosanquet
Lawrence House
Lawrence St.
Chelsea Embankment S. W.

H. Walpole
16 Hallam St.
Portland Place

MacIlvaine
32 Portland Place

Marie Lee Childe
16 rue de l'Élysée
Paris

Francis Viélé-Griffin [1]
16 Quai de Passy
Paris

H. Mackinnon Walbrook Esq (the
P. M. G. [2] critic of the "Saloon.")
20 Old Buildings
Lincoln's Inn
W. C.

Dr. Christopher Wheeler
35 Queen Anne St.
Cavendish Square
W.

Mrs. (Braddon) Maxwell
Litchfield House
Richmond Surrey

Mme. Duclaux
10 Place St. François Xavier
Paris

Gertrude Abbey
C. L. 42 Tite St.
S. W.

---

1. Viélé-Griffin (1864–1937), born in the United States of American parents but raised and educated in France, was a poet associated with the French Symboliste movement.
2. The *Pall Mall Gazette*.

J. B. Pinker's country address:
The Oaks
Worcester Park.
Surrey

Harry[3]
Warren Hoague James and Bigelow
84 State St.

Wilton Rix (Remington)
45 The Drive
Tunbridge

Mrs. Van Rensselaer
23 Glebe Place
Chelsea. S. W.

Mrs. Sutro
31 Chester Terrace
Regent's Park
N. W.

Hon. Secretary R. N. Lifeboat Institution. Salisbury Branch Major Arthur
T. Fisher
Bemmerton, Salisbury

Clare and Wilfred Sheridan
Mitchen Hall
Godalming
Surrey
Telegraph Elstead

Colonel Irving
22 Westgate Terrace
Redcliffe Square
S. W.

May Gaskell
14 Lower Seymour St.
Mayfair S. W.
Tel. 3539

Gertrude Kingston
24 Victoria Square
Grosvenor Gdns. S. W.

Edward Sheldon
44 W. 44th St.
New York

1912

Joseph Conrad
Capel House
Alstone nr. Ashford.
Kent

Prof. W. M. Sloane
105 East 69th St.
New York City

Royal National Lifeboat Institution
Capt. Sir Fredk Henry Bathurst
Naval and Military Club
Piccadilly

Mrs. Van Rensselaer
Tel 6517 Western

Prothero's
telephone N. 1495 City

Henry Head Esq. F. R. S.
4 Montagu Square
W.

1913

The Henry Whites
1624 Crescent Place
Washington, D. C.

Henry James jr. Esq
12 West 44th St.
New York City
U. S. A.

Mrs. Crackanthorpe
65 Rutland Gate
S. W.

3. WJ's eldest, and the address of the New York business firm with which he was associated.

Mrs. Wells
Charlston Laundry
Packington Road
Acton. W

Swedish Masseur (Crackanthorpe's)
Mr. Edward Johanson
Carlisle Place
Victoria St.
S. W.

J. B. Pinker
Broomills
Holmwood R. S. O.
Surrey

Des Voeux's[1] Swedish Masseur Lind-
quister
25 Carlisle Mansions
Victoria
S. W.

W. M. Fullerton
15 (?) Rue du Mont-Thabor
Paris

Miss Hogarth
64a Kenway Road
Cromwell Road
S. W.

Stuyvesant Morrises
16 East 30th St.
New York

Alice Edgar[2]
433 Kane Place
Milwaukee

Caroline James
191 Prospect Avenue
Milwaukee. Wis. U. S. A.

Florence Pertz
72 Prince's Square
W.

Stephen Olin
Glenburn
Rhinebeck N. Y.   U. S. A.

Thomas Meteyard
155 King Henry's Road
South Hampstead
N. W.

"Ernest" E. Connell
33 Redburn St.
Chelsea, S. W.

Miss Clara Smith
28 Hunter House
Hunter St.
W. C.

Herbert Dunster[3]
14 Jerningham Road
New Cross
S. E.

Ruth Draper
18 West Eighth St.
New York

H. Dunster
56 Santos Road
Wandsworth
S. W.

Edith Bigelow
Orchard House
Great Austins
Farnham

Bill and Alice[4]
39 Chestnut St.
Boston, Mass.

Edward Warren's Electric Light
Fixtures Faraday
Wardour St.

1. Dr. Des Voeux was HJ's last physician.
2. Alice, née James (1875), daughter of HJ's brother Wilky, in 1910 married David Alexander Edgar, a Canadian.
3. This name and address are crossed out.
4. WJ's son and his wife.

Price Collier
57 Seymour St.
W.
Gerrard *5440*

Emile Boutroux
Membre de l'Institut de France
Fondation Thiers
Rond-Point
Bugeaud
Paris

1914

Comte Joseph Primoli
Palazzo Primoli
Via Zanardelli 1.
Rome

Benjamin May, Chiropodist
31 King's Road S. S.
home 3-7. Tel. No. Kens. 3592

Miss Heynemann
117 Ladbrooke Road
Holland Park
W.

W. Morton Fullerton
8 rue du Mont-Thabor

Laura Wagniere
Petit Sully
Tour de Peilz
Suisse

Alice Edgar
433 Kane Place
Milwaukee, Wis.

Sir Edward Elgar
Severn House
42 Netherhall Gdns.
Hampstead N. W.

Herbert Dunster
43 Rose Crescent
Perth
[HJ here crosses out "(June 14:) 1
Fairfield Road Crouch End N"]

Albert Whiteman
76 Brayerbrook Road
Hastings.

Barber. Maison Jean Strobeau
Kens. 5771

Mrs. Vernon Boynton
28 Cavendish Square
W.

John J. Chapman
325 W. 82d St.
New York City
U. S. A.

1915

Alice Edgar
191 Prospect Avenue
Milwaukee, Wis.

Oliver Elton
Wensted
Grassendale Park
Liverpool

The Sam Abbotts
Villa Lontana
Via di Ponte Molle
Rome

Aurist:—Harold Barwell F.R.C.S.
etc. etc.
39 Queen Anne St.
W.

T. Bailey Saunders
The Knoll
Staveley Road
Eastbourne

George Henschel
Alttnairiche Aviemore N. B.

Logan Pearsall Smith
Telephone No: Kensington 4872

Harry's *cable* address
Rokstitute New York

and

Rockefeller Institute
66th St. and Avenue A.

American Embassy.
Tel. Mayfair, 4866

Mrs. Smalley
328 West 57th St.
New York City

The Protheros' Doctor
Dr. Gayer
33 Stanhope Gdns.
S. W.

Index